TO RISK IT ALL

TO RISK IT ALL

* * *

*General Forbes,
the Capture of Fort Duquesne,
and the Course of Empire
in the Ohio Country*

Michael N. McConnell

UNIVERSITY OF PITTSBURGH PRESS

A JOHN D. S. AND AIDA C. TRUXALL BOOK

Published by the University of Pittsburgh Press, Pittsburgh, Pa., 15260
Copyright © 2020, University of Pittsburgh Press
This paperback edition, 2023
All rights reserved
Manufactured in the United States of America

Cataloging-in-Publication data is available from the Library of Congress

ISBN 13: 978-0-8229-6726-2
ISBN 10: 0-8229-6726-x

Cover art provided by historical artist John Buxton, www.buxtonart.com
Cover design by Joel W. Coggins

For Alice

And to the memory of
Jean D. Speer (1921–2018)
Fred N. McConnell (1924–2018)
Peter (2002?–2019)

CONTENTS

Acknowledgments	ix
Prologue	3

* * *

Introduction
    An Empire at War … 7

One
    New York and Philadelphia, Winter–Spring 1758 … 29

Two
    Friends and Enemies, Winter–Spring 1758 … 62

Three
    Preparations, May 1758 … 90

Four
    Moving West, June 1758 … 111

Five
    Raystown, July 1758 … 143

Six
    Forbes's Road, July–August 1758 … 173

Seven
    Loyalhannon and Fort Duquesne, September 1758 … 198

Eight
    Loyalhannon, October 1758 … 222

Nine   242
    Easton and the Kuskuskies, October–November 1758

Ten   261
    Loyalhannon and Fort Duquesne, October–November 1758

Eleven   280
    November 1758–March 1759

Conclusions   292

   *   *   *

Notes   299
Bibliography   359
Index   381

Acknowledgments

❋ ❋ ❋

This book is complete thanks to the generosity and assistance of a number of people and institutions. Foremost among those individuals who gave me much advice and who spent much time listening to my ideas is Marty West. I first met Marty years ago when he was director of the Fort Ligonier Association. Since then he has become a valued friend, a font of knowledge and information on all things pertaining to the Seven Years' War, and a guide through the world of museum collections. He was kind enough to read an earlier version of the manuscript and offered valuable comments. Our (sometimes) semiannual talk fests have been made even more congenial thanks to the warm hospitality of Marty's wife, Penny.

I met Brian Dunnigan when he directed the Old Fort Niagara Museum in New York. I benefited from his generosity and knowledge then and later when he moved to the Clements Library, retiring as associate director of the library. His unmatched knowledge of British military records and cartography allowed him to point me toward a particular elusive plan of Fort Ligonier.

Our son, Michael, an accomplished historian of modern Germany, made a number of suggestions, offered encouragement, and helped his technophobe father wrestle with computer issues. Doctor Gerald Norris took time away from his busy practice to read through many pages of references to General Forbes's health and to offer his professional insight into the causes of Forbes's illnesses and lameness. David Lindroth generously made available a map he had produced for another publication. I thank Timothy Shannon for reading the manuscript and offering insightful comments. Also thanks to David Preston for his comments and encouraging remarks. Peter rarely had much to say on the matter but was always willing to listen or rearrange my desk—as the mood suited him. At the University of Pittsburgh Press, editorial director Sandy Crooms took an early interest in the work, shepherded it through the editorial process, and provided the title. Managing editor Amy Sherman helped make my first time reviewing copyediting on-screen not only manageable but enjoyable. My thanks to them both. Another stroke of good fortune was having Pippa Letsky as copyeditor; her skill and suggestions have been most valuable.

A number of institutions were generous in providing illustrations and permissions. I thank the Tracy W. McGregor Library, University of Virginia, and the Scottish Records Office, Edinburgh, for having earlier provided copies of the Forbes papers, which form the backbone of this study. The Association of Environmental and Engineering Geologists kindly granted permission to use a plan of Forbes's Road. McGill-Queen's University Press and the University of Virginia Press both granted permission to use maps appearing in their publications. I would also like to thank Bridgeman Images, the Historical Society of Pennsylvania, the American Philosophical Society, the William L. Clements Library, the Fort Ligonier Association, and Erica Knuckles, curator of collections, the Geography and Map Division of the Library of Congress, the Gilcrease Museum, the Heinz History Center, Pittsburgh, Johnson Hall State Historic Park, Johnsontown, New York, Macpherson-Grant Papers, Ballindalloch Castle, Banffshire, Scotland, the Metropolitan Museum of Art, the Morgan Library & Museum, the Philadelphia History Museum at the Atwater Kent, Royal Collection Trust, London, University Collections of Art and History, Washington and Lee University, Yale Center for British Art.

I owe special thanks to Alice. She would occasionally ask about my progress, but mostly created a warm loving environment within which to pursue this project. The past couple of years have been hard on both of us, but she has managed to keep an even keel—for both of us. It was a good day when I met her over forty years ago, and I continue to count myself most fortunate for having her in my life.

TO RISK IT ALL

Prologue

* * *

Viewed from on high, the army would have looked like a giant undulating serpent making its way across mountains, bogs, and meadows. It would stretch for miles. And as it pushed itself ahead, the creature would diminish in size and strength. A ground-level view would reveal this reptilian mass in all its complexity. Amid the noise of shovels, axes, wagon wheels, and livestock, voices would suggest the polyglot nature of this Anglo-American army as it headed toward its goal in the summer of 1758: French Fort Duquesne. Along with English, one could also hear Dutch, German, French, Cherokee, Catawba, Broad Scots, Irish brogue, Afro-English, and Gaelic. The speakers were a particolored collection of professionals and amateurs: red-, blue-, or green-coated men, men in the somber "government" tartan worn by Highland troops, others in linen shirts, buckskins, and trade cloth, or no shirts at all. Plodding along with them were hundreds of horses pulling freight wagons, artillery, and sutlers' carts as well as flocks of sheep and herds of cattle. These were tended by some of the many civilians—contractor's agents, craftsmen, slaves, and most of all, women and children—who belonged to the army. From nose to tail something close to seven thousand people were following a single narrow track through what is now south-central Pennsylvania.

Their leader, however, could not be found among this mass of soldiers and civilians. Sick—so sick he was often unable to walk, ride, or write—

Brigadier General John Forbes followed his army. He and his escort were days, even weeks, behind the head of the column.

The weather, much of it bad; the road, poor and crossing some of the worst terrain in British America; and above all, time, too much already gone, perhaps not enough left; all of this gave Forbes cause for endless anxiety. So too did the French and their native allies, somewhere over Sideling Hill, Allegheny and Laurel Mountains, and occasionally nipping at his army's flanks. How many were they?

What did they plan? Had they been reinforced? Forbes knew none of this. Try as he might, he could not gain accurate information. He was marching blind. This ate at him, adding to the burdens of command.

And beyond the mountains, beyond the French, there were the Ohio Indians: Delawares and Shawnees mostly, living at places like the Kuskuskies, Saukunk, and Logstown. At war with Virginia and Pennsylvania since 1755, they were also the key to British victory and peace on the colonial borderlands. As the region's dominant force, they could rally behind the French and stop Forbes in his tracks. Or they could make their own peace with the British, stand aside, and let his army drive the French from the Ohio Country. No one could be sure which way these people would turn, though Forbes was determined to support Pennsylvania Quaker efforts to negotiate peace and end a horrifying border war, even as his army continued to push west.

Perhaps worst or all, though, Forbes found himself battling not just rain, mountains, the seasons, and an unseen enemy but also his own army. Petty politics within the governments of Maryland, Virginia, and Pennsylvania threatened to deprive him of men and supplies. High-ranking officers, both regular and provincial, put their own egos and their governments' parochial interests ahead of the army and its mission. Soldiers, many ill-trained, poorly equipped, and indifferently led, were thinking more about going home than going to Fort Duquesne. And native allies—Cherokees and Catawbas—whose support was considered crucial to success were going home to the Carolina mountains in droves, put off by the army's late start, slow pace, and general stinginess, not to mention the violent reception from Virginians through whose territory the warriors had traveled to reach the army.

* * *

General Forbes, his army, and the campaign they waged have long been a part of local and state history. Pittsburgh was named by Forbes in honor of William Pitt, and the modern city is full of places associated with people and events surrounding the campaign: Forbes Avenue, storied Forbes Field, Grant's Hill, Mount Washington, and Duquesne University, among others.

To the east there is the town of Ligonier, originally the encampment at Loyalhannon and renamed by Forbes after his patron general Sir John Ligonier. Farther east is Bedford, named for the duke of Bedford and in 1758 site of the Raystown camp. U. S. Route 30 is still known locally as Forbes Road, though it only approximates the route of the original military road. In 2008, during the 250th anniversary of the Seven Years' War in America, new markers were planted at important sites along the highway and accompanied by a splendid guidebook that traces the general's moves from Philadelphia to the Forks of the Ohio. At the same time the Fort Ligonier Museum, housing one of the largest collections of artifacts and art dating from the war, completed reconstruction of the fort that was built as a camp and depot in 1758 and mounted stunning new exhibits about the site and the global Seven Years' War.[1]

Histories of the Seven Years' War also include the Forbes campaign, but usually as an aside to the main story. For military historians the campaign holds little of the drama associated with the siege of Louisbourg, with the slaughters associated with Braddock's defeat and Abercromby's failure at Fort Carillon (Ticonderoga), or with Wolfe's penultimate triumph at Quebec. More general studies of the war, its causes, and consequences tend to treat the campaign as something of a sideshow. Perhaps with reason. Even Forbes believed he had been all but forgotten, even as he pushed across the Allegheny Mountains. And his death, not on the battlefield but at the end of a lingering, painful illness, did not provide the heroics that might have guaranteed him a seat in the pantheon of heroes. The image that often emerges is one of a plodding, unspectacular march amid the swirl of events elsewhere.[2]

The chapters that follow necessarily deal with purely military events, but their larger purpose is to place Forbes, his army, and their experiences within the context of Britain's eighteenth-century empire. This empire was still evolving when the Seven Years' War broke out in America, and the Forbes campaign offers insight into how British soldiers such as Forbes and the colonists he dealt with coped with an ill-defined relationship between peripheries and center. One of the arguments here is that we can learn something important about empire by examining the stresses of war as experienced by one group of men in one place at a particular moment in time. The overland nature of the campaign imposed demands on soldiers and civilians that the amphibious operations on Lake George or in the north Atlantic did not. The campaign and the army that waged it raised conflicts between competing interests that ran the gamut from raising troops to hiring wagons to enlisting native allies.

Those would-be native allies remind us of the complex web of Indian affairs that lay at the heart of Forbes's strategy and of the larger war itself. The

Forbes campaign represents one of the earliest British efforts to raise large numbers of native auxiliaries. Opting to fight fire with fire in countering the deadly hit-and-run tactics of the French and their native allies, Forbes and other British leaders attempted to fashion a "British and Indian War." Yet, British–Indian relations were just as tangled and conflict ridden as were other facets of the campaign. Forbes ultimately found himself having to deal with two royal Indian superintendents and provincial governments as well as private groups and individuals, notably Philadelphia Quakers and the Moravian missionary Christian Frederick Post. Put another way, General Forbes found himself waging a coalition war against his French enemies, with all the attendant cross-purposes, ill will, and competing interests that have come to define military coalitions. How he succeeded, and what his success meant to the subsequent history of the mid-Atlantic colonies, native inhabitants of the Ohio Country, and the empire he represented are at the heart of what follows.

INTRODUCTION

An Empire at War

* * *

The war that brought Colonel John Forbes to Halifax in mid-1757 was already three years old. It began in the volatile Ohio Country where Virginia land speculators collided with local natives and the French. At issue was ownership of the upper Ohio Valley and, specifically, the Forks of the Ohio. Open warfare there quickly spread to the other contested borderlands between British America and New France: Lake Ontario, the Champlain Valley, and the disputed boundary between Acadia and Nova Scotia. By the end of 1755 both Britain and France had committed their regular armies to America, and France formally declared war the following year. Colonial border disputes led to war wherever the rival empires were close enough to collide: the Mediterranean, West Africa, India, and, finally, in northwest Germany, where France, loosely allied with Austria and Russia, faced off against Prussia, supported by Great Britain. The American "French and Indian War" and the European "Seven Years' War" had, in effect, become one huge conflict.[1]

The results of three years of fighting had been dismal for Britain and her American colonists. Colonel George Washington's humiliating surrender at Fort Necessity in 1754 was followed by the near destruction of General Edward Braddock's army near Fort Duquesne one year later, exposing Virginia, Maryland, and Pennsylvania to devastating raids by Ohio Indians, French irregulars, and their Great Lakes and Canadian Indian allies. An effort to cut

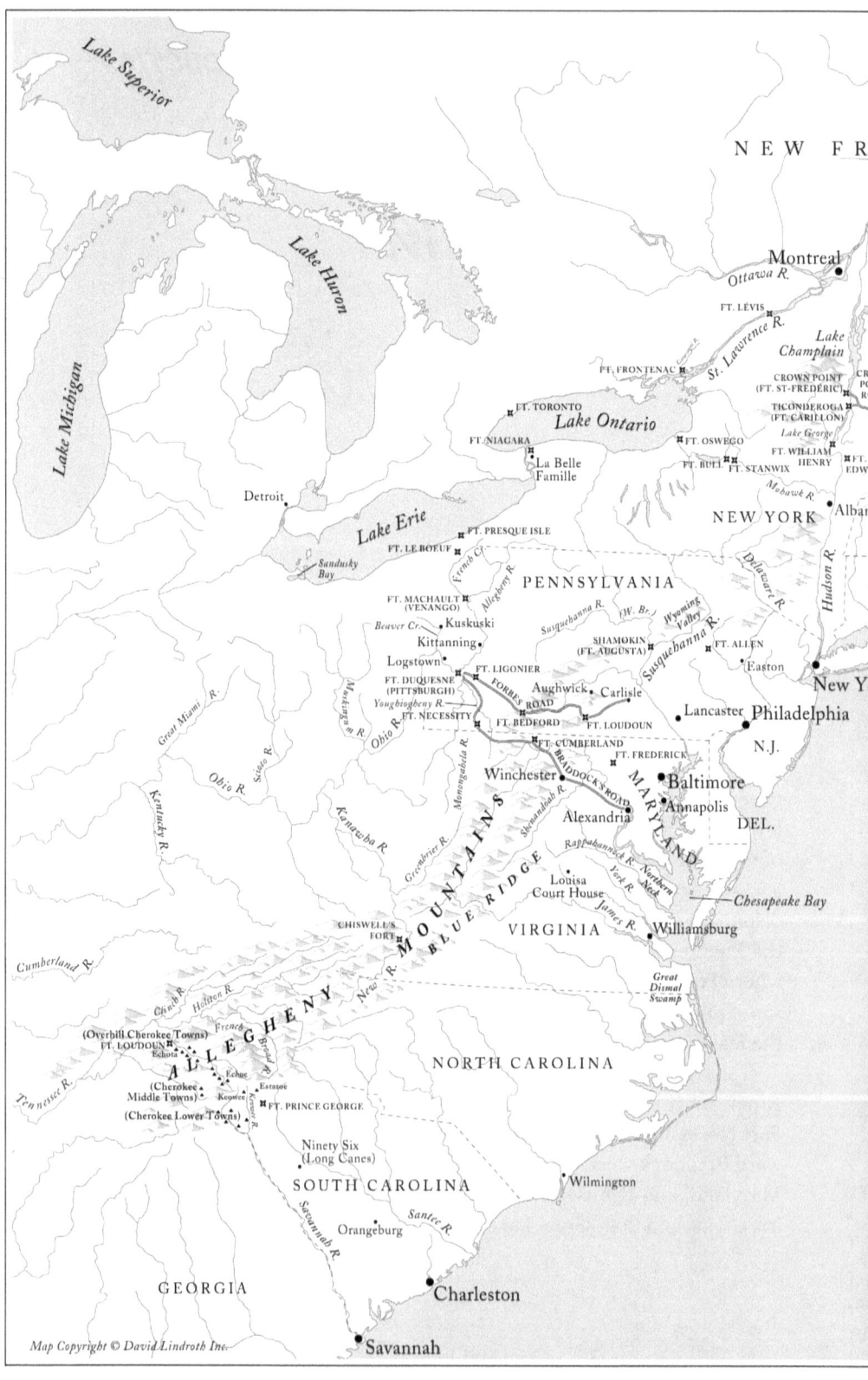

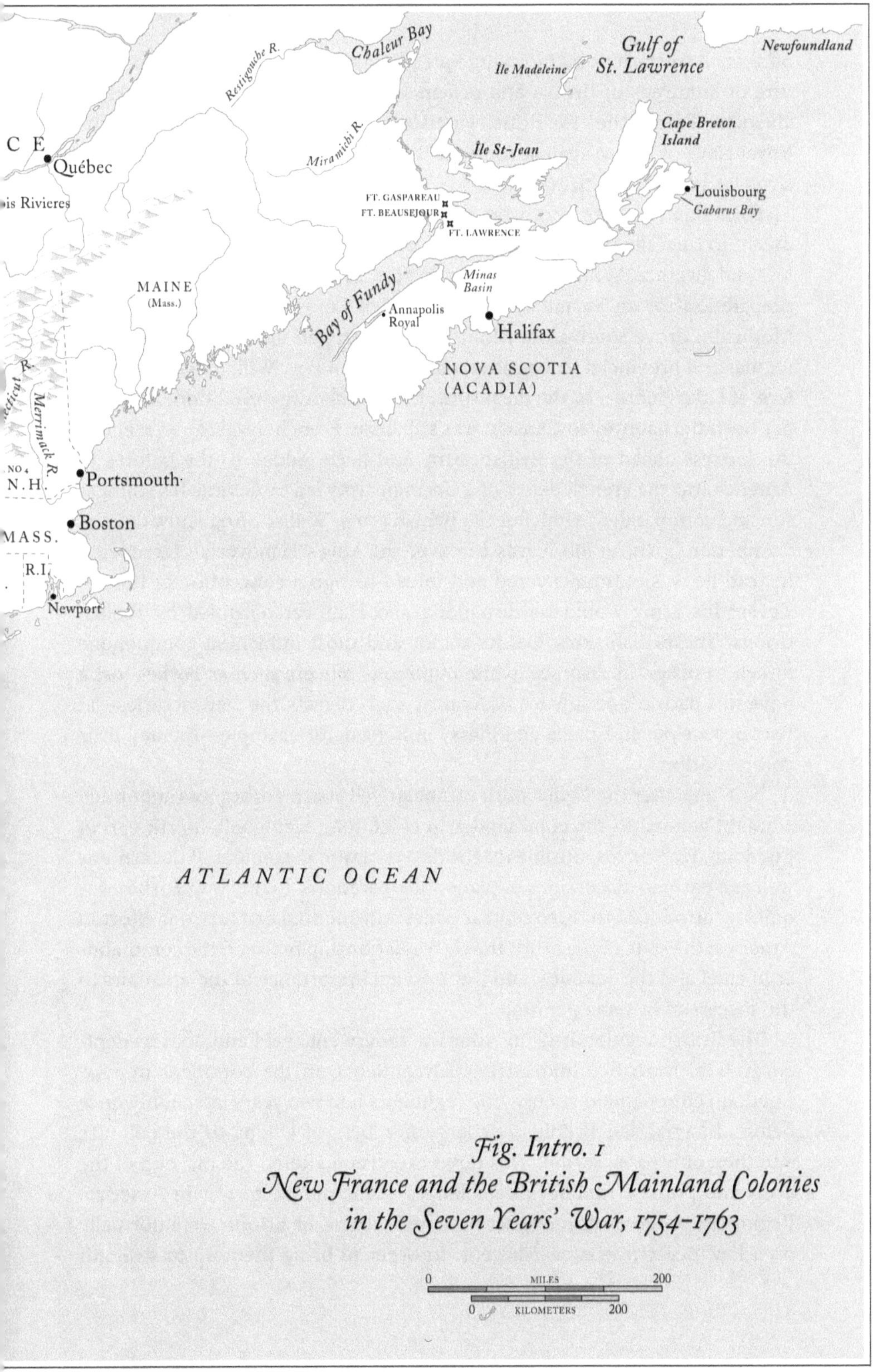

Fig. Intro. 1
New France and the British Mainland Colonies
in the Seven Years' War, 1754–1763

off French western posts by taking Fort Niagara ended instead with the capture of hundreds of British and provincial troops at Fort Oswego. Farther afield, the French took the British garrison on Minorca in 1756, depriving the Royal Navy of a base against southern France and costing Admiral Sir John Byng his life before a firing squad.[2]

Forbes and his 17th Foot were part of a massive buildup of British forces meant to turn the tide in 1757. Instead, British forces faced only further defeat and disgrace. While most of Britain's forces were gathering in Halifax in preparation for an assault on the fortress of Louisbourg, the marquis de Montcalm drove south from Montreal and snapped up over two thousand regular and provincial troops after a brief siege of Fort William Henry at the foot of Lake George. In the meantime, the Louisbourg expedition, meant to pry open the gateway to Canada, was still born; French naval forces reached the fortress ahead of the British army and fleet. Added to the failures in America was the French defeat of a German army led by George II's younger son and commander in chief of the British army, William Augustus, duke of Cumberland, whose job it was to cover the king's Hanoverian territories. Instead he was outmaneuvered and forced to sign a convention at Kloster Zeven: his army would be disbanded and Hanover occupied by French troops. The British army lost its senior and most influential commander, forced to resign in disgrace, while numerous officers such as Forbes lost a powerful patron and advocate. Against such defeats the few victories—at Fort Beausejour in Acadia and Plassy in Bengal, for example—seemed little compensation.[3]

Not long after the Louisbourg campaign fell apart, Forbes was appointed adjutant general to the commander in chief, John Campbell, fourth earl of Loudoun. He was responsible for the day-to-day management of the army as well as a party to discussions of plans and operations. In this way, Forbes was quickly introduced to three central issues surrounding Britain's war effort in America: the state of the army, the testy relationship between the commander in chief and the colonies, and the growing importance of Indian affairs to the success of British operations.[4]

The British regular army in America underwent rapid and unprecedented growth; from five understrength regiments on the continent in 1755, Loudoun commanded twenty-one regiments just two years later. Only once before, in 1711, had Britain sent large numbers of troops to the colonies and then only for a season. This rapid expansion altered the makeup of the army and posed a number of challenges, some unique to war in America. Regiments ordered on active service from Ireland or Britain were normally on a low, peacetime establishment. In order to bring them up to strength quickly, the army resorted to the time-honored practice of drafting: drawing men from regiments at home to fill those going abroad. At the end of 1757, for example, Forbes was busy preparing a draft for those regiments left to garrison in Nova Scotia. Aside from giving regimental officers an opportunity to discard unwanted men (troublemakers, slackers, or misfits), drafting weakened the bonds of comradeship that came from long service in the same regiment. Indeed, at the very beginning of the war, General Braddock, whose two regiments absorbed hundreds of drafts and colonial recruits, was compelled to alter the tactical organization of his army, "that the Officers and Men might know one another." A year later, Loudoun found the 35th Foot very disappointing, its new men "unruly." He hoped the next campaign would allow him to make better soldiers of the "pressed Men" that filled its ranks. The Highland Regiment (42d Foot), though a good regiment, "have not near two hundred" veterans left out of nearly a thousand rank and file. British troops may have been reasonably well-equipped and disciplined, but they were often strangers to each other; only active campaigning in the face of the enemy would re-create reliable regimental communities. In addition to drafting, the army recruited heavily in Ireland, Britain, and America. The resulting influx of men meant that the army got younger. Veterans—the "old standers" as they were known—were matched and outnumbered by inexperienced recruits whose officers would not have the luxury of peacetime duty during which to turn them into acceptable soldiers.[5]

The American army was also augmented by new regiments, notably the Royal American Regiment, later the 60th Foot. Huge by army standards, its four battalions, numbering over four thousand men, would be raised largely in the colonies. Its officers included a large number of "foreign Protestants": Swiss, German, and Huguenot professionals whose commissions were a gift of the king, instead of being offered through purchase. These were joined by Scots, English, and provincial officers. The enlisted men were drawn from New England and the mid-Atlantic colonies as well as from Protestant states in northern Germany, and they ran the gamut from native-born colonists to immigrants from all across the British Atlantic. Finally, and with the encouragement of William Pitt (now head of the government), the army began raising new regiments from the Scottish Highlands. In addition to the veteran 42d, the American army would include two new Highland regiments: Lieutenant-Colonel Montgomery's First Highland Battalion (later 77th Foot) and Lieutenant-Colonel Simon Fraser's Second Highland Battalion (later 78th Foot). Although led by cadres of professional soldiers, including men such as Major James Grant of the 77th, who had been serving in the Scottish regiments of the Dutch army, these new regiments were composed of inexperienced troops who would learn their trade on campaign.[6]

The army's officer corps also posed challenges. British officers were notoriously prone to indiscipline, motivated by class, personal honor, hunger for advancement, and, in the case of Englishmen, a profound dislike of Scottish officers. This last issue involved Forbes directly when Captain Charles Lee of the 44th Foot complained of the large number of Scots, and alleged that Forbes earned his colonelcy by toasting the Pretender. Forbes, as adjutant general, also had to cope with Major-General Lord Charles Hay, whose insubordination led Loudoun to order him home. When Hay refused to leave, Loudoun, through Forbes, placed him under arrest. In the meantime, officers angered at the failure of the Louisbourg expedition blamed Loudoun and openly questioned his fitness for command. Forbes, no stranger to the frictions of high command, became determined that no such behavior would be tolerated in any force under his command.[7]

Overshadowing the challenges of raising and training an army and coping with a fractious officer corps there was a more basic and much greater issue: what modern soldiers would call "logistics." Eighteenth-century armies never used the term and it does not appear in contemporary dictionaries. Nevertheless, the British army needed everything from ammunition to wagons. Without supplies and equipment, training was impossible, morale would suffer, and the army would simply be unable to move. Moreover, the fact that the redcoats were operating on friendly soil in the colonies created as many problems as it solved. Yes, the colonies had an abundance of people, most of them engaged in agriculture. Yes, there were ports such as Boston, New York, and Philadelphia that could be used as bases for operations. And, yes, American settlements, like their counterparts in Britain or Europe, relied on animal power and water transportation, which could be turned to the army's advantage.[8]

On close inspection, these became questionable assets at best. An abundance of people, yes, but spread out through provinces that, taken together, dwarfed Britain in size. Moreover, as one moved west or north (toward the enemy), the population thinned out. Even large towns lacked the capacity to house thousands of soldiers and their dependents, and declining population density created other problems in finding shelter and resources for troops. Although most colonists did make their livings directly or indirectly from the land, not all agricultural assets were useful to the army; slave-based economies of tobacco or rice were less an advantage than general farming or raising livestock. Those settlers who did produce foodstuffs did so with an eye to their family needs and the market but maintained only enough horses, oxen, and wagons for their present needs; they had little in the way of surplus in any of these precious assets, which the army needed in quantity and was notorious for wantonly destroying.[9]

Port facilities were of little use unless reliable means could be found to transport goods and men to where they were needed. Not only were distances a problem, but the colonies simply lacked the infrastructure that could allow an army of thousands of people to move efficiently any distance at all. The Hudson River–Lake Champlain corridor did offer an advantageous route to the heart of Canada. The passage up the Mohawk River to Lake Ontario and from there to Fort Niagara lay through the lands of the Six Nations: there were no towns to serve as depots and no roads to carry artillery and supply wagons. In the absence of towns the army built forts, along with roads connecting them, and these were tasks that consumed time, money, and manpower. South of New York, any attempt to reach the Ohio Country would run headlong into the Appalachian Mountains—the "endless mountains" of local lore. The navigable rivers ran north–south and not east–west, except for the Mohawk and Potomac. Alternatives consisted of trading paths that were adequate for packhorse trains, but not an army.[10]

The mid-eighteenth-century British army was, in fact, a collection of regiments of several hundred officers and men. Each had a surgeon and a surgeon's mate plus farriers in the cavalry. Other than these specialists the army lacked any sort of institutional "tail" designed to support fighting troops. Support was entirely ad hoc and fell under the control of long-serving bureaucrats, members of the permanent government, whose collective experience allowed them to quickly create the necessary system to maintain an army. These men—commissaries, muster-masters, artillery conductors, and others—were an obscure but vital part of the "sinews of power" that allowed Britain to finance and manage a global war. Parliament, aside from voting the annual army estimates and renewing the Mutiny Act (without which an army could not legally exist), had little to do with these arrangements. In addition, regiments on active service drew upon their own manpower for specialized labor. Soldiers found themselves transporting supplies, as well as building storehouses, barracks, and fortifications. Colonel Henry Bouquet, stationed in South Carolina in 1757, was able to find 149 skilled labors representing fifty different trades in his five companies of the Royal Americans. These men included blacksmiths, wheelwrights, and bakers. Those without skills found themselves cutting timber or mending roads.[11]

Three government departments were crucial to the creation of a support system for the army. The Board of Admiralty undertook to carry troops overseas, feeding them from their own victualling agency. The Board of

Ordnance controlled ammunition—the Royal Artillery and the engineers, neither of which was part of the army. Overshadowing both the Admiralty and Ordnance was the Treasury, responsible for securing supply and transportation contracts, providing funds through its Paymaster's Office, and issuing bills of exchange that army commanders could use to raise cash for contingencies. The Treasury's agents could be found throughout the army: men to arrange contracts for local materials and labor, commissaries of stores, commissaries of wagons, and mustering agents, the latter responsible for ensuring that the number of troops on the ground corresponded to the monthly returns before pay and allowances were issued to regimental agents. Meanwhile, the War Office continued to cope with the blizzard of paperwork associated with a rapidly growing army. The Secretary at War issued orders from the king or commander in chief, dealt with the various legalities that went with raising new regiments and recruiting those in service, and fielded the seemingly endless requests for commissions and favors. Orders creating hospitals and their personnel were reminders that essential medical services were also created as needed. A Physician-general, Surgeon-general, and Apothecary-general for the American army were appointed by commission from the crown. Additional surgeons, mates, hospital matrons, apothecaries, and nurses were hired, often through patronage networks. The army's general hospital in New York supplied manpower to hospitals with field armies and controlled the flow of medical stores.[12]

Providing the mountains of foodstuffs, forage, wagons, and livestock was the task of civilian contractors. Unlike the Royal Navy, whose yards contained a ready supply of naval stores and whose Victualling Board maintained permanent depots of foodstuffs, the army needed to accumulate supplies when and where needed. Drawing on a century of experience supplying military forces, contractors submitted bids and signed contracts with Treasury agents, based on the projected number of men and horses needed over a specified period of time. Contractors also benefited from the dense network of trade and credit that characterized the British Atlantic world. British contractors, foremost among them the firm of Kilby and Baker, subcontracted with provincial firms and individual merchants such as Plumstead and Franks, DeLancey and Watts, and Adam Hoops, the latter from Carlisle, Pennsylvania, and others located in or near the major distribution points. Other, transatlantic firms such as Greg and Cunningham, took advantage of partnerships rooted in both Britain and America. And in the case of Kilby and Baker, one of the partners (Christopher Kilby) resided in the colonies, working in New York and Philadelphia. Contracting, as well as the presence of large numbers of soldiers themselves, guaranteed that by 1757 the colonies were awash in specie and bills of exchange, which further stimulated local, frequently cash-poor, economies.[13]

* * *

Managing the flow of material from ports and contractors to troops—linking supply and demand—was the task of the American army's deputy quartermasters general. Officially, their tasks embraced far more than the title would imply. A contemporary definition of the post emphasized that the "duty is to mark the marches, and encampments of the army" and to designate sites for each regimental camp in the field, while coordinating the movement of vital supplies. A quartermaster general was to be a man of "great judgement and experience." In the colonies one such man was Lieutenant-Colonel Sir John St. Clair, who had directed the organization and march of Braddock's army and survived its destruction, though with a serious wound that bothered him for the rest of his life. Loudoun retained him even though St. Clair was often bedridden. As the army grew and its operations expanded, so, too, did the number of deputy quartermasters general. Of these men—including Captain John Bradstreet, Captain Gabriel Christie, and Major James Robertson, along with St. Clair—none was a specialist in what he did. They all, like Forbes or any other staff officer, undertook a job deemed suited to their talents and experience—yet another example of the army's ad hoc arrangements.[14]

The tasks and difficulties these men faced went well beyond the definitions offered by military dictionaries, however. According to Loudoun, St. Clair had "a great deal of Business," more, in fact, "than in any Service I ever was in." St. Clair himself readily admitted that "what was looked on at home as easy" was, in fact, a daunting task. Especially challenging to him and the army was moving through "this vast tract of Mountains." If the army could support itself in America as it could in Europe, "the Thing [Braddock's march] wou'd be easy." Planning marches through such "vast tracts" was only one problem; the need for far-flung garrisons was another. Holding forts that guarded vital waterways or roads while safeguarding frontier towns demanded that St. Clair oversee the building of hospitals, storehouses, and barracks and ensure that garrisons of regulars and provincials were provided with necessary supplies in the face of poor roads and civilians reluctant to rent horses and wagons. America, in other words, was turning into a very different "school of war" from the familiar ones in Flanders and Germany. It was a theater of war unlike any that Forbes, St. Clair, or their comrades had ever before encountered.[15]

The American commander in chief, Loudoun, arrived in the colonies to face and sort out a ramshackle operation that had produced little beyond waste, fraud, and defeat. Arriving in July, 1756, Loudoun immediately superseded William Shirley, governor of Massachusetts and acting commander in chief since Braddock's death. There was no overarching plan for war in America and little in the way of capable staff. Melding provincial and regular war efforts was a challenge in itself, particularly since the king ordered that "all General and Field Officers" commissioned by colonial governors "shall take Rank as Eldest Captains" when serving with regular forces; a decision, first made in 1755, that rankled status-conscious provincials such as George Washington and only added to already tense military relations. That, and ongoing issues of supply, organization, and training consumed much of Loudoun's energy until he was relieved by Pitt at the end of 1757. Yet, Loudoun did succeed in creating the administrative structure that allowed British and provincial troops to campaign successfully in the years ahead. Even so, Loudoun found himself locked in a war of words with colonial politicians and soldiers, whose ideas of war and, especially, empire, were at odds with everything that Loudoun and his fellow Britons held to be true and correct; conflicts that hinted at the cross-currents and latent tensions that defined relations between Britain and her mainland American colonies.[16]

Loudoun found himself frustrated at every turn. His officers enlisted indentured servants and immediately found themselves detained for theft of property by local magistrates. Demands that colonies provide quarters for troops or build barracks for them were met with foot-dragging and arguments about the rights of Englishmen, local usage, and precedent. In one incident, Bouquet was refused quarters for troops by Philadelphia magistrates; the sheriff likewise refused to enforce the colonel's orders. Only an appeal to the governor William Denny and the threat of quartering additional troops in the city broke the impasse. After only three months in America, Loudoun was driven to complain that "the backwardness of the People of this Country . . . is incredible." Others—such as Admiral Sir Charles Hardy, now governor of New York—chimed in. Hardy referred to "unhappy divided America" and was particularly frustrated by the jealousy that prevented individual colonies from raising their quotas of men until they knew that their neighbors were likewise raising troops. If these were British dominions, they seemed to behave in decidedly un-British ways and were as wary of imperial authorities as they were of the French.[17]

Hardy's comments suggest what may have been the greatest obstacle to cooperation between colonists and the army: a deepening sense of "otherness." Metropolitan and provincial Britons were not alienated from each other, but were nevertheless inclined to emphasize differences as much, or more than, similarities. Many Britons on both sides of the Atlantic found provincials to be "mysterious and paradoxical people." And, within the growing armies taking shape in America, with regulars and provincials living and working cheek-to-jowl, familiarity could easily breed contempt. The first hints of this surfaced with the arrival of Braddock's troops in 1755. Reporting to Braddock in early February, St. Clair not only reminded him that colonists were "totally ignorant of Military Affairs," but "Their Sloth &Ignorance is not to be described." He suggested that treating the Germans among them like the peasants of Europe might have a positive effect. Three years later, at Louisbourg, General James Wolfe made similar observations, accusing provincials of being "in general the most contemptible cowardly dogs" he could imagine. On the other hand, some officers, including Bouquet and Colonel Thomas Gage, were willing to see past colonial faults, at least far enough to seek their fortunes through landed estates or advantageous marriages. Meanwhile, civilian visitors, such as the Reverend Andrew Burnaby, avoided scathing remarks only to use condescension instead. While in Philadelphia, Burnaby found the women "exceedingly handsome and polite," but he quickly added that, "since their intercourse with the English officers, they are greatly improved" and would "not make bad figures even in the first assemblies in Europe."[18]

Colonists then were lazy, slovenly—and selfish. British officers were angered at the openness with which colonial merchants engaged in smuggling with the Spanish and French, especially when they used "flag of truce" vessels, designed to repatriate prisoners of war, as an excuse to trade in enemy ports in the Caribbean. Others, including Forbes, were equally upset at the price-gouging of farmers and tradesmen who held back needed wagons and supplies until prices went up. And, of course, there was the king's directive regarding commissions—another hint, perhaps, that Britons found the colonists somehow unequal and unworthy.[19]

Some colonists met these attitudes with bemusement. Writing to inform a friend of military affairs in America in 1755, Marylander Daniel Dulany made a point of suggesting that, perhaps in another hundred years, Britons would finally learn that "we live in houses, speak English, wear clothes, and have some faint notions of Christianity," while laughing at questions from newcomers such as "have you any cows, or horses in Maryland?" Things would change, Delany concluded, "as our importance begins to be understood" thanks to the war.[20]

For provincial soldiers swept into the war and into British-led armies, though, "otherness" was no laughing matter. For them, encounters with redcoats and their officers raised the specter of draconian discipline and order largely unknown in the colonies outside of slave-based plantations. Close observation convinced many that British troops were "but little better than slaves to their Officers." One provincial soldier who witnessed his first military execution described it in great detail in his diary, as something hideously outlandish. Colonists used to local self-rule and personal autonomy found courts-martial and the humiliating sentences they handed down a shock, disturbing proof of the gap between provincial notions of English "liberties" and those expressed by the king's troops. Many colonial officers seem to have agreed; when presenting men to a court-martial, they often deliberately reduced the charges just to avoid the capital punishments common among the regulars. Yet, over time, others such as George Washington of Virginia and Joseph Shippen of Pennsylvania, for example, came to embrace the regular army's professionalism and codes of conduct, even to handing out severe punishments to their own men. These conflicted views of Britons and colonists, however, reflected the complex state of the empire they were trying to defend.[21]

* * *

The British Atlantic was less an empire in the traditional sense than it was a vast collection of territories and peoples stretching from slaving stations in West Africa through Caribbean islands to lumbering and fishing settlements in Maine and Newfoundland. From the viewpoint of any traditional imperialist, it would have seemed a ramshackle assortment at best. Colonies and trading stations arose from the initiative of private individuals, companies, and corporations; the result was that, over a century and a half, the British Atlantic consisted of a patchwork of places each with its own history, legal foundation, and social character. Two things bound these places together. One was a common allegiance to the monarchy that had given its approval to the founding ventures; what has been called "reciprocal sovereignty." The other was the growing network of trade, the transatlantic flow of people, goods, cash, and credit.[22]

Soldiers such as Loudoun looked to Parliament for the legal underpinning of their profession, but it played a limited role in defining how colonies viewed themselves as part of a larger British world. Indeed, the mainland colonies, many of which played only a small role in Britain's global economy, enjoyed considerable self-government and only limited interference from abroad, largely through the Navigation Acts, which merchants found ways of avoiding, including smuggling.[23]

When war broke out, the American colonies continued to reflect the rapid territorial and population growth that sustained regional diversity and localism. Colonists were busy moving into the piedmont borderlands of Virginia, Pennsylvania, the Carolinas, and Georgia. The latter, founded in 1733, was barely two decades old when Virginians and Canadians began killing each other in the Ohio Country. Much of this growth was fueled by a white population that quickly reproduced itself thanks to abundant resources. Added to this was continued migration. The war in America erupted in the middle of a wave of migration that saw thousands of Germans and Ulster Scots arrive in the colonies during the middle decades of the century. Moreover, the use of slave labor, especially in the staple economies of Virginia and South Carolina, steadily increased throughout the eighteenth century. Altogether, the mainland colonies that played host to Loudoun's army held over one and a half million people, one-third of them African or African American.[24]

New England, with its largely native-born population of English ancestry, most reflected England ethnically and culturally. The so-called middle colonies—New York, New Jersey, and Pennsylvania—were far more diverse. New York City, the American army's headquarters, was home to English, Scots, Dutch, Africans, and French, as well as colonial creoles. Reporting to his superiors, one early governor found the city and colony a bewildering mix of Quakers, Catholics, Baptists, Huguenots, Dutch Reformed, Anglicans, and Presbyterians. As the list implies, this colony, as well as neighboring New Jersey and Pennsylvania, perhaps came closest to our modern concept of an American "melting pot." "Fruit salad" might be a better term for colonies that contained large numbers of self-consciously Welsh, Ulster Scots, Dutch, Germans, Africans, as well as English. Here, ethnicity and religious persuasion often went together: Scottish and Irish Presbyterians, Welsh Quakers, and German Lutherans, Moravians, Baptists, and Mennonites. These people tended to cluster near others of the same background and persuasion and created a landscape punctuated with names like New Rochelle, Bryn Mawr, Ephrata, Donegal, and Strasburg as well as Lancaster, York, and Reading.[25]

Farther south, in Maryland, Virginia, and the Carolinas, the cultural landscape's most noticeable characteristic would be the stark contrast between Europeans (mostly free landowners and renters) and the large population of African slaves and their American descendants that characterized plantation economies. By 1755, in fact, slaves were a numerical majority in much of Tidewater Virginia and coastal South Carolina. In addition, the Chesapeake colonies absorbed many of the British convicts who arrived in America.

Numbering some fifty thousand from 1717 to the eve of the Revolution, these men and women were sent to the colonies as bound laborers as an alternative of capital punishment in Britain.[26]

Finally, native peoples continued to live within many of the mainland colonies, either as individuals trying to earn a living on the margins of society, or as communities with at least a tenuous hold on land and collective identities. "River Indians" along the Hudson River, Stockbridge Indians living in the town of that name, Munsees holding on in the upper Delaware Valley, Delawares at Shamokin on the edge of Pennsylvania, Conestogas living outside Lancaster, Pennsylvania, as well as remnants of Powhatans, living in Virginia on America's oldest reservations, all stood as reminders of the human cost associated with the rapid expansion of British America. With all of this wild variation, coupled with widely varying military traditions (from well-established militias in New England, to no military at all in Pennsylvania), to newcomers such as Loudoun or Forbes, "British" America was a very strange world indeed.[27]

These polyglot provinces thrived on equally varied economies. Geography, climate, resources, and the conscious choices of the founding generation of settlers guaranteed that the colonists would find a wide array of solutions to the challenges of making a living and making money in their new worlds. From the cod fisheries of the north Atlantic to the rice plantations of the South Carolina lowlands, no two colonies developed in quite the same manner. While several provinces depended on the production and sale of staple commodities: such as rice, tobacco, fish, or furs, others relied on more mixed economies based on subsistence agriculture and resource extraction. Virginia, with its slave-based tobacco production, for example, differed considerably from Pennsylvania's mixed farming, iron production, and deer-hide trading. The colonies also supported a handful of cities and dozens of small towns serving regional and local markets. And, by the 1750s, the growth of "backcountry" regions like Virginia's Shenandoah Valley or the Cumberland Valley of Pennsylvania with their subsistence farms and desire for access to eastern markets and political power, added to the complexity of what Governor Hardy characterized, with an ironic hint of truth, as "divided America."[28]

Not everyone enjoyed the benefits from the continued growth of British America. Slaves remained below the bottom rung of colonial society generally, producing wealth but never permitted to share it. As the colonies became more tightly enmeshed in an Atlantic—indeed, global—economy, they were more affected by cycles of economic boom and bust often triggered by the numerous wars of the long eighteenth century. Port towns were especially vulnerable in this regard: economic dislocation hit them hardest and lasted longer than elsewhere. Moreover, seamen and those dependent on the shipping trades faced seasonal, as well as war-related shortages of work. And in port towns, as points of entry, immigrants, including servants and unskilled laborers, competed for what jobs were available. In the countryside, especially in New England, population pressure meant that land was becoming scarce and with it the economic and political independence that were the goals of sons and grandsons of farmers less able to transfer working farms to the next generation. Those unable to learn a skilled trade or find steady work became the pool from which both British and provincial officers found recruits after 1755. At the same time, the Great Awakening and a spreading consumer culture were challenging traditional ideas of authority and place, producing dissention within churches and further underscoring divisions of wealth and power. These were societies that, in complex ways, were becoming both more British-like and more distinctively American at the same time; societies born of tensions between Old World traditions and New World possibilities. Colonies were home to more and more American-born people, who were nevertheless tied to a global economy driven from London, an economy that at once both encouraged emulation of British ways and widened gaps between rich and poor.[29]

These were, then, societies in a state of flux, and never more so than in the middle decades of the eighteenth century. As Loudoun, Forbes, and other Britons soon discovered, the colonies were not only home to complex, sometimes very un-British, social landscapes, these provinces also had their own methods of raising troops and dealing with the demands of the commander in chief. Simply put, Loudoun found himself in a British Atlantic world largely shaped by processes of negotiation between center and peripheries, where colonists enjoyed considerable self-government and economic independence. Unable to impose their will on distant and poorly understood subjects, metropolitan officials had been content to tolerate a good measure of local autonomy in return for colonial acceptance of London, king, and Parliament as legitimate sources of power and patronage within the empire. Under such circumstances, jealous localism, resistance to outsiders' demands, and the "divided" character of the colonies were, in fact, the norm. Where Hardy expected to find a uniform system of law and governance akin to that of British shires, he found instead hallowed traditions of local rule based on elective legislatures—even in those "royal" colonies, like New York, where governors were appointed by the king.[30]

From an American perspective, the empire resembled a loose coalition of coequal parts whose interests sometimes coincided and sometimes clashed.

The colonies could not even agree on any form of common defense; the famous Albany Plan of Union, promoted by Benjamin Franklin, was dead on arrival before the provincial assemblies. Consequently, British commanders, their agents, and their superiors at home, found themselves negotiating colonial participation in a war that, ostensibly, was being waged for the colonists' benefit. Everything from recruiting servants to quartering regulars and raising provincials had to meet with the approval of not only the army, but also local custom, legislatures, and political interests, the latter including many of the same men who sought and signed supply contracts with the army. As early as Loudoun's arrival in 1756, it was clear that the war in America would be a cooperative effort among equals. Validation of this came in 1758 with a decision by George II to allow provincial officers to hold rank equally with regulars in the same grade, subject only to seniority and the decision by Parliament to reimburse colonial governments for the costs of raising and supporting their troops.[31]

* * *

Although the war in America was waged on the margins of the British colonies, it was often fought in the heart of Indian country. In 1755 most of North America was still occupied and controlled by numerous peoples whose lives were no more simple or static than those of their colonial neighbors. In fact, the middle decades of the eighteenth century found native peoples wrestling with an array of issues that now included the ever more disruptive and deadly struggles between Britain and France. Iroquois, Delawares, and Cherokees, among many others, were no more likely to be coerced by imperial powers than colonists. Indeed, natives were only too adept at using geographic position, economic influence, and military clout when it came to dealing with imperious colonists and imperial government. If authorities in London and America ever hoped to promote a "British and Indian war" against the French, they would have to do so through careful negotiation and coalition building. This would not be an easy task: long histories and long memories left natives either leery of dealing with colonies or outright hostile. By late 1755 both Pennsylvania and Virginia were embroiled in a bloody border war with Ohio Indians that paralleled, but was not part of, the wider Anglo-French conflict; it was a war the colonists were losing, and one with no end in sight when Forbes assumed his new command in 1758.

The eighteenth-century Indian world beyond the Appalachian Mountains was shaped by events stretching back to the initial contact between natives and newcomers nearly two centuries earlier. In one sense, Iroquois, Cherokees, Creeks, and Shawnees were among the beneficiaries of the disasters that swept over coastal people from Florida to Nova Scotia. Living farther inland they had time to learn about and adjust to the French, Spanish, Dutch, and English who began to populate the margins of Indian country. This does not suggest that inland peoples somehow escaped the epidemics, population collapse, and other disruptions that followed encounters with the Europeans. The Iroquois, for example, were swept into a destructive cycle of warfare for much of the seventeenth century, triggered by population loss that led to the resulting grief and anger being projected outward against others who could be classed as alien and enemy: the so-called mourning war. At the same time, Cherokees moved into the mountains and river valleys of western North Carolina and east Tennessee, filling the void left by the collapse of the mound-building chiefdoms that had dominated much of the Southeast, a collapse triggered in part by the arrival of Europeans, with their goods and diseases.[32]

Warfare was not new to Indian America, although encounters with Europeans spawned more widespread and destructive conflicts. Mourning wars as well as struggles to control resources and trade routes reflected the growing importance of European technology—metals, cloth, firearms, for example—in native lives. Other wars grew out of the need for slaves; English settlers in South Carolina after 1670 were eager to acquire native captives for use at home and as commodities to be traded to the West Indies.[33]

Wars, whether for captives, goods, or slaves, proved a constructive as well as a destructive force in native societies. New peoples emerged in the late seventeenth century from refugees and the descendants of once powerful chiefdoms in the Southeast. Such peoples emerged as the "Creeks" and "Catawbas" who began to enter British colonial records in the early eighteenth century. Meanwhile, Jesuit missionaries and continued unrest at home prompted some Iroquois, especially Mohawks, to relocate to the Saint Lawrence Valley close to French settlements. These Christian Iroquois, or Kanawakes, joined other refugees, such as the western Abenakis who founded the town of Odanak in order to escape the expansion of New England settlements. Finally, land fraud and dispossession, rather than warfare, compelled natives from the Delaware Valley to turn their backs on William Penn's colony and head west. There, in the 1720s, they pioneered the empty upper Ohio Valley. Joined by others from Iroquoia and the Great Lakes, these people forged a distinct identity as "Ohio Indians." They would play a central role in Forbes's effort to drive the French from Fort Duquesne.[34]

By the middle of the eighteenth century evolving native societies confronted an enlarged colonial world. In some respects, colonies and Indian country reflected similarities. Both were dynamic places and participants in an "empire of goods," the London-based Atlantic system of trade and credit. New peoples—either American-born British colonists and slaves or Catawbas and Ohio Indians—characterized both worlds. And, if British Americans had reason to cast a wary eye toward Spanish settlements in Florida or French towns and forts to their north and west, so, too, did natives worry about increased colonial expansion. For natives, the problem was literally all around them. By the 1740s and 1750s Indian country east of the Mississippi River occupied the center of a ring of colonial claims and settlements from Pensacola and New Orleans, north to the Illinois Valley and Great Lakes, and to the British colonies to the east.[35]

Rather than surrender the initiative to the Europeans, however, native peoples persisted in defending their identities, sovereignties, and frontiers. They did so by engaging in what one colonist called "modern Indian politics": playing off rival colonies and empires to native advantage. This strategy was a risky one: Indians could seldom know or influence policies crafted at the heart of European empires. Nevertheless, such a strategy, in its many manifestations, worked for two generations after 1700 because both natives and colonists could benefit. Natives could keep settlers at bay while maintaining access to valued markets—and political influence. Colonies gained valuable commodities and might gain allies or neutralize potential enemies in the event of renewed imperial conflict.[36]

The best-known example of this play-off strategy was the elaborate diplomatic arrangement created by the Iroquois Confederacy, known as the Covenant Chain. Originally a pact between New York and the Mohawks in the 1670s, the Covenant Chain continued to grow into the next century. It worked because colonists—New York, then Massachusetts, Virginia, Maryland, and Pennsylvania—could turn to their allies within the Confederacy to help keep the peace on western borders, and the Confederacy increasingly assumed the role of favored ally. Moreover, standing between the British and French, the Iroquois asserted official neutrality while permitting constituent villages to pursue relations as best suited them, thus helping to keep the peace at home. By mid-century, however, the Covenant Chain had also become a tool for British expansion. Pennsylvania, for example, used their alliance with the Iroquois to coerce and dispossess natives in the Delaware Valley. Iroquois headmen who made bold claims to having "conquered" other natives found colonial officials more than willing to agree, especially when the Six Nations cooperated in removing the "conquered" from lands coveted by settlers and the Penn family. This led to enhanced influence for the Six Nations while allowing them to protect their own territory. It was the Covenant Chain and fraudulent treaties like the now infamous Walking Purchase that compelled Pennsylvania natives to look to the Ohio Valley for security and autonomy. They would not welcome attempts to extend the Chain westward in the 1750s and, indeed, began to shape their own version of "modern Indian politics."[37]

To the south, Cherokees and their neighbors pursued similar strategies in their efforts to manage the French, British, and Spanish, and to jockey for advantage against each other. Even small nations could parley reputation and location to advantage. The Catawbas in the foothills of the western Carolinas turned their reputation for aggression and their deft understanding of British legalities into a secure homeland, complete with deed and colonial neighbors who could be counted on to help the Catawbas deal with their inveterate northern enemies, the Iroquois. This new Indian politics was an inherently unstable arrangement, based as it was on networks of agreements between numerous autonomous native societies and diverse, independent colonies. If natives like the Delawares suffered dispossession at the hands of self-interested Iroquois and Pennsylvania leaders, so, too, did individual colonies run the risk of seeing vulnerable borderlands caught in the crossfire between rival natives. Moreover, subtle and not so subtle shifts in imperial power could compel Indian people to reassess their alliances and trading partnerships with nearby colonies.[38]

The moment of reckoning came when the governor of New France decided to occupy the upper Ohio Valley in the face of both Pennsylvania's traders and Virginia speculators calling themselves the Ohio Company. An anemic British response, coupled with the alienation of the Mohawk Iroquois that jeopardized the Covenant Chain, threatened to unravel alliances at a time when French moves were threatening to reignite imperial warfare. In a striking example of how, by 1755, Indian affairs and Indian power had become critical to the British in America, the home government moved to take Indian affairs away from individual colonies. In what proved to be a first, controversial, step in crown efforts to reign in colonial independence, William Johnson of New York, land baron and adoptive Mohawk, and Edmond Atkin, successful South Carolina Indian trader and negotiator, became superintendents for Indian affairs in 1756: Johnson responsible for the colonies north of Virginia, and Atkin, for Virginia, the Carolinas, and Georgia.[39]

War with France was now a reality, and Johnson and Atkin were expected to deliver Indian allies both to defend colonial borders and to carry the war to the enemy in the fashion of the Canadian French and their native allies. This would be a difficult challenge. In the first place, the superintendents represented merely another level in the already complex and contradictory system of Indian affairs in British America. Colonies were as reluctant to surrender local control over their relations with natives as they were to cede control of their defense to British military commanders. Especially in Pennsylvania, local politics and Indian affairs merged in ways that guaranteed continued provincial involvement in efforts to end the war with the Ohio Indians.

In the second place, success in recruiting native allies had to face the daunting obstacles of both colonial history and the present war. To gain allies, colonists and Britons would have to set aside long-standing assumptions about Indian "savagery" and the compelling urge to reduce natives to the status of subordinates within an imperial system. Even those who maintained close, amicable relations with particular Indian people—such as William Johnson, Conrad Weiser, Christian Frederick Post—never seriously imagined a world in which natives and colonists shared the continent as equals and where Iroquois or Cherokees could remain politically and culturally sovereign. Yet native societies living west of the Appalachians were determined to remain independent and would accept nothing less. The gulf between peoples was a wide one even before the war began; mistakes in negotiations could prove costly. In 1755, Ohio Indian leaders, hoping to help General Braddock drive the French from their land, made a point of asking that the British also leave when the campaign was over. Braddock's equivocal replies cost the British valuable assistance and cost the general his life.[40]

Open warfare only complicated British efforts to rally natives. Aside from the "massacres" of British troops at Forts Oswego and William Henry, the war unleashed a devastating wave of frontier attacks, most coming from the Ohio Valley. During the first three years of the war Penn's "peaceable kingdom" was especially hard hit, as well as settlements living in the exposed western counties of Virginia. Attacks were not as random as they appeared, and more colonists were taken captive than killed, but the wide-ranging attacks spread panic and a rising tide of Indian-hating as border settlers refused to distinguish between enemies, friends, and those natives who were simply caught in the war's crossfire. One ominous reflection of changing colonial attitudes was the scalp bounty.[41]

Cash bounties for the scalps of Indian enemies were nothing new, of course. Massachusetts had offered bounties during Metacom's War (King Philip's War) in 1675–1676. Taking a page from this colonial history, in 1755 Braddock also offered a cash bounty for enemy scalps. In the wake of his defeat, however, the practice quickly spread. By 1756 even Pennsylvania was offering bonuses for the scalps of enemy men, women, and children. Although meant to further stimulate reluctant colonists to become soldiers, the bounties only fueled Indian-hating and indiscriminate violence. By 1758 some provincials were enlisting just for the bounties and were not at all particular as to where they took the trophies. Moreover, colonial attitudes toward Indians sooner or later spread to British professional soldiers who augmented bayonets with tomahawks and scalping knives. Britain's Indian allies soon found that they needed passes and agreed-upon peace signals if they hoped to avoid falling victim to scalp hunters while attempting to meet colonial officials or work with the army. And, perhaps predictably, the indiscriminate, hate-driven response to border raids produced an equal reaction among native enemies. The time when intercultural relations were shaped by actions and a willingness or ability to conform to others' expectations was passing. Now, negotiable frontiers gave way to hard racial categories, "red" and "white"—where Delawares, Mohawks, or Cherokees became the feared and hated "other."[42]

*   *   *

Colonel John Forbes's arrival coincided with a massive increase in the British war effort in America. Something close to seventeen thousand regulars were now in the colonies; with provincial troops, the numbers were approaching forty thousand. The challenges involved in managing such an army were immense. The colonies presented British professionals with a theater of war unlike any they had previously encountered. There were settlements without the centuries of infrastructure and experience with warfare common in the Low Countries or Germany; armed forces separated from London by an ocean, not the English Channel; geography that more often hindered than helped advancing armies. Complicating the purely military issues of organization, supply, and movement was the character of British America. Colonies with their own particular histories, customs, and interests insisted on being treated as cobelligerents, not subordinate parts of an empire. Those colonies also guaranteed that any quest for a "British and Indian War" would be complicated. Native peoples living on the margins of British America would view any offers of alliance through the lens of a century or more of often testy, sometimes violent, relations with colonies, even as the sources of conflict began to include not just the age-old arguments over land and trade, but new, race-based hatreds and identities.

Any British commander leading provincial or regular troops, or any British general eager to attract native allies would necessarily find himself engaging in what amounted to coalition warfare. Coalition armies were certainly not new to British soldiers; virtually every war they had fought since 1689 saw redcoats fighting alongside Hanoverians, Hessians, Dutch, and Austrian soldiers. But the wars fought by Marlborough, or more recently by Forbes and Loudoun, engaged professional armies provided through treaty with sovereign governments and embracing the same set of military standards and ethics. Even then, misunderstandings, confusion, and mistakes were common. Coalition warfare in America was of another kind, involving jealously independent colonies and wary Indians, as well as regular forces frequently composed of untried soldiers. Any campaign into the Ohio Country, moreover, would be complicated by intercolonial squabbles, as well as political battles within provinces, intertribal hostilities, and two separate wars, one involving the French and their Great Lakes native allies and the other pitting Ohio Indians against colonists. An army commander facing these realities would find himself coping with multiple "frictions" of war: the enemy, to be sure, but also the land, weather, colonial subjects, alien peoples with their own agendas, and the character of his own army. It would not be easy; certainly not like contemporary war in Europe.

ONE

New York and Philadelphia

* * *

WINTER–SPRING 1758

I shall lose no time in getting everything in readiness to move forward.

—FORBES TO PITT, MAY 1758

The letters went out on December 30, 1757. One went to Lord Loudoun informing him he was relieved of command in America; another appointed General James Abercromby the new American commander in chief; circular letters to colonial governors outlined campaign plans and the number of troops each was expected to raise. Others were directed to the Admiralty, the Treasury, and the Board of Ordnance. William Pitt, secretary of state for the Southern Department, was about to begin his first military campaign as head of Britain's government.[1]

The military forces at Pitt's disposal in 1758 were impressive. Indeed, Britain had never supported so many troops and ships so far from home. In North America, the all-regular army to be led by General Jeffery Amherst against Louisbourg numbered 14,215; at Albany, Abercromby was assembling an Anglo-American force of 6,884 regulars and anticipated another 17,680 provincials—roughly half that number would accompany him to Fort Carillon (Ticonderoga). Regulars assigned the job of retaking the Ohio Country numbered 1,854 along with 5,000 provincials. Add to this the garrison in Nova Scotia and the total came to over 47,000 men. On the other side of the Atlantic, Pitt was preparing amphibious raids against Rochefort and St. Malo in France that would occupy another 17,000–20,000 regular troops. In addition to these land forces, the Royal Navy committed 43 warships and nearly 15,000 men and well over 100 transports and supply vessels to the

Fig. 1.1 General James Abercromby, c. 1756, by Allan Ramsay. (Courtesy Fort Ligonier Association.) Appointed to replace Loudoun, and charged with taking French Fort Carillon at Ticonderoga, Abercromby wasted his regulars in a frontal assault that failed. His redeeming act was to order Colonel John Bradstreet to attack Fort Frontenac. In doing so he greatly aided Forbes's efforts to take Fort Duquesne.

Louisbourg operation while keeping others on station along the North American coast, the Caribbean, and the Gulf of St. Lawrence. The assaults on the French coast would require nearly three dozen more warships and additional transports. In 1755, Parliament voted a little more than £285,000 for all of Britain's overseas land forces, including the Braddock expedition; by 1758, the supplies voted for overseas land forces had grown to nearly £670,000.[2]

Although the force directed against Fort Duquesne was the smallest of the British armies in America, the French occupation of the Ohio Country had been on the minds of British and colonial leaders since the Braddock catastrophe. The most compelling issue was the wave of enemy attacks threatening Virginia, Pennsylvania, and Maryland. Although Shawnees had begun raiding Virginia in 1754, the real onslaught began in the autumn of 1755 when western Delawares launched their own war against the colonies with raids against Cumberland County, Pennsylvania. Caught by surprise and wholly unprepared for the assaults that followed, Virginians and Pennsylvanians saw their western borders rolled back; by 1757, Carlisle and Shippensburg were now the outer edge of settlement in Pennsylvania, the new town of Winchester stood alone in the lower Shenandoah Valley, while Maryland forces clung to Forts Cumberland and Frederick. With scores of settlers either dead or captured, panicked neighbors fled east, leaving behind a large swath of territory from Shamokin through the Shenandoah Valley that was a wasteland, a "vast Tract of Territory," now a "howling wilderness" populated only by the "blackened ruins of houses and barns."[3]

Frontier settlements quickly collapsed into a Hobbesian world of what has been called "soul-wrenching, family-destroying chaos," Indian hating, and political unrest as victims turned their anger on the seemingly unresponsive provincial governments. Responses were certainly feeble enough. The Virginia Regiment under Colonel George Washington clung to a line of forts past which raiding parties moved with impunity. Pennsylvania adopted the same strategy, but that colony did manage to mount an attempt to carry the war to the enemy in Colonel John Armstrong's raid against the Delaware town of Kittanning in September 1756. Although the raid had some immediate impact on the enemy, it was never repeated, despite Pennsylvania's declaration of war against the Ohio Indians and the passage of a scalp bounty to encourage enlistments. In the meantime, as French and Indian attacks continued, the military potential of Virginia and Pennsylvania would be tied up in local defense, and their ability to contribute to Pitt's plans was severely limited. Such realities made it a certainty that Fort Duquesne would be high on Pitt's list of objectives. In addition, there was the army's morale to consider: Braddock's defeat simply had to be avenged.[4]

* * *

While such matters were being considered in Whitehall, Forbes, when Pitt's instructions arrived, was occupied with routines of army management. Winter was the season when premodern armies went into quarters and began the process of rebuilding for the next campaign; North America was no exception. Forbes found himself largely consumed with maintaining the dis-

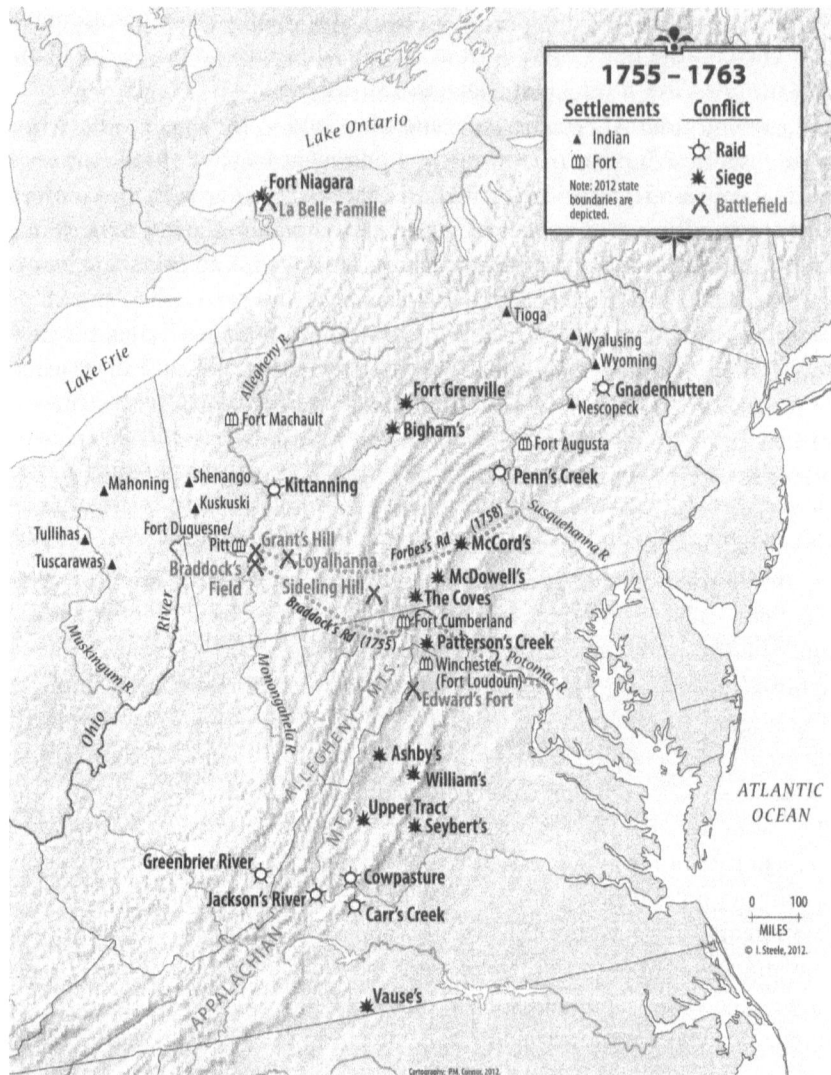

Fig. 1.2 "Map of Allegheny Country, 1755–1763." Steele, *Setting All the Captives Free*, 75. Ian Steele. Montreal: MQUP, 2013.

cipline and well-being of nearly twenty thousand regulars stationed from Halifax, Nova Scotia, to Charles Town, South Carolina, in regiments that required food, shelter, supplies, and replacements. It was a tedious job, one marked by much paperwork and very little else. Ominously, as Forbes worked, he began to mention symptoms of the illnesses that would plague him throughout the coming year. Calling his condition "really no joke," the fifty-one-year-old complained of swelling in both legs and blistered feet that kept him housebound through much of the holiday season.[5]

Forbes learned of his new command in early March 1758. Two weeks later he wrote to the governor of Maryland, announcing that Abercromby had "appointed me to the Command of the King's Regular Forces and provincial Troops" for the coming campaign "to the Southard." More specifically, Forbes would hold the rank of brigadier general in America: a local rank that allowed him to exercise an independent command. In this he was one of a group of young officers including Jeffery Amherst, George Augustus, Viscount Howe, and James Wolfe, who were promoted ahead of senior commanders deemed too hidebound or of limited talent. And, like his peers, Forbes enjoyed the patronage of Field Marshall Sir John Ligonier who, since Cumberland's disgrace, had taken on the role—if not the title—of commander in chief of Britain's land forces and Pitt's principal military advisor. Forbes had served as one of Ligonier's staff officers in the last war and had clearly left a strong impression. In a letter regarding the departure of troops for America in 1757, Ligonier told Loudoun: "I wish you joy of John Forbes." Forbes also served the duke of Cumberland both in Flanders and Scotland in 1745–1746 while holding rank in the 2d Dragoons, which he had first joined in 1735. By 1750 he was lieutenant colonel of his regiment and received the king's approval for promotion to colonel of the 17th Foot just prior to his departure for America.[6]

In his service prior to 1758, then, Forbes followed the trajectory of emerging professional British officers marked by long service, broad experience, and a self-taught grasp of regimental and army affairs. Forbes and others like him marked an important transition between an army led by officers whose military service was merely a step in a larger political or economic life and men who made the military a career and slowly professionalized both the officer corps and the army as a whole. They were men whose skills and experiences were highly valued by George II and by Cumberland, who both devoted much effort to raising the quality of the army.[7]

Forbes arrived in Philadelphia within six weeks of receiving his command. He hoped for an early start; as soon as sufficient grass appeared to support the horses, he would begin his march west. Speed was important; by getting to the Ohio in mid- to late summer, Forbes would be able to move beyond Fort Duquesne, perhaps even threatening Fort Niagara, France's link to the western interior. The year's campaign was to be a coordinated effort. With Abercromby threatening Montreal and Amherst besieging Louisbourg, the French would be hard-pressed to send substantial reinforcements to the Ohio Country, making Forbes's task that much easier. However, speed would elude him, and time would become one of his worst enemies. So, too, would decisions made by superiors and provincial governments. Forbes's first problem surfaced even before he set out for Philadelphia for, as yet, he had no army.

According to the plan of campaign, Forbes would lead an army of nearly seven thousand men, and a yet undetermined number of civilian employees and dependents. The core of this army would be four companies of the first battalion of the Royal Americans and thirteen companies of Highlanders, ten of which belonged to Lieutenant-Colonel Archibald Montgomery's 77th Foot. Together they were supposed to provide just over eighteen hundred trained men. Forbes never thought he had enough regulars, and the ones he led were mostly untested. At one point in mid-June, Forbes expressed the hope that Amherst had already taken Louisbourg and that "he will send us back a few regulars," telling Abercromby, "I have not so many as to keep my irregulars in due decency and order." Those "irregulars" consisted of the Pennsylvania regiment, Washington's veteran 1st Virginia regiment, and William Byrd's new 2d Virginia regiment, and several companies from Maryland and North Carolina together amounting to five thousand men—on paper.[8]

The number of troops allocated for the campaign meant that Forbes's army, unlike those gathering to the north, was largely colonial in composition. This unusual arrangement meant that Forbes would have to rely even more on his small force of regulars to set the standards of discipline and the proper management of troops in the field. Moreover, these redcoats (only one-quarter of his army) would be expected to shoulder the most dangerous and exacting work of the campaign: facing the French in battle and conducting a successful siege. In addition, William Pitt's announcement that henceforth "all Officers of the Provincial Forces . . . are to have Rank according to their respective Commissions," although welcome news to colonial field officers who had chaffed under the old orders that ranked them no higher than regular captains, created further challenges as Forbes attempted to organize his army. Now he would have to carefully consider the abilities of men such as Colonels Byrd and Washington as well as James Burd, and John Armstrong of Pennsylvania who would be in a position to issue commands to any regular officers below them in rank. Friction between testy professionals and equally rank-conscious provincials was a real possibility. It placed Forbes in the uncomfortable position of having to negotiate between his own subordinates in ways that neither Amherst nor Abercromby had to consider.[9]

For the moment, however, issues of rank could be pushed aside as Forbes grappled with a more immediate problem: he did not yet have an army to command. When Forbes reached Philadelphia, provincial legislatures were locked in debate about how to raise troops and how to fund them. Worse, his precious regulars were scattered along the coast from Charles Town to New York and out in the Atlantic. Forbes arrived on April 18, 1758; the first of his troops turned up within a week—three sickly companies of Highlanders, worn out by their trip from Glasgow to Philadelphia. These troops, referred to as "additional companies," were raised from the overflow of recruits for the two new Highland regiments. Nine companies all together, they were to be attached, three each, to the 42d, 77th, and 78th Foot as part of the general reinforcement sent to America for 1758. These additional companies seem not to have been of very high quality; one officer found the companies assigned to the 78th Foot "not so good bodys of men" and concluded that "most of the men of these 3 companies are really by no means fit for immediate service."[10]

Nearly a month later four companies of the 1/60th Foot arrived. Their odyssey had begun a year earlier when they and their commander, Lieutenant-Colonel Henry Bouquet, were sent to South Carolina in anticipation of French attacks there. After months of relative inactivity in the malarial lowlands of Carolina, Bouquet received orders to take his troops by sea to New York. Upon arrival, he was told by Abercromby that he would serve as Forbes's second in command and to march his men overland to Philadelphia.[11]

When he departed South Carolina, Bouquet also left Lieutenant-Colonel Archibald Montgomery's 77th Foot behind. They, too, were to join Forbes, but delays in hiring ships and the unpredictable weather meant that by the time Bouquet got to Philadelphia the Highlanders had still not sailed. Still worse, the ship dispatched from England by the Ordnance Board carrying Forbes's artillerymen and the train of guns, ammunition, and additional small arms was still unaccounted for. By late May, Forbes, Bouquet, and a handful of staff officers had only seven under-strength companies of regulars, hastily raised Pennsylvania troops still gathering, no artillery, no engineers, and a campaign season that threatened to slip by before an army could be properly assembled.[12]

Neither Bouquet's Royal Americans nor Montgomery's Highlanders would begin the campaign at full strength or in good health. Both suffered from what southerners casually called "seasoning," the inevitable sickness and death that occurred when Europeans first arrived in a region rife with humidity, poor water, and tropical diseases. Bouquet told South Carolina's governor in February that his officers were facing "great difficulties to repair the losses occasion'd by death and desertion." Three months later Forbes reported to Pitt that the Royal Americans "are very Sickly, Coming from Carolina." He did not dare send them beyond Philadelphia until they were given several days to recover from hard travel and lingering illness. Indeed, by the time they arrived at Philadelphia, Bouquet's four companies totaled only 339 enlisted men: at full strength they would have numbered 400.[13]

The story was much the same with the Highlanders. They were "all very robust" upon arrival at Charles Town in early September, 1757, though "quite raw men" with little training; the author of a drill manual aimed at Highland troops warned about panic among men who "never saw a Cat killed in their Lives." Disease, unseasonably cold weather, and the effects of a long ocean voyage quickly thinned their ranks. Within a month of their arrival, fully half of the battalion was sick, and 60 would die over the winter. Montgomery's had arrived over-strength, with 113 "supernumeraries" carried along as replacements; by the time the battalion reached Philadelphia most of these men were either dead or invalids. Only the three "additional" companies, with "one third sick" and the rest still recovering from weeks aboard transports, would bring Montgomery's near to full strength. By March, 1758, the Highland officers were anxious to move north, fearing that the return of hot weather would decimate their troops. As it was, they were delayed in sailing to Philadelphia; still embarking in late April, they did not reach Forbes until June 9, 1758.[14]

Some losses were, of course, inevitable. What concerned Bouquet, Forbes, and Montgomery was that matters were made worse by South Carolina's disappointing attempts to provide adequate quarters. Although Bouquet reported that he "met with the same difficulty as in Philadelphia" in his effort to get quarters, he quickly added that Carolinians did not show the same "unwillingness." In fact, the colony was simply overwhelmed in its effort to secure housing, firewood, and other barrack stores for nearly two thousand new arrivals. This said, Bouquet still had to petition provincial officials, reminding them that the troops were in Charles Town "for no other Purpose but the defence of this Province," while asking that food shipped to the regulars continue to be unloaded duty-free in order to spare the contractors the added cost. Loudoun also got involved, accusing Carolinians of foot-dragging and vowing to seize whatever quarters were required. By the time Loudoun's threats reached the colony, barracks were being erected for both soldiers and officers. Yet, it was too little and too late to save scores of men who died or whose health gave out altogether. By February 1758, the officers (and doubtless the enlisted men) "begin to despair to go back to Pensilvania" even though about two-thirds of the men were now in proper barracks.[15]

While Bouquet's troops were anxious to be away from South Carolina, Forbes was wrestling with colonial Britons in Pennsylvania, Maryland, and

Virginia. Within days of arriving in Philadelphia, the general sent what he thought was a routine demand that Pennsylvania's Governor Denny turn over several hundred muskets in the colony's possession, citing the "great Scarcity of Arms," and noting that the province would still have weapons enough to equip its own troops for the campaign. Just one day later, Forbes wrote again, this time to express his disappointment that "any just request of mine to you" should "met [sic] with obstructions," reminding the governor that he was refusing "what is the Undoubted Right of the King to demand." This may have been the issue that prompted a letter from the provincial secretary Richard Peters to Forbes. Denny learned of the letter and deeply resented what Peters referred to as Denny's "disrespectful behavior" and the hint that he was not fully committed to supporting the campaign. Denny, like Forbes, was a professional soldier, and he was not inclined to accept anything impugning his character. This dustup over a few hundred weapons was a pointed reminder that dealing with colonists would not be easy and could involve personalities as well as politics.[16]

Before the war, Pennsylvania had no militia, and no military tradition of any kind; its only foray into colonial defense was Benjamin Franklin's Association—volunteers who provided their own weapons, and whose officers' commissions came from the governor, not from the Quaker-led Assembly. Raised in 1747, the Association quickly went out of business the following year. By 1758, however, the government had managed to raise, pay, and equip a force of long-service troops. These were provincials whose numbers and organization continued to fluctuate since troops were first raised in 1755. The colony also moved away from short-term enlistments to terms of at least three years. This offered some stability and meant that Forbes would find at least a small number of experienced officers and men in the regiment.

What became, the Pennsylvania Regiment in 1758, was the result of partisan politics and the rising anger of western farmers who demanded protection from raiding parties and who threatened the government. One issue was the long history of Quaker political dominance in the colony and with it a refusal to take up arms as a matter of principle. The local politics of faith had been a part of Pennsylvania's experience since its founding when settlers and William Penn collided early and often over political power and exactly how the "Peaceable Kingdom" should develop. With Penn's death, a new issue surfaced in the form of the huge land grants owned by his sons, the current Proprietors. The Penns consistently refused to approve any laws that allowed their estates to be taxed; the Assembly was loath to approve public funds unless the Proprietors paid their share. And, with the sudden, unanticipated Indian war many Quakers were inclined to point the finger at the

Penns and their generation-long effort to separate local Delaware people from their land.¹⁷

Open warfare, frontier defense, and British commanders' demands for provincial money and manpower ultimately fractured the Quaker political bloc, with most Quakers stepping away from government by 1756 rather than compromise their principles. This had two important consequences for Forbes and his campaign. First, the Assembly and governor could act without the threat of internal bickering and deadlock. Yet, money—and the Penns—continued to be a problem. Having spent thousands of pounds on defense already, the Assembly feared that "we have not Money to Recruit" without taxing the Proprietors. Second, "weighty Friends" (influential Quakers) led by Israel Pemberton turned their attention to the Indian war. They were particularly interested in the Penns' land dealings and treaties with Delawares and Iroquois and were determined to set things right and end a war nobody wanted. In the end, Forbes would be the beneficiary of both what the Friends refused to do and what they did accomplish.¹⁸

Despite a slow start, by early 1758, the colony had built and manned a line of forts east of the Susquehanna River, and had established a permanent force of provincial troops. Moreover, Armstrong's raid against Kittanning in the autumn of 1756, though of limited value, was the one time that troops from any of the "middle colonies" managed to carry the war to the enemy. In response to Pitt's call for troops, the colony was prepared to augment its standing force substantially, by adding some seventeen hundred "New Levies" to the existing regiment of roughly one thousand men. These new men agreed to serve only until the end of the year. Local recruiting officers told the men they would serve until "Winter Quarters." Prospective enlistees, however, insisted that "it should be a certain number of Months," finally agreeing to serve through December. Among these troops, moreover, was a unique military unit that arguably allowed Forbes to get his army started in a timely fashion. "Obliged to scrape together some guns" to fill the void left by the absence of the Royal Artillery, Forbes asked that the Pennsylvania Regiment identify anyone with experience with or interest in field artillery. The result was a provincial "train" led by Ensign Martin Heydeler (Heideler) and sixty men from his second battalion of the regiment. Equipped with guns belonging to the colony, Heydeler's men were ready to march from Lancaster in late May 1758, with "the two 6-pounders with all their train," ensuring that the army's advance had at least a modicum of artillery protection.¹⁹

Maryland's contribution to the campaign posed equally thorny problems. The colony had voted men to defend the frontier as early as 1755. By early

1758, however, this effort was in total disarray, thanks to localism and a power struggle between the lower and upper houses of the Assembly. Maryland troops were initially raised to occupy Fort Cumberland on the upper Potomac River. Issues of command and insistence that Maryland troops defend only what was indisputably Maryland soil, led to building Fort Frederick, sixty-odd miles east of Cumberland. The Assembly throughout 1756–1757 also cut the number of troops from an initial three hundred to barely half that and threatened to disband them altogether. Frugality was one issue; another was insistence in the lower house that Maryland raise and spend no money for defense until or unless its neighbors, Virginia and Pennsylvania did likewise. Stalemate was the result, with the lower house passing defense bills that the upper house refused to accept, while the governor, Horatio Sharpe, held out for results that would be in line with the king's interests, blaming proprietary government for much of the problem. Caught in the middle were Captain John Dagworthy and four companies of Maryland provincials who, by late 1757, were without pay and provisions. The earl of Loudoun, desperate to keep Fort Cumberland secure, privately suggested to Sharpe that, if his Assembly did not fund the troops, Loudoun would take them into British pay.[20]

This was the situation that Forbes encountered when he turned his attention to the colony and its troops in March 1758. The Assembly would not even meet until April, and although Sharpe pledged to do what he could to get the money, he warned Abercromby that his legislators were not inclined to support a garrison at Fort Cumberland, where the troops were threatening to go home if they were not regularly paid and supplied. By early May things remained at a standstill. A clearly frustrated Sir John St. Clair, now Forbes's quartermaster general, begged, "For God's sake tell me what I am to do," since he could see nothing but "a deal of Vexation" in trying to support the Maryland troops. Faced with the Assembly's refusal to vote funds, all Sharpe could do was blame the proprietary government for making it impossible for "Money for His Majesty's Service" to be raised as readily as in other colonies.[21]

As the ordeal dragged on, Forbes lost his temper. He wrote St. Clair: "I really think that province [Maryland] ought to be treated as Enemys, and not friends." He suggested that impressing Maryland wagons—and ordering the Assembly to pay for them—would only be the right thing to do. Forbes wanted Dagworthy's men with his army. Yes, there were at best only three hundred of them, but "they have been used to the Woods and the Indian Manner of fighting." Given how few of his troops could boast such experience, Forbes was not about to allow the Marylanders to disband. He also urged Dagworthy to hang on, assuring him that his men would be paid (by whom and when Forbes did not say) and told him that as a reward, Abercromby was prepared to offer Dagworthy a captaincy in the Royal Americans. The best Abercromby could offer Forbes was the suggestion that he take them into regular service as "rangers." By late June, Forbes broke the impasse and agreed to abide by Loudoun's original promise and pay the Marylanders out of his contingency funds, while hoping that his superiors, including Pitt, would understand.[22]

While Forbes endured the prolonged confusion and frustration that was Maryland politics, Virginia was busy doubling the size of its forces. Like Pennsylvania, it tried to do this quickly by offering short enlistments; like the Pennsylvania New Levies, the new Virginia Regiment would serve only until 1 December—time enough, everyone thought, for the campaign to run its course. Washington's veterans in the frontier forts now became the 1st Virginia, and William Byrd III's regiment became the 2d Virginia. On paper they would add two thousand men to Forbes's army, half of whom had been in service for at least two years and could be considered seasoned troops. Raising new troops was made easier by Pitt's promise of Parliamentary reimbursement; the colony immediately raised the enlistment bounty and rapidly filled up the 2d Regiment. Virginia was between governors; Robert Dinwiddie had left the colony and his replacement, Sir Francis Fauquier, would not arrive until summer. The president of the governor's council, John Blair, served as acting governor, or president, tackling the myriad issues arising from recruiting and fielding Virginia's enlarged army. In the rush to complete Byrd's new regiment, officials discovered that there were not enough uniforms for them all. Byrd solved the problem by deciding to dress his men "after the Indian Fashion" and asked for blankets and match-coats. In mid-June a privateer turned up with a load of French uniforms taken from a prize ship. These blue-and-yellow coats were turned over to Byrd's men who, if they wore them at all, would have turned them inside out while on work duties, as was customary in the army.[23]

The campaign plans made in London also called for North Carolina provincials to join the army. Forbes, however, quickly discounted any aid, telling Pitt that "there is nothing expected from the Carolinas." Nevertheless, Forbes learned that Governor Arthur Dobbs had indeed raised three hundred men and was sending them to the army by land and sea. By the time they began to turn up at the end of June, the three companies under Major Hugh Waddell were in no condition to be of much use. By mid-July two companies mustered only 151 men between them, including those who were sick. When St. Clair encountered them, he simply dismissed them as "an Army in the

Clouds" and "good for nothing." They arrived short of everything: weapons, clothing, and camp equipment. Bouquet reported they "are in pitiable condition, and lack health, uniforms and everything." Perhaps worse, the new arrivals brought a letter from Dobbs telling Forbes that his colony had no means to pay these troops, asking Forbes to use his "credit" to pay them until Parliament's funds arrived, otherwise the companies would disband.[24]

*   *   *

While Forbes was struggling to gather his army, he was also mustering his own staff—his "family" in eighteenth-century military terms. Like much else about the British army, a field army's administrative staff was an ad hoc affair. In most cases it appears that Forbes had a role—if not the final say—in these appointments. This was certainly the case with his brigade major, Major Francis Halkett of the 44th Foot. Forbes may have known him through his father, the late Colonel Sir Peter Halkett, from whom Forbes once solicited help in getting a commission for his brother. Evidently the initial encounters between Major Halkett and Forbes did not go well with the latter complaining to Abercromby that he could not get any clear insight from Halkett regarding orders from Loudoun. In fact, he warned Loudoun, "I am therefore affraid, you will have a bungled work unless better explained to him." When asking that Halkett be assigned to him as a secretary, he told Abercrombie: "you well know that . . . Halkett although honest & willing is rather slow." Yet, Halkett evidently proved himself; six months later Forbes said that "Frank Halkett, alone . . . is the most diligent." Halkett did indeed prove his worth many times over. He was Forbes's adjutant, private secretary, sounding board, and the one man the general came to rely upon as his health continued to deteriorate. Much of Forbes's correspondence and many of his orders were written by Halkett who also continued to look after his commander's fragile health.[25]

Forbes also secured the services of Doctor William Russell, a surgeon from the army's general hospital in New York. Russell's official role was as Forbes's medical director: the head of the "flying hospital" created to support the army and its regimental surgeons. How much Russell looked after Forbes's personal health is unclear since the general also relied on the services of Lieutenant James Grant of the 77th Foot as a personal physician. He also asked for, and received, the services of Sergeant Morton of the 48th Foot; Morton remains otherwise anonymous, though he may have been responsible for Forbes's baggage and transportation, since Forbes mentioned that "they say he or some such is absolutely necessary for the Roads, etc." Forbes also asked for "either a Secretary or a Clerk," and Morton may have done this work as well. These few men were Forbes's inner circle: men with whom he spoke and interacted on a daily basis.[26]

Beyond this group, Forbes relied on other staff officers. Captain Harry Gordon, 44th Foot, was Forbes's chief engineer: Bouquet referred to him as "the 1st Engineer" of Forbes's army. In that capacity he would plan and direct the works undertaken by the army, principally road and fort building along the line of march. In addition, Gordon would be responsible for the army's siege operations once it reached Fort Duquesne. Gordon was a seasoned engineer; he appears to have trained as an engineer and served in Flanders during the previous war. In 1751 he was engaged in road building in the Scottish Highlands and prepared a map of the road system for the Board of Ordnance. By 1755 he was a "sub-engineer" and held equivalent rank as a lieutenant in the 44th when it accompanied Braddock to America where he laid out that army's route of march. He was, in 1758, one of perhaps a dozen engineer officers serving in America. These men, under command of the Board of Ordnance, were part of a small corps of officers—the only engineering force in the British army. Indeed, one of Gordon's main responsibilities would be to organize the gangs of soldiers drawn from their regiments to undertake necessary construction tasks. It is unclear whether Forbes asked for him specifically; Abercromby refers to "Mr. Gordon, The Engineer under your Department," suggesting that perhaps the assignment came from army headquarters. By late February, 1758, Forbes was asking that Gordon be sent to New York and, two months later, wanted Gordon "with any other engineers that are to Serve under him" be sent to Philadelphia "as there is plenty of business for them."[27]

Captain Lieutenant David Hay would direct Forbes's artillery once it arrived. Hay was already in America in the spring of 1758; he had arrived the previous year as part of the reinforcements for Loudoun's abortive Louisbourg expedition. Like Gordon, he was a veteran. As a second lieutenant he had taken part in the defense of Fort St. Philip on Minorca in 1756. In an undated letter to Forbes in 1758, the engineer Matthew Clerk recommended Hay to command "your detachment of Artillery," saying that he was the most capable officer for such an assignment. By May 25, Hay was in Philadelphia awaiting the tardy ordnance vessel so that he could organize his train. He seems to have brought some men with him from New York, perhaps including a Dr. McLean (McCleane), the surgeon appointed to the train. When everything finally arrived, Hay would command a force of roughly one hundred men, regulars, Pennsylvanians, soldiers, and civilian employees. Gordon and Hay were true professionals in the modern sense of the word. Trained at the Woolwich Arsenal, they were masters of engineering and gunnery while the other officers in the army accumulated professional expertise through learning on the job. The real test of Gordon, Hay, and the men they led would come if and when the army attempted to attack Fort Duquesne.[28]

Making certain that the army did arrive at its objective was the responsibility of two men who were not with Forbes on a daily basis but who nonetheless were vital to his success: Lieutenant-Colonel Henry Bouquet and Lieutenant-Colonel Sir John St. Clair, Forbes's second in command and quartermaster general. These three men would need to work together if the campaign was to succeed. And, as Forbes's health continued to deteriorate, the burdens of command would fall more heavily on these two senior subordinates, especially Bouquet.

Bouquet's appointment as Forbes's second in command underscored his already favorable reputation among officers in America. Aside from raising the first battalion of the Royal American Regiment, Bouquet was given command of troops in South Carolina. Months spent in Charles Town put him in touch with Virginia soldiers, such as Major Andrew Lewis, and tested his abilities to organize and manage a force that consisted of largely untried troops, a mix of provincials and regulars, including Montgomery's new regiment of Highlanders, while acting as a diplomat of sorts in his dealing with colonial officials and civilians. Although a thoroughly professional soldier of long service in Swiss regiments in the Sardinian and Dutch armies, Bouquet, like his British counterparts, faced a steep learning curve when it came to service in America.[29]

Bouquet's successful American experiences before 1758 provided additional vindication for the crown's experiment of enlarging its American forces by inviting foreign Protestant officers to accept commissions in the new Royal American Regiment. Bouquet was one of many such men—Swiss, Germans, and French Huguenots—who accepted the offer, hoping to make their reputations and careers in British service. Yet Bouquet and others also found that accepting British commissions also carried risks and potential problems. In the first place, the king gave commissions without purchase to these volunteers, and what the king gave, no man could subsequently sell. Not only were these men placed "in the only regiment where we can serve," Bouquet and others like him could hope for promotions only within their regiment, and since they could never sell their commissions they could not enjoy the financial benefits that came with "selling out" and retiring with a substantial sum of money. At the same time, the sudden influx of so many continental officers raised resentment among their new British comrades. In a long, plaintive, almost cloying, letter to Sir John St. Clair, Bouquet com-

Fig. 1.3 Colonel Henry Bouquet, c. 1758–1759, attributed to John Wollaston. (Courtesy of the Philadelphia History Museum at the Atwater Kent/ Bridgeman Images.) The consummate professional soldier, Bouquet assumed much of the day-to-day management of the army, earning Forbes's trust despite his role in Grant's defeat outside Fort Duquesne.

plained about how British officers frequently found fault with the foreigners, asking him if "a foreigner deserve[s] some indulgence, if in so short a time he could not become acquainted with all your customs and unwritten rules?" More generally, Bouquet and others like him felt profoundly vulnerable, both socially and professionally. As a result, these foreign officers spent a good deal of time cultivating British officers, such as St. Clair, who might advocate for them, and, looking beyond the army to well-connected civilians or colonial economic opportunities. For example, Bouquet made a point of telling Provincial Secretary Richard Peters that he looked upon Pennsylvania "as my Mother Country in America, and feel myself still prejudiced in its favor," this while aggressively pursuing investments in South Carolina rice plantations.[30]

Bouquet received his orders to serve with Forbes shortly after he arrived in New York from Charles Town with his Royal Americans. It is unlikely that the two men had met; Bouquet was in South Carolina for much of 1757, and by the time he reached New York, Forbes was already in Philadelphia. They certainly knew of each other. Loudoun's orders to Bouquet were transmitted by Forbes, and each may have learned something of the other through mutual acquaintances or from army news and gossip. As he had with St. Clair, Bouquet assumed a properly subordinate tone when writing Forbes: "I congratulate myself very much, Sir, to have the honour of serving under your command," assuring Forbes that "no assignment could have been more agreeable." Their professional relationship seems to have blossomed quickly. As early as June, when the army was just beginning its long trek west under Bouquet's direction, Forbes told him that he and the public "are obliged to you" for carrying out duties that were both "troublesome and disagreeable." By August, Forbes had come to rely ever more heavily on Bouquet's judgment and experience. Bemoaning his recurring illnesses, Forbes nonetheless said: "I dare say my presence is no ways necessary where you have the Command." Yet on one very important occasion, Bouquet's decisions would deeply disturb Forbes and threaten the campaign.[31]

While Forbes enjoyed a cordial, even close, association with his second in command, the same cannot be said of his relationship with his quartermaster, Sir John St. Clair. Forbes knew him and seems to have regretted St. Clair's appointment from the outset. The choice of quartermaster general for Forbes's army lay with Abercromby who initially thought of Lieutenant-Colonel John Bradstreet who had made a name for himself as creator of a boat service that kept British posts supplied west of Albany. Abercromby, set to lead an amphibious campaign along the Champlain corridor, decided to keep Bradstreet and his unique skills for himself. His subsequent choice of St. Clair was based on that officer's American experience since 1755. During the Braddock campaign St. Clair traveled widely through Pennsylvania, Maryland, Virginia, as well as the backcountry. Moreover, his travels were only one indication of how seriously he took his work; almost from the moment he landed in Virginia he began collecting maps and intelligence on the Ohio Country, working tirelessly to organize and equip provincial troops, collecting wagons and livestock, and planning the army's march. Braddock called

Fig. 1.4 Sir John St. Clair, 1758, miniature by John Singleton Copley. (© The Metropolitan Museum of Art.) A veteran of the Braddock campaign, St. Clair boasted experience and expertise on matters involving the raising of troops and supplies. His abrasive personality and failures to properly manage the army's vast supply system—both aggravated by persistent illnesses—placed additional burdens on both Forbes and Bouquet.

him "indefatigable," saying that St. Clair had done "all that could possibly be expected," sentiments echoed by Virginia's governor Robert Dinwiddie.[32]

Indefatigable, yes, but also abrasive and impetuous. Where Bouquet was correct, deferential, even diffident, Sir John took a much more direct approach to people; he did not suffer civilians—especially provincial politicians—lightly. In one notable episode in 1755, he confronted Pennsylvania commissioners regarding the military road they were to build. It was now April, and he angrily reminded them he had requested that the road be started in January. So upset that he refused to listen to any explanations, St. Clair, according to the civilians, "treated us in a very disagreeable manner," while he "stormed like a Lion rampant." Insisting on the primacy of military needs over civilian excuses, he then threatened to march troops into Pennsylvania and compel civilians to work at sword point if necessary. Three years later, President Blair of Virginia found himself the object of St. Clair's wrath. Upon learning that Blair would not be attending a meeting at Winchester, Sir John dressed him down in a letter, accusing Blair of wasting his time and reminding him that Forbes expected affairs regarding Virginia's troops to be dealt with quickly. Adding insult to injury, he further reminded Blair that Pennsylvania had already settled issues of subsistence, pay, and equipment for its men.[33]

This same impetuosity carried over to his dealing with fellow officers. At a council of war held shortly before the disastrous battle on the Monongahela, St. Clair urged that Braddock's "flying column" halt and await the arrival of the rest of the army slowly struggling with the heavy baggage and guns. Although he "strongly" advised doing this, his fellow officers quickly rejected the idea "with great indignation." Yet, in the aftermath of Braddock's defeat, in which St. Clair was badly wounded, the quartermaster general continued to urge a new advance while there was still time, arguing the "moral certainty" of success; this too, was ignored as the remnants of Braddock's army made haste to put distance between themselves and the French.[34]

Complicating St. Clair's personality and behavior was the state of his health. He was already suffering from kidney problems, including the "gravel," or painful kidney stones. The chest wound he received on the Monongahela—the bullet remained lodged under the skin—would have done nothing to ease his condition. By early 1757, St. Clair was beset by "many complaints" and told Loudoun that *"he found he must die."* The general, in turn, reported to London that "violent Fits of the Gravel" led to "Nervous Complaints" that had left St. Clair's health "totally broke." In April he was diagnosed with ulcerous kidneys that, by the end of the year, were "supperating"; in his doctor's opinion "if he recovers" he should go home. Instead, St. Clair took on the job as quartermaster general to Forbes's army. It would be a formidable challenge, even for a veteran. Abercromby's instructions were comprehensive. St. Clair was responsible for everything from the state of the roads and setting up a chain of couriers to mustering newly raised provincials and maintaining adequate stocks of provisions and forage. He was required to travel from New York to Philadelphia, Annapolis, Winchester, and points in between. He seems to have relished the chance to get into the field once more. He was certainly back in form; by June, Forbes was complaining that, added to poor wagons and roads, he had to cope with a "cross hot headed Madman" who almost "disobliged the whole Virginians with their new Governor in to the bargain."[35]

Whether a result of his poor health or a natural inclination, St. Clair also seems to have had a vindictive streak. He revealed this in the course of a dispute with Lieutenant-Colonel Adam Stephen of the Virginia Regiment. The two had served together with Braddock, and by the autumn of 1755 they were at odds over a report from St. Clair to Governor Dinwiddie regarding an alleged breach of military discipline by Stephen stemming from a dispute over rank and authority between Stephen and Captain Dagworthy at Fort Cumberland. An already angry Stephen then learned that St. Clair had complained to Dinwiddie; Stephen wanted to talk with St. Clair directly. By this time in Albany, St. Clair would only say that his complaints were rooted in what he had heard when he first arrived in America the previous winter; moreover, St. Clair was upset that Stephen had not followed his orders to discharge a Virginia soldier known to be Catholic. Hinting that Stephen's character was at issue, St. Clair then told him that if he had wanted to hurt Stephen he could have done so. This incident added yet another source of friction in the army; Stephen and St. Clair would have to work closely together during the campaign and each of them had a long memory.[36]

Bouquet, St. Clair, Halkett, Gordon, Hay; these men were Forbes's key subordinates, men who were expected to do much of the day-to-day planning and to make decisions that would both further their general's plans and keep the army moving, fed, and secure. More by accident than design, perhaps, Forbes took with him several veterans of Braddock's campaign who were familiar with the geography, the potential routes, and the enemy: St. Clair, Halkett, and Gordon. Both St. Clair and Gordon carried wounds from that earlier campaign. In addition, several of Forbes's field officers were also veteran campaigners. Washington had famously been one of Braddock's aides in 1755, and Adam Stephen had also been in the fight on the Monongahela. Colonel James Burd of Pennsylvania knew much about the region west of the Susquehanna thanks to his road building in 1755. Colonel John Armstrong had the distinction of actually taking the war to the enemy with his Kittanning raid in 1756. Montgomery, sometimes referred to as "Archie" by Forbes, was an old campaigner, as was Major James Grant of the 77th. Of the latter, Forbes said that his "parts as a Military man are inferior to few." When Grant was taken prisoner in a poorly planned and executed raid on Fort Duquesne, Forbes could only lament that "he was my only plight anchor and support."[37]

These, then, were the men who would help Forbes create an army where none existed, pulling together troops from western Virginia, the Carolinas, and the wider Atlantic world. Although several had the shared experience of battle in 1755, others, including William Byrd III and Hugh Mercer, were strangers and without military experience. Some of these men would prove troublesome during the course of the campaign, in part because of their own bullheadedness and selfishness.

* * *

The principal challenge facing Forbes and his staff was the fact that their "army" defied the term as understood by professional soldiers. Not only was it a potentially volatile mix of provincials and regulars, it was also a "young" army; its component units were newly raised and lacked the experience of campaigning in the field that marked a seasoned, professional force. The largest single unit, Montgomery's 77th Foot, had only been raised in early 1757; by late summer it was on its way to South Carolina and what turned out to be months of tedious garrison duty. Bouquet reported near the end of 1757 that "the Highland Battalion being a new Corps, & not yet formed, cannot be employed before the Month of February next." Bouquet's own Royal Americans had been raised beginning in late 1755, but had spent their time building fortifications at Carlisle, Pennsylvania, and shoring up the defenses of South Carolina while absorbing new recruits to offset losses to disease. Most of the provincials were also "young." Pennsylvania's regiment included hundreds of New Levies and even the veterans seldom had more than a year or two of largely inactive service behind them. Byrd's new Virginia regiment and the Carolinians were likewise new to the service. Perhaps the most seasoned troops were Washington's Virginians. Many officers and men were veterans by the spring of 1758 thanks to the three-year enlistment period mandated by the Burgesses. They and Dagworthy's Maryland companies were the most experienced force in the army, but even they had spent most of their time in static garrisons, occasionally chasing after raiding parties that had already done damage to border settlements.[38]

Fundamental to being "young" regiments and companies was the fact that they had not yet learned to operate as parts of large units. Bouquet hinted at this when he referred to the 77th as not yet "formed": it had yet to learn proper discipline, let alone tactics and camp routines. Ideally, this process would be undertaken in stages as soldiers learned to use weapons and equipment, operate in small groups, then in company and regimental formations. Time and circumstances, however, meant that this was seldom the case; the army would have to learn its collective trade while on the move. Moreover, different units might be trained according to different manuals and methods. Washington purchased a copy of General Humphrey Bland's *A Treatise of Military Discipline*, the best-known British drill manual. He studied it intently and urged his officers to do the same, though to what ends is unclear since his regiment was scattered in penny-packets along the line of forts in western Virginia. In the meantime, the duke of Cumberland had underwritten a new drill regimen that appeared in 1757. This manual, *A New Exercise to be observed by His Majesty's Troops*, may have been used in newer regiments like Montgomery's. Most provincials would certainly have made do with whatever they could lay hands on—if they trained at all. At the same time, basic training of the kind advocated by Bland or Cumberland also included such fundamentals as laying out encampments in a manner that would preserve the army's health while enabling it to organize a line of battle quickly and effectively.[39]

The varied state of training was only a hint of the challenges that came with putting the army together. Weapons, for example, were as diverse as the troops themselves. The regulars, of course, each had a "stand of arms" consisting of a government-issued musket with sling and muzzle cap, its seventeen-inch bayonet, and either a cartridge box (a wooden form with a leather flap, drilled for paper cartridges and worn on the front of the waist) or the more familiar cartridge pouch suspended from the left shoulder and resting on the right hip. Beyond this, uniformity was the exception, not the rule. Virginia troops were often armed with antiquated muskets; William Byrd complained that his men were given old dog-lock muskets that had been in store since the reign of King William III some sixty years earlier. These and other provincial weapons were also in "bad order" from sitting in a colony's magazine or governor's mansion for years. The weapons held by Washington's regiment were fast wearing out from use and his insistence on musketry exercises to ensure that all of his regiment's arms were "straightened" before the men took the field. At the same time, new recruits from Pennsylvania showed up with whatever they could lay hands on: foreign muskets, antiquated British weapons, or the German "grooved rifles" (the famous Pennsylvania rifle) as well as antiquated Dutch weapons. Bouquet recommended supplying the riflemen with bar lead, since each weapon took its own particular bullet and, in any event, these recruits knew nothing about making paper cartridges. He also warned that rifle-equipped troops, aside from having no bayonets, would need "fine powder FF" for their weapons, not the gunpowder normally issued for muskets. Yet, even this was better than the condition of the North Carolina companies when they finally arrived: one contingent "has not one Gun among them."[40]

North Carolinians were not the only ones short of firearms; weapons were in short supply all around, thanks in part to the tardiness of the store ship with its load of muskets. The colonies had received small numbers of older arms from London in 1756, but these had long since been issued, lost, or damaged. St. Clair was kept busy trying to scrounge additional weapons, often relying on his experiences from the Braddock campaign. For instance, he reminded President Blair that there were weapons in the "Government House" (the governor's mansion), and he ordered them sent forward immediately. He also borrowed weapons from one colony to equip another's troops, as when he asked Governor Sharpe to send up four hundred muskets from Maryland's store so they could be issued to Byrd's new regiment, though Washington worried that Byrd's troops would be "sadly distressed" for weapons should these Maryland arms ever be taken back. As late as June, Bouquet was still distributing a late arrival of newer arms to Burd's Pennsylvanians while taking their old, Dutch muskets, "for the most part unfit for use," and giving them to the New Levies. The colony also encouraged recruits to bring their own weapons of whatever type. Altogether, the provincials in Forbes's army carried "an incredibly mixed lot" of firearms, many of which were antiquated, untested, or broken. Meanwhile, cartridge boxes and bayonets were distributed as they were made or became available, or else men were issued powder horns, shot bags, or animal skin pouches along with hatchets and knives.[41]

As varied as their weapons, the appearance of the army ran the gamut from regulation uniforms to civilian clothes and makeshift "Indian" dress. Bouquet's companies of Royal Americans were fortunate to have received new uniforms before they set out on campaign, made necessary, said Bouquet, since "our old Coats [are] in Rags." Montgomery's men were still wearing the clothing issued to them in Scotland before their journey to South Carolina. Months of rain, sweat, and labor had turned coats to a dirty brick-red color or faded to something resembling pink, while tartans were already beginning to wear thin.[42]

Provincials were also issued uniforms by their provinces. Washington's Virginians wore blue coats with red facings, waistcoats, and breeches, which were also wearing out; Washington apologized to Forbes in advance, saying that his regiment would doubtless make a "shabby appearance" when it joined the main army. Admitting that his regiment was "very bare" of regimental clothing and encouraged by both Forbes and Bouquet, Washington let his men dress as they wished during the warm months; most, of them seem to have adopted buckskin or cloth leggings, breech cloths, and blankets. Byrd's new regiment did the same, their colonel insisting that, in the absence of uniforms, "I intend to dress them After the Indian Fashion," though some of Byrd's men evidently continued to wear their civilian clothes. Pennsylvania's veteran troops were dressed in a variety of uniforms, some blue, others green; Forbes insisted that the New Levies be dressed in short green coats faced with the same color. This prompted at least one local magistrate to tell recruits near Fort Allen not to buy uniforms "as it only putts money in their officers' pockets." Others also questioned the need for uniformity, suggesting outfits of stocking, "Petticoat Trowsers," and "sailor's Frock" would do just as well. Little is known about how the North Carolina and Maryland troops looked; besides having few serviceable weapons, the Carolinians were "in want of Everything," including clothing. They and the Maryland companies likely appeared in what they were issued or could bring from home: blankets, coats, and any other gear of whatever color or description. Captain Evan Shelby's company of Maryland volunteers agreed to serve as rangers without pay, but insisted on being issued moccasins instead of standard leather footwear. By early June, Forbes was ready to concede that his provincials could not be uniformed and "to save time dispenses with uniformity alltogether."[43]

Keeping soldiers shod over the mountainous terrain was a constant concern. Bouquet recommended that instead of one pair each man be issued three pairs of shoes for the campaign, but even this proved inadequate. Troops also lacked tents, knapsacks, blankets, and essential camp equipment such as kettles, hatchets, and mess utensils. Philadelphia manufacturers and suppliers suddenly found themselves swamped with orders for these materials as well as sets of harness, packsaddles, and horseshoes. Pennsylvania's troops seemed especially short of essential equipment. Colonel James Burd, inspecting troops in garrison along the frontier, submitted a lengthy and numbing list of shortages: few serviceable weapons, little or no ammunition and accoutrements, no blankets, no tomahawks, no kettles, no tools. Virginians seemed little better off. St. Clair inspected the new Virginia regiment and found that, besides weapons, they needed blankets, kettles, tents, and canteens. The shortage of tents was particularly worrisome, and everyone searched for enough canvas to accommodate several thousand men. While these troops were undeniably short of needed equipment, their lack of complete uniforms and accoutrements may have been a long-term advantage. One Royal American officer later calculated that a fully equipped regular, complete with ammunition and a week's ration, would carry just over sixty-three pounds of clothing and gear and this did not include things like hatchets, kettles, or other cooking equipment.[44]

* * *

Confronted with the task of creating an army out of widely diverse units, Forbes and his staff labored to bring some order to what must have seemed to them less a military force than a collection of men in an ill-equipped mob. Near the end of the campaign, Forbes famously remarked that his army was "collected from all parts of the Globe," from Highland Scotland, Europe, and several colonies. Yet there was more commonality than such comments imply. Indeed, had the general and his subordinates looked closely at the enlisted ranks, they would have readily agreed that these men shared more than just being parts of a British army.[45]

The common British soldier in the Seven Years' War was, nominally, a volunteer who agreed to serve his king for either a fixed term of years or "life" in return for wages. These soldiers were not the scrapping of jails and taverns, but did represent what contemporaries would have known as "the lower sort": men who practiced marginal trades or were simply laborers, picking up what work they could in town or country. Most of those who ended up in red coats were themselves caught in the destabilizing currents of war, embargo, and the early signs of what would later be called the Industrial Revolution. The army offered an alternative to short wages and little or no food. And, as the war went on and outright volunteers grew fewer, the government resorted more frequently to the "press." The term is most often associated with notorious naval press gangs who swept Britain's waterfronts looking for anyone who could fill a berth in a man-of-war. But the act of pressing extended to the army as well. Parish and shire officers were encouraged to identify those men who practiced no useful trade or were otherwise a drain on local resources; these were rounded up and turned over to recruiting parties. The army these men joined was growing younger as the war dragged on. As the "old standers" left the ranks because of death, wounds, or age, the average age dropped as younger men stepped into the ranks. By 1758, then, Britain's land forces were increasingly manned by economic unfortunates, men desperate enough or, perhaps, daring enough to trade their civilian lives for the army. This was equally true of colonists who enlisted in the regular army. The 50th and 51st Foot were both raised in North America and drew heavily from New England and the Middle colonies. Cities like Boston or New York proved fertile recruiting grounds; both cities, especially Boston and the surrounding towns, were still recovering from loss and dislocation caused by the last war and the generally declining opportunities for young, single men.[46]

Forbes's regulars were no exception to this profile. In mid-1757, Colonel Bouquet provided army headquarters with a detailed account of his companies of the Royal Americans then in South Carolina. The five companies with

Bouquet had 407 noncommissioned officers, drummers, and privates. A slight majority were English, Scots, or Irish; 155 were "foreign"; the majority came from the colonies reflecting the battalion's recruiting area of Pennsylvania, Maryland, New York, and New Jersey. Only 44 were "American." Although the battalion enlisted a few old soldiers, the men in this diverse lot were young: 258 were teenaged or in their early to middle twenties, and in length of service, 313 had served at most one year. Finally, of these 407 men, only 149 were skilled workers, and even these were drawn from the more marginal trades: tailors (21), weavers (18), along with shoemakers, button makers, dyers, wool combers, and plasterers. Altogether, these 149 men represented fifty-two trades ranging from bakers to watch chain makers. The largest number were presumably unskilled, men listed simply as "labourer."[47]

Bouquet's men seem to have been overwhelmingly volunteers. According to one soldier's memoir, however, Montgomery's regiment was recruited on a different basis. Robert Kirk, who enlisted as a volunteer noted that the regiment was "mostly composed of impress'd men from the Highlands," suggesting that these men had been pushed into the army by local elites anxious to cater to the government or were idlers swept up by civil officers. These men, according to Kirk, were also "in the prime of their youth." While classed as British, these Highland Scots might just as well have been "foreign" troops. Forbes, a Scot, compared them to Indians, referring to Cherokees and "their Cousins the Highlanders." Their dress—tartan plaids, short red jackets, checkered stocking—clearly set them apart from "English" or colonial forces, and few of them could speak or understand English. This language barrier could prove fatal; on at least one occasion a Highlander, "coming out of the wood, with his hair hanging loose, and wrapped up in a dark-coloured plaid" was shot to death by a sentry who had ordered him to halt—in English, a language the soldier did not understand.[48]

By the spring of 1758, both Virginia and Pennsylvania were well on the way to creating their own "regular" forces, whose composition and treatment bore a striking resemblance to British regiments. Both colonies faced the challenge of putting reliable forces into the field, and both ultimately looked to the regulars as a model. Using the militia was never an option; in Virginia the militia, made up of landowners, could not serve outside the colony, and Pennsylvania had no militia at all when the war began. Instead, each colony created "provincial" regiments made up of men enlisted to serve outside the colony. In doing so, Virginia and Pennsylvania, like the British, cast their eyes on the economically and socially marginal. And, like the British, the rationale was largely political and economic: provincial politicians were loath to place taxpaying voters in harm's way especially when many Virginians were lukewarm about the war and so many Pennsylvanians rejected carrying arms out of religious scruple.[49]

The resulting forces were composed of men who were economically vulnerable or from outside provincial society altogether. In both colonies, the majority of enlistees identified themselves as laborers or artisans plying marginal trades such as weaving or shoemaking; they apparently enlisted in the hope of earning money and gaining entry into the civilian economy. They were also young; the majority in each case were under the age of thirty. Since short-term enlistments made it hard to train and discipline provincial regiments, both colonies extended the term of service to three years, and, when recruits balked at that, both colonies resorted to pressing or drafting vulnerable men or began to take up newly arrived immigrants. Less than half of Virginia's troops came from the colony and more than three-quarters of Pennsylvania troops hailed from someplace else, notably Britain or Europe. Moreover, Pennsylvania filled its regiment with both recently arrived immigrants and indentured servants. The colony that strenuously objected to the regulars' recruitment of servants as theft of property now eagerly enlisted them, reimbursing owners against the arrival of Parliamentary funds as promised by William Pitt. One modern account concludes that Pennsylvania's troops were little short of mercenaries, men hired to fight but with few or no ties to the society they were expected to defend with their lives. Finally, as enlistments grew longer, so the terms of service became more akin to those of regulars. Men served for long periods in isolated frontier garrisons, had their meager pay docked to pay for uniforms, arms, and equipment, and faced increasingly harsh discipline. Colonel Washington demanded, and received, the power to inflict both corporal and capital punishment on defaulters, especially mutineers and deserters—both more common as service conditions deteriorated. Virginia and Pennsylvania adopted the British Mutiny Act, subjecting their troops to the same disciplinary regime faced by the redcoats, with Lieutenant-Colonel Adam Stephen boasting to Washington that he had "wealed" captured deserters "'till they pissed themselves." The discipline imposed on colonial soldiers echoed that of the regulars, and, in their composition the provincial regiments, like the regulars, reflected the social and economic structure of the British Atlantic world, with poor men in the ranks being led by those men drawn from the governing classes.[50]

The Virginia Regiment and the Pennsylvania troops then, reflected patterns of enlistment and discipline much closer to the regulars than to the popular idea of American volunteer troops. Indeed, in the case of the Virginia Regiment, this was by intent, not just accident. Washington was anxious to get a regular commission and saw his regiment as a means to this end. He and his officers lobbied the commander in chief, asking that their regiment be taken into British service, and arguing (with some truth) that it was at least as good as any regular battalion. Sir John St. Clair would have agreed; having reviewed several companies of Washington's troops he concluded that the "Regt does Honour to its Coll." and believed that if the rest of the regiment looked as good as these, Forbes could "expect a great deal of Service from them." Such men, along with Dagworthy's long-serving and long-suffering Marylanders, stood in stark contrast to the short-service men who filled the New Levies and Byrd's Virginia Regiment, let alone the North Carolina companies.[51]

* * *

These troops shared one additional feature: more out of necessity than design, regular and provincial soldiers were routinely accompanied by their families. Women and children were a fixture in all European armies of the time. Along with civilian employees such as commissary agents, teamsters and sutlers, for example, women and children were characterized as "followers" of the army. Indeed, early modern armies, whether in Europe or America, took on the characteristics of "walking cities" made up of thousands of men, women, children, servants, and, in the colonies, slaves. Forbes's army, with seven thousand troops and hundreds of such followers was larger than any town in the Middle Colonies aside from New York and Philadelphia; it dwarfed places like Carlisle, Winchester, Williamsburg, and Annapolis.[52]

By the middle of the eighteenth century, women and children were permanent fixtures of regimental and army life. Although soldiers were discouraged from marrying, some did nonetheless, and others enlisted with a wife or family already in tow. In the absence of any support system, these dependents had no choice but to follow the army, taking their chances along with their husbands and fathers. They were subject to regulation just as the soldiers themselves. Officially, regiments were permitted to take up to six women per company; officially on the strength these women would work for their rations. In practice, the numbers of women exceeded the prescribed limit and often by a considerable number; with children these dependents could number more than one-quarter of the men in a regiment. The difference between the stated allowance and the actual number of dependents reflected both the determination of these folks to stay together as families and reluctance on the part of the commanders to see women and children left behind with no means of support. Colonel Samuel Bagshawe, whose regiment was bound for India in 1754, told a superior that "there is no part of the Expedition I so much dread as the parting of the Soldiers from their Wives and

Children," noting that nothing was "more discouraging to the Men" who knew their families would have few or no means of support and would face "real distress." Many men like Bagshawe simply bowed to necessity and carried many more dependents than permitted; indeed, the entire military command seems to have winked at this, torn between regulations and simple humanity.[53]

Life for soldiers' families was difficult, even by the standards of the day. Women normally drew one-half the normal ration allotted to men, and children were given quarter rations or none at all. Privacy was nonexistent: in barracks, wives and children shared bedding with their husbands and fathers in rooms full of other men, women, and children. In camp, the same circumstances would prevail, except under canvas. In exchange for room and board, women worked as laundresses, officers' cooks and servants, in return for which they could expect to earn a few pence, and nurses in hospitals, the latter perhaps one of the most dangerous duties in any early modern army. Women who refused such chores were simply cut off from rations. Children who could not work productively simply had to keep out of the way and were constantly at risk of sickness and accident. In one horrific episode a boy "about 10 years of Age," on a navy transport while his father's regiment prepared to make a landing on the coast of France, was caught between the ship's side and a landing barge, which "Crush'd him to death in a moment."[54]

Aside from the inconvenience of constant movement, crowded quarters, and the ever-present threat of diseases such as typhus, smallpox, or influenza, dependents, especially women, also ran the risks of battle and siege. Several soldiers' wives died with Braddock's men at the Monongahela in 1755, others were with the garrison that surrendered at Fort William Henry. Wolfe's army, trapped in Quebec during a bitter Canadian winter, included 569 women in a garrison of some 6,300 men. They and their children faced the constant threat of losing their husband or father and becoming utterly destitute as a result. While officers' wives might expect small payments from a regimental fund or the sale of their husbands' effects, soldiers' dependents had to rely on whatever they might receive from charitable organizations.[55]

Determining the numbers of wives and children who followed the army is a challenge; mention of them in official records is spotty at best, and what numbers do appear reflect particular units or work assignments. Taking as a basis the six women per 100-man company that was the standard used in North America during the war, Forbes's army may have included 382 women, allowing for only three for each of the forty-eight Pennsylvania companies, ten for the Maryland companies, and six for the artillery, but making no allowance for the North Carolina troops. This exercise is complicated by the available records. For example, Dagworthy's four Maryland companies included only ten women; the three "additional companies" of Highlanders took fourteen wives with them, while nothing at all is said about Montgomery's regiment, which may have had the normal six per company. Fifteen companies of the 2d Pennsylvania battalion had only twelve women drawing rations. At the Raystown camp in August, Bouquet, in an effort to lessen the strain on logistics, ordered that no more than three women per company be allowed to draw rations. Finally, six companies of the 1st Virginia Regiment listed four women per company.[56]

Information on women in the British army during the American Revolution suggests that the officially stated numbers may be off by nearly one-half. The 31st Foot allowed 105 women to embark for America, but only 60 were permitted to draw rations—6 women per company. If we assume that regiments during the Seven Years' War also took along many more women than were officially on ration lists, then it would seem prudent to take the figure of 382 women as a median number. Increasing it by 40 percent would give 536 women with the troops; taking the much smaller number reflected in Bouquet's orders would reduce the total to 270 women.[57]

This exercise is further complicated by any attempt to determine the number of children with these women. Certainly not all wives had children, but what constituted a "household" in the abnormal conditions of army life is unknown and must have varied widely over time and place. References to children in Forbes's army are enigmatic at best. The Reverend Thomas Barton, marching west with the army, tells us that in August he baptized at least three children, two of whom belonged to soldiers. Again, figures from the Revolutionary era may give at least an indication of numbers of children with the regiments. A decade after the Forbes campaign, the 31st Foot was in garrison at Pensacola, West Florida. A list of dependents revealed that the regiment supported 80 women and 68 children. All were part of enlisted men's families; the largest of these families included four children, and five more had three children each with the remaining 49 families having one child each. Lists compiled for British regiments during the Revolution also suggests that the number of children per family was low: overall less than one per couple. Based on this evidence, men like Reverend Barton would have seen between 200 and 300 children following the army.[58]

Getting beyond numbers is equally difficult; children turn up in records if they died, while their mothers would normally attract attention only for some infraction and, even then, were rarely mentioned by name. Charlotte Brown, the matron for Braddock's hospital, did keep a journal, and her experiences can suggest something about those soldiers' families. She traveled in an army freight wagon with hospital stores and complained about "Great Gusts of Rain" pouring in, with roads "so Bad that I am almost disjointed." Other army women must have traveled in similar conditions, but the majority probably walked, either with their men or at the end of the column. In April 1759, Colonel Bouquet paid two pounds seven shillings to "Texter's Wife" and one pound sterling to "Heil's widow." Both were probably from his Royal Americans and may have reflected a dead husband's remaining wages. A month later, we learn of Mrs. Middleton, "the Matron," and Mrs. Robinson, "the Nurse," attached to the hospital that accompanied the army in 1758. Nothing more is written about these two except the hope that they would be paid their salaries.[59]

Some of these women were certainly experienced army wives; Texter's and Heil's spouses may have followed the army for several years, and Middleton, Robinson, and Brown, not only followed the army but served in what were undoubtedly the most taxing jobs in the field: attending to the sick and wounded. Middleton and Brown, as matrons, and Robinson, as skilled nurse, were also responsible for organizing and supervising the shifts of army women who were assigned as nurses and cooks while assisting the hospital staff of surgeons and apothecaries. One woman who was certainly a veteran campaigner was Martha May, whose husband was in Bouquet's Royal Americans and who very likely made the long march to the Ohio. We know of her only because she ran afoul of her colonel. Bouquet had placed her husband under arrest. May herself ended up in the Carlisle jail in early June 1758, having been "Put ... in Such a Passion" by her husband's treatment that she confronted and, in her own words, "abused" Bouquet. Deciding to show contrition, she humbly petitioned on her own and her husband's behalf. Yet she also took the opportunity to remind Bouquet that "I have been a Wife 22 years and have Traveld with my Husband every Place or Country the Company Marcht to and have worked very hard ever since *I was in the Army*" and hoped to carry water to her husband "and my good Officers in the Hottest Battle *as I have done before*." In a "young" army of often raw troops, Martha May and other women like her were seasoned veterans, and for all that they and their children were seen as a necessary evil, they had skills and insight that their husbands and possibly officers such as Bouquet would find valuable in the days ahead.[60]

If we are able to catch brief glimpses of army women through Charlotte Brown's journal or Martha May's letter, the servants, free blacks, and slaves with whom they marched remain virtual ghosts. Officers, whether regular or provincial, were entitled to at least one servant, frequently a soldier, or "batman" who drew rations and earned additional pay from the man he served.

And while we cannot know for certain, some officers certainly had civilian servants such as cooks, grooms, barbers, or body servants. African Americans and people of mixed race were also part of the army, and some may have served in the ranks. The British army certainly enlisted Africans, or Afro-English, and a few even applied for pensions from the Royal Hospital at Chelsea. At least one black soldier, Henry Wedge, deserted from Bouquet's Royal Americans later in the war. Most people of African descent, however, served as labor. In 1755, Braddock informed his superiors that he would not allow his troops to act as teamsters or batmen but hired "Numbers of Mulattoes and free Negroes." Such folk may also have turned up among the civilian teamsters and packhorse drivers in Forbes's army. We catch a glimpse of one such man, a "French Negro" who deserted from Fort Duquesne. He eventually took the name Frank and claimed his freedom in Williamsburg. Meanwhile, Washington recommended him to St. Clair as a "Shrewd, Sensible Fellow" whose knowledge of the Ohio Country might be useful. This may have been "Sir John's Negro" who was paid one pistole out of Bouquet's accounts for unknown services. At the same time, provincials probably brought slaves with them. Slaves may well have been on Washington's mind when he asked Bouquet if officers' servants "who are not Soldiers" could draw rations in his regiment. Beyond such vague references we can only assume the likelihood that Virginia, Maryland, and Carolina planters would have brought slaves with them, and that they, along with free Blacks, mulattoes, women, and children added noticeably to the size and character of Forbes's already complex army.[61]

*   *   *

On May 19, 1758, Forbes wrote a report to Pitt telling him, among other things, that he hoped to have at least one thousand Pennsylvania troops together by June 1, but when the rest would join "I can scarce form any Judgement." In the meantime, the "Virginians are going on slowly in compleating their Quota." Forbes hoped he could get at least half of their two thousand men by the beginning of June. Yet, as late as mid-June, Bouquet reflected on "how far we are from being ready." Pennsylvanians continued to drag their feet about paying their forces, the Assembly having declared that it would not pay for camp equipment since they were only required to raise and clothe the troops—not equip them for the field. This same attitude also meant that the colony would refuse to buy medicines and other equipment needed for Dr. Russell's hospital. With Montgomery's regiment and the ordnance ship nowhere in sight, the best Forbes could do was to send the three Additional Highland companies and Bouquet's Royal Americans into the backcountry along with Heydeler's small artillery train. It was a meager show of force, but the best he could do.[62] All of this stood in stark contrast to Pitt's optimistic declaration at the end of December 1757 that he expected Forbes to take the field by May 1, "if possible, or as soon after as shall be any way practicable." Now, more than two weeks late, and unlikely to get even a portion of his army on the road for nearly a month, Forbes waited while the campaign season ticked away. Perhaps an indication of his growing frustration was his health. Since the debilitating problems that had beset him in New York, he mentioned nothing about his health until late May. Then, in a letter to Colonel John Stanwix, he revealed that he had "been at death's door with a severe Cholick."[63]

The mounting friction threatened the campaign in another, important, way. Forbes was determined to enlist Cherokee and Catawba warriors. Already, French and Indian raiding parties were in the field—they were one reason that it was hard to gather Pennsylvania's regiment together. With the enemy in the field, Forbes was once again reminded he was fighting two enemies: the French and their western native allies and the Ohio Indians. Making peace with the latter would make defeating the French much easier, but this depended on the cooperation of colonial and imperial officials. Getting to the Ohio would nonetheless require men who knew the woods, who could collect intelligence and at the same time shield his army from the enemy's prying eyes; in short, he too understood the pressing need for native allies. Unfortunately, getting the Cherokees into the field proved much easier than mustering regulars and provincials. The natives expected to join an army when they arrived in Virginia and Pennsylvania. What they found was chaos enough to force them to think twice about joining Forbes.[64]

TWO

Friends and Enemies

* * *

WINTER–SPRING 1758

I think the Cherokees of Such Consequence that I have done everything in my power to Provide them in their necessarys.

—FORBES TO ABERCROMBY, APRIL 1758

The search for Indian fighters to join the army against Fort Duquesne began even before Forbes was appointed to the command. This effort represented only the latest attempt by British commanders to enlist native allies; by 1758 the results had been disappointing at best. Several hundred Iroquois, mostly Mohawks, had joined Colonel William Johnson's army at the foot of Lake George in 1755. Heavy battle casualties, including the death of the important Mohawk sachem, Hendrick, put a damper on further Iroquois assistance. So, too, did decisions by western Iroquois villagers: Onondagas, Cayugas, and Senecas, avoided involvement in the Anglo-French war, opting instead for armed neutrality. By August, 1756, Loudoun could only report that "we have no support" from Indians. Without active scouting to forewarn of attacks, without any intelligence whatever of the enemy and his intentions, Loudoun and his troops were effectively blind. They were facing an enemy that was a master of *la petite-guerre* (little war), the irregular warfare of ambushes, raids, intelligence gathering, and harassing of supply lines. Its American variant, *la guerre sauvage* (savage war) was even more effective when raiding parties included native fighters whose attacks became a form of terror raid, designed to destroy property and drive the civilian population away. Its success could be measured by the increasing size of the "wilderness" created in the backcountry as settlers fled eastward.[1]

The British, like their French enemies, knew all about guerilla warfare.

Loudoun himself, along with Forbes, St. Clair, and other officers had seen at firsthand the value of hussars, Croat and Serb irregulars, and Piedmontese mountaineers. What they lacked were men who could engage in such warfare with the same skill and success as the French. For two generations, Canadian militia and native fighters from mission towns in Canada and from the Great Lakes region had carried war and disruption to the British colonies from Schenectady and Deerfield in New York and Massachusetts to Penn's Creek in Pennsylvania and isolated settlements in western Virginia. These raiding parties continued to operate with impunity, easily slipping past static garrisons in the line of forts that defined the much contracted Pennsylvania–Virginia borderland. Aside from killing and burning, these raiders also took prisoners who could be valuable sources of information. Loudoun's army, on the other hand, could only react, most often belatedly. As a result, French forces easily snapped up not only Fort Oswego in 1756, but also Fort William Henry in 1757; their garrisons and potential relief troops lacked native scouts who could gather intelligence and shadow French forces. Indeed, Loudoun was forced to admit that he had no "certain Accounts of the Road to Ticonderoga, as it has never been reconoitred properly." It was a stunning admission, given that Fort Carillon (Ticonderoga) was a major British objective and the base from which Montcalm's army descended on Fort William Henry and threatened Albany.[2]

Instead, and since the French "are so superior in Irregulars," Loudoun was forced to rely on "our Rangers" drawn largely from New England provincials. These men and their leader, Major Robert Rogers of New Hampshire, were expected to fill the gaps in intelligence created by the lack of native allies. The results were disappointing; while providing information on the activities of French and Indian forces around Forts Carillon and Ste. Frederic, Rogers's command was twice decimated in encounters with the enemy. In the meantime, the expense of these special units and the difficulty in subjecting them to regular discipline led to the creation of the 80th "Light-Armed Foot" for Abercromby's 1758 campaign. A regular regiment, it was the brainchild of Colonel Thomas Gage, another veteran of the Braddock debacle. Abercromby hoped that the regiment—recruited from among the regulars in New York and led by British volunteer officers—would fill the need for irregular troops while avoiding the cost and friction associated with the rangers.[3]

In the foothills and mountains of the Carolinas the prospects for enlisting natives seemed much brighter. As early as January, the new royal superintendent of Indian affairs for the South, Carolina trader Edmond Atkin, received directions from Loudoun to recruit as many Cherokees as possible. A month later, not satisfied with the pace of Atkin's efforts, Loudoun urged South Carolina's Governor Lyttleton to "spur him on." Loudoun dispatched "a particular Friend of mine," Colonel William Byrd III of Virginia, as his personal emissary to the Cherokees. Captain Abraham Bosomworth of the Royal Americans, a Georgian who claimed to be well versed in Indian affairs, would soon join Byrd. Their efforts, and Atkin's, would, Loudoun hoped, recruit as many as five hundred Cherokees for the campaign.[4]

The Cherokees seemed the best source for native fighters. They had a peaceful, if strained, relationship with South Carolina and had provided men to patrol the frontiers of Virginia earlier in the war. In 1758, the Cherokees comprised four clusters of towns: the Lower, Middle, Valley, and Overhill, together home to roughly nine thousand people. This population included perhaps as many as three thousand men able to bear arms, making the Cherokees a potent force in the Southeast. Geographical location, like that of the Iroquois in the North, also made the Cherokees worth courting; their towns extended from the Carolina foothills as far west as the Tennessee River valley, giving them ready access not only to British colonies but the growing French settlements in the Illinois Country and Louisiana. They had the potential, therefore, of serving as an early warning system and frontier guard for the plantation settlements. Cherokee towns also sat astride two important trading paths that connected the natives to markets for deer hides and sources of manufactured goods from Virginia and South Carolina.[5]

Their relative isolation in the Piedmont and Smoky Mountains protected the Cherokees from the steep population loss and accompanying political and social dislocation that came with the collapse of Mississippian chiefdoms and the slave-raiding provoked by new, labor-hungry Carolina colonists. Nevertheless, they, too, were products of what has recently been called the "shatter zone" created by unpredictable encounters between natives and newcomers all along the Piedmont from New York to Georgia. Like natives throughout eastern America, Cherokees felt the effects of the growing proximity to Europeans. Since the founding of South Carolina in 1670 and the appearance of French settlers to the west thirty years later, the Cherokee population had fallen from an estimated thirty-two thousand to only nine thousand when Byrd arrived seeking fighting men. Imported diseases were the worst enemies, regularly eating away at native societies; the nine thousand Cherokees in 1758 were the survivors of the latest smallpox epidemic in 1738. Deer-hide traders, their servants and slaves might carry smallpox but also brought in horses, chickens, and pigs that began to alter domestic economies, while muskets, ammunition, metal goods, and cloth increasingly tied the Cherokees to wider Atlantic markets. Expanding Carolinian settlements began pushing against the Cherokees, threatening the agreed-upon bound-

Fig. 2.1 Cunne Shote, 1762, by Francis Parsons (The Thomas Gilcrease Institute of American History and Art). Painted from life, Cunne Shote would have been a contemporary of the many Cherokees who left the Overhill Towns to join Forbes's army. Cunne Shote's dress suggests what Cherokee fighting men expected to receive in return for their work with the army.

ary of native lands, Long Cane Creek. And although the Cherokees and their colonial neighbors had been at peace for two generations with the boundary officially recognized by both crown and colony, there was always the potential for misunderstandings and violence that could plunge the region into war. The smallpox epidemic and the rapid growth of a rice-and-slavery economy meant that, by 1758, the demographic scales had already tilted against the Cherokees; those nine thousand natives now faced nearly seventy thousand African and Anglo-Carolinians.[6]

Colonists, their microbes, and their merchandise were not the only issues facing Cherokee society. It is easy to forget that colonists were not the only, and on occasion not the most important, people with whom any native society had to contend. The Cherokees inhabited a world filled with other native peoples: Creek, Choctaw, Chickasaw, Catawba, as well as the distant Iroquois and Ohio Indians. Adding to the losses from disease, for example, was the warfare between Cherokees and Creeks as well as a long-standing conflict between Cherokees and the Six Nations. Such conflicts were rooted in age-old animosity, fueled by the mourning war and made more lethal by the widespread use of firearms and the desire to secure access to valuable resources such as deer hides and the French or British markets. There were also political costs: warfare raised the profile of war leaders and their followers while challenging the influence of town elders dedicated to maintaining peace and consensus. Cherokee society, then, was not stable, peaceful, and unchanging, and the recent experiences of disease, warfare, and settler encroachments, along with trade would define how Cherokees responded to the British call for fighting men.[7]

Kinship was, according to one authority, "the adhesive that bound Cherokee society together." All Cherokees were members of one of seven matrilineal clans, members of which could be found in all of the towns. Not only did kinship define self and place within family and town, it also guaranteed that decision making was local and tied to the interests of kinfolk. This localism was heavily reinforced by the town-based nature of Cherokee identity and politics. Despite efforts by colonial and imperial officials to define and work with a Cherokee "nation," no such entity actually existed. Instead, over fifty towns loosely affiliated by region pursued their own political agendas. Individual colonies were jealous of their identities, rights, and interests; so too were the Cherokee towns. There was nothing unique about this localism among the Cherokees; it was a feature they shared with native societies throughout eastern North America. And, if Cherokees coalesced into larger bodies in order to negotiate with outsiders, this process was generally regional in nature.[8]

Peace within towns, among towns, and between Cherokees towns and outsiders was a product of consensus, negotiation, and reciprocity. Town headmen and chief warriors could lead only as far as others were willing to follow; coercion was not a part of Cherokee politics. Instead, leaders or would-be leaders gained respect and support through negotiating agreements while setting examples by listening, carefully considering differing points of view, and attempting to arrive at an agreeable solution. Those who remained dissatisfied with the outcome of such negotiations could decide to follow their own course or, in extreme cases, even split off from the town. At the same time, respected leaders were also generous, giving in order to receive the support and respect needed to negotiate differences and find consensus. This process extended beyond Cherokee towns as well. What Europeans called "diplomacy" was consensus politics directed toward other peoples.[9]

Likewise, "trade" was, for Cherokees and their neighbors, more than the simple act of buying and selling. Although natives certainly desired cloth, metal wares, and weapons, for example, they viewed exchange as a symbolic act of friendship between equals. Goods served to animate and reinforce friendship and alliances. Underpinning this view of social relations was reciprocity, not necessarily a one-for-one equality of value, but an acknowledgment that an amicable relationship was alive and well. For natives, in other words, alliances and treaties were not one-off events or pacts. Rather, they were relationships that demanded continual renewal and affirmation. This made perfect sense in the face-to-face world of Cherokee towns, clans, or war bands where personal relationships and not abstract laws made by distant authorities, shaped everyday life. When dealing with Creeks or Iroquois, who shared these values, understanding was relatively easy. When Cherokees applied the same standards and values to their relations with colonists, however, there was always ample room for misunderstanding. British officials frequently saw the exchange of gifts at councils as a form of bribe or, at best, a generous donation to subordinate peoples. Nevertheless, Cherokee leaders were not above gently reminding their colonial neighbors of the right meaning of generosity and reciprocity. Only two years before Byrd's mission, the headman of Chota, then the dominant Overhill town, made the point to recently arrived provincial soldiers who had come to build a fort the Cherokees had requested. Although "we have little amongst us," Connecortee said, "your people may also have a part of what there is . . . as we do, one from another." Any Cherokee would have understood the generosity and the implied reciprocal obligations it established; unfortunately, the British often did not.[10]

Cherokees, then, would face Byrd and Bosomworth with certain expectations and assumptions clearly in mind. Threatened by pressure from expanding settlements, and attempting to recover from population loss aggravated by war with the Creeks, Cherokees above all strove for both stability at home and autonomy in the face of rival colonies and empires. Among those anxious to achieve these goals were the leading men of the towns, especially the "mother towns," sacred sites that also served as a focus for the surrounding communities. In a world where all politics were town based and clan based, these men had to balance contending forces. Usually defined as "pro-British" or "pro-French," it would be better to see these contending groups as all equally "pro-Cherokee" but differing in ideas about how to maintain autonomy and peace. Towns vied with each other for influence within regions and among the Cherokees as a whole. The tactic used—courting nearby colonists—further complicated the political landscape. Leaders in Chota, the mother town of the Overhill Cherokees, for example, had actively sought a special relationship with Virginia by asking that a fort be built near their town. The town of Keowee lobbied South Carolina. In each case the Cherokees were engaged in a local variation of the "play-off" strategy familiar to other native societies in eastern America. By striving "to be at Peace with all Kings," Cherokee headmen hoped to keep their people secure and their options open.[11]

No less than the Cherokees, British officials also understood their world as seen through the lens of their own experiences. South Carolina's royal governor James Glen, not only insisted on seeing Indians as naturally subordinate people, but also aggressively attempted to extend Carolinian authority over natives. His competitor for influence among southeastern Indians, Governor Robert Dinwiddie of Virginia, pursued much the same goal. What Cherokees heard as invitations to equals were seen by Glen and Dinwiddie as opportunities to manipulate or control native societies. By accepting invitations to post garrisons in rival Cherokee towns, each hoped to use his clients to extend influence by naming the town headman "king" of a Cherokee "nation." Neither office nor entity existed in the Carolina mountains, at least not until the late eighteenth century and then only in ways that were based on Cherokee interests, not those of outsiders. In 1758 Glen, now former governor of South Carolina, would take his experience in Indian affairs to Pennsylvania, where he would join his cousin, John Forbes, as an unofficial advisor.[12]

Cherokee decisions to offer or withhold support for the British also turned on recent political developments. Overhill Cherokees from the town of Tellico (Great Tellico), concerned that Virginia and South Carolina were gaining too much influence among their people, sent a delegation to the French in Louisiana offering peace and a trading alliance. This posed a serious challenge for Cherokees from other towns and regions, Chota in the

Overhills, and the Lower and Middle towns, whose leaders quickly moved to counter this threat to their own influence at home based on ties to the British. That this issue pitted some Overhill Cherokees against those from farther east only underscored the power of localism and the limits of pan-Cherokee unity. At the same time, leaders of Chota not only moved to undercut Tellico's threatened French connection, but also consolidated an ongoing shift in power from the Lower Towns to the Overhills. Symbolic of this was the emergence of Attakullakulla (The Little Carpenter) as spokesman for Overhill warriors and those who continued to embrace alliance and trade with the British. By answering the British call for fighters, Attakullakulla and his followers both shored up support for their British ties and further cemented the Overhills' command over external affairs.[13]

In the end, the extent of Cherokee participation in Forbes's campaign would turn on issues of power and balance within the Cherokee nation, couched in terms of equality and reciprocity. Responding to a call to serve in the "common cause" in response to French attacks on their "elder Brothers" (the British), warriors exchanged wampum and calumets with Bosomworth and other agents. Cherokee fighting men took these words seriously along with the implied meaning behind them—equality and partnership. They saw themselves as brothers helping brothers. These men certainly had much to gain by going to war in the Ohio Country, the chance to strike traditional native enemies while enhancing their own reputations back home. At the same time, however, warriors ran severe risks. In this regard, British pledges of arms, ammunition, and trade goods seemed only fair compensation for men who were abandoning the important spring hunt in order to join the army, and who, placing themselves in harm's way, would leave behind families that might be the object of enemy retaliation. Yet even here, a certain doubt shows through. Governor William Henry Lyttleton of South Carolina made a point of warning Loudoun that "If the promise" that Carolina's agent, Colonel Howarth, "[m]akes to the Indians is not performed it will exceedingly embroil us with them." What he meant was reflected in an exchange between Attakullakulla and William Byrd. Attakullakulla's insistence that he and his followers be given the gifts promised for services already rendered included the assertion that, "if he gets what he expects," he would collect men and follow Byrd to the army. Although Byrd found "that little savage" "very insolent," the message was clear: Cherokee fighters expected reciprocity and would accept nothing less of their so-called brothers. Moreover, Attakullakulla had staked his reputation on the value and benefits of cooperation with the British.[14]

Attakullakulla's words may have rankled Byrd because they struck a nerve.

The Virginian and the other agents active in recruiting Cherokees were, after all, trying to enlist hired guns, mercenaries who would do the army's bidding in return for the promise of payment. Forbes needed trained, skilled eyes and ears if he was to make his way west in the face of French, Indians, and the *guerre sauvage*. The Cherokees seemed willing and able to supply the need. This was no "alliance" but a marriage of convenience. Those Cherokee men who offered to join the army did so in the expectation that they would be treated with respect and compensated for their skills and risks; for the general, these men were, at best, auxiliaries of the kind that the British army had long employed in Europe under the heading of "subsidy troops"— soldiers kept on retainer like the Brunswickers and Hessians fighting in "His Britannic Majesty's Army" against the French in northern Germany. And Attakullakulla may not have been the only one to raise questions about British reliability. Although Byrd could announce that he was able to send over 600 warriors, including a band of Catawbas, to join the army, the scope of Cherokee participation was nevertheless limited. Of some fifty towns, only sixteen provided the 652 men who followed Byrd to Virginia. Much was riding on their reception, for both Attakullakulla and Forbes.[15]

Four other issues emerge from this British effort to recruit southern fighters. First, the evidence suggests the confused and complex nature of British Indian affairs by 1758. To say that British diplomacy suffered from too many cooks may be an understatement. Colonial governors James Glen and Lyttleton, the crown superintendent of Indian affairs in the south Edmond Atkin, Loudoun's and Forbes's agents, William Byrd and Abraham Bosomworth, and Colonel Howarth acting for South Carolina, all of these had a hand in negotiations. Waiting in the wings were Sir William Johnson, Atkin's counterpart in the northern colonies, President John Blair of the Virginia Council and acting governor, the soon-to-arrive Virginia governor Francis Fauquier, governors William Sharpe of Maryland and William Denny of Pennsylvania, not to mention other self-styled authorities such as George Washington. Forbes would not lack for voices on Indian affairs, and this would be a problem.[16]

Second, was the voluntary nature of Cherokee involvement: choosing to go to war on their own terms and for their own ends meant that warriors believed they could come and go as they pleased. Should any individual or group decide that enough was enough or that the British were not fulfilling their agreements as brothers, leaving the army was not only an available option, but one that carried with it no stigma of cowardice or fecklessness. All of this made perfect sense within the cultural world of the Cherokees, but it flew in the face of everything professional soldiers were taught to value about subordination and loyalty.[17]

Third, the eagerness with which many Cherokee men took up arms was predicated in large measure by assurances that a vast army was ready to march. Told that "a great Number of Soldiers & a Train of Artillery" were being prepared, Cherokee warriors were "very desirous" that Forbes's army "may be assembled as soon as conveniently may be" so that "our young Men may not be tired with Waiting" and perhaps go home. Groups of Cherokees were already marching north toward Winchester in March and April, while Forbes and his staff were still collecting troops and supplies east of the Susquehanna River.[18]

Finally, no one, either Cherokee or British, reckoned with the rise of indiscriminate Indian-hating engendered among border settlers by three years of terrifying raids. By custom and necessity, Cherokee fighters would have to travel along the "warriors' paths" that led from the Smoky Mountains though the western Carolinas and north through western Virginia. Frontier settlers had always been wary of Indians, whether strangers or neighbors, but they and natives had worked out a rough accommodation and traveling bands of Indians might even expect hospitality from farmers. The war suddenly—and permanently—changed all that. Now, Cherokees would have to run a gauntlet of fear, anger, and pure hatred even before they reached Forbes's army. By mid-spring, Forbes's search for docile Indian auxiliaries was already complicated and would only become more so as the campaign progressed.[19]

*   *   *

While Cherokees argued among themselves about the wisdom of cooperating with the British army, hundreds of miles to the north, near the far end of the warriors' paths, the stress of war was provoking discussions within many Ohio Valley towns. At the Kuskuskies, Saucunk, and smaller hamlets, the Delawares were entering their fourth year of war with neighboring Pennsylvania. Their Shawnee neighbors at Logstown and villages down the Ohio River near its confluence with the Scioto River had been on the offensive against Virginia even longer, since before Braddock's defeat.

The Delawares had arrived in the Ohio Country less than thirty years before the war. Coming west from their original homes between the Delaware and Susquehanna Rivers, the natives hoped to escape the colonial land grabbing that led to their dispossession and that of their Shawnee and Munsee neighbors. This migration, which Delawares hoped would put distance between them and the Penn family and its land agents, was not a mad flight of disorganized refugees. The move was planned and carried out by kin groups under the leadership of what one captive later styled the Delawares' "royal family": three nephews of the headman Sassoonan/Alumapees, whose family dominated negotiations between Delawares and Pennsylvania. These three men—Pisquetomen, Tamaqua, and Shingas—were little known in the late 1720s when the migration began, but would quickly emerge as leaders in both war and peace.

The Delawares' chosen destination, the upper Ohio Valley, seemed an ideal place to establish new towns. Swept clear of its original Erie and Monongahelan inhabitants during the Five Nations' mourning wars of the seventeenth century, the region began to beckon Iroquois, Wyandots, even Mesquakis (Fox) from the western Great Lakes, as well as Delawares, Munsees, and Shawnees from Pennsylvania. All were drawn by the prospect of unused land, ample game, and, most of all, distance and security from turmoil at home and pressures from expanding and contending French and British empires. The Six Nations maintained a claim to the land and by the 1740s had established two local men—the Oneida Scarouady and the Seneca Tanaghrisson—to oversee the Iroquois Confederacy interests in the region. Dubbed "half-kings" by colonists, their real authority was nominal, and they neither directed nor oversaw the new influx of peoples. By the late 1740s towns stretched from Buckaloons on the upper Allegheny River to Scioto on the Ohio River. All told, by 1748, there may have been as many as four thousand people in the upper Ohio Valley, in addition to settlements of the Miamis confederacy farther west. Pennsylvania traders followed their old customers west, reestablishing trade at Logstown, the Kuskuskies, and as far west as Cuyahoga (modern Cleveland, Ohio) and Pickawillany in present-day Ohio. More ominously, after 1748 these peddlers were joined by other men looking for land—agents of the new Ohio Company of Virginia.[20]

What many natives envisioned as a haven instead became a cauldron of competing and increasingly violent interests beginning in the last years of the War of the Austrian Succession (King George's War in America). Trouble began in 1747 when local Iroquois, calling themselves "Warriors, living at Ohio," sent messages to Pennsylvania requesting an alliance against the French. In return, the colony sent its Indian agent, Conrad Weiser, to the Ohio in order to make contact with these natives. This initiative came at a dangerous time; Ohio Iroquois were attacking French traders while a splinter group of Wyandots from Detroit moved eastward to be closer to British supplies and support. At the same time Piankashaw members of the Miami confederacy, led by a man known to the French as La Demoiselle and to the

Fig. 2.2 Tishcohan, 1735, by Gustavus Heselius. (Courtesy of the Philadelphia History Museum at the Atwater Kent.) No known images or descriptions exist for either Pisquetomen or Tamaqua, but this portrait of a Delaware man taken from life suggests what the next generation of Delawares might have looked like.

British as Old Briton, did the same, threatening to destabilize the Great Lakes–wide alliance system upon which New France depended as a buffer against British expansion into the important but vulnerable region west of the Ohio River. Despite a peace treaty between Britain and France in 1748, these events virtually guaranteed that the Ohio Country would become less, not more, peaceful in the years to come.[21]

The Ohio Iroquois and their neighbors were engaged in a local variation of modern Indian politics: attempting to counter French influence with support from nearby British colonies. They badly miscalculated. By 1749 Virginia agents had entered the region, looking for men with whom they could arrange a land deal for the newly organized Ohio Company, a group of wealthy speculators who hoped to obtain a grant of some two hundred thousand acres in a region that Virginia claimed on the basis of its original charter from James I. Fearing an expansion of British trade that would undercut their alliance system, and now faced with the prospect of settlements in the Ohio Country, the French responded to Pennsylvania and Virginia delegations with military force. In 1749 Captain Céleron de Blainville led an expedition from Montreal to Detroit. Passing through the Ohio Valley, he asserted French claims to the region, telling British traders to leave and telling their customers of the wisdom of a French alliance. Nevertheless, by 1752, Virginians, working with the local Ohio Iroquois half-kings got their treaty and land cession at a council at Logstown, raising the specter of new settlements. In the same year, French forces out of Fort Michilimackinac destroyed La Demoiselle and his settlement at Pickawillany, killing and seizing British traders into the bargain.

The Logstown treaty marked a new phase in regional developments. By giving in to Virginia pressure, the half-king Tanaghrisson might have hoped to counterbalance increasing aggressive French efforts to dominate the Ohio Country. In fact, events were to prove that neither Virginia nor Pennsylvania was capable of confronting the French on equal terms. More important, whatever influence the Iroquois may have exercised began to fade as first the Delawares, and then the Shawnees began to chart their own paths through the increasingly dangerous terrain they now inhabited. Of particular note was the emergence of Shingas as the designated Delaware spokesman, or "king," marking that people's determination to act independently in the face of rival empires. By 1758, the western Delawares and their "royal family" would dominate affairs in the upper Ohio, facing both French and British threats to their sovereignty. And although they distanced themselves from the half-kings and their treaties, they surely would have agreed with Tanaghrisson that upper Ohio natives now found themselves living "in a Country between" rival empires and were even more determined than Scarouady to "keep our country clear of settlements."[22]

Tanaghrisson's words proved all too true, while Scarouady's pledge rang hollow by 1754. Less than a year after the Logstown conference, an aggressive new governor general of New France, Ange de Menneville, marquis de Duquesne, trumped the Ohio Company—and the Ohio Iroquois—by sending forces into the region to build a line of forts asserting French claims. Rejecting out of hand Virginia claims to the Ohio Country and that colony's demand that they depart, the French kept building, from Presqu'Ile and Fort Le Boeuf to an outpost at Venango (later Fort Machault). Finally, in April, 1754, they bloodlessly ejected a small Virginia force bent on building the Ohio Company fort at the Forks of the Ohio, replacing it with Fort Duquesne.

The bloodletting came soon enough. While Ensign Edward Ward was marching his would-be fort builders back to Virginia, Colonel George Washington was marching north with a relief force. Little more than a month after the French occupied the Forks, Washington's small force, augmented by some Iroquois led by Tanaghrisson, found and attacked a small detachment of French near a place called the Great Meadows. Whether Ensign Joseph Coulon de Villiers de Jumonville came to deliver messages to Virginians or whether he was intent on spying—or worse—hardly mattered. After a brief fight in a rain-soaked forest clearing, Jumonville and most of his party lay dead at the hands of British provincial troops and their Ohio Iroquois friends. Diplomats and politicians on both sides of the Atlantic, French and British, would attempt to put their own twist on events; nevertheless, hostilities had erupted and only escalated in the coming months as French troops led by Jumonville's brother set out to drive the Virginians out of the Ohio Country. The well-known climax came at the Great Meadows where Virginian and regular British troops from South Carolina found themselves surrounded and forced to capitulate at Fort Necessity on July 4, 1754. For all practical purposes Virginia and New France were at war, soon to be joined by their mother countries.[23]

Although Britain and France were now at war thanks to their colonial proxies, the conflict did not yet involve Ohio Indians other than Tanaghrisson's band of Iroquois. The Indians who assisted the French in surrounding Washington's force at the Great Meadows came from the Great Lakes and Iroquois mission towns in New France. It would take other events, all of them from outside the region, to send Ohio Country warriors against British border settlements. The first of these arose in distant South Carolina in 1753 where six Shawnees had been captured and imprisoned as they attempted to raid their traditional Catawba enemies. Their treatment infuriated Shawnees in the Ohio Valley towns who interpreted the imprisonment as a violation of friendship, indeed, an act of war. Two of the prisoners were subsequently returned home and three others managed to escape, but Shawnees chose to retaliate; by the autumn of 1754 they were attacking outlying settlements in western Virginia, which became the opening phase of a campaign that would continue in earnest for the next four years.[24]

The western Delawares' march to war followed another path and took somewhat longer. From the outset, what most concerned Delawares in the Ohio Country was the integrity of their towns and land. They were not about to be dispossessed twice in a single lifetime. French forts were a problem, but posed little immediate threat compared to what the natives feared most: British settlers with their plows, livestock, and hunger for ever more land. Indeed, as the Delaware Ackowanothic said, local natives could "drive away the French when we please" but not the more numerous British. Fear about land and security came to the fore when news arrived that a grand council held at Albany, New York, had produced new real estate deals. The council was called to repair the badly frayed alliance between the colonies and the Mohawk Iroquois in anticipation of increased French military activity. In the background, however, private negotiations gave the Penn family, as their colony's Proprietors, a deed for a vast tract of land west of the Susquehanna River. In effect, the distance Delawares had hoped to put between them and colonial farmers had been erased, raising the specter of a new round of dispossession. While Delaware headmen and their people were digesting this news and its implications, the British government decided to meet force with force by sending regular troops to America and made a plan to attack New France simultaneously from several directions at once and put an end to the French threat to British colonies and their land claims. One of these armies, led by General Edward Braddock, provided the final provocation that led many Delawares to join their Shawnee neighbors in going to war. Braddock's army, much more imposing than anything the French could muster, entered the Ohio Country in June, 1755. According to one captive's later account, the Delaware "king," Shingas, approached Braddock and offered assistance against the French in return for a pledge that the British would leave after taking the Ohio Valley forts. According to Shingas, Braddock was dismissive, telling him that "No Savage Should Inherit the Land." The veracity of this particular account has recently been called into question, but it does reflect Delaware efforts to use one army to rid their land of another and the stark realization that Braddock's imposing army was determined to occupy the region. Moreover, documents captured at Braddock's defeat included a rough plan of the "New Work at Fort du Quesne" showing a sprawling work that bears a striking resemblance to the later Fort Pitt. Perhaps the French showed the plan to local Indians, confirming their worst fears and giving rise to Shingas's account. Nevertheless, by the fall of 1755, Pennsylvanians were beginning to experience the horrors of frontier warfare; Delaware fighters from the Ohio Country hit isolated settlements west of the Susquehanna River on Penn's Creek and elsewhere while eastern Delawares from the Susquehanna Valley and their headman, Teedyuscung, launched their own, independent, raids against the colony.[25]

In the Ohio Country, what has been labeled a "French and Indian" war was, in fact, far more complicated, with implications for both the French themselves and for Forbes's plans to drive them out of the region. While the French and their allies from the Great Lakes and St. Lawrence Valley (Odawas, Ojibwas, Potawatomies, and Iroquois from Kanawake and other mission towns in Canada) launched their own campaigns against British colonies and forces, two other parallel wars—one Shawnee and the other Delaware, rooted in different issues—sent warriors east as well. The latter groups might have been accompanied by French officers and cadets, but they selected their own targets and attacked according to their own interests and time tables. For the beleaguered colonies of Virginia, Maryland, and Pennsylvania, though, all these raids and attackers quickly merged into one unanticipated and increasingly horrible border war. Provincial governments hurriedly raised troops and built forts, but border settlers responded in their own way: they fled, allowing French, Shawnee, and Delaware attackers to push colonial settlements back more than one hundred miles by 1758.[26]

Warfare disrupted the lives of all those involved. Most obviously, it upended colonial backcountry settlements and society, erased years of labor, destroyed families, triggered political unrest, and spawned virulent Indian-hating all along what one scholar characterized as the "ragged, bloody edge of empire." Readers of newspapers in Philadelphia, Williamsburg, and Annapolis were treated to a litany of accounts of killing and, just as terrifying, the capture of men and especially women and children by Indian raiders. The raids started early and continued for months until fall hunting by native men brought them to a halt, temporarily. In April 1756, Pennsylvanians learned that M'Cord's fort was destroyed with twenty-seven casualties, including at least one "little Girl" taken prisoner. Also that month a Virginian reported that the "Indians have returned in greater Numbers" and "have drove in the Inhabitants on the Frontiers for fifty Miles." Between flight and concern for their own families, no local militia could be collected to go after the attackers. By summer, the *Pennsylvania Gazette* reported two more missing children near Fort Henry; a week later the paper advised its readers that the two children had been found dead. The following year brought more of the same: four people taken on the South Branch of the Potomac while three entire families were "cut off" at Conococheague in Cumberland

County, Pennsylvania. At the same time, rumors spread that Winchester itself would be attacked while Virginia's provincial troops stayed in their forts and "panick" took hold of local civilians. There was no letup the following year, either. As Forbes was attempting to assemble his army, reports came in from York County of farm families killed and scalped or taken captive by raiders.[27]

A recent thorough examination of such accounts and other sources suggests that the French, their native allies, and the Ohio Indians accounted for 1,587 civilian casualties, of whom 822, mostly women and children, were taken prisoner. At the same time, frontier populations plummeted as thousands fled eastward; Augusta County, Virginia, lost one-fifth of its prewar population while hard-hit Cumberland County, Pennsylvania, seems to have lost over 90 percent of its people with nearly a thousand farms abandoned. These unprecedented losses created chaos on the frontier and generated political and economic turmoil in the colonies. Lancaster and Philadelphia, became magnets for refugees, which led to overcrowding and an outbreak of smallpox in Philadelphia in the summer of 1757. Meanwhile, the Virginia governor Robert Dinwiddie worried about "The Villany of the Negroes" who might take advantage of war to foment rebellion. Worse still, the collapse of border societies happened to coincide with the arrival of substantial numbers of "French neutrals," the French Acadians who after 1755 were systematically uprooted and dispersed throughout the mainland British colonies as a government-sponsored attempt to secure the contested borderlands of Acadia/Nova Scotia.[28]

Confusion and panic bred anger, which in turn was directed at both provincial governments and native enemies. In Virginia, settler anger was fueled by knowledge that the war grew from the private affairs of the great men of the Ohio Company. Resistance to militia duty and enlistment in the colony's new provincial regiment were both driven by a sense that somehow the war was forced upon innocent people by selfish speculators. To the north, Pennsylvania's government was threatened by people who blamed the defenseless condition of the frontier on the colony's Quaker establishment, which many believed was more willing to side with Indians than with hard-pressed colonists. In both provinces, a stark division in political power also fueled anger and threats of violence against authority by people in newly settled frontier regions who enjoyed far less representation and political influence than did the older, more developed eastern counties.[29]

Colonists reserved much of their anger, though, for their Indian enemies and, in the process, risked treating all native peoples as enemies. In the chaotic atmosphere created by raiding parties, border settlers deemed *Indians*, of whatever society, as threats and enemies, generating what has been termed a "blind hatred" that ultimately drew a stark line along the frontier, with "white people" on one side and "Indians" on the other. It was a line reminiscent of the chasm created by racial slavery in the colonies, and it became just as pervasive and just as rigid.[30]

Manifestations of this were the attempts at retaliation. These took two forms; one was the government-organized counterattack represented by the Kittanning raid of 1756 and the abortive Virginia attack on Shawnees in the same year. The other was the vigilante-style hunt for enemies characterized by Thomas and David Cresap. According to one report, these two collected sixty like-minded men living near Conococheague who, "dressed and painted like Indians," went out to "kill the Women and Children in the Indian towns, and scalp them" in retaliation for "their Warriors . . . committing the like Destruction on our Frontier." The act of scalping had come to symbolize the inherent "savagery" of native peoples. Yet scalping, a culturally sanctioned facet of warfare deeply rooted in native societies, became, in the hands of men like the Cresaps an act of atrocity. There was no talk here of taking captives—which native fighters also did—but only of killing and mutilating in a fashion not in keeping with European ways of war. And, thanks to provincial bounties, the hunt for Indian scalps only grew. Virginia's Governor Dinwiddie urged the Burgesses to enact a scalp bounty in 1755, one modeled on "the Measures taken by our Brethren of New England" nearly a century earlier. Pennsylvania was not slow to follow; by 1756 the Peaceable Kingdom had adopted its own bounty to accompany a formal declaration of war against the Delawares. Bounties were a way to encourage otherwise reluctant men to strike back, as either soldiers or freebooters. Substantial sums were offered for scalps of adult native men, and money was also offered for those of women and children, discouraging captive taking and further distinguishing colonial retaliation from native practice. Predictably, colonial retaliation only spurred native warriors to increase their level of violence in a cycle that grew worse as the war went on. At Kittanning, for example, Colonel Armstrong's men took no Delaware prisoners, but did take the time to scalp the dead men, women, and children. More problematic was the scalp bounty itself. Virginia's new governor, Francis Fauquier, perhaps best summed up the problem in 1758 when he told superiors that the bounty "was found to produce bad Consequences, by setting our people on to kill Indians whether Friends or Enemies, for the Sake of the Reward; by which we must fear the Cherokee Nation are incensed against us; it was thought advisable to repeal it."[31]

*   *   *

Ohio Indians, the French, and their native allies enjoyed considerable advantages in waging war. As the attackers, they could choose the time and place of raids. Often traveling in large groups, these fighters would then break down into smaller raiding parties, striking several isolated farms or forts, and depart before any colonial response was possible. Indeed, Shingas characterized colonists as a "Parcel of Old Women" for their lack of fighting skills. As a result, native losses were minimal. The one notable exception was Armstrong's raid against Kittanning in 1756. The Pennsylvanians burned much of the town on the east side of the Allegheny River and killed fourteen Delaware men, women, and children, including the noted (or, for colonists, notorious) war leader Captain Jacobs. This raid, with the killing of noncombatants, led natives to make attacks in kind; instead of destroying farms, and livestock (hated symbols of settler expansion) and taking captives, warriors now concentrated on killing settlers and spreading terror along the frontier as "blind hatred" took hold on both sides of the cultural divide.[32]

Although they successfully carried war to colonial frontiers, Ohio Indians were no more immune to the costs of conflict than were their enemies. In addition to casualties, warfare changed the landscape of the Ohio Country just as it did the colonial backcountry. By the end of 1755, those Ohio Iroquois who had sided with the British since 1748 had all but abandoned the region; the half-king Tanaghrisson died an exile in Pennsylvania where Scarouady and others found a haven at Augwick, the home of trader and Indian agent George Croghan. Those who did not go east drifted back up the Allegheny River to the Seneca towns there and in the Genesee River Valley. Still others, notably Wyandots, moved back toward their towns near Detroit and Sandusky. In the process, the cultural dynamics of the region changed dramatically. The Delawares and the Shawnees emerged as the dominant people. The earlier, multiethnic towns known to Conrad Weiser and Ohio Company agents were now either abandoned or, as in the case of the Kuskuskies and Logstown, home to wholly Delaware or Shawnee families. This sorting out of people and places would shape the region for the next generation. At the same time, the Delawares founded new towns farther to the west in the Muskingum Valley of modern Ohio while Shawnees also began to relocate up the Scioto River from their older towns at the confluence of the Ohio and Scioto Rivers.[33]

The movement of peoples out of the Ohio Country was matched by an influx of strangers to the region who, beginning in 1753, came as French allies from as far away as the mission towns of Odanak (St. Francis) and Kanawake in the east to the Straits of Mackinac and the Chicago River to the west. Some came with women and children, but these Odawas, mission Iroquois, Abenakis, Ojibwas, and others came not to settle but to fight with their French allies. These were the warriors who drove Washington from the Great Meadows and crushed Braddock's army, and they, with French officers and Canadian volunteers, were among the first to carry war to the British colonies. They tended to stay seasonally and remained close to French forts; some remained in the Ohio Country for an entire campaigning season and others went east to join French forces in the St. Lawrence Valley and Lake Champlain. These folks, like the French, only added to the pressures on local resources and heightened tensions with resident peoples.[34]

Pressure on resources and the disruption of normal subsistence patterns were two ways in which warfare played havoc with Ohio Indian lives. Delawares and Shawnees were more secure in their access to land, but no less immune to the costs of war than the now landless settlers flooding the roads to Winchester and Philadelphia. Young men who spent most of the year waging war had less time to devote to clearing new fields and hunting. Colonial captives later told of how the Indians had "neglected their Corn planting," with predictable results. Indeed, by the end of 1758, some local natives were on the verge of starvation, and local French garrisons, themselves chronically short of supplies, could do little to help. Moreover, nutritional deficiencies may have made Ohio Indians more vulnerable to diseases, including smallpox, which surfaced in 1757. The cause seems to have been the Great Lakes Indian fighters who passed through the region on their way home in the late summer and autumn. They had taken part in the siege of Fort William Henry where they were exposed to the disease. There is no evidence of a widespread outbreak among the Delawares, or Shawnees, but Senecas to the north were affected as likely were the smaller villages and hunting camps west of the Ohio River through which Odawas and others passed.[35]

Another war-related feature of Ohio Indian towns was the rising number of captives and refugees. Young men and women such as Hugh Gibson, Marie Le Roy, and Barbara Leininger found themselves working for and, in some cases, adopted into Delaware and Shawnee families. Others were younger. On May 28, 1756, the chaplain at Fort Duquesne baptized an infant, the daughter of a woman taken captive, and then gave the child to the fort's commandant. Living among these captives were others who appear to have arrived voluntarily, such as Catholics John Candon, his wife, and his infant daughter, captured by Shawnees while attempting to "join the Catholics" at the French forts. Losses from war and disease made these people especially valuable as potential adoptees; others were ransomed to the French for money and merchandize. Delaware headman Tamaqua, for example, eventually returned two women whom he identified as "my Mother" and "Sister," clear indication of the roles these nameless captives now played in one native family. Indeed, so firmly embedded were many of these people, especially young women and children, that their repatriation would be a sore point between natives and British authorities for years to come. How much these captives affected Ohio Indian society is difficult to say; however, their numbers and concentration in a few towns like the Kuskuskies or Logstown may have provided skills and knowledge that Indians could use, and certainly provided needed intelligence on the state of colonial frontiers.[36]

War had never been the overwhelming choice of Ohio Indian peoples, especially among the Delawares. The emerging factional struggle within their towns proved the most important result of the war; it would provide Forbes an opportunity to separate these native fighters from the French. Refusing to be driven to war by the French, Delawares elected to fight the British based on their own understanding of threats posed by redcoats and the swarm of civilians that would follow them into the region. Shingas, Jacob, and others who opted for war, deliberately targeted Pennsylvanians as the historic enemy of Delaware autonomy; by destroying farms and livestock they both took satisfaction for earlier dispossession and targeted the specific threats to their security. One measure of their fear of renewed dispossession was the emergence of rumors that the British—maybe with French cooperation—were bent on nothing less than destroying the natives, rumors that took on new immediacy in the aftermath of the Kittanning attack. At the same time, other young men accepted invitations—in the form of scalps, calumets, or wampum—to join raids by Great Lakes Indians and the French. Those opposed to war, however, chose the traditional path of standing aside and biding their time until opportunities arose to offer an alternative. In this way, warriors could fight while others worked quietly in the background for peace, which threatened neither consensus nor social harmony.[37]

The Kittanning raid had a telling effect on the Delawares, by demonstrating the vulnerability of towns east of the Allegheny River. By the end of the year, the natives had occupied the Kuskuskies (New Castle, Pennsylvania), and other towns on the upper Mahoning, Shenango, and Neshannock Rivers, well west of the Allegheny. By bringing the war to the natives, the raid also shook the confidence of some, and provided a vital opening for men such as Tamaqua, Menatochyand (Delaware George), Pisquetomen, Netawatwees (Newcomer), and Custaloga, among others, who sought to bring an end to the warfare that threatened to disrupt their societies.[38]

These men were animated by rumors of a different kind: rumors of British efforts to negotiate peace with eastern Delawares. The reality proved encouraging. In 1756 Pennsylvania's governor, joined by influential Quakers, opened talks with Delawares living in the upper Susquehanna Valley. At the center of what became a complex process of negotiation stretching over the next two years was a man called Teedyuscung. Known to some colonists as Honest John, this hard-drinking sometime Moravian convert had once waged war against the colony but now turned to negotiation. At the heart of the ensuing talks was the Delawares' insistence that the Proprietor and his government accept responsibility for earlier land frauds, including the now notorious "Walking Purchase" of 1737 that defrauded natives out of thousands of acres. Supported by Quakers only too happy to weaken the Penns and reestablish peace with Indians based on fair treatment, Teedyuscung pressed the issue at Easton in 1756.[39]

Meanwhile, George Croghan, now Sir William Johnson's assistant, sent wampum belts to the Ohio Country in an effort to test western Delaware interest in joining negotiations. The wampum arrived at Venango. While the Delawares "seem'd desirous of peace," this trial balloon fizzled when native leaders, notably Tamaqua, expressed caution and rejected the belts, allegedly because they were not "proper Belts on this Occasion" and not made of "old [genuine] Council Wampum." Nevertheless, a way to the Ohio Indians had been opened, even if communications had to rely on Teedyuscung, whose erratic temperament made him increasingly difficult to manage, and upon crown Indian agents closely linked to the Six Nations. The western Delawares did not place much trust in Teedyuscung, and the newly formed Quaker Friendly Association for Regaining and Preserving Peace with the Indians by Pacific Measures remained wary of Sir William Johnson. A significant step forward, however, came in the wake of the 1757 Easton Treaty, when "three Indian Men and a boy" from the west approached Teedyuscung with messages from two western Delaware headmen, Menatochyand (Delaware George) and Netawatwees (Newcomer), both of whom would become vocal supporters of peace. In response, Governor William Denny sent word of his colony's willingness to negotiate to native headmen who were anxiously "waiting at Venango for a reply."[40]

*   *   *

French commanders in the Ohio Country may not have known about these developments and they continued to do all they could to encourage native raids against Pennsylvania, Virginia, and Maryland. The results were gratifying; Great Lakes and Ohio Indian fighters, joined by French colonial regulars and Canadian militia ensured that the British would not be able to mount effective counterattacks while creating a growing no-man's-land between the Ohio Country forts and the nearest colonial forces. By 1758 this uninhabited region, stretching from the Susquehanna River south into western Virginia and west to the Allegheny River had become one of the French military's main assets in the face of the mounting number of British troops in America. Another asset was the continuing native campaign against the colonies keeping this no-man's-land clear while putting British provincial and regular forces on the defensive. Forbes's campaign threatened both. By marching an army overland, Forbes and his superiors were prepared to cope with the challenge of distance and carry the war once more to the enemy. At the same time, British efforts aimed at making peace with the Delawares threatened to rob the French of fighters who, unlike the Great Lakes Indians, would remain in the region year-round and had a strong incentive to protect the region. Should the French be deprived of either the security of distance or reliable native defenders, their hold on the Ohio Country would be severely, if not fatally, weakened.

Native support was crucial to the defense of the Ohio Country. New France could send only limited numbers of men to the region compared to the forces arrayed against them; in fact, the French military in the west was positively anemic. Soldiers in the west were drawn from two sources: the *compagnies franches de la marine* and the *milice*. Despite their name, the marine troops did not serve aboard ship, instead serving as colonial garrison troops administered by the French Ministry of the Marine, which directed the navy and France's American colonies, hence the term "marines." Wearing off-white woolen coats with dark blue facings, waistcoats, and stocking, these troops were regulars, recruited in France for long-term service in overseas garrisons. Organized into independent ("free") companies in New France, these troops were led by creole elites and their sons: the seigneurs who owned much of the land in the colony. These companies of marines could be found not only in New France, but also in Louisiana and Ile Royal (Louisbourg); those in New France numbered (on paper) some fifteen hundred men before the wartime augmentation of 1757. Most were stationed in Quebec and Montreal with detachments scattered from Michilimackinac to Fort Duquesne in the west to Acadia in the east. These men bore a striking resemblance to the British provincial troops: young, single, outsiders with limited economic prospects. In the west, they rarely numbered more than two hundred men at any given fort, and often fewer than fifty. Since they served primarily as garrison soldiers, their soldiers' skills were rudimentary at best. Only occasionally would they augment native raiding parties and take part in *la petite guerre*; they numbered only about one hundred of the approximately seven hundred men who defeated Braddock.[41]

While the marines were expected to hold the line of forts in the Ohio Country on a year-round basis, their numbers were augmented by detachments of militia from the settlements of New France. These men, drawn from the farmers and tradesmen (the *habitants*), were subject to annual service, unlike their British counterparts, who only formed a pool of potential recruits for provincial regiments. Once touted as the real defenders of New France, men bred to the woods from childhood, recent studies suggest that, like the British militia, these Canadians were also poorly trained and equipped: a shortage of usable firearms was a constant complaint. The true woodsmen, who took most readily to *la petite guerre* were the hired men, the voyageurs, who worked in the Great Lakes fur trade. What the militia did supply was manpower, not just for raiding parties but also for the all-important labor involved in building and maintaining frontier posts. Some could be sent to outposts for several seasons, while most mustered in the spring and returned in late autumn in order to reduce the pressure on precious supplies. The biggest problem surrounding the militia was not its lack of fighting experience or weaponry, but the fact that the men who manned the bateaux and canoes in the west were the same who grew the food upon which New France depended. Unlike British New England, for example, New France had no "surplus" male population that could be expended on military campaigns; every militiaman sent west in the spring was one less to man a plow team or tend livestock.[42]

For all that Governor-General Duquesne believed that fortifying the Ohio Country was the best way to secure the frontiers of New France and its vast inland alliance system, Fort Duquesne and its outposts quickly proved a greater burden than an asset. The Ohio Valley forts were built to keep the British out of the Ohio Country; the region was of no economic value to the French who valued beaver pelts and other furs, not the deer hides that were abundant in the area. More important still, if distance helped buffer the forts from British attack, distance was also the Achilles heel of French efforts to defend the region. A distant appendage of a distant colony, Fort Duquesne's garrison was tied to New France by a slender supply line that stretched from the Gulf of St. Lawrence, through Quebec and Montreal, to Fort Frontenac (Kingston, Ontario) on Lake Ontario, across the Niagara portage (Lewistown, New York), along the south shore of Lake Erie to Presqu'Ile and across a boggy portage to Riviere aux Boeufs (French Creek) and the Allegheny River. In practical terms, this meant coordinating supply convoys that could take months to reach the Ohio Country while French garrisons lived a hand-to-mouth existence; unlike Detroit or Michilimackinac on the Great Lakes, there were no civilians and no farms around Fort Duquesne.

For a colony whose population only approached sixty-five thousand by 1760, supplying distant forts tasked men, animals, and other resources to the limit. The problem of building and maintaining such distant outposts began in 1753 when the French began to fortify the upper Ohio Valley. Captain Joseph de la Malgue, sieur de Marin, led over two thousand men, mostly conscripted Canadian militia, into the region in early summer; by the end of the year only two of the planned three forts were built and the expedition stalled with hundreds dead from disease and malnutrition, including their commander. The 1753 expedition was only a hint of how much manpower could be consumed in sustaining the western posts. During the 1750s thousands of men, most of them Canadian farmer/militia were occupied with shipping and hauling supplies for garrisons that, at best, numbered a few score troops apiece. By 1758, the colony's intendant (chief administrator) claimed that three thousand men were busy operating boats and canoes loaded with stores for the frontier. Official reports hinted at how contingent the logistical operations were. *If* wheat was planted at Fort Duquesne and *if* the harvest was good, then sufficient food would be available. In the meantime, however, the only corn being grown by local garrisons was for the families of native men who were going to war. In 1757, the governor general informed his superiors that "I have this year *luckily* surmounted" the problems of supplying the Ohio forts. But in the next paragraph he also mentions that the "extreme scarcity" felt throughout the colony "cannot fail to make itself felt in the region of the Belle Riviere [Ohio]."[43]

The Ohio Country forts could, alternatively, be supplied from the Illinois Country, the northern extension of the Louisiana colony. The Illinois villages were, by mid-century, already producing wheat and other foodstuffs for export to New Orleans and promised to be the breadbasket of Louisiana. Yet, again, geography thwarted the plans of colonial administrators. To reach Fort Duquesne, supply convoys from the Illinois had to travel 1,164 miles, upriver, against seasonally powerful currents on the Ohio River. Such trips generally lasted months instead of weeks. About midway between the Illinois farms and Fort Duquesne's garrison lay the Falls of the Ohio (Louisville, Kentucky), formable at any time, but especially in periods of low water. On one occasion, a convoy worked for twenty days just passing this obstacle.[44]

The spectacle of French soldiers, short of supplies themselves, tending cornfields for native allies underscores just how dependent the garrisons were on Indian fighters. As the war went on, that dependency only grew. While the governor general might dispatch as many as two thousand troops to the Ohio Country each summer, moving supplies, maintaining wooden forts in a constant state of disrepair or threatened by seasonal floods, and the need to keep a body of troops together to defend against a British assault meant that Great Lakes and Ohio Indian fighters continued to bear the brunt of actual combat on the frontiers. This, in turn, required not only that those warriors' families be fed and protected, but also that the French continue to supply the cloth, firearms, ammunition, and metal wares that natives expected and needed. With no access to British traders, Ohio Indians were especially dependent on the French for necessities.[45]

By 1758, the French in the Ohio Country were facing a double crisis, both of them logistical and neither of which they could in any way resolve. First, New France experienced a poor harvest, which severely limited the amount of food that could be sent west, especially when thousands of troops were concentrated in the colony's heartland to defend against British invasions. Of even greater immediate consequence to Captain François le Marchant de Lignery and the troops he led in the Ohio Country, the British naval blockade of New France and the siege of Louisbourg effectively constricted the flow of manufactured goods from France. Existing stockpiles in places like Fort Frontenac would not last forever, and were safe only as long as the British concentrated their forces elsewhere. As early as 1757, signs appeared that the French-Indian alliance and the cooperation of the Ohio Indians were headed for trouble. Reports came from Fort Rouillé (Toronto) that "several drunken Mississaugas [threatened] to destroy the fort." At the same time, other natives were openly challenging French claims that they were driving back British armies, saying that "they were now resolved to turn the hatchet" on their onetime allies. Reports of "great unrest" among Indians in the far west, and that relations were "on the decline" underscored how serious and widespread the crisis had become. Closer to home, a party of Miami fighters, denied both food and liquor by the badly strapped garrison, threatened to fire on Fort Duquesne and did kill some of the garrison's precious livestock. Forbes later learned that Shawnees were so "disobliged at the French" that they were moving out of the Ohio Country altogether.[46] In the meantime, one Delaware made it clear that, once they defeated the British, "we may do . . . what we please with the French . . . and may cut them off at any time." These defections and mounting anger also came at a moment when western Indians, in particular, were having serious doubts about the wisdom of returning to the French camps. Smallpox exposure during the siege of Fort William Henry in 1757, sickened and killed Great Lakes warriors and their families. Some 1,799 Indians were then with the French army, but a year later, only 15 appeared at Fort Carillon to face General Abercromby's army, as more and more natives chose discretion over valor. Equally important, this mounting unrest served Delaware peace advocates well by pointing out the vulnerability of the French and those who supported them.[47]

* * *

Developments beyond Philadelphia and the Middle Colonies by the spring of 1758 would both help and complicate Forbes's campaign. The Cherokees' willingness to join the army meant that the British would have the opportunity to gain essential intelligence about French numbers, movements, and intentions. Forbes boasted that the seven hundred Cherokees pledged to his army would be "by far the greatest body of Indians that we have ever had to join us." At the same time, however, Cherokee cooperation was not the result of an alliance rooted in mutually agreed-upon interests. Instead, the arrival of native fighters in the British camp was largely the result of Cherokee politics and expectations. British misunderstanding about what native fighters expected and ignorance of the complexities surrounding Indian affairs ensured that cooperation would be fragile at best. Indeed, amid his enthusiasm for newfound native warriors, Forbes had to acknowledge that at least "one Warrior and thirty of his tribe" had already left that spring, disappointed when they found no great army massed to take the field.[48]

West of the Susquehanna, three years of Indian and French raids guaranteed that Forbes's army would be traveling through a desert: no farms, no livestock or wagons, and no sources of information about what lay ahead. Forbes was painfully aware of this, noting that his army would be moving through a region "uninhabited for more than 200 Miles [because] our back inhabitants being all drove into Carlisle," forcing him to plan a more deliberate advance over the great distance. The raids continued, preventing Pennsylvania troops from mustering on time and setting back Forbes's timetable, which, in turn, discouraged his new Cherokee partners. In the meantime, those Cherokees had so far failed "to get Intelligence of the strength of the French and Indians in those parts," meaning that Forbes would have to proceed with no clear idea of what lay in front of his army.[49]

Yet, even as Forbes wrote of his frustrations and concerns, Pennsylvania Quakers—in defiance of royal officials such as Loudoun and Johnson, but encouraged by Forbes—continued their overtures to the eastern Delawares led by Teedyuscung. Wampum belts and accompanying messages of peace and a willingness to listen to native grievances not only allowed the Friendly Association to make headway in the east; word of negotiations was filtering back to the Ohio Valley where the news convinced men such as Tamaqua to make overtures of their own. As the army prepared to march, Pisquetomen and other western Delawares would come east to learn for themselves what the British were willing to give in return for peace. It seemed that Forbes's determination to separate Ohio Indians from the French might happen. Yet problems remained; the appearance of Cherokee warriors only reinforced native fear that the British meant to destroy them and take their lands. The challenge for Forbes was to convince western Delawares to make peace while leading an army into their country, an army that would bring along scores of southern Indians who were longtime enemies of those on the Ohio.[50]

The army that Forbes was assembling would more than overwhelm whatever forces the French could muster in the Ohio Country, and Fort Duquesne was never built to withstand a determined siege. Nevertheless, despite the severe logistical challenges facing the French, time and distance were still on their side. Crossing mountainous territory holding nothing but abandoned farms would necessarily slow Forbes's advance and, coupled with spoiling attacks and continued frontier raids, might keep him from reaching the Ohio before winter. It was this last challenge that occupied Forbes in the late spring and early summer of 1758. Before he could attack Fort Duquesne or make peace with the Ohio Indians, he would have to confront the many tasks involved in getting his yet incomplete army on the road west of the Susquehanna River.

THREE

Preparations

* * *

MAY 1758

It is now time to form our Magazines.

—FORBES TO BOUQUET, MAY 1758

There was an undertone of frustration in Forbes's report to William Pitt on May 19, 1758. Twice he emphasized his determination to put his army on the road by June 1 and promised to "lose no time" in getting his force ready to move. Nonetheless, Forbes's letter was a catalogue of problems and delays: Pennsylvania and Virginia troops were late gathering and underequipped, and Pennsylvanians had already consumed one-half of their financial levy to pay down past debts; Maryland's Assembly still refused to fund the colony's troops, forcing him to take them into royal pay for the campaign; Montgomery's regiment was who knew where between Charles Town and Philadelphia; and Forbes had no word at all about the ship with his artillery and all important weapons and stores. Forbes told Pitt only that he had managed to collect a few guns locally along with a handful of men and one regular officer, Captain Lieutenant David Hay. With few regulars available, Bouquet's Royal Americans and the additional Highland companies, still recovering from sickness, were being sent to Carlisle as a show of force to impress Cherokee warriors. At the same time, Forbes decided that he needed to keep large garrisons in the forts east of the Susquehanna River so as to secure his rear and the vulnerable frontier. This ultimately meant culling the Pennsylvania Regiment of 15 men per company; these 720 men would consist of those who were not fit enough for a long campaign but who were able to do garrison duty. This would mark the beginning of the inevitable process by which Forbes's army would become smaller as it moved west. Forbes assured Pitt that he had collected three months' provisions for 6,000 men, and these supplies had been collected "on the back Frontiers of [Pennsylvania]." These provisions were at Lancaster and Carlisle—"west" to be sure—but had yet to be carried toward the mountains and the Ohio Country. In the meantime, Forbes scrambled to collect a "sufficient number of Waggons and Pack-horses" to move these stores from "one deposite to another." Even then, his rate of march would depend on how quickly he could muster enough troops to "prepare those stockade deposites."[1]

Forbes's army, like all others in the eighteenth century, operated by the seasons. In winter they went to ground or disbanded; in early spring they saw feverish activity in anticipation of consistently warm weather with the dry roads and green forage that made operations possible. By late May conditions were improving to the point that Forbes was anxious to get started, even if snow still fell in the western mountains. Sluggish provincial responses to the call for men and equipment included, each delay risked a late campaign and the likelihood of facing the unpredictable autumn weather or, worse, being trapped in the Ohio Country over the winter. Given the myriad difficulties he outlined to Pitt and the immense work required of getting past these obstacles and on the march, it is perhaps small wonder that only a week later he told a colleague that he had "been at deaths door with a severe Cholick."[2]

*   *   *

Forbes's instructions to Colonel Henry Bouquet, who would serve as his second in command, provide some insight into the complicated process involved in moving even a small army. "As it is now time to form our Magazines," Forbes told Bouquet to arrange the hire of 120 wagons, "to be ready to enter into the Kings pay at Carlisle . . . in order to transport the provisions from thence backward [westward] to Rays Town." There, Bouquet was to erect storehouses for supplies as well as clear a "good large spott of Ground" as an encampment for the troops destined to occupy the site. This last required specific orders to the deputy quartermaster St. Clair and to the engineers Captain Harry Gordon, Lieutenant Thomas Basset, and Ensign Charles Rhor. They would have to select the proper ground and direct the work of carpenters and others drawn from the troops. What followed were details concerning the march of regulars to Carlisle, and how wagons were to be organized and their drivers paid; all this in the hope of quickly forming "the head of ane army" at Rays Town. By looking closely at these provisions and the wagons to haul them we can gain some insight into how complex the army's logistics really were.[3]

Each British and provincial soldier was entitled to weekly rations consisting of seven pounds of bread, eight pounds of salted beef or five of salted pork, three pints of peas or one and a half pints of rice, a pound of cheese, and smaller amounts of oil, salt, and other condiments. In the complicated calculus of army supply, oatmeal and butter could be substituted for flour and cheese. By custom, officers could expect to receive more food in proportion to their rank: two daily rations for an ensign and up to a dozen or more for a commanding general. Beginning with the 1758 campaign, however, General Abercromby, worried about the strain of feeding hundreds of provincial as well as regular officers, ordered that each officer, regardless of rank, receive only one ration per day. At the same time, although regular enlisted men would normally be charged four and a half pence per day for food, Loudoun and his superiors declared that rations would be freely provided in recognition of the higher cost of food in the colonies. This small financial boon would continue throughout the war in America. Complicating these calculations was the inevitable dustup with provincials who thought themselves ill-provided with the king's rations. Virginians, in particular, were indignant over the amount of food issued by the army since they were currently drawing from their colony one-third more in rations than the regulars.[4]

Foodstuffs were delivered to field armies in bulk and were stored in barrels and hogsheads weighing as much as two hundred pounds apiece. Each container was numbered and inventoried, with the oldest food issued first. Civilian contractors and commissaries managed the purchase of these supplies and oversaw their distribution to individual regiments in amounts that were to correspond with recent returns or musters. Spoilage, whether accidental or deliberate, was a given, and agents ordered more food as a way of compensating for the predictable need to condemn rotten supplies. Barrels of flour might sit in damp conditions for weeks, resulting in an outer crust of worthless material, with occasional whole barrels ruined. The shipping of meat, packed in brine as a preservative, was paid for by weight; unscrupulous shippers or wagon owners might tap the hogsheads, draining the brine, lightening loads, spoiling the meat, but still claiming full shipping rates. Finally, lax oversight, distance, and time meant pilfering and the issuance of food that had not been properly inspected. For example, Draper Wood, the commissary of stores for Forbes's army, warned that pork shipped from North Carolina and Virginia was of poor quality, of a "fishy & oily nature" and warned that it would trigger fluxes among those who ate it. He also warned Forbes to watch the contractors' agents closely so as to avoid similar problems in the future. As a result, field armies routinely convened boards of officers and commissaries to periodically inspect—and, if necessary, condemn—food stores during a campaign.[5]

The rations for six thousand men over three months were substantial: 504,000 pounds of flour, 216,000 pounds of beef, 164,000 pounds of pork, 108,000 pounds of rice, plus cheese, oil, salt, sugar, molasses, and alcohol in the form of rum and whiskey, altogether about 1,000 tons or more. In addition, the army took beef on the hoof, some 400 head, each of which was calculated to yield about 550 pounds of meat. Yet the army would likely be on the road for considerably longer than three months, which meant that similar quantities of food would need to be collected and shipped at later dates. Nowhere in the correspondence is there any indication of how bulk flour was to be processed and issued. Soldiers might expect to carry at least a part of their weekly bread ration (7 pounds) in the form of biscuit—what a later generation would call "hard tack." These could be baked in advance, stored in canvas bags, and weighed out as needed. Alternatively, armies in the field would erect beehive-shaped ovens and bake bread, usually in 6-pound loaves, for issue to the troops. By the outbreak of the Seven Years' War the Prussian army, for example, was using portable ovens built around riveted iron frames. These were superior to brick ovens; the latter required that the bricks be carried (an additional drain on wagons and horses) and required days to build. In 1755 St. Clair recommended that Braddock buy bar iron in Virginia sufficient to make "portable Ovens" of the kind he had undoubtedly seen while serving in Germany during the last war. There is nothing to suggest that Forbes's army carried tons of bricks or the iron for ovens. Evidence instead points to the army making temporary ovens from local wood and clay as they were needed, as well as in large encampments such as those at Raystown (Bedford, Pennsylvania) and Loyalhannon (Ligonier, Pennsylvania). At those two camps, calls went out for bakers and oven makers, soldiers with the required skills to produce this basic ration. Whether the army marched with a supply of biscuits is also unclear, and the troops and regimental women may well have done their own rough-and-ready baking whenever they could.[6]

Moving this mountain of provisions could only be done by horse and wagon. Commissary agents concluded that it would require nearly five hundred wagons (each with a four-horse team) to carry all the supplies; a single week's worth of rations would need forty-one wagons. If amassing huge quantities of edible provisions was one challenge, moving food with or to the army was clearly going to be another. Forbes began advertising for wagons in early May, offering fifteen shillings per day in Pennsylvania currency and stipulating that each wagon would be expected to travel twenty miles a day. The advertisements were quite specific about requirements: four horses and a driver for each wagon; each wagon to be equipped with a drag chain, grease bucket, a brush knife for cutting forage, an axe, two shovels, hobbles and extra shoes for the horses, and a canvas cover for the wagon. Forbes also needed teams for his artillery and offered ten shillings a day for anyone willing to make four "good strong Horses" available to the army. Forbes was certainly offering competitive terms; Braddock offered ten shillings for a wagon and two shillings each for horses. Forbes thus hoped to quickly collect the necessary rolling stock; in this as with much else in this campaign, he would face frustration and disappointment.[7]

Directing his appeals to Pennsylvania farmers, Forbes and his officers hoped to tap into one of the richest agricultural regions in the colonies. One contemporary traveler estimated that the colony had some nine thousand wagons on hand. But this number, even if accurate, did not necessarily translate into vehicles available to the army. Farmers' first responsibility was to their families; many were reluctant to part with equipment and teams that were needed for tending crops and taking surplus to market. Not every landholder had a spare wagon and team to lease. Benjamin Franklin recognized as much in 1755 when he tried to collect wagons for Braddock's army. In an advertisement directed at the people of Lancaster, York, and Cumberland Counties, Franklin urged "three or four of such as cannot separately spare . . . a Waggon and four Horses and a Driver" to combine their resources and divide the proceeds accordingly. This particular problem was also compounded by the flight of many families from the frontier who simply abandoned farms and equipment in their haste to avoid French-Indian raiders.[8]

Another complicating issue was that the memories of the Braddock fiasco hung like a cloud over new appeals for transport and horses. The army's defeat and precipitate flight in 1755 meant that many wagons were captured or deliberately destroyed and horses either taken by the French or lost in the woods. Cumberland County was said to have had "very few" wagons by 1758. Moreover, as civilians discovered at that time, dealing with the army was not a simple business transaction; the value of wagons and teams had to be appraised to the satisfaction of all concerned, which evidently rarely happened. Values set were disputed by angry owners who threatened to take their teams home, only to be reminded that what the army could not buy it might be forced to seize outright. Franklin reminded his fellow subjects in 1755 that lack of cooperation would be taken as disloyalty and that the quartermaster general Sir John St. Clair, "the hussar," would simply take what the army required at the point of a bayonet. Owners who did rent their teams and equip-

Fig. 3.1 Civilian wagons, Fort Ligonier. (Courtesy of the Fort Ligonier Association.) On the left is the "Virginia" wagon whose shape gives it the look of the classic "Conestoga" wagon. On the right is a Pennsylvania wagon, its more boxy shape setting it apart from its Virginia contemporary. Each proved able to haul about fifteen hundred pounds of cargo and was pulled by a four-horse team, with the driver walking alongside the team.

ment were still faced with the likelihood that these would be destroyed by hard service and neglect by soldiers. Others were drawn by the promise of specie in a perpetually cash-poor society and, however reluctantly, offered themselves and their teams to the army.[9]

The wagons that began to gather at Lancaster, Carlisle, and Shippensburg are often called "Conestoga wagons," the term conjuring up popular Hollywood images of the prairie schooner of the mid-nineteenth century. Forbes was paying for farms wagons of varying age and condition, known locally as "Dutch" or "Pennsylvania" wagons or the Virginia variation, "the Shannando" (Shenandoah) or "Virginia" wagon. These wagons all displayed certain characteristics in common: a bed of about twelve feet in length with the distinctive angled ends that made a cargo space about three feet in depth, with front wheels of about forty-five inches in diameter with the rear wheels some sixty inches in diameter. The wheels were considerably narrower than those on heavy army wagons or gun carriages whose iron tires were as much as three inches wide. The wagon beds could also be fitted with ribs to support a canvas cover. Experience suggested that these vehicles could carry about fourteen or fifteen hundred pounds of bulk cargo. Forbes and his subordinates apparently based their logistical calculations on wagonloads of a ton apiece and were upset to learn otherwise, this despite Braddock's experience and evidence that the European wagons routinely used by field armies had about the same capacity.[10]

The total number of wagons employed during the campaign is hard to determine; no comprehensive list seems to have survived, unlike for Braddock's army. What is clear, however, is that the numbers fluctuated throughout the campaign, and the army found that far more transport was necessary than was originally calculated. Northampton County alone provided 201 wagons and nearly 700 draft horses, but St. Clair decided that Lancaster County might provide 100 wagons. In early June Bouquet was satisfied that "we shall have enough wagons" since he thought 120 would get the army as far as Raystown, and he had recently added 47 wagons from Lancaster to the numbers already contracted for. What concerned him was moving beyond Raystown, since he assumed all of his wagons would by then "be unfit to use on the expedition." At the time of his report Bouquet may have had over 300 wagons ready to march. One very rough method of estimating Forbes's need would be to compare his army's size to that of Braddock in a plan written by Bouquet for a march to the Ohio in 1757. Braddock's column included some 2,100 troops and at least 150 wagons. Bouquet proposed a column of 2,160 men and an artillery train and concluded that he could make the trek with 300 wagons. Forbes's army, initially numbering some 6,000 men (after deducting the Pennsylvanians left as garrisons), would therefore require closer to 1,000 wagons, adding nearly as many men to his army's logistical tail. More wagons would be needed later in the campaign to replenish supplies of food and as replacements for those that, by August, would be rated as "extremely bad" because of overuse and the poor road. Moreover, Forbes's artillery train—when it arrived—would ultimately require another 120 freight wagons in addition to such specialized vehicles as a traveling forge, powder carts, and tool carts. As the campaign continued and wagons fell victim to the mountainous terrain, the army began to rely more on packhorses to carry bulk foodstuffs. Braddock had advertised for as many as 1,500 pack animals in 1755, and Bouquet began advocating their use, noting that 8 horses could carry more than a wagon and could do so more quickly and cheaply. The army managed to collect 600 packsaddles by early May, but many more would be needed as the campaign continued.[11]

Wagons, drivers, and teams may have promised to move the army's stores, but they all presented challenges of their own. Farm wagons, used for local travel and light loads, were never designed for the punishing service they faced with the army. Breakdowns were frequent, wagons were wrecked, and owners decided to cut their losses after only one round-trip between the settlements and the army's forward encampments. Wagon drivers, who may or may not have been the owners, demonstrated the same sort of contrariness that met Franklin and Braddock. Bouquet complained that they "seem so obstinate and so unfriendly," and local magistrates would not impose any order for fear of offending the "country folk." Along with other provincial civilians, wagon owners with long memories were quick to say that "they were afraid of being ill treated," while even provincial officers found them "saucy." As the campaign wore on, officers found drivers quick to desert and an affront to good order. Moreover, many of these men arrived unarmed, assuming that it was the army's business to protect them on the road. All told, these civilian contractors would add to the consumption of rations and would need to be closely supervised and guarded. Drivers could be irritating, but their horses also presented a burden that the army could neither escape nor dare ignore. Even 120 wagons meant 480 horses. And while a soldier—or civilian follower—was supposed to consume less than three pounds of food each day and a quart or more of water, each horse required up to twenty-four pounds of feed each day and up to eight gallons of fresh water. Half the feed would have to be in the form of oats, while the balance could hopefully be made up with green forage along the line of march. Thus, the animals that the army needed to move imposed their own logistical demands: grain would have to be carried by each wagon and replaced as needed; drivers or soldiers would need to cut forage, and the army would have to ensure adequate water, anything less risked stranding several thousand men and women without food of their own. The arithmetic of consumption rates for hundreds of horses was one more thing that St. Clair and his assistants would need to consider.[12]

The quartermaster's calculations meant that the army would have to move an estimated 252,000 bushels of oats to feed 1,600 horses pulling 400 wagons over a three-month period; these oats would weigh some 756,000 pounds and themselves require over 400 wagons to move over the same period. In effect, the army would have to double its transport in order to keep both men and animals fed. The good news in all of this was the abundance of grass along the line of march. St. Clair had ordered hay to be sent to Shippensburg, but Bouquet stopped this and claimed it was a waste of wagon space "as there is enough grass everywhere." On the other hand the longer the army or any portion of it stayed in one place the sooner it would run out of grass. The quartermasters in the meantime were busy collecting as much feed as possible: 10,000 bushels were available at York by mid-May. Such amounts might sustain the transport system for a while, but by midsummer, "greatly diminished" pastures had Forbes and others discussing the possibility of substituting rye and straw for the now scarce oats.[13]

Most of this grain and many of the foodstuffs for the army would come from Pennsylvania or, in the case of barreled beef and butter, from Britain and Ireland through the port of Philadelphia. As the campaign continued, the colony would be a critical source of forage for hardworking animals and liquor—especially whiskey—for overworked soldiers. Maryland, Virginia, and North Carolina would also supply beef, both barreled and on the hoof, as well as flour. Yet agriculture in the newly settled Shenandoah Valley, like that of Cumberland County, Pennsylvania, was badly damaged by French and Indian raids and would not be able to supply the army until *after* that threat was eliminated. North Carolina was too far away to be a convenient base of supply, which left the older well-developed farms of southeastern Pennsylvania, Maryland, and northern Virginia as the sources of much of what the army consumed during the campaign.[14]

The men charged with tapping these resources were the civilian Adam Hoops and the army's quartermaster general St. Clair. Hoops, an Ulsterman, was an established merchant in Carlisle and had contacts throughout southeastern Pennsylvania. Joshua Howell and Christopher Kilby, representing the British army's London contractors, identified Hoops as best suited for the task of locating and arranging contracts for any and all available wagons and teams; they confidently assumed that he could get at least 300 wagons on two weeks' notice. Hoops was also familiar with the backcountry, having served on a committee appointed in 1755 to lay out a road from Pennsylvania to Braddock's army. As wagon master Hoops would become an important member of the expedition.[15]

St. Clair was responsible for collecting adequate amounts of forage, identifying where more could be collected when needed, and shepherding wagons, horses, and their drivers to supply bases ahead of their journey west. At the same time, he was busy mustering and inspecting provincial troops so that the shortages in equipment could be made good. At one point, on May 31, 1758, he complained to Governor Horatio Sharpe of Maryland that "I have wrote Eleven hours this day and tired with that and Vexation." The writing of orders, requisitions, contracts, and reports may have proved the easiest part of his job. As he told Colonel Washington: "I am busy about Roads, Hay, Oats, Indian Corn, Waggons," as well as meetings with local officials. From early April through the end of May St. Clair was constantly on the move: at Philadelphia on April 9, Lancaster by May 7, then Winchester by May 24, all the while meeting with civilians, provincial officers, and their troops. In early May he could report he had managed to deal with forage and learn about the roads west from Lancaster, but he still awaited word on how Pennsylvania was going to raise the necessary wagons. On May 24, he assured Forbes he was preparing the Virginians to take the field in sixteen days while trying to scrape together the weapons and equipment for their troop of light horse. Complicating his efforts was a shortage of muskets. He could get 700 from Maryland but tried to keep President Blair of the Virginia Council out of the loop for fear he would refuse to send them on to Winchester. This latter issue made St. Clair feel as if "I am bound here [Winchester] in Chains," trying to cope with touchy and uncooperative provincial officials. And through all of this, he still had to keep one eye on possible routes for the army. For example, he concluded that a road from Raystown to Fort Cumberland could be cut in as few as four days, less if work gangs started cutting from each end. Meanwhile, Bouquet wanted him back at Carlisle in order to get convoys on the road west of the Susquehanna River.[16]

As busy as St. Clair was with his many duties, he still found time to collide with his superiors. The quartermaster general had a reputation for confrontations and violent outbursts, most of them directed at provincial civilians who failed to meet his expectations. Now, however, he challenged Bouquet's authority. At issue was the chain of command and St. Clair's insistence on acting as he saw fit, regardless of orders from above. In a written dressing-down, Forbes attempted to set him straight, reminding him that "You know very well" that Bouquet had authority as second in command of the army "by the Government" and "commands everywhere in my absence," while as quartermaster St. Clair had no command authority despite his rank and seniority. Furthermore, Forbes angrily pointed out that he would never issue orders without communicating them to Bouquet and that Bouquet had his complete trust: therefore St. Clair could have no reason ever to assume that Forbes and Bouquet worked at cross purposes. Several days later Bouquet wrote Forbes suggesting the general send St. Clair copies of all further orders concerning the army "so that the service will not suffer." This was the first hint of problems with St. Clair over command authority and responsibilities that would plague Forbes throughout the campaign.[17]

*   *   *

While Forbes and his subordinates worked to collect troops, supplies, wagons, and horses, they also needed to collect something at least as important: accurate information about what lay beyond the mountains. The men who were to have supplied this intelligence, the Cherokee and Catawba fighters, were inadvertently creating more problems than they solved. Forbes's comment to Abercromby that he could "foresee an immensity of trouble to manage the Indians" proved to be an understatement. The trouble came from all sides. In the first place, Captain Abraham Bosomworth and his friends among the Cherokees had done their work too well; parties began going north in early spring, fully expecting to meet a real army. What they found, of course, was the confusion and time-consuming efforts to pull troops, equipment, and supplies together. Although the Cherokees were at present "in tolerable humour," they were "impatient to see our Army, Artillery, and their own presents," none of which Forbes could readily display. In the meantime, thirty warriors prepared to leave for home "a little displeased," that they had found neither an army nor the muskets promised them, calling the British "Cowards and Liars." Catawbas were also "beginning to get impatient" and were anxious to know when the army was planning to march. Indeed, "all the Riches in Virginia," according to St. Clair, would not be enough to keep the natives with the army under the circumstances. Washington, at Winchester, warned that delays would continue to alienate the Indians and worried that, though "hearty in our cause," they would abandon the army. At the same time Washington complained about natives who seemed completely mercenary and willing to go anywhere to get supplies and trade goods since "their cravings are insatiable." Cherokees and Catawbas began to depart even as others were on the way; instead of a dependable force of some 700 men, Forbes worried that he could well end up with far fewer men that would make reconnaissance and intelligence gathering more difficult. More ominously, native warriors were prepared to take matters into their own hands: if the British would not release goods promised to them, they would simply take them. Bosomworth warned that it was an "absolute necessity of making a shew" that the expected goods were at hand, since Bouquet directed the Cherokees to Fort Loudoun in Pennsylvania "to receive the Presents," gambling that they would not be disappointed since, he said, "If that measure miscarried, we are in a bad situation."[18]

Complicating efforts to cope with the Indians was a complete lack of any knowledgeable men who could help manage Indian affairs for the army. Forbes expected assistance from the two royal superintendents of Indian affairs, Edmond Atkin and Sir William Johnson. Neither, as it turned out, showed any enthusiasm for the campaign or provided any assistance in creating a viable Anglo-Cherokee army. As he prepared to set his troops in motion, Forbes wrote angrily: "It is amazing to me that neither Sir William Johnston [sic] nor Mr. Atkin have either come themselves, nor have they sent any one person to look after the Indians." This, despite repeated requests for their help. To Johnson he had written that "these affairs have somehow been cruelly neglected," telling him that things "are at Present in the Greatest Confusion." The underlying problem, as Forbes came to understand, was that his army would be moving through a vacuum between two Indian departments, with neither Atkin nor Johnson eager to take the initiative. Bosomworth wrote complaining about a "Cock & Bull" treaty between a band of Cherokees and Croghan (Johnson's deputy). Forbes was faced with confusion and uncertainty at every turn and had to confront Johnson's own efforts to aggrandize Indian affairs north of the Potomac as well as the superintendent's own war with the Pennsylvania government and Pemberton's Quakers.[19]

Johnson complained to anyone who would listen about the "Party spirit" (factionalism) generated by the Quakers and their meddling. What he seems to have meant by this was that, by supporting Teedyuscung's grievances against the Penns, Pemberton and the Friendly Association were threatening to sideline Johnson, who insisted that all negotiations to end the war in Pennsylvania should be conducted through his Iroquois allies. By promoting the centrality of the Six Nations in peace talks, Johnson tried to ensure his own control over events for his own ends. He had equally unkind words regarding the provincial government's role in Indian affairs, suggesting that the government was intent on usurping his authority. He urged that northern Indians should join Forbes's army, noting that the Cherokees were the enemies of the Indians living in the Ohio. In this he was not entirely wrong, and the long-standing conflicts between the two peoples were never far from the surface. Yet here, too, Johnson attempted to extend his own influence even though he sent no Indians nor hastened to provide personnel from his department. Indeed, Abercromby's own campaign against Fort Carillon meant that Johnson's interests were drawn to recruiting natives for that army, not Forbes's.[20]

Forbes's problems with Johnson did not stop with the superintendent's aloof attitude or the meddling of his subordinates. Forbes understood that Cherokee cooperation with the army was dependent on his ability to provide the goods the warriors expected: the "presents" mentioned by Bosomworth. These ran the gamut from clothing and weapons to beads, paint, silver brooches, and kettles to cook the food the army was expected to supply. Forbes found buying the necessary goods a challenge. Philadelphia should have been a rich source of such material, but Forbes quickly learned that Johnson was busy outbidding and outbuying him. Forbes complained to Abercromby of the "underhand way" Johnson was busy "engaging all the Indian goods" through agents (what Forbes called "Myrmidons") sent specifically for that purpose. Angrily, he wrote Johnson directly, pointing out that Johnson's agent had recently bought up goods already set aside for St. Clair to distribute to the Cherokees in Virginia. To compensate for this Forbes placed an embargo on all Indian supplies until such time as he could collect enough for the Cherokees and Catawbas—and was only notifying Johnson as a matter of courtesy. As his opinion of Johnson plummeted, Forbes finally heard from Atkin, who decided in late May to write and inform the general that Atkin had received orders in late March to cooperate with Forbes's army. With that Atkin proceeded to promote his own choice to manage the Cherokees, his own deputy Christopher Gist, while questioning Bosomworth's experiences in Cherokee affairs.[21]

Snubbed by the supposed experts, Forbes and his staff tried to manage affairs as best they could. Bouquet, for example, sought out "George McGuy" (Thomas McKee) "a man well recommended" even though (or because?) he was "disagreeable" to the Pennsylvania Indian commissioners. Bouquet also drew up a list of what he thought to be commonsense guidelines for managing the army's native allies. He suggested that Forbes convince them to wait "without impatience" until the army was collected and ready to march; not to demand gifts until the expedition was over and to "cooperate with us in the necessary arrangements for the safety of our communications," by which he meant assigning warriors to posts as Forbes and Bouquet saw fit, while keeping raiding and scouting parties active. What seemed only common sense to Bouquet, however, made no sense to the Cherokees. They had been promised an army and none had yet materialized, which called into question British determination to strike the enemy. Withholding presents smacked of selfishness and threatened to put the Cherokee and Catawba fighters on a par with British or provincial wage-earning soldiers. And, "cooperate" implied little but native subordination—not the equality warriors had every right to expect based on their own cultural values. Each of these issues, and more, would strain relations until a viable British and Indian war seemed virtually impossible.[22]

The future of Indian affairs in the army relied on men like Johnson, Atkin, Bosomworth, and Croghan; it also depended on people Forbes never met but whose actions were ultimately more threatening than agents' spending sprees or lack of cooperation. While Forbes was attempting to put Indian affairs in some kind of order, St. Clair, in Winchester, sent along more bad news. Not only had some Cherokees returned home in disgust, they had also "plundered all along the Road" through the Shenandoah Valley. Worse, settlers in far-off Halifax County, Virginia, "had a scuffle" with these same warriors, resulting in deaths on both sides. Added to this was news that Winchester inhabitants had mistreated Indians. In particular, St. Clair noted that a shopkeeper had horsewhipped a Cherokee fighter.[23]

For generations Cherokee men had traveled north down the valley on their way to raid traditional enemies in the Great Lakes and Iroquoia just as these enemies moved south on similar missions. This low-level warfare was a rite of passage for young native men and also projected violence outward, away from hometowns, a characteristic of the mourning war. By the eighteenth century, raiders were more likely to meet newly arrived settlers along the way; conflicts were inevitable, but over time natives and newcomers reached a tense accommodation: warriors would occasionally take a stray cow for food or horse for transport motivated by a sense that the road was theirs and the settlers, not natives, were the intruders, and local farmers might engage in trade for pelts, deer hides, or booty taken in raids. A rough live-and-let-live policy helped keep the peace even in the face of hard words or periodic physical violence. By 1758, however, Cherokees moving up or down the valley ran head-on into the fear and hatred sparked by three years of border warfare. Settlers who might have made distinctions between Cherokees, Senecas, or Catawbas now saw only "Indians," all equally capable of killing or capturing the unwary, all deemed enemies merely by dint of being natives. When William Byrd III reported his arrival with fifty-seven Cherokees at Bedford, Virginia, as being "without incident" he was remarking on how unusual his trip really was; by late May, violence was far more common.[24]

The likelihood that Cherokees and Virginians would meet and kill each other rather than exchange hard words or throw punches had grown considerably by 1758. As early as March, Atkin informed Loudoun that settlers had killed some Lower Town warriors in Virginia; by May, Byrd was complaining that "skirmishes" were threatening to undo his attempts to recruit men for Forbes's army. To call them "skirmishes" makes these set-tos seem insignificant; they were not. On May 12, for example, "several" Indians were killed by settlers along the valley roads, and it was all that Byrd could do to prevent native retaliation. Less than two weeks later President Blair of Virginia reported that sixteen or seventeen Cherokees had been killed in "some battles" in Bedford County; three of the victims had been scalped. The scalping and reports that local farmers were acting without orders suggest the spontaneous and hate-filled nature of these encounters. Adding to the volatility were attacks by natives "which Cald them selves Sum times Cherokees & sumtimes Shonees" as they moved through the valley, "Robing & Stealing Plundering houses Puling men of their horses" as well as "Beating with Tomahawks & stoning many People." Attack and retaliation: these encounters bore all the hallmarks of the fear- and race-fueled violence that came to typify life on the border between settlements and Indian country. As St. Clair was quick to point out, even if the Indians initiated trouble, scalping three of these men and leaving their bodies to be found by other Cherokees was just asking for trouble. By the end of May, Forbes was desperate to keep "The Country people and the Cherokees from massacring one another."[25]

Forbes and his subordinates were well aware of how serious the problem was. As word filtered in that Cherokees had been attacked and killed, natives already with the army might feel compelled to leave and exact revenge on the killers. St. Clair found it beyond his power to prevent native fighters from leaving Winchester, even as he tried to get scouting parties out to Fort Duquesne, telling Bouquet that "Numbers go home every day from hence," while Forbes spoke of the Indians' "anxiety and unease." The obvious solution was to get them moving west, away from the settlements and, hopefully, the rumors. But with the army yet to march, this seemed unlikely; in the meantime St. Clair said he simply did not know what to do with the Indians already at Winchester since he could not put them in the field and allowing them to remain idle would only encourage more to leave, adding to the risk that they would run afoul of settlers.[26]

This situation was not helped by the fact that many of Forbes's troops were of the same disposition as the Bedford County settlers. Most could not tell friendly Indians from the enemy and were, in any case, disinclined to see much distinction between Cherokees and Shawnees. Forbes was worried enough about the possibility of bloodshed that he issued orders that all Indians with the army were to sport a distinctive sign: pieces of yellow cloth held on the ends of poles or muskets. The hope was that this would serve "to distinguish" friendly Indians and thus "prevent accidents." The worrisome part of this, however, was that it was up to the natives to remember to display the accepted signal and not to respond if soldiers still insisted upon shooting whether by accident or design.[27]

Those southern Indians who remained with the army proved unable to serve as Forbes had intended. While numerous small parties went toward the Ohio, they returned with little or nothing in the way of useful intelligence. As early as March scouting parties had been to Fort Duquesne, but they were unable to secure any prisoners. Major Francis Halkett was excited by the news—later proved false—that a Catawba party had arrived at Winchester with prisoners, saying that Forbes was "extreamly desirous of knowing" what the captives had to say. By late May Cherokee and Catawba parties were coming in with scalps, but no captives from the French garrison. Forbes and others, desperate for fresh information, grew increasingly impatient with natives who never seemed capable of seizing French soldiers but did manage to return with scalps.[28]

The problem, like much else involving Indians and the army, was cultural; in this case two very different warrior cultures were colliding. For native warriors, scalps or captives were marks of success in battle and added to personal prestige. For the army, live enemies were at a premium, and dead ones were of little account. In early May a scouting party did return with captives, but Forbes worried that he might never learn anything since the Indians might refuse to part with them. Warriors who did bring in captives, then, ran the risk of having them appropriated by the army, never to return; better to take scalps as a mark of battlefield success. Moreover, native fighters could look forward to additional payment for the scalps, at a time when the army was equivocating on releasing the goods that warriors expected for joining the British. Bouquet began attaching provincial volunteers to scouting parties in the hopes that they could insist on taking prisoners. On at least one occasion, however, Bouquet reported the warriors "compelled" the soldiers to return, "as they wished to be alone," either from lack of trust or from fear that inept colonists would threaten the party's security. By the time Forbes finally put the army in motion, he still lacked even the most basic information about French and Indian forces to the west, and his officers were reduced to sending out scouts with the admonition to take prisoners "if possible."[29]

*　　*　　*

Since his Indian allies were unable to provide the prisoners who could supply Forbes with the information he needed, he turned elsewhere. To Governor Denny he suggested that a provincial officer or soldier pose as a merchant or deserter in order to find his way to the Ohio and spy on the French garrison. Forbes also contacted Israel Pemberton, bane of the proprietary government, and Johnson. Recognizing Pemberton's contacts with eastern Indians, especially Teedyuscung's Delawares, Forbes asked him to persuade several Indians to travel to the Ohio, each "unknown to the other" so that Forbes could compare their reports and make a determination of what lay ahead. The questions put to Pemberton suggest just how little Forbes knew of his enemy as the campaign began. He needed to know the number of Indians at Fort Duquesne and the state of the garrison—its numbers, whether it had been recently relieved, and how its own logistical situation stood. Could the garrison be supported from the Illinois Country? Did the French expect an attack this year? And how much artillery was mounted at the fort?[30]

Forbes also managed to collect sixteen men to serve as guides, each of whom allegedly knew something about routes to the Ohio River. Their qualifications varied widely, from John Walker who "knows the roads, a good woodsman & hunter," to Lazarus Lowry and Ralph Sharrett, men "not very Sufficient for a Guide." In 1755 St. Clair complained of a lack of information about the country through which Braddock's army traveled, finding that no one knew the whole route. Most of the purported guides then and in 1758 had worked in the deer-hide trade before the war, and most of them knew only the areas in which they had worked; Samuel Brown, for instance, knew only the Frankstown Path, and a man named Stalnecker only knew the Lower Shawnee Town far down the Ohio River.[31]

Beyond such men and the hoped-for cooperation of Pemberton's native contacts, Forbes had recourse to maps and information accumulated by the provincial government. The problem here was that there were few accurate maps; many were based on traders' information such as John Patten's map, made in 1752 for Pennsylvania's governor and one that Forbes would have seen. Along with maps, governmental papers included testimony from men familiar with the West who offered estimated distances from Carlisle to Raystown. One important exception was *A Map of the Middle British Colonies* by Lewis Evans, published in 1755. The map covered all of Pennsylvania, the Ohio Country, and the lower Great Lakes, as well as Maryland and Virginia. It provided the most detailed and accurate rendering of the trans-Appalachian region then available to British officials. St. Clair obtained what might have been a preliminary unpublished copy in 1755 and likely recommended it to Forbes. Despite the lack of intelligence from the field, Evans's map and commentary allowed Forbes and his officers to understand the geography between Carlisle and Fort Duquesne along with the location of native towns and former trading posts such as Raystown and Loyalhannon. Evans's map, along with other information, indicated that an army might be able to follow the trading path west from the Great Virginia Road to Raystown near the head of the Juniata River and may have influenced Forbes's subsequent decisions about his army's route and where best to establish advanced posts.[32]

Had any French prisoners been interrogated, Forbes might have learned that the Ohio garrisons were facing challenges of their own. Supplies continued to be a problem; since the previous summer only food brought in from Detroit and from the Illinois had prevented starvation at Fort Duquesne and its outposts. To reduce the number of men needing to be fed, detachments had been sent to both the Great Lakes and the Illinois Country, leaving the Ohio Country with small housekeeping garrisons. The French also discovered that Fort Duquesne's location at the Forks of the Ohio all but guaranteed that it would suffer repeated floods, especially in late winter and spring when sudden thaws on the Allegheny River sent torrents rushing downstream. The previous autumn there had been an inundation that, according to a French soldier, did little immediate harm to the fort but did sweep away native huts along the banks of the Allegheny River. More encouraging would have been news that French relations with the Ohio Indian continued testy. Delawares were becoming disgusted with the usage they received from the French. This would have hindered French efforts to gain information about British intentions. Even though it was common knowledge that eastern and western Delawares were talking with each other, French officers could not assume that natives would share information with them. Delaware towns were also increasingly divided over the issues of war and peace, potentially limiting their attacks against settlements and military convoys, and the emergence of Tamaqua and his allies ensured that talks with eastern natives—and through them, with the British—would continue.[33]

Despite growing Delaware interest in peace negotiations, the sudden appearance of Cherokee and Catawba fighters in Virginia and Pennsylvania raised concerns among Indians in both Pennsylvania and the Ohio Country and threatened Forbes's chances of ending the border war and taking away potential French support. Ohio Indians first raised the alarm when, in March, they sent messages to Teedyuscung about the approaching southern warriors. The eastern Delaware headman quickly sent word to Governor Denny asking him to stop the Cherokees and Catawbas—warning that the British would be blamed for any attacks on the Ohio Indians and that the arrival of southern Indians threatened contacts with Tamaqua's supporters. His reasons were quite clear: the Cherokees, traditional enemies of the northern Indians, according to Teedyuscung, "hate" the Delawares and Shawnees. He also insisted on knowing how many warriors were then in Virginia and how many more were expected. The issue now became one of steering the southern warriors away from Pennsylvania Indians without alienating either people. The simplest solution would be to quickly get the Cherokees and Catawbas moving west, away from Delawares and other local Indians; with the army not ready to march, this seemed unlikely. At the same time, Virginia provincial officers expressed concern that news of negotiations between Teedyuscung and Denny would alienate the Cherokees. Johnson agreed and urged that the Cherokees and Catawbas be told nothing of negotiations. Cherokee delegates were heading for Philadelphia and from there to the Six Nations. Should they be stopped and, if so, on what pretext? Such were the unintended consequences of seeking southern Indian participation in a British and Indian war.[34]

* * *

The preparations during May reveal much about eighteenth-century warfare in general and Forbes's army in particular. Like the armies fighting in northern Germany or Bohemia, the British army in America was dependent upon civilians for food, fodder, wagons, and horses. Unlike those other armies, however, Forbes's command could not simply take what it needed, gathering up supplies, impounding wagons, and requisitioning horses at will. Custom and, above all, British law made that impossible. Provincial officials may have warned of the dreaded "hussar" St. Clair, but by 1758 the threat, if it ever took hold, had worn thin; what the army was not prepared to seize in 1755 it could not take three years later. Instead, it had to bargain with scores of independent farmers and merchants who weighed their own particular interests against the public good. In the end, by appealing to patriotism and above all the pocketbook, Forbes got his wagons and teams, at least enough for the first leg of his trip west. And, like all contemporary armies, Forbes's was hostage to weather and time, neither of which could be predicted; by late May the largest part of his regular forces had still not arrived nor had his all-important artillery with its specialist gunners, tools, and munitions.

Wagons were needed to carry the mountains of supplies that even a small army needed to survive for weeks away from friendly territory. Hundreds of tons of bread, meat, grain for both men and horses, ammunition, hospital supplies, tents, and personal baggage belonging to the army, its suppliers, and followers would have to moved, guarded, secured, and distributed in order to keep the troops moving toward their objective. The lack of reliable information on what lay beyond Carlisle or Shippensburg only made the task more difficult. The French and their native allies would surely attempt to raid the columns, slow them down, and inflict what damage they could, but where these attacks would likely materialize, or in what numbers Forbes could not say. The fact that enemy parties were already hovering around the army proved troublesome, but as yet, Forbes and his subordinates could do little about them.

The arrival of hundreds of Cherokee and Catawba fighting men should have eased Forbes's problems with both intelligence and security, but in fact it did not. Instead, misunderstandings and alienation quickly surfaced as native and British warriors met at Winchester and Carlisle. On the one hand was the expectation of friendship and generosity; on the other hand was an insistence on subordination, discipline, and obedience. Indian men quickly learned that their British partners held a very different set of military values: for example, warriors were expected to turn over their prisoners, the living manifestation of a man's martial prowess, instead of carrying them home.

Fig. 3.2 Ammunition wagon, Fort Ligonier. (Photo by author.) Ammunition wagons like this were widely used by the army for hauling not just explosives but also rations and, if need be, casualties. The "GR" cypher on the red-painted wagon cloth indicates its government ownership. Note the wagon is designed to be pulled by horses in tandem.

Little wonder, then, that southern fighters preferred to kill Frenchmen and take scalps as trophies, robbing Forbes of vital sources of information. For their part, British officers expected the natives to follow orders and await payment until the campaign ended, which was reasonable from their perspective but a serious violation of the reciprocity and generosity expected by native fighting men, who began going home disgusted with the treatment they received. The fact that warriors and border settlers attacked each other only underscored the tensions inherent in British-Indian cooperation; such violence even threatened to spill over into the army itself. And lacking skilled negotiators, men who understood cultural differences and could try to bridge them, Forbes was at a loss to cope with his native fighters even as their appearance in Pennsylvania threatened to undo negotiations with Pennsylvania and Ohio Indians. In the meantime his officers began to openly express not just doubts about Cherokee support but growing contempt for people seen as demanding and troublesome, and utterly mercenary.

As Forbes's army prepared to move beyond the settlements and establish its forward magazines, then, much remained to be done. The army would need to be completed with troops and supplies and would need to learn much more about its enemy. It would have to move as quickly as possible by whatever route its general chose. And, in the process, what amounted to a mass of several thousand men, women, and children needed to be transformed into a reliable force able to defend itself as well as attack the French.

FOUR

Moving West
* * *
JUNE 1758

Operations are clogged with many Difficultys.
—FORBES TO PITT, JUNE 1758

The tempo picked up in late May and early June. Bouquet was finally able to get wagons, men, and supplies on the road from Carlisle. The long-awaited Highlanders and Royal Artillery finally appeared in Philadelphia. The arrival of these last parts of the army did nothing, however, to make up for lost time. Instead of moving at the beginning of May, the army was just beginning to march at the end of the month. The recently arrived troops would take even longer to catch up, as would provincials still being raised and equipped by cash-strapped governments.

Montgomery's Highland battalion finally appeared on June 8, but then it took several days for all the transports to get upriver to Philadelphia and for the troops to disembark. Their trip north was marked by delays: weather, tides, and above all a lack of transports; Bouquet's troops had apparently taken up all available shipping and left nothing for the 77th. The Highlanders would also need a few days to recover their land legs before moving west. Despite the long trip north, the troops were evidently delighted to be actively campaigning. They were heartily tired of garrison duty as well as the unfamiliar weather and sickness of the South Carolina lowland. Prior to embarking, the regiment was 39 men short and had 39 more sick of its 1,000 rank and file. By mid-June, soon after arriving in Pennsylvania, they were down to 848 rank and file fit, with 86 men sick and another 68 on detached service. By the end of the month things had improved a bit, with 934 men fit, 64 still sick, and 4 dead. With the still sickly additional companies, though, Montgomery could count on nearly 1,200 officers and men. Like the rest of the army, except for Washington's Virginians, the Highlanders were untried and unused to the rigors of campaigning. Like their regular and provincial comrades they would have to learn their trade on the march.[1]

From the standpoint of the army's mission, the arrival of the Ordnance stores and the Royal Artillery were even more important. Without heavy guns and the specialized equipment that came with them, Forbes stood little chance of taking Fort Duquesne by any means other than a costly direct assault or a lengthy siege that could put his army at risk. The Ordnance stores ship also appeared on June 8 but evidently did not get to Philadelphia until June 11, having first stopped at New York with stores for Abercromby's army. Coming on the heels of Montgomery's regiment, the docks at Philadelphia were suddenly very busy and, for day laborers, profitable. The artillery assigned to Forbes technically consisted of two parts: the train and its personnel. The "train" consisted of the guns, howitzers, mortars, and all of their necessary stores. These ranged from at least one traveling forge to a gin, a tripod with block and tackle for lifting gun tubes onto carriages, and mountains of supplies from portfire sticks that were used to fire the pieces to sheet lead to protect the touch holes against damp, to rope, fuses, ammunition of all sorts, linen cartridges, sandbags, and other engineering gear, along with powder carts, carts for tools, tents, and "ammunition wagons," the four-wheeled vehicles used for carrying everything from bread rations to wounded men and artillery supplies. And, as a reminder of the artillery's wider importance to the army, the train included cartridge paper, twine, and flints. The Royal Artillery was also responsible for making and issuing small-arms ammunition to the troops. For this army, supplying munitions would be a problem because provincial troops were armed with an array of muskets of different sizes and calibers; the gunners would need to ensure that the bullets, flints, and powder charges would actually fit the myriad weapons held by Forbes's men.[2]

The artillerymen who cared for and used this array of specialized equipment included Captain Lieutenant George Anderson, Lieutenant Fireworkers Walter Michelson (Mitchelson) and George Wright, and thirty-four enlisted men—miners, bombardiers, gunners, matrosses (gunners' mates), and a drummer. Twelve other men also disembarked. These were members of the so-called civil branch of the Board of Ordnance, specialist tradesmen needed to keep the train functioning. Included were conductors (who arranged for moving the guns and equipment), carpenters, wheelwrights, smiths, a collar maker, and a cooper. Altogether the army's regular artillery detachment included these forty-nine men, in addition to their commander, Captain Lieutenant David Hay, and five other men sent down earlier from New York. The numbers were small, given the number of pieces assigned to Forbes. Even allowing for Heydeler's provincials and drafts from the infantry to do the heavy lifting, Forbes felt that he was being short-changed. Abercromby assured him, "You had all [the men] I cou'd give you," adding that one hundred artillerymen had to be sent to Halifax from New York, "so that I am no better provided, in Proportion, than you are."[3]

The weapons, the heart of the train, were an assortment designed to support the army in the field as well as to allow it to lay siege to Fort Duquesne. Exactly what Forbes carried with him to the Ohio is unclear. The train shipped from Britain consisted of four light twelve-pounder guns, six light six-pounders and a dozen coehorn mortars—that is, stubby pieces fixed to solid woodblocks that threw explosive shells of roughly four-inch diameter in a high arc so as to reach over enemy defenses. All of these pieces were of brass—what we would now call bronze. Forbes wanted howitzers, similar to mortars but of larger (five-and-a-half-inch) caliber and mounted on field carriages. He told Abercromby that he wanted at least eight of these, believing that they would be far more useful than regular field guns. He may have been acting on the advice of engineer Matthew Clerk in New York, who advised Forbes to take an eight-inch howitzer with him and as many "royal" (five-and-a-half-inch) howitzers as possible, being far superior to guns for demolishing earth and wood fortifications like Fort Duquesne. Forbes never received that many. Not one was apparently shipped from Britain, and Forbes spent contingency funds getting howitzers cast in the colonies for his army. The best indication we have of what the army actually took with it comes from the journal of Reverend Thomas Barton, who served as a chaplain with the Pennsylvania Regiment. At the camp at Raystown, in August, Barton saw the arrival of at least a part of the artillery, consisting of six twelve-pounder and six six-pounder guns, an eight-inch mortar, two eight-inch and two royal howitzers, and a dozen coehorn mortars. In addition, Governor Horatio Sharpe of Maryland wrote of "a small Train" consisting of "some Cannon & Mortars" that Forbes had collected from New York and Philadelphia as a hedge against the late arrival of the stores ship. These may have been included in Ensign Heydeler's Pennsylvania train. Finally, Forbes left some weapons behind in Philadelphia, specifically six six-pounder guns along with an array of ordnance stores. It seems the army took a respectable train with it: at least thirty-one guns and mortars. To operate these weapons, he had fewer than one hundred men who could be classed as trained or semi-trained artillerymen.[4]

Fig. 4.1 Fascines, battery, and howitzer, Fort Ligonier. (Photo by the author.) Fascines—bundles of saplings—served to shore up temporary works such as this earthen battery erected in the fall of 1758 at Loyalhannon. The howitzer, with its stubby tube, was also used as a siege weapon, but with its ability to fire explosive shells and antipersonnel shot it also proved to be a versatile weapon.

These weapons would serve specific purposes, depending on their type and size. The twelve-pounder guns would have been concentrated in batteries in a field army, though Forbes may have planned to use their solid shot to help batter down French defenses. The six-pounder guns would have been used in a similar fashion in Europe—as battery guns in the field. They could also be assigned as "battalion guns" at a rate of two per infantry battalion and again for service in a line of battle. They would have been light enough for the army to use in the field if they ever encountered a large enemy force. Howitzers and mortars, of course, were largely siege weapons, though howitzers could cause havoc to an enemy army by firing explosive shells or antipersonnel shot at its line of battle; they would be particularly effective at shattering the morale of untrained troops or, in Forbes's case, native fighters unused to such weapons. Although Forbes had no news about the current state of Fort Duquesne's defenses, the British had known since 1754 that the main fort was built entirely of wood with only a portion having earth-filled ramparts capable of absorbing cannon fire. Based on this information, the

Fig. 4.2 Artillery gin and coehorn mortar, Fort Ligonier. (Photo by the author.) The gin, used in lifting heavy artillery tubes onto their carriages, was just one item inthe vast store of materials under the control of Captain-lieutenant David Hay's Royal Artillery. The coehorn mortar, designed to fire explosive shells into an enemy fortification, would have been the workhorse of any siege batteries erected against Fort Duquesne.

army had an adequate train to deal with the fort; the question (one of many) was what kind of guns the French had to defend the fort.[5]

The artillery also had to be organized for the trip west. Customarily it would move in "divisions," each with a proportion of weapons, ammunition, and supplies. This ensured both that the road would not be clogged with slow-moving guns and that the weapons would be distributed along the line of march so the army would always have artillery available if the need arose. This organization was also designed to ensure adequate road space for the train, along with the scores of general supply wagons. The artillery vehicles, at least, were pulled by teams harnessed in tandem (one horse behind another, not in pairs as we might assume), thus creating very long convoys. In Forbes's case, the train moved in three divisions, the composition and pace of each determined by the quartermaster general and the artillery conductors. In one respect, however, Forbes decided to break with tradition. In Europe the Ordnance Board would normally hire civilians to drive the guns and wagons; the problem was that when a battle began, as one officer reported, "the Drivers taking fright, when the action began, cut the traces & ran off with the Horses," resulting in the loss of both guns and equipment. Forbes directed that provincial soldiers from Pennsylvania serve as drivers, hoping to avoid such costly and dangerous problems.[6]

Organizing the artillery was easy; moving it proved far more challenging. When he saw one division of the train arrive at Raystown, Reverend Barton counted 138 wagons along with the guns; 70 of these wagons belonged to the artillery. The twelve wheeled guns of this division plus the necessary wagons would have required over three hundred horses. Authorities like John Muller felt that two horses were sufficient to pull a six-pounder gun or a royal howitzer, and three horses for a twelve-pounder. Traveling forges and two-wheeled carts (tumbrels) hauling tools and other equipment could also move with a pair of horses; wagons hauling ammunition, mortars, and other heavy gear would, like the civilian carriages, require four horses. But such calculations were based on the relatively flat open terrain of England and northwest Europe. Captain Robert Orme, one of Braddock's aides, found that moving across the Alleghenies required much more horsepower. Seven horses were assigned to each howitzer and five to each gun. All told, the artillery train would add considerably to the number of wagons and horses that had to be provided and cared for and would also add to the length of the marching column. In one case, for example, Forbes arranged to have no fewer than 140 wagons (560 horses) available at the start of the campaign for artillery stores, and this was in addition to the teams for the guns themselves.[7]

The arrival of Montgomery's regiment and the Royal Artillery provided more than men and equipment for the army; they also brought hard cash and bills of credit to both workers and merchants. Dockworkers, including sailors idled by the war at sea, earned wages for unloading the mountains of gear brought in by the regulars. At the same time, regimental officers would have been buying up everything from spare shoes to blankets and pallets for their men. Captain Lieutenant Hay was busy contracting for a range of material: eight-inch shells, bushels of coal for the smiths, harnesses, candles, tar, tents, and assorted hardware for the train. In June alone, Hay spent over four hundred pounds sterling on these and other items, and purchases continued throughout the summer as the artillery made up for material damaged, lost, or forgotten.[8]

* * *

While Philadelphians were enjoying the fruits of military spending, more than 120 miles to the west Colonel Henry Bouquet was busy getting the army on the move. Carlisle would be the army's jumping-off point; the previous

Fig. 4.3 Artillery forge Fort Ligonier. (Photo by the author.) Forbes's artillery train would have included at least one of these portable forges, allowing Royal Artillery artificers to make necessary repairs and spare parts. Freight wagons would have hauled the tons of charcoal needed to feed the forge.

Fig. 4.4 Twelve-pounder field gun and limber, Fort Ligonier. (Photo by the author.) The twelve-pounders were the heaviest field pieces with Forbes's army. At ranges of from five hundred to one thousand yards, they would have severely damaged Fort Duquesne.

year, five companies of Royal Americans and the engineer Thomas Bassett had built a large fortified camp there that could serve as a secure base. At the same time the new town, founded in 1751, sat at the intersection of roads and paths that connected it to the Allegheny Mountains, Maryland, Virginia, and the Delaware Valley. It was, in the words of one historian, a town "in-between" that sat on the main road used by immigrants traveling south to the Shenandoah Valley and beyond. "Road" might be too formal a term for what was in fact a wide stretch of level ground following the valley of Conococheague Creek east of the first range of the Allegheny Mountains. It was the northern end of what was then known as the "Great Virginia Road," which carried German, Scots-Irish, and others into western Maryland, the recently settled Winchester, southwestern Virginia, and the newly opened lands in western North Carolina. By 1758, however, refugees had created a backflow as recent settlers fled the frontiers. The advantage of this route for Forbes lay in the fact that his army could either move due south down the Concocheague Creek to the Potomac and then west or link up with the trading paths that ran west—from Cumberland County to the Ohio Country. Forbes seems to have contemplated the former track when he ordered Pennsylvania's troops to rendezvous at the Conococheague. By the end of May, however, his attention was drawn to the Raystown Path, a decades-old traders' route that ran along the Juniata Valley. Although the route from Carlisle was well traveled, it was not suitable for army transport. Forbes ordered that existing roads be widened to accommodate artillery carriages and the surfaces cleared of stumps and other debris that could damage his wagons. Nevertheless, this was a small matter. The real "Forbes Road" would begin later.[9]

Despite the conflict generated later in the campaign by his choice of roads, Forbes's initial decisions were based on both the army's past experience and his own insistence on keeping his options open for as long as possible. Philadelphia and southeastern Pennsylvania provided an almost ideal base of operations. Thickly settled and producing plenty of food, leather, iron, and other supplies, Philadelphia and its hinterland also enjoyed a well-developed port and a road system tying it to neighboring Maryland, New Jersey, and Virginia. Moreover, Philadelphia merchants could supply money and credit. By contrast, neither Maryland nor Virginia enjoyed such assets. Even in 1755 most of Braddock's wagons and much of his food had come from Pennsylvania even though he campaigned in western Virginia. Forbes's quartermaster general, St. Clair, also knew from experience that Pennsylvania was a better base; in early 1755 he ordered that colony to cut a road to intersect Braddock's march, accepting Braddock's conclusion that this "is the Road we ought to have taken."[10]

Fig. 4.5 Lewis Evans, "Map of the Middle British Colonies," 1755. (Courtesy of the Geography and Map Division, Library of Congress.) Forbes would have seen, if he did not own, a copy of this latest map, which illustrated the daunting overland route to the Forks of the Ohio.

This new road—known as "Burd's Road" after its builder, Colonel James Burd—was never finished but could still be used. The road was cut because St. Clair was concerned that moving men and supplies over existing routes from Philadelphia to Winchester were too roundabout and time-consuming. Instead, a new road running west to the Forks of the Youghiogheny (known as the "Turkey Foot") could then link up with a planned road north from Fort Cumberland. Such a road, said St. Clair, would provide both security in the event of retreat and also "facilitate the Transport of Provisions, [for] the supplying of which we must greatly Depend on" Pennsylvania. The new road, then, would be designed to support wagon traffic; St. Clair ordered that it be cut "at least 30 Feet" wide. James Burd, Adam Hoops, John Armstrong, along with George Croghan and William Buchannon were to lead the road builders; Burd, Hoops, and Armstrong would all join Forbes's army in 1758. As they moved west, Burd and company generally followed the Raystown trading path. By mid-June they had reached the crossing of the Juniata River and were headed to Raystown. At that point they were joined by a covering party of Virginia troops sent by Braddock. Burd managed to get to the top of Allegheny Ridge before his workmen, very short on food and fearing enemy parties, decided to turn back. Word of Braddock's defeat put an end to further attempts to complete the road to the Youghiogheny. Nevertheless, Burd and his men had determined that a good wagon road could be cut at least as far as Allegheny Mountain; they told Provincial Secretary Richard Peters that they had "a general Satisfaction" in their work. Indeed, one wagoner found it as good as any road he had seen and claimed that a fully loaded wagon could easily cross the mountains.[11]

Burd's Road, called the "North Road" on a 1758 map, provided Forbes with an optional route not available to Braddock and one that could be reached from existing roads on the west side of the Susquehanna River. Moreover, Forbes had to assume that the French would expect him to use Braddock's Road and would be watching it closely, eager for a chance to inflict another defeat on the British army. Burd's Road, unfinished and unused, would likely be of less interest to the enemy, at least until the British had a firm base from which to drive west. Following St. Clair's advice, then, Forbes elected to move by the new road, at least for the time being. Doubts lingered, however. Telling Bouquet that "As to the Roads, I can say nothing," Forbes worried that "after I was advised by everyone to go by Raes town [I would be] sorry if it proves impracticable." His comment is another reminder that the army would be moving without any clear sense of what lay ahead.[12]

By following the Great Wagon Road south from Carlisle toward Shippensburg and then to Pennsylvania's Fort Loudoun, Forbes's army could then turn west to pick up Burd's Road. Marching west along the Juniata Valley to the abandoned traders' site at Raystown, the troops could continue due west or move south toward Fort Cumberland at the head of navigation on the Potomac River by way of a road to be cut from Raystown to that fort. There, Washington's Virginia Regiment was standing guard at the southern end of Braddock's Road. As far as Raystown the army could avoid the worst of the Alleghenies and Forbes would still hold the option of tackling the mountains or following the old road to the Ohio. The final decision could be held for a later date, though Forbes's long-range thinking may have been reflected in his choice of guides, all of whom claimed knowledge of routes through Pennsylvania to the Ohio County. By the end of May and early June, however, the crucial issue was getting troops and supplies on the road and safely to Raystown, the army's "magazine."[13]

Moving from Carlisle to Raystown also fit well with another aspect of Forbes's plan for the march to the Ohio: what he called the "protected advance." This plan came from the widely read *Essay on the Art of War*, written by Lancelot, comte Turpin de Crissé. Forbes, like many of his contemporaries, read and followed Turpin's maxims for moving an army. In a letter to Pitt in October 1758, Forbes cited the work and wrote that he had adopted a cautious advance, "by having posts along my route" and referring Pitt to the final chapter of Turpin's fourth book for details. Turpin used the metaphor of the siege to explain how an army ought to move in the field. A besieging army moved carefully against a fortress, digging its way forward, covering its methodical advance with trenches, redoubts, and batteries. If Carlisle is thought of as the start of the approach trench to Fort Duquesne (what Turpin called the "tail of the trenches"), then Raystown would be the site of the army's first parallel—the line of trenches and batteries built parallel to the enemy works at extreme range. From there, men, guns, and stores could be amassed so the army could continue sapping forward to the second and, if need be, third parallels before the final assault on the enemy fortifications. The "protected advance" mimicked this methodical operation as the army covered its advance with magazines and forts from which it could draw supplies and to which it could, if necessary, retreat. Since he would be moving through broken and mountainous country, Forbes could not use mounted patrols to cover the front and flanks of his army. Instead, fortified camps, defended storehouses, and redoubts would serve this purpose: the army would build as it advanced in much the same way that besiegers dug their way toward an enemy fortress.[14]

By adopting Turpin's maxims, Forbes had decided to trade time for security. As he told Pitt, "altho' I advance but gradually, yet I shall go more Surely." Braddock had done the opposite in 1755: anxious to get to Fort Duquesne, he had eschewed a protected march, divided his small army and moved ahead rapidly with only a portion of his troops, and then suffered a catastrophic defeat. By contrast, Forbes's plan emphasized the safety and unity of his army. The danger, of course, was that the protected advance would cost too much time, putting him on his objective so late in the year that getting home would be impossible. It was imperative that his army keep moving and this required ample transport and a steady supply of food and forage; any unanticipated delays could prove costly.[15]

The move from Carlisle to Raystown was the sort advocated by Turpin. Declaring that "the Great Channel of Communication to Virginia to be entirely by Carlisle and Shippensburgh," Forbes told Pitt that he would establish a large fort "at every Forty Miles distance" while ordering that "several Posts should be made of the Provincials to secure it, at about six Miles distance." These way stations would then form "a Chain for the protection of that Road." From Shippensburg he would move as quickly as possible to Fort

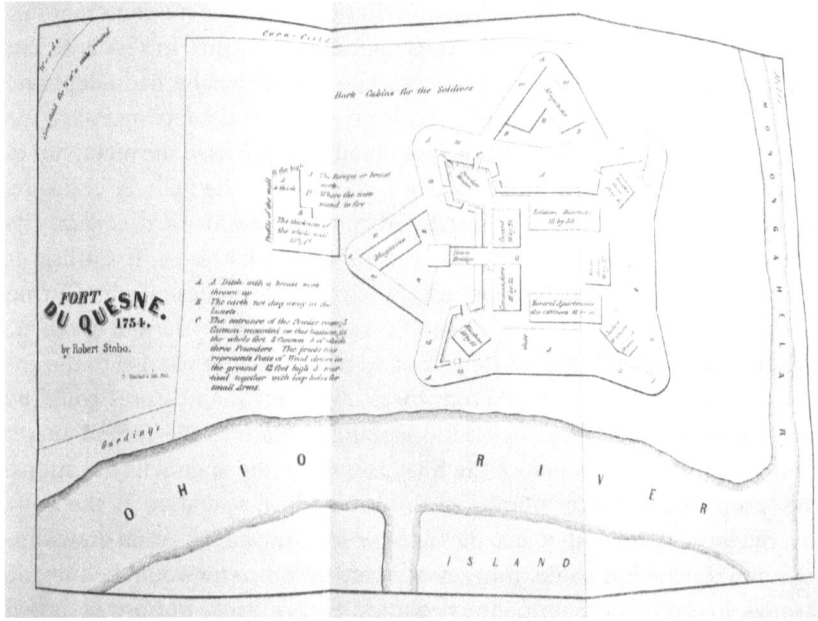

Fig. 4.6 Fort Duquesne. (Courtesy, of the William L. Clements Library, University of Michigan.) A mid nineteenth-century copy of Major Robert Stobo's plan, made while he was a prisoner at the fort in 1754. The object of Forbes's campaign and the linchpin of French power in the Ohio Country was, in fact, a modest work of earth, timber, and palisades. The French garrison understood its vulnerabilities and chose to blow up the fort rather than face a formal siege.

Loudoun, from there to Fort Littleton, then on to the Juniata crossings and Raystown. Once he was at Raystown the tasks of establishing a defended magazine would begin as well as cutting a road to Fort Cumberland and Washington's Virginians. Instead of Turpin's cavalry, Forbes intended to use his Cherokees to create a chain of patrols along the mountains ahead of the army and along its flanks to cover the advance. On paper the plan made sense and was relatively simple: Forbes would push as many men and supplies as possible to Raystown, establish his base (Turpin's "first parallel"), pull the army together there, and then plan the next stage of the advance. Meanwhile, wagons would continue to move foodstuffs and forage along the road, replacing what the army used and providing the stores necessary to continue the march.[16]

Forbes planned to move his troops in stages. Once Bouquet with two companies of his Royal Americans reached Carlisle in late May, he was to advance Armstrong's Pennsylvanians to Fort Loudoun, and Burd's battalion would be sent from Carlisle to Shippensburg. Having thus formed a "Chain for the protection of that road," the remaining Pennsylvanians were to move to Carlisle and then Raystown. Forbes would send forward divisions of artillery escorted by the remainder of Bouquet's regulars, joined by the additional Highland companies. He hoped to have Montgomery's regiment on the road by mid-June. Bouquet would command what amounted to an advance force of provincials, including five companies of the 1st Virginia Regiment under Lieutenant-Colonel Adam Stephen who would join on route. This force would secure Raystown and prepare it for the balance of the army, which would arrive in stages along with the all-important supply convoys. On paper the plan was simple and easily within the capabilities of men such as Forbes, Bouquet, and St. Clair. Reality on the ground would be another matter entirely.[17]

The army's march was plagued with problems from the start. Bouquet discovered that "the roads between Lancaster and Harris's Ferry are very bad" and needed to be widened, a task the Lancaster County magistrates were loath to do. Heavy rains restricted traffic across the Susquehanna River since "they have only two Flats [ferries] on Each Side." The only immediate solution was to reduce the wagon brigades from forty to thirty vehicles each, easing congestion at the ferry but complicating schedules. And, with unintended irony, St. Clair told Bouquet that he would cut the intended road from Fort Cumberland to Raystown then added that "I am afraid you will have a deal of work, from Fort Loudoun, to Rays Town, which I am afraid will be Troublesome."[18]

"Troublesome" proved an understatement. The existing road from Carlisle to Shippensburg was both longer and worse than Bouquet imagined; he fumed about being "deceived" about a road that proved to be twenty miles longer than necessary. As he asked after alternative routes across Tuscarora Mountain, "a very steep mountain," he learned that "no one in this country can be relied on." Then, thanks to the rain, the road from Fort Loudoun to Fort Littleton was impassable because of rock slides, and a lack of top soil made it nearly impossible to repair the road. He was seriously considering making a new road from Loudoun through Maryland to Fort Cumberland when he finally decided that he could make do on the present route but only "by employing the troops on it constantly." For the rest of the campaign, scores of provincial soldiers would be busy repairing and maintaining the road, drawing more men away from the main army. After reading this, Forbes conceded that the main road from Shippensburg was "very bad Indeed," but he was determined to push on by that route since, as Bouquet reminded him, "the season is too far advanced to consider any other communication." What angered Forbes, though, was that his chief engineer was still in Carlisle instead of busy making necessary improvements to the road. The army's vanguard continued its march to Fort Littleton by way of Path Valley and Cowan's Gap over the mountain, avoiding a stretch of Burd's Road that was prone to flooding. Conditions did not improve; beyond Fort Littleton, Bouquet found the road to Juniata Crossing "so hilly that it will never be good."[19]

The same foul weather that created "this hellish road" also meant that the Juniata River was in flood. With over four feet at the crossing site, the troops and wagons would have to wait for the water to subside before they could ford the river and build a post there to secure the crossing. But between Bouquet's column and the Juniata River lay Sideling Hill, the first real obstacle to confront the army. There was no convenient pass like Cowan's Gap; the only recourse was to move across the mountain. John Potts's map of the army's route illustrates the result: a series of switchbacks that allowed the wagons to make the ascent. These "zig-zags" as they were known were only a hint of the labor that would be needed to push the road across the mountains. In the meantime, lowlands and secondary streams had to be made passable; Virginia Captain Thomas Bullitt, with Bouquet's advanced force, warned that he might be late in scouting the road to Raystown since "we have Severell Bridges to raise" before reaching Sideling Hill.[20]

All of this proved to be a sobering lesson. Bouquet had originally planned on taking the vanguard of his army from Shippensburg to Raystown in five days, during which he would erect stockades at Juniata Crossing and "cut the brush" that might have grown up along Burd's Road. Instead, his troops faced rock-strewn roads, impassible streams, steep climbs over not one but two mountains, and an extended south-to-north loop around high ground on the way to Cowan's Gap. Instead of marching with a clear idea of what lay ahead, Bouquet was forced to conclude that "the little knowledge we have about the whole route" could only be remedied by making accurate surveys; scouting parties were sent out and engineer Bassett was ordered "to start work immediately."[21]

Surveys implied charts or plans, and we might expect that Forbes's campaign produced its share of maps of the region beyond Carlisle. Harry Gordon, for example, produced a detailed map of Braddock's march, noting each campsite, and accompanied this with a detailed journal of encampments and obstacles. Nothing comparable has ever surfaced for the 1758 campaign. In fact, in the numerous letters and reports there are no references to suggest that commanders such as Bouquet even consulted maps, though they certainly had detailed journals from scouting parties, which included estimated distances and compass bearings. The only existing map was made by a Pennsylvania provincial officer, John Potts. It is titled "General Forbes marching Journal to the Ohio by John Potts." Not a journal, it is a map of the route, not unlike modern travelers' strip maps that show the route followed with very little of the surrounding geography. Its value lies in its detail of the route, marked by a dotted line, covering the entire march from Fort Loudoun to Fort Duquesne, as well as Potts's notations of the distance in days between points such as Fort Loudoun and Raystown. His three-day estimate of travel between those two points conforms to Bouquet's information that sixty miles separated these two posts, an unrealistic marching rate of twenty miles per day. Potts also notes where and how the army's route deviated from Burd's Road and the Raystown Path as well as details such as the switchbacks across Sideling Hill.[22]

Chastened by his experience thus far, Bouquet had to admit that "the farther I go away from the settlements, the more I see that this expedition, which is believed so easy, is full of almost insurmountable difficulties." Among those difficulties was the state of his supply wagons. As early as June 11, wagons were breaking down; "of the 73 wagons I had at Littleton," reported Bouquet, "there are 33 to be repaired." This level of attrition was made worse because the "wagons are old and the horses worn out," thanks to the bad faith of Pennsylvania farmers. By the time he reached the Juniata Crossing, Bouquet estimated that the army would need at least 400 wagons; he reported that "we now have 250 wagons Contracted for," but these were still not enough. This matter of wagons was all the more troubling and urgent because, "for want of stores prepared in advance," the army would be consuming as much food and forage on the way to Raystown as could be carried over the road. Without the means to replace what had been used and create sufficient magazines, the army would either starve or be forced to retreat. Forbes's army thus confronted a variation of a logistical problem faced by all eighteenth-century armies: the longer they operated away from secure bases of supply, the more they would depend on wagons and horses for food, munitions, and other stores. Distance was an enemy no army could control or manage. Moreover, the lands between Carlisle and Fort Duquesne could provide no logistical support aside from grass for fodder. Whereas, in Europe, armies could forage an area, collecting all they could, and then move on, Forbes's army was moving through a desert. And even if frontier farmers had stayed on their land, they were far too few to sustain an army of several thousand people and animals for even a few days, let alone weeks or months.[23]

The shortage of wagons was only part of the problem. Bouquet calculated that "a wagon cannot go from Loudoun to Littleton in less than a day and a half, and two days from Littleton to Juniata," and will only carry fifteen hundred pounds—not one ton as he and Forbes had assumed. Three and a half or four days' travel just to get to Juniata Crossing meant that only more wagons could keep pace with the need to amass stores there and at Raystown, eighteen miles farther west. What also worried Bouquet was the cost: several days' worth of forage and feed for the horses, food for the teamster, and an estimated three pounds for the trip, on top of the costs from Carlisle to Fort Loudoun at a time when the army was already hard-pressed for cash. Faced with these disturbing facts, Bouquet's interest turned to packhorses. These sturdy beasts had been used for a generation by trans-Appalachian traders and had proved capable of crossing mountains on narrow trails loaded with trade goods or deer hides. By Bouquet's reckoning, eight of these animals could carry sixteen hundred pounds of stores and make the same trip from Loudoun to Juniata in only two days. They did not need expensive feed such as hay or oats, whereas the army had to provide both of these for wagon teams, requiring yet more transport. Another advantage was that these eight horses would only cost thirty-two shillings per day, a bargain compared to a wagon and team. He pointed out to Forbes that 840 packhorses could carry 168,000 pounds of flour; the same load would occupy over 100 of the more expensive but less reliable wagons and teams.[24]

Forbes's response was equivocal. He told Bouquet that "I have ever been of opinion that the Advanced part of the army in order to make the deposites [magazines], ought to have nothing else [that is, only packhorses] with them," but he quickly added that "I thought that after taking post, and making of the roads that Waggons would be the most expeditious method" for moving supplies. He ended by throwing the matter back into Bouquet's lap, telling him "as you are upon the spott and see the nature of the roads, you must certainly be the best judge what is properest to be done." He added that St. Clair and Colonel John Armstrong were already hiring horses. On the one hand Forbes's assessment of the continuing need for wagons was correct: packhorses could not carry artillery stores, the flying hospital, and much of the heavy gear such as tents and tools. On the other hand, if he did believe that the army's vanguard should have relied entirely on pack animals, this was not reflected in his initial call for transport, when every effort was spent to get adequate wagons, with no mention of providing packhorses for Bouquet's initial advance. As the campaign wore on, the army, while using packhorses, continued to rely on wagons and teams, which in turn made the collection of ample supplies of hay and grain as important as providing bread and gunpowder to the troops. Forbes was all too aware of the logistical conundrum he faced. He explained that "making the Waggons carry their forage for two or three days is in reality cheating ourselves, as they carry infinitly less provisions in proportion," which, if allowed to continue, meant that Forbes would be unable to create adequate magazines and the campaign would end for lack of food. This same unforgiving calculus applied to men as well as horses. The troops had already consumed a month or more of rations, and from Raystown they would still be only halfway to their goal. With each day's march away from its base at Carlisle, the army would become more dependent on a constant, predictable convoy of wagons hauling the all-important flour and salt meat. The solution was clear: the wagons could not carry two or three days' worth of forage; oats, yes, but hay would have to be found and stored on route so that hungry teams could be fed on the road through a magazine system like the one that was to sustain the rest of the army.[25]

It was here that Forbes discovered that the frontier might not be all desert after all. Growing on the scores of abandoned farms between Shippensburg and Raystown was hay, which "rots upon the Ground for want of Hands & Scythes to cut it down and make it." The individual responsible for harvesting this unanticipated bounty was the quartermaster general, St. Clair. Collecting forage was not his only duty, of course, and in May and June he was occupied with mustering, arming, and equipping Virginia troops, keeping increasingly disgruntled Cherokees in good humor, planning the new road to Raystown from Fort Cumberland, and balancing the army's myriad needs against its diminishing ability to pay suppliers. On this latter point, though, Forbes was quick to complain that "my Friend Sir J. St. Clair does not value what expence he runs into," leaving it to Forbes to "moderate as much as possible." In the meantime, St. Clair's abrasive personality, directed against all who stood in his way, was already causing problems. The result was that "Waggons and roads are the Devil," with "Sir John having almost disobliged the whole Virginians with their new Governour in to the bargain." Forbes was also forced to compel St. Clair to act on positive orders regarding the posting of provincials and Indians to screen the army as it moved through the mountains, telling St. Clair that he did not want to micromanage but had to insist that his orders be followed. St. Clair was inclined to behave as though he enjoyed a field command, arguing with Bouquet and attempting to exercise authority that he did not possess. Much of this would come to a head later; but already, in late June, Forbes was beginning to regret the appointment of his quartermaster. He told Abercromby in early July that St. Clair was serving him as he did Braddock, promising everything but delivering nothing, and Forbes cited as an example his provision of packsaddles of such poor quality that they threatened to maim the horses. These were merely the opening salvos in a barrage of complaints that would grow as the campaign continued.[26]

* * *

Despite all of the issues in front of him such as wagons, roads, weather, money, and St. Clair, Indian affairs were never far from Forbes's thoughts. It could hardly have been otherwise, given how important natives, both enemies and allies, were to the success of the campaign. As early as June 7, Forbes "very near" lost the Cherokees who, having come north expecting an army, saw nothing but the confusion that plagued Bouquet. Forbes had to work hard to convince the natives that he had an army and would attack the French. At the same time he knew that "our Negotiation with the Delaware Indians upon the Ohio has come to a pretty good length" now that Christian Frederick Post and the Quaker Charles Thomson were headed north to Wyoming to talk with the natives ahead of the planned peace conference at Easton later in the year. Forbes's relations with Cherokees and Ohio Indians as well as his efforts to penetrate the screen of Indians that covered Fort Duquesne were tied together by a web of relationships rooted in recent history, native diplomacy, and French success in keeping their Indian allies in the field. That Forbes moved west carrying both the sword and offers of peace only further complicated his relations with friend and foe.[27]

The risk of losing the Cherokees and Catawbas was very much on Forbes's mind in May and June. He knew that the Indians "are Impatient and want to go home" in the face of the army's inertia. Worse, "they begin to grow Extreamly licentious" going so far as to "seize the presents designd for them," which the warriors felt were their due whether the army moved or not. The Catawbas proved less worrisome than the more numerous Cherokees; of the Catawbas' leader, Captain Bullen, Bouquet told Forbes "I have adopted him as my son" and the Catawbas "will not leave us." Yet the Cherokees gathered at Winchester were said to express much "anxiety and unease." Colonel William Byrd said they were "restless" and would not stay with the army indefinitely. St. Clair tried to persuade them to stay, but some had already left and "plundered all along the Road," perhaps to get even for their treatment on the road north. At the same time, St. Clair told Bouquet that "it is the greatest curse which Our Lord could pronounce against the greatest sinners, to have to do business with Indian friends." St Clair was also worried about the eight hundred unarmed Virginia troops at Winchester should the warriors decide to exact a measure of revenge for the killings in Bedford County. Bouquet warned that those Cherokees at Shippensburg exhibited a "bad humour." By early June, the goodwill that seemed to animate both natives and British was beginning to wear dangerously thin. Native fighters felt cheated on two counts: they had taken the long and dangerous trip north to discover that there was no army on the move and that their so-called allies were bent on treating them as just another sort of enlisted soldiers whose pay, the promised "presents," would be distributed as wages and not as a symbol of friendly generosity. The reception accorded the Cherokees in southern Virginia did not help, of course, nor did the short tempers of officers such as St. Clair. Anxiety, restlessness, and a growing measure of mutual contempt would grow as June wore on and the army made only a fitful advance.[28]

Forbes did what he could to ensure that those warriors who joined the army did so without fear of trigger-happy soldiers, most of whom had never been face-to-face with natives. Along with the yellow cloth mentioned by Bouquet were "silver arm plates & 50 bracelets" for native leaders, all designed to serve as recognition signs. Even so, soldiers were ordered not to shoot at Indians unless fired upon, since some Cherokees and Catawbas might not yet have "the proper Marks to distinguish them." Sutlers and other civilians traveling with the army were specifically forbidden to sell alcohol to Indians; any civilians in the army's path who did so risked having their houses razed and goods impounded. Yet orders to the troops still placed the burden of proper identification on the Indians, and the prohibition against liquor could be seen by thirsty men as another example of British disdain for their friends. While there are no examples of friendly fire between British and Indian soldiers, the orders only served to underscore latent distrust and insecurity on both sides.[29]

Amid this growing friction some Cherokees and Catawbas did go out to scout near Fort Duquesne, and a few managed to take *la petite guerre* to the enemy. Natives returned to Fort Loudoun (Virginia) in mid-May without the prisoners that Forbes wanted, but they did kill two French soldiers; at the end of the month, another party came in to Winchester with a French scalp, while several more parties were still in the vicinity of the French fort. June brought more of the same: Cherokees arrived at Fort Littleton after six weeks having killed one Frenchman on the portage road near Fort Presqu'Ile, an encounter that also cost the natives one dead. A reminder of the problems facing Forbes's army in the task of dealing with its native warriors surfaces in Lieutenant-Colonel Hugh Mercer's report of this scout; the information he sent was the best he could get from "their Signs, for We have no Interpreter here." On another occasion, a Virginia provincial with a Cherokee party was forced to return alone after an encounter that left one Frenchman dead and scalped and the Virginian bitten by a rattlesnake; he survived when the Cherokees "gave him a root which he was to chew" and apply to the wound. He headed for Raystown when he could no longer keep up with the natives.[30]

Cherokee attempts to get prisoners were unsuccessful despite Forbes's admonitions about "endeavouring to get particular Intelligence of Fort du quesne" as well as to scout the routes ahead. By mid-June, as frustration mounted, Pitt learned that Forbes had "used every art and Means to get Intelligence, . . . but to little purpose." By early July, Forbes still knew "little or nothing" about the enemy and complained of moving "in the dark." Southern warriors' efforts to screen the army from unwanted attention also failed. As early as May 25, Bouquet reported from Carlisle that "we can no longer move a step without an escort, as there are several small parties of enemy Indians all around us." The same problem plagued the army's outposts. In mid-June, for instance, Thomas Cresap sent news to Bouquet that four Indians had attacked a party of thirty or forty men near Fort Cumberland, killing and wounding four soldiers. By contrast, Delawares from the upper Allegheny Valley were able to tell the French commander at Fort Duquesne that the British were collecting large numbers of troops and cattle at Lancaster and planned to attack the fort once the grass was growing. Governor-General Vaudreuil at Montreal could tell his superiors in France that he was able to keep raiders out as far as Fort Augusta (Sunbury, Pennsylvania) who continued to collect both scalps and prisoners. These and other reports suggest that French and Indian parties were able to maintain pressure on Pennsylvania's borders through the summer. Yet the French also may have been in the dark: they evidently knew little or nothing of Forbes's advance beyond Lancaster, and one French officer, Bougainville, held the opinion that the British would not attack Fort Duquesne before October; there was still ample time to see to the defense of the Ohio Country.[31]

The problem, Forbes knew, was that by early June as many or more Cherokees were leaving the army as were arriving. Moreover, those who remained were proving unreliable and reluctant to exert themselves for "allies" who were so close-fisted—men who treated Indians like subordinates rather than equals. Resentment had festered since Byrd's and Bosomworth's initial efforts to recruit Cherokee fighters. Along with fine words about friendship and cooperation, warriors were reminded, for instance, that Forbes expected them to remain with the army and not leave without his permission—in return for which they would receive goods. Talk about the "common cause" began to ring hollow when natives arrived in Pennsylvania only to discover that there was no army and that provincial officials were anxious to send the Cherokees on their way out of the settlements before their presence could threaten delicate negotiations with Teedyuscung's eastern Delawares. Finally, promises of goods had been freely given to induce warriors to abandon their spring hunt in favor of joining the army; now it seemed that the promised compensation would be given only at the end of the campaign since the British saw these goods as wages instead of gifts. Only when Cherokee fighters demonstrated their dissatisfaction and "had blackened themselves & were going off in a bad humour" at not receiving goods when they arrived did Bosomworth ask that the "Indian Presents" be sent to Shippensburg, "to Satisfy the Indians that we have Provided the necessary Goods for them." Bouquet also told St. Clair that he had sent Bosomworth to convince the Indians to go to Fort Loudoun (Pennsylvania) "to receive the Presents," adding, "if that measure miscarries, we are in a bad scituation."[32]

The British were indeed in a "bad scituation," and it was about to get worse. The epicenter of the collision between Cherokees and the army was Fort Loudoun. On June 5, Bouquet learned that Cherokees had decided to go home but wanted the promised goods before they left. When William Trent, Pennsylvania trader and sometime Indian agent, tried to stall them, several men took off their shirts and threw them at Trent, saying they were for Bouquet since he evidently loved such things so much he would not share with the Cherokees. Worse, the warriors threatened to plunder settlements on their way home if that was the only way to get the materials promised them; some talked of joining the French and their Creek allies. Clearly shaken, Trent told Bouquet that he and Forbes needed to make clear what they expected of the Cherokees, adding that without proper interpreters he was reduced to using an Indian, "Anthony," suspected of stirring up Cherokee anger in the first place. By now, "a great number" of warriors had already left the army and more were to follow; less than a week after their confrontation with Trent, Maryland's governor predicted that fewer than one hundred fighters would probably remain with the army.[33]

Matters finally came to a head in mid-June. In the middle of moving the vanguard of the army to Raystown, Bouquet went to Fort Loudoun and from June 14 to June 16, met with the warriors in an effort to salvage the British-Cherokee war effort. After rehearsing their friendship and the threat the French posed to both natives and British, Bouquet told the assembled warriors they needed to be patient and ridiculed those men who had already gone home by saying they were more eager to see their wives than fight the French. He added that Forbes was an experienced "warrior" and would not move the army forward until he was ready. Further, the natives were told that Forbes had indeed collected a very large supply of presents for them, part of which they had seen at Shippensburg, but that these would only be given out at the end of the campaign. Then, perhaps in an attempt to avert another showdown while the army was moving, Bouquet reminded the Cherokees that such a large body of goods was difficult to carry with the army; it was best to leave them in one place (Fort Loudoun) secure against harm (and against Indians eager to take what was theirs). There is no record of the natives' reply to any of this. Since the only interpreters present were Bosomworth and Trent (neither of them fluent in Cherokee), we cannot know how much of what was said was understood. Nevertheless, Bouquet felt satisfied that he had averted a disaster, telling Forbes that "After two days of intrigue, dinners, and public councils," he had convinced the natives to stay with the army.[34]

Whatever Bouquet thought of his council skills, it is clear he said nothing that would make native fighters think twice before leaving the army. Patience? Cherokees and Catawbas had begun arriving in April and had run the gauntlet of Virginians, losing men into the bargain. It was now mid-June and still the army was not ready, which left these men the choice between cooling their heels until the warrior Forbes decided it was time to move or going home to look after families who depended upon them for trade goods as well as security in a time of war. And those trade goods—blankets, shirts, tools, weapons, powder and shot, silver brooches, beads, and countless other things—were now to be locked away until some vague moment in the future. Finally, whether he knew it or not (or cared), Bouquet also drew a stark distinction between native and British views of cooperation. Cherokees and Catawbas who were already risking their lives scouting ahead of the army had good reason to expect their "brothers" to exhibit appreciation by releasing the goods on demand, as an act of reciprocity between equals. Moreover, Bouquet's refusal to release the goods undermined Forbes's standing as both "warrior" and leader in the eyes of the natives. Forbes and his officers, on the other hand, only reinforced the assumption that native fighters were subordinate members of the army, men whose cooperation would be rewarded with "wages" when their services were no longer needed. It was the sort of cultural disconnect that plagued British–Indian relations for generations and never more so when the two peoples attempted to cooperate militarily. Neither natives nor British were willing to surrender what they thought was right and proper for the sake of a "British and Indian" war.[35]

The problem went deeper still. While Trent and Bouquet were struggling to overcome the warriors' mistrust and sense of betrayal, Forbes was expressing an all-too-common assessment of his erstwhile allies. To Pitt he spoke of the Indians' "natural fickle disposition" and resented his inability to compel them to act as he thought they should. On the eve of the confrontation at Fort Loudoun, Forbes told Bouquet that the Cherokees "are most certainly a very great plague," while telling the earl of Loudoun of their "natural wavering disposition." These sentiments were not his alone but were shared by others in the army. William Byrd, the de facto superintendent of Forbes's native fighters, also found them "insolent," "restless," and by extension not to be trusted. Washington, while acknowledging that the "unfortunate arrival" of the Indians before the army was ready caused the natives to "be tired of waiting," nonetheless attributed their impatience to their "naturally . . . discontented Temper." The only notable exception was Bouquet. Coming away from his first encounter with natives in a formal council, he marveled at their speeches and "was amazed to See So much of true understanding, dignity, and Strength of argument in their Propositions." Yet he did not preserve their speeches and added that he did not know how much "we can depend upon their Sincerity, or their steadiness," only conceding that "I never Saw better appearances."[36]

Cooperation between southern Indians and the British army had always been fragile and prone to misunderstanding. There was clearly no middle ground here, no cooperation based on shared interests that could transcend the differences among individuals and particular events. Instead, Cherokees and Catawbas who converged on Winchester and Carlisle did so more from the dynamics of local politics than a sense that cooperation with the British could serve any larger purpose. For the Cherokees, in particular, competition between towns and headmen for power at home led some to embrace the British call for fighters, hoping to bolster their own prestige and that of their kin groups. The British army simply needed men with the training and experience to combat an enemy whose woods craft and ability to damage the army—perhaps fatally—were well known and respected. In fact, it would not be too much of an exaggeration to say that Forbes needed native fighters far more than they needed him. Forbes's initial enthusiasm for Cherokee and Catawba warriors was rooted in the assumption that they would give him the edge needed to successfully cross hostile territory and take Fort Duquesne. The goods ("presents" or "trade goods") seem to have been the only issue the two sides had in common, but even here cultural differences and misunderstandings resulted in hardware and clothing becoming symbols of greed or betrayal, depending on the point of view. And, if Forbes and others could readily label natives as "insolent," "fickle," or "naturally discontented," Cherokees could have rendered the same assessment of the British. They, after all, were the fickle ones: promising goods, then changing the terms of distribution; Bouquet was insolent in chiding warriors for wanting their women more than martial success; native treatment overall might have suggested that the soldiers and civilians were naturally slow and discontented. Not all Cherokees left the army, and others, not yet aware of what awaited them upon arrival, were still on route. But the rift between Forbes and his native fighters, manifest in the contention over gift-giving, was now a fact.[37]

Faced with native defections, Forbes sought explanations for his problems in the behavior of others. He had been hard-pressed to collect the necessary Indian goods in the first place, thanks to Sir William Johnson's buying spree in Philadelphia that spring and Johnson's continuing tendency to "intermeddle." Forbes still needed a trusted Indian advisor and thought Byrd "would be the properest," assisted by Bosomworth, but quickly added that he did not "know how far we can trust" Bosomworth. He would continue to rely on Byrd while leaning more and more on his cousin James Glen, the former governor of South Carolina and a member of the general's official "family." It is doubtful, though, that even a gifted negotiator, someone of Johnson's stripe, could have averted the problem now facing Forbes, the differences were simply too wide to be easily bridged and the distrust that grew from close association too powerful. In the end Forbes could only put the best face on what was yet another setback, saying that only a couple of hundred loyal natives were worth more than three times that number who could not be relied upon. Forbes also turned to ways of compensating for the departure of Indians; at one point he noted that the experienced Maryland companies had to stay with the army since he needed such men. Finally, he held out the hope that relations with the Cherokees would improve with the anticipated arrival of that most pro-British leader, Attakullakulla. When he appeared, all would be well.[38]

Deprived of most of his native fighters and convinced that Forbes was "very much detached from the prejudices of the past," Bouquet suggested making "Indians of part of our provincial soldiers." He argued further that the expense would be minimal, that the troops themselves "are very willing," and since the army found itself "groping into an unknown country," the advantages of such men "would be very real." What evidently made the soldiers so willing was the thought of discarding regimental clothing in exchange for breech clouts, moccasins, and shirts. Forbes readily agreed, saying that "I have been long in your opinion" of equipping provincials "like the Savages" and pointed to Byrd's Virginians, most of whose men were without uniforms and thus already "equipt in that manner." Since the army was moving toward the mountains and enemy country, and since his efforts to collect intelligence had so far been futile, Forbes concluded that "in this country, wee must comply and learn the Art of Warr, from Enemy Indians or anything [sic] else who have seen the Country and Warr carried on in itt." The fact that few if any provincial troops in the army were seasoned woodsmen or had ever heard a shot fired in anger seems not to have entered the discussion. And although Forbes may have had in mind the veteran rangers that served in New York and Nova Scotia, it remained to be seen whether letting his soldiers play Indian would work. Indications certainly suggest that enthusiasm was no substitute for hard experience of the sort that the provincials—and regulars—lacked. One Virginia soldier out on a scout to Fort Duquesne only survived when he was rescued by a party of Cherokees after he wandered aimlessly for eight days without food. Two months later Bouquet complained about the failure of another large party that lost its way and never did accomplish its mission.[39]

Having in mind the rangers he saw in New York, Forbes also took steps to engage men who were experienced in border warfare. As early as May, Maryland's Governor Sharpe appears to have discussed "a new kind of Company" with St. Clair. This turned out to be fifty volunteers led by Captain Evan Shelby. According to Forbes, the men agreed to serve for rations, moccasins, and "the liberty to keep all the scalps they shall take to sell them to their Assembly" for the stipulated bounty of fifty pounds sterling per scalp. Needing good scouts and men who could wage *la petite guerre* as the French did, Forbes shrugged off whatever qualms he may have had and accepted the now widespread use of scalp bounties as an enticement for recruits. By early September these men, according to Forbes, were "out upon the hunt so I wish them a good harvest," though he worried that these scalp-hunters might kill the wrong "enemy" Indians, such as Delawares who might be traveling with Christian Frederick Post. Meanwhile, Forbes also promoted Captain John Dagworthy to lieutenant colonel and commander of the Maryland companies who were "some of the briskest people I have seen." Along with the three companies from the lower counties of Pennsylvania (now Delaware) and the few North Carolinians, Dagworthy's men would serve Forbes's army as light infantry.[40]

*   *   *

While Bouquet was busy trying unsuccessfully to keep the Cherokees with the army, Christian Frederick Post was delivering a report on his recent trip to the eastern Delaware town of Wyoming. Located at present Wilkes-Barre, the town was home to Teedyuscung and the center of Pennsylvania's effort to restore peace on its frontiers. Fond of alcohol, Teedyuscung boasted by 1758 of leading a coalition of ten "nations" on and near the upper Susquehanna River. The coalition may have been a myth, but Teedyuscung's role as a link between the British and the western Delawares was real enough. Post was sent by Governor Denny at Forbes's insistence to gain information about Indian affairs, especially in the Ohio Country. At the same time the mission was intended to further the colony's still evolving and complicated relationship with Teedyuscung whose accusations of fraudulent land sales now pitted the Penns and their agents against the antiproprietary movement led by Israel Pemberton and the Friendly Association, whose support the general needed. At stake was not just peace with those Delawares living near the colony but also negotiations with the western Delawares in the Ohio Country, something that Forbes wanted very much to encourage.

The current state of Indian affairs as presented by Post and his companion Charles Thomson was, at best, complicated and volatile. First, Post's group never made it to Wyoming. Reports that "strange Indians were thick in the woods," men "whose Language none of the Delawares understood," as well as rumors of pro-French Senecas bent on attacking local Munsee towns prevented the men from going much farther than Fort Allen on the Lehigh River. Instead, Teedyuscung met them on the road, refusing to take them to his town for fear of an attack. He also told Post and Thomson that a "Report" had spread to the Iroquois towns that the British were building a fort at Wyoming "with 800 men." In fact, a small number of civilians were building houses for Teedyuscung's people. Such rumors and reports of "strange Indians" were indications of how clouded relations were among different natives and between native groups and the colony. Moreover, though western Delawares had contacted Teedyuscung months earlier in order to learn whether the colony was truly interested in peace, no direct meetings had yet taken place between the emerging peace faction at the Kuskuskies and either Teedyuscung or Pennsylvanians. War and rumor had effectively blocked the roads—both metaphorically and literally—preventing communication between east and west. Post's mission also faced the Indian-hating that was now a common feature on the frontier. The commander of the provincial garrison at Fort Hunter, Captain Neilson, "expressing himself with great Bitterness against Teedyuscung," threatened to kill the Delaware headman and any of his people "without asking any Questions." The immediate source of Neilson's diatribe may have been the recent killing of a member of the house-building party at Wyoming; those unnamed Indians in the woods seem to have been responsible, but the captain was quick to blame the Delawares and expressed his wish to attack and destroy Wyoming, telling Post that "we have no friends among the Indians.[41]

Faced with rumors, fears, and visceral Indian-hating, Post nevertheless carried on with his mission, delivering Forbes's and Denny's messages to Teedyuscung and stressing their desire for peace. At the same time, Post "endeavoured to gain some more Intelligence," especially "News from the Westward." This news included information that the French at Fort Niagara were short of food and were relying on local Senecas for whatever corn they received. Since Fort Niagara was the transshipment point for supplies meant for the Ohio Valley and the Great Lakes, this would be encouraging news for the general. So, too, would information that the commandant at Fort Duquesne was at odds with his allies and local Indians. Wyandots and other Indians from the Great Lakes refused to accept French invitations to strike pro-British Iroquois; the Wyandots "kicked the Wampum" offered them rather than accept it. According to Teedyuscung's information, western Delaware warriors had begun to attack French stragglers near the fort leading to a confrontation in which the natives threatened the French, telling them "The English are coming up" and as soon as they "strike you on one side" the Delawares would join in. Yet suspicions lingered. The Delawares were cautious and wanted to know the truth behind the rumors of a fort at Wyoming. This insistence on clarity was driven home by Nenacheehunt, "a Chief of one of the Towns on the Allegheny." He had come to Wyoming days earlier wanting to know if the British were willing to include his people in any peace negotiations and in return offered to surrender all colonial prisoners in his town.[42]

Post also learned that while the "Chief Man of the Senekas" living near Fort Niagara and in the Ohio Country "was affected to the English," he and other headmen had little influence over followers, men who were still "in the French Interest," and that "the nation in general" was "exasperated against the Pensilvanians." The picture of Indian affairs that began to emerge was one of continued divisions among native societies. Delawares remained opposed both to the French in the Ohio Country and to British expansion and forts on the upper Susquehanna, the lands that many still claimed as their homes, but some among them were clearly interested in opening negotiations with the British. Delawares and, presumably, other natives were clearly aware that a British army was on the march, yet there was nothing in Teedyuscung's information to suggest that the French were aware of the route the enemy would take or how far advanced they were. The French as well as Forbes and his men were operating with, at best, fragmentary intelligence. Finally, roads blocked by war led to the growth and spread of rumors that could cause confusion, miscalculation, and further violence. Captain Neilson's desire to wipe out Wyoming because he heard that local Indians were responsible for killing a colonist was matched by western Delawares' hesitancy to commit themselves to peace until they learned what was behind the story of British fort building at the same town.[43]

Forbes received a summary of Post's report at his Philadelphia headquarters and wrote to Bouquet that "our Negotiations with the Delaware Indians upon the Ohio, has come to a pretty good length," adding that he had been "positively assured" that numbers of these people were already moving back east and away from the French. He, too, may have succumbed to rumor or misinformation; perhaps he was grasping at straws. Western Delawares were not resettling to the east of the mountains, and he may have confused this movement with that of the Seneca warriors or the "strange Indians" lurking around Wyoming. Forbes's lingering concern emerged when he told Bouquet he hoped the army would have no encounters with Indians "to the north of the west branch of the Susquehannah, . . . least [sic] we mistake friends for foes."[44]

Uncertainty continued to dominate discussions with and about the Delawares. So far, all negotiations had been with Teedyuscung. His demand that fraudulent land deals be investigated and made right had become the centerpiece of talks aimed at making peace with those Delawares and Munsees living in the upper Susquehanna Valley. Teedyuscung's access to colonial authorities and Wyoming's role as a crossroads connecting east and west meant that Delawares from the Ohio Country would seek him out as they also explored the possibilities of peace. Yet the British remained in the dark about what individuals and groups lay beyond Teedyuscung and what exactly they wanted. Did Nenacheehunt speak for others as well as himself? He was a "chief man" in the Ohio Country, but what exactly did that mean? Who were the ten "nations" for whom Teedyuscung allegedly spoke? Denny admitted his own lack of certainty on these and other questions when he told Johnson that "it is impossible for me to obtain this necessary Knowledge, since every thing is transacted by Teedyuscung," whose close ties to Pemberton's Quaker Association also rattled the governor. One thing was certain. By the time Post tendered his report in mid-June, no western Delawares had yet made face-to-face contact with British officials or their agents. Until this happened there was little likelihood of any negotiations aimed at separating these people from the French.[45]

Western Delawares faced their own quandary. Working through Teedyuscung might have been convenient at first, but indirect contact raised more questions than it answered. The western Delawares also had to contend with garbled messages carried along paths that were easily blocked. In one notable example, Johnson's assistant Croghan attempted to send wampum belts with messages of his own to the Ohio Indians. The belts got as far as Venango and the Munsee headman Custaloga, who "seem'd desirous of Peace." Local Senecas, though, advised against responding to the belts, which did not clearly indicate who exactly Croghan wanted to talk with. In other words, from the Indians' perspective, Croghan's belts conveyed gibberish and could not be taken as a serious or trustworthy offer to negotiate.[46]

The belts only added to native confusion. If the British genuinely wanted peace, why was a large army—many times the size of Braddock's—moving west? And why did this army include a multitude of southern Indians who infested the woods? If Teeduyscung and the British were alarmed by news of "strange Indians" threatening the roads between Wyoming and Philadelphia, so too were western Delawares worried about the appearance of their old enemies the Cherokees and Catawbas. If the British meant peace, why send men whose actions could potentially widen an already costly war? What exactly did the British offer in return for peace and what would they demand? In June, no one in the western Delaware towns knew the answers to these and other questions. An effort to contact the British a year earlier had not produced the desired results: Croghan's clumsy attempt to negotiate was not to be trusted, and Nenacheehunt's mission never got past Teedyuscung. And, like Denny or Johnson, western Delaware leaders were reluctant to place too much confidence in Teedyuscung whose own agenda might not mesh with their own. None of this boded well for the emergent peace faction led by Tamaqua. They, like the Seneca headmen, were not able to control the actions of their own warriors, who had been shadowing Forbes's army and were certainly among the "small parties of Enemy Indians" who were "all around us" forcing Bouquet to conclude that his convoys "can no longer move or stop without an escort." Indeed, Tamaqua's own brother Shingas was notorious among Pennsylvanians for his raids on the colony's frontier. In the face of a profound lack of trustworthy information and with factionalism roiling in Delaware towns, Tamaqua and his handful of supporters might have done well to simply await events. Instead, they chose to act, with profound consequences for General Forbes and his campaign.[47]

At about the time that Post and Thomson were returning from their aborted trip to Wyoming, a small party of Delawares left the Kuskuskies headed east. Led by Pisquetomen (Tamaqua's brother) and Keekuyscung, their ultimate destination was Philadelphia and a meeting with British officials. It was a bold move: the future of Tamaqua's diplomacy rested on the outcome. These two men and their escort arrived at Wyoming sometime during the last week of June 1758. By sheer accident, their trip east happened to coincide with yet another trip to the town by Post and Thomson, who left Philadelphia on June 20. On June 27 the Pennsylvanians arrived at Wyoming to find "a great Number of Indians," "many with painted Faces" and "upwards of 40 Strangers of Different Tribes," some of whom Post recognized. The

Delawares were "upon their Guard, and have Scouts out" as if expecting trouble. Post's mission was to deliver a message from the Cherokees assuring the Wyoming Indians that they had nothing to fear and that the southern warriors were bent on taking the war to the French and their allies. Not long after delivering the message, "Teedyuscung shewed me Two Chiefs and several other Indians from Allegheny."[48]

Pisquetomen and Keekyuscung were palpably relieved to meet Post, calling him "brother" and telling him "we are very glad to see you and have long time wished to see some of the Inhabitants of Pennsylvania with whom we could speak ourselves," reminding him that "we cannot believe all we hear and know not what is true and what is false." The two men "came early" to speak with Post the following day and invited him to eat with them. It was then that the pent-up suspicions and confusion began to surface. "They asked me many Questions," said Post, and told him that "thro' many idle reports they had heard from time to time" they grew worried that the British would not make peace with their people and "hence were resolved to stay with the French." Emphasizing that they were sorry for having gone to war against the colony, they also "wished often to have seen some Messengers from the Government with whom they could have spoken." The problem, they told Post, was that "they never heard any Satisfactory Account" of the peacemaking that had already occurred at Easton and had received no messages, a criticism of Teedyuscung's less than reliable role as intermediary. Finally, Kutaikund (Keekyuscung), "one of their Chiefs, who lives this side [east] the Allegheny," urged the colony's governor "to send somebody with them at their return Home," saying that "it would be of great consequence to them [western Delawares] to hear the Governor's mind from their own Mouths." And, to underscore their seriousness, Pisquetomen and Keekyuscung told Post that the French in the Ohio Country were in a bad way. Although they estimated about eleven hundred men at Fort Duquesne, most were "almost starved with Hunger," and had their allies not helped them "the most of them must have left the place." This was the sort of specific intelligence that Forbes badly wanted but was unable to get on his own.[49]

The meeting at Wyoming was the breakthrough that Tamaqua and his allies hoped for. It was also a boon to Forbes. He now had clear evidence that at least some Ohio Indian headmen were inclined toward peace; moreover, they were willing to provide information on the French that he could not get by any other means. Informed by Israel Pemberton that the western Delawares were expected in Philadelphia, Forbes also learned that the Friendly Association wanted Forbes to attend the anticipated council with Pisquetomen and Keekyuscung, stressing that his presence would "relieve us from a painful anxiety" about the meeting's outcome. It was a reminder that other interests were at work; not only did Pemberton believe it would be best for all concerned if Teedyuscung remained at Wyoming, but with Denny, the Proprietor's representative, Richard Peters, and Sir William Johnson's agents, there would be ample room for conflicting agendas that might alienate the Delawares. Though, "extreamly Bussy" with military matters, Forbes, now at Carlisle, readily endorsed the meeting and agreed to send a representative to the western Delaware towns. It now appeared that his plan of military action and diplomacy might work after all.[50]

* * *

Forbes left Philadelphia at the beginning of July and arrived at Carlisle on the evening of July 4. He had finally arranged for those parts of the army still east of the Susquehanna River to join Bouquet's advanced guard as quickly as possible. In the meantime, the general tried to sort out the chaos he found among the provincial troops gathered at Carlisle. In the process, he had been "obliged to go through a great deal of Rideing and walking." Contrary to the fears of his staff, especially Major Francis Halkett, Forbes seemed better "than I have seen him since his coming to the Continent." Taking command of troops in the field rather than sitting at a desk in Philadelphia seemed to have "reestablished his health." Moreover, by the time Pemberton's letter with the good news from Wyoming reached him, the van of Forbes's army had been in its Raystown camp for two weeks. The first stage of his "protected advance" had been a success, with small garrisons covering the road and enemy actions confined to scouting parties. And the army's logistics, makeshift under the best of circumstances, had thus far held up. From a military point of view the campaign was off to a good, if very tardy, start.[51]

The other, equally important, facet of Forbes's campaign, Indian affairs, had produced very mixed results by the end of June. While Bouquet's regulars and provincials were covering the last few miles up the Juniata Valley toward Raystown, many of the Cherokees were heading home, angry and disillusioned with the British. A seemingly unbridgeable gulf had opened between natives and redcoats as the issue of goods promised to southern warriors exposed profound differences in the ways each party defined war and friendship. If Bouquet and Forbes felt betrayed as Cherokees packed up and left Fort Loudoun, so too did the warriors, who believed they were joining an army as equals only to be treated as hirelings and subordinates. The army was not completely bereft of native fighters: Catawbas remained as did the persistent hope that once Attakullakulla appeared with the army, his Cherokees would rally and once again join the British against their mutual enemy. As complex and difficult as British–Cherokee relations had become, this was offset by the news coming from Teedyuscung's town and the Ohio Country. There, western advocates of peace with the British finally made contact with officials who could provide the encouragement that Tamaqua and his allies had been seeking for nearly two years. It seemed that Forbes's insistence on negotiating with the Delawares and his increasingly close association with Israel Pemberton and the Friendly Association were beginning to bear fruit.

Yet, by the end of June, no deals had been struck, no official embassies launched, enemy Indians (including western Delaware warriors) were still in the field, and the army had yet to master the Endless Mountains. Indeed, neither Forbes nor Bouquet had yet completely mastered their own army, which was more a collection of poorly disciplined individuals and units scattered over one hundred miles from Raystown to Lancaster than the organized force needed to seize Fort Duquesne and occupy the Ohio Country. The new camp at Raystown would allow the general and his officers the chance to assess the route ahead and begin turning provincial levies and raw redcoats into an army.

FIVE

Raystown

* * *

JULY 1758

I... shall then proceed 100 miles further to Raestown.
—FORBES TO PITT, JULY 1758

"I set out from Philadelphia with the Highland Battalion of Montgomery and the train of Artillery which marches into Camp here this day, all well and in good order." So Forbes informed Pitt on July 10 from "Carlisle Camp west of Susquehannah." He admitted that he could not get away from Philadelphia for nearly two weeks after the Scots and artillery arrived; it took him that long to put them in "some Order" before leaving the city on June 30. Bouquet with the army's advanced guard, "1500 of the Provincials" along with parts of the Royal Americans and additional Highland companies, was establishing a camp and depot at Raystown. Aside from that post and Forts Littleton and Loudoun, Forbes told Pitt, his troops had to make their way through "an immense Forest of 240 miles of Extent," along with the first of the "Endless Mountains." Forbes's bitterness over Cherokee affairs was still evident when he wrote that this wilderness was as "impenetrable almost to any thing humane save the Indians (if they be allowed that Appellation)." He was also quick to blame the Cherokees for their defection, noting that "they are like Sheep, where one leaps, all the rest follow," except for the estimated two hundred who remained with the army. The weather was also beginning to wear on the army. Aside from the rains that continued to ruin the roads and make life miserable, Forbes complained about the "excessive hot weather," which made crossing the Schuylkill and Susquehanna Rivers more burdensome than usual. Yet, in Carlisle, he reckoned that his portion of the army was only one hundred miles from Bouquet at Raystown. Once united, the army could prepare for the next leg of its protected advance.[1]

The hot weather aggravated Forbes's chronic poor health. While in Philadelphia he complained of "Cholicks" and sought permission to "come home to save my life after the campaign." By early July he suffered the flux and a return of "violent pain" that made it almost impossible to urinate for several days. Yet, whether it was the anticipation of finally joining the army or merely a temporary respite from his illnesses, by July 9, the "great deal of Rideing" and walking involved in organizing the troops seemed to have revitalized Forbes for the first time in months. A relapse occurred in late July, however, and Forbes found himself "taking Physick" and unable to write; the flux returned and in early August, still at Carlisle, he was "still extreamly weak."[2]

While Forbes was in Philadelphia gathering together the remainder of the Pennsylvania troops and his newly arrived regulars, Bouquet was taking steps designed to turn a collection of raw recruits and their officers into an effective army. Even the veteran companies from Washington's regiment and the few regulars Bouquet commanded had never served on campaign in the field; the rhythms of operations in the field were altogether different from life in a garrison. More important, none of these troops had ever served in units larger than companies—or, in the case of the Royal Americans, half battalions—and they simply had no experience with the complex evolutions and maneuvers required in the face of the enemy, whether in siege or in battle. Forbes's army was coming together on the march, and it would begin training in the same way, on route to its initial base at Raystown. The lessons began when the army left Carlisle for Shippensburg, Fort Loudoun, and the Juniata Valley.

Bouquet's troops started west without their full complement of arms and equipment; many did not have complete uniforms, tents, or blankets, and none had any foul-weather gear to protect them against the frequent rains that marked late June and early July. Surgeons assigned to the Pennsylvania troops marched without sufficient medicines, and the companies of the 1st Virginia Regiment that had joined the army had to build bark lean-tos since they had no tents. The Pennsylvania New Levies were so poorly armed that about half of those on the road "Walks with Sticks" instead of muskets. The chronically damp weather made matters worse. The rain turned the road into a quagmire of mud and loose stones; wool coats quickly absorbed water, adding to the weight each man carried, while green, blue, and red dyes ran and bled into the rest of the clothing. Rain also ruined shoes, accelerated the rusting of old and poorly maintained weapons, and threatened what little ammunition the troops carried. Hard marching took a toll on everyone, regular and provincial alike. The Royal Americans and Highland companies were still adjusting to the change of climate and fighting malarial fevers and the ills that came from confinement aboard ship. Pennsylvanians also fell sick, and there were "Many with Sore Legs." Discipline also became a casualty of the hard march. By the end of June Virginians were refusing to do extra work unless paid for it, prompting Bouquet to draw the line by refusing them more than what everyone else received: one gill of rum per man per day of labor.[3]

Despite the poor weather, hard going, and shortages, Bouquet insisted on imposing order and discipline on his raw troops and giving them some rudimentary training. Forbes clearly felt the need to balance training against the overwhelming need to keep the army moving. He instructed Bouquet, "in going along" with the provincials, to occasionally "drop them a barrel of powder" so they could practice shooting. At the same time, though, he instructed the colonel to leave "one good Officer" at Carlisle to drill the New Levies "in firing at Marks" and "to observe the strictest Discipline." Bouquet placed his emphasis on this last point: turning what was little more than a poorly armed mob into an army. We can follow this process through his orderly book covering the last stretch of the vanguard's move from Carlisle to Raystown.[4]

The surviving portion of Bouquet's orderly book begins on June 17, 1758, at Fort Littleton. By then his troops and convoys had been on the road for about three weeks and were well over halfway toward their destination. We can assume that orders appearing on that date were already becoming part of the daily routine. The troops were commanded that "When the General [a drum signal to assemble] beats all the Troops to appear immediately under Arms," ready for any emergency. Company officers were ordered to inspect their men and weapons daily. To discourage straggling and desertion, the rolls were to be called "three Times a Day ... if any Soldier is absent he must be reported and confined." In addition to this last order, on June 19 Bouquet commanded that "The Articles of War be read at 12 o'Clock," especially those portions dealing with mutiny, desertion, and the treatment of government property. These orders were intended to remind the troops, regular and provincial alike, that they were now under martial law.[5]

Provincial officers began to learn their new trade as well. Field officers such as Lieutenant-Colonel Hugh Mercer of the Pennsylvanians, a physician by training, found themselves appointed as "field officer of the day," responsible for camp discipline and security for a twenty-four-hour period. These men, in turn, directed officers of the guard, making sure that they and their men knew the daily "parole" or password and countersign. The maintenance of proper march discipline and camp routine were also the officers' responsibilities. Company-grade officers suddenly found themselves serving on courts-martial dealing with offenses ranging from disorderly conduct to desertion while trying to learn the fine points of military law. Officers, like the men they led, struggled to grasp the rudiments of military drill as well as the more complex maneuvers that allowed companies and regiments to operate together against the enemy. Some, like Washington, may have relied on popular texts, like General Humphrey Bland's treatise on military training and camp discipline. Others may have followed a not uncommon practice among British professionals and found an enlisted man with enough experience to teach them the manual of arms and other basics.[6]

By the time Bouquet's force reached Raystown on June 24 the troops were growing accustomed to following schedules and procedures. Assembling at four in the morning, packing tents and other gear, and being ready to march an hour later was now part of the daily routine, as was the marching order that Bouquet imposed. A "Corporal & 6 Woods men" would march a half mile ahead of the main column, followed by a sergeant and a dozen more "Woods men" who were to march abreast to cover as much ground on either side of the road as possible. One reason for this was to detect lurking enemy scouts; another was to catch "Men stragling in the Woods" so they could be returned to their units. These detachments were in turn, covered by two piquets, each of thirty-two men, "marching in two Indian Files" on the sides of the road. Behind this advanced guard came the "Hatchet Men," one per company led by a sergeant. These men, also called "pioneers," were responsible for clearing obstructions from the road and filling gullies or small streams ahead of wagons and artillery. Indeed, following these men were two guns, probably a pair of light six-pounders, "with a Cart of Ammunition." Finally, there came the main force: the two Pennsylvania battalions, Stephen's Virginians, the detachments of regulars, as well as the all-important supply trains. Once they arrived at Raystown, the emphasis would be on the creation of a regular encampment, one that could not only accommodate the whole army but also be defended from any sudden attacks.[7]

Upon arrival, soldiers traded muskets for picks, shovels, and axes, and there was plenty of work to go around. Normally, selecting encampments was the job of the army's quartermaster general, but with St. Clair overseeing the movement of men and supplies at Carlisle, Bouquet probably made arrangements himself; he chose a wide, relatively flat piece of ground on the site of the earlier traders' camp. One of the first tasks was to build the storehouses that would hold supplies for the next stage of the campaign. These were surrounded by a simple stockade—set three feet into a trench, the stockade posts would rise another eight or nine feet, tied together near the top with traverse strips of wood. The enclosure, an irregularly shaped pentagon with projecting bastions at the corners, was located on high ground near the Juniata River and called at the time the "fort at Raystown." Bouquet also sent off a brief letter to Colonel Washington at Fort Cumberland telling Washington that "Nichols the Pilot [guide]" had begun to mark the route from Raystown to Cumberland, and Bouquet expected that the Virginians "will begin to cut the Waggon Road to open the Communication between us." In the meantime, Bouquet and his staff began to organize a proper cantonment sufficient not only for the troops at hand but for those who would follow.[8]

*   *   *

Establishing an encampment for several thousand men, their dependents, wagons, heavy guns, and livestock was never as easy as pitching tents. Like virtually everything else the army had a method for establishing what amounted to sizable towns; when complete, Raystown would be one of the largest settlements in Pennsylvania after Philadelphia. Encampments were laid out according to precise rules in order to create a rational, ordered space for soldiers, which mirrored the neat grid-based plans that had come to dominate towns ranging from the small new settlements of Carlisle and Winchester to large cities such as New York, Philadelphia, Charles Town, and Sir Christopher Wren's new London itself. Rooted in the townscapes of imperial Rome, these ordered spaces were designed to project the wealth and power of those who governed them. Central to colonial townscapes were courthouses and governors' mansions; in military encampments it was the standards and drums posted prominently at the head of each regiment. Equally important, uniformly ordered encampments made it possible for troops to move quickly into either a line of march or a line of battle. By 1758 the army was guided by manuals written by British officers; General Humphrey Bland's *A Treatise of Military Discipline* provided a guide in words and diagrams of how troops in the field should encamp as well as organize their daily routine. Forbes, Bouquet, Washington, Montgomery, and others certainly knew Bland's work and used it to guide their own schemes, adapting his observations to the unique geographical conditions of warfare in America.[9]

The first step in establishing the camp was to clear sufficient ground for the army. This task fell to the "hatchet men": at one per company these pioneers used not just hatchets but shovels, crowbars, and block and tackle to clear the site of trees, deadfall, and large rocks, all the while filling in any

Fig. 5.1 "Encampment of the Allied army under Duke of Cumberland, near Maestricht," 1747, by Paul Sandby. (Courtesy of the Yale Center for British Art, Paul Mellon Collection.) This is what Bouquet must have had in mind as he assembled Forbes's army in the early summer of 1758. Note the bell-of-arms tents in the foreground sheltering weapons and the neat rows of tents and sentry assigned to keep order in camp.

ravines that could impede or damage wagons and gun carriages. Under the direction of an engineer, they could also be put to work building bridges or filling in low-lying ground and collecting the wood and bark necessary to build covered racks for muskets. Normally, these would be stored in "bell-of-arms" tents; Forbes's army seems not to have had sufficient numbers of these conical shelters, hence the resorting to bark substitutes.[10]

The actual layout of the camp was in the hands of the regimental quartermasters, assisted by "camp-color men." These soldiers—one per company, equipped with a "camp color," a small square flag of the regiment's facing color marked with its number (a dark blue square marked "LX" for 60th Foot/Royal Americans, for example)—would mark the tent lines of their regiments. When properly organized, each regiment would occupy a piece of ground on which a company's line of tents would face those of another company across a precisely laid-out street; for a regiment of ten companies, there would be five streets. Normally, these company streets would be lined with tents holding up to seven men each. At Raystown, however, and in the absence of sufficient tents, many of the troops had to erect wooden or bark huts, but still on the same plan as outlined in Bland. At the end of each street there would be a separate tent for the company sergeants and at the head of each regiment—that is, facing the likely approach of an enemy—would be the arms tents or sheds, the drums, and the colors. To the rear of the enlisted

encampment in each regiment would be separate rows of tents for subaltern officers, captains, and field officers. Each regiment would be arrayed in like fashion, differing only according to the number of men. Custom dictated that the senior regiment in the camp took a position on the far right of the cantonment area, the next senior on the far left, then alternating with the most junior regiments in the middle of the line. In creating this regimented space, the quartermasters would be careful to maintain prescribed distances between rows or tents and between the enlisted men and their officers.[11]

While Bouquet used Bland's recommendations regarding camp organization as a guide, he also felt free to modify these to fit the army's peculiar circumstances. Unlike the neatly arranged training camps in Britain at places such as Coxeheath or Hyde Park, Forbes's troops found themselves in enemy country, vulnerable to *la petite guerre* raiding as well as full-scale attack. Bouquet established an encampment that emphasized defense as well as order. J. C. Pleydell's plan of the Raystown camp clearly shows this. To the west of the fortified storehouses, Bouquet's troops built a chain of fortified encampments each within musket range of the others. They would provide a strong line of defense facing the most likely avenue of an enemy attack while covering the army's source of water and the all-important road back to Carlisle. Since each camp was fully surrounded by defensive works, the troops were secure from raids or attacks from any direction. These camp fortifications or "retrenchments," were not made of stockades but, rather, consisted of logs laid horizontally, beginning with a course of three or four logs as a base, followed by two, then one log. The resulting walls were proof against small arms fire and could even deflect light artillery. Each camp's fortification was regularly designed and built: almost all were in the form of squares, with projecting bastions—the exception being the small camp for the Royal

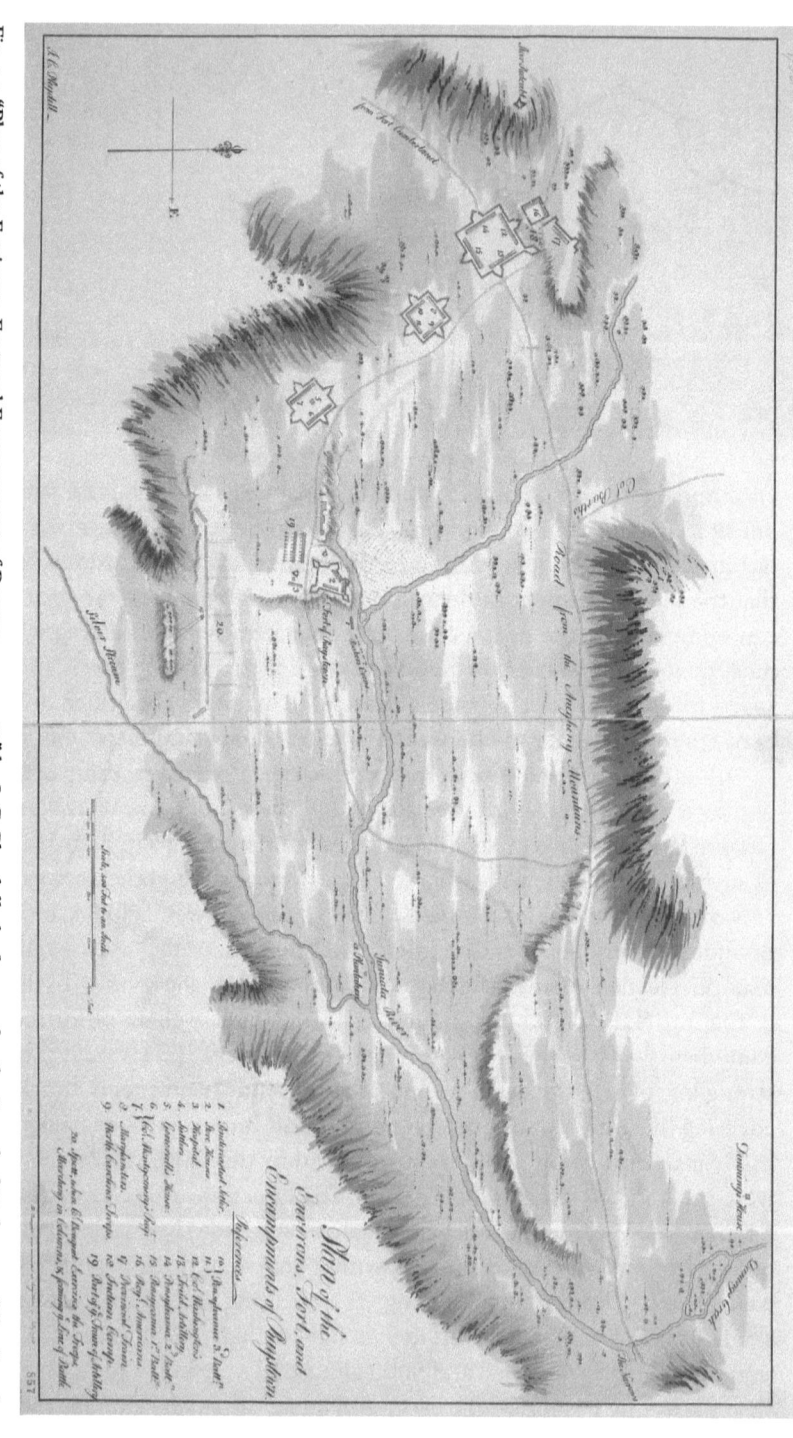

Fig. 5.2 "Plan of the Environs, Fort and Encampment of Raystown, c. 1758," by J. C. Pleydell, draftsman for the Board of Ordnance. (The Royal Collection Trust/© Her Majesty Queen Elizabeth II 2019.) This is the only plan of the details of Bouquet's encampment. Note the small pentagonal fort on the right—later Fort Bedford. At the bottom (south) of the plan is the cleared field used by Bouquet to tactically train his force.

Americans. Within these fortified camps, which varied in size according to the number of troops in each, regiments were arranged in regular fashion along the sides of the retrenchments. Despite the separate fortified camps, the army maintained regimental seniority as best it could, given that the bulk of the troops were recently raised provincials. On the right of the line was the camp of the Royal Americans, the senior regular regiment, and the far left was occupied by Montgomery's Highlanders, next senior in the line. The provincials occupied the center, but it is notable that Washington's 1st Virginia, longer serving than any of the others, was located next to the Royal Americans.[12]

Had they paused to look around amid the seemingly endless labor at Raystown, most of the provincials and regulars would have found this camp unlike anything they had experienced. The fortifications, growing numbers of troops, emerging artillery parks, as well as the continuous guards that patroled in and around the site, all served as a stark notice that they were now at war. And while the camp routines were broadly familiar to the regulars, they might have baffled, even irked, many of the colonial troops and civilian followers. Orders began to flow from Bouquet's headquarters as soon as the troops arrived. Soldiers were forbidden to "bark any Trees" in the camp or along the road, to prevent dying trees from falling with fatal results; tree bark for shelters was to come from the surrounding woods or from deadfall. No soldier out hunting in the hope of supplementing monotonous army rations was to shoot within hearing of the camp, and hunters had to first obtain permission to go beyond the lines. Soldiers with complaints about provisions had to seek redress by going through proper channels, not by pilfering or badgering officers. Each soldier was to take his rightful turn on duty, however onerous; their regimental orderly officers were told to prevent any partiality or exemptions. Soldiers were reminded that muskets were weapons, not convenient poles to carry "any Bundle or Kettle," and this additional gear was to be carried on the men's (or women's) backs. Soldiers were forbidden to gamble, "that pernicious Custom," nor were they or their dependents to give or sell liquor to Indians; guards were placed "at the Indian Camp" in order to prevent this traffic. Finally, in mid-July, soldiers were ordered "to Attend divine Service every Morning at Revalee Beating."[13]

Other orders are a reminder of just how dependent the army was on its own labor and skills for survival. Little more than a week after arriving, Bouquet put out a call for "all Tradesmen" including "Carpenters, Joyners, Bricklayers, Masons, Oven Makers, Sadlers, Millrights, Coalmakers, Coopers, Tin Men, Sawyers, Mealmakers," as well as general labor. Following army custom, skilled men were paid additional wages. In this case they had a choice

Fig. 5.3 Retrenchment, Fort Ligonier. (Photo by the author.) Substantial log walls such as this would have surrounded the regimental encampments at Raystown. The section shown here surrounded the inner fort and much of the encampment at Loyalhannon.

of working for nine pence and a ration of rum or whiskey per day, or one shilling "without Liquor." They were promised their pay each Saturday. The "Common Labourers" received a liquor ration "when they work." The skills advertised suggests just how much went into creating this fortified camp. The army would need ovens for baking fresh bread in camp and biscuits for the march; building hospitals and storehouses would occupy joiners, sawyers, carpenters, and masons; the artillery and supply wagons would have to rely on coopers, saddlers, and "coalmakers" (men skilled in making charcoal for blacksmiths and gunsmiths). The call for millwrights suggests that Bouquet planned to build a sawmill on the Juniata River, or perhaps a gristmill—hence the reference to "mealmakers." The result of this work was to turn an abandoned traders' establishment into a large and complex military town. Close to the river, and next to the fortified storehouses was what might be imagined as the town center, the artillery park, a line of "Bake Ovens," the hospital, and even a commercial district—the "Settlers" (sutlers), men and women licensed by the army to sell all manner of consumer goods from foodstuffs and alcohol to articles of clothing, shoes, buttons, and buckles. Operating out of tents, they may also have hired soldiers to build crude cabins to secure their goods. To the west of this town center were the regimental camps and outposts and, beyond these, the fields that supported livestock and woods that provided building material and fuel. And, running through the whole settlement were the two crude roads that linked the army to its base at Carlisle and to Washington's garrison at Fort Cumberland and Braddock's Road.[14]

The population of the encampment at Raystown would continue to fluctuate throughout the remainder of the campaign as troops came and went, though over time the troop returns reveal that the army continued to diminish in size as it moved west. This would not have alarmed Forbes or Bouquet and the losses were not due to casualties, yet, but to the inevitable sickness and injuries coupled with the need to garrison the chain of posts that was central to the protected advance. A "Sketch of the Number of Troops under Brigadier General Forbes," made on July 17 at Carlisle showed 6,362 soldiers assigned to the army; these included the 1st Virginia companies still at Fort Cumberland with Washington, but did not include the 552 Pennsylvanians detached to occupy forts east of the Susquehanna River. All told the army included slightly more than 7,000 men, ranging from the 2,828 men of the Pennsylvania Regiment to the 221 officers and men of the recently arrived North Carolina companies and the forty-four-man detachment from the Royal Artillery.[15]

These figures were intended to give Forbes and his superiors a general view of the army. In reality, the army was never collected together at any one place or time. At the same time that this return was made, for example, Bouquet commanded fewer than 2,308 men at Raystown when he arrived in late June. A closer look at the "Daily Return of the Troops" at Raystown, taken on July 21, reveals that the number of "effective troops" (those who were available for strictly military duties) was considerably less. No fewer than 282 men were listed as "on command," a label that denoted men detached on duties away from the army. Of these men, 252 were Pennsylvanians, part of the detachment of 15 men per company ordered by Forbes to remain east of the Susquehanna. Another 133 men were returned as sick, either left behind at other posts or present at Raystown. The largest number of these sick men (49) belong to the 515 men of Montgomery's Highlanders, suggesting that the regiment was still struggling against sickness picked up in South Carolina or aboard ship. Bouquet's call for skilled labor was answered by 83 men, and these "artificiers" were also serving away from their units under the command of the engineers. Another 102 men were listed as "batmen," that is, officers' servants who were all drawn from the provincial regiments, not the regulars then in camp. Deducting those men sick, detached, or on some other special duties, Bouquet could call upon 1,708 men for military duties such as mounting guards, manning patrols, and escorting supply wagons coming from the Juniata crossing.[16]

The numbers grew as more troops joined Bouquet's force. A return made on August 10 shows 3,770 troops, including a number of small detachments and artificers. An additional 244 men included wagon drivers, packhorse men, tradesmen, a small provost guard to watch over prisoners, and the sick from the "Highland Hospital" and the "Virginia Hospital." This list was made to determine the number of daily rations consumed by this force (8,475) and would have excluded people not drawing their food from the army: additional civilians along with some women and children. A week later, Major Joseph Shippen of the Pennsylvania Regiment told the colony's secretary that about 2,500 men were then encamped at Raystown, "exclusive of" the 1,400 men working on the new road, and that many of the Virginians including most of Byrd's regiment had not yet arrived. Again, these numbers provide only a snapshot of what was in fact a very fluid situation, with troops, wagon teams, and others coming and going as Forbes attempted to build up his base of supply at Raystown while continuing to push troops west across the mountains.[17]

By mid-July, Raystown was taking on the appearance of a regular military encampment. Bouquet was especially proud of the "18 ovens built" and the supply of charcoal already on hand. He was satisfied with the progress, considering the rocky ground that slowed work as did the cutting of lumber, even though "we have 10 saws at work." Nevertheless, he told Forbes that storehouses were now available for three months' provisions and that the remaining work would go quickly, especially, as Bouquet recommended, "a little indulgence" was shown toward the provincial troops who did most of the labor. To outsiders, the camp was already impressive; the Reverend Thomas Barton spoke of "a fine Fort," and the former South Carolina governor James Glen was effusive when telling Washington that the "beauty, regularity, and cleanliness of this camp will charm you." He went into detailed descriptions of the fortifications before observing that "such wonders does the admirable Bouquet work in the Wilderness." Yet the work continued well into August, with a new ditch around the fortified storehouses, while men continued to improve fortifications as well as building "a storehouse for hay."[18]

* * *

Adding to the necessary work of making and maintaining a large encampment was the growing emphasis on military training: basic drill and more complex evolutions. Now that the army was entering the mountains it could expect contact with the enemy, and inexperienced men needed to be immersed in the soldier's trade. Moreover, Bouquet had to plan for the possibility of a formal battle or siege once the army arrived at Fort Duquesne. By early August, therefore, orders to drill became more frequent. On August 2, for example, "All the Troops not upon duty are to be under Arms in their Camp . . . and to Rendezvous in the Plain below the Fort, where they are to be drawn in a Line of Battle." Pleydell clearly drew this large open area on his plan of the encampment, labeling it the "Spot where Col. Bouquet Exercises the Troops. Marching in Columns, & forming ye Line of Battle." Both provincials and regulars were ordered out for training. For hard-pressed men, this must have been an onerous exercise. Soldiers just returned from days working on the road could look forward to little rest; their "off-duty" time now consumed with battle training as well as camp routines.[19]

The orders provide some idea of how Bouquet intended to train his command. Regiments were first arranged in a proper line, according to seniority: "The Americans & Highlanders on the Right and left, The Virginians next to the Americans, The N. Carolina Troops next to the Highlanders the Pennsylvanians & Marylanders in the Center"—not unlike the layout of the camp itself. This was the "Line of Battle," and every officer was expected to know where his troops stood. Bouquet evidently organized his line according to the standards laid out by authorities such as Bland. On August 7, the troops were to be "divided into Plattoons of 20, with an officer or a Sergt. to each Plattoon." The "platoons" were part of an elaborate drill meant to keep up a constant fire by having the troops discharge their weapons by groups—platoons—in a prescribed order. These platoons only existed in the line of battle and were not part of a regiment's administrative organization. In one particular, though, Bouquet clearly deviated from the norm. Instead of arranging his men in three ranks, he ordered that "The Troops to be formed two deep." This resulted in a longer line and allowed him to create "wings" on each flank. Together, this longer battle line and the wings would lessen the likelihood that his troops could be flanked by the enemy; the wings could turn on any attempt to get around the ends of the line. In fact, it was here, on the field at Raystown, that Bouquet began to experiment with tactics and formations to cope with the broken country and the skillful native fighters his men would face. These innovations would serve him well in the western campaigns of 1763 and 1764. What Bouquet had in mind comes to us from Reverend Thomas Barton, who watched the training. On August 10, Barton tells us that "This Afternoon was spent in exercising the Troops, in running & firing *in the Indian Manner.*" He provided additional details, noting that "They are form'd into 4 Columns 2 Men deep," each column fifty yards from the next. "After marching some Distance in this Position, they fall into one

Rank entire forming a Line of Battle with great Ease & Expedition," after which each platoon fired three rounds, beginning at the right of the line, then the left, and alternating until the entire line had fired, by which time those on the ends had reloaded and were ready once more. The climax came when the troops made "a sham Pursuit with Shrieks & Halloos in the Indian Way."[20]

Since the troops were "very raw," Bouquet and his officers spent a good deal of time on basics. Very few of these soldiers had ever fired a shot in anger, and they all (even those who had) needed basic training in the use of muskets and bayonets; only repeated practice could result in the running fire described by Barton. Initially, this training would have been limited to the manual exercise, the different steps necessary to effectively handle a musket. Next, the men would have fired "squibs" (blank paper cartridges) in order to feel the weapon's discharge and get used to the sparks and flash produced by a flintlock. Finally, troops practiced volley fire by platoons with live ammunition and became accustomed to the noise and billowing smoke that such volleys produced. In addition, Bouquet had his men fire at "marks" (targets), training not confined to this army, but widely adopted by British forces throughout North America. The smoothbore musket was famously inaccurate at ranges exceeding one hundred yards, but the men were nonetheless trained to identify a target and shoot at it until they scored hits. Those men who consistently scored well were rewarded with an additional liquor ration. We cannot know how proficient these men became as marksmen, or even ordinary infantry in the line, but the drill, with its noise, smoke, and the sound of lead striking wooden targets at least gave them some idea of what they might face and gave them some confidence that as a group they could stand their ground against the French and Indians.[21]

With the training also came a greater emphasis on discipline. The orders regarding noise and latrines certainly underscored this point, but so, too, did the recurrent warnings about behavior and the recurrent notices of courts-martial that were held to try any malefactors. The fact of being under the Articles of War and, with it, what provincials saw as a swift, arbitrary, and brutal military punishment may have served to keep most men in line. Forbes's men learned through general orders, for instance, that anyone firing a weapon in camp would receive five hundred lashes, many times more than a similar offense would earn in a civilian court. For infractions of camp discipline and ordinary rules, regimental courts-martial tried the offenders and handed down justice. These regimental courts among the provincials often acted as a buffer between soldiers and the worst punishments demanded under the Articles of War. For example, a regimental court could find a defendant guilty of a lesser charge, or let him off with a warning. In one such case, a wagoner was to be tried by a court-martial at which the "Deputy Waggon Master [a civilian employee] is to Prosecute him." Capital cases, on the other hand, were in the hands of general courts-martial, which could, and frequently did, hand down death sentences for men convicted of theft, homicide, or desertion. This last offense was a constant problem for the army. Bouquet initially lacked an official warrant authorizing him to call such courts, but he told Forbes he needed one, in the general's absence, since "An example must be made to stop deserters." He noted that "We have a man here who has offered his services to do the hanging." Bouquet also made it clear that he would treat any sort of theft as a capital offense.[22]

Desertion remained a problem throughout the campaign. In mid-September, Reverend Barton wrote of "a Number of Men" held for the crime. The courts showed a measure of discretion when handling deserters but also handed out the full measure of military justice. Washington's orderly book cited eight soldiers tried for the crime; two of the guilty were given five hundred lashes, one received nine hundred lashes, but five (one each from Maryland, Virginia, and Pennsylvania, two from North Carolina) suffered the death penalty. Capital punishment in the army, as in civilian life at that time, was a moment of public theater. Executions provided an opportunity for the condemned to admit his sins and plead with his audience to obey the law; authority, whether civil or military could extend mercy at the last possible moment, dramatically driving home the terrible penalty to be paid for crime and the mercy that lay with magistrates and, through them, the monarch. For those soldiers who were denied clemency or pardon (usually repeat offenders), execution could be a terrifying ordeal, both for the victim and those soldiers mustered to witness the punishment. Offenders could be hanged or shot. Barton witnessed one such execution by firing squad and recorded it in detail. At Raystown, on September 26, a soldier of the Pennsylvania Regiment (perhaps one of those noted by Washington) "is to be shot to Death for Desertion." In characteristic fashion, the condemned man, who "behav'd with uncommon Resolution," asked his "Brother-Soldiers to take Example by his Misfortunes" and to "live sober Lives" and "beware of bad Company." "But above all he charg'd them never to desert." Kneeling in front of the firing party, he asked that they "do your Office for God's Sake do not miss me, & take Care not to disfigure me." At the sergeant's signal, they fired, "but shot so low that his Bowels fell out, his Shirt & Breeches were all on Fire" as the deserter fell to one side and "soon expir'd. A shocking Spectakle to all around him."[23]

* * *

Glen's comments about the "regularity" and "cleanliness" of Raystown as well as Barton's observation of new hospital buildings serve as reminders that good health, like rigorous training and discipline, was vital to the army's success. Early modern armies were notorious for their sickness. These walking cities were incubators for a range of often highly contagious, and lethal diseases: chronic dysentery ("flux"), smallpox, typhus, tuberculosis, influenza, syphilis, in addition to pneumonia, pleurisy, strep, and rheumatic disorders. Closely confined for months at a time in unsanitary conditions, consisting of men and women from widely diverse backgrounds and medical histories, and including children who were ideal carriers of crowd diseases such as smallpox, armies characteristically lost far more lives to germs than to bullets; disease could hollow out an army faster and more efficiently than any military force. Soldiers ate and slept in close proximity on what they called "our ground," and tent mates would frequently stitch blankets together to make a sleeping bag, lying head-to-foot in their clothes. Inevitably, any disease carried by one man would likely affect his tent mates, then those nearby. These perambulating germ factories readily infected neighboring civilians, triggering local or regional outbreaks that lasted long after the troops themselves had passed through. By the middle of the eighteenth century, soldiers' health and camp hygiene became a growing issue not just for medical men but also for general and regimental officers. The British army, for one, began to inoculate soldiers against smallpox, while a growing body of literature appeared identifying illnesses, the conditions that spawned them, and the ways of treating them or at least of lessening their impact.[24]

Foremost among these was *Observations on the Diseases of the Army*, by Doctor John Pringle, who had served as hospital director for the British army in Flanders and Scotland during the previous war. In the process, he made particular note of the relationship between environment and health: the effects of climate, weather, wetlands, uplands, and river valleys. He also explored ways of combating illness through better treatment and hygiene. Among other conclusions he came to, Pringle argued there was a correlation between the crowding so typical of military encampments and diseases such as typhus, which in the eighteenth century was known variously as "jail fever," "hospital fever," and (tellingly) "barracks fever." Aside from good food, and clothing suited to the environment and season, Pringle advocated hospitals, attention to sanitation, and the dispersal of troops when possible. He also revealed just how devastating disease could be. Serving with the duke of Cumberland's army in Scotland in 1745–1746, he noted that in 1746 (the year of the Battle of Culloden), some two thousand men fell sick from "hospital fever" and "near 300 died"; this from an army that numbered no more than ten thousand men. Such observations, made in the field on campaign only reinforced commonsense recommendations.[25]

With several thousand people at Raystown occupying an encampment that covered no more than a couple of square miles, sanitation and health were persistent concerns, and Bouquet's orders clearly reflected this. "Necessary Houses" were to be built and "Cleanlyness of the Camp Recommended." The interior guard that mounted daily was to ensure that "no Body wash either Meat or Linnen in the Springs about the Camp," which were to be kept strictly for "use of the soldiers"; all washing was to be done in the Juniata River whose current would carry waste away from the camp. Bouquet also followed Bland's and Pringle's recommendations by seeing that new latrines were dug at least once a week and the old ones "carefully stopped up," duties that fell to the camp-color men. The army's livestock was another health concern. Cattle were taken out daily to graze under the care of "grass guards" and were penned up under guard at night. The scores of horses, without which the army could not move, presented their own problems. Most were owned by civilian wagoners who were reluctant to take them far from the security of the camp. Consequently, they roamed at will dropping manure as they went and keeping the camp awake at night with the incessant rattling of their bells. Bouquet insisted that any horses found loose during the night were to be taken up by the guard and released only when the owner paid one shilling per animal to the camp guard. In addition, owners were told to graze their teams beyond the camp.[26]

Sanitation remained the most serious health issue, and orders on the matter were often repeated. Hundreds of soldiers fresh from civilian life and used to relieving themselves when and where convenient were not inclined to walk any distance from their own tents to the latrine line. However, the problem was not confined to provincial enlistees who simply did not know better. One British veteran made no secret of the fact that the regulars were just as prone to ignore orders, noting that soldiers would not use latrines at night but, instead, relieved themselves right outside their tents on the company streets. Soldiers were also actively discouraged from butchering animals within the camp areas; meat had to be issued from butchering areas located well away from tents, hospitals, and the camp's water supply. In addition, "kitchens," little more than the fire pits used by troops to prepare their rations, were also to be located at least one hundred yards from the tent lines, both to avoid the spread of fire and to keep food remains at a distance from living areas.[27]

Even if these various orders were meticulously obeyed, and repeated notices suggest they were not, sickness would still have appeared. Soldiers carried with them not only their arms and equipment but also whatever ailments may have plagued them upon enlistment; men arrived in camp with rashes, tuberculosis, respiratory ailments, and some had been exposed to smallpox. Wives, children, servants, and slaves were equally prone to infectious disease. The weather certainly failed to cooperate. The rains of June continued through July; "very heavy rain" alternating with "dark, cloudy weather" and "excessive hot weather" made life in the camp miserable. And muddy. Thousands of feet and hooves churned Raystown into a filthy quagmire, a ripe mixture of human and animal waste and food remains. These conditions, added to poor drainage and the need to move away from garbage, meant that regimental camps had to be periodically relocated.[28]

The 133 men listed as sick on July 21 represented less than 6 percent of the troops with Bouquet, making this force remarkably healthy. These figures, though, should not be taken as the norm. Rather, they offer a portrait of one portion of the army at a particular moment. A closer look at individual regiments reveals variations among units and changes over the course of the campaign. The condition in the two Virginia regiments is a case in point. Five companies of Washington's regiment were with Bouquet's force on its march to Raystown; the remainder of the regiment did not join the army until mid-fall when Washington, his own troops, and Byrd's 2d Virginia left Fort Cumberland.

The difference in health between the two Virginia regiments is striking: from early summer to late fall, Byrd's 2d Virginia had a sick rate that was considerably higher than that of Washington's regiment: 16 percent on average as opposed to 11 percent. Moreover, from July through September, the sick rate in Byrd's regiment climbed from 13 to 27 percent while Washington's regiment saw an increase from 4 to 13 percent from July to mid-November. Byrd's regiment certainly entered the campaign under less than ideal circumstances, with no uniforms, little in the way of camp equipment, and antiquated weapons. Such conditions might have contributed to the sick lists, but the central explanation was the regiment's recent origins. Raised quickly from whatever manpower was available for twelve months' service, indentured servants, out-of-work laborers, recent immigrants, even men from outside the colony, Byrd's regiment consisted of troops who were wholly unused to military service. By contrast, Washington's regiment had seen three years of continuous service on the frontiers. It, too, experienced initially high sick rates, but by 1758 conditions had improved as men in poor health either died or left the ranks, as the survivors adapted to life in garrison and in the field, and as officers took greater responsibility for their men's health. Put another way, the contrast between seasoned troops and new recruits is clear. For example, in August, Washington reported that Byrd's men "know little of the service." As a result, "a fifth of them" were sick. He also observed that even the healthy men "become low Spirited and dejected," suggesting that they showed signs of the disorientation and anxiety that veteran troops had learned to overcome.[29]

The health of Pennsylvania's troops should also have reflected the influx of new recruits: the New Levies enlisted for one year's service. Nevertheless, the few returns of the Pennsylvania battalions suggest levels of health more akin to Washington's long-serving regiment. Prior to 1758, the sick rate of the Augusta Regiment, based at the fort of that name on the Susquehanna River, topped out at only 10 percent, less than the 16 percent rates that plagued Washington's regiment in its early days. By August 1758, when some 13 percent of Byrd's regiment's men were sick, the 2d battalion of the Pennsylvania Regiment had only 47 of its 656 men (7 percent) on the sick rolls. Again, "seasoning" seems to have made a difference. Each of the three Pennsylvania battalions contained a leavening of long-service men; a return of part of the 1st battalion shows a total of 389 men who had enlisted for three years (or the whole war) and only four recent recruits. Another reason for the relative health of the Pennsylvanians was Forbes's decision to cull the regiment of its worst men to provide garrisons for the line of forts in the colony at the rate of 15 men from each of the forty-eight companies. It seems likely that officers took the opportunity to detach those men who were most obviously unsuited to the rough service that lay ahead, ensuring that the balance of the regiment consisted of healthy, if not entirely veteran, troops. The three companies raised by the "Lower Counties" of Pennsylvania (now Delaware) also underscore the difference between veterans and new men. These companies, raised for the campaign, at one point had a sick rate of 27 percent, comparable to Byrd's regiment at its poorest.[30]

Forbes's regulars present a somewhat different picture. The three additional Highland companies struggled with poor health into the fall; in mid-September there were 303 enlisted men on the rolls, but 61 of these were listed as sick. By the time they landed in Philadelphia, Montgomery's regiment carried with it 86 sick noncommissioned officers and privates out of 1,058 in the ranks. They subsequently lost 4 men dead, though the number of sick continued to decline once the regiment was off the crowded transport ships. Bouquet's Royal Americans also had a number of sick; 31 of 371 rank and file in late August. Taken together, Forbes's regulars were not suffering high levels of illness, though with differences among the units; both Montgomery's and Bouquet's regiments seem to have improved once they were out of the malarial lowlands of South Carolina. Regardless of these variations among regiments, though, the army not only got smaller over time, it also became less healthy as summer gave way to autumn. Rainy weather persisted, complicating matters for men trying to recover from bouts of malaria or dysentery. By September frost, fog, and freezing nights accompanied the rain; by November troops without adequate clothing were also facing the first snowfalls west of the mountains as ice replaced mud on the road. Again, even the incomplete returns that have survived suggest the trend. A partial return from late July shows 133 sick from a total of 1,479 privates; by September there were 458 sick present or "left behind" from 4,538 private soldiers. Two weeks before the army's final push to Fort Duquesne, out of a total of 4,611 enlisted men, 602 were listed as sick or recovering from the fighting that took place in September, October, and November.[31]

Numbers on the field returns offer a glimpse of trends: veteran troops and newly raised levies, men exposed to the colonial subtropics, and those who were not, and the seasonal nature of the army's overall health. But what sicknesses did soldiers actually suffer from? We know that smallpox appeared in midsummer. Its impact, however, was distinctly limited because of the quick actions of Bouquet and other officers, who isolated the sick—and kept the threat of epidemic a secret in order to avoid a feared mass exodus of frightened men. Typhus seems not to have visited Forbes's army, but other illnesses did. Flux was common and especially enervating and spread through the Raystown camp during the summer; by early August Bouquet reported it was widespread among the troops. Reverend Thomas Barton reported nearly 400 "persons" down with the flux, "diarrheas" and other ailments, suggesting that civilians were suffering as much as soldiers. Forbes also reported that the flux was "a general Distemper" at Carlisle, and he blamed it on the high amount of lime in the local water supply, the same complaint made three years earlier when flux struck Braddock's army.[32]

Fluxes, either from bad water or bad food, were only one aspect. Pringle discussed a range of ailments, from fevers to "the itch" and rheumatism. Pringle treated soldiers in Flanders and Scotland for "autumnal diseases," rheumatic pains, as well as coughs, fevers, and "pleuritic pains." Soldiers at Raystown complained of "Ague & Fever," commonly used terms for what was likely malaria, with its cycles of chills and fevers. These were particularly prevalent among the Virginians, many of whom lived or worked in the humid Tidewater region where malaria was endemic. John Peebles, surgeon for the 2d Virginia Regiment, listed the following complaints in early September: flux, fevers, "sore legs," "pains," pleurisy, and venereal disease. He was caring for 112 men, with flux the single biggest cause of illness. Mostly, soldiers were identified as just "sick," with no attempts made to identify the illnesses, though Pringle's and Peebles's lists are suggestive. In August, for example, Bouquet reported that so many men were sick he was no longer able to provide proper escorts and guards while a Virginian merely observed that "Soldiers here [Raystown] very sickly & die fast." Similar reports continued through summer and into autumn. Bouquet noted that the Virginians' camp was "very Sickly." Colonel Armstrong only mentioned "having Sundry Officers & Soldiers Sick" at a road-building camp in September. Of the Pennsylvanians, Bouquet reported "the greatest number of them are Sick," so many in fact that he suggested calling in the invalids assigned to the Pennsylvania forts as replacements. Moreover, illness was no respecter of rank, and many of the officers in the additional Highland companies were sick by mid-August; Armstrong was reported to be "very Sick."[33]

Identifying specific illnesses from reports of "sick" or "sickly" is, of course, impossible. However, rain, hot and humid days of work followed by chilly, or freezing, temperatures at night would probably have triggered a variety of respiratory complaints including colds and allergies. Along with the "sore legs" that confounded troops unused to long marches, rheumatic complaints likely increased as well. With colder weather came influenza, and pulmonary diseases. Along with these complaints came sore throats and aches, which might have led to complications accelerated by exposure along with poor diet, triggering cases of food poisoning. And in fair weather or foul, soldiers suffered from broken teeth, cavities, and abscesses. Even nature conspired against soldiers' health. Getting lost in the woods meant the risk of starvation as one express rider discovered. "Having lost his way" and after wandering for several days he was finally rescued but "was a perfect Skeleton." Sweaty, sick men sent into the woods to cut wood or scout for the enemy faced the painful irritation of deer flies, ticks, and poisonous snakes; equally toxic plants such as poison ivy, poison oak, or sumac only added to the misery. With roads to cut, wagons to load and unload, security patrols to mount as well as the normal duties of the camp, soldiers already suffering from a variety of ailments—perhaps several at once—found their physical and mental strength further taxed. Reverend Barton saw another dimension of the strain experienced by the troops. He reported in his journal that "It is said that some of our Grass-Guards upon hearing the Cackling of Wild Geese at Night ran into Camp & declar'd they had heard the Voice of Indians all around them." Fear, heightened anxiety, depression, a longing to go home, all added to the misery of common soldiers and threatened a cycle by which poor physical health triggered a psychological malaise that made illness more likely.[34]

Sickness, then, followed Forbes's army like a dark cloud from Raystown to Loyalhannon to Fort Duquesne. And, as more men fell sick, the burdens of the campaign fell to those who were still well enough to work or fight. Yet disease was not the only threat that plagued Forbes's men. "Aches" could refer to almost anything, but most often to what has been called "biomechanical strain": the wear and tear on the human body that comes from hard, physical labor. Much of this was hidden from doctors and other observers who could only see outward manifestations such as bruising, swelling, or severe limps. The skeletal remains of soldiers, however, are more revealing. Some of the dead recently discovered at Fort William Henry suffered not only simple fractures, but also fractures resulting from intense stress. They manifest signs of tearing where muscles attached to bone, the result of labor such as carrying heavy weights or of work associated with digging and hauling. Others displayed signs of infections and poorly healed fractures, which, in the arms or legs, would have interfered with normal motion and added to physical stress. Finally, there would be accidents. Men cutting timber might miscalculate and be hit by the tree causing concussions or broken skulls; even deadfall was dangerous, as a member of one of the Lower Counties companies learned when a dead tree fell on him. A misstep on a wet, rocky stretch of road could result in life-threatening lacerations or broken bones. Men wielding tools were particularly at risk. One soldier broke his leg while working; another "cut himself much" with an axe or spade. Even attempts to stay clean could end badly when soldiers drowned while swimming or bathing.[35]

Doctors treated accidental injuries in much the same way as they confronted illnesses: using what amounted to folk remedies or sovereign cures. Surgeons dosed men with Dr. James's Powder to treat symptoms of illness; they likewise applied various elixirs and nostrums to everything from minor burns to open wounds. Dr. John Buchanan, surgeon to the Royal Horse Guards, treated "lacerated skin" or "slight wounds" with *balsam universal* and recommended candle wax as a suitable treatment for severe sunburn. The universal cure, though, was brandy. Buchanan prescribed internal doses and also applied it to bruises, sprains, and "smarting eyes." As surgeon to a mounted regiment, Buchanan was as adept at medicating horses as he was troopers, a reminder that regimental surgeons might be called upon to perform a variety of tasks. The same man who treated smallpox or gunshot wounds was just as likely to extract a tooth or assist midwives at childbirths.[36]

Another danger lay in the fact that the encampment brought together a volatile mix of soldiers, many new to the army, and firearms. Reports of accidental shootings abound. Braddock had to convene at least one court-martial to deal with the case of one regular having shot and killed another under circumstances that the court found to be accidental. In another case, the adjutant of a battalion of Royal Americans was shot and killed by a sergeant whose weapon accidently discharged. Soldiers might go to close order drill forgetting that their muskets were charged; one such man killed a comrade and severely injured another in a "Melancholy Accident" when his double-charged musket went off; another man was killed on the same day in a similar incident. At Juniata Crossing "Some Dispute hapned," and Thomas Wills was shot in the leg, suffered a broken bone, and was "in a languishing Condition" for lack of medical care. Enlisted men were not the only source of gunshot wounds. Captain Hambright of the Pennsylvania Regiment took a ride with a volunteer named Clayton, who was "unfortunately shot" when Hambright's weapon went off. Adam Davison of the Highland Regiment was acquitted by court-martial of shooting another man; Ensign Kirkpatrick of the Lower Counties was "accidently shot thro' the Knee at the Loyal Hannon Camp." Not even the artillery was immune. After remounting a six-pounder gun on a new carriage, the crew decided to test fire the piece, and, according to a witness, "The Wadden struck thro' a Sutler's Tent & made a great Hole."[37]

For those whose injuries or illnesses were beyond the capacity of regimental surgeons to treat, the only recourse available was the army's hospital. The establishment at Raystown was intended as the principal facility for the army, a "general hospital" that could treat patients before sending them back to the settlements and, perhaps, the army's main hospital in New York. The term "hospital" as then understood included both the physical structure and the personnel—physicians, surgeons, mates, apothecaries, and nurses. The hospital with Forbes's army was no small organization: it occupied twenty freight wagons that served to carry medical gear as well as shelters for the personnel. Once built, the hospital complex contained buildings serving as wards for the sick, kitchens, and, eventually gardens for fresh herbs and vegetables. Nevertheless, it was not capable of accommodating all the men who needed medical attention, especially as the sick lists grew during the autumn months. By early September, for instance, Bouquet was warning Washington to leave his sick men behind at Fort Cumberland since the Raystown hospital could not possibly handle them. Once established, the hospital required a daily detachment of guards, not so much to keep intruders away but to keep patients from leaving before they were properly discharged. Along with guards the army routinely assigned a number of women to serve as cooks and nurses and washerwomen; they were paid for their service but were also not permitted to refuse this duty since they were carried on regimental ration strengths and therefore considered part of the army. Refusal meant loss of food and the possibility of being turned out of camp. By late August six women from the regiments then in camp were being ordered to work at the hospital for two weeks before being relieved; these women could expect to receive six pence a day—comparable to the daily wage of a private soldier.[38]

Despite the facilities, food, and assistance, the hospitals were no more effective in caring for the sick and injured than the regimental surgeons. Eighteenth-century medical men treated symptoms and knew little or nothing about the underlying causes of diseases. Sick men were given purges or "physick" to cleanse the body of excess humors or to treat fevers—provided, of course, that adequate medicines were available. The hospital at Raystown seems not to have had any drugs or other medicines for weeks after the army arrived. When medicine did arrive, it consisted of Dr. James's Powder (the all-purpose medication of the period) and various decoctions of mercury, sulfates, Peruvian bark (quinine), rhubarb, and camphor used as purgatives, laxatives, or (in the case of mercury) to treat syphilis. Surgeons also made use of bleeding and compresses. For the injured there were splints, salves, sutures, and—for badly damaged limbs, fingers, or toes—amputation. Any wound to the abdomen, head, or chest was likely to be fatal since such wounds did not respond to medication and surgery was considered too dangerous. Doctors might also decide to treat gunshot wounds by leaving the shot in the body and hoping either that the wound would heal or that the ball would work its way out of the body. And, while camp women washed linen, the hospital, like the camp in general, was far from clean. Antiseptic medicine and germ theories of disease were generations in the future, so that even simple wounds could easily turn septic, leading to gangrene. Small wonder, then, that soldiers "have such a dislike to the confinement of the hospital," that they "endeavour to secrete [sic] their disorders" rather than risk the experience.[39]

Doctors and surgeons knew the value of cleanliness in keeping soldiers healthy. Pringle taught that dirty skin prevented proper perspiration and that soldiers who were bathed (in a solution of vinegar and water) upon entering the hospital and given clean linen were more comfortable and less likely to contract the "itch" (psoriasis), which Pringle called "the most general distemper among soldiers." He also advocated the use of "ventilators," most likely fans or skylights, since "pure air" was absolutely necessary in a hospital. Experienced soldiers also understood the value of sanitary bodies and camps, hence Bouquet's orders regarding the washing of clothes, the placement of latrines and their use, the periodic relocation of regimental camps, and the routine airing-out of tents.[40]

How deliberately officers and men looked to their own hygiene during the campaign is unclear. Labor on the road or escorting convoys as well as incessant rains, mud, and insects made cleanliness difficult if not impossible. Soldiers came from diverse backgrounds, both rural and urban where personal hygiene and grooming were not always a priority. Robert Webster, serving in New York in 1759, noted that "I washed" on July 10—the first time he had done so since he left home in mid-May. We know that soldiers with Abercromby's army on Lake George occasionally drowned while they attempted to wash themselves, but we do not know how often Forbes's men tried to bathe in the Juniata River or Loyalhannon Creek. The orders concerning the washing of clothes suggest that Bouquet and others anticipated that soldiers would do this, but to what degree is impossible to say. Most men had their uniforms and maybe spare stockings or an extra shirt, but little else. And even if they were inclined to do laundry, soldiers must not have done so very often. Captain William Sweat, a member of Abercromby's army, kept a detailed journal in which he noted "Washing my cloes" exactly three times from his arrival at the army in early May until his unit was dismissed in November.[41]

Nutrition was critical to soldiers' health, yet daily rations often compounded, rather than lessened, health problems. The prescribed diet—one pound of salt meat (pork or beef), one pound of bread (or flour) supplemented by small quantities of butter, dried peas, and cheese—would have provided close to three thousand calories a day. This may have been adequate for normal activity, but fifteen-to-twenty-mile-a-day marches or the work of road building, cutting timber, or mounting scouts and patrols demanded much more. Forbes's men would have quickly lost weight and stamina. The daily ration lacked complex vitamins and minerals, resulting in physical disorders such as night blindness or poorly healed injuries and, perhaps, behavioral manifestations including anxiety or irritability; in all likelihood these men felt constantly hungry, which helps explain orders attempting to regulate hunting around the Raystown camp. Issued food was monotonous and frequently tainted from poor packing and shipping, which, in turn, added to the risk of food poisoning. The salt that infused most foods as a preservative only increased thirst and may have contributed to soldiers drinking contaminated water if beer or liquor were not available. Soldiers were also expected to prepare their own meals, in part to ensure that they ate properly and regularly. Each company within a regiment was routinely divided into "messes" of up to eight men who took turns collecting and preparing rations. Consequently, cooking, and sanitation could vary widely; undercooked pork, for instance, risked trichinosis, and badly prepared food certainly added to the list of those suffering from the flux. As bad as subsistence might have been for common soldiers, dependents fared worse, since they received less food:

one-half-ration for women, at best one-quarter ration for children. Basic nutrition, then, in this as in any early modern army would have depended on pooling meager resources, foraging for whatever wild foods might be available, and planting gardens. Barton wrote of "a large Piece of Ground" planted with turnips at Raystown; he also found "several fine Gardens fenc'd in" at Fort Cumberland, whose garrison enjoyed "all Kinds of Vegetables." Gardening was also a form of recreation; soldiers enjoyed time tending their crops and took offense when duties or officers intruded into what they considered to be their own time and space.[42]

Rations were also a matter of morale; viewing their service in contractual terms, soldiers expected a full and proper ration in return for the duties they performed. Complaints about the quality and quantity of food were evidently common. Corporal William Todd, serving in Germany during the war, made no secret of his own feelings on the matter. His journal contained a number of remarks such as "We are in the utmost want of all kinds of provisions, & many of our men begin to fall sick," and "our Bread Waggons comes very Uncertain." That troops in Germany were expected to buy food on the open market with their meager "subsistence" of six pence a day only made matters worse, especially for those with wives and children to support. In America, British and provincial soldiers received their rations gratis, but they still found reasons to complain of shortages and poor quality, thanks in part to the inexperience of commissaries such as Adam Hoops. Shortly after arriving at Raystown, for instance, Bouquet was faced with a serious protest from provincial troops who were angry at what they saw as skimpy allotments of food. Before joining the army, these Virginians and Pennsylvanians had enjoyed much more ample rations from their own governments; now, according to Bouquet, "they complain continually that the ration is not enough for them." Bouquet conceded the point, though he likely did not consider that colonial working men were used to more, and a more varied diet, than that provided by the army. Bouquet did acknowledge that the "general discontent" arose from the hard labor for which soldiers received no additional monetary compensation, soldiers who expected a larger portion of food. He also offered Forbes a way out of a dilemma that could have caused delays, even mutiny: give them the additional food while the army remained at Raystown. Once they were into the mountains, rations could be pared back under the pretext of transportation difficulties. The widespread unhappiness was also expressed in Bouquet's orders reminding soldiers that only complaints about food sent through the chain of command would be investigated.[43]

*   *   *

Both the quantity and quality of rations were dependent upon the army's logistical system. In mid-July the new storehouses at Raystown along with those at Fort Loudoun (Pennsylvania) and Fort Littleton held bulk flour (250 tons) sufficient to provide ninety-three days of bread or biscuit. The contractors had also sent forward over 500 barrels of pork. The army was receiving its supply of alcohol, and the work crews were receiving their daily ration of whiskey or rum. Nevertheless, there were signs of problems ahead. As the army continued to move west, its supply line grew longer; with mountainous terrain and the incessant rains this would add days to the time required to get rations from Carlisle to the troops. Moreover, while the army labored to open the next section of road beyond Raystown, the troops would have to remain in place, consuming food but making no substantial progress on the march to Fort Duquesne. These facts were clearly on Forbes's mind. In late July he told Abercromby that "till I am able to keep up constantly three months provisions at Raestown," while keeping pace with consumption there, he would keep his troops distributed along the road from Carlisle; otherwise, he concluded, "it would not be safe or expedient to proceed." Unless adequate stores could reach Raystown, then, his army might never be collected together.[44]

The quantities received look impressive, but they paled when set against the army's projected needs. On July 8, the commissary calculated that three additional months' worth of food meant accumulating 2,520 barrels of flour, yet only 1,700 barrels were then "supposed to be a Posts & on the Road," leaving a deficit of 820 barrels. The same held true of pork, the other essential of the daily ration; 900 barrels were needed, but only 330 were on hand. To supplement the pork, commissary Draper Wood and his agents were busy buying livestock in Pennsylvania and Virginia. By mid-July, for instance, some 300 oxen and 818 sheep were either at Raystown or "on the road." An additional 550 cattle and more sheep were due to arrive in early August. These animals would have to be fattened before slaughter by putting them out to graze at Raystown. Even so, the cattle were only expected to provide about 300 pounds of meat per head, representing less than a thirty-day supply. More ominously, Wood also purchased 196 barrels of cornmeal, suggesting that supplies of wheat flour were getting scarce. The danger here was that the troops, told that they could expect certain foods in certain amounts, would not take well to substitutions, especially if this meant accepting lesser quality rations: cornmeal for wheat flour, for example. Further complicating matters was the poor quality of some of the foods received. As early as June,

Wood, had to condemn virtually all of the pork purchased in North Carolina, keeping only 120 barrels for emergency use only. In mid-July, he received cornmeal but found most of it sour and unfit to distribute to the troops.[45]

The army, then, faced the possibility of a hand-to-mouth existence. Until it could cut a road and establish the next base of supply along the "protected advance," troops would remain in Raystown consuming supplies. When the army did move forward, its pace of advance and numbers would be governed by the ability of Forbes, Wood, and others to stockpile food and other supplies over a road now longer and crossing the worst stretch of mountains. Transport and time were key: the army had to maintain serviceable wagons and teams and ensure that convoys kept moving to Raystown and beyond. In July, the number of wagons was not yet a problem; St. Clair reported that 200 wagons loaded with provisions were on route from Carlisle to Raystown in early July. The problem, rather, was their condition, and that of the teams. St. Clair, for example, worried that the road from Carlisle would not accommodate more than the 200 wagons he ordered forward since it was full of narrow defiles, badly rutted, and eroded from the rain. Bouquet echoed this when he told Forbes that "The roads are strewn with broken wagons," but he added that part of the problem lay with the wagon masters who, in his opinion, "are good for nothing." That many of the drivers lacked firearms only added to the problem since the convoys required escorts, and the drivers themselves were showing signs of quitting the service rather than risking ambush along the road.[46]

Forbes and his staff also discovered that the available wagons took far longer to reach Raystown than they had anticipated, based on estimates provided by the commissaries. Bouquet found that a round-trip of eighty miles between Fort Loudoun and Raystown based on a rate of sixteen miles a day would take five days—not including the time taken to load and unload the cargo. Experience proved that this was "another one of Mr. Hoops [Adam Hoops, commissary of wagons] dreams, like his estimate from Carlisle here." In reality, Bouquet found, a round-trip from the Carlisle depot to Raystown would take fifteen days. Given this simple arithmetic, Bouquet concluded that he could never accumulate adequate food and stores; he once more urged the use of packhorses to supplement the inadequate wagon convoys. He was appalled by the awful condition of the wagon teams. Bouquet railed against farmers "who had good horses when they were appraised" but then sent "nags who are unable to drag themselves along." Forbes agreed, telling Abercromby that the horses at Raystown were hardly able to keep on their feet, let alone pull wagons. The poor quality of horseflesh was only compounded by a mounting problem with forage. A horse required twenty pounds of green forage every day, besides six gallons of grain per team each day; by July the army was increasingly pressed to deliver this essential ration because food for men competed with food for horses. Forbes concluded that the army was "like to be at one Intire Stop for want of provender." At Raystown, local pastures "are greatly diminished" though there was enough for "some time." Of greater concern was the lack of oats; Bouquet was hoarding whatever shipments he received "as if they were gold." And the longer the army remained at Raystown, the worse the problem would become; by early August when a division of the artillery arrived the nearest grass for the exhausted teams was six miles from camp, leading Bouquet to conclude that it was the lack of forage—not the road—that was ruining the horses. Yet ironically, the very "desert" created by war provided one asset: abandoned farms near Fort Loudoun would provide an estimated 2,000 tons of free fodder for the army.[47]

In casting about for an explanation for their current problems, both Forbes and Bouquet pointed to the usual suspect: Sir John St. Clair. As quartermaster general he was responsible for overseeing the collection and shipment of supplies and, above all, for ensuring adequate stocks of food and forage. Forbes, worried that the army would be stranded for lack of forage, said that "Sir John had only made an Imaginary Provision," since in fact there was no hay nor any prospect of getting any at Carlisle. He also blamed St. Clair for the "heap of Confusion" at Carlisle. St. Clair was, according to Forbes, "at Variance with every mortall, [. . .] most disagreeable [he] impedes Every Thing," leaving Forbes to sort things out while hoping that "God grant I may Keep my Temper." Bouquet said simply that "It was a great Neglect in the Quarter Master General" not to have arranged for the collection of forage at Fort Cumberland, saying that the "omission is Sufficient to ruin the Expedition" since grass was now scarce along the road, and as a result, the army "will not be able to Carry all supplies at once" and must rely "by Deposites" and a continual resupply—both time-consuming and dangerous.[48]

That St. Clair had a volatile temper and was prone to intimidate or alienate people was well established by 1758. Yet, we also need to consider his responsibilities as the army reached Raystown. He not only had to oversee the movement of men and supplies as well as the civilian commissaries and contractors while attempting to collect intelligence of French activities, he was also responsible for selecting the army's route west and directing the work of building a road. To carry out these duties—and the immense amount of correspondence and other paperwork—he had the assistance of just two officers, the assistant deputy quartermasters Lieutenant Lewis Ourry and Lieutenant James St. Clair (Sinclair). In July 1758, the new road west of Raystown occupied most of his time. Sent to the camp from Carlisle on July 25, by July 31 he was discussing plans with Bouquet and preparing to leave on a survey of the route as far as Loyalhannon beyond Laurel Mountain. By the end of the month, as Forbes and the balance of the army were preparing to leave Carlisle for Raystown, pressure mounted to get the road marked and opened. From this point on, the army's success—and St. Clair's reputation—would depend on selecting the best route forward and in cutting a road sufficient to support an army.[49]

SIX

Forbes's Road

* * *

JULY–AUGUST 1758

I am in hopes of finding a better way over the Alleganey Mountain, than that ... which General Braddock took.
—FORBES TO PITT, JULY 1758

The best route to Fort Duquesne had been on Forbes's mind from the beginning. Nothing was more important than securing a route that was both adequate to the army's needs and defensible against anticipated French attack. On the surface the choices facing Forbes were simple and straight forward: he could either opt to use Braddock's Road by marching through Maryland or Virginia, or he could seek a new route that would take him over the mountains through Pennsylvania. Each option posed challenges that might stymie the campaign. Braddock's Road and the available encampments were known and its southern end was guarded by the Virginians at Fort Cumberland. But Forbes had to assume that the French would be expecting him to take that route and would be prepared to contest his advance. Moreover, before mid-1758 no road able to support wagon traffic existed between Fort Frederick (Big Pool), Maryland, and Fort Cumberland, and the Braddock campaign had revealed how limited the resources were in western Maryland and northern Virginia; it was this fact that prompted both Braddock and St. Clair to conclude the proper route should have been through Pennsylvania.

The Pennsylvania route also presented problems. The first and most daunting was the topography: the army would have to march across the grain of the Appalachian Mountains, facing in turn a series of steep, rugged ridges—Sideling Hill, Allegheny Mountain, Laurel Mountain, Chestnut

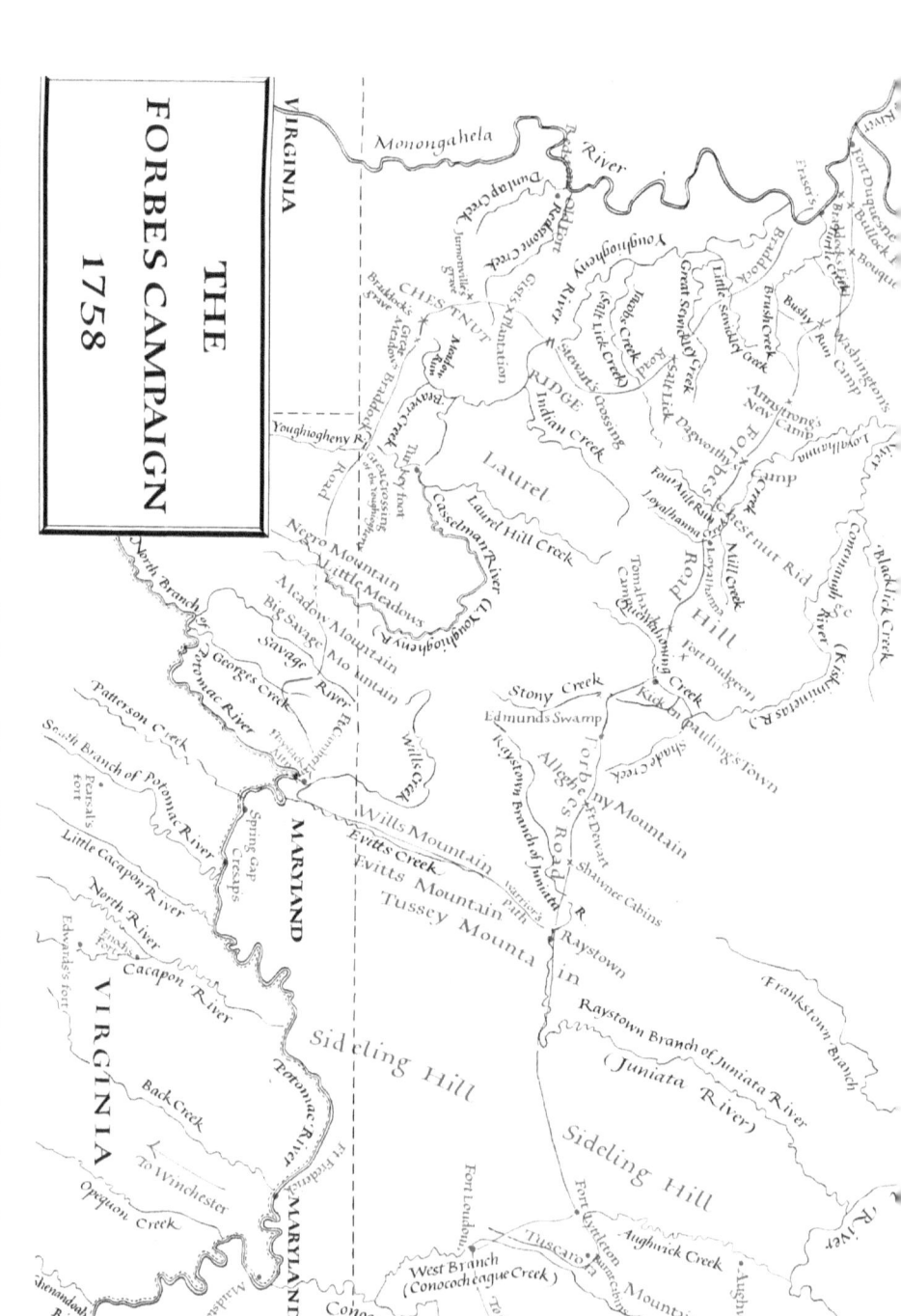

Fig. 6.1 "The Forbes Campaign." In George Washington, *The Papers of George Washington, Colonial Series*, vol. 6, *September 1758–December 1760*, edited by W. W. Abbot. 28–29. © 1988 by the Rector and Visitors of the University of Virginia. Reprint by permission of the University of Virginia Press.

Ridge—that would play havoc with logistics. Despite using the far richer and better developed Pennsylvania settlements as a base, just getting wagonloads of food, forage, and munitions over the mountains would be an unprecedented challenge. Unprecedented simply because, beyond Raystown, no one knew where the best route lay, what obstacles lay beyond the next ridge, and whether there were adequate resources such as water and grass for an army more than double the size of Braddock's in numbers of men, animals, artillery, and wagons. Those guides retained by Forbes proved about as ignorant of the land beyond the colony as the general himself. Mostly deer-hide traders, they viewed the mountains, their passes and obstacles, from the perspective of short strings of packhorses, not armies.

The choice of which road to take also raised tensions within the army. Forbes may have been concerned only with the most safe, reliable, and expeditious route of march, but others saw the road from the standpoint of their particular colonies and the local advantages that access to the West would bring. The running debate over the road stands as a prime example of how easily colonial localism could interfere with military and imperial interests and how volatile the coalition armies that fought the war in America really were.

*   *   *

Even before the army began its march toward Raystown, Forbes had clearly decided on a different route to Fort Duquesne. At the beginning of May he told Pitt he was prepared to move "fifty or sixty Miles" beyond the Pennsylvania settlements. Later that month he spoke of his design to "open the road across the Allegany Mountain towards the Yohagany [Youghiogheny]," the road pioneered by Colonel James Burd in 1755. Indeed, there is little reason to think Forbes was not already set on opening a new route to the Ohio River. In late June, for example, he wrote Abercromby: "I shall take my Departure across the Allegany Mountains" once a firm base at Raystown was established. The impression of indecision well into the campaign comes from plans to open secondary roads that would give the army flexibility in the event the mountains did indeed prove too great an obstacle. The Maryland road from Fort Frederick to Fort Cumberland proposed by Governor Sharpe was one of these, as was the new road opened between Fort Cumberland and Raystown. His orders to Bouquet, who was leading the army's advance, are clear. Bouquet was to scout ahead at least as far as Laurel Mountain. Despite his own misgivings Bouquet sent out two survey parties and assigned engineer Lieutenant Thomas Basset to direct these but also conceded: "The season is too far advanced to consider any other communication." Finally, on July 6, Forbes made it clear that "most Certainly wee Shall now all go by Raes town." Yet he insisted in keeping his options open. As he told Abercromby just three days later, the army would either move "directly across the Allegany" from Raystown or "by Fort Cumberland and take General Braddock's road," which he already ordered "opened the length of the Crossing of the Yohageny." The new road from Raystown to Fort Cumberland would thus serve as a detour—if needed—and a way to bring Washington's Virginians up to the rest of the army. If activity on Braddock's Road drew French attention away from Raystown, so much the better.[1]

Forbes admitted that the choice of a route through Pennsylvania was at best problematic, telling Bouquet in June that "As to the Roads, I can say nothing, only I was advised by everyone to go by Raes town." Saying that "I shall be sorry if it proves impracticable," he revealed his own lack of information and underscored the need for alternatives. He certainly did nothing to dispel Bouquet's own worries about the army's march beyond Raystown. Who "everyone" was is not clear. Forbes would have seen Lewis Evans's map and accompanying narrative and may have talked with Pennsylvanians including officials such as Richard Peters and the guides who claimed knowledge of the Juniata Valley. The one individual who certainly advised Forbes was his quartermaster general, Sir John St. Clair, whose duties included selecting and marking the army's routes of march. St. Clair had eagerly sought assignment to Forbes's army by promoting himself as an authority on the country the army would cross. Forbes in fact made it clear that "Sir John St. Clair was the first person who first advised me to take the road to Raestown" rather than follow Braddock's Road. On this vital issue, as with the shortage of forage, St. Clair appears to have failed his general. By early July St. Clair was having second thoughts about his earlier suggestion, now telling Forbes that the army would never find a way across Allegheny Mountain: "That he says its impossible wee can pass, without going into Braddock's old Road," compelling Forbes to take the precaution "to have the Communication opened from Raestown to Fort Cumberland." Yet, on the choice of route, Forbes held to his earlier decision, gambling that he could yet make it across the mountains and convinced that the direct route west was shorter than the alternative. Angry that St. Clair had not bothered to make his doubts known earlier instead of advocating a route he now condemned, Forbes could only wish that the quartermaster general would "hold his peace now." Indeed, it was in light of St. Clair's second thoughts that Forbes ordered Bouquet to push ahead with a survey of possible routes over both Allegheny and Laurel Mountains.[2]

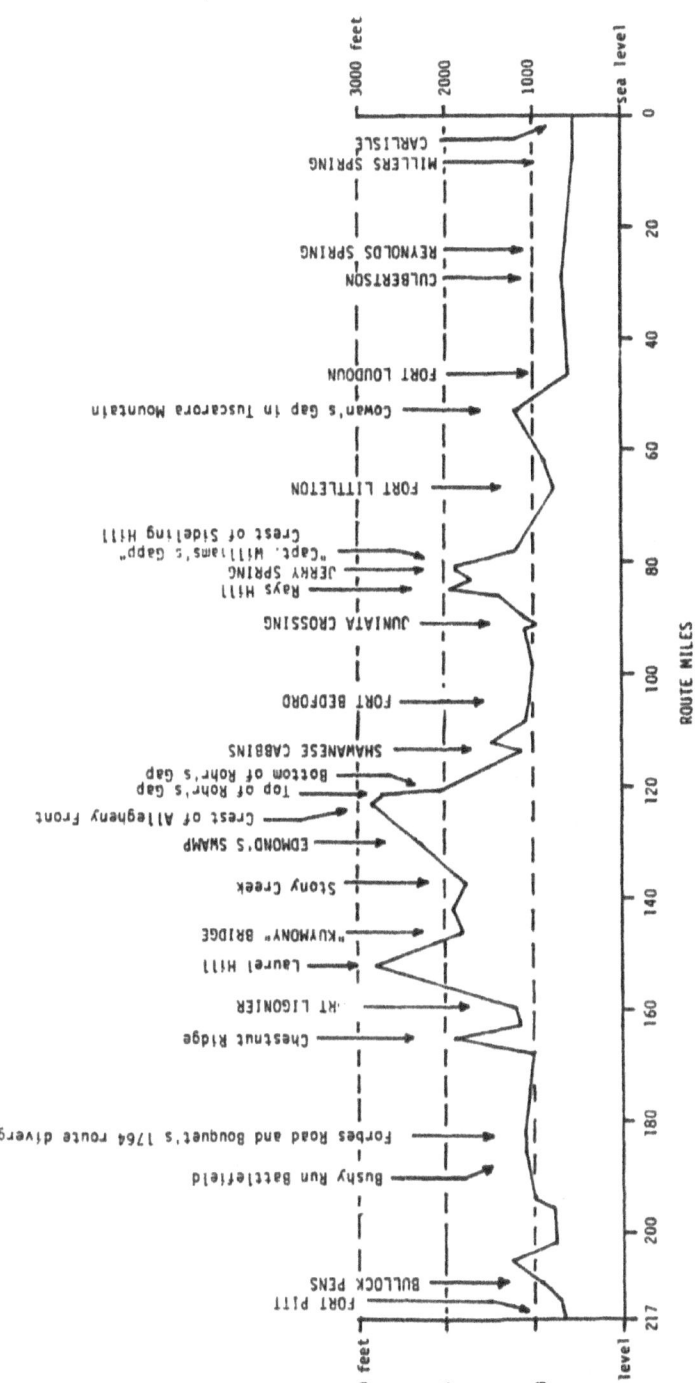

Fig. 6.2 Reginald P. Briggs, "Conquest of the Allegheny Mountains in Pennsylvania: The Engineering Geology of Forbes Road, 1758–1764," *Environmental & Engineering Geoscience* 4, no. 3 (1998): 403. By permission of the Association of Environmental & Engineering Geologists.

In a letter written to Bouquet on July 23 in which he railed against what he saw as his quartermaster's incompetence, Forbes also suggested another possible motive for St. Clair's sudden change of mind. In reviewing the whole issue, Forbes concluded that "Sir John I am afraid had got a new light at Winchester," which led him to advocate a new road from Fort Frederick and diverting the army to Fort Cumberland. "Winchester" referred not only to the Virginia town where St. Clair had spent considerable time organizing and equipping new provincial troops; it was also an allusion to the Virginians themselves, in particular the officers of the Virginia regiments and their colonels, Washington and Byrd.[3]

Forbes was referring to the mounting opposition of these men and the politicians behind them to any route other than Braddock's Road. Since at least April, speculation had been building about the army's route. In the absence of any information to the contrary, colonial officials it seems had assumed that Forbes and his troops would naturally follow Braddock's Road; in 1758, it remained visible and was well-known. Rumor and idle speculation were not helped by the fact that Forbes kept his own counsel, never discussing his options and decision with his regimental officers and communicating only with Bouquet, whose own professionalism prevented him from divulging official correspondence with others. Yet it seems Bouquet's own doubts about a route across the mountains fueled the hopes of those who espoused the Braddock Road. In such an atmosphere, men were free to draw their own conclusions. For example, Governor Sharpe of Maryland could tell the Maryland Proprietor in June that "I find that the Army is to march thro Pennsylvania to Raystown & not to Fort Frederick as I expected." Only two weeks later, Colonel John Armstrong of Pennsylvania told Bouquet that he had learned that "Raes Town is not to be the place of General Rendezvous, but C——d [Fort Cumberland]." Then contradicting his earlier report, Sharpe wrote: "I understand that the General intends to march part of the Army this way [i.e., through western Maryland]."[4]

For these colonists the choice of route was of more than passing interest. Everyone understood that, whichever road the army adopted, commerce and settlement would surely follow and the colony through which the road advanced would enjoy considerable economic advantage. This was certainly on the minds of Virginians, in particular Colonel George Washington. For him and others, the Ohio Country had been calling since the late 1740s. Then, an association of land speculators—including Washington's half-brother Lawrence—organized themselves as the Ohio Company and sought a royal patent for several hundred thousand acres near the Forks of the Ohio. The French spoiled the plan by occupying the upper Ohio Valley beginning in 1753; the subsequent campaigns to drive them out were as much about private profit as imperial security. Despite the years of collapsing frontiers and French and Indian raids, the lure of the Ohio Country persisted among planters anxious to invest in fresh lands and draw rents from the settlers who would inevitably enter the region once the French were gone. Governor Sharpe, for example, clearly had his sights set on the future, telling Lord Baltimore, the eldest member of the Calvert clan, that "It would give me great pleasure to see [the new road from Fort Frederick] compleated because it will hereafter be of vast advantage to this Province." If Forbes did as expected and followed Braddock's Road, Virginia and its planter elite would stand to reap the rewards.[5]

Washington's increasing advocacy for the Virginia route thus had less to do with strategy than with land speculation; there was much at stake both for the colonel personally and for his province. These considerations, not the military effort, increasingly influenced his judgment on the matter. Not that the Virginians were alone in putting local interests ahead of those of army and empire. Sharpe was convinced that Pennsylvanians "would not wish to see a better Road made from the Inhabited Parts of Maryland . . . than can be made through that Province [Pennsylvania]." Edward Shippen, landowner and merchant, was certainly interested in Forbes's decision. Writing from Lancaster to his son, an officer in the Pennsylvania Regiment, he made a point to ask if the road was to be cut from Raystown to Loyalhannon. According to Barton, although Virginians argued that "it will be extremely difficult" to make a road from Loyalhannon to Fort Duquesne, Pennsylvania captain Robert Callender "and some others" said "that an Excellent Road may be made" and his troops could prepare a road for wagons and artillery in just five days. By autumn, Colonel John Armstrong was delighted to tell Peters that "The Virginians are much chagrin'd at the Opening of the Road thro' this Government."[6]

The most persistent—and strident—advocate for Braddock's Road, though, was Washington. His partisanship began at the outset of his military career. He confidently reported in 1755 that "the eyes of the General [Braddock] are now open," and he will take his army through Virginia. At that time Washington was particularly concerned that Maryland might enjoy the fruits of the army's road building, but he was relieved that Braddock would march by way of Fort Cumberland, "which gave me infinite satisfaction." Little had changed in three years. As early as April 1758, he was offering unsolicited advice on routes, urging that Fort Cumberland be the army's advanced base. Moreover, Washington told St. Clair that the southern Indians would refuse to follow the army if it went by Pennsylvania, telling him that using

Fig. 6.3 "George Washington as Colonel of the Virginia Regiment," 1772, by Charles Willson Peale. (Courtesy of Washington and Lee University, University Collections of Art and History.) This is how Washington would have looked in full dress in 1758.Tucked into his waistcoat pocket is a piece of paper labeled "Plan of March." This detail suggests that Washington was particularly conscious of his contribution to the successful campaign, even though the portrait was done as Britain and her American colonies were approaching a political crisis.

Maryland or Pennsylvania as a rendezvous for the army "will give [the Indians] some disgust" because, "from long use," they were more comfortable with Fort Loudoun, Winchester, and the road to Fort Cumberland. By early

June, based no doubt on further conversations with Washington and his officers, St. Clair reported that "The Virginians are dissatisfied with the Whole Army taking the route of Pennsylvania."[7]

Washington persisted in his lobbying throughout July. On July 7, he was telling Bouquet he had been told "by all hands" that the army would use Braddock's Road and again warned that the Cherokees would "absolutely refuse to March any other Road than this they know." Then Colonel William Byrd began to chime in, echoing Washington's warning about the Indians. Officials back in Williamsburg were monitoring reports about the road, and Washington received letters from allies at Raystown and Alexandria telling him of how bad the new road was: "Steep, Stony & of very difficult access," while lamenting "our injur'd Colony," the victim of the "Torrent of headstrong prejudice" by "Crafty Neighbors" who were guilty of "Injustice." Washington needed no prompting. He wrote to remind Bouquet that he had taken "particular pains" to have Braddock's Road scouted and concluded that it would require "such small repairs" an army could easily see to them while on the march. He repeated the same subtle hint a week later, being careful not to seem "officious." Officious or not, Washington continued to press. "Chearfully" willing to do whatever he was commanded, Washington pledged never "to have a will of my own where a point of Duty is required," but at the same time he also told a correspondent that "I shall warmly urge" the adoption of Braddock's Road.[8]

* * *

Washington's persistent drumming in favor of Braddock's Road was becoming tiresome to those who had to listen to him or read his letters; by late July the colonel was skating on very thin ice. Major Francis Halkett, Forbes's principal aide and Washington's friend since 1755, tried twice to warn him to back off but to no avail. As early as June 25, Halkett told Washington that he personally respected his point of view and knowledge, which gave Washington "very good *pretentions to advise the General*" and assured him that Forbes "puts that Confidence in your way of Thinking, *which your merit deserves.*" The word "pretentions" was a reminder that Washington's views and comments were wholly unsolicited and that Forbes was being courteous in considering them. To Bouquet, Halkett also reported that, having made his decision about a new road that would be shorter and with fewer "inconveniences" than Braddock's Road, Forbes was "at the same time extremely surpris'd at the partial disposition that appears in those Virginia Gentlemans sentiments." Bouquet certainly agreed, telling Forbes in early July that "All the letters I receive from Virginia are filled with nothing but the impossibility of finding a passage across Laurel Hill, and the ease of going by Braddock's Road." He added: "This is a matter of politics between one province and another, in which we have no part." Yet he also urged Forbes to "act with double caution" in the face of Virginia opposition, "that we may answer their outcries convincingly in case of an accident," while not missing the chance to dismiss "these Gentlemen" who "do not know the difference between a party and an army."[9]

Forbes decried factions: "As I disclaim all parties myself. Should be sorry that they were to Creep in amongst us." As Loudoun's adjutant general he had seen, and been the object of, divisions within the army and would have none of it in 1758. This was the source of his mounting anger and frustration over the Virginians' incessant efforts "to drive us into the Road by Fort Cumberland." He as well as Bouquet understood the source of provincials' "parties": Virginia opposition to Pennsylvania "who by Raestown would have a nigher Communication to the Ohio." Saying that "I utterly detest all partys and views in Military operations," Forbes not only rejected the advice "that some foolish people have made" but also dressed down his own quartermaster general for succumbing to such behavior. At the same time Forbes clearly resented the second-guessing of his decisions; his insistence on taking the new road from Raystown was simply reinforced by Virginia resistance. As he later said: "I told them plainly, that, whatever they thought, yet I did aver that in our prosecuting the present road, we had proceeded from the best Intelligence that could be got for the good and convenience of the Army." He may have been less than comfortable with his choice and only time would tell if his intelligence was really the best "that could be got" and whether the army would benefit from his decisions. This uncertainty, which hovered over the campaign from start to finish, could be dispelled—or at least held at bay—by making decisions and holding to them. Persistent indecision of the kind exhibited by St. Clair simply would not do.[10]

A showdown was brewing by late July and became inevitable. On July 27 Bouquet asked Washington to meet him for a face-to-face discussion about the road, this after receiving letters from Washington again urging Braddock's Road and insisting that "every other Person who has knowledge of that Country" thought the old road was the best choice. Bouquet evidently expected Washington to either present concrete evidence or let the matter drop in the face of Forbes's decision. Their meeting, at a blockhouse midway along the new road from Raystown to Fort Cumberland, was disappointing for both. Bouquet accepted what he called Washington's "generous dispositions for the Service [and] the candid Exposition of your Sentiments." Yet neither man changed his mind; Bouquet stood by Forbes's decision, and

Washington continued to press his now predictable arguments. Something of the outcome is reflected in Bouquet's letter to Forbes in which he reported," I have learned nothing satisfactory," and that the Virginians "find every thing easy which agrees with their ideas, jumping all over the difficulties."[11]

Washington, on the other hand, responded by writing a rather hysterical letter to his friend Halkett, where he conceded that "I find him [Bouquet] fixd upon leading you a new way to the Ohio" and quickly added his old refrain about "the beaten Tract, universally confessd to be the best Passage through the Mountains." Not content to rest there, Washington then painted a picture of impending doom, telling Halkett that if Forbes insisted on the new road "all is lost!—All lost by Heavens!" Driving the point home, he insisted that the result would be "our Enterprize Ruind," the "Southern Indians turn against Us," insisting that "These are the Consequences of a Miscarriage." He ended by reminding Halkett: "I am uninfluenced by Prejudice . . . that be assured of." Only a week later Forbes declared that he was "now at the bottom of their Scheme against this new Road, a Scheme that I think was a shame for any officer to be Concerned in." Forbes had his proof "[b]y a very unguarded letter of Colonel Washington that Accidently fell into my hands"—most certainly the letter to Halkett. He shared this not only with Bouquet but also with the commander in chief in America, General Abercromby. Although no letters exist from Forbes to Washington or any other Virginia officers, he made a point of telling Abercromby: "I have now got the better of the whole by letting them *very roundly* know" that their "Judging and determining of my actions and intentions" were such that "I could by no means suffer it." His worst condemnation of Washington's behavior, however, came in a letter to Bouquet. Forbes told him that, in finally uniting the army at Raystown by bringing in the remaining Virginia troops at Fort Cumberland, Bouquet should "consult" Washington "although perhaps not follow his advice, as his Behaviour about the Roads, was no ways like a Soldier."[12]

Forbes's anger was made worse knowing that even his professionals had succumbed to "parties"—certainly, in his mind, St. Clair and perhaps also Captain Harry Gordon. Of all the men in a position to know about Braddock's Road, Gordon would have been the reigning expert; he had mapped Braddock's march and kept a meticulous record of each encampment from Fort Cumberland to the ill-fated battle of July 9, 1755. Gordon rarely appears in the records at this point, though in June Forbes complained that he ought to be busy on the roads rather than remaining in Carlisle. Gordon, too, may have been a vocal champion of the old road. In a remarkable document entitled "Memorial Concerning the Back Forts in North America," written in December 1765, Gordon launched into a diatribe against Forbes's decision.

According to Gordon: "[I] thought myself obliged to remonstrate in the strongest Terms to the Brigadier" though he evidently received no reply. In Gordon's view the new road, by no means superior to Braddock's, was built "by the immensist Labour & as great Expence." He concluded by blaming "politicks" for the decision and also the vanity of "particular Commanders" (a clear reference to Forbes and Bouquet) who acted against the interests of the country and attempted to "screen their Blunders and support their foolish Proceedings." The tone of Gordon's "Memorial" strongly suggests that at some point during the summer of 1758 he and Forbes crossed swords over the choice of roads and that, having no tolerance for the partisanship and perhaps prevarications of his quartermaster general, Forbes was not about to tolerate the same behavior in his chief engineer. Gordon's accusations are remarkable, though by that time neither Forbes nor Bouquet was alive to answer them. Had they done so, they might have produced Gordon's own 1755 journal in their defense; of the eighteen campsites listed, nine carried notations of "no water," "Bad water," or "poor forage," and one other had only "tolerable" water. Bearing in mind that Forbes marched with over twice the number of men, wagons, and animals as Braddock, it is hard to see how these sites could have served the army. Indeed, these were precisely the conditions that Forbes was most worried about; he may have known enough of Braddock's route to decide that a new road was worth the gamble.[13]

Despite Forbes's censure of St. Clair, the Virginians, and perhaps also Gordon, the choice of a road remained a festering sore and the sniping continued into the autumn. Bouquet, for example, lost no opportunity to show the Virginians just how wrong—and wrong-headed—they were, telling Washington at one point: "We find happily less difficulty in opening the Road than we imagined." He told Pennsylvanian William Allen that taking Braddock's Road "would have been our destruction." For his part, Washington began referring to the new road as "your" road in correspondence with Bouquet. He continued openly to blame Pennsylvania for what Virginia Captain Robert Stewart called "our once well grounded hopes" now "blasted" by Virginia's rivals.[14]

The "parties" that Forbes despised reflected what Virginians and Pennsylvanians alike saw as their legitimate interests. Not unlike his disappointing experience with the Cherokees, Forbes's problems with Washington, Byrd, and their supporters grew out of fundamental differences about how the campaign should be conducted. Cherokee fighters, whose lives were rooted in regional and town identities, thought nothing of abandoning Forbes when he would neither treat them as equals nor conduct the campaign according to their schedule, or when he would insult their values and self-esteem. In the same way, merchants such as Edward Shippen or speculators such as Washington saw the campaign from parochial points of view; province trumped empire here, just as the ongoing quests for profit and status trumped the military discipline and professionalism that Forbes cherished. Washington never for a moment believed he was doing anything other than acting as a responsible gentleman to whom others looked for leadership in an effort to secure his colony's interests. His values and Forbes's, though, were on a collision course from the outset: Forbes demanded loyalty, obedience, and cooperation from his officers while the Virginians expected a respectful and sympathetic hearing of their particular concerns. Put another way, Forbes was once again reminded of the limits of authority in waging a coalition war. The complicity of professional soldiers such as St. Clair and Gordon in creating divisions within the army only made matters worse.

* * *

The effort to find a way across the mountains began in June when St. Clair informed Bouquet that he was relying on the advice of one John Walker in locating a suitable route from Allegheny Mountain. Walker's comments—that the way would take "a great deal of labour & time" and should be scouted in autumn when there were no leaves on the trees—evidently forced St. Clair to rethink his advice to Forbes. Beginning in early July and convinced that "I have been too often deceived by the reports of others," Bouquet sent out additional parties under trustworthy officers both to look for a passage over the mountains and to observe Fort Duquesne. These were no small affairs: one detachment numbered 104 officers and men; another consisted of at least 30 soldiers and as many Cherokees. The commanders of these parties were ordered to keep a record of how far they traveled and what they saw, "observing the Road & the Bearings."[15]

The most detailed report came from a scout led by Captain Edward Ward and Captain Asher Clayton, both of the Pennsylvania Regiment. Bouquet provided them with very specific instructions for a trip that was to take them over the Allegheny and Laurel Mountains to the Forks of the Youghiogheny. On their return they were ordered to pick up Byrd's Road, follow it to a cache of tools left in 1755, and return with these to Raystown. Ward and Clayton were told to "consider attentively" whether "a road can be made across Laurel Mountain," to scout gaps in the mountains, and to take accurate bearings and distances—all in anticipation of setting crews to work on the new road. The result was Ward's journal giving distances and directions. Ward found, for example, that the Shawnee Cabins were nine and a half miles from Raystown and the crest of Allegheny Mountain eight miles farther. Laurel

Mountain was thought to be forty-six and a half miles from Raystown, and a source of water at Quemahoning Creek was only four miles beyond Laurel Mountain. By his own reckoning Ward's party traveled about 138 miles from Raystown to Loyalhannon Creek, then south to the Three Forks of the Youghiogheny before turning back north to pick up Byrd's Road. They also brought back other important information. Ward and Clayton found only one difficult piece of ground on their way up Allegheny Mountain and reported that it could be avoided. The ground to the west was stony and covered in thickets; the way up Laurel Mountain was also stony. However, they did find the land east of Laurel Mountain to be well watered and full of forage. On the west side of Laurel Mountain, in the valley of Loyalhannon Creek, they found "vast glades" and meadows as well as swampy ground. The army would eventually build its last major encampment in this area. Once they got to the forks of the Youghiogheny, though, the party encountered ground that would be bad for horses and hills and that, in their opinion, wagons could not manage. Over a two-week trek they were free of enemy parties but had to contend on occasion with heavy rain before retrieving the tools and carrying them back to Raystown. The only mishap occurred when one soldier, named Myers, left camp without permission and did not return. The party even risked firing muskets every few minutes to guide him back, but without success.[16]

While returning to Raystown, the scouting party encountered Captain James Patterson with his party of eighty men on a scout to Fort Duquesne. On his return Patterson provided Bouquet with his "Observations on the Road from Fort DuQuesne to Reas Town." These included glowing accounts of "fine level ground," "a fine Ridge," an area where a good road could be made without difficulty, and "A beautiful Place for an army to encamp." All of these observations were of land west of Laurel Mountain; Patterson found his route a good one and claimed that Chestnut Ridge, west of Loyalhannon Creek, was not formidable. It is not clear where exactly Patterson traveled; his brief account merely refers to "runs" crossed, three "little Ridges," "two other Ridges," and so forth, with mention of "Cock Eye's Cabin," "Two Licks" and "Big Bottom." Nevertheless, his account, taken with Ward's, suggested that a new road over the mountains was possible and would go through country that could support an army with its transport. Later that same month Major George Armstrong of Pennsylvania reported on a scout he led from Raystown to Loyalhannon. He told Bouquet that Quemahoning Creek was both ample and surrounded by cleared ground and that the route they followed was "pretty Good." As if to underscore the point, Armstrong said he wanted to mark out "a very Good Plantation or two upon this Creek."[17]

Other reports offered more detail but reinforced Ward's conclusions. Lieutenant James Baker, a member of Ward and Clayton's party, found the ascent of Allegheny Mountain "very Steep & Stoney" and doubted if a loaded wagon could "be got up this Mountain." He agreed, though, that it was possible to make a road over Laurel Mountain, though he described much of the route they took as "very stoney." Major Armstrong agreed about the quality of the ground the army would have to cover but also said that even the Virginians with his party agreed that a "Tolerable" road could be cut across Laurel Mountain to Loyalhannon. He noted good grass in clearings made years earlier by Indians. Finally, a regular engineer, Ensign Charles Rhor, traveled to the top of Allegheny Mountain along the "Old trading path" and found hills "which are quite practicable," though he found little forage available at the foot of the mountain. Reports were so favorable, in fact, that Forbes even had the satisfaction of learning that St. Clair conceded that the general was right and that a road was "very practicable." Bouquet was also sold on the new route, observing to Forbes, "how right you were in preferring this Route."[18]

None of this would have pleased the Virginians, but it seems these reports confirmed Forbes's decision to march due west from Raystown rather than by Fort Cumberland and Braddock's Road. Forbes was also particular about the kind of road he wanted. In addition to the main road, broad enough for freight wagons and artillery, he ordered that a "small Road" be cut on either side and one hundred yards from the main track. He insisted that these did not have to be perfectly cleared but merely wide enough to accommodate two men abreast. The additional labor would serve two important purposes: first, it would keep the main road clear of troops and available for heavy transport; second, it would permit the army to cover the road and lessen the likelihood of ambush. This latter issue was not unique to Forbes; Braddock had organized his march to include flanking parties on each side of the road for precisely this purpose.[19]

While their senior officers argued about the road or evaluated reports on what lay ahead, common soldiers were trading muskets for saws, shovels, chains, and crowbars. Some of these men were already adept at roadwork, having made improvements to the miserable road from Fort Loudoun to Raystown over Sideling Hill. Beginning west of Raystown, however, the immense task of cutting a new road over the mountains would occupy the army for the rest of the summer and into autumn. As they set out, working parties confronted two formidable obstacles: Allegheny Mountain and Laurel Mountain. The former rose twelve hundred feet from the camp at Shawnee Cabins, its crest a full three thousand feet above sea level. Laurel Mountain was almost as high and the western slope dropped sixteen hundred feet to the valley of Loyalhannon Creek. Farther west, beyond what would become the Loyalhannon encampment, was the final high ground: Chestnut Ridge, less than one thousand feet high. Once across Allegheny Mountain, the army would enter the Ohio River watershed, a signal milestone for Forbes and his troops. The mountains, though, were only one—albeit the most daunting— challenge. Old growth forest that resisted axes and saws was another. Moreover, throughout July and early August, rain and heat continued to plague the army, making work both miserable and dangerous. The rains added to the problems of moving across low ground like Edmund's Swamp near Stony Creek. By mid-August the rain continued but now with cooler temperatures, fog, and frost—sure signs that Forbes was leaving the best campaigning months behind. The absence of maps meant that working parties had to proceed at the pace of the surveying and scouting parties. Finally, once in the mountains they were much more vulnerable to raids by French and native fighters. Major Armstrong's party, encamped between Allegheny and Laurel Mountains, heard "Indian halloes" in the night, a reminder that they were now in country known to and controlled by the enemy.[20]

Roadwork began even as the scouting reports were being submitted and discussed. By the first week of August Bouquet could report that some twelve hundred men were assigned to the road including four parties totaling seven hundred men busy opening the way between Raystown and Major Armstrong's camp at Kickenpauling's Town, a former native settlement on Quemahoning Creek at the eastern foot of Laurel Mountain. They did so by following blazes on trees left by the scouting parties. One party of nearly six hundred men was mustered on August 4 and provided with three days' worth of rations and ammunition before joining the road crews. The ammunition is a reminder that not all of these men would be wielding tools; a substantial number would be scouting along the route and serving as covering parties in case of attack. Whatever their particular task, the work was physically and mentally demanding. Rain and fog in early August made marching, watching, and working both uncomfortable and dangerous; the "stoney" ground along which the men were working became slippery and unstable in wet weather and destroyed shoes already worn out from weeks on the march. In the meantime, the bakers at Raystown were busy turning flour into biscuit in an effort to keep these parties supplied; this, in turn, required other detachments to cover men detailed for woodcutting.[21]

There was a clear sense of urgency as soldiers toiled on the new road. Bouquet was anxious to establish a base closer to Fort Duquesne. He wanted the road opened quickly to Kickenpauling; at that point he would march fif-

Fig. 6.4 Tool cart, Fort Ligonier. (Photo by the author.) These relatively lightweight vehicles were vital for hauling not only road-building tools but the rations and liquor required by the road builders. These carts could be equipped with wagon cloths. The mortally wounded General Braddock was taken from the battlefield in one such wagon.

teen hundred troops to Loyalhannon without cutting a road, planning to work back toward Laurel Mountain once he had a new camp established. Forbes urged him on, saying he hoped the "new Road advances briskly" by working on Laurel Mountain "at the same Time that you are making the pass of the Allegany practicable." Time was now important as autumn approached. Troops just arrived at Raystown such as Montgomery's Highland regiment were quickly organized into work parties and sent out to assist those already working.[22]

The pace of road building depended on a number of variables: weather, the number of men working, adequate tools, and the nature of the terrain. Building the famous military roads through the Scottish Highlands revealed that a soldier working a ten-hour day could clear no more than two yards of roadway, and this in country that was mountainous and cut by numerous rivers and streams but largely devoid of the forests and swamps such as those facing Forbes's men. Virginia Colonel George Mercer discovered that old-growth forest might look promising, with the trees widely spaced, but their size was a formidable challenge for men equipped with axes and two-man saws. In the span of four days, Mercer's men working on the road from Fort Cumberland to Raystown were able to clear six miles. He learned that "A Road for one Waggon might be cleared as fast as it could drive," yet this road needed to be cut thirty feet wide—enough to accommodate two wagons—a fact that Mercer blamed for the slow pace. And there was no predicting how fast his men could work." We only cleared half a Mile the day before Yesterday. Yesterday we made out more than two." And, *clearing* the roadway was not quite the same as making it free of stumps, roots, or rocks—nor did this work account for the footpaths that Forbes wanted cut parallel to his main road. Moreover, work crews needed to eat and expected a daily ration of rum or whiskey, all of which had to be brought forward from the nearest depot.[23]

Bouquet planned to make the road from Raystown to the foot of the Allegheny Mountain "in five or six days" but conceded that "the hardest work will be" going over the mountain. To speed up the work, Bouquet arranged to have large parties working from each end of a stretch of the road, cutting toward each other and all under St. Clair's direction. Major George Armstrong's party, for example, was on the west side of Allegheny Mountain, busy cutting three miles of road in the direction of Laurel Mountain; in the meantime, Virginians were working eastward from the base of Laurel Mountain. These parties would also be responsible for maintaining the "protected advance" by creating fortified way stations: at Shawnee Cabins, on the crest of Allegheny Mountain (Fort Dewart), Edmund's Swamp, and Kickenpauling.[24]

The process—and troubles—of road building are revealed by the experiences of the workmen led by Lieutenant-Colonel Adam Stephen of Virginia. By August 8, Stephen's Virginians were already hard at work on the road at Edmund's Swamp. He found the pace of advance slow mostly, he claimed, because the tools were "extreamly troublesome to Carry." Nevertheless, his men were busy clearing ground for a camp and building a reservoir at a nearby spring to ensure a good supply of water for the horses. Their next obstacle was the "Shades of Death": a generic term used to describe heavily wooded lowlands where light rarely penetrated. Stephen found it "a dismal place." His men fought not only old-growth forest and the swamp but also rocks, high weeds, and brambles. Frustrated, Stephen told Bouquet that he needed more men, saying: "I shall not believe you are in earnest about the Road, until you Employ more men on it," supervised by good sergeants. What evidently ate at Stephen, as it did Bouquet and Forbes, was the thought that the army might still completely surprise the French. Indeed, Stephen believed it would be "glorious" if they could reach Loyalhannon before the French became aware of their advance.[25]

Two days later Stephen reported that he was through the "Shades of Death," but only because he had shifted the roadway a mile to the right of the planned route. His way through the swamp is a reminder that the army was essentially making the road as it went; the only master plan was to get over the mountains to Loyalhannon and detours such as this were not uncommon as the realities of road building trumped scouting reports and "expert" guides. The workmen were also learning that the forests were more than a match for the tools they carried. Axes shattered when they struck tree trunks, and according to Stephen, old logs along the route were as hard as iron. This problem was, in fact, predictable. Governor Sharpe of Maryland told St. Clair in early July that the "Felling Axes" the quartermaster sent to troops cutting the road from Fort Frederick "are easily broken nor are they half heavy enough." Cross-cut saws quickly wore out and crowbars and spades gave way before the rocks and gravel on the roadway, all suggesting Bouquet's boast—that with the two hundred axes he had available at the beginning of August, "I hope in five or six days to open the Road as far as the gap [that is, Allegheny Mountain]"—was overly optimistic. By August 12, St. Clair could report that a good road had been made from Raystown to the "Foot of Allegheny." Nevertheless he, like Stephen, found the work "immence" and that it required far more workmen than originally assumed. By mid-month, Bouquet had fully sixteen hundred men "over the Mountains" opening the road, leaving him with barely eight hundred men to hold Raystown and the outposts.[26]

On August 13 Stephen reported that his men were within two miles of the crest of Allegheny Mountain. St. Clair had men working on the other side of the mountain, and he pledged that no one would rest until the road was open from Raystown to Quemahoning Creek. He complained once again to Bouquet about the immensity of the task. It was at this point, as workmen faced Allegheny Mountain from east and west, that the troubles began. Any hope of moving wagons from Raystown to Stephen's men near Edmund's Swamp depended upon finding a way over the mountain. The original route was simply too steep for loaded wagons; once again the encouraging reports of small parties on foot fell short of reality. Not entirely convinced of initial reports, Bouquet sent Ensign Charles Rhor, his engineer, to take a look at the planned route. Rhor's report was "very different." The engineer found Allegheny Mountain worse than Sideling Hill with all of its switchbacks, and he did not believe a wagon road could be made. Rhor did, however, find a pass about two miles north of the original route along the Indian trading path. This alternative, now known as Rhor's Gap, offered a much more manageable climb to the crest. St. Clair later confirmed this new route was indeed better, but it was not until mid-August that work on the pass began. Even then, it was not easy. Bouquet told Forbes that "It is a difficult and long Task to build the Road," especially when work was hampered or delayed because of rain. Once again, Bouquet tried to speed the process by having multiple crews out cutting the road in four places eight miles apart, covered by Armstrong's Pennsylvanians and the additional Highland companies. The slow going and delays preyed on Forbes, who confessed that the "slow advance of the new Road . . . touch[es] me to the quick." And once again he blamed St. Clair. Forbes reflected on how hard he had tried to stop St. Clair's appointment as quartermaster general but, in the end, "was resolved to make the most I could of a wrong head." This, on top of the lack of forage that threatened to stop his wagons, "makes me suspect the heart as well as the head."[27]

The pace of road building was determined by the lowlands as well as the mountains. Stephen's men at Edmund's Swamp had to build a bridge through the Shades of Death and other low spots. Although no one provided details of what was undoubtedly seen as a common solution to poorly drained land, the bridging probably consisted of a makeshift affair. Fascines, six- or nine-foot-long bundles of sticks and saplings, were placed on the ground over which men laid a corduroy road of whole or split longs, placed perpendicular to the direction of the road. Never intended as a permanent solution, these "bridges" did allow wagons and gun carriages to pass and could be readily repaired with the means at hand such as felling axes, brush knives, and shovels. Such bridging would become more common on the west side of Allegheny Mountain where the road either crossed or came near a number of watercourses such as Shade's Creek, Stony Creek, and Quemahoning Creek, as well as the wet lowlands in between. Bridging also added to the workload of the road crews. By August 12, Stephen told Bouquet that large rocks would be easy to remove with the "essence of Fat Beef gradually mixt with a Puncheon of Rum": a subtle reminder that his men needed more food and, especially, more liquor. A week later he was more direct, asking simply that more rum be sent to men who expected a daily ration and were reluctant to work without it.[28]

With all of this physical labor, men began to suffer from both fatigue and injuries. Again, we lack any reports from surgeons or others that would allow a detailed assessment of how these troops fared. Nevertheless, we can easily imagine that the roadwork quickly increased the cases of sprains, hernias, herniated discs, ruptures, and lacerations, as well as sore or infected eyes from dirt, dust, and smoke. Axes that shattered when used were more dangerous to the user than the trees; careless use of brush knives, saws, or other tools would have resulted in wounds that could quickly turn dangerous even with medical treatment. Moreover, as Stephen's comments suggest, the men were not getting much more than the barest of rations; troops were ordered to carry three or four days' worth of food when they left Raystown, but the monotonous diet of salt beef or pork and biscuit would not have kept pace with the amount of calories being consumed in digging, chopping, and hauling. Little wonder, then, that workers expected a regular issue of alcohol. Finally, sickness, especially dysentery and other digestive disorders, would have increased as soldiers boiled their salt meat in bad water or ate poorly cooked food. The constant activity and noise also made it virtually impossible for the men to hunt since available game scattered as the troops advanced. Not only was his army getting smaller as it moved west, but Forbes's troops were probably getting sicker and sorer as the labor involved in moving forward increased.[29]

Despite the problems, though, the work continued, and by August 20 Bouquet could tell Forbes the road was open for wagons from Raystown to Edmund's Swamp, and he anticipated that this day the crews would finish the road from there to Kickenpauling. Rhor had evidently improved on Stephen's road through the Shades of Death, the road crews working from east and west had met, and Bouquet was encouraged enough to send troops ahead to Loyalhannon and establish a major camp at a site called by one scouting party "a very pretty place." The next day Bouquet also wrote to Washington, taking the opportunity of telling the Virginian that he had been to the "top of Allegheny Hill where I had the Satisfaction to See a very good Road," this despite the "Alpine difficulties" that Washington had been told the army faced in conquering Allegheny Mountain. Instead of being able to accommodate lightly loaded wagons on a "Steep, Stony & very difficult access," as his informant reported, Washington learned from Bouquet that twenty loaded wagons made their way to the crest with double teams of horses. In the meantime, crews were moving ahead to the next obstacle: Laurel Mountain. Based on scouting reports in July, Forbes had referred to it as "that Bugbear or tremendous pass of the Laurel Hill." By August, though, he could tell Peters: "we have got entirely the better of that impossible Road, over Allegany Mountain & Laurell Ridge." Bouquet and those around him believed the army could make short work of that portion of the road—provided there were enough men. On August 23, St. Clair predicted he could cut the road over Laurel Mountain in three days and in three more days could be at Loyalhannon, but with only 150 workmen available, he would need at least 600 more men.[30]

In late July St. Clair, on foot, made his own reconnaissance of Laurel Mountain and the valley of Loyalhannon Creek. Calling his trek a "party of pleasure," he emerged from the forests appearing, in the words of one witness, "somewhat grotesque, a long beard, a blanket coat, and trousers to the Ground." St. Clair assured Forbes that there were no major obstacles other than the western decent, which was both stony and steep. The eastern flank of the mountain appeared to offer no great difficulties. In fact, however, the road that was eventually cut proved a struggle for both men and wagons; like much else on Forbes's Road, this passage was an improvisation, determined more by time than anything else. Bouquet was eager to get his troops and supplies to Loyalhannon and was pushing everybody to move ahead as quickly as possible. On August 26, for example, the first division of artillery was crossing Allegheny Mountain even as the road was being cut from there to Laurel Mountain; the second division of the train was to follow as soon as the teams of horses returned to Raystown. Colonel James Burd of Pennsylvania joined by Major James Grant of the Highlanders led over a thousand men ahead to Loyalhannon, the road to be cut behind them. Something of the pace can be gathered from a report on August 29 that the final three-fourths of a mile between Quemahoning and Laurel Mountain would be cleared in two hours. Anxious to maintain momentum, Bouquet risked going over Laurel Mountain on the hastily cut road, though hoping to find "a less frightful pass" up the eastern flank. He and Forbes ultimately chose to cut a new road—yet another detour—rather than spend time and labor trying to improve what already existed. This was another reminder that the road was a wartime expedient and one that required constant adjustment and maintenance almost from the time it was made, with significant implications for the army's logistics.[31]

While Bouquet was occupied with road building and moving the army forward, St. Clair again threatened both the army's progress and its harmony. Like the Virginians' insistence on Braddock's Road, St. Clair's latest behavior once more risked pitting regulars against provincials and producing those "parties" that Forbes hated. What precisely triggered the confrontation between St. Clair and Lieutenant-Colonel Adam Stephen is not clear. Stephen had earned Bouquet's praise for his efforts on the road, and St. Clair had made no prior complaints against the Virginian until their collision in late August. The two men had a history of friction going back to the Braddock expedition, and Stephen later told Washington that he and his troops had been "greatly harassed" by the quartermaster general since early summer in Winchester. Whatever the truth of this, in August Stephen defiantly rejected deference to a superior and stood his ground, infuriating St. Clair, embarrassing Bouquet, and angering the already overtaxed Forbes.[32]

The immediate trigger was evidently St. Clair's vocal criticism of how and how hard the Virginians were working when he met them at Quemahoning on August 26. Stephen wrote two versions of the encounter to Bouquet; one addressed to "my Commanding Officer," the other "to my Friend." In the first report Stephen said that, when his officers challenged St. Clair's criticism, he shouted "Mutiny" and promptly arrested Stephen, "flew into a passion," and "Usd me extreamly ill." This ill-usage extended to St. Clair's insistence on taking command of the Virginians by posting sentries and issuing the nightly password. The second report, to Stephen's "Friend," provided a day-to-day log of encounters with St. Clair. As early as August 16, St. Clair had not inspected Stephen's camp despite receiving a report on the work in progress. He deprived Stephen's men of their expected liquor, despite the fact they had been at work without it for eight days. Shortly after, Stephen received orders "in a very Odd manner" from St. Clair to build shelters for provisions at Edmund's Swamp. Instead, Stephen chose to keep his men busy on the road as per his original instructions. Faced with a very difficult stretch of road to construct and with his men falling ill, Stephen suggested to St. Clair that loaded wagons could get from the Swamp to Quemahoning without the need to unload, only to be met with "important Looks and Evasive answers." Stephen bristled when St. Clair ordered his exhausted men back to Stony Creek in order to build fortifications; he objected on the grounds that St. Clair had an entire battalion of Pennsylvanians there who could do the work. By August 24, St. Clair was taking control of Stephen's troops, keeping two companies with him, thus costing the Virginian five days' work. Adding insult to injury, St. Clair then, according to Stephen, declared the road unusable—even though wagons were passing through on route to Loyalhannon. The last straw, from Stephen's perspective, came when St. Clair bypassed him to give orders directly to the Virginian officers and men. When the officers resisted these "arbitrary" orders, St. Clair accused them of mutiny. The officers urged Stephen to maintain command, even though St. Clair was intent on posting the nightly guards and issuing passwords—what Stephen termed the "peculiar Behaviour of the Qtr. Master General." It was when Stephen insisted on exercising command over his own men that St. Clair ordered him under arrest, upon which Stephen, according to St. Clair, told him that "rather than receive any Orders from me he woud brake his Sword in pieces."[33]

St. Clair's version of events was much shorter and differed from Stephen's report, stressing the mutinous behavior of the Virginians, especially Stephen. In arresting Stephen, St. Clair said, he was facing down what amounted to a "general mutiny," which was averted only through the efforts of Major Andrew Lewis. St. Clair also revealed his own state of mind when he told

Bouquet: "As I had not sufficient Strength to take him by the neck from amongst his own Men," he allowed Stephen to remain with his men rather than go, presumably under guard, to Raystown. It was then that Stephen threatened to "brake his Sword to pieces" rather than receive orders from St. Clair. If Stephen found St. Clair's behavior "peculiar," St. Clair saw Stephen's as "most Extraordinary."[34]

For both Stephen and St. Clair, the conflict was personal. Stephen's resentment was certainly fueled by memories of his first collision with St. Clair. At the same time Stephen's reputation with his own troops and, by extension, with Virginia society was also at stake. St. Clair's attempt to take control of the troops and usurp Stephen's powers of command were a direct affront to Stephen's personal honor, hence Stephen's vow to break his sword rather than obey St. Clair. For his part St. Clair seemed to be incensed with the defiance of provincial officers; his comment about his desire to publicly take Stephen by the neck suggests the sort of treatment one would mete out to a social inferior. But at bottom this was a recurrence of St. Clair's inclination to intrude into affairs that were outside his authority. He had attempted to ignore Bouquet and had received a sharp rebuke from Forbes who reminded him that as quartermaster general St. Clair had no command authority other than what Forbes chose to give him. A veteran officer, St. Clair should have known this, but he persisted in ignoring Stephen's rank and independence. Moreover, at a time when provincial and regular officers of equal rank were to be accorded the same respect, St. Clair's actions threatened to reintroduce a very sore point among provincials such as Stephen or Washington and thus threaten colonial cooperation.[35]

It was ultimately up to Bouquet and Forbes to deal with an embarrassing and potentially divisive confrontation. Bouquet, learning of the affair, told St. Clair bluntly that it "gives me much uneasiness," especially since St. Clair accused the Virginians of mutiny. Bouquet went on, saying: "I am afraid, My Dear Sir, that there has been Some heat in this affair, and that you will have a good deal to do to justify Such a violent measure against an officer of his Ranck, Commanding a Corps." He then reminded St. Clair that as quartermaster general he had "no right to command as such," that "you do not act in the Expedition as Colonel, but as Q.M.G. only," and that he could have no other pretentions. Bouquet ended by advising St. Clair, "as a Friend," to "make up the matter" with Stephen. Bouquet told him he would not write to Forbes until he learned of St. Clair's intentions but reminded him that the general expected harmony between regulars and provincials and that he would doubtless see St. Clair's actions as "precipitate and unseasonable." St. Clair refused to back down even after both Burd and Grant tried to intercede. Stephen was equally stubborn, saying that "he is right" and was content to remain under arrest unless he had "public justification." Given the impasse, Bouquet, as good as his word, reluctantly wrote Forbes, telling him that he tried "to spare you from hearing of this disagreeable affair" and that the issue now dominated camp talk and gossip. Indeed, one of Washington's correspondents at Raystown referred to St. Clair as "Sir John Wildair" and the "B—ly," while Reverend Barton only observed that St. Clair "seems much dissatisfied with some Field-Officers [who] contended with him about Rank." On September 14, in the absence of a speedy reply from Forbes, Bouquet took it upon himself to order Stephen to resume his duties, promising to seek redress for any insults offered to the Virginia officers. It appears that Forbes did contact St. Clair directly. On September 23, the general told Bouquet that St. Clair had agreed to acknowledge his error if Forbes told him he was wrong. Forbes took him at his word and there the matter rested, but not before personalities and matters of rank, authority, and honor once more threatened the integrity of Forbes's army and further damaged the reputation and authority of one of the most important members of the expedition.[36]

* * *

The army in late August was smaller and more physically taxed than when it arrived at Raystown. Nearly two thousand provincials and regulars had moved ahead of the road crews in order to take possession of a new encampment at Loyalhannon. These soldiers had yet to meet the enemy and any training they received between camp duties and road building was as yet untested, though by modifying tactical formations and emphasizing firing and charging the enemy, Bouquet must have hoped his men could face whatever the French and their Indian allies could bring against them. The army was also not the unified command that Forbes hoped to maintain. Virginians, notably George Washington, had repeatedly challenged the decision to make a new road to the Ohio, exposing particular political and economic interests within the army. To this "party" St. Clair had raised the specter of conflict between regulars and provincials. Both insubordination and colonial resentment of partisan and high-handed behavior could tear the army apart even as it finally overcame the worst of the mountain barrier between the army and Fort Duquesne.

SEVEN

Loyalhannon and Fort Duquesne

* * *

SEPTEMBER 1758

My advanced post consisting of 1500 Men, are now in Possession of a strong post 9 Miles on the other side of Laurell Hill.

—FORBES TO PITT, SEPTEMBER 1758

As hundreds of soldiers toiled on Forbes's new road amid the bickering between regular and provincial officers, to the north a small party was slowly making its way west. These men had been traveling since mid-July; their destination was the western Delaware towns lying north of Fort Duquesne. Leading this group was Pisquetomen, the Delaware headman who had come to Pennsylvania on behalf of his brother Tamaqua and his supporters in order to "Know the truth of affairs" in the face of garbled and unreliable news from the east. The little information that did come to Ohio natives suggested that Pennsylvania officials were willing to talk about ending their war with the Delawares and to address the natives' central concerns—land and sovereignty. At the same time, however, a large army was making its way toward the Ohio Country, building forts as it advanced. The eerie feeling of many of Forbes's men that they were being watched was not wrong. Whether for the French or, more likely, for their own satisfaction, western Delawares had been shadowing the army since it reached the mountains. What the natives wanted to know was how the British planned to reconcile a desire for peace with the actions of war.[1]

Traveling with Pisquetomen was Christian Frederick Post, who was frequently employed as an emissary by Pennsylvania's Governor Denny. Post had been deeply involved in negotiations between the colony and Teedyuscung's eastern Delawares; now he was asked to make contact with the Ohio

Indians. Specifically, Denny wanted Post to open negotiations for the release of scores of Pennsylvanians held captive in native towns. Post was also to learn from the western Delawares what the natives expected from any peace talks. Finally, he was to gauge the mood of the people living at the Kuskuskies, Saucunk, and other towns along the Beaver River. Before leaving, Post had been given a British flag as a sign of friendship—a passport of sorts— that the governor hoped would protect him and his companions.[2]

Post left a colony that was divided and unsettled by the war. Backcountry refugees blamed eastern politicians for the violence and for their losses. Quakers squared off against the Penns on the issue of Indian affairs, and crown officers such as Sir William Johnson tried to wrest frontier diplomacy from the colonial government. Once across the Allegheny Mountains, however, Post entered a native world that was equally divided, inhabited by people struggling with the costs of war and questions of peace. Arriving at Shingas's town at Saucunk (Beaver Falls, Pennsylvania), Post found the Delawares "much disturbed at my coming" and quickly noticed "their faces were quite distorted with rage." His reception at Tamaqua's settlement at the Kuskuskies, upriver from Saucunk, was vastly different. There, Delaware headmen anxiously awaited his arrival; Menatochyand (Delaware George) greeting the emissary by saying that "he had not slept all night, so much had he been engaged on account of my coming."[3]

Post thus discovered firsthand the divisions that ran throughout Delaware society, differences that would make it difficult to reach a consensus on peace. Indeed, the subsequent talks between Post and native headmen revealed just how much distrust, anxiety, and confusion prevailed among the Delaware and other native towns in the Ohio Country. Post's own instructions only added to the turmoil. Told to negotiate a release of captives, Post found his initial attempt met by anger and disbelief. Insisting that such negotiations could only happen *after* peace was restored, Delaware leaders thought it "unreasonable that we should demand prisoners before there is established peace" and that "such an unreasonable demand makes us [the British] appear as if we wanted brains." Instead, the natives were eager to learn something accurate about British intentions, saying "We never expected to see our brethren the *English* again." The Delawares also quickly dispelled any idea that they would negotiate through Teedyuscung. Rejecting Post's report that Teedyuscung had agreed to go to war with the French on the advice of the western Delawares, Tamaqua insisted "they had never sent him such advice." Moreover, when Post first tried to tell them of the 1757 Easton Treaty, his audience "presently stopped me, and would not hear of it," saying "they had nothing to say to any treaty . . . made at Easton, nor had anything to do with Teedyuscung" and, if Post had no messages from the governor specifically to them, "they would have nothing to say to me."[4]

Insisting that the British negotiate directly with the western Delawares as autonomous people, native headmen also reminded Post that they would not make peace alone but only with the other nations "from the sunrise to the sunset" with whom they were allied: Wyandots, Ohio Iroquois, and Shawnees. Nevertheless, several headmen wanted to pursue peace talks. Post noted that "*Delaware George* is very active in endeavouring to establish a peace," acting on behalf of his brother Tamaqua. The latter, emerging as leader of the western Delawares, needed to maintain a noncommittal stance until he could bring others into negotiations. There were also the French and their native allies to consider. When Post arrived at the Kuskuskies a French officer and fifteen men were building houses for the natives as a further way of cementing cooperation; still others were in nearby towns. The Delawares lost no time in pointing this out, telling Post that the French were generous, giving them food, clothing, and ammunition: what would the British offer? At the same time, however, the natives were testing the French. Tamaqua invited the French officer to his home and then "said before the *Frenchman*, that the Indians were very proud to see one of their brothers, the *English*, among them." According to Post, the officer then appeared "low spirited, and seemed to eat his dinner with very little appetite."[5]

Post delivered his messages at a large gathering across the Allegheny River from Fort Duquesne. French attempts to seize Post were once again rebuffed, though French soldiers were among the three hundred people who Post estimated were present; the French even went to far as to set up a table so that scribes and interpreters could take down his words. After opening with the expected words of condolence to set a proper atmosphere, Post conceded that the natives had only "a slight, confused account of us" and could not know of the peace made between Teedyuscung and Pennsylvania the previous year. He then offered "The large peace belt" and promised that "Every one that lays hold of this belt of peace, I proclaim peace to them from the *English* nation." These words, of course, did not correspond to British actions, and Post then ventured onto more dangerous ground by acknowledging that his king had sent a great army to the Ohio Country—but "not to go to war against the *Indians*" but only the French, emphasizing that "We do not come to hurt you." In reply the Delawares gave the belt and other wampum to the Ohio Iroquois. They, in turn, reminded Post that they did not start the war and accused the Shawnees of first taking up arms against the colonies.[6]

Having delivered his messages and informed the Ohio Indians of his government's intent, Post, escorted again by Pisquetomen, turned north toward Saucunk and the Kuskuskies. Passing through nearby Shawnee towns, Post found these people "very proud to see me return," and upon reaching Saucunk he received a reception very different from his earlier encounter. Two nephews of Netawatwees (Newcomer) "accepted my hand, and apologized for their former behavior." Yet there were pointed reminders of lingering suspicion. Shingas, whose scalp commanded a large Pennsylvania bounty, worried that if he ever went to the colony he would be killed, though he spoke in a "very soft and easy manner." When Post tried to reassure him another member of Shingas's escort, Shamokin Daniel, erupted. Interrupting Post, Daniel told Shingas that the emissary "tells nothing but idle lying stories." When Post denied this, Daniel struck back, saying "G-d d-n you for a fool" and "D-n you, why do not you and the *French* fight on the sea." You come here only to cheat the poor *Indians*, and take their land from them."[7]

Although Pisquetomen and others "appeared sorry" for Daniel's outburst, the anxiety behind his words lingered among the Delawares. Closely questioned by Shingas, Tamaqua, Menatochyand, and Pisquetomen, Post found himself facing native leaders still skeptical of British intentions despite the offer of a peace belt. Asked "why do you come to fight in the land God has given us?" Post again denied that the British had any interest in taking native lands. Nevertheless, the Delawares continued to press, telling Post that "they knew better" since British traders and others had told them that "the *English* intend to destroy us, and take our lands." Insisting that "the land is ours and not theirs," they suggested that Post and his masters make peace and let the Ohio Indians drive the French from the region, since "it is plain that you white people are the cause of this war." Echoing Daniel, the headmen again recommended that the British and French "fight in the old country and on the sea."[8]

The Delawares' suspicion and the uncertainty that preyed on them were clear, as was their insistence on what Post would call sovereignty. From their rejection of Teedyuscung's initiatives to the emphatic reminders that the Ohio Country belonged to them alone, Tamaqua's people were determined to chart their own way and maintain their independence both from other natives and from rival empires. Complicating native efforts, though, was a recent history that underscored just how fragile Indian sovereignty could be. Less than a generation earlier, Pennsylvania's Proprietors with help from the Six Nations had leveraged Delawares out of their ancestral homelands, setting many, including Tamaqua and his family, on the road to the Ohio Valley. They were determined not to be expelled again. Moreover, the Delawares were keenly aware how vulnerable they were, facing the closing jaws of an imperial vise with the French on one side, the British on the other, and their own homelands now a battlefield. Collective survival and identity rested on the Delawares' ability to accurately read the strengths and weaknesses of these imperial foes, to manage their own version of "modern Indian politics." Finally, in order to make peace with the British there had to be consensus at home. Tamaqua's emergence as the driving force behind the Delaware quest for peace was by no means complete or assured. He had support from his brothers, most notably Shingas, whose reputation rested on his aggressive raiding of the Pennsylvania borders but who was now inclined toward peace. Nevertheless, the angry faces at Saucunk, the snubs from Killbuck, and Shamokin Daniel's rage were all pointed reminders that many natives remained unconvinced that the British—or the French—could be trusted. This was what Post detected when he wrote in his journal that the Delawares seemed to be "wavering."[9]

Post's embassy to the western Delawares ended with less than he expected to take away. Native leaders admonished the British to "be strong, and exert yourselves" so that the friendship that once existed between them and the natives "may be well established and finished between us." In other words, the next move was up to Pennsylvania's governor and General Forbes: both would need to clearly demonstrate that native fears were misplaced. Delawares further reminded the British of the contradictory messages being offered: "all your young men [Forbes's army] . . . are now standing *before our doors*" even while "you come with good news and fine speeches. This is what makes us jealous, and we do not know what to think of it." It would have been better, they said, if word of peace had arrived before "your army had begun to march." As things presently stood, however, "We do not so readily believe you" and "we cannot conclude, at this time, but must see and hear you once more." With that, negotiations ended for the moment, but not before Pisquetomen once more agreed to escort Post and see him safely back to Pennsylvania, especially since the French seemed determined to seize Post.[10]

* * *

While Pisquetomen led Post back to the colony, Colonel James Burd and over a thousand Highlanders, Royal Americans, and provincials were setting up post in the Loyalhannon Valley west of Laurel Mountain. This latest move by Forbes's army certainly added to Delaware worries about British intentions; from their new camp the troops were only about fifty miles from the Forks of the Ohio and the site of Post's recent council. If Armstrong's Kittanning raid two years earlier had surprised the natives, hundreds of men busy turning woodland into fortifications must have genuinely alarmed them.

Moreover, while Burd and his men marched ahead of the road builders, Forbes's new road would soon link them to Raystown and settlements to the east and south. Loyalhannon would be the last major encampment of Forbes's army short of Fort Duquesne and the last in a chain of fortifications that maintained the "protected advance" from Carlisle, through Shippensburg, Fort Littleton, Fort Loudoun, Juniata Crossing, and Raystown. Smaller posts and redoubts had been hastily built to cover the new road and its convoys: Shawnee Cabins west of Raystown, Fort Dewart at the eastern base of Allegheny Mountain, Edmund's Swamp, Stony Creek, and Fort Dudgeon covering the approach to Laurel Mountain.[11]

Loyalhannon Creek had been considered as the site of an encampment since July. At that time Bouquet learned that there was no adequate place for a depot on the east side of Laurel Mountain but that the west side would prove better. A strong post there would, Bouquet argued, serve several purposes. First, it would put the army within fifty miles of its goal; if the French proved too strong or aggressive, the army could still hold the new camp and "we shall have already accomplished something by gaining 140 miles of lost ground" and by occupying the passes through the mountains. Finally, an advanced post at Loyalhannon would provide further cover for Washington's Virginians when they moved from Fort Cumberland to join the main army.[12]

The detachment sent to Loyalhannon was substantial. With at least fifteen hundred men drawn from Montgomery's Regiment, the Royal Americans, the 1st Virginia Regiment, the Pennsylvania Regiment, as well as a division of artillery, this force was equal to what Bouquet initially led to Raystown. Given its size the detachment would require a senior field officer as commander, and here Bouquet found himself with few to spare. Both Stephen and Armstrong were directing roadwork, Montgomery was with Forbes, and Colonel Hugh Mercer of Pennsylvania was only recently appointed and lacked experience. The command fell to Colonel Burd whose battalion of the Pennsylvania Regiment would form a large part of the force. Burd was the senior colonel available, and he also knew the area from his activities in 1755. Yet he was also a provincial, and despite royal orders confirming field-grade rank for American colonials, Bouquet was evidently concerned about Burd's capabilities. He therefore assigned Major James Grant of the Highlanders as second in command. Grant, a professional soldier "whose parts as a Military man are inferior to few," would see to the detachments of regulars with Burd's force. Forbes and Bouquet evidently assumed that military matters would be Grant's charge, yet at the same time Forbes insisted "one must save appearances with Col. Burd" who was Grant's superior.[13]

Bouquet gave Burd detailed instructions. Logistics took paramount im-

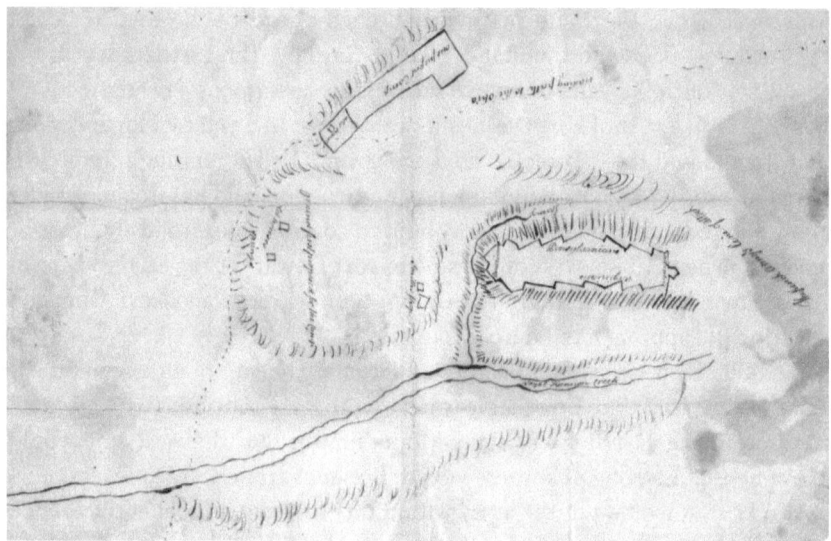

Fig. 7.1 Colonel James Burd's rough sketch of his encampment at Loyalhannon. (Courtesy of the Heinz History Center, Pittsburgh, Pennsylvania.) Of particular interest is a note indicating the original site chosen for the camp, to the west of the zigzag trace of what would be the outer retrenchment. Burd also indicated the direction of the French attack in October—from the east. The small squares indicate the locations of a small smithy and cabins once used by Pennsylvania deer-hide traders working along the Juniata Path.

portance; Burd was to erect storehouses and set his men to work making charcoal and gathering hay. Security was also on Bouquet's mind, and he emphasized that Burd's men were to sweep the ground beyond their camp each night and post advanced guards that were to be relieved every hour, "without noise," to assure that sentries would be alert. Burd was also to prevent anyone from wandering away from the camp. With only fifty miles separating Burd's men from an unknown number of French and Indians, Bouquet was determined to prevent surprises.[14]

Locating and occupying a suitable encampment at Loyalhannon proved anything but simple. In the first place Burd's force would move ahead of the road builders, and the road that did exist was less than ideal. Arriving at Fort Dewart, Burd reported that only a portion of his wagons and artillery had succeeded in getting over Allegheny Mountain. Burd also learned from his engineer Ensign Rhor that less than a mile of road had been cut beyond Quemahoning Creek; Burd could only hope that more would be opened by the time his troops arrived. In response Bouquet ordered him to leave his artillery and wagons at the foot of Laurel Mountain and push ahead with his troops, ensuring that each man had three days' rations. When Bouquet traveled to Loyalhannon in early September, he found the road "a most infernal one," so bad that it was wearing out both wagons and packhorses. He also became increasingly "uneasy" about provisioning a large force west of Laurel Mountain unless he could get better wagons and fresh horses.[15]

Even more troublesome was evidence that Sir John St. Clair had once again misinformed Bouquet and Forbes about the ground he had chosen along Loyalhannon Creek. Bouquet was beside himself when he learned that the site was completely dominated by high ground to the north and south. In a private letter to Major Grant, Bouquet now worried about "my poor commission, my honour, and my head," since he had "taken a lot on" himself by authorizing the advance on the strength of St. Clair's now discredited report. "It is impossible to undertake or execute with such a man," Bouquet said, adding that "I am exasperated by the faux pas." Acting quickly Bouquet decided that the detachment should "lightly" retrench the site while using most of the men to cut the road back to Laurel Mountain. The only other hope was that a new site, nine miles to the west near Chestnut Ridge, might be better. This place, according to both Rhor and Burd, would be a far superior location for a major encampment. After venting to Grant, Bouquet reluctantly wrote Forbes on August 26, to report the problem. Evidently St. Clair had given Bouquet "verbal and written assurances ... that the Post of Loyalhannon was very suitable for a depot." It was this report that prompted Bouquet to dispatch Burd's force, but now he was receiving reports from Rhor and Burd that the chosen site was anything but "very suitable." A furious Bouquet could only say that "the blunders of the Quartermaster General totally change the shape of things"; he wondered "what is to be done to relieve these mistakes" now that fifteen hundred men were well beyond recall or relief, their work on the new post so much wasted effort.[16]

Forbes agreed that Rhor's choice of ground was "founded on good sense and good reasoning" and felt that the additional nine-mile march was "nothing." He was more concerned about the "slow advance of the new road" saying that the "cause of it touch[es] me to the quick"—the cause being Sir John St. Clair. Bouquet acted to "relieve these mistakes" as best he could. He ordered Burd to dig in at the original site while occupying Rhor's new post only after the road was opened to Loyalhannon. Days later he amended his orders by urging Burd to put most of his men to work cutting a road to the new post at Chestnut Ridge. Burd was also to do his best to protect his encampment from the high ground by erecting "traverses," earthen walls designed to prevent artillery fire from sweeping the camp. Burd, on his own authority, also moved the campsite to cover a small stream and some good ground for livestock near abandoned cabins built by traders. By September 11, then, Burd's force, under the direction of engineer Lieutenant Thomas Basset, was busy building what would become the army's encampment at Loyalhannon, later known as Fort Ligonier. They did so in weather that was turning cold and raw with rain, fog, and cold nights. The troops woke up to frost on September 11. The onset of cold weather and falling leaves were yet more reminders that the best campaigning season was now behind them.[17]

The camp occupied rising ground along Loyalhannon Creek on the site of the present reconstructed fortifications. In composition the encampment was very much like that at Raystown. On the highest point Burd's men built what Bouquet called a small fort to protect the new storehouses. Surrounding this at a distance was a line of log retrenchments meant to protect the troops' encampments. This area ultimately proved too cramped, and most of the regiments made their camps outside these lines, covered by a chain of redoubts along the eastern and northern perimeters of the encampment. Below the retrenchment were the small stream and cattle pens on ground that would also be occupied by ovens and hospitals. The road, when finally completed, would skirt the fort to its north and then cross Loyalhannon Creek to the southwest.

Loyalhannon evolved over a period of roughly three months. Colonel Burd's rough sketch of the site provides an idea of what he initially hoped to accomplish. This plan, dated September 3, clearly showed St. Clair's choice of camp on the low ground occupied by the traders' cabins and Burd's new site on the higher ground to the east. At the time Burd's force was encamped to the north of the site while his men labored to cut timber for the irregular retrenchment he outlined. On September 25, Burd received new orders from Bouquet that required "a Fort of Logs" to be built around the storehouses. Bouquet also included the three redoubts he wanted built and the number of men that each should hold in an emergency. As an added precaution against an attack, he also sent Captain Evan Shelby's Maryland volunteers and part of Colonel Dagworthy's battalion to help scout around the encampment. Finally, all the skilled workmen—smiths, carpenters, oven makers, and other workmen—would take their orders from Basset, the senior engineer at the site.[18]

A plan by engineer Richard Dudgeon and redrawn by Ordnance Office draftsman J. C. Pleydell shows the works and encampment as finally completed in late autumn. The plan identifies newly built hospitals, a cattle pen, and the inner fort holding storehouses, a small barracks for officers, and an aboveground magazine. In addition to the log retrenchment, the troops built two substantial batteries, one on the east side of the camp, the other directly west of the inner fort. Dudgeon included Bouquet's three redoubts covering the encampment and cattle pens. Much of this work was completed shortly before the army began its final march to Fort Duquesne and little of these elaborate works survived for more than a year or two. At least one indication of future plans is the dam across Loyalhannon Creek, built for a planned sawmill. Dudgeon's plan also shows the odd construction of the inner fort. Although it conforms to the standard plan of a simple square with four corner bastions, it is of hybrid construction. The eastern curtain wall and one and a half bastions were constructed of a cribbing of horizontal logs filled with earth and rubble to provide a defense against artillery fire. The remainder of the perimeter is a simple palisade of the kind erected at Raystown. The fort's composition is a testament to the different ideas of "fortification" held by Forbes and his chief engineer, Captain Harry Gordon. Bouquet's instructions clearly envisioned a stockade work, or "Fort of Logs," one that could be quickly and economically built from the trees being cleared around the site to create open fields of fire. But the term "fort of logs" apparently caused some confusion. To Gordon this evidently meant the more substantial ramparts that he began to erect. Bouquet seems to have said nothing to him, but when Forbes arrived at Raystown, he learned "to [his] great surprise" that what Gordon "was building at Loyal Hannon [was] fit to stand a siege." "You know we want nothing but a strong post," he angrily told Bouquet, adding, "for Gods sake think of both time money and Labour and put a stop to all superfluitys."[19]

Another plan of the encampment, made in 1759, suggests that Forbes—or more likely, his engineers—continued to make additions and improvements throughout the fall. In addition to the small officers' barracks, for example, part of one storehouse was turned into a barrack or guardroom for a small garrison. Numerous small huts for officers appear on this plan as well as foot bridges over the stream at the foot of the encampment. By November 1758, artillery batteries built of sods and fascines had been built at the eastern and western ends of the inner fort, with the western battery complete with its own ditch and palisade. Yet all of this construction could not overcome the site's prevailing weakness: it was dominated by high ground. At a council of war in early November, when asked about the fort's ability to withstand a regular attack, engineer Gordon replied by suggesting that the inner fort could be completely destroyed if one explosive shell from a mortar hit the exposed magazine.[20]

The new encampment at Loyalhannon was important for reasons other than its proximity to Fort Duquesne. Like all early modern armies, Forbes's force needed to move in order to survive, even though each mile forward put

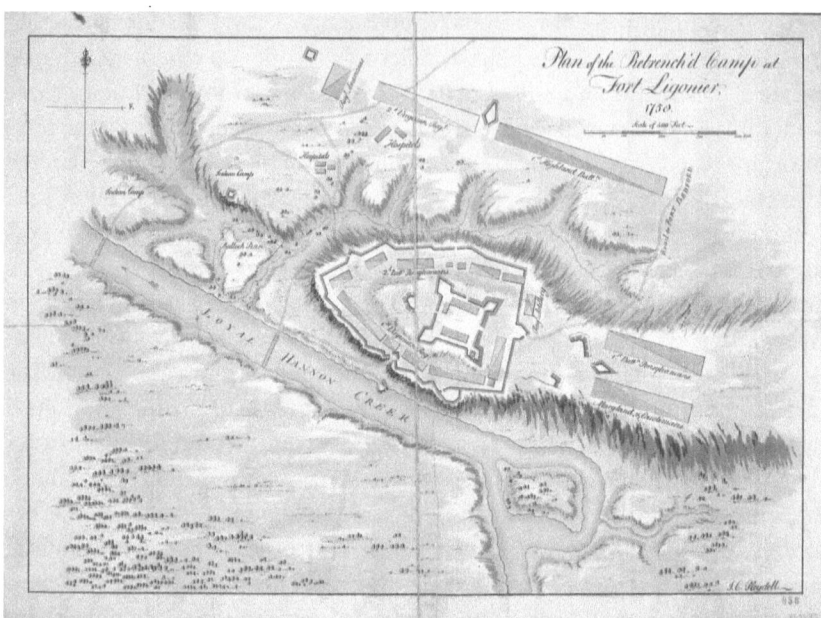

Fig. 7.2 "Plan of the Retrench'd Camp at Fort Ligonier," c. 1758 by J. C. Pleydell. (The Royal Collection Trust/© Her Majesty Queen Elizabeth II 2019.) The layout of the Loyalhannon camp is clearly shown here, along with the campsites of the various regiments. Note also the native encampment west of the livestock pen as well as the western battery, fully surrounded by its ditch and stockade and the peculiar arrangement of the inner fort, half earth-filled cribbing and half simply a stockade, testimony both to engineer Gordon's intended plan and Forbes's insistence on simplicity and speed.

additional strain on an already overtaxed supply system. Several thousand people and their animals occupying the Raystown camp for weeks posed risks and problems. Even with a good supply of water close by, pollution and subsequent illness increased over time with the accumulated waste including everything from old clothing to offal from slaughterhouses. Soldiers would also have to travel farther, with greater risk of attack, in order to gather firewood as well as forage for livestock. Cutting ground cover, in turn, added to erosion and runoff into local water supplies. Bouquet was already worried about food for the animals, telling Forbes in late July that "Our pastures are greatly diminished" and that he was hoarding all the oats that came to hand. Forbes also mentioned his distress and took steps to ease the pressure on available forage by ordering troops on the road not to proceed to Raystown so that their horses would not add to the problem there. By the time Forbes issued these orders in early August, the army's "grass guards" at

Raystown were having to take livestock six miles from camp in order to locate adequate forage. These distances only compounded the army's difficulties; troops now had to be away for up to four days, and large guards of close to two hundred men were necessary to cover the foragers and the animals. This, in turn, risked having a large detachment cut off and destroyed by enemy raiders as well as encouraging desertion. By late August these grass guards were taking on the appearance of the "grand forage" used by large European armies to sweep up all available fodder, with encampments, guards, and "ranging parties" employed to sweep the desired ground to prevent ambush. Yet there was no alternative. Horses "suffered a great deal" from hauling wagons and artillery along the miserable road and needed several days to recover before moving on. In effect, the army was caught in a vise: forward movement was necessary but forward movement only lengthened supply lines and placed troops in greater jeopardy.[21]

Reports of "excellent pastures" and good water at the new camp selected by Burd were a godsend at a time when packhorses were able to carry loads of only 130 pounds (not the 200 pounds originally thought) and when cattle driven in from Virginia produced only a scrawny 170 pounds of meat per head. The wagons were also wearing out from hard use, neglect, and accidents. Convoys of overworked horses pulling wagons that one witness said were "extremely bad" continued to make their way slowly up the road toward Raystown. A logistical crisis was brewing just as Forbes and Bouquet were pushing large numbers of troops across Laurel Mountain. Both men found supplies interrupted by disputes over money and poor planning by contractors. Forbes assumed that the contractors would always have at least three months' worth of salt meat for eight thousand men available in reserve, but such was not the case. At the beginning of September Bouquet had only one month of provisions in store at Raystown, and he worried that this would not support Burd's force as well as those troops left behind. Days later, Forbes told Pitt that, although he was pleased with the progress his force had made, his "real hindrance" was not the road or any threat from the French but the "distress" over shortages of provisions. As if to underscore the point, Washington arrived at Raystown in mid-September and "surprised" Forbes by reporting that Fort Cumberland was low on food; the Virginians there expected to be resupplied by Bouquet who was then wondering how he would provide rations for his forces along the road. Finally, wagon owners and drivers compounded the logistical problems—some wanting to take their rigs home, others by refusing to move unless paid and provided with adequate forage. Forbes, who calculated that one large convoy would be able to carry enough supplies forward to sustain the army, now threatened to simply confiscate the wagons and teams he needed and to send St. Clair to Pennsylvania to personally direct the seizures.²²

Thanks to St. Clair's efforts, Forbes did get his additional wagons and horses. Perhaps chastened by the reaction to his earlier missteps, St. Clair also managed to put the collection of forage "on a better footing," or at least on one good enough to satisfy the wagoners. Forbes conceded that his quartermaster general "used diligence and application" in rounding up enough transport to carry the necessary supplies. This was all a pleasant change from the seemingly endless difficulties St. Clair had raised—from arresting Adam Stephen to failing to provide adequate forage along the road, "a neglect," Forbes vowed, "that Sir John St. Clair can never answer for." Yet despite his good showing in Pennsylvania that fall, St. Clair and Forbes remained at odds. The "immense confusion of Waggons and roads" were, according to Forbes, "entirely Sir John's creating," and he further characterized him as a man "who by a certain dexterity has you in fresh Dilemma's every day," adding that "his solemn face will tell you when he has done the worst that he really acted for the best and can justify it." Taking everything together, Forbes could only conclude that "he is a very odd man," and he regretted having "any Concerns with him."²³

The combination of logistical and command problems coupled with the need to make decisions quickly while still being days behind his army's advanced forces all began to tell on Forbes. "One must be sick to be thoroughly sensible of the affinity there is betwixt the mind and the body," he told Bouquet in late August, noting that "whenever your Directions and orders goes smooth & easy I am all Tranquility and full of Spirits, but the Reverse happening disturbs my whole frame." There was certainly much to disturb him by September. In the middle of his debate with army contractors, Forbes admitted a mistake and offered no excuse except "pain, want of health and a flux that has reduced me to nothing." He refused to become embroiled in the conflict between Stephen and St. Clair, citing poor health. His ailments were also causing "excrutiating pain," which laid him so low that he could "scarce bear Motion." Flux and the return of what Major Halkett simply called his "most painful symptoms" led to relapses that, in early September, "have been worse" as the campaign's "disappointment was greater." Forbes admitted to Pitt that "My Health, that has been extreamly precarious these two years," had now "of late been very near brought to a close." To Abercromby, Forbes confided that he had been attacked "with most excruciating pains in my Bowells," and wondered if he would be able to travel from Shippensburg to Raystown and beyond. Men who saw him wrote as though they expected him to die at any time, and Abercromby told Colonel John Stanwix that the last letter he had received from Forbes was written in early August, "but by Reports he is dead."[24]

At a time when Forbes was, in his own words, "as feeble . . . as a child almost," the latest news from Loyalhannon came as a profound shock. Early reports told of a serious setback: Major Grant and nearly eight hundred men had been routed within a mile of Fort Duquesne, the major was a prisoner, and a yet unknown number of men were killed or missing. Forbes had no reason to anticipate that Bouquet, Grant, or anyone else would, on their own authority, send a force against the French, especially when the troops at Loyalhannon were still isolated and vulnerable. To understand what has been referred to as "Grant's defeat" or the "Grant affair" on September 14, it is necessary to appreciate the mounting frustrations within the British camp and the extent to which the French continued to dominate *la petite guerre*.[25]

By early September it was clear that the British were failing in their efforts to collect intelligence and were losing *la petite guerre*. Typical of the army's experiences was an incident at Fort Cumberland in mid-July where two men were killed and one was taken captive only a mile from the fort. Washington's best efforts to retaliate came to nothing. Indians and soldiers sent to locate the attackers picked up the trail of an estimated six men but found no one. Washington feared that "we shall be pestered with their Parties" all month, "haunting our Camps, & watching our Motions." A month later, Colonel Adam Stephen spoke about a "golden Opportunity lost" when he sent a force out to ambush raiders who had been lurking near the road-building parties. Despite orders his men lit fires, which alerted the enemy, who brazenly passed the troops in broad daylight. Stephen believed that the Indians "no doubt would have Cut" his men "to pieces" had the detachment not been so large. In the meantime, Forbes had his Highlanders chasing Indian parties near Shippensburg—but without success.[26]

Enemy parties continued to hang on the flanks of Forbes's army, and British efforts to penetrate the forest and collect intelligence on the French failed completely. Five of the army's few remaining Indians returned to Raystown on August 2 without the prisoners they were expected to bring in, despite staying near Fort Duquesne, as no Frenchman came near enough for the natives to seize. In early August another failure occurred when a party returned empty-handed, despite seeing tracks of an estimated one hundred men, though in this case the British did manage to retrieve food, tobacco, and paint from the trail. Worse, fog at the Forks was so heavy it was impossible for scouts to even see the French fort. Forbes was convinced that small scouting parties could not provide the necessary intelligence; moreover, he simply did not trust information supplied by Indians who had been out on their own. "Therefore," he told Bouquet, he was "still of opinion that a Strong party" that could defend itself would do better. He may have had in mind a suggestion from Colonel John Armstrong that a force of three hundred of his Pennsylvanians be sent against the small French fort at Venango—in effect, a repeat of Armstrong's successful raid on Kittanning. While Forbes conceded that "I have had that long in view," he remained cautious, wondering how proper such an attack might be since "a repulse to any of our partys may be of bad consequence." He also asked Bouquet for his opinion on the matter. In the meantime, scouting parties continued to depart from Raystown, only to return without success. One, led by Armstrong's brother, returned "from their unsuccessful Scout" and were "coldly received by the Commanding Officer [Bouquet]." All Bouquet could do was make commonsense suggestions to his officers about keeping noise and light discipline, telling Burd that "the Indians having So acute a hearing" that otherwise they "would soon find scouting parties from Loyal Hannon." Clearly frustrated, Bouquet also reminded Burd that, while French prisoners were desirable, "[as] for the Indians let them be knocked on the head."[27]

By contrast, the French and their native allies owned the woods. Small raiding parties—of the sort Forbes believed to be of little good—routinely sniped at the army's vulnerable communications. On August 1, for example, wagons traveling between Forts Loudoun and Littleton were attacked, a driver killed, and a sutler taken captive. One wagoner was killed and three more taken on Sideling Hill. Troops as far back as Shippensburg were not safe; Major Halkett told of Indian parties that "now infest us," and Forbes also reported that "they are scalping within a mile of this." Even when driven off, the attackers still managed to inflict casualties, as they did near Fort Littleton when they wounded two men before retreating. By mid-August St. Clair reported from Allegheny Mountain that "The Enemy are all round us in partys of 6 and 10" and wondered how long this would continue, promising that "I shall take all the care I can." From Raystown Bouquet made a similar report, telling Washington that the "woods about us are full of little Partys of Indians" while forced to concede that "they have discovered our New Road." Washington was only surprised that the enemy had been quiet for so long. Christian Frederick Post also attested to enemy success; while he was at the Kuskuskies in early September he witnessed the return of a raiding party with three "German" prisoners and two Catawba scalps. The scalps may have belonged to two prominent Catawba war leaders serving with the army: Bullen and Captain French. They and other native fighters had escorted a supply convoy to Fort Cumberland on August 24. The two leaders advanced ahead of the convoy, against the advice of Virginia officers. Both were shot down in an ambush, allegedly by Delawares who called out that they were Cherokees. Both Bullen and French were given funerals "with Military Honours" by Washington, who was worried about the effect the deaths would have on his few remaining Indians.[28]

Not only were the French and their Indian allies able to keep the British on the defensive, they were also able to collect information. To be fair, perhaps one of the most important revelations was handed them by Post who, at his council opposite Fort Duquesne, made it clear that a large British army was advancing. Prisoner interrogations and close observation, though, allowed the fort's commander to report in late August that Bouquet had occupied Loyalhannon with two thousand men and that Forbes himself was expected soon. Captain Lignery was even able to tell his superiors that the Loyalhannon force included eight field guns and some mortars, as well as describing the post's construction. Governor-General Vaudreuil would not venture to predict whether Fort Duquesne would be attacked before the end of the campaign season, but he did note that many of the provincial troops would be discharged at the end of the year, making an attack less likely. He therefore encouraged Lignery to harass the enemy as much as possible to slow them down until the weather brought their march to a halt and their army disintegrated.[29]

Lignery needed no encouragement. French forces were already testing the latest British advance. Only two weeks after Burd's force arrived at Loyalhannon it was the target of raiders who attacked vulnerable grass guards, leaving one soldier dead and taking another captive. Some forty Indians had got to within a mile of the new camp; three British parties went out in pursuit, Bouquet commenting that "I expect some scalping if they find them." They did not. The single road that supplied Loyalhannon was so vulnerable that Bouquet ordered convoys to be completely covered, front, rear, and flanks, "as there are Strong Parties of the Enemy upon the Communication."[30]

These incidents, especially attacks on troops at Loyalhannon in early September, convinced Major James Grant that a bold counterstroke was needed. Bouquet apparently favored sending out "parties" to pursue attackers and set ambushes, but Grant disagreed, arguing instead for a strong force "to reconnoiter the roads and the forces of the enemy" and, in Bouquet's words, "To check the boldness of this Indian rabble." The two men had discussed possible retaliation soon after Grant arrived at Raystown. Bouquet was at Loyalhannon on September 9 when the subject came up again. Grant once more argued that only a large force could be effective, and Bouquet reported, "as he insisted . . . I consented" to what Grant later referred to as "a long projected Scheme." This plan echoed what Armstrong had suggested to Forbes when the latter demurred, worried about the risks of a defeat. Bouquet rationalized his decision by pointing out that his men were afraid of the enemy and such a raid "will be a good lesson for the Troops." He also ordered the engineer Rhor to join Grant's force, hoping to finally get an accurate and professional report on the French defenses. In his report to Forbes, Bouquet made a cryptic reference to "secret orders" for Grant, which Bouquet would relate to Forbes in person. Given what transpired, the orders may have been for a "coup de main" that Grant later mentioned: not a reconnaissance but an attempt to seize Fort Duquesne by a surprise attack, despite having no clear information on the size of the French and Indian force that awaited the British.[31]

Bouquet gave Grant a "large party." Indeed, Grant took with him "the pick of the troops" at Loyalhannon, some eight hundred men, both regulars and provincials. The former consisted of four companies of Highlanders and a company of Royal Americans. The bulk of the provincials, led by Major Andrew Lewis of the 1st Virginia, were from that regiment, augmented by Marylanders, Carolinians, and Pennsylvanians. This picked force represented half or more of Burd's command, though Bouquet also summoned Dagworthy's Maryland battalion to bolster the Loyalhannon garrison. Grant and his men departed on September 9, and Bouquet expected them to return a week later. They first marched about three miles from camp "where," according to one participant, "we were taught the art of bush fighting by our commander, Maj. Grant." The force then marched to what was now being called "Grant's Paradise," the advanced post on the west side of Chestnut Ridge. Bouquet arrived on September 10 to find Grant still there, "detained by an oversight regarding his provisions." Building a proper breastwork at the advanced camp occupied the men on September 10. Despite the delay, though, Bouquet was clearly pleased with what he saw, later telling Forbes that Grant's men left "in splendid order" since the soldiers "have the air of going out to do their best," calling the mission "somewhat hazardous" but "absolutely necessary." No one seemed the least concerned that this column also included a small herd of cattle meant to supplement rations.[32]

Bouquet and Grant were also satisfied that none of the detachment knew where the force was going and, if captured, could not alert the enemy. Nevertheless, word leaked out. Reverend Barton at Raystown was told by Captain Allen McLean of the Highlanders that the force planned to lure the French into an ambush and then destroy the Shawnee settlement at Logstown. In fact, Grant's actions at Fort Duquesne were meant to provoke just such an ambush and to attack native fighters living near the fort. Meanwhile, Ensign Thomas Gist of Virginia recalled that on September 11, "we all paraded, with different opinions concerning our *Adventur*," some believing they would go to Braddock's Road. But "Major Lewis determined the matter, he being before consulted in the whole secret." The expedition's objective, then, appears to have been widely known by the time Grant's force left; if so, the breach of security may help explain what happened on September 14.[33]

They arrived within ten miles of Fort Duquesne on September 12, and the following morning Major Lewis was sent ahead with three hundred provincials to set up an ambush "within five miles" of the fort, while sending a smaller party ahead "to find out if we was discover'd." Unable to do more, Lewis sent word to Grant who, "about sun setting" on September 13, ordered that every man should put on a white shirt over his cloaths" while those with no shirts were sent back with the baggage guard. The main force then proceeded "by the light of the moon," which, according to Gist, allowed the men to see "the glistening of the firelocks against the moon." The white shirts caused some to comment "that we look'd more like ghosts than soldiers." Meeting Ensign Chew of Lewis's force, Grant learned that Indians were encamped near the fort. Reaching the crest of a hill within a half mile of the fort, Grant's men saw fires "which was supposed to be the Indian camp." Gist recalled that the force "halted for a considerable time." And here, on what became known as Grant's Hill, things started to go wrong.[34]

Lewis led four hundred men—half the command—down the hill toward the fort with the Royal Americans in the lead, followed by Highlanders, Marylanders, Pennsylvanians, and the Virginians bringing up the rear. Grant and the rest of the troops held a defensive position on the hill, providing a rallying point for Lewis's force. In the dark they moved "each holding his leaders shirt tail, and keeping the most profound silence." The regulars in the van "began to cock their pieces" then unexpectedly retreated "with such violence that we was obliged to give them the road" until they reached Grant's position. By that time it was nearly daylight on September 14, and a "very thick fog" prevented anyone from clearly seeing what lay ahead. Gist noted that the panic among the regulars occurred after "some Highlanders got lost and strayed into the woods, one of which got to the French camp." Another participant, Robert Kirk of the Highlanders, recalled in his memoirs that this plan to approach the fort at night "proved abortive" since "two of the Royal Americans deserted and informed the enemy of our strength and councils." It would appear, then, that at least some of the regulars, deliberately or not, found their way to the native camp outside the fort. With the general plan known to many of the troops, it is at least possible that the French learned of Grant's force, perhaps its size, and its objective. The original aim to attack and destroy the Indian encampment was no longer possible. In the meantime, Grant sent Ensign Rohr with an escort of Royal Americans down toward the fort in order to make a plan of the works. At some point during all this activity, Grant decided to attempt a "coup de main" according to what he had called his long-projected scheme.[35]

Grant's version of events, written later that day in French captivity, sought to shift the blame for the confusion and delay onto Lewis, also a prisoner at Fort Duquesne. According to Grant, Lewis was ordered to attack the Indian camps identified by their fires seen by scouts a day earlier. Lewis's men saw no fires this night and became disoriented in the dark. Grant admitted that, fearing discovery by the French and "with no time to be lost," he ordered Lewis to move quickly to the fort. The disorderly retreat that followed may have been a result of this hasty order. Unfamiliar with the ground and with no fires indicating where the native camps were, Lewis, according to his own report, told Grant that "it was impossible to do anything, that the Night was dark, that the Road was bad, worse than anything I had ever seen, that there were Lots of wood across it, that their [sic] were fences to pas that the Troops had fallen into Confusion." He believed they were lucky to get out alive given the noise they were making. Unconvinced, Grant ordered Lewis and his Virginians to the rear.[36]

Subsequent events unfolded quickly. Grant ordered Ensign Rhor and his covering party toward the fort since the fog was still so thick that the French works could not be seen from the hill. Then, apparently to inspire his troops, Grant ordered his pipes and drums to play reveille. If the French and Indians still had doubts about what lay beyond their camps, the racket from the hill would have quickly settled the matter. And if soldiers did stray or desert into French lines, it is likely that an attack was being planned for daybreak and that Lewis's men had been allowed to retreat rather than spoil the surprise. However it occurred, the French attack was sudden and overwhelming. Grant, Lewis, and Kirk all agreed that the enemy struck from several directions at once, with Kirk remembering that Indians came up the Monongahela River to overrun the British left flank. Some of the regulars seem to have stood against the first attack; both Gist and Kirk heard what Gist called "platoons" and what Kirk called "regular platoon firing"—the measured volleys of men firing by command. Nevertheless, the British lines were quickly broken with soldiers making for the rear. According to Grant, "I was told a number of the Americans [60th Foot] and Highlanders had gone, my party diminished sensibly, every Souldier taking the Road he liked best." Lewis, Captain Bullitt, and the rearguard came forward, but it was too late, Lewis was taken prisoner, as were Gist and Kirk, and survivors headed east toward Loyalhannon and safety. The last anyone saw of Grant, he was sitting on a log and allegedly said "My heart is broke ... I shall never outlive this day." It was this sentiment that seems to be what prompted Grant to borrow pen and paper from his captors in an effort to justify himself to Forbes. He was gentleman enough, though, to show his letter to Lewis before it was carried to Loyalhannon and included Lewis's assertion that he had not ordered the initial retreat, but that "Capt. Launder [Landers of the Royal Americans] who was the next Officer to him can best account for that Step." Grant then acknowledged that he may have been mistaken about Lewis's behavior. If Lewis's version is correct it would suggest another conflict over command authority that was likely to occur when regular and provincial officers served together.[37]

While the French accepted the surrender of officers and some enlisted men, their native allies were less generous, and Gist witnessed a number of prisoners killed and scalped, the bodies thrown into the nearby river. The total cost of Grant's battle was 273 men killed or missing out of 803 in the detachment; at least 40 wounded officers and soldiers were able to make their way back to Loyalhannon. Among the dead was engineer Rhor who may have been among the first to die when the French and Indians charged out of the fog upon hearing the bagpipes. Also killed was Lieutenant Billings of the Royal Americans whose widow would later enlist the aid of Rebecca Franklin in trying to secure her husband's effects and any money due his family. Washington's regiment took heavy losses. Out of only 186 officers and men engaged, the Virginians lost 7 officers and 62 men killed or taken. Grant's companies of Highlanders also lost heavily, 10 officers and 187 men listed as dead or missing and another 26 wounded among those who returned to Loyalhannon. Altogether, this first engagement between Forbes's army and the French was a disaster, made worse by Grant's assumption he had achieved surprise. In fact, evidence points to the contrary: Colonel Stephen, who was not present, learned from survivors that Grant was summoned to surrender by the French who "called him frequently by his Name to Surrender."[38]

Another potential casualty of Grant's defeat was Henry Bouquet. Having authorized Grant's expedition, Bouquet now had to answer to Forbes for the consequences. Clearly worried, Bouquet sent Forbes the best account he could of what happened, though stragglers were still arriving at Loyalhannon. He then told Forbes that "I make no apology regarding the part I have in this affair. I leave it to an account of the facts to condemn or justify me." If this was meant as reassurance, it failed. Forbes was already "very uneasy" and was said to have been in shock over the defeat. Forbes replied that he read Bouquet's report with "no less surprise than real Concern, as indeed I could not well believe that such an attempt would have been carried into execution without my previous knowledge, and concurrence," reminding Bouquet that "you well know my opinion, and dread, of the consequences of running any risqué of the troops meeting with the smallest check." Concern for the morale of his green troops was matched by his worry that the defeat could cost the army its few remaining native fighters. More worrisome still was the impact the defeat might have on the Delawares. If Bouquet had only followed orders, Forbes said, all would now be well. As things stood, however, Forbes feared that the defeat could prove costly and perhaps even prevent him from completing the campaign just as his army seemed to be gaining momentum. Behind this concern was Forbes's expectation that the French would not remain idle but would attempt to strike his advanced force in order to keep the army off balance. Forbes's frame of mind was not helped when two wounded Highland officers arrived at Raystown—having come directly from the battlefield—carrying a "lame" account of the action. As for Grant, "his thirst for fame brought on his own Perdition" while risking the entire army. Grant's poor judgment cost the army perhaps its most capable engineer, Ensign Rhor. Forbes could only say that "I am extreamly sorry for your loss of De Rhor, nor can I well conceive of what he had to do there" that put his life at risk. Forbes wrote to Abercromby and Pitt in a similar vein, telling them of the "Severe check" his army had suffered and, to Abercromby, he wrote of Bouquet's "Endeavours . . . to apologize." With his second in command and Grant clearly in mind, he concluded that "the rashness and ambition of some people brings great mischief and distress upon their Friends." Major Halkett, in a private letter, mentioned Forbes's unhappiness with Bouquet's conduct and also concluded that Grant was "spurr'd on by Ambition," a view that seems to have been widely shared. Colonel Armstrong referred to "our Quixot Expedition"; Washington told Virginia's governor that the expedition was either "very ill-concerted, or very ill-executed . . . perhaps both" and added that "it seems to be general acknowledged, that Major Grant exceeded his orders in some particulars."[39]

French accounts of the battle were more muted. Lignery gleaned some remarkably good information from his prisoners, even learning of the death of "an engineer who had gone ahead to reconnoiter the fort." French participants also understood how much they owed to Grant's decisions. Lignery admitted that the British might well have caught the garrison by surprise had Grant not ordered his men to burn buildings outside the fort. What disturbed the French, though, was the certain knowledge that the British came "very secretly" "by a very different road from General Braddock's" and that they had built "a chain of posts from Pennsylvania to the Ohio" that might allow them to spend the winter west of the mountains. Uncertain about the route taken by the enemy suggests that, despite scouting parties that reported on an army advancing over the mountains, the French as Forbes suspected still had their eyes fixed firmly on Braddock's Road as the most likely avenue of attack. Now, however, there was no doubt as to the direction of the British advance. One French officer at Quebec evaluated this news and could only conclude that Forbes's "success is more than probable," all the more so since many of the Great Lakes natives who had crushed Grant's force were now going home. Laden with captives and plunder, Ottawas, Wyandots, Ojibwas, and others began to depart, taking with them any hope the French had of monitoring Forbes's advance and further damaging his army. The French were forced to admit that "this fortunate *adventure* has ... produced an unfortunate and inevitable effect." One party of Wyandots from Detroit took Ensign Gist with them, his "lott was to carry about fifty pounds of plunder that they had got chiefly from the Highlanders." This party stopped at the Kuskuskies where they could rest and obtain food for the trip home. It is uncertain whether any of the Delawares who hosted Post participated in the fight, but Gist did remark that they and the Wyandots held a council as a "confirmation of friendship."[40]

The only good news came from beyond the Ohio Country. On August 27, Colonel John Bradstreet had taken the key French post of Fort Frontenac (Kingston, Ontario) at the head of Lake Ontario. This was the main supply depot for all French forces in the west including the Ohio Valley. Acting under orders from Abercromby, Bradstreet led a force of provincials up the Mohawk River and across the lake and took the fort with "an immense quantity of provisions and goods to be sent to the Troops gone to oppose Brig. G. Forbs." The "goods" mentioned included supplies for native allies and diplomatic gifts; without these, French hopes of keeping native fighters in the field or influencing the wavering Ohio Indians began to fade. This was a major success for the British; it guaranteed that the French and western Indians would not be resupplied or reinforced from Canada, just as the head of Forbes's army came within striking distance of Fort Duquesne. Forbes received the news in mid-September before learning of Grant's defeat, but he admitted that news of Bradstreet's victory "has been a good deal damped" by Bouquet's report from Loyalhannon. Indeed, news from Fort Frontenac may have added to Forbes's anxiety; he now had a chance to take the Forks of Ohio knowing that the French would be hard-pressed to stop him. At the same time, though, Grant's battle might threaten the negotiations with the western Delawares begun by Post. Forbes was also uncertain whether his army's morale would allow him to take advantage of Bradstreet's coup. On this latter point, he might have rested easier if he had known that, according to one Pennsylvania officer, troops at Raystown "now breathe nothing but Revenge & are in high Spirits." Moreover, as Washington discovered, the defeat had done nothing to harm relations between regulars and provincials despite Grant's effort to shift the blame onto Lewis and his Virginians. Washington noted that "Highlanders and them [Virginians] are become one People, shaking each other by the hand wherever they meet tho. Perfect stranger's."[41]

* * *

By early September, the "protected advance" had carried Forbes's army to Loyalhannon and within reach of its goal. Despite not being the location that Forbes, his engineers, and other officers would have selected, the Loyalhannon camp offered fresh water and plentiful forage for jaded horses and cattle that had eaten through whatever was available at Raystown. Moreover, the army was effectively now out of the mountains that had caused so many delays and so much worry. With Allegheny and Laurel Mountains behind them, the road ahead would only have to traverse Chestnut Ridge, a minor impediment given what the troops had already faced. Yet, instead of continuing on to Fort Duquesne, the army had stalled.

Part of the problem was logistical: the continuing issue of too few wagons carrying too few supplies for man and beast along a wretched road. The problem was also one of miscalculations and ambitions of subordinates, which resulted in an embarrassing and costly setback less than a mile from the French fort. Forbes was struggling to keep everyone and everything moving, battling a new round of illness as well as contrary subordinates. He would only catch up to his army at Raystown on September 15. Now, with Bradstreet's victory, it seemed the most opportune time to push ahead and complete the campaign. In the meantime, the bulk of the troops prepared to leave Raystown for the new camp at Loyalhannon; it would be the army's home for the next six weeks.[42]

Grant's defeat revealed two things. First, neither Grant nor his troops were able to cope with a French-Indian attack. Far from becoming woodswise like the Indians, Forbes's men from commander down to privates showed a distinct lack of skill in waging *la petite guerre*; no one thought to reconnoiter a way to the fort from Grant's Hill and the resulting confusion disrupted the night attack and possibly alerted the French to the enemy's presence. Not until men like Kirk heard war yells and shooting did anyone realize that the Indians could easily flank their attackers simply by moving along the banks of the Monongahela River.

Grant's defeat also threatened to undo the fragile work of peace that began with Post's arrival at the Kuskuskies. Not only was Post sent home without any commitments from the western Delawares, but these same people played host to, supplied, and may have joined the western Indians who destroyed Grant's force. Clearly, any steps toward peace with the British were still very tentative and Tamaqua could not assume the support of his people. While he, his brothers, and others anxiously awaited the return of Post and Pisquetomen with more substantial British commitments, many other Delawares may have hoped that Grant's defeat would mark the end of Forbes's march, leaving the French to be dealt with as opportunity arose.

Nevertheless, Grant did manage to catch the French by surprise. Fixed on Braddock's Road they seem not to have considered that the British might come from another direction. Only the sight of soldiers fleeing *east* instead of *south* confirmed that Forbes's army had succeeded in crossing the mountains. One explanation for this lies in the fact that Forbes decided to keep a force (Washington's) at Fort Cumberland. Their patrols and other activities may have confirmed French assumptions about the importance of Braddock's Road. Another explanation rests with those small parties of Indians that so irritated British commanders. They were probably less the eyes and ears of the French than opportunistic raiders who, instead of going to the border settlements of Pennsylvania or Virginia, picked off stragglers and small working parties from Forbes's army without providing details of what they saw and without making a connection between these victims and a much larger threat.

What Forbes learned was that his army was of questionable value in any future battles and men he trusted for their professionalism and experience had bungled an ill-advised attempt to seize Fort Duquesne. Virginians continued upset at Forbes's choice of road, and his quartermaster general, normally an army commander's righthand man, had both failed him and created unwanted friction with provincials. As he made his way from Shippensburg to Raystown, Forbes knew that time was slipping away. In addition to the rain that bedeviled him and plagued his road builders, the best campaigning weather was now behind him. In this part of the country, as some provincials likely knew, winter came early. Already, soldiers who had left their uniform coats and other equipment behind to lighten their loads were facing colder nights and hard frosts, while the summer grass was dying and, with it, cheap forage for worn-out horses. Forbes either had to push on to Fort Duquesne or see his campaign collapse in the face of bad weather and, possibly, short rations. He would collect his army at Loyalhannon and try to take advantage of Bradstreet's success, all the while hoping that the upcoming Easton council would help further undermine the French.[43]

EIGHT

Loyalhannon

* * *

OCTOBER 1758

> *I am this Moment in the greatest distress, . . . If the Weather does not favour, I shall be absolutely locked up in the Mountains, . . . I cannot form any judgement, how I am to extricate myself, as every thing depends upon the Weather, which snows and rains frightfully.*
>
> —FORBES TO PITT, OCTOBER 1758

Grant's defeat was more than a tactical setback. Forbes's hope of a swift advance from Loyalhannon to Fort Duquesne evaporated when news arrived at Raystown of the debacle and the losses. Forbes was clearly stunned by Grant's impetuous behavior; in late September, Colonel John Armstrong reported that Forbes "has been very uneasy," though "he is getting over the Shock." The loss of over 270 men was, Forbes told Pitt, "a most terrible check to my small Army" just as he was to "have marched to the Enemy," since his troops then had sufficient supplies with only a short march to the Forks. Forbes was especially worried about the effect that Grant's defeat would have on delicate negotiations with the western Delawares. He had "suspended all military Operations against them and their villages" hoping that the Easton conference would draw the natives "entirely to our Interest." Now, however, Forbes and his army were at a standstill while he pondered how to limit the damage Grant had caused and how to carry the campaign to completion.[1]

Neither his health nor the weather made Forbes's task any easier. Clearly depressed, he wrote to Abercromby asking him to send compliments to Sir Jeffery Amherst on his successful siege of Louisbourg, saying: "I should be obliged to him if he will send me a small sprig of his Laurels" since Forbes's own campaign "produces nothing but briars and thorns" without much hope of improvement. Weighed down by these "briars and thorns," such as Grant, poor roads, an unreliable quartermaster general, and dissention within the army, Forbes's health continued to deteriorate. Colonel Hugh Mercer learned that the general's health "exceeds our Expectations." If so, then expectations must have been especially low. Halkett reported only a day after Mercer that Forbes was "greatly fatigued." The general himself admitted to Washington that he was "quite as feeble now as a child." After arriving at Raystown in October, Forbes told Governor Denny and Abercromby that his health "continues precarious" but insisted that he could complete the campaign. His mission had now become a reason, perhaps the central reason, for staying alive.[2]

Good weather tended to bring Forbes out of his brooding. Near the end of October he wrote Bouquet that the "few days of fine weather last week raised my spirits and flattered my hopes that everything would go easy and well." Unfortunately for Forbes and his army, fine weather was at a premium. Warnings of a change in seasons had been appearing since mid-August when troops at Raystown awoke to "a cold Morning" with their tents "cover'd with Hore-Frost." Bouquet was then asking for blankets and warmer clothing for his men, and St. Clair asked that he be sent "my Down Quilt" since "the weather is cold." At the same time, Andrew Stephen was urging Washington to send his men's regimental coats from Fort Cumberland, along with their bayonets, saying that "The Season approaches which require the Use of Both." The short spells of dry warm weather of the sort that reinvigorated Forbes were now the exception rather than the rule. The frosts and cold foggy mornings in September increased the use of firewood as men fought off the cold and damp. Washington remarked in mid September that "the frosts have changed the face of nature" and predicted that there would be no more than one month left for the campaign since the grass was dying and fodder was scarce.[3]

During October the army slowly gathered at the Loyalhannon camp. Using Turpin de Crissé's metaphor of the siege to explain the protected advance, Loyalhannon was now Forbes's second parallel (Raystown being the first), meaning that he had pushed his way much closer to the enemy's works. From here Forbes would marshal his forces and decide whether to continue the slow deliberate march to the Forks or to launch a quick attack against Fort Duquesne. Grant's defeat had for the moment ruled out the latter; the former choice meant gambling with the seasons. Despite the pressures of time and weather, moving deliberately seemed the best course. Forbes was still hampered by a lack of information about the French, their numbers and intentions. Clearly, they were capable of resisting an attack, but Forbes knew nothing certain beyond that, complaining to Richard Peters as far back as August that "I can learn nothing that is to be depended upon." In the meantime, "the number of posts that I must occupy to preserve the Communication" sapped his available forces. It would take time to call in some of these troops. One such force—roughly half of Washington's Virginia Regiment—had been kept at Fort Cumberland to draw French attention toward Braddock's Road. Grant's assault had alerted the enemy to the threat from the east, however, and Forbes could now pull the Virginians back, directing them to march by the new road to Raystown as soon as they were relieved by Maryland militia. To the Virginians, the prospect of a more secure source of provisions was a relief. For Washington, their colonel, the move to Raystown meant he would not languish in a backwater while the army moved ahead and that he would have the opportunity to reunite and rebuild his regiment after the Grant debacle. Washington also learned that army contractors had been ordered to collect rations at Loyalhannon sufficient for four thousand men for the winter: an ominous indication that the army might be stalled in the mountains after all.[4]

While the Virginians were marching to Raystown, much of the rest of the army was moving to Loyalhannon over the newly opened road across Laurel Mountain. The pace was slow and the trek difficult, especially for the artillery. As early as July Forbes was complaining about moving his guns and their equipment, swearing that his small train was more troublesome than that of the whole allied army in Flanders during the previous war. His frustration arose from knowing that, even with the best equipment and horses, the artillery's rate of march was maddeningly slow: in ten days the train had not completed the trip from Carlisle to Raystown. A month later he urged Bouquet to get the artillery—specifically Captain Lieutenant David Hay—to "putt all things to right" and to "keep them close at it," since "their dilatory doings putts me madd."[5]

Determined to get guns and equipment up to Loyalhannon to support Burd's troops, Bouquet arranged for the first division of the train to leave Raystown on August 23. This was no small undertaking. The division consisted of four guns and eight coehorn mortars, which, with their ammunition and gear, would require forty-two wagons and limbers. Aside from the number of horses required (as many as 168), this convoy needed a large escort. Earlier in the summer all four companies of Bouquet's Royal Americans, over three hundred men, were assigned to this duty. By October half of Washington's regiment would be protecting additional artillery as it made its way to the new encampment. Only on September 11 did this first artillery division finally reach Loyalhannon. Burd had reported optimistically that the train was at the Clear Fields on September 6 and would be at Loyalhannon the following day. It is doubtful that the train left Raystown on time, and even if it had, the gunners and their escort would have been delayed by roadwork; in his haste to get men to Loyalhannon, Bouquet had pushed Burd's troops ahead of the road-building crews laboring over Allegheny and Laurel Mountains. The dead weight of guns and howitzers also caused problems as axle trees gave out and needed to be replaced or a new gun carriage needed to be built, keeping the train's carpenters, smiths, and conductors busy. More frustrating—and embarrassing—was the discovery that the train did not carry adequate spare parts. Major Halkett was compelled to write to Maryland's governor asking if there "are any spair Wheels or carriages for Hobtzers [sic]" in the colony, "Captain Hay having brought no spair ones with the train." Then there was the ongoing problem with horses, they were too few, underfed, and overworked. Horses were in short supply by late summer, and Bouquet was forced to use his teams in relay. Once the first artillery division reached the top of Laurel Mountain, the horses were to be sent back to Raystown to pick up the next division, and whatever horses were with Burd would pull the guns to Loyalhannon. By mid-September, moreover, a hundred horses belonging to the train had been commandeered as pack animals in order to carry flour.[6]

The artillery would continue to set the pace for the rest of the army throughout September and October. Since each division of the train required escorts, Forbes's army arrived at Loyalhannon in bits and pieces over a period of several weeks. Orders announced, for example, that "A Detachment of Artillery" was to leave Raystown on October 6, escorted by "all of the Troops belonging to the Pennsylvania Regt & Compys of the Lower County's" then in camp. Other detachments were sent off a week later guarded by that portion of Washington's regiment not already assigned to escort convoys. Only on October 24 did the remainder of the Highlanders and Byrd's Virginians leave Raystown for Loyalhannon; on November 3 the last of the artillery finally cleared Raystown. For over a month, then, small detachments slowly made their way west, moving no faster than the slowest of the artillery transports. And, long before the last convoy prepared to leave Raystown, Forbes was already far behind schedule. As he told Abercromby on October 8: "It is now ten days past, when I proposed to have marched from [Raystown], and to have marched directly for the banks of the Ohio," a march that he thought would take only eight days, provided that all of his artillery was already at or near Loyalhannon.[7]

Instead, Forbes found himself delayed by the usual circumstances. His troops needed food, and sending up rations and other supplies stalled his advance for several days. The original road cut over Laurel Mountain proved less than satisfactory, and a detour had to be cut, adding to the delay. Finally, heavy rains threatened to ruin a road already heavily used and poorly maintained; the foul weather would prove to be among Forbes's worst enemies. The last half of September had been dry, if colder, and the road was beginning to improve. Optimists like Colonel Armstrong believed that if "this month [October] happens to be dry weather, it will be greatly in our favour." Within a week of this comment, the skies opened once more, bringing downpours that lasted for days at a time. Traffic was at a virtual standstill by mid-October while sodden men and animals waited for the rain to stop so that road repairs could continue. Delays occurred again by October 20 as streams flooded and the road washed away. Killing frosts destroyed the grass; the army would now have to rely on whatever forage it could transport. By October 24 Forbes reported that "two days of rain with carriages upon a deep clay soil" made the road impossible for artillery, and "the Baggage horses are so weakly animals, that they cannot get along." These "extraordinary," "quite unexpected," and "unusuall" rains were followed by "frightful" rain and snow by late October.[8]

The new encampment, then, offered little to inspire newly arrived troops who had just struggled over the mountains. By early October the ground in and around the site was already churned into a thick mud, and soldiers busied themselves digging ditches around their tents in a frantic effort to avert flooding. Those on the high ground were best off; the tent lines on the western slope of the encampment caught the worst of the flooding from both rain and the overflow from Loyalhannon Creek. Flooding and erosion were made worse by the clearcutting of trees and brush for fortifications and to create clear fields of fire; cutting sods to build artillery batteries also added to the problems. Since Burd's force was reduced by half in mid-September because of Grant's expedition, work on fortifications, ovens, fences for cattle, and supply buildings had slowed down and only began to regain momentum as new troops arrived and as the men assigned to defend the "advanced post" to the west were recalled after Grant's defeat. Loyalhannon was the site of half-completed log retrenchments, storehouses, and the inner fort. The growing encampment created a tent city extending in a rough ellipse from the new road in the east to the low ground near the stream to the west. To anyone unfamiliar with an army on the move, the scene would have been one of chaos: men, women, children, wagons, horses, cattle, and dogs, all jostling for room in an area that ran some fourteen hundred feet east to west and eight hundred feet north to south. By late October only Washington's Virginians and one battalion of Pennsylvanians occupied the retrenched lines surrounding the inner fort. The bulk of the army pitched its tents on high ground to the north and east, guarded by a chain of redoubts and batteries. The hospitals were also outside the defenses; most were on the west side of the camp covered by the Royal Americans, though the Maryland hospital was on the east side near the tent lines of the Maryland and North Carolina companies.

Whether anyone noticed, amid the hurly-burly of camp life and work, the army that gathered at Loyalhannon was substantially smaller than the force that had occupied Raystown weeks earlier. One battalion of the Pennsylvania Regiment, led by Colonel Hugh Mercer, was left behind at Raystown to provide security for the army's hospital there as well as the road toward Loyalhannon. J. C. Pleydell's plan of the Loyalhannon encampment shows only one camp for the Royal Artillery, suggesting that Heydeler's provincial train had been left behind as well. There were also the numerous small detachments that made up the "protected advance" in addition to those Pennsylvanians "idling in the Forts" east of the Susquehanna River. Grant's defeat and the persistent sniping by Indian parties had also taken a toll: a return from late September listed 249 men dead or missing. It is clear that by the time it arrived at Loyalhannon Forbes's army was beginning to disintegrate. Specific figures are difficult to find; during the press to cut a road and the final advance of the troops, accurate returns were a rarity, and Forbes himself might have had no clear idea of how many men he commanded. Bouquet had to admit at the beginning of September that the nearly three thousand Pennsylvanians were now "reduced to 1,000 [at Raystown]," and "I cannot account for the rest." Even an official return of the army made on September 1 acknowledged that the numbers of Pennsylvanians reported "greatly exceeds their real numbers," since no monthly returns for these troops had ever been turned in to army headquarters, making this "General Sketch of the number of Troops" of little value. Forbes only spoke in general terms about his "little" army and by late October was worried about having so few regulars: by his count, the army contained only twelve hundred "King's Troops" from the 60th and 77th Foot. An accurate assessment of the army's size is further made more difficult by what we must assume was a growing list of sick men in the face of persistent bad weather, falling temperatures, and poor rations.[9]

On September 5, for example, Byrd's 2d Virginia Regiment reported 112 men sick—perhaps as much as 15–20 percent of its manpower. At roughly the same time, the "greatest number of" the 1st Battalion of the Pennsylvania Regiment were sick. Most were laid low with the flux and fevers. By late October, Forbes was urging colonial governments to take steps for "making the

Soldiers' Lives Comfortable in this severe Climate" as winter approached. These urgings included providing a second blanket for each man in addition to a flannel jacket and new shoes and stockings. Although we can know only the status of those men who reported sick either in their camps or at the army's hospitals, we can say nothing about men who simply decided they had had enough and who drifted on home, part of a backflow of men, wagons, and horses along Forbes's road.[10]

Desertion became a more serious problem as the army marched to Loyalhannon. In what appears to be the largest single prosecution, eight men (all provincials) were tried for desertion by general court-martial at Raystown. All were found guilty, and Forbes ordered three of them to be shot. Even this seems not to have stopped desertion. Washington heard that there was "considerable desertion" among the Lower Counties (Delaware) companies, five of whose men deserted at one time from an engineer's working party. Officers continued to openly quarrel among themselves, making camp discipline more difficult. Enlisted men guilty of noncapital offenses found themselves taken under escort "to Cut firing [firewood] for the General," as well as other unpopular fatigue details. Court-martial reports only deal with men caught attempting to desert and tell us nothing about the numbers who were successful in running from the army. The references in daily orders to desertion, fighting and other disciplinary issues, and the punishments meted out are also a reminder that many of Forbes's men were suffering from what a later generation of soldiers would call "short-timer's disease." Enlisted men knew little about the army's operations, but they did know when they had enlisted. For the men of Byrd's Regiment and the Pennsylvania New Levies, this meant knowing that their terms expired on December 1, and as that date drew closer, some men, such as those deserters from the Lower Counties, may have decided to risk leaving early in the face of defeat, the threat of continued enemy attack, deteriorating camp conditions, and threats posed by disease. The desire to go home was also a symptom of declining morale. On September 4, before Grant's defeat, Bouquet warned Forbes that "the army is beginning to become visibly bored and impatient, their ardor is cooling." Reverend Barton echoed this report when he observed that "we found the Troops much dejected" and that men "dispair'd" of completing the campaign before winter trapped them in the mountains. By late October Forbes learned from Bouquet that "the prevailing spirit in the army forecasts other storms." Bouquet complained further that disgruntled men "are making trials on me," but he tried to dismiss this as simply the behavior of men who were "without education or principles." By October, then, Forbes's army was beginning to unravel.[11]

*   *   *

In the midst of the activities at Loyalhannon and the deteriorating morale, regiments also took part in a ritual common to all armies of the time: drawing up inventories of personal effects left behind by soldiers known to be dead or missing in Grant's battle. In some cases, these goods would be auctioned to any and all bidders and the money used to pay outstanding debts or sent on to the next of kin. In the Royal American Regiment, company commanders drew up the lists and certified them. These included the belongings of three officers and thirty-three enlisted men. These inventories are all that survive from the battle, though each regiment involved would have compiled similar lists as time allowed. The information contained in these lists is quite complete: Lieutenant John Billings, for example, left "One small diel [deal] box, One Port Mantle [portmanteau] One pair of Boots & a horse with Sadle & Brydle." Fellow officer Edward Jenkins, owned a "Matras," blankets and sheets, a "Regimental Coath [coat]," as well as shoes, stockings, nightcaps, boots, and a portmanteau meant to be carried on a "Mare which is lame." By contrast, the common soldiers owned very little: among five men missing from Bouquet's company, there were only "4 Knapsacks" and "2 old West coaths [waistcoats]." The stark contrast reinforces the popular image of the wide social and economic gulf that separated officers and private soldiers in Britain's professional army. The reality was more complex, and the camp at Loyalhannon provides a unique opportunity to examine the material lives of Forbes's army. Amid the construction, the mud, and the tented encampments, men, women, and children left a rich and varied material record of their lives on the road. Since the early 1960s, some twenty thousand artifacts ranging from bullets and buttons to wagon hardware have been recovered and preserved and now form what is one of the largest artifact collections from the Seven Years' War in America.[12]

Among the most evocative items are shoes: nearly a hundred pairs and fragments of many more all preserved, along with other leather, wood, and metal objects in the anaerobic environment of the dried-up creek that once ran along the west side of the encampment. The shoes run the gamut in quality and styles—from the locally made to the imported—and include women's and children's footwear as well as those belonging to soldiers. With their soles worn completely through, or mended, or covered with hobnails, the shoes are mute testimony to the rigors of walking from eastern Pennsylvania or from the lower Shenandoah Valley to Loyalhannon. Evidence also suggests that some people insisted on maintaining appearances even in this rough, mobile society. The wooden heel from a woman's shoe survived as did a number of metal shoe buckles ranging from steel and brass to some that were silver-plated; many were plain, but others carried stamped or incised decorations or filigree designs. The fancier buckles and those washed with silver might at first be associated with officers or other nominally well-to-do individuals. Yet, ads for runaway servants suggest that brass and silver buckles, presumably carrying decorative marks, were commonplace. For the wearers, in fact, they may have been a form of social "signaling" meant to convey a sense of taste or status in a colonial world in the throes of a consumer revolution by the mid-eighteenth century. Indeed, one engine driving that consumerism was the appearance of mass-produced items like shoe buckles or the numerous fancy cuff links found at Loyalhannon that allowed the owners to project a persona beyond what their station in life may have allowed.[13]

One striking example of this widespread consumerism is the sole of a woman's shoe that would have included an embroidered cloth upper. Unlike Martha May and other women with the army who made do with plain leather shoes, whoever wore shoes of this style either was or aspired to be of genteel status. Such embroidered shoes were a mark of refinement and would have been distinctly out of place in the muddy confines of the Loyalhannon camp, yet the wearer seems to have persisted in maintaining appearances, at least until the shoes either wore out or simply fell apart.[14]

At the other end of the gamut of footwear, archaeologists also found in the streambed a slightly burned moccasin, which featured a separate sole. This colonial-made version of native footwear would have been quite popular with troops and civilians alike; with their flat soles they were more comfortable than heeled shoes or boots and, if properly treated, would have been water resistant as well. Again, who may have used this specimen is beyond determination, but it does remind us of Captain Evan Shelby's Maryland volunteers who agreed to join the army in return for scalp bounties and moccasins. Forming part of an ad hoc light infantry battalion composed of Maryland, North Carolina, and Delaware troops led by Colonel Dagworthy, these volunteers were as close as Forbes came to realizing his goal of turning soldiers into Indians. Indeed, their value was such that Bouquet made a point to remind Forbes that these men, "Our best woodsmen," were "accustomed to moccasins" and could not be employed "for lack of footwear." He requested "500 prepared deerskins be sent from Philadelphia" in order not to lose the services of such valuable troops.[15]

Scores of worn-out shoes remind us of the mobility inherent in this army; wooden tent pegs and a mallet to drive them home also highlight the impermanent nature of this mobile society. Tools of all sorts—axe heads, iron

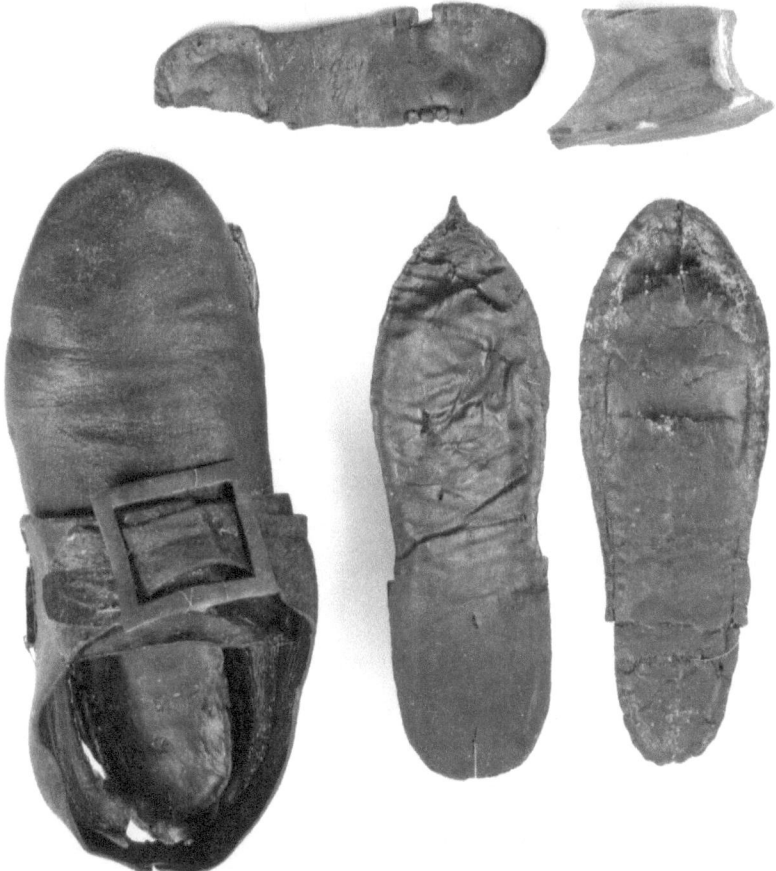

Fig. 8.1 Man's, woman's, and child's shoes from Fort Ligonier. (Courtesy of the Fort Ligonier Association.) Mute testimony to the movement of the thousands of men, women, and children, free and slave, who made up the "walking city" that was Forbes's army.

shovels, augers, and a grindstone for honing cutting tools—conjure up images of woodcutting, ditching, as well as the constant road building that occupied Forbes's troops. Numerous clasp knives turned up at Loyalhannon, enough to suggest that this item was a commonplace among soldiers of all ranks, a useful tool for paring fingernails, preparing rations, or repairing firearms. Those firearms are well represented on the site as well and speak to the variety of weapons, good, bad, and indifferent, that required frequent mending by the artillery smiths. The poor state of these weapons is hinted at by the number of cocks, frizzens, ramrod pipes, and strap buckles that ended

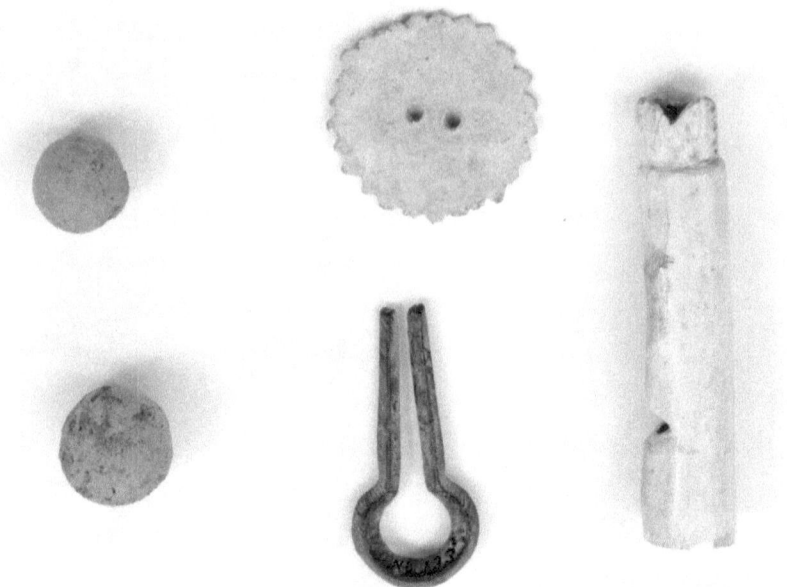

Fig. 8.2 Items lost or discarded at Fort Ligonier. (Courtesy of the Fort Ligonier Association.) Clay marbles, bone whistle, Jew's harp, and the lead portion of a toy known as a "whizzer," all suggest how soldiers and civilians—particularly children—passed their time in camp.

up being lost or discarded. The array of weapons—from government-issued Tower muskets to Dutch or German arms bought by provincial governments, to personal firearms—are also reflected in the wide array and caliber of lead shot uncovered. For many provincials carrying nonstandard weapons, bullet molds were a necessity, while those without cartridge boxes or pouches made do with leather bags and powder horns.[16]

Wagon parts—hundreds of them—underscore both the importance of transport to the army's success and the deteriorating state of rolling stock. Like myriad gun parts, the metal hubcaps, pieces of chain, wheel rims, and other detritus were broken or otherwise worn out. Along with the shoes for both horses and people, harness leather, numerous nails, canteens, tin cups, tools, lead shot, buttons, and buckles, the impression these artifacts give of Loyalhannon is one of a vast junk yard, strewn with castoffs of all kinds. Although the physical evidence is lacking, there is no reason to think that Raystown or other sites occupied by the army looked any different.[17]

Yet, amid the rusting metal, torn leather, and fragments of barrels that once held powder, flour, or salt meat, other objects such as an embroidered shoe speak to attempts to maintain a semblance of normalcy and civility amid the organized chaos and chronic filth of camp life. Children as well as soldiers and other civilians played with jaw harps, ceramic marbles, and toys like a "whizzer" made from scrap lead. Letters to family, superiors, or subordinates were composed using lead pencils as well as quill and ink. At least one individual carried his or her own chamber pot in an effort to maintain a small measure of privacy and avoid fetid common latrines. Eventually broken, this ceramic vessel was simply tossed into the ditch of the newly built western battery. Officers, entitled to transport their own provisions, owned wooden boxes for glass case bottles, as well as candleholders, while sutlers peddled liquor from common bottles. The site of the encampment and fort was strewn with fragments of stoneware, delftware, earthenware, and porcelain; how much—if any—belonged to Forbes's army rather than later occupants is impossible to know, but the variety and quantity would suggest that some soldiers and civilians as well as sutlers and officers' batmen carried mugs, bowls, and plates on the trek west, along with forks and spoons and the ubiquitous knives. There are even reminders of the constant battle against camp diseases and wounds: a delftware tile used for rolling pills and fragments of medicinal vials.[18]

*   *   *

The astonishing collection of materials from Loyalhannon indicates that the camp's occupants were occupied with the quotidian rhythms of military life. These included the baking of bread or biscuit, the slaughtering of livestock for fresh meat, and the issuing of salt rations, as well as unofficial foraging as men and women attempted to fill out otherwise monotonous menus. By early October, even as more troops arrived, the army had little trouble feeding itself. True, gardens of the sort planted at Raystown had long since given up the last of the harvest and officers were beginning to worry about collecting sufficient supplies of oats and fodder for horses and oxen. Few members of the army beyond Forbes and his senior officers were aware that a logistical crisis was looming. As Forbes was making his way to Raystown, his army was perched on the heights overlooking Loyalhannon Creek at the end of a precarious supply line that stretched back over the mountains to Carlisle, and across the Susquehanna River to Lancaster and Philadelphia—a one-way trip of over two hundred miles. No other British army in America or Europe had to face such circumstances.

To be sure, the quantity of supplies was not the problem, even though in early September Forbes admitted that "My greatest distress ... is the provisions." Just six weeks later he was able to assure Bouquet that "we have now plenty of provisions betwixt this [Raystown] and Loyal Hannon," and he reported to Abercromby that "I am now Master of provisions to the 20th November" for his men and horses, in no small part due to the efforts of his quartermaster St. Clair to muster the needed supplies and wagons with "such diligence and application." Indeed, so happy was he over his logistical situation that Forbes begged leave of Abercromby "to retract my reflections upon" the quartermaster and his staff.[19]

The problem had less to do with quantities of supplies than it did with the relentless overland logistics and natural forces that Forbes could neither predict nor control. All summer long, for example, he had to wrestle with the persistent conundrum of army logistics: given the finite number of wagons available, should he carry provisions for men or provender for his horses? Without horses to pull wagons, men would starve, but any decision to haul more food to forward magazines risked destroying the army's very means of movement. Forbes recognized the problem, at one point observing that, by having wagons carry forage for teams, he was limiting food for his troops since such convoys "carry infinitely less provisions in proportion." This predicament only got worse as the campaign continued: wagons wore out or broke down; natural fodder began to disappear, requiring more loads of oats and corn; and civilian drivers became increasingly reluctant to stay with the army, both out of fear of the French and out of concern for their own families as the harvest approached. Despite St. Clair's success, Forbes was still forced to impress at least fifty wagons in order to get supplies from Raystown to Loyalhannon, while an assistant quartermaster was compelled to use both "fair means" and "Compulsion" in order to get a new train of wagons moving from Lancaster to Loyalhannon. The fair means was an offer of a generous fifteen shillings per day, though anyone who refused faced the threat of having driver and rig impressed. Even at that, though, the pace was maddeningly slow. By late October Forbes found that loaded wagons took a whole day to move across Allegheny Mountain along the "best made road of the whole" and then had to "halt a Day to refresh" teams exhausted by the trip.[20]

The passage over Allegheny Mountain may have been the "best made" part of the road—though hard enough on animals and wagons—but the greatest part of Forbes's road was turning into a disaster. The original passage across Laurel Mountain was deemed "absolutely impracticable," and work began on a bypass in mid-October. In the meantime, rain, frost, and overuse were turning large stretches of the road with its clay soil into a quagmire that slowed progress and destroyed valuable horses. Even turning to packhorses did not help; the five hundred animals sent from Carlisle were loaded with forage (about two hundred pounds per horse), but their arrival at Raystown and Loyalhannon was blocked by wagon trains held up by the poor road. The quartermaster at Raystown, Lieutenant Sinclair, spoke of wagons "from below . . . Crowd[ing] so fast upon us [that] *if the weather continues favourable*," he believed wagons could be sent forward to Loyalhannon every day. Mother Nature did not cooperate, however, and Forbes's hope of moving his army to Loyalhannon dissolved as quickly as the road itself in the continuing rain. For every bit of good news (Bouquet reported some good forage north of the road on route to Loyalhannon), there followed bad news: rains had swollen Quemahoning Creek to such an extent that more time would be needed in attempting to bridge it. By late October, Bouquet was compelled to remind Forbes that the road was so bad he risked the artillery in sending it forward. He pointed out that "you cannot leave troops and feed them at this distance" and suggested that Forbes urge Pennsylvania to undertake to garrison and feed its provincial troops along the road.[21]

Forbes was trying to cope as best he could, but he complained that "with Disorder, Indians, Waggons, Provisions & Provendor my life has been a perfect Burthen to me." The logistical snarl was literally making him sick, adding pressures and anxieties to his already frail health; when he wrote about the "Disorder," he also told Bouquet that he needed to have Lieutenant Sinclair write his letters since he was unable to hold a pen. Learning just a few days later that the Allegheny Mountain road "is broke to pieces from down right neglect," all Forbes could do was assign more men to repair it and hope for better weather. That hope would continue to fade, though, as the days grew shorter and colder and continued wet. The realities of supporting an army along a single road still held: time, distance, and weather were now Forbes's biggest enemies. His worst nightmare, as Bouquet suggested, was having his men caught on the far end of the road as rain, snow, flooding, and exhausted draft animals kept rations from reaching them.[22]

By early October Forbes's logistical crisis was building. For the garrison of Fort Duquesne, however, the crisis was both real and immediate. Ironically, the victory over Grant produced a major problem, as more and more native allies left for home loaded with booty and prisoners. By early October Captain François-Marie le Marchand de Lignery, a fifty-five-year-old veteran of campaigns on the margins of New France, also knew that Frontenac had fallen. Supplies of dry goods and ammunition were drying up and making it more difficult to support the parallel war of the western Delawares and Shawnees. French troops could look forward to less corn and game as the natives left; indeed, the Shawnees abandoned their settlement at Logstown (Ambridge, Pennsylvania), leaving fields of corn unharvested. Worse, the colony itself was in the midst of an economic crisis. While New France could normally feed itself and even export some grain, the influx of thousands of French regular troops (*troupes de terre*) and the ineptitude on the part of civilian officials meant that by 1758 the colony was running out of food. And although the Illinois garrisons provided reinforcements under Captain Charles Philippe Aubry, these French troops and Illinois natives carried only limited supplies and merely added to the logistical burden facing the Ohio garrisons. The Illinois Country was simply too far and the trip up the Ohio River too time-consuming to be a viable alternative source of food and other supplies.[23]

Time and distance were as much the enemies for Captain Lignery as they were for Forbes. Unless the French acted soon, they would be unable to act at all, since hundreds of miles separated Lignery from supplies and reinforcements from either Canada or the Illinois Country. Thanks to Major Grant they had undeniable evidence that the main British threat would come from the east. Thanks to native scouts and ambush parties, Lignery also knew that the British were strung out along a narrow road through the mountains. If he could stall the enemy's advance, even for a few weeks, it might be enough to save Fort Duquesne for another year when, hopefully, more men and supplies would make British success impossible. Lignery also knew specifically where the British were and that they were for the moment stationary. A quick strike, with limited aims, might keep the British from moving any farther west. Logistics, both French and British, would shape the events of the next several weeks. In the metaphor of the siege Lignery would lead a sortie designed to disrupt the besiegers' works: not so much to break the siege but throw it off schedule.

* * *

Forbes, Bouquet, and others assumed that the French would retaliate for Grant's raid. Yet when the attack came, on the morning of October 12, it caught the Loyalhannon encampment by surprise. Although British patrols were out, none found any trace of the attackers until after they retreated; rain, perhaps mixed with fog, may have encouraged sentries and pickets to seek shelter rather than keep watch. According to the report of the camp's commander, Pennsylvania's Colonel Burd, the first indication of the enemy came at eleven in the morning when "the enemy fired 12 Guns to the South west of us," perhaps an indication that the French had run into a foraging party or a grass guard. Burd's statement is vague: "Guns" might imply artillery, but no other source suggests the French carried any with them. The reference to the southwest indicates that the approaching force might have been attempting to shield themselves from view by moving beyond high ground south of Loyalhannon Creek (today occupied by a cemetery). If so, their scouts may have found that any attack directly from the west was impractical; not only was this avenue crowded with animal pens and hospitals and covered by redoubts to the north but the rising ground on which Fort Ligonier was being built acted as a natural *glacis*: open ground up which any attacker would have to move exposed to defensive fire. The plan of the encampment drawn in 1760 by Theodosius McDonald clearly shows the French attack as coming from the *east*, a more vulnerable part of the camp that was still largely undefended in October and a position that allowed the French to cut the road from Raystown; Burd's own plan of the encampment also indicates that the attack came from the east. If this was the plan, then the initial firing to the southwest could have heralded the French move toward the eastern end of the encampment.[24]

Burd responded to the firing by sending out small parties and then "a large party of 500 men," but these were "forced back to the Camp" by the French advance. If Burd's figure is correct, his force would have been almost equal to the force with Aubry and Lignery, which has been put at about six hundred French and Indians, though Burd and others in the camp thought the enemy numbered about fourteen hundred. Having driven in the British forces, "a regular Attack Issued which," Burd thought, "lasted a long time I think above two hours." What he meant by "regular" attack is unclear; it is doubtful that the French commanders would have risked their force in an open fight. Perhaps Burd was referring to "regular," disciplined volley fire of the sort heard by survivors of Grant's battle, of just persistent shooting. If so, it may not have lasted for long; rainy conditions would have led to numerous misfires and obscured the enemy, and once the British pulled back to their retrenchments it is likely that the French and Indians simply fired at whatever targets presented themselves. It is clear that they never attempted to rush the defenses. One big reason for their caution was the presence of British artillery. Although few in number, "the cannon & cohorns [mortars]," Forbes later reported, "were well served"; the guns were directed by senior engineer Captain Harry Gordon. The cannons may have been five-and-a-half-inch howitzers, and firing explosive shells, canister, or grapeshot from howitzers and mortars would have kept the French at a distance. The gun crews kept up a deliberate fire during the day and night, since the French still kept to the tree line at least until dawn of October 13. This was to be the Royal Artillery's only combat experience during the campaign; it cost them only one casualty, Lieutenant Fireworker George Wright, who was listed as "wounded slightly in the head."[25]

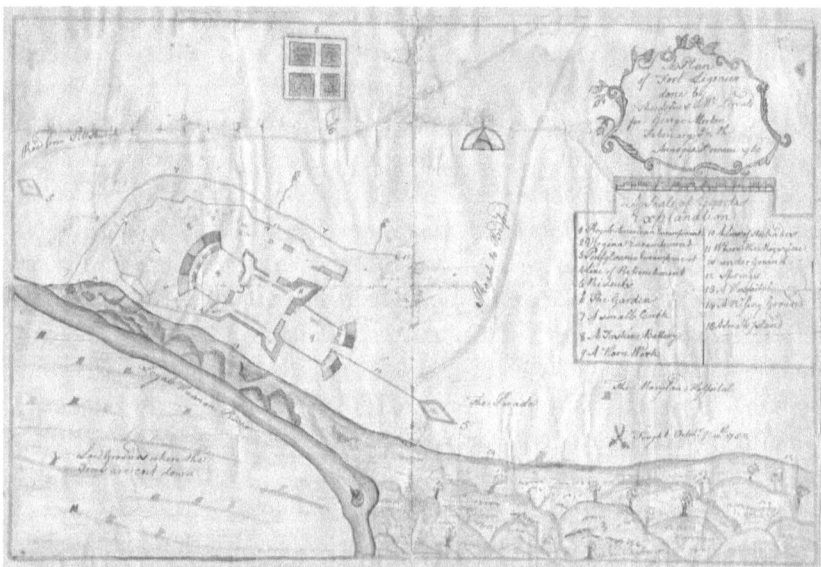

Fig. 8.3 Plan of Fort Ligonier, drawn by Theodosius McDonald, 1760. (Courtesy of the William L. Clements Library, University of Michigan.) This plan clearly shows where the French launched their attack on the Loyalhannon camp. The crossed swords in the lower right indicate the point of attack.

An attack that lasted for a long day produced few casualties. Aside from Lieutenant Wright, Burd's force of some fifteen hundred regulars and provincials lost sixty men—half of them listed as missing, with only twelve killed. The Maryland companies absorbed the worst losses: two dead, six wounded, and eleven missing, and among the casualties were three of their officers. Pleydell's plan shows the Maryland and Carolina companies encamped to the east of the fort; the Maryland hospital was also in this camp, covered by a small redoubt. Next to these troops who, with the Lower Counties companies, constituted the light infantry was the 1st Battalion of the Pennsylvania Regiment, whose men went out to support the Maryland troops. These Pennsylvanians lost twenty-one men dead, wounded, or missing, while the Carolinians suffered three missing, and the Lower Counties reported only one man missing. As McDonald's plan of 1760 indicates, this was the focal point of the French attack, and these troops suffered forty-four of the sixty British casualties. These provincials clearly impressed Forbes; in his report to Pitt, he made a point of commending "the spirit of some of the provincials, particularly the Maryland troops," glad that he had retained the latter in service. French losses are unknown. Captain Pierre Pouchot, commandant at Fort Niagara, claimed that the attackers lost only three men, which may understate the reality, though scouting parties from the camp did recover three French dead. Burd would only say that, when the French departed on October 13, they carried their dead and wounded with them, all except one wounded man who was taken into the camp, where he was questioned and later died. Given the volume of fire, the defenders naturally assumed they had inflicted heavy casualties on the French; Bouquet, who heard mortar fire while on Laurel Mountain, also assumed the attackers suffered heavily. Nevertheless, aside from three bodies and the badly wounded prisoner, we simply do not know anything about the French losses; the artillery fire, while vigorous and steady, occurred in rainy weather and at night and probably had little effect other than to keep the French at a distance.[26]

Later that day a scouting party returning from Fort Duquesne stumbled on an enemy encampment and found a bloody bandage but Burd's troops failed to intercept or overtake any of the attackers. Bouquet sent some of his own troops in that direction, but they too found nothing. Some of the French force may have remained in the vicinity for several days. A fragment of a diary entry evidently kept by someone on patrol mentioned "Indians that went past them" on October 19. In fact, evidence suggests that British parties, including the patrol sent before October 12 to Fort Duquesne, actually crossed the French line of march. That patrol found tracks of a large force marching in columns moving away from Loyalhannon; these traces were enough to put the soldiers on alert as they approached the encampment on October 13, since they did not know whether it was occupied by their army or by the French. At the same time, the troops heard men yelling at the British. There was, however, clear evidence of what the French had attempted to do. Forbes reported on October 16 that the French made off with many of the camp's horses; he later told Pitt that "they carried off all the Baggage Horses belonging to that post." Pouchot claimed that some two hundred cattle were also killed, though Forbes insisted that "we saved all our Oxen." The attack, for all of its noise and duration, was a spoiling raid designed to cripple Forbes's army; given their numbers and their own logistical situation, the French leaders could do nothing more. The lack of any evidence of French artillery further suggests that the plan was to disrupt the camp, do as much damage as possible, and depart quickly under cover of night and poor weather.[27]

If this was, in fact, the French objective, it seems to have worked. Bouquet was chagrined when he learned the details of the attack, finding the outcome "humiliating to me," especially since some fifteen hundred troops had been kept at bay by fewer enemy troops who succeeded in carrying off the horses and escaped unscathed with their dead and wounded, as well as British prisoners. He wrote of the "audacity of the enemy" and expressed concern for the campaign's loss of livestock. Forbes was equally upset at the disappointing outcome, sarcastically calling the fight a "great action," though he was not convinced that French aims were so limited, believing they had planned to attack and seize the fort. Both officers, however, agreed to put the best face on the affair for the sake of morale. Bouquet pointed out that it was necessary "to try to pass this off as an advantage in order to maintain the courage of the Troops," courage shaken by recent events. And, in order to keep the colonies in ranks behind the army, Bouquet also thought that public news of the attack would convince settlers "that the enemy is strong enough to attack us nearly fifty miles away," and that the campaign was far from over. For his part, Forbes confessed to Pitt that he was "extreamly angry" that Bouquet had not pursued the French, but told the colonel he was "very glad" that the French attack "has turned out near as fruitless to them as ours was to us" under Major Grant. Forbes was optimistic enough to suggest that the attack indicated just how worried the French were and predicted that they would make further attempts to destroy the encampment, but under no circumstances would he consider a withdrawal.[28]

One outcome of the Loyalhannon attack was that Forbes's troops finally had a live French prisoner. For most of the campaign, Forbes was moving without any clear sense of his enemy's strength, circumstances, or plans. Now, ironically, the French by attacking Loyalhannon gave the British what they had needed for months in the form of a badly wounded Martin Discentio. His name would imply that he was not a Canadian *habitant* but, rather, a member of the colonial regulars, the independent companies of marines whose ranks were filled from volunteers recruited in France and elsewhere in Europe. Before he died Discentio provided some valuable—and troubling—information. He claimed that the attacking force consisted of seven hundred regulars and Canadians as well as three hundred Indians, nearly the same size as Burd's garrison. Clearly, then, the French could still mount a formidable attack. Moreover, Discentio told his captors that five hundred additional troops were expected from the Illinois Country. When asked, he provided details on Fort Duquesne, saying that the fort mounted fifteen guns, the largest six- and four-pounders, hardly sufficient to withstand Forbes's artillery. He confirmed that the target of the attack was not the encampment itself but its outer guards and its livestock.[29]

The prisoner also seems to have provided information on the state of the garrison at Fort Duquesne. Having read the deposition, Bouquet discounted Discentio's account of further reinforcements due to arrive, arguing that the season was "too far advanced for a reinforcement to be sent to them." He also dismissed any thoughts that the marquis de Montcalm would send any part of the main French army from Quebec to the Ohio, especially after the destruction of Fort Frontenac. It was clear that the French were neither as numerous nor as well-off as the British feared; the only questions remaining were whether and how the army could move toward the Ohio as the seasons turned and the weather continued to deteriorate.[30]

By mid-October Forbes's army had reached a point some fifty miles from its goal; whether it could successfully make its way to Fort Duquesne, though, was still an open question. Two encounters with the French had provided little evidence that the British troops could fight and win a battle or siege. Indeed, neither Grant's battle nor the attack on Loyalhannon could have given Forbes much reason for optimism. True, portions of his army had fought well on October 12, but reports and casualty lists also indicate that large numbers of troops—including the regulars upon which he placed so much reliance—had simply stayed behind their works; the Highlanders reported only one killed and one wounded, the Royal American no losses at all. And although Forbes was now certain that his enemy had limited numbers and resources, his own force continued to shrink as he faced the potential for a major logistical crisis. Ending the campaign at Loyalhannon was still a realistic alternative. Finally, while Forbes and his subordinates were wrestling with lost battles, poor morale, and a precarious line of communication, to the east the long-awaited Easton conference was beginning. Convened on October 7, the council would last for over two weeks and might mean the difference between success and failure for the men, women, and children settling in at Loyalhannon.[31]

NINE

Easton and the Kuskuskies

* * *

OCTOBER–NOVEMBER 1758

I had Some time before that [Grant's defeat], suspended all Military Operations against [the western Delawares] and their Villages, in hopes of gaining them entirely to our Interest, which I hope is now in a great Measure done, in a solemn meeting With their Chieffs at Easton upon the Dellaware, ... but as yet I Do not know the result of their deliberations.

—FORBES TO PITT, OCTOBER 1758

From his headquarters at Raystown Forbes was wrestling with the myriad problems of an army whose advance had all but stalled. A stinging defeat in September was followed by the embarrassing spectacle of his advance force motionless within its defenses at Loyalhannon in the face of a French attacking force of inferior numbers that inflicted casualties, drove off valuable horses and other livestock, and returned to Fort Duquesne without incident. With his own health uncertain ("precarious," then seeming to "mend a Pace"), Forbes began to wonder if he would live long enough to take Fort Duquesne. His ability to complete his mission also depended increasingly upon forces over which the general exercised little control: deteriorating weather, a rickety supply system that still functioned but no one knew for how long, and the western Delawares. Although Forbes could not know for certain, it is likely that some of the fighters who attacked Loyalhannon had come from the Kuskuskies, Saucunk, and other Delaware towns. As he sat at Raystown reviewing his circumstance and prospects, Indian affairs remained paramount to the success or failure of his campaign.[1]

Securing Ohio Indian neutrality had been at the heart of Forbes's strategy from the beginning, and the Delawares had been on his mind for months. He became convinced that peace with the numerous and influential people would remove a critical obstacle as he continued to move west. Governor Denny only reported the obvious when he told Sir William Johnson that Forbes "has been instrumental in bringing about" the impending Easton conference, and "is very anxious for the Success of it." Determined to separate Ohio Indians from the French, Forbes had consistently urged Pennsylvania to make peace with the Delawares, and he found in Quaker Israel Pemberton's Friendly Association men who were prepared to further that goal.[2]

Forbes knew about Post's mission to the Delaware towns, obtained a copy of Post's journal, and heard directly from him as Post returned to Pennsylvania. The news was not encouraging. Post spoke of "many difficult times" and could only pray that "God will make everything to turn out for the best," while his journal made clear how divided the Delawares were, even as Pisquetomen headed east with a message for the British. Forbes's relentless march west was at the root of much that troubled the Delawares. Shamokin Daniel and others clearly blamed the British for the war and questioned the sincerity of peace overtures when an army was busy occupying their country. What were the colonists' and soldiers' real intentions? Post spoke about peace, but Forbes came for war; the alleged interference by the Six Nations in communication between Pennsylvania and the Ohio towns and the glaring lack of any definite statements from the colonial leaders themselves only added to uncertainty and division and guaranteed that at least some Delaware fighters would have joined the attack on Loyalhannon.[3]

Circumstances were equally complex and uncertain for Forbes. Aside from the information supplied by Post, Forbes knew nothing about what was happening in the Delaware towns. Moreover, for the past six months, the general had been responsible for his own Indian affairs, for example, naming Abraham Bosomworth and William Byrd III as his Indian agents. Without clear orders from his immediate superior, General James Abercromby, and virtually ignored by both Johnson and Atkin, Forbes had to fashion his own strategy; hence his cooperation with the Quakers in trying to secure what he believed was crucial to his army's success—the neutrality of the western Delawares and their neighbors. For all that he complained about Johnson's refusal to provide agents and information to his army, Forbes received nothing in return. Abercromby offered excuses for Johnson: he was too busy rallying Indians for Abercromby's own army or was uncertain about just how far his authority ran as opposed to Atkin's. In effect, Abercromby made it clear that Forbes was entirely on his own. Abercromby reminded Forbes that he was the commander in chief in the south but that Abercromby would "support and assist you to the utmost of my power." Abercromby stopped well short of providing direct orders and did not attempt to take Johnson in hand. If Tamaqua and other western Delawares were frustrated by the mixed signals from the British, Forbes was equally perplexed by the lack of support he received from those in a position to give him the aid he required. Hence his willingness to embrace the Quaker effort to promote peace, even at the risk of being drawn into the vortex of provincial politics that pitted the Friendly Association against the Proprietors and further alienating Johnson into the bargain.[4]

* * *

The exact schedule of the meeting could not be fixed in advance. Although invitations to the interested parties had gone out, time, distance, and unforeseen obstacles ensured that no one would arrive at Easton precisely when intended. The formal conference began on October 7, with opening words from Governor William Denny. Simply put, the Easton conference aimed at drawing the western Delawares and their neighbors into the peace already made with Teedyuscung's people as well as settling outstanding differences over land, trade, and the colony's expansion, which, Forbes and others hoped, would be enough to convince the Ohio Indians to stop fighting, abandon the French, and craft a new peace with the British. Yet, nothing at Easton was simple. This large gathering of tribes, colonies' representatives, and crown officials—over five hundred Indian men, women, and children were in attendance—meant that the treaty grounds would also become an arena in which competing and sometimes hostile interests would collide.[5]

Aside from Denny's party and that sent by New Jersey's government, the large gathering included Israel Pemberton and other prominent Quakers, the often inebriated Teedyuscung and other Delawares from Wyoming, and a large contingent from all of the Six Nations, along with George Croghan, Johnson's deputy. Denny, of course, wanted to reaffirm the peace made with Teedyuscung the previous year and, more important, to open negotiations with the distant and still hostile Delawares, Shawnees, and other Ohio Indians. New Jersey's delegates likewise wanted to settle outstanding differences with the eastern Delawares who had attacked that colony during the war. In both cases the crux of the matter was land: for the eastern Delawares some acknowledgment of their claims and a secure place to live; for the western Delawares and their neighbors the assertion of their independence and insistence that their new homes west of the mountains would not be subject to the same invasion that had dispossessed their people a generation earlier. The Six Nations attended for two closely related reasons: what they took to be a fraudulent land sale at Albany in 1754 that allegedly ceded the lands between the Susquehanna River and Allegheny Mountains to the Penns and, by settling that sore point, to reassert their political dominance over not only the irksome Teedyuscung but the distant Ohio Indians as well. Pemberton and his Friendly Association were there to see that Teedyuscung's people received compensation for the infamous Walking Purchase as well as an acknowledgment from the proprietary representatives that the natives had been defrauded of their lands and that this was the real reason for the present war. The Quakers recognized the crucial link between these land claims and the restoration of peace. By insisting that they wanted peace with the Indians based on "just" and "rational" principles, they put themselves on a collision course with Johnson by challenging his authority. Finally, Croghan was there to ensure that everyone—particularly Pennsylvania officials and the Quakers—clearly understood that Indian affairs were Johnson's province, not theirs. Croghan supported the Six Nations, thus reinforcing the Covenant Chain and, through it, Johnson's paramount authority. Taken together, there was a cacophony of voices striving to be heard at Easton and many interests, not all of them compatible. Moreover, both Indians and colonists brought with them memories of recent and much earlier relations. History would be as much on display at Easton as the wampum belts and gifts.[6]

Animus was also just below the surface at Easton. The Six Nations, for example, relished the opportunity to abase Teedyuscung and dismiss his boastful claims of leading ten nations or more by implying that the Iroquois looked to him as well. Johnson also cast doubt on Teedyuscung's authority, noting that while he was reputed to be a "leading Man," Johnson himself had his doubts, though he was certain that the Delaware headman was really Pemberton's puppet and a tool of the "Party Spirit [that is, opposition]" that characterized Quaker behavior. The Quakers wanted nothing more than to expose the Penn family's land deals over the past generation, both as a way to restore peace with natives such as Teedyuscung and Tamaqua who were dispossessed and as a way to further undermine the proprietary regime that influential Pennsylvanians, including Benjamin Franklin, hoped to replace by a new royal charter and government.[7]

The Quakers, in turn, were reviled by provincial and royal officials alike. Aside from the distrust of avowed pacifists in time of war, the Quakers had stepped into Johnson's jealously guarded territory by inserting themselves into Indian affairs, something royal officials such as Johnson and Abercromby viewed as an affront to the king's prerogative. Johnson was equally upset that Pennsylvania's governor—at Forbes's urging—had issued invitations to Easton that included the Six Nations, something that he characterized as "Counter Workings." Pointing to Quakers and Denny, Johnson complained that they "entirely interfere with my Management" of Indian affairs. And, of course, there was Pennsylvania's political leadership. Governor Denny and Provincial Secretary Richard Peters wished to stop both Quaker meddling in Indian affairs and their attacks on the Penn family, their land-grabbing, and refusal to pay taxes to the colony on any of their holdings. At the close of the conference, for example, Denny could congratulate himself that he and others were able to "counteract the designs of the wretched and restless faction." Four years later, facing yet another Indian council, Peters continued to accuse the Quakers of "playing the same Game" they had at Easton and that they wished only to make "mischief."[8]

Anticipating such mischief Johnson chose to stay away, offering as an excuse that he was too preoccupied with recruiting Indians for Abercromby's army and worried about what he saw as a hasty rush to negotiate. Yet, by late August it was abundantly clear to everyone that Abercromby's army was not going to renew its campaign against the French. In reality Johnson may have been reluctant to involve himself in a potentially volatile meeting whose outcome "I cannot take upon me to say." He originally sent messages to the Six Nations "forbidding" them to accept Denny's invitation, but he quickly backed down when Abercromby received "warm Applications" from both Forbes and Denny for Johnson's cooperation. The Six Nations did attend, and Croghan stood proxy for his superior. In the meantime, Johnson might have been up to "mischief" of his own. He acknowledged sending his own messages to the Ohio Indians, though the latter denied every receiving them. Moreover, Post learned that western Delawares were not prepared to act according to Johnson's and the Six Nations' bidding. Not only tired of receiving garbled and conflicting messages from the east, the western Delawares were particularly upset that the Iroquois messages, endorsed by Johnson, urged them to return to their old settlements in the east, closer to the Six Nations and colonial settlements. Rejecting this out of hand, the Delawares insisted on negotiating on their own, as sovereign people, not as subordinates to the Covenant Chain.[9]

*   *   *

Before following the course of the Easton conference, we might pause and briefly consider an issue central to the exchanges that began in earnest on October 8: the talks adhered closely to native, not British, protocols. These included private meetings and even more secretive discussions "in the bushes"—the off-the-record discourse and arguments that often helped move agendas forward. For example, as the host, Governor Denny was expected to speak first, and when he did, he reprised the Condolence Ritual so

Fig. 9.1 Sir William Johnson, 1772, by Matthew Pratt. (Courtesy of Johnson Hall State Historic Site, Johnstown, NY, New York State Office of Parks, Recreation and Historic Preservation.) As crown-appointed superintendent of Indian affairs for the northern colonies, Johnson exercised considerable power with both the British military and the colonial governments. He was a thorn in Forbes's side throughout the 1758 campaign.

familiar to his Indian audience. Using strings and belts of wampum, Denny metaphorically created the proper atmosphere for discussion by wiping "the Sweat and Dust out of your Eyes, that you may see your brethrens Faces, and look cheerful." In addition, he took "all Bitterness out of your Breast, as well as everything disagreeable that may have gathered there" so that the natives "may speak perfectly free and open to us." And, finally, he symbolically removed the blood (the lingering animosity) from the council "that your Clothes may not be stained, nor your Minds any Ways disturbed."[10]

Denny's initial speech, his words and the wampum that gave substance to them, as well as the governor's reliance on Conrad Weiser as an interpreter all remind us that, however much the colonists may have controlled land and trade, the council fire was still very much part of Indian country. The Delawares, Iroquois, and others insisted that time-honored protocols be strictly adhered to and delivered in the natives' languages. It was a small, but powerful, reminder that peace required *British* conformity as well as Indian acceptance. In the days that followed, all important proposals, counterproposals, and agreements would be accompanied by wampum that in effect breathed life into words and served as reminders of what had passed long after the words themselves had been spoken. This fact helps explain why meetings like Easton lasted as long as they did, even though officials such as Denny might have wished for a faster pace. Custom dictated that respondents take the time to discuss what they had heard and carefully prepare a reply. In the give-and-take of native discussions, arriving at the required consensus could take time, and even then, those who continued to disagree with any proposals were not under any obligation to accept them. At the same time, wampum strings and belts had to be prepared to accompany the replies, and this too would take time, as native women busily assembled the beads according to instructions. This slow and deliberate back-and-forth was the very essence of native council proceedings, aimed at calm persuasion rather than confrontation, demands, and dictates.[11]

Exactly when the western Delawares arrived in Easton is not clear, but their presence was acknowledged in the minutes for October 13. Pisquetomen and his party arrived alone; Post had taken a detour in order to report his proceedings to Forbes at Raystown. Told by his brother Tamaqua to place Post "into your bosom" and take him home safely, Pisquetomen insisted that their party take a wide detour to avoid both French parties looking for Post and British colonists looking for Indian scalps. They reached the comparative safety of Fort Augusta on September 20 after a tension-filled trip from the Ohio. For Pisquetomen this journey may have been particularly exhausting. Britons who met him in 1767 estimated his age then at eighty-six; if so, he would have been seventy-seven when he made not one but two trips across the mountains on behalf of his younger brothers. Pisquetomen's subsequent speeches and the message from the western Delaware leaders were made at Denny's invitation and, though not part of the original agenda, underscored the Delawares' independence. Pisquetomen's presence for the remainder of the talks ensured that his people would have a trusted and independent report on proceedings; Pisquetomen could also carry messages from the governor directly to the western Delaware towns.[12]

*   *   *

Once they had listened and responded to Denny's greetings, the assembled native headmen consumed two days "deliberating on Matters necessary to be adjusted" before the next public session. Evidently knowing how impatient the British could be, they "desired [that] the Governors [Denny and recently arrived Francis Bernard of New Jersey], would not be impatient" as deliberations continued into a second day. On October 11, the Six Nations were prepared to respond. The Iroquois were to speak first and had already "laid some Belts and Strings in Order on the Table," when Teedyuscung, interrupting the Six Nations, asked to speak. Croghan quickly asked if what he had to say was on behalf of the assembled Delawares and if *they* wanted to speak first; getting no reply from Teedyuscung or the assembled Delawares, Governor Bernard rose to offer greetings to the natives. The abrupt dismissal of Teedyuscung was only a hint of what was to follow. From the moment the Seneca headman Tagashata began speaking, the Iroquois dominated the assembly, shaping the agenda and ensuring that their (and Johnson's) interests prevailed. Having answered both Denny and Bernard, the Seneca speaker reserved his substantive remarks for the following day.[13]

When Tagashata spoke on October 13, he made it plain that the Six Nations were acting on behalf of their "nephews," the other nations at the conference, particularly the Minisinks (Munsees) and eastern Delawares. On behalf of the Delawares he formally made peace and blamed hostilities on the French. Having assured Denny that their nephews "have, at last listened to us [and] laid down the Hatchet," he also informed the gathering that the Iroquois had sent similar messages to "our Nephews" (the Delawares and Minisinks) living "on the Ohio." The use of the term "nephew" was meant to underscore the subordinate role of these nations. Then, suddenly, the Six Nations turned on Teedyuscung. Their orator "spoke for some Time, with great Vehemence, pointing frequently to Teedyuscung." The tone and substance of the speech was such that Pennsylvania's official interpreter, Conrad Weiser, "desired to be excused, as it was about Matters purely relating to the Indians themselves" and suggested that the speech was best interpreted in a private conference. At that private meeting, on October 15, the Iroquois complained that Teedyuscung had long boasted of being a great man, telling Denny that "we do not know he is such a great man," and if he was such a great man they wanted to know who made him so. When, on the following day, Denny responded in open council, he told the Iroquois that "I never made Teedyuscung this great Man, nor ever pretended to give him any Authority over you" and assured them that Teedyuscung had always referred to the Six Nations as "Uncles and Superiors." From that moment, Teedyuscung lost all standing at the conference. Drunk or sober, he continued to demand a voice in the conference, but at one dramatic moment, as he rose to speak, the Iroquois headmen quietly, one by one, walked out of the meeting. It was abundantly clear that Teedyuscung not only had lost all credibility with the assembly but was of no further value to the Friendly Association members who hoped to pursue their case against the Penns. Moreover, by both words and action, the Six Nations emphatically reasserted their authority over subordinate peoples; they had restored the Covenant Chain and, with it, Johnson's authority in Indian affairs.[14]

For Pemberton and Denny, Pisquetomen's appearance was the high point of the conference, the first time that western Delawares and colonial authorities had come face-to-face since the border war erupted three years earlier. In the context of the conference, the Delawares' response to Post's messages delivered that summer was brief and to the point. On behalf of his people, Pisquetomen shook hands with Pemberton, Denny, and Teedyuscung as a way of acknowledging their role in making the meeting possible. The message from the western Delaware peace faction made it clear that "we long for that Peace and Friendship" that had previously existed between natives and the colony and that, even in the midst of war, "we will not let that Friendship quite drop." They were also heartened by news that Pennsylvania had restored peace with Teedyuscung's people, though Tamaqua and his followers stopped short of offering peace. Instead, they repeatedly admonished the governor to "be strong" and move ahead with peace offers, at the same time telling him to "make Haste, and let us soon hear of you again." For a fragile coalition of village leaders this was an important point: the risk that these men took in contacting the British had to be reciprocated, and soon, since Forbes's army was now in their country. And though they also understood that negotiations took time and required good faith from all parties, they placed the burden of making peace squarely on the British, telling Denny: "When you have made this Peace, . . . then you will be pleased to send it to me at Allegheny." In return, Tamaqua and his followers would readily work toward peace that embraced "all the Nations of my Colour"—that is, all of those living in the Ohio Country.[15]

The Delawares' message was also important for what it did not include. There was no reference to the Six Nations—and by implication, the Covenant Chain. Instead, Pisquetomen spoke for those "at Allegheny" and acknowledged only those whom they believed had made this meeting possible. Nowhere in the message was there a clear offer of peace. A desire for peace, yes, but no talk about what the *Delawares* would do to make that happen; it was the British who were expected to make the initial gestures, since, as the natives saw things, it was the British and not they who had begun the war. The natives expected to hear directly from Denny on the all-important matters of security of native lands and a resumption of trade. Moreover, they would not accept any insulting demands—like the return of prisoners—before a formal peace had been made. Hence their repeated calls for Denny to "be strong; if you do so, every Thing will be well." In closing, they asked that the British king "know what our minds are" and once more urged haste.[16]

Three days later, on October 18, in a lengthy speech that only reinforced the arguments Post had earlier heard from the Delawares about the causes of the war, Six Nations warriors reminded the British that the conflict had many causes, all of which could be set at the feet of the colonists. Among their strongest indictments was the colonial effort to take native lands. They told the conference that "The Governor of Virginia took Care to settle on our Land for his own Benefit" and that this was "the very Cause why the Indians at Ohio left you." And, to drive home the point, the Iroquois warriors demanded that the 1754 Iroquois sale of the land between the Susquehanna and the Alleghenies be nullified; the "Warriors, or Hunters" had never agreed to it and the Six Nations would no longer confirm land cessions since "they are our hunting Grounds."[17] Telling the natives that since Johnson had "represented this Matter" to the Penn family, Denny agreed to return these lands and told them that they could negotiate with Richard Peters and Conrad Weiser in order "to settle the Boundaries between you." This latter comment was the first suggestion of a point that would become critical to peace in the Ohio Country: the fixing of boundaries that would keep colonists out of native lands. Denny then turned his attention to what Pisquetomen awaited: his formal reply to the western Delaware message.[18]

Pisquetomen was anxious to depart for the Ohio Country. On October 21, before the official end of the conference, Pisquetomen and his Delaware companion, Thomas Hickman, "came to take their Leave of the Governor"; they would be accompanied by the Delaware Isaac Stille and two provincial officers, Captain John Bull and Lieutenant William Hays, "the Persons appointed to attend them to the Ohio." Pisquetomen carried a number of wampum belts and strings to accompany the written message from Denny. To ensure that the messages were properly related, "The Belts and Strings were numbered, as well in the written Paper containing the Messages, as on labels tied to each of them" along with passports that would hopefully allow the delegates to travel west unmolested. In the midst of this leave-taking, Christian Frederick Post arrived with news from Forbes about the recent attack on Loyalhannon.[19] "Having received the orders of" governor Denny, Post also made preparations to return to the Ohio; on October 25 he left Easton, overtaking Pisquetomen's party near the town of Reading where the Delaware headman embraced him and learned that Post would accompany the group to the Delaware towns. The subsequent journey was a taxing one; at one point Pisquetomen was drunk and nearly too sick to travel. They were joined at the end of October by two Cayugas—all that remained of a party of Iroquois, most of whom were reluctant to proceed west. Their reasons became clear when, near Chamber's Fort (Chambersburg, Pennsylvania), "some of the Irish people, knowing some of the Indians, in a rash manner exclaimed against them." The travelers "had some difficulty to get them off clear." At Fort Loudoun, they were met by Cherokees "in a friendly manner" who expressed satisfaction in learning of the Easton conference.[20]

The trip west—the second for both Pisquetomen and Post—was challenging, between Indian-hating settlers, the effects of liquor, and the miserable weather as October ended and November began. Yet, both men knew that the real work would begin once they arrived at the Kuskuskies. The governor's message was certainly encouraging. Throughout, he addressed the Delawares as "brethren," equals not "nephews" or "children." Moreover, he offered to restore peace, inviting the natives to Philadelphia, "to your first old Council Fire" and that he would metaphorically "clear and open [the] Road for you saying that he would be glad to see them once more." In none of this was there any mention of Six Nations' authority or the Covenant Chain. In effect, Denny was prepared to treat the western Delawares as autonomous people, capable of negotiating for themselves and standing as equals with the Iroquois and others of Pennsylvania's friends and allies. The news that the 1754 Albany cession had been given back to the Iroquois meant little under the circumstances; arrangements would have to return as they were before the war began. Given how reluctant the Six Nations were to embroil themselves in Ohio Country affairs, the natives living there could continue to chart their own course, without the interference or mediation of the Covenant Chain. The only ominous note was sounded when Denny told them "If you are Earnest to be reconciled with us" to keep their warriors at home and, above all, keep "at a Distance from Fort Duquesne." This last would be a sensitive point for Tamaqua and his people. Some Delaware fighters had certainly been at Loyalhannon and were probably still shadowing Forbes's army. And, if the Delawares were to protect their sovereignty, that army would have to leave the Ohio Country. On this point Denny said nothing, and there were no messages from General Forbes, only several thousand British troops poised to move into the heart of native territory.[21]

Post intended that his group should go directly to Forbes first, in order to receive his messages to the Delawares. Their route by way of Carlisle and Fort Littleton followed the military road and made the natives extremely uneasy. Telling Post that "you have led us this way, through the fire," Pisquetomen made it clear that "if any mischief should befall us, we shall lay it entirely to you; for we think it was your doing to bring us this way." One reason for Pisquetomen's anger was that Post had not confided in him: that Post "should have told us at Easton, if it was necessary we should go to the general." Worse, Pisquetomen got into an argument with the provincial officers, wondering "whether the general would claim the land as his own, when he should drive the French away" and whether the British intended to settle the land. The Delaware reminded Post, Bull, and Hays that "we are always jealous the English will take the land from us," wondering "what makes you come with such a large body of men" making "such large roads into our country" when the Delawares "could drive away the French ourselves, without your coming into our country." Anger and suspicion rose to such a level that Post had to warn the officers "to be careful how they argued with the Indians," since "it may prove to our disadvantage, when we come amongst them." The hope and trust of the previous summer had clearly evaporated, and Pisquetomen, on whom Post must rely, was expressing doubts about peace.[22]

Moving along what Post called "one of the worst roads that ever was travelled," the party made its way to Loyalhannon, overtaking part of the artillery as it struggled over Laurel Mountain. Pisquetomen was clearly unimpressed by the soldiers and the road, telling Post that if he "had not come to us before, . . . we could have destroyed all this people on the road, and great mischief would have been done." It was a chilling reminder of just how exposed and vulnerable Forbes's army was and how little still stood between the western Delawares and the soldiers' destruction. And, while Pisquetomen and the rest were "gladly received" by Forbes "and most of the peoples" at Loyalhannon, a number of provincial officers approached the Indians and "spoke very rashly" to them "in respect to their conduct to our people." Angry at "such usage" directed to men who had "come upon a message of peace," Pisquetomen and his companions "were much displeased, and answered as rashly," reminding the British that "they were not afraid of us." These exchanges occurred on November 7; the next day the mood changed when Forbes spoke directly to Pisquetomen. This would be Forbes's only encounter with the people who could make or break his campaign. How the two men assessed each other is not known. Forbes, visibly ill, wrapped in blankets and perhaps too weak to stand, faced Pisquetomen, an older man, but robust despite having nearly completed his second trip over the mountains this year and seeing or hearing little that would have impressed him about Forbes, his army, or their chance of success. Stalled at Loyalhannon, facing deteriorating weather and mounting talk of turning back, Forbes found the meeting with Pisquetomen and Post marked a turning point in the campaign. Convinced that the Delawares were acting in good faith and perhaps reassured by Pisquetomen, Forbes determined to push negotiations ahead.[23]

At a public council that included those few Cherokees and Catawbas who were still with the army, Forbes welcomed Pisquetomen's party and "expressed his joy to see them." Then, cutting quickly to what most concerned him, Forbes "desired them that had any love for the English nation" to withdraw from the French, warning that he would treat as enemies any natives found with the French as his army advanced. Then, having offered a toast to the Delaware leaders and their warriors, Forbes convened a private meeting with the Delawares and Iroquois at which he offered a more fulsome message and the necessary wampum to support it. The written copy of the message was not ready until midday on November 9, upon which Pisquetomen, Post, and their companions left Loyalhannon escorted by one hundred provincial troops, making camp that night at the now abandoned post at Grant's Paradise. Still worried about enemies, both native and colonial, Pisquetomen then insisted that an advanced party of twenty men cover the rest, in case, according to Post, "any accident should happen" as Pisquetomen feared that "the enemy will follow the smallest party." The precaution proved unnecessary, though the travelers had a brief scare when they sighted three men, "in Indian dress." With Isaac Stille displaying white wampum as a sign of peace and Pisquetomen giving "an Indian halloo," the trio dropped their packs and fled. Close inspection of the gear revealed that they were soldiers, perhaps lost, perhaps deserting.[24]

The cold rain that followed Pisquetomen and his party from Loyalhannon might have seemed a bad omen. Unlike their summer trip Post and Pisquetomen faced one problem after another. One Delaware's horse stumbled on the wet ground "and rolled down the hill like a wheel." In the meantime the party struggled through "weeds, briars and bushes" at the site of the former Shawnee town of "Keckkeknepolin [Kickenpauling Old Town]." Lieutenant Hay's party of provincials, ordered to escort the party to the Allegheny River, insisted on turning back since they were short of provisions. Meanwhile, the Delawares and Cayugas "grumbled" at Post, complaining that if they had traveled by way of the native town at Shamokin, they might have received goods from the British stationed there. Although Post chided them for complaining about gifts while undertaking an important mission of peace, he privately agreed that the "Indians were so slightly fitted out at Easton," and Forbes evidently had nothing at all to give them. Adding to the generally sour attitude that settled over the party, Pisquetomen found a white wampum belt given by the Pennsylvania Quakers who managed the Indian trade but "could find no writing concerning the belt" and thus he could not accurately explain it in council with the other Delaware headmen. Pisquetomen and his companions "seemed much concerned" to know what the belt meant.[25]

Worse followed. As they neared the Kuskuskies, Pisquetomen recommended sending messengers ahead to alert the town of their arrival "as the French live amongst them." Upon meeting two natives on the road, though, they learned that "no body was home, at Kushkushking," and that 160 men had "gone to war against our party [the army]." Only Menatochyand (Delaware George), who had welcomed Post's arrival that summer, was available to talk; Post and Pisquetomen told him of Forbes's message, upon which Menatochyand decided to visit the general himself. Before he could leave, however, word arrived that Lieutenant Hay's party had been attacked by Delawares; Hay and several men were killed and others captured, one of whom "was to be burnt." The incident threatened to poison an already difficult and dangerous undertaking. By killing the provincials the Delawares had, by accident or design, disrupted any peaceful discourse, staining the road just opened by Pennsylvania's governor to the natives with the blood of his soldiers. Upon learning that the prisoners were part of Post's party come to discuss peace, and upbraided by Post, the returning warriors could only say that "it is a hard matter, and we are sorry for it hath happened so." Only with difficulty was Post able to get a messenger to Saucunk, where the prisoners were held, telling the natives that he and Pisquetomen had come "with good news." The Delawares again regretted the attack and surrendered the prisoners, but they asked that Forbes do the same with any of their people held in his camp. By November 19, "a great many of the warriors came home." They evidently told Post that the French had incited them to attack the British, including Hay's party, by telling them that Forbes's ultimate aim was to "fall upon the Indians, and destroy them" after disposing of the French.[26]

Pisquetomen's and Post's experiences on the way west exposed negotiation for what it was: dangerous and both physically and mentally exhausting. Once they were at the Kuskuskies, moreover, the full extent of Delaware factionalism and distrust became clear. True, Post was not greeted by the "murdering spirit" of men and women that had threatened his first embassy to the town. Yet, neither was he embraced by those few Delawares, like Menatochyand, who were still at home. Virtually all the leading men were absent, and large numbers of young Delaware fighters had joined the French. The warriors' actions, in particular, underscore how angry and worried the Delawares were at Forbes's continued advance. As the men charged with defending towns and families, they reacted to the British advance as one might have expected; not knowing anything of Easton or of Pisquetomen's mission, all these men knew for certain was that their land had been invaded and their towns placed under threat. Those facts, rather than anything having to do with the French, encouraged these warriors to take the field. In the meantime, other Delawares had opted for a different response. One reason that Tamaqua, Shingas, and other headmen were absent in November was that the Delawares were once again preparing to relocate in the face of invasion. These men and many others were doubtless in the Mahoning Valley near modern Youngstown, Ohio, and farther west in the Muskingum Valley, scouting suitable lands for new towns. As happened at Kittanning in the aftermath of Armstrong's raid, natives from the Kuskuskies, Saucunk, and neighboring towns had decided to move deeper into the Ohio Country, putting distance between themselves and the oncoming British troops. Their decisions to do so suggest that even among those people like Tamaqua who were committed to negotiation, trust of the British was in short supply. The natives acted without hearing of the outcome of talks in Pennsylvania.[27]

For Post the first three days at the Kuskuskies "was a precarious time for us." The British were "warned not to go far from the house" provided for them, since returning warriors, "having been driven back" at Loyalhannon, "were possessed with a murdering spirit." Indeed, the Delaware Isaac Stille was "dubious of our lives." When summoned to speak before them, Post conveyed to the natives the messages from Forbes and Denny, "with great satisfaction to them." Indeed, a day later, on November 20, a messenger came in from Fort Duquesne and attempted to rally the Delawares, telling them on behalf of the French commander that the British wanted nothing less than to destroy both the garrison and the Indians. In the first sign that attitudes were beginning to change, however, one by one the Delaware war leaders refused to accept the accompanying wampum; one of them "threw the string to the other fire place," and others "kicked it . . . as if it was a snake" and replied that the French should fight their own battles. Those few French still at the Kuskuskies were "mortified to the uttermost," and their leader "looked as pale as death." As Post spoke, Forbes's troops were getting closer to Fort Duquesne and the end of the campaign.[28]

Speaking to assembled warriors was one thing, presenting formal messages to western Delaware leaders quite another. Post, anxious to be on his way to Forbes with a report of his proceedings, was forced to wait while the native headmen slowly appeared; Keekyuscung arrived on November 22, Tamaqua did not appear until November 24, Shingas came in the following day. These men, along with Menatochyand and other leaders, were vital to the peace process; it was their collective message that Pisquetomen presented at Easton and only they could sway a still divided people to accept British terms. The headmen were expecting a response; Tamaqua told Post that "as soon as I heard of your coming, I rose up directly to come to you." Shingas also "saluted us in a friendly manner." When asked if the talks should be held in front of the French, Tamaqua tersely replied that "it was no matter, they were beaten already." Indeed, the Delawares were so certain that the French, shorn of their Great Lakes native allies, could not hold the Ohio Country that Pisquetomen made the point that Forbes's vast army was wholly unnecessary: the natives could easily deal with the French in their own way. A British army in the Ohio Country was neither needed nor welcome.[29]

These sentiments would set the tone for the council. The Delawares, accepting Denny's and Forbes's messages, quickly made it clear that they would not tolerate any further invasion—by French or British—and expected to remain undisturbed on their lands in the Ohio Country. While Denny, Forbes, and the Cayugas insisted that the Delawares remain quietly at home and not interfere with the army's advance, Tamaqua and his followers were equally adamant that the British turn around and go home. Post conceded that the "Indians concern themselves very much about the affair of land," noting that they were persistently "jealous, and afraid the English will take their land." And, in his response to Forbes's message—one represented by two white strings of wampum tied together, a symbol of peace and unity— Tamaqua calmly but firmly warned the general, "in a most soft, loving and friendly manner, to go back over the mountain, and to stay there." In return Tamaqua pledged that, "if you do that, I will use it for an argument to argue [for peace] with other nations." Employing council metaphors, Tamaqua repeated the British message of "opening a road" between the Delawares and Pennsylvania—an act of peace. By taking his army back east Forbes would literally clear the road he had made and ensure that nothing stood in the way of peace. Others were more direct. Keekyuscung, "one of the chief counsellors," flatly stated that "all the nations had jointly agreed to defend their hunting place at Allegheny, and suffer nobody to settle there." And, since the natives "are very much inclined to the English interest," he urged both Denny and Forbes to prevent settlements beyond the mountains because "if they staid and settled there, all the nations would be against them; and he was afraid it would be a great war." In the middle of this sometimes tense discourse, on November 25, Tamaqua informed Post "that the English had the field": Forbes had occupied the burning ruins of Fort Duquesne.[30]

The news of Forbes's arrival at the Forks of the Ohio excited the British and Iroquois but seems not to have convinced the Delawares they ought to quickly make peace. Indeed, on November 27 "while we waited all day for an answer" to Denny's and Forbes's messages, Post learned that the Indians were "busy all day long" in discussions among themselves. Noticing Post's eagerness to be on his way, Tamaqua told him "it [peace] is a great matter, and wants much consideration." Explaining that all three of the Delaware clans in the Ohio Country "must separately agree among ourselves," Tamaqua asked for a private rereading of the messages.[31] Having heard from Denny, Forbes, Pisquetomen, and the Cayugas, on November 28 the assembled natives offered a positive response to the offer of peace. Having stressed their determination of keep the Ohio Country as their own and enjoining the British to treat them with the same respect and generosity as had the French, the Delawares agreed to sit by and not interfere with the army. They embraced the "chain of friendship" that formerly linked them to Pennsylvania. Yet Tamaqua also made it clear that peace was a process, not a decision reached in a moment. He pledged to carry his "good news" to surrounding natives but urged the British to "be strong" and not jeopardize peace efforts by any rash or foolhardy actions like keeping an army in the west or permitting settlers west of the Alleghenies. This was Tamaqua's supreme moment; after months of promoting peace at home, supported by his brothers and other headmen like Keekyuscung, he had brought warriors and headmen to agreement that they should accept British peace offers. Moreover, he had positioned himself as the region's peacemaker. In this, he and his people were certainly gambling that the British would recognize native sovereignty over their lands; that both Denny and Forbes would be as good as their words and that those words would be translated into meaningful actions. In effect, what Tamaqua and his people sought, and appeared to obtain, was an agreement to honor the status quo antebellum; an agreement to turn the clock back to 1750, before the Ohio Company, before the French militarized the region, before Braddock, Penns's Creek, and Kittanning. That the Iroquois had secured the western lands that the Delawares and their neighbors occupied mattered little. Unlike Teedyuscung's people, who lived at Wyoming at the sufferance of the Iroquois, the Delawares and other Ohio Indians, including Senecas, had pioneered the region and taken it as their own, regardless of the Six Nations' expansive claims. Before the Albany sale, the land west of the Susquehanna River and especially land lying beyond the

Alleghenies had been acknowledged as Iroquois territory by colonial governments hoping to someday profit from them. The peoples living there, especially the western Delawares, had acted and gained recognition as separate nations, turning distance into de facto sovereignty, unlike in the case of Teedyuscung and his people. The Iroquois were careful to stay out of Ohio Country affairs, and indeed, at the Kuskuskies, the Cayugas had addressed the Delawares as "cousins"—not "nephews."[32]

Implicit in the messages and discussions at the Kuskuskies was the idea of a boundary. By warning Forbes to go back east and not stray into lands "beyond the mountains" or "at Allegheny," Tamaqua and his supporters were drawing their own line on their mental map of the Ohio Country, insisting that the region be occupied exclusively by natives. Remembering the efforts by the Virginians to buy and settle land near the Forks and with Forbes's now victorious army at the ruins of Fort Duquesne, the Delawares did their best to underscore the point that land was not negotiable, forts and armies were unacceptable, only traders offering good terms would be welcome in Ohio towns. This issue of boundaries—first raised at Easton and the Kuskuskies—would remain the central issue in British-Indian affairs for over a decade.[33]

Post promised that he would convey the Delawares' declaration that the Ohio Country was off-limits to the British. Laden with messages and wampum belts, Post and his companions set off for the Forks of the Ohio where they hoped to find Forbes and submit a report of all they had heard and seen. Stray horses and bad weather conspired to delay them; on December 3, while he waited to cross the Allegheny River, Post "saw the general march off from Pittsburg." His attempts to overtake and speak to the dying Forbes failed, and Post had to be content with leaving a copy of his journal and memoranda. With Forbes gone, Indian affairs fell to Henry Bouquet, who held a council with the Delawares at the Forks on December 4. Only later did Post learn of Bouquet's "displeasure" with the Delawares' insistence that the army go home. Bouquet wanted the Indians to "alter their mind," but, according to Post, the Delawares "had no inclination" to do so. The Delawares did agree to the small garrison established on the Monongahela River, not far from Fort Duquesne, but only after Bouquet had reaffirmed British intent to open a "large and extensive Trade with you." Tamaqua also confirmed his commitment to spread news of peace to other nations to the west. At the same time, however, he subtly underscored the Delawares' position when he replied to Bouquet's request that the Indians keep the garrison informed of any French moves against them. Tamaqua assured him that "No Body can come across our Country without our Knowledge." He hastened to add that he could not answer for those nations still at war with the British. He pointedly insisted "that None of your People straggle out in the Woods." The garrison would be responsible for its own security against any raiding parties that escaped Delaware notice.[34]

While traveling south toward the Forks, Post passed through Saucunk and outlying hamlets. Saucunk was where the emissary had found the Delawares visibly angry on his first visit. He still encountered skeptical people in December. He also discovered that the Shawnee towns in the vicinity, notably Logstown, were "empty of people," and large fields of corn "stands ungathered." And while the British had "come themselves" to make peace, there was still the matter of the soldiers who also arrived. Bouquet's repeated assurances on Forbes's behalf that "We are not come here to take Possession of your hunting Country" and his observation that Forbes had indeed turned around with the army (less the garrison at the Forks and those along the road) and "marched away . . . out of your hunting Country" sounded good, but once again words and actions clashed. The Delawares had made a point to emphasize that the mountains were the border between them and the British; but Bouquet only promised not to cross the Ohio River. And, of course, there were those garrisons. The "road" to the council fire at Philadelphia continued to be occupied by soldiers, and they, not the promised trade, were the reality as the year 1758 ended.[35]

TEN

Loyalhannon and Fort Duquesne

* * *

OCTOBER–NOVEMBER 1758

I do myself the Honour of acquainting you that it has pleased God to crown His Majesty's Arms with Success over all His Enemies upon the Ohio, by my having obliged the Enemy to Burn and abandon Fort Du Quesne.
—FORBES TO PITT, PITTSBOURGH, NOVEMBER 1758

While the Easton conference slowly moved forward, Forbes was facing the crisis of the campaign. His army was stalled at Loyalhannon, and he admitted to William Pitt that he could not "form any judgement, how I am to extricate myself," pointing out that "every thing depends upon the Weather, which snows and rains frightfully." To make matters worse, Forbes was still at Raystown, several days behind the bulk of his army. He candidly admitted to Pitt that what he needed most of all was time, "a thing at present so precious to me, that I have none to spare." With his army sitting in a rain-sodden camp at the end of a supply line that could snap at any moment, Forbes faced three choices, each of which carried its own risks: "to risque every thing, and march to the Enemy's Fort, to retreat across the Alleganey if the provincials leave me, or maintain myself where I am to the Spring." Deciding to leave Raystown, even though "the weather did not mend," he added a short postscript from "Camp Top of the Alleghaney Mountain" on October 20, telling Pitt that "I thought it necessary to march forward, to embrace the first opportunity."[1]

* * *

The army that Forbes reached on November 2 was not the aggressive force he expected to lead. Having been bested twice by smaller French and

Indian forces, Forbes's regulars and provincials were not as sure of victory as they may have been when they began their march when the weather had been warm, if rainy, and the food adequate, if monotonous. Now, nearly six months later, these troops were deep in enemy country, effectively blind since the disappearance of most of their southern Indian allies, slowed to a crawl by the snow and rain of the coming winter, and beginning to feel the pinch of dependence on a supply line that now stretched for two hundred miles. Defeat, boredom, fear of what lay beyond the retrenchments at Loyalhannon, and for some, the certainty that in one more month their enlistments—and ordeals—would be over, all hung over a force of men, women, and children also faced with the sickness that came from poorly healed wounds, overcrowding, cold weather, and exposure. This army was noticeably smaller than the one that had set off from Lancaster and Carlisle months earlier. Normal attrition, occasional desertions, some battle casualties, but most of all the need to maintain garrisons and working parties on the road meant declining numbers, with correspondingly more work for those still in the ranks.[2]

Forbes notified the governor of Virginia of his arrival at Loyalhannon, telling him that "I am now here with all the Army I can expect." That army, according to the last surviving return, now consisted of 4,674 officers, staff, and enlisted men. Of that number only 2,528 enlisted men were available for duty; 351 more were sick but still in the ranks, and 251 others were in hospitals at both Loyalhannon and Raystown. Another 970 men occupied Raystown and the forts on Pennsylvania's frontier, and 572 were "on command" assigned to road repairs or the garrisons of the hastily built small posts like Fort Dewart along the road. More revealing were the numbers available from each of Forbes's regiments: the Highlanders had only 582 men fit, the Royal Americans just 256—just 838 regulars in all as against 798 men in the two Virginia regiments and 589 from Pennsylvania and the Lower Counties. There were a mere 41 men from North Carolina still available for duty. The artillery, which would have been counted separately, may have added about 100 officers and men, including the Pennsylvanians. With the 602 men listed as sick, more than 1 in 10 of Forbes's soldiers were unfit for serious duty. To accommodate the rising number of sick, soldiers were busy building "an Hospital" that was to adjoin "The Virginians and Opposite to the Pensilvania Hospital." They also helped relocate the men from the Maryland hospital. It had been overrun on October 12; now the inmates would be housed within the inner fort. There are no comparable figures reflecting the numbers or health of the army's many civilians: wives, children, servants, slaves, contractors. The sick list, both military and civilian, would only grow while the army continued to occupy the wet, filthy encampment.[3]

How to proceed? How to make the best use of whatever time remained was the issue foremost in the minds of Forbes and his senior officers. None of the choices Forbes outlined for Pitt was without risk. Moving ahead meant mustering enough men and supplies to give such a risky undertaking a reasonable chance of success. Not only would the attacking force need food, transport, and munitions, but so would any troops left to occupy Fort Duquesne once the French were beaten. The magnitude of such an undertaking was reflected in some calculations made by Bouquet. Planning to use three thousand troops for a winter attack on Fort Duquesne, Bouquet calculated that he would need six weeks' worth of food for the expedition and another six months' supply for whatever garrison was left at the fort once the French were driven out. In addition, he wanted each man to have extra clothing, including an overcoat, shoes, and stockings. A detailed breakdown revealed that he planned to supply his force on half rations (only 3–4 pounds of bread and meat per week); even so he estimated that he would have to carry some 75,600 pounds of provisions—not including what would be left behind for a new garrison. Finally, to compensate for the lack of reliable draft and packhorses, he wanted to dam Loyalhannon Creek for a sawmill that would turn out the necessary lumber for flat-bottomed boats called bateaux that could carry the expedition by water to the Kiskiminetas River, then into the Allegheny River above Fort Duquesne.[4]

Forbes reported on October 24 that he now had enough food to last until November 20, but he did not have nearly enough forage, and securing these supplies meant relying on civilians to make good their agreements with the quartermasters. Beyond this assessment, there is no detailed information about how much food was on hand at Loyalhannon or on the road. Moreover, a prolonged spell of bad weather could mean disaster if wagons could not get through. Bouquet himself later calculated that five thousand men (roughly the size of Forbes's army) would consume 45,000 pounds of flour and 25,000 pounds of salt pork per week. On December 15, the provisions contractors had on hand at Lancaster 263,000 pounds of flour in bulk and barrels, but only 21,600 pounds of pork and 25,000 pounds of beef. By early December, then, the logistical pipeline would be running dry with little or nothing more to be expected until the next harvest. Clearly, any advance by a large force risked running low on food, let alone the forage to power the animals intended to carry provisions for the troops, as well as their ammunition, medical supplies, and other necessaries.[5]

The same relentless arithmetic would also hold if Forbes decided to keep any part of his army in the west at Raystown and Loyalhannon over the winter. The attraction, of course, was that he would not lose ground—or time— once the 1759 campaign season opened. The threat, again, was starvation. His troops would be virtually immobilized by winter weather, dug in at the end of a road that would be impassable until the following spring. And not only would food become a serious problem, so too would clothing and equipment, especially cutting tools like saws and axes that would be needed to harvest the acres of firewood needed by the troops. The third option— retreat "across the Alleghaney"—was, from every standpoint, the worst. Forbes would have to surrender the initiative and hope that the French and Indians would be as winter-bound as his own troops. He would need to maintain garrisons from Loyalhannon back to Carlisle in order to protect the road; here again, logistics would be a nightmare. Worse, his army would literally vanish: his precious few regulars would be in the forts while many of his provincials would go home as their enlistments expired in December. It had taken all of his energy to collect men, materiel, and supplies for the current campaign; there was no guarantee he would be able to do the same the following year. Many provincials, having had a good long taste of military life, might refuse to reenlist. Provincial assemblies, jealous of their prerogatives and sensitive to the need for raising more revenue through loans and taxes, might simply refuse to cooperate, as the Maryland Assembly had done this year. With these possibilities in mind, Forbes was already writing to colonial governors, entreating them to extend the service of their troops in the event that he could not complete the campaign before December.[6]

Bouquet's plan evidently gained little traction, though his emphasis on a continued advance meshed well with Forbes's own ideas. Nearly a week after Bouquet's proposals, on November 11, Forbes called a formal council of war that included all of his regimental commanders as well as St. Clair. Forbes offered three brief arguments in favor of an advance: "The hope of driving the enemy from the Ohio" and securing the country for Britain; "the hope of getting rid of the Indians . . . who continually overrun and ravage our provinces" (here Forbes was referring to the Great Lakes Indians and mission Iroquois who "have settled along this [Ohio] river"); and finally, "the hope of justifying the expenses of the expedition" to the colonial governments and taxpayers. Some of his subordinates enumerated no fewer than seven reasons not to proceed. Among these logistics loomed large: the "scarcity of provisions and uncertainty of obtaining any" and the consequent "impossibility" of providing this post with provisions for the winter should the army continue consuming food at the present rate. Some also questioned whether they could hold Fort Duquesne if they were lucky enough to take it with troops who lacked winter clothing. Moreover, a march to the Ohio risked losing much of the army's artillery if the weather or a defeat caused the army to return to Loyalhannon. The final argument against an advance was the risk of defeat, "which would cause us to lose the advantages we had acquired" and which "would bring down upon us" not only the Great Lakes Indians, "but also those who have made peace at the Treaty of Easton." Without explicitly mentioning a retreat, the council concluded that "the risks being so obviously greater than the advantages, there is no doubt as to the sole course that prudence dictates."[7]

As if to underscore the problems outlined by his council of war, on November 12 Forbes ordered the quartermasters to begin issuing half rations. He was, according to public orders, "apprehensive that the Stock of flowr at Loyall Hannon may fall Short," and he directed that each man now received "½ lb. flower & 1 ½ lbs fresh Beef . . . each day." The slight increase in the meat ration offset the reduction in bread but even that might not last beyond mid-November. Underscoring the unsettled prospects for the immediate future, the adjustment in rations could also reflect a prudent economy in anticipation of a move forward or it may just as well have been an effort to stretch supplies as long as possible in order to maintain a garrison at Loyalhannon as provincial enlistments expired. In either case, the order confirmed that critical supplies were now becoming scarce as contractors' stores ran low and as winter weather made shipment difficult if not impossible.[8]

Should he decide to hold what he had gained this year, Forbes faced another problem. The hastily built forts of wood and earth were deteriorating quickly from the weather and neglect. As the army moved forward, the Forts Littleton, Loudoun, and Raystown were left to small garrisons without the means to make the necessary repairs. Even the army's main camp at Loyalhannon was of questionable value as a defensive bastion in the event of a French attack. Still not complete in mid-November, the works were, in the opinion of his engineers, in such a state that "it was Impossible to put this Place in Such a Condition" that it could withstand a serious attack, regardless of how many men were put to work. Indeed, Captain Gordon offered the opinion that the present works could not withstand "a Battery of Six Six Pounders," light field guns not normally effective against fortifications. The engineers did suggest that hasty repairs could be made so that the fort "might be Able to Resist and be proof from Shot of Small Pieces of Cannon," but they quickly added that "One Coehorn Mortar would be Sufficient to Destroy the Place by Blowing up the Magazine."[9]

There was much to discourage both Forbes and his senior officers, and the decision not to press forward may have been a foregone conclusion. Two of the participants in the council of war, Colonels Washington and Byrd, may nevertheless have felt a sense of vindication. Both had been actively advocating for Braddock's Road, and the council's views seemed to underscore their arguments that the new road was a failure and a waste of time and resources. Even after Forbes had discovered Washington's "unguarded" comments about him, both Virginians continued to agitate for the Virginia route. By October, however, it must have been clear to Byrd and Washington that Forbes would stick to his original plan; Washington and the rest of his regiment were ordered to Raystown and from there marched with the balance of the army to Loyalhannon, arriving at the camp by October 23. By pulling Washington's troops out of Fort Cumberland, Forbes signaled that he had decisively turned away from Braddock's Road, hoping only that the few troops there had kept the French guessing about his real plan. At the same time, by ordering Washington to join the main army, Forbes sent a message to the colonel: however much Washington had violated proper behavior by placing Virginia's interests above the army's, Forbes still valued his presence. In effect, he was offering Washington a chance to redeem himself. The message was not lost on the colonel who had repeatedly asked to join the main army, fearing that he would be stuck in a backwater while the campaign reached its climax.[10]

In a letter to Abercromby Forbes complained that "this small body of people" (his army) was subject to "frequent skirmishes and allarms," reminders that the French were still active and perhaps intent on another effort to cripple his advance. These annoyances were of little consequence, except for the events on the late afternoon of November 12. Forbes mentioned it only as part of a larger report to Abercromby. On that day, according to Forbes, some two hundred French and Indians "came to attack our live Cattle and horses." When they were detected by outposts or the grass guards, Forbes immediately "sent 500 men to give them chace" and an equal number to attempt to surround the enemy. What happened next is unclear and still open to interpretation. According to a letter sent from Loyalhannon and reprinted in the *Pennsylvania Gazette*, Washington led the initial party of Virginians and encountered the French some three miles west of the encampment. The resulting gunfire prompted the second sortie, also Virginians from Washington's regiment led by Lieutenant-Colonel George Mercer. In the gathering dusk and mist along the creek bottom, the two forces collided and fired into each other. Before Washington could get between the parties and stop the firing at least thirteen soldiers were killed, including Lieutenant Evans of the Royal Americans, and an unknown number wounded. Despite the confusion

Washington's men managed to take three prisoners. It was these prisoners, in fact, that triggered the shooting: seeing people dressed as Indians, Mercer's people assumed they were the enemy and opened fire.[11]

While his report attempted to downplay the severity of the encounter, saying that only "a few Shot were exchanged," Forbes reported that two officers—one of whom was Evans—and some thirty-eight soldiers were either killed or reported missing, along with an unspecified number of wounded. Washington recorded nothing at the time regarding the incident. The only reference is in his orderly book, that on November 12, his regiment was warned that a 450-man detachment would depart the next morning "to the Ground where the Skirmish was this Evening." They were to carry "a proportion of Spades in Order to Enter the Dead Bodies." Decades later, in 1787, he provided a short account of his service during the war. He then referred to the incident as "a circumstance," which "involved the life of G.W. in as much jeopardy as it had ever been before or since." According to Washington, it was Mercer's detachment that marched first, and their firing on the French prompted Washington to ask Forbes for permission to lead out another party to Mercer's support. These "Volunteers" must have included Evans of the Royal Americans. Following the sound of the skirmish in the gathering dark, Washington said he sent men ahead to alert Mercer of his arrival but, "it being near dusk, and the intelligence not having been fully dissiminated among Colo. Mercers Corps," the latter mistook Washington's force for the French and "commenced a heavy fire upon the relieving party which drew fire in return." Only after Washington stepped between the two detachments "knocking up" their muskets "with his sword" did the shooting stop. His only other comment was that there "several privates" killed "and many wounded."[12]

In many respects, the skirmish on November 12 was yet another example of how Forbes's troops remained unreliable. Some of these Virginians had been with Grant and witnessed the French attack in October, and although Washington remembered that both detachments involved had properly "presented" arms with their muskets (the position just prior to leveling the weapons to fire), this bit of parade-ground exactitude belied a persistent nervousness, perhaps unreliability, among the troops that echoed what had occurred in September and then again the following month. Indeed, these Virginians may have inflicted more casualties on themselves than the French did on those two earlier occasions. It was certainly a traumatic experience that no one wished to recall in detail either at the time or for years afterward. For Forbes, at least, it was a further reminder of the risks he ran in bringing his army of "raw" troops to a climactic battle with the French.[13]

As much as this skirmish again raised troubling issues about the army, the British did manage to secure three prisoners: two native women and a colonist named Johnson. However Johnson found himself at Loyalhannon (as a slave or adoptee of one of the Indians, as a turncoat, or as someone who sensed an opportunity to flee his captors), the news he offered was electrifying and changed the course of the campaign. According to Forbes, "we have had the only Intelligence of the Enemys strength" thanks to Johnson who told his new captors that most of the French and Indian forces had indeed left Fort Duquesne after the October attack "imagining," according to the version picked up by Governor Sharpe, "that General Forbes would not be able to proceed . . . for want of Horses," which the French had either killed or driven off. Emboldened by this news and by awareness that the Delawares would pursue the peace initiatives, Forbes lost little time in acting. Within a day he had ordered out large detachments of provincials under Lieutenant-Colonel John Armstrong to open a road beyond the old advanced camp on Chestnut Ridge. On November 13, he ordered "The line [the army] to hold themselves in readiness to March at an Hours warning" and required that officers strictly inspect their troops' ammunition and to replace anything found defective. The following day orders explained that "the Circumstances of the times require that a Disposition be immediately made of the Troops" and set out a new tactical organization, ordering that the troops leave their tents at Loyalhannon under guard. Events of November 12 marked the second critical turning point in the campaign. Finally, the army was told that the selected troops would march on November 15.[14]

The new organization for the troops in the field suggests that Forbes had in mind a swift march with a select force whose aim was to seize the fort or at least isolate it. Again, using Turpin de Crissé's analogy of a military advance and a siege operation, Forbes would be launching a sortie designed to gain the enemy's works. Such an advance put a premium on speed. The troops would carry a maximum amount of ammunition (each enlisted man was allotted eighty rounds) and only eight days' worth of food; heavy wagons loaded with tents and other camp gear would be left behind in favor of packhorses and necessary ammunition wagons from the artillery park. The artillery itself would also be limited. Bouquet wrote of a "light-train of Artillery" in case they met the French in the field. Later evidence mentions only a single howitzer at the Forks. The number of guns would in any event be limited by the availability of draft horses. The force, some twenty-three hundred men representing the fittest men available in each regiment, was organized into three brigades. That on the right would be led by Washington and consist of his own Virginia Regiment, two companies of workmen to help cut a road, and the ad hoc light infantry battalion led by Lieutenant-Colonel Dagworthy. The center brigade was Montgomery's with his Highlanders and Byrd's Virginia Regiment; they would also escort the artillery. The left brigade would be led by Bouquet and consist of his Royal Americans and the Pennsylvania Regiment. Engineers were assigned to each brigade to supervise construction. Each brigade was also given a "brigade major," the senior administrative officer and assistant to each commander. A small reserve, commanded by Colonel James Burd, would include two hundred of his Pennsylvanians, along with equal numbers of Highlanders and Virginians.[15]

The organization of the army hammered out by Forbes, Bouquet, and Halkett was made easier by a plan submitted by Colonel Washington. Over a month earlier at Raystown, Forbes had asked his regimental commanders to submit proposals for a march to Fort Duquesne. If others did tender plans, they have not survived; Washington's did, however, and it offers a detailed proposal for an "Order of March" that Forbes adopted. Drawing on his own and others' experience fighting the French and their native allies, Washington designed a march that took into account the likelihood of attack and ambush as well as the need for a rapid advance: he eschewed wagons except those attached to the hefty artillery train included in his organization. He deliberately organized the force so that the troops could quickly move from line of march to line of battle. Washington also emphasized the need for close control all the way down to sergeants' and corporals' commands and that marching discipline would include flanking parties and scouts to provide early warning of the enemy. In the event of a French attack he proposed that the troops advance and surround the enemy: Braddock's defeat in reverse. Vivid memories of what had happened to Braddock's army seem to have been at the heart of Washington's plan. For example, calling for the army to advance and surround the enemy, Washington noted that such a move is "a practice different from any thing they have ever yet experience'd from Us" and would therefore succeed. It was a well-conceived plan, and Forbes made only minor adjustments: instead of Washington's four thousand men, Forbes could muster a little over two thousand. Forbes also deliberately ordered the artillery to follow as best it could; he took little ordnance with him fearing that the lumbering train would only slow the march. By reaching and surrounding Fort Duquesne, he could secure the field until his big guns arrived under escort; in the meantime, a single howitzer or a couple of light field guns would be sufficient to threaten the fort.[16]

Even with a practicable plan from Washington and the captive Johnson's news regarding the French garrison, Forbes was still uneasy, telling Abercromby that "I am in the greatest anxiety how to proceed in case of Success." Now thinking beyond the capture of Fort Duquesne, Forbes faced a new

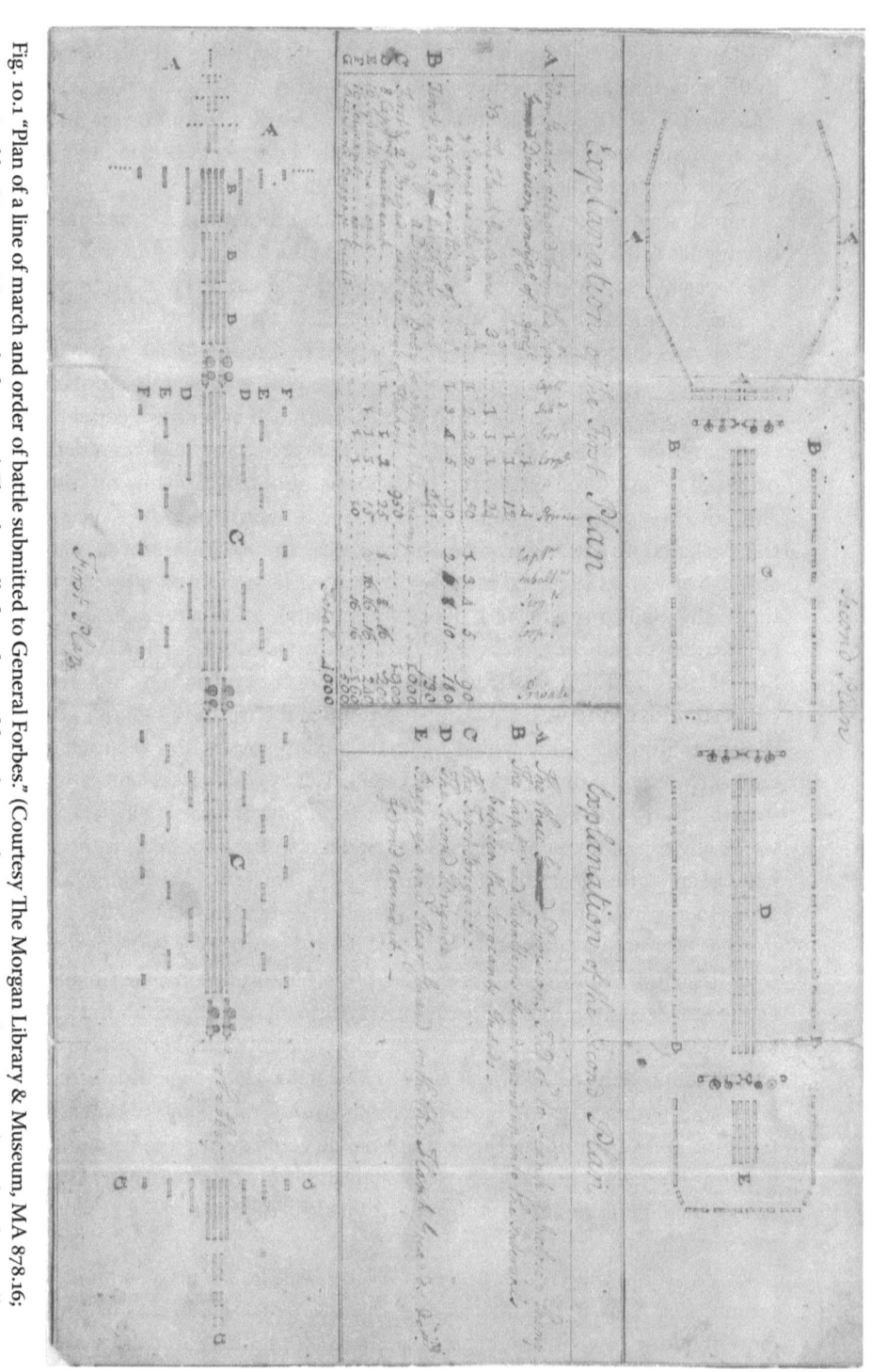

Fig. 10.1 "Plan of a line of march and order of battle submitted to General Forbes." (Courtesy The Morgan Library & Museum, MA 878.16; acquired by Pierpont Morgan before 1913.) The plan calls for a force of four thousand men, suggesting that it was adapted to the smaller force that finally set off for Fort Duquesne in November 1758. At the top and bottom are diagrams for two alternative lines of march; the bottom plan resembles the order of march of Braddock's force on July 9, 1755.

challenge. What, if anything, should he do after taking the fort? Should he attempt a further advance up the Allegheny River and aim at the French forts at Venango, Le Boeuf, and Presqu'Ile? Or should he remain where he was? His worries were driven by a lack of positive orders but also by his own failing health. By mid-November Forbes was so weak he could only travel any distance in a litter carried between two horses. If observers like Colonel Burd thought Forbes was on the mend, the general admitted that his "State of Health continues precarious," but he thought he could continue on despite his ailments. Yet he began to hedge, telling Abercromby that "in the present situation of my health" he had done all he could to complete the campaign. He also began to doubt he would survive, telling Denny "that *if* I get to Philadelphia," he hoped to be able to restore "a Health that I run the risque of ruining" in completing the campaign. He also asked his commanders to erect small shelters with chimneys for him along the line of march. By the time he reached the Forks, he had been "seized with an inflammation in my stomach, Midriff and Liver, the sharpest and most severe of all distempers."[17]

The weather refused to cooperate. The threat of snow on November 11 was enough to cause worries about losing the artillery as it tried to make its way from Raystown to Loyalhannon. The following days brought cold raw weather as the troops struggled to move ahead. As they neared their objective, the soldiers faced deep snow and cold so severe that regiments had to encamp in the woods rather than face exposure on open ground. And, as the army worked to cut a road and keep itself together, the combination of snow and cold finally broke its supply line, forcing the men to go without regular rations "for several days."[18]

* * *

Since June, when most of his Cherokee fighters had rebelled against their treatment and left for home, Forbes had continued to hope for a restoration of British-Cherokee cooperation. That hope came to rest on one man, Attakullakulla, known to the British as the Little Carpenter. This most British-leaning of all the Cherokee headmen would certainly arrive and put things to rights. In June, as cooperation withered away, Forbes and others anticipated Attakullakulla's impending arrival at the army. Forbes hoped that he would arrive sooner than later and help rally disaffected warriors, believing that his presence would have the desired effect on natives who were openly defying the British. Those hopes were frustrated as weeks turned into months and still Attakullakulla failed to appear. In August Colonel William Byrd learned that Attakullakulla was at Winchester and that he and his men planned to join the army in the autumn for four months; only a shaman who warned of sickness and death if they arrived any earlier kept the Cherokees back. Finally, Forbes learned that Attakullakulla with some sixty-three of his men, joined by an equal number of Catawbas led by their headman, Hagler, had left Winchester for Raystown, setting up what would be Forbes's last encounter with his native fighters.[19]

The natives arrived at Raystown by October 15, and any hope Forbes may have had for reconciliation were quickly dashed. Instead of a cooperative ally Forbes met a native leader who, along with his followers, "appear to be bullying us in to a mean complyance with their most sordid and avaritious demands," threatening to go home if their terms were not met. It was May and June all over again, with natives insisting on gifts and treatment as equals, while Forbes still insisted on treating them as auxiliaries. Although nothing was decided at Raystown, Forbes began to refer to Attakullakulla facetiously as "the Famous Little Carpenter," while to Abercromby he complained about having to listen to Attakullakulla's "stupid speeches" and referred to him "as great a Rascal to the full as any of his companions." A temporary improvement in his health may have raised Forbes's spirits enough for him to believe he had, after all, persuaded the Cherokees to remain with the army. Yet, in reality, nothing had changed on either side: the British and Indian war was still held hostage by colliding expectations and vastly different meanings of cooperation. Forbes tried once more to impress Attakullakulla and his followers. Asking them to join the main army at Loyalhannon, Forbes arranged that the garrison should fire "Seven Guns" to honor the Cherokee when he arrived on November 2.[20]

Attakullakulla and his men stayed with the army for another two weeks, encamped near Loyalhannon Creek to the west of the army. Whatever the natives heard or saw while they were there is now lost, but it is clear that the friction between them and Forbes only grew worse. Perhaps, as one historian has recently suggested, Attakullakulla, discovering so few natives with the army, simply decided that his services were no longer required. We do not know whether the Cherokees were involved in operations with the army or how they received the news of the accidental collision of the Virginians only a few miles farther west. By November 13, the army was rapidly making arrangements to march to the Forks, and no more notice would have been taken of these Indians any more than the handful of Iroquois that arrived with Croghan. Forbes, consumed by the impending march and his own continuing doubts, may have refused to have any more to do with negotiations over how and when Attakullakulla and his followers would participate in the campaign. The general left Loyalhannon on November 18, and one day later, while at the "New Camp" on the way to Fort Duquesne, Forbes gave vent to his pent-up frustrations when dealing with Indians. In a letter to Colonel James Burd he railed at the "villainous desertion" of the Cherokees. The letter is mutilated but clearly expresses rage at what Forbes believed was Attakullakulla's betrayal; he was "Astonished and amazed" about "the methods he [Attakullakulla] had used" "under the Cloak of Friendship" and resented being deprived of native help "at so very critical a time." The word "deserted" holds a key to Forbes's thinking and the inherent weakness in British-Cherokee cooperation. Instead of treating these men as equals, as they expected, Forbes continued to view them as common soldiers, no different from the regulars or provincials he commanded. Moreover, while Attakullakulla expected to be handsomely rewarded for his participation, Forbes saw only a sham, an attempt to collect goods under false pretenses; he believed the headman and his followers were no better than thieves—indeed he was explicit in saying that they "robbed" him.[21]

We cannot know what exactly passed between Forbes and Attakullakulla during their few days together, but Forbes's long effort to recruit and use Cherokee warriors had clearly failed. As Attakullakulla and his men left the army, Forbes issued orders that the natives were to be pursued and arrested. He also insisted that these "deserters" be stripped of the horses, blankets, weapons, and all other goods they had been given. Forbes broadcast his confrontation to colonial governors; Governor Fauquier mentioned "the scandalous Behaviour of the Little Carpenter" in a letter to the governor of South Carolina. Less survives from the natives themselves. A Presbyterian missionary, Samuel Davies, living in the Cherokee towns, offers some insight. Writing in early 1759, he spoke of dreading Attakullakulla's return because of the way he was treated "to the northward." News of the confrontation with Forbes traveled quickly. Davies also learned from another headman, Hop, that Attakullakulla had gone north not to make war but to broker a peace between British and French. Hop openly "railed much agt Virginia," saying that the Cherokees "hate all that comes from it." Attakullakulla may, in fact, have been trying to keep peace at home. The Cherokees continued to be divided over cooperation with the British, especially in the face of continuing mistreatment by Virginia traders and the still fresh experiences of warriors running a gauntlet of angry settlers just to join Forbes's army. Attakullakulla may have hoped that Forbes would show a different attitude toward his native partners, one that the headman could take home with him in discussions with those like Hop who were of a different mind. If so, he was clearly disappointed. Indeed, Forbes's treatment of Attakullakulla served only to reinforce anti-British sentiment in the Cherokee towns, especially when the natives learned firsthand from the headman that "his arms had been taken from him; that he was like a child & no man." By disarming Attakullakulla and his followers the British had unmanned them; confiscating the other gifts was simply salt rubbed into an open wound. As the army pushed on to Fort Duquesne, then, the British and Indian war in the Ohio Country had completely collapsed; by the time he reached the Forks, Forbes's army included only a handful of warriors under Croghan and a small number of Catawbas.[22]

* * *

When Forbes left Loyalhannon on November 18, much of his army had been on the move for several days; he hoped to move quickly, making a systematic orderly advance. On November 13 he had ordered Armstrong's Pennsylvanians to move ahead and build a new camp for the army about ten miles beyond the now abandoned advanced post of Chestnut Ridge. This was the "New Camp" where Forbes and Attakullakulla had their final showdown. In the meantime, men from Washington's brigade began cutting a crude road following an old trading path that passed through Loyalhannon toward the Forks—the same path followed by Grant's force in September—until they met Armstrong's troops. At the New Camp, thought to be twenty-two miles from Loyalhannon, a rude encampment would be cleared and protected by hastily built redoubts. The "road" that was created by this rapid march was little more than a strip of roughly cleared ground. With time now the pressing issue, workmen cut down trees, but left stumps and brush in their haste to advance. So quickly and poorly was this work done that Forbes had to order his slow-moving artillery train to make the necessary repairs, clearing stumps, widening the path to accommodate gun carriages, and building whatever bridges were needed over low ground. In the meantime, an escort of eighty-three officers and men was sent from Loyalhannon with a herd of cattle for the advancing force, whose own rations were about used up. Compared to the slow methodical advance from Carlisle to Loyalhannon, this final phase of the campaign began as more of a mad dash, animated both by knowledge of the greatly weakened French and by the onset of winter and the looming end of provincial enlistments. Time, as Forbes reminded Pitt, continued to be his greatest enemy.[23]

Inevitably, problems arose and the march slowed down. Armstrong's men cut the road in the wrong place, which led Bouquet to order Shelby's Maryland volunteers to blaze the correct route and to redirect Armstrong's men accordingly. Dull and broken tools, miserable weather, and simple exhaustion also slowed the pace. Washington's brigade only made it as far as the advanced camp on the first day and continued to lag behind Armstrong's force; lack of saws and axes accounted for much of the delay. Bouquet learned on November 16 that Armstrong's camp was only sixteen miles from Loyalhannon. Convinced that such slow progress "does not answer our purpose," Bouquet urged that Washington join forces with the Pennsylvanians to push the road ahead at a faster rate. Washington admitted that "I have been sadly puzzled for want of a guide," remarking that "the Service has suffered by it." Other commanders were worried about diminished rations, especially beef. Yet the troops continued to make headway; by the evening of November 17, Washington could report that he had "opened the Road between 7 & 8 miles to-day" and was nearing Armstrong's force. More ominously, desertion began to increase. It was particularly rife among the Lower County companies, and some of those who ran had been working with Lieutenant Bassett on the road. Accidents, sickness, and exposure also took a steady toll of the men.[24]

Washington finally caught up with Armstrong's workmen on November 18. His slow march from Chestnut Ridge was partly because of the confusion over the route Armstrong was taking but also because of the need to stop and issue rations, including fresh beef from the cattle sent on from Loyalhannon. Washington reported that his men were in "high spirits" and "anxious to get on." Despite the miserable weather, hard work, and threat of short rations his troops began to sense that this was the last haul—for better or worse the campaign was coming to an end. Yet all the goodwill in the world would not make headway with dull, broken, or missing tools, all of which complicated roadwork, even with parties from Armstrong, Washington, and Montgomery behind him cutting toward each other. On the day Washington arrived at the "New Camp," the army's rendezvous, his brigade had only ninety-eight axes and two saws, with only two grindstones to keep them in repair. Moreover, the colonel discovered that "we have been greatly deceived with regard to the distance," telling Forbes that men in the ranks familiar with the region claimed they were still a good thirty miles from the Forks. Having reached Armstrong, Washington's brigade would now take the lead and establish a new encampment," Washington's Camp," near Turtle Creek and close to the old Braddock battlefield. Forbes, on the other hand, made good time from Loyalhannon. Having left on November 18, he arrived during the night of November 19–20 at "the Camp where they are Building the Redouts" (Armstrong's camp), nearly midway between Loyalhannon and Fort Duquesne.[25]

As they cut the road, Armstrong, Washington, and others were becoming acutely aware they were being watched; scouts reported seeing signs of a forty-man party "making toward Kiskamanetes [Kiskiminetas River]" north of the troops. Washington was glad to learn that "Mr. Croghan is so near at hand," though the agent brought few Indians with him, and Forbes wrote to tell Washington that the Cherokees "are not come up." In the absence of native trackers, "The Carolina & Maryland Companies [Dagworthy's men] are to be Exempt from Guard Dutys and Fatigues on Acct of their being us'd as Scouts." Forbes "never doubted of the enemys scouting partys discovering us," though he insisted that it was "highly necessary that wee discover them likewise." Secrecy was impossible; what Forbes and his senior officers feared most was an ambush. Washington's daily orders constantly reminded officers and men that they needed to be vigilant; as his brigade moved closer to Fort Duquesne, he had his forces camp in line of battle, sleeping "on their arms"—dressed and fully equipped to move at first notice.[26]

The French indeed were well aware of Forbes's advance. By November 19 their scouting parties could hear British troops at work on the road and also reported hearing cannon fire. Knowing the size of Forbes's army, Captain Lignery was under no illusions about the outcome of any confrontation. With Fort Frontenac gone, the garrisons in the entire Upper Country would "fall of themselves." At best, the French hoped to slow the British advance until the weather stopped it. Clearly, though, that was no longer possible. Despite the October raid the British were coming in the face of deteriorating weather. Moreover, Lignery undoubtedly wished for native allies as much as Washington did. The inability to acquire goods from Canada to serve as pay and gifts for allies helped alienate the Ohio Indians and weakened the French in the eyes of the formerly dependable Great Lakes warriors. By the time Armstrong's men began the final stretch of road, Lignery, with few native fighters and no hope of supplies, had to disband his forces. Those who came from the Illinois Country went back home; others, for lack of food, headed for Fort Niagara, Detroit, or the Canadian settlements. What remained was a skeleton force of no more than three hundred men, not nearly enough to stop Forbes before he reached Fort Duquesne. The French could only hope to marshal their forces early the following year and drive the British out of the Ohio Country.[27]

Logistics weighed on Forbes as well as the French; the difference lay in the fact that Forbes was in a better position to meet his army's short-term needs. He did so by taking some risks. Having decided that rations would have to be carried on packhorses, he cut down on the need for slow heavy wagons but this was at the cost of carrying less food. By November 19, Forbes took another calculated risk; with a poor road virtually unfit for heavy traffic and with many of his wagons immobilized at Loyalhannon, he ordered "40 of the Waggon Horses" just arrived at that post and "very fine" to be used as pack animals to push forward additional stores. A quick assessment of what was on hand and what could be carried satisfied Forbes that "wee have flour enough," and with several dozen scrawny cattle on the road, he would also have enough meat for his troops. His gamble worked. By November 21, Washington was able to order his men to draw three days' full rations (one pound of flour and one pound of meat), adding that "those that have received but half a Pound of Flour are to be Completed . . . with half a pound more." Forbes was able to restore full rations at a moment when his hard-pressed men were working furiously to cut their way to the Forks.[28]

Forbes organized his small army for battle while it remained at Washington's Camp on November 21. Washington's orderly book noted that the three brigades had been "newly formed and Divided" into tactical units. On November 22 the army continued its march, going as far as Bouquet's Camp on the northwest side of Turtle Creek. The route deliberately avoided the ground over which Braddock's troops had moved but suggests that Forbes may have been following a plan similar to the one devised by Braddock. In 1755 the plan called for British troops to cross the Allegheny River at Shannopin's Town while another force went straight to the Forks, surrounding the fort ("investing" it, in contemporary military language). Forbes had a general idea from scouting reports that the French had enlarged the fort along the Allegheny River, but how much and how strongly he did not know. Crossing part of his force would allow him to cover these new works. Yet, knowing that the French were few in number, he may also have planned to drive ahead and attack the fort, following the route taken by Grant's force, while sending troops toward Shannopin's Town to cut off the French retreat north to Lake Erie. Given his lack of heavy artillery and his insistence on a rapid march, the latter case seems more likely if what Forbes envisioned was a quick attack—an "escalade" that would seize the works before the French could mount much resistance. Whatever he had in mind, his final decision would have been dictated by the size and strength of the enemy works. Advance parties were already closing in on Fort Duquesne. One such detachment, following the Monongahela River, crossed Grant's battlefield where it found the still unburied dead from the September encounter. As word of this spread through the army, Forbes's untried men must have begun to worry about the possibility of yet another battle against the French and Indians, this time in the freezing and snowy weather.[29]

The scouts who crossed the grisly scene less than a half mile from Fort Duquesne also thought they heard sentries firing, an indication that the French seemed alert. These men also saw boats loaded with firewood, but no indication that the garrison had been reinforced. What the garrison might be up to was still unclear as the army made camp only about ten miles from the fort at what was now called "Bouquet's Camp." Anticipating both a battle and the behavior of edgy troops, orders went out that threatened two hundred lashes to any soldier who "fires his piece without his officer's orders." Washington had earlier forbidden any of the women attached to his troops to accompany the force, and this may have been an army-wide order. Women and children could only slow the advance and add to the army's burdens. Nevertheless, the army was plagued by other unwelcome followers in the form of dogs. These animals—pets, strays that simply followed a likely source of food, or trained to herd sheep—were clearly out of hand by the time the army got within striking distance of the Forks. Moreover, their barking and semiferal behavior became added irritations on the march. Army orders on November 24, therefore, decreed that "as the number of Dogs that follow the Troops are become a great Neausance," the army's provost was now authorized to hang any animal he might find running loose. The principle culprits were officers' pets, and the order encouraged these men to take advantage of horses going back to Loyalhannon to send their dogs down country or else keep them on a tight leash.[30]

A member of the Loyalhannon garrison reported that "on the 22d a heavy Firing was heard from [Fort Duquesne] at Loyalhanning." No one with the army that day heard any such noise or, if they did, left no record of it. The "firing" may have been the French destroying military stores, and acoustics may account for the odd fact that Forbes's men, only ten miles from the fort, failed to hear what was picked up at Loyalhannon, some fifty miles to the east. The French commander, Lignery, reported that, with the British so close and with only three hundred men, most of them sick and all of them hungry, he decided to abandon the post on November 23. Whatever happened on November 22–23, the campaign, now in its seventh month, ended on a decidedly anticlimactic note. Forbes had "the pleasure" of informing his superiors of the success of his "little Army" on November 26. His light troops under Dagworthy had occupied the burning ruins the previous evening, evidently just hours after the last of the French garrison departed. A day earlier Bouquet sent news to Pennsylvanian William Allen, boasting that the army had covered some fifty miles in five days, "a great diligence considering the Season, the Uncertainty of the Roads intirely unknown," as well as the labor involved in making a road. The feeling among the troops was reflected in a letter Washington sent on November 28, announcing the victory to Governor Fauquier. In it, he wrote that "the possession of this fort has been a matter of great surprize to the whole Army." While Forbes, Bouquet, and Washington congratulated themselves, each other, and their friends on what Bouquet called "the Reduction of this important place," many others probably felt a huge relief: the campaign ended without further fighting and losses, and with it now over, men could go home. The heavy artillery finally arrived on November 30. Having played but a small part in the campaign, the Royal Artillery would have been the center of attention had a siege taken place. Instead, the gun crews "fired some Howitzer Shells into the Face of the Works," remnants of earthen walls faced with wooden timbers nine inches thick. To their own satisfaction, if no one else's, the gunners "found that in firing but a few Hours, we must have destroyed the entire Face."[31]

Twenty-five hundred men gathered around the smoldering ruins, happy that the ordeal was over, many doubtless picking through Fort Duquesne looking for loot or souvenirs. The weather continued miserable with the deep snow and freezing temperatures characteristic of winter in the Ohio Country. All the more reason, then, for officers and men, soldiers and civilians, to look forward to the trip home. Yet there was still much to do. Forbes, as desperate as anyone to get back to Philadelphia, needed to remain for several days in the hope of meeting Tamaqua and other Ohio Indian leaders and to try to convince them that his victory was good for them as well as for the colonists. Fort Duquesne was an utter ruin, not worth the time and effort to rebuild; in order to hold the Forks, men would have to be assigned to the garrison and a new, albeit temporary, fort built to house them. These men would also need food, clothing, ammunition, and tools, which meant that the long chain of posts stretching back to Shippensburg and Carlisle would need to be held—and supplied. In the midst of planning all of this, Forbes knew that large numbers of men would insist on going home on December 1, regardless of the army's needs. For them (mostly Virginians and Pennsylvanians), the ruins of Fort Duquesne marked the end of military service, discipline, road building, and wondering when or where the French would strike next. For others, though, the campaign was not yet over.

ELEVEN

November 1758–March 1759

* * *

Give me leave therefore to congratulate you upon this Important Event, of having expelled the French from Fort Duquesne.
—FORBES TO ABERCROMBY AND AMHERST, NOVEMBER 1758

The days following the army's arrival at the Forks were busy ones. The army's mood is hard to gauge from the sources but probably included a mixture of relief—no siege, no enemy, and no chance of being killed while shivering in siege lines—and, for many, anxiety about wanting to go home. Whether the troops cheered or otherwise spontaneously celebrated is uncertain. One witness did, however, report that Forbes set aside November 26 as "a Day of publick Thanksgiving to Almighty God for our Success," followed by the traditional *feu de joie* as the army assembled in line of battle and fired a volley to mark their victory. There were also less pleasant tasks to perform. As the army marched to the Forks, the troops had passed through Grant's battlefield where the soldiers saw "Numbers of dead Bodies, within a Quarter of a Mile of the Fort." Parties were detailed to bury these remains, and others marched up the Monongahela to Braddock's field "to bury the Bones of our slaughtered Countrymen," including Major Halkett's younger brother and his father, colonel of the 44th Foot. Both the celebrating and the somber burial details were performed by officers and men who were already suffering from cold and exposure since, as one participant wrote, "We left all our Tents at Loyalhanning, and every Conveniency, except a Blanket and Knapsack."[1]

While his soldiers were exploring the remains of Fort Duquesne, burying the long-dead, or thinking about home, Forbes was grappling with other matters. One of these was his own deteriorating health; he started a long report to Pitt on November 27 but was unable to complete it until January 21, 1759. He also made known his desire to return to Britain, since, as the army's doctors told him, only a return home would offer a chance to save his life. Halkett wrote other letters that Forbes dictated. To Abercromby and his newly named successor, General Jeffery Amherst, Forbes announced his success and pressed again for orders or some direction given regarding what he should do next. He wrote to Pennsylvania's governor Denny asking that barracks in Carlisle, Lancaster, and Philadelphia be put "in good repair" for his dwindling numbers of regulars, who required "Comfortable Winter Quarters" to begin the work of rebuilding after "so hard and tedious a Campaign."[2]

Declining health, lack of instructions, and a deteriorating army, all weighed heavily on Forbes. So too did other issues. He still hoped to meet with Ohio Indian leaders and expand upon the message he had sent them before leaving for the Forks. He also knew that his mission was still incomplete: given its present condition and the poor weather there was no way for the troops to advance up the Allegheny River to the French garrisons at Venango, Fort LeBoeuf, and Presqu'Ile. Even though he had taken Fort Duquesne, the French remained within striking distance and posed a threat to his hard-won victory. The most immediate challenge was also the most visibly obvious: his army was falling apart. As he reminded Abercromby and Amherst, "The Pennsylvania, Maryland, Virginia, and North Carolina troops may all disband tomorrow," since the terms of many men were set to expire on December 1, and "their provinces will pay them no longer." This complicated any plans to hold the Forks and cover the communication to Pennsylvania, especially since he was determined to send his few precious regulars to the settlements to refit. He finally used his authority as commander in chief in the region to "detain 250 of them," mostly Pennsylvanians under command of Colonel Hugh Mercer, but he worried that even such a small garrison might be impossible to support over the winter "considering 400 miles of land carriage thro an immense Wilderness, and the worst roads in the world."[3]

*   *   *

The army had reached the end of its endurance. While detailed returns from this period have not survived, it would not be an exaggeration to suggest that the troops at the Forks were cold, hungry, and suffering from a variety of illnesses. Colds and other respiratory ailments along with rheumatism from the cold and wet weather sapped men's strength but were not serious enough to force them into hospitals. The troops had been subsisting on bread, biscuit, and salt meat for days. Coupled with the disappearance of whatever vegetables they had planted at Loyalhannon and Raystown, such a diet would produce the early signs of scurvy. Since that part of the army left at Loyalhannon and Raystown was in equally bad shape, getting bulk supplies to the Forks became a slow, tedious process. Moreover, the costs of transportation in terms of carriage fees and loss of horses steadily increased. By early January Forbes was offering as much as four pounds in Pennsylvania currency (more than two pounds sterling) for each hundredweight of flour carried to the Forks garrison. He also encouraged farmers to use packhorses instead of the slower wagons. Even at that, Forbes estimated that it would take forty-two days to make a trip from Carlisle to the Forks and back. In addition, the small garrisons along the road would also need to be fed. Others also took a hand in urging supplies westward. Washington, while he objected to keeping provincial troops at the Forks and along the road, did issue a circular "to the back inhabitants of Virginia" (the new settlements in the Shenandoah Valley around Winchester), reminding them of the many advantages of British victory and calling on them to carry foodstuffs along Braddock's Road, now considered safe to travel. At the same time, though, he doubted whether the small garrison at the site of Fort Duquesne could hold on for the winter; once the weather improved the French would surely attempt to strike back.[4]

Forbes was especially concerned about his regulars; without them as a reliable core no new army could be raised. The Royal Americans and Montgomery's Highlanders had borne much of the fighting and had done their share of the labor on the campaign. Bouquet reported the loss of "nearly all our officers" during the campaign; his four companies of the 60th were now left with three captains and only two subalterns along with Lieutenant Ourry who was serving as an assistant quartermaster under St. Clair. These six were all that remained of some fifteen officers who had begun the campaign; the others had been killed, captured, or in the case of Lieutenant Emanuel Hesse left behind mortally ill. Moreover, the rank and file "are also greatly reduced" and in need of clothing and shoes, though "without means of getting any." To the uncle of one of his remaining officers, Bouquet admitted that "we are ourselves reduced to a sad state of affairs." Returns from early 1759 suggest the magnitude of the losses. At York, Pennsylvania, in late March, the four companies totaled only 318 men, including 59 still stationed in the west. Those in the York quarters included 46 sick and the detachment was short 12 officers. With just 79 men per company, sick and well, the 60th was far below its established strength of 100 men per company, plus 16 officers. These companies would spend all winter and spring rebuilding. They could expect no help from the six companies in New York; these were in even worse shape having suffered heavy losses in officers and men during Abercromby's attack on Fort Carillon.[5]

Reports from the field also suggest the problems facing Bouquet's troops. Ensign Archibald Blane, one of the three surviving subalterns, led thirty-two sick men east in mid-December, and Colonel John Armstrong told Bouquet that even more men were "falling Sick" at Fort Bedford from exposure. Less than two weeks later Armstrong reported that "the residue" of the Royal Americans had finally started down country. Heavy losses, sickness, and falling morale also led to disciplinary problems. Blane, writing from Fort Ligonier, was troubled to learn "that our Men behave so bad in their Quarters" at York and elsewhere in Pennsylvania. This poor behavior seems to have pervaded the ranks. In late January the sergeant major of the Royal Americans attempted to evict a sergeant of Forbes's 17th Foot from his quarters, provoking a fight and a court-martial. Friction and bad feelings were not confined to the enlisted men. On November 30, Bouquet received a written request from Captain Francis Lander for "leave to sell out of the Army." His only explanation was a cryptic reference to the decision making "two Persons happy who are at present extreamly Miserable." Whether this referred to a conflict between Lander and another officer or with Bouquet is not clear.[6]

Montgomery's regiment was at least as badly off as the Royal Americans, in some respects more so. The 77th had borne the brunt of Grant's attack in September; 10 officers and 187 rank and file were killed, captured, or missing, and another 24 men were wounded but managed to make it back to Loyalhannon. Another man was killed and one wounded at Loyalhannon in October. An unknown number were casualties in small skirmishes along the road. In addition, Montgomery's regiment had also begun the campaign under strength because of malaria contracted in South Carolina; those who remained in the ranks included many who suffered the lingering effects of this disease as well as the respiratory problems, colds, and rheumatism brought on by winter weather. The suffering may have been greater due to the fact that these men were clad in kilts; by mid-December their clothing was in a "deplorable condition" with some men "almost naked" and the regiment short of tents and camp equipment. Major Halkett took it upon himself to order those men passing though Fort Loudoun to take blankets from the stores in order "to Cloath these Men who are quite Naked." It took literally months to correct the clothing problem: as late as August of the following year one captain was forced to report that his men "have scarcely a Stitch of Cloathes, their Coats were all in Raggs before the End of the last Campaign." As a result, sickness tore through the regiment. In late December, 357 Highlanders passed through Fort Bedford on their way to better quarters in the east, many "Scarce able to drag their Leggs after them." For all practical purposes Montgomery's regiment had ceased to exist as a functioning regiment.[7]

The provincial troops likely fared even worse, if only because of their lack of training and seasoned officers and the fact that they bore the brunt of the hard labor needed to build roads, forts, and encampments. Like the regulars, they were getting sicker as the campaign reached its end; one man "found great numbers of Sick" at Loyalhannon as the army set out. Both Washington's and Byrd's Virginia regiments had left their heavy clothing and equipment behind at Loyalhannon before the march to the Forks. Now, eager to go home, they could not take what they deemed the shorter route along Braddock's Road but had to backtrack to Loyalhannon in order to pick up their gear, then go home or (in the case of Washington's regiment) into garrisons by way of the Raystown–Fort Cumberland Road. These troops, particularly Washington's, were also depleted from desertions, sickness, and the deaths produced by exposure and poor food. Indeed, Washington warned Virginia's governor that his regiment would soon be ineffective and worried that he would be unable to find the same quality of men to fill the ranks. Certainly, all of the provincial forces, like the regulars, had worn-out uniforms, shoes, tents, and other equipment; the North Carolina companies had, in fact, arrived at the army without much of this material in the first place. The unpaid Maryland volunteers probably had the easiest time: seasoned woodsmen, they would have simply collected whatever gear they owned along with whatever scalp bounties they could claim and turned homeward.[8]

How badly decimated the provincial units were is difficult to assess. Washington's Virginia regiment suffered heavy losses with Grant and during the accidental shooting outside Loyalhannon in November. Surviving material for the Maryland companies led by John Dagworthy does offer a glimpse of one of these units and its losses over the course of the campaign, though we should bear in mind that Dagworthy's troops formed the core of Forbes's ad hoc light infantry battalion and were more active and more consistently engaged than many other troops. Dagworthy's four companies, averaging 357 men, suffered 32 killed—of which 21 were lost with Grant, another 10 lost during the October attack on the encampment—and an unknown number of wounded in both affairs. Their battle casualties alone certainly amounted to considerably more than 10 percent of the companies. Noteworthy, however, are the 56 men listed as having deserted. Dagworthy lost men throughout the campaign, but the numbers began to grow in the autumn—12 in October, 9 in November, with desertions spiking at 20 in December. As clothing and shoes finally gave out just as winter began and as men faced short rations and no certain end to the campaign, not only did the sick rates likely increase but so too did the number of men who made their own decisions to end the campaign. Moreover, the fact that many of the Marylanders who deserted in December apparently did so in groups, suggests that both officers and fellow soldiers turned a blind eye to those who sought to escape.[9]

The rise in desertions, which began even before the final march to the Forks, was one sign that the army was unraveling. Plundering by homebound soldiers was another. Those men who had enlisted for one year—the 2d Virginia Regiment, the Pennsylvania New Levies, and the Carolinians—knew to the day when their time was up. By the time December arrived, many of these men were already on the roads; by mid-month what began as a trickle became a flood as one-year men went home. In the process they helped themselves to whatever stores remained along the road. At Raystown, Colonel John Armstrong expressed "great Mortifycation" at the "disorder" "respecting the Stealing & Carrying off of horses and Sundry Other things," which was evidently widespread both there and elsewhere along Forbes's Road. Assistant quartermaster Lewis Ourry told his friend Bouquet that he had lost "all Patience" with the "plundering Hands of unjust & ungratefull Men." Even men still in the ranks joined in stealing from the king's stores. "Nothing," wrote Ourry, "is spared, Horses, Saddles, Wagons, Provisions, Hay, Planks" were stolen "every Day, Night, & Hour." He was even worried that the small amount of forage and food set aside for Forbes on his return trip would be plundered. Adding insult to injury, one of Bouquet's own horses was stolen, only to be recovered the following day. Horses to carry men home more quickly, forage to keep the animals going, and food for hungry ex-soldiers were the favorite items taken. Each stolen horse or plundered wagon made it that much harder to maintain those troops left behind at the Forks and along the communication.[10]

Desertion, sickness, and rampant theft only complicated Forbes's plans for western garrisons. The provincial troops, even those still legally in service, were proving difficult to manage. In early January at least 40 out of 75 officers belonging to two Pennsylvania battalions were absent, this in addition to the large number of troops unfit for active service. As finally settled, Forbes decided to keep 350 men at the Forks and planned to add 50 more "when we can Supply them with provisions." Fort Ligonier would hold 400, Fort Bedford (Raystown) 300, with 160 divided among Juniata Crossing, Fort Littleton, Fort Loudoun, and Shippensburg; 100 men would hold Carlisle and, hopefully, these posts would "support one another & forward all Convoys with proper Escorts." To the east of Carlisle there would also be a small garrison each at Wright's Ferry and York, as well as William's Ferry and Cresap's in Maryland. Will's Town "on the Pottomack" and Fort Cumberland would also be kept up.[11]

With numbers dwindling and their officers absent, finding adequate numbers of Pennsylvania troops to hold all the posts along Forbes's Road proved impossible, and reluctantly Forbes ordered detachments of both the Royal Americans and Highlanders to march back to Bedford, Ligonier, and the new fort being built on the Monongahela River near the Forks and commanded by Colonel Hugh Mercer. Confusion arose here, too, since Colonel Armstrong misunderstood Forbes's intentions and had hurried the regulars down country. Now, expresses had to be sent out to intercept these men and get them on the move to the Ohio. Altogether, 200 Highlanders and 50 Royal Americans found themselves heading back into the wilderness and away from the anticipated winter quarters among the settlements. The Scots, in particular, must have been crestfallen at having to march west again in the remnants of kilts and coats. Their officers were no less unhappy, especially when attempts to get some kind of clothing for their men met with army red tape. Captain Alexander McKenzie, leading men "distressed for want of Shoes & Clothes," was told that he could take blankets out of the storehouses at Bedford and Ligonier "to Suply the party with Jackets." Armstrong, at Fort Bedford, refused this on the grounds of not having written authorization to distribute any supplies. Only a hastily written order from Forbes through Halkett overcame Armstrong's "Puzellanimity." All of this only served to delay the Highlanders' march in the snow and freezing temperatures. In the meantime, Colonel Mercer made do with his troops, whom he termed the worst of his regiment, and the few tools and equipment he had to build what was called simply "Mercer's Fort." Made strong enough to withstand French or Indian raids, it would be replaced the following year by the new and much more elaborate Fort Pitt.[12]

*   *   *

Ohio Indians watched the activities at the Forks with mixed emotions. Curiosity, certainly, perhaps even amusement as they watched what must have seemed the chaotic movements and behavior of the invaders—cannons firing at a burned-out fort and soldiers coming and going, either in organized groups, or singly, or in small groups heading east or south. The natives must also have had a sense of unease. Yes, the French had destroyed their fort, but they were not far off in the Allegheny Valley, suggesting that the war in the Ohio Country was not yet over. Then there were the British. Instead of seeing the ruins, turning around, and going home, they were preparing to stay, building new fortifications, and laying in supplies even though the word from Easton was that the country belonged to the natives and the British would stake no claims beyond of the mountains. Forbes's message, delivered by Frederick Post in mid-November, was conciliatory but at the same time carried ominous undertones.

Nevertheless, the western Delawares were not content merely to react to British initiatives. Their world was changing and becoming more—not less—unpredictable. The large Shawnee settlement at Logg's Town was now abandoned, and other neighbors had pulled back to the upper Allegheny or to the Great Lakes. The Delawares themselves were relocating to the Muskingum Valley. Changing settlement patterns and social networks that went with them were part of the cost of the war that headmen hoped was finally coming to an end. With the French in retreat one source of needed goods and services was disappearing, and although the British promised to open trade and provide gunsmiths and blacksmiths, these were still only a promise. War had disrupted normal routines: fields went untended, young men were out hunting enemies instead of deer and other sources of protein and hides. Towns now held dozens, perhaps hundreds, of British American captives whose futures were still unclear: would they be adopted to replace the wastage of war, or would they have to be returned as the price of peace? The Delawares certainly needed peace but were not prepared to surrender.[13]

Post quickly discovered as much when he finally arrived at the Kuskuskies in mid-November. As the Delaware headmen slowly convened to learn about Easton and the status of Forbes's army, it was clear that Delawares were still divided. Post noted that he was "gladly received" by "most of the people," but others were alarmed that he had come with an armed escort. Some were inclined to listen to French agents who continued to warn the natives that talk of peace was simply a trap: the real British design was to first rout the French, then fall upon the natives. This internal tug-of-war continued even after Tamaqua, Shingas, and other leaders of the peace movement returned to listen to Post's messages. Encouraged that the British would reopen trade provided the natives stayed out of the Anglo-French war, the Delawares had demands of their own. They were, according to Post, "afraid the English would come over the river Ohio," underscoring the central issue with the natives: their sovereign control over the land they had settled and fought to protect. Tamaqua went further, telling Forbes to return to the east, explaining that the only way the Delawares could persuade their neighbors to embrace the peace offered by the Easton Treaty was if the metaphorical road to peace and brotherhood was kept open "and that is the reason that maketh me tell you to go back over the mountain again, and to stay there." More to the point, Keekyuscung, "a noted Indian," told Post that "all the nations had jointly agreed to defend their hunting place at Allegheny and suffer nobody to settle there." Only by accepting this could the British look forward to peace. Knowing that the French were beaten, moreover, the Delawares dismissed the idea that the British needed an army to defend themselves, pointing out that the few French troops along the Allegheny River were of little importance and impotent in the face of native resolve to embrace peace and have no more war in their country. Nothing about the future of the Ohio Country would be quite so simple.[14]

In response to Forbes's invitation, Delaware headmen arrived at Fort Duquesne on December 4 expecting a face-to-face talk with the general and a fair exchange of views. Instead, they found Bouquet prepared to speak for the general, whose health had finally compelled him to leave for Philadelphia just hours before the natives arrived. The resulting meeting was brief, and both sides skirted the potentially explosive issues of British garrisons and colonial captives. For his part, Bouquet acted the good host by warmly welcoming the delegates. He then quickly tried to assure them that "We are not come here to take Possession of your hunting Country in a hostile manner" but were only interested in restoring trade and peace. Mercer's Fort and the garrisons there and at Forts Ligonier and Bedford had now become merely a security force "to protect our Traders" from the French. Bouquet also took the opportunity to provide a subtle lesson in modern Indian politics by reminding the natives that "your Brethren the English are not only the most powerful People on this Continent" but also the wealthiest—and best able to provide Indian wants—now that the French were in full retreat. He alluded to the expectation that prisoners would be returned, referring to an earlier discussion between Delawares and Johnson's man Croghan. In response, Tamaqua vaguely agreed that the prisoners would be repatriated and that the Delawares would use their "Interest" with other nations to do likewise. Expressing satisfaction that the British would reopen trade, Tamaqua pledged that his people would assist these men in every way that they could. On the matter of garrisons, "we recommend it to you that None of your People straggle out in the Woods" since "a few Indians" may attempt to kill or seize such men "without our Knowledge." Tamaqua also accepted Forbes's urgent request that the Delaware headmen meet him in Philadelphia, assuring the natives that "Provisions will be laid on the Road for you." No repetition of the Delawares' message through Post that the British depart entirely seems to have been made, at least not publicly. Indeed, the council reflected two peoples who eyed each other warily but were cautious about provoking a confrontation. For both British and Delawares, actions would speak louder than words, and each side was content for the moment to sit and await events.[15]

Forbes, though unable to meet the Delaware headmen, nevertheless tried to hammer home the point that only by honoring the Easton Treaty and its promises regarding trade and settlement could Britain and her colonies maintain peace with the Ohio Indians. The general certainly had no illusions about the nobility of "savages," but he still understood that peace required all sides to keep faith and perform the actions they pledged, whether it be returning captives or keeping the land-hungry at bay. To Denny, whose colony was most directly affected by the negotiations, Forbes pointed out that "the Conquest of this Country is of the greatest Consequence to the adjacent Provinces, by securing the Indians, our real Friends, for their own Advantages." The advantages Forbes had in mind certainly included peace along a vulnerable frontier and the economic benefits of trade. General Amherst, the new American commander in chief, received several letters from Forbes underscoring the necessity of honoring the terms offered at Easton. Forbes wrote on January 6 admitting that "many things are left at sixes and sevens," especially Indian affairs, which he identified as "of a delicate nature," warning Amherst that Indian matters "requires your immediate personal presence" at the anticipated council in Philadelphia, a point he repeated only a week later. Near the end of January, Forbes wrote again, saying that "I dare venture to say you will think highly necessary" to have Indian affairs settled "on some solid footing," since "the preservation of the Indians, and that Country, Depends upon it." He tried to stress the tentative nature of peace by telling Amherst that while the Ohio Indians were "now well Disposed to us and easily secured," Forbes continued to worry about French influence and feared the "greatest confusion" that would result if Amherst and other authorities ignored Indian affairs. Then, noting the arrival of western Delawares for the Philadelphia council, the general reminded Amherst that he needed his commander's guidance before he spoke with the natives—assuming his health would permit him to attend the talks. Finally, on February 7, Forbes wrote Amherst to express his worry that "The State of the Indians all along the Ohio, Shawnees and Delawares, is I'm afraid not generally understood," or worse, manipulated "to purposes serving particular ends" by which he meant "Sir William Johnstone and his Myrmidons" and the ongoing contest between Pennsylvania and Virginia for control of the Forks. To all of this, Amherst's only recorded reply was to Forbes's letter of January 26 and the minutes of the Fort Pitt council of December 4. Having read the document, Amherst concluded that "like most other conferences with those Scoundrels," the December meeting "ends with their asking for Rum." He did concede that necessity required the British to "try to make them our friends," but he quickly added that this would only happen when the natives accept that "we are superior to the French." As a harbinger of things to come, Amherst's dismissive comments did not bode well for the Ohio Indians, the army, or the colonists.[16]

*   *   *

By the time he received Amherst's letter, Forbes may have been beyond caring. As much as he stressed the need to carefully manage Indian affairs, he also repeatedly mentioned his health. Amherst and Abercrombie as well as Pitt learned of his deteriorating health, the "inflammation in my stomach, Midriff and Liver," and his inability to write or even dictate letters. "If I get to Philadelphia," he told Denny, "I shall yet run a good Chance of reestablishing a Health that I run the risque of ruining." Having reached Lancaster in mid-January, he asked Amherst to send Dr. Richard Huck to Philadelphia. But since he was "weaker than a child and recover no Strength," Forbes wondered whether the doctor's ministrations would do him any good. Finally arriving in Philadelphia on January 17, he was still suffering from "infirmity & Distemper."[17]

The journey east offered little rest and must have been agonizing for a man who could neither walk nor ride but had to be carried in a litter. With garrisons to fix and with the balance of his army moving off as fast as feet, wagons, and stolen horses would permit, Forbes continued to be occupied with the details of army administration. We hear little of his quartermaster St. Clair. Instead, Forbes had to immerse himself in such issues as moving supplies forward, restocking magazines, and collecting forage for those animals still under army control. Halkett tried to ensure that warm dry accommodations—what Halkett termed "Chimneys"—awaited his general at every fort on the road. On at least one occasion, however, Halkett spoke of "our disappointment" upon arriving at Tomahawk Camp, "to find that the Chimney was unclay'd, no fire made, or any Wood cut," forcing Forbes to sit for some two hours without a fire "expos'd to a snow storm," which "had realy very near distroy'd him intirely." Nevertheless, Forbes rallied; by the time he reached Fort Bedford on December 31, Halkett could breathe a little easier since "the General stands his Travling tolerably well" and insisted on continuing on the next day. The trip, which began on December 4, did not end until January 17 in Philadelphia; the very next day Forbes was busy dictating a long letter to the Lords of the Treasury about his accounts for the campaign.[18]

Too ill to meet the Ohio Indians in Philadelphia, Forbes continued to work as best he could through January. His last letter to Bouquet once again stressed the need to prevent renewed conflict with the natives, complaining of the "rubs and hinderances" that made better relations difficult. His general health continued to deteriorate. On February 13 he made his will, naming his cousin James Glen his executor. Bouquet arrived in Philadelphia anxious to speak with his general, but as he told Amherst, by March 1 he was "So far gone that I could not see him." Less than two weeks later, on March 11, Forbes died. He was escorted to his grave in Christ Church by his own regiment, the 17th and, appropriately, two companies of the Highlanders that had escorted him from Carlisle to the Ohio. On March 15, William Pitt wrote a letter telling Forbes that George II approved of his application for leave in Britain.[19]

Conclusions

* * *

The Seven Years' War in America did not end in the winter of 1758. Campaigning in the Ohio Country continued into the new year and beyond. A small garrison stood watch during the cold and anxious winter, convinced, as were its leaders, that the French would be back in force as soon as the weather improved. Meanwhile, plans went ahead in London and colonial capitals for yet another attack at what was left of French North America.

Captain Lignery, from his winter quarters at Fort Venango, certainly anticipated an attack on the Forks once the Allegheny River opened in the spring. He and other French officers in the Ohio Country and the *pays d'en haut* spent their time gathering men and materiel. Yet when the time came, Lignery and his men would advance north—not south. By midsummer 1759, a new British-provincial army led by General John Prideaux was making its way to Fort Niagara, the final link between French settlements in Canada and the West. Lignery responded to an urgent appeal from Fort Niagara's commander who was now faced with a formal siege. Despite warnings to travel down the west side of the Niagara River, thus avoiding the British forces, Lignery's force of over a thousand marines, militia, and native allies elected to take the shorter route along the east side. On July 24, 1759, Lignery and his men were overwhelmed and routed in what was a Braddock's Defeat in reverse; among the casualties was Captain Lignery, who died of his wounds as a British prisoner four days later. Fort Niagara's surrender on July 25, 1759, followed by Wolfe's victory at Quebec in September, spelled the effective end of French Canada, though its formal surrender would wait until the fall of 1760.[1]

* * *

Lieutenant-Colonel Henry Bouquet was instrumental in fixing Britain's hold on the Ohio Country. Indeed, his reputation would become inseparable from the region. He oversaw the occupation of the region as de facto commander of British forces. As such, he was compelled to act as his own quartermaster general and avoided having to work with Sir John St. Clair who was occupied clearing accounts from the Forbes campaign. Among Bouquet's staff was his brigade major in 1759, Captain Horatio Gates of the British army. Bouquet's fame was assured when he succeeded, despite heavy casualties at Bushy Run on August 5 and 6, 1763, in getting relief to Fort Pitt during the conflict popularly known as "Pontiac's War." The following year he led an expedition into the Muskingum Valley of Ohio and began the process of negotiating an end to the Ohio Indians' involvement in the war. In the meantime, he created a systematic scheme of tactics to help British troops face what he called "this infamous war of scalps." In doing so, he drew on his own and others' experiences during the 1758 campaign and his efforts to train Forbes's army at Raystown. Promoted to brigadier general in America, he was given command of the fractious garrisons of the new colony of West Florida. He contracted typhus on the voyage to his new command and died upon arriving at Pensacola in 1765.[2]

Exhausted from the recent dash to Fort Duquesne and suffering from a bowel disorder—likely flux brought on by a steady diet of bad food—George Washington left the army in December and headed for Virginia and his beloved Mount Vernon. Carrying letters from Forbes to the colony's governor, Washington passed through Winchester on his way to Williamsburg where he formally resigned as colonel of the 1st Virginia Regiment. Through four years of tough campaigning he had gained a military education that few in the colonies could rival. First under Braddock, then Forbes, he had seen how armies were organized, supplied, and administered during war while at the same time developing a respect for the British army and its leaders. These experiences, as well as other qualities, would serve him well when, in 1775, he was appointed commander in chief of the American Congress's new Continental Army.

One of the lessons he may have learned from his months with Forbes's army was the danger of what Forbes called "parties" within an army. Washington certainly faced his share of sniping from subordinates and politicians during the Revolution, all while remaining in control and projecting an image of calm and professionalism that might have impressed Forbes. At the same time, Washington never turned his back on the Ohio Country. As a landholder and as a Virginian, he remained convinced that the future was linked to access to the Ohio Valley. Although not as strident as in his duels with Bouquet and Forbes, Washington continued to espouse Virginia's claims to the region, continued to worry about the evident advantages enjoyed by Pennsylvania thanks to Forbes's road, and continued to promote the region by advocating what later became the C&O Canal, and by his frequent visits.

Perhaps there some irony in Washington's subsequent careers as commander in chief and his country's first president. Throughout, he had to constantly face down the pressures of localism and particular interests for the sake of unity. In ways that Forbes could not have imagined but with which he could easily have sympathized, Washington found himself waging his own coalition war for independence and national unity. His last association with the Ohio Country came in 1794 when, as president and commander in chief, he led an army west in order to impose the national will on localist antitax protesters who had fomented the "Whiskey Rebellion."[3]

When James Kenny encountered him at Fort Pitt in 1762, the Quaker storekeeper remarked that Tamaqua and those with him were "half Snow'd with Rum." It was a side of the Delaware headman that never appeared in council negotiations. We might wonder why he was traveling along the Forbes Road in such a state. Perhaps it was the recent council in Lancaster. There, predictably, talk of finalizing peace was pushed aside as colonists once again attempted to separate Delawares from their lands; equally predictable was the sniping that took place between Quakers and representatives of the Penn family. Or maybe it was the fact that in going to and from Lancaster, Tamaqua had to travel on the army's new road and pass through or near several garrisons, including the massive Fort Pitt. Certainly, the Delawares' demeanor suggested that, when Kenny met them, the natives were "not so cheerful as befor."[4]

For Tamaqua, other Ohio Country natives, and for that matter the border settlers who were even now cautiously moving back to abandoned farms, the war seemed not to have ended. Despite British promises and despite his clear urgings that Forbes take his army and go back east of the mountains— and stay there—the road was still busy with troops, peddlers, and wagons. In place of the rickety Fort Duquesne the British were busy finishing an earthen and brick Fort Pitt: a silent but clear statement of their intent to stay and develop native lands. To the south, squatters were already moving down the

Monongahela River looking for likely farmsteads, so many of them that the region around Fort Pitt would soon be organized as Westmoreland County—Virginia. What was good news for landowners and speculators such as Washington spelled nothing but trouble for officers such as Henry Bouquet whose brief included keeping unauthorized colonists out of the region.

Violence, or the threat of it, was never far from the surface. A native might be murdered by a sentry at Fort Venango. A soldier from Fort Le Boeuf out hunting to augment his rations could be stopped, forcibly disarmed, and pointedly told "not to come out there any more." Theft was commonplace between natives and newcomers; Delawares might target a stray cow or horse; soldiers and squatters tried to confiscate wampum or anything else that struck their fancy. The best that commanders such as Bouquet could do was punish soldiers and browbeat civilians.[5]

Perhaps the most pressing issue was the growing difference in power between natives and the oncoming British empire. By "knocking the French on the head" (in Bouquet's words), Forbes's victory as well as those that followed completely overturned the "modern Indian politics" that had helped Ohio Indians and others to navigate their way through imperial conflict for two generations. Now with the French gone, there was no other European power in the region. Delawares had received hints of this as early as December 1758, when Bouquet announced that British forces would remain in the region—albeit to "protect" the promised reopening of the deerskin trade. More dramatic was the news in 1763 that Britain and France had decided the Ohio Country's future without consulting its native owners. When word reached the Ohio Valley that France had ceded the region to Britain, Netawatwees, one of the rising generation of Delaware leaders, was "struck dumb" at the news. Meanwhile, out on the Great Lakes, a loose coalition of peoples decided to act when they learned that their French "father" (mediator and generous partner) was now gone, replaced by tight-fisted and arrogant British soldiers and traders.[6]

The immediate response was renewed warfare. Assessing the British threat from their own regional perspectives, Great Lakes Indians launched attacks, some led by Pontiac, aimed at driving the British from the west. Ohio Indians did the same, but to protect their lands. One of the last recorded actions taken by Tamaqua was to warn British traders in his towns of the coming storm. Beyond that he could only step aside, perhaps disgusted with false promises and his own mistakes in trusting the fair words of men such as Frederick Post. By the end of 1763 the West was in turmoil, a majority of British garrisons were overrun, and General Amherst's American career was in shambles. At the same time Ohio Indians reenacted a well-rehearsed strategy and began to move west again, this time to the Muskingum River, once more putting distance between them and the oncoming settlers. It would be up to a new generation, typified by Netawatwees, to determine how best to cope with a new political and economic landscape.[7]

Equally ominous, not just for natives but for imperial managers at home and in London, was what one historian has called the emerging "racialized landscape." Two wars within a decade had convinced many, perhaps most, living on the margins of the colonies that Indians were an existential threat. Conestoga Indians were massacred in 1763—not because they were at war with Pennsylvania but because they were Indians, unarmed, and handy. Others were prepared to take their hatred of Indians and of those who supposedly coddled them a big step further. Calling themselves the "Black Boys" and led by a former Indian captive, James Smith, these men from the Pennsylvania borderlands attacked a convoy of trade goods headed to Fort Pitt, determined that their enemy not receive aid and comfort from crown Indian agents such as George Croghan. And when the wagoners sought the protection of Fort Loudoun, the Black Boys began shooting at its British regular garrison, an act of defiance—to some, treason—that would only grow over the years as stamped paper, taxed paints, and tea joined frontier security on the list of provincial reasons to suspect the motives of their imperial leaders.[8]

* * *

The ramifications of the Forbes campaign thus extended well beyond the Forks of the Ohio and the Seven Years' War. Not that the campaign actually caused the 1763 Indian war or the American Revolution; no-one living at the time could have imagined such a thing. The campaign—the way it was organized, its goals, and its participants—nonetheless produced a host of unintended consequences and exposed fault lines that would plague the British Empire and the new United States for years. The inherent frictions between native and colonial interests, though not inevitable, were on full display in 1758, first with the Cherokee fighters, then with the Delaware negotiators. Forbes was only being realistic when he urged Amherst to adhere to the hard-won results of the 1758 Easton Treaty: peace with Ohio Indians was much preferred over the costs of war, whatever Forbes and others may have thought about real Indians.

The campaign pushed the boundaries of empire far to the west, at a moment when planners in London had yet to consider the consequences of their victories. A period of political instability in Britain only made it more difficult for American officials such as Sir William Johnson or General Thomas Gage to find a solution to the perennial threat of border warfare.

Gage was particularly anxious to remove troops from distant outposts and return them to eastern cities where their presence could, hopefully, dampen colonial unrest in the years after 1765. The only workable solution seemed to be lines on maps: boundaries between "Indian country" and settled colonies. But the first such line, that of 1763, was dead on arrival. A second attempt, at the famous Fort Stanwix Treaty of 1768, served only to benefit Johnson, the Penns, other speculators, and the Six Nations, who negotiated away a large portion of Pennsylvania and what is now West Virginia and Kentucky without consulting the peoples who lived on, or used, the land. For a time, the Iroquois secured their own lands by selling out Delawares, Shawnees, and others. The outcome was predictable—new settler expansion, border friction, and Dunmore's War in 1774.[9]

Dunmore's War, which pitted Virginia interests against those of the crown, only further exposed not just colonial-imperial differences but the inherent localism that shaped each colony's approach to wider affairs and that was openly on display during the Forbes campaign. Virginians, Marylanders, Pennsylvanians, they all had agendas and were not shy about pursuing them despite calls for unity. It was a problem that would shadow the new United States for another century.

The Forbes campaign, then, reminds us that contingencies and unintended consequences matter in understanding history. Forbes's success turned on the willingness of Delaware leaders to risk their reputations on peace, while a blunder in the twilight provided Forbes with crucial information that made pressing ahead seem like a gamble worth taking. A campaign designed to drive the French from British-claimed territory and set right Braddock's defeat, produced long-term results that no one, native, colonist, or Briton, could have anticipated—or welcomed.

NOTES

Abbreviations

AM	*Archives of Maryland*, vol. 9, *Correspondence of Horatio Sharpe*, ed. Browne
APS	American Philosophical Society
BP	*The Papers of Henry Bouquet*, ed. Stevens et al. 6 vols.
CO 5	National Archives, Kew Gardens, England, Colonial Office Papers, Class 5: America and the West Indies (microfilm)
Correspondence of Pitt	*Correspondence of William Pitt*, ed. Kimball
EAID	*Early American Indian Documents*, vol. 3, *1756–1775*, ed. Hirsh
EWT	*Early Western Travels*, ed. Thwaites. Vol. 1.
FAP	Friendly Association Papers, Bryn Mawr College, Bryn Mawr, Pennsylvania
FHQP	Headquarters Papers of John Forbes, Alderman Library, University of Virginia, Charlottesville. Microfilm, 3 reels
Forbes/SRO	Papers of General John Forbes, Scottish Records Office, Edinburgh, Scotland, Dalhousie Muniments, GD 45/2, 2 reels
GWLC	George Washington Papers, Library of Congress, Washington, D.C.
GWP	*The Papers of George Washington, Colonial Series*, ed. Abbott et al., vols. 5–6
HSP	Historical Society of Pennsylvania, Philadelphia
Malartic Journal	*The American Journals of Comte Maures de Malartic*, ed. Raffle
Military Affairs	*Military Affairs in North America*, ed. Pargellis
NYCD	*Documents Relative to the Colonial History of the State of New York*, ed. O'Callaghan and Fernow
PA	*Pennsylvania Archives*, ed. Hazard (with series, volume, and page numbers)
PCR	*Colonial Records: Minutes of the Provincial Council of Pennsylvania*
PFF	*The Official Papers of Francis Fauquier*, ed. Reese
SWJP	*The Papers of Sir William Johnson*, ed. Sullivan et al.
WO 34	War Office Papers, Class 34: Papers of Sir Jeffery Amherst
Writings of Forbes	*Writings of General John Forbes*, ed. James

Prologue

1. Kummerow et al., *Pennsylvania's Forbes Trail.*
2. On the purely military aspects of the campaign, see James, "Decision at the Forks," in James and Stotz, *Drums in the Forest*, 3–56; Leach, *Roots of Conflict*; Cubbison, *British Defeat of the French*; Brumwell, *Redcoats*. Indian affairs during the campaign are discussed in Jennings, *Empire of Fortune*. On the campaign as part of the wider war in America, see Gipson, *Great War for the Empire*; Anderson, *Crucible of War*; Ward, *Breaking the Backcountry*; Baugh, *Global Seven Years War*, 256–75.

Introduction. *AN EMPIRE AT WAR*

1. On the global character of the war, see Anderson, *Crucible of War*; Baugh, *Global Seven Years War*. For the European phase of the conflict, see Savory, *His Britannic Majesty's Army*.
2. Anderson, *Crucible of War*, chs. 12–13. Canadian officials were hardly exaggerating when they submitted reports that repeatedly mentioned their ability to "devastate" the Pennsylvania frontier. Indeed, they even apologized for not having fresh reports to submit, since, according to one of them, Pennsylvania's backcountry was "pretty bare" by the beginning of 1757. "Abstract of dispatches from Canada [1756]," and "January 15, 1757," in O'Callaghan and Fernow, *Documents Relative to the Colonial History of the State of New York* (hereafter cited as NYCD), 10:490 ("devastate"), 518 ("pretty bare").
3. Anderson, *Crucible of War*, chs. 12–21.
4. On Forbes's career before 1758, see Ian K. Steele, "Forbes, John," in Brown, *Dictionary of Canadian Biography*, 3:218–19; Whitworth, *Lord Ligonier*, 152, 154, 213, 241. More recently, Oliphant, *John Forbes*.
5. For 1711, see Graham, *Walker Expedition*, esp. 23, 178–79; Brumwell, *Redcoats*; Brumwell, "Rank and File." On the number of troops in the colonies by 1758, see Brumwell, *Redcoats*, 19–21. On drafting, see Forbes to Captain Cosnan, New York, December 27, 1757, in James, *Writings of General John Forbes* (hereafter cited as *Writings of Forbes*), 28–29; Braddock to Napier, Alexandria, Virginia, April 19, 1755, in Pargellis, *Military Affairs* (hereafter cited as *Military Affairs*), 83; Loudoun to Cumberland, Albany, October 2, 1756, *Military Affairs*, 235 (on 35th and 42d Regiments). The king directed that the "worst men be drafted" in order to provide reinforcements for Loudoun's army. Whitworth, *Lord Ligonier*, 215. The corrosive effects of repeated drafts of manpower from regiments is best illustrated by the plight of the 93d Foot. Its lieutenant colonel reported that, after the regiment lost over two hundred men to drafts, the transfers "have tore the Regt. To pieces" rendering it unfit for active service. Windus to Bagshawe, Cork, March 17, 1761, in Guy, *Colonel Samuel Bagshawe*, 236. See also "The Journal of a British Officer," in Hamilton, *Braddock's Defeat*, 42 ("old standers").
6. Campbell, *Royal American Regiment*. On the age of the army, see Brumwell, "Rank and File"; "A Report on the Service, Size, Age, and Country . . . of Five Companies of the First Battalion . . . Royal American Regiment of Foot," July 24, 1757, in Stevens et al., *Papers of Henry Bouquet* (hereafter cited as *BP* with volume and page), 1:152.

On the corresponding decline in the ages of officers, see Houlding, *Fit for Service*, 110, table 3. In addition to the 60th, 7th, and 78th Foot, in 1755 the army also raised Shirley's 50th and Pepperell's 51st Foot. Their existence was brief: the majority of both regiments were captured at Oswego in 1756, and the remnants were disbanded and drafted the following year. On raising the Highland regiments, see Dziennik, *Fatal Land*, chs. 1–2.

7. Guy, "That Stubborn English Spirit." On Lee, see Pargellis, *Lord Loudoun*, 349. On Hay, see Pargellis, *Lord Loudoun*, 241–42; Forbes to Loudoun, Halifax, August 6, 1757, and Forbes to Hay, Halifax, August 7, 1757, in *Writings of Forbes*, 7–10.
8. The one notable work on the subject is D'Aulney, *Traité General*.
9. On road systems in the colonies, see Hornsby, *British Atlantic*, 158, 166, 210; also Lemon, *Poor Man's Country*.
10. Shy, "Logistical Crisis."
11. Brewer, *Sinews of Power*, ch. 3. On the routine maintenance of the army, see Guy, *Oeconomy and Discipline*. On British logistics, see Bowler, *Logistics*; all European armies faced similar challenges.
12. On logistical administration, see Scouller, *Armies of Queen Anne*, chs. 1, 5; Bowler, *Logistics*, ch. 1; Schumann and Schweizer, *Seven Years War*, 92–101. On the War Office, see Hayter, *Eighteenth-Century Secretary at War*. On medical services, see Pringle, *Observations*; Cantlie, *Army Medical Services*, vol. 1, ch. 5; Von Arni, *Hospital Care*; Kopperman, "Medical Service"; "The Journal of Charlotte Brown, Matron of the General Hospital with the English Forces in America, 1754–1756," in Calder, *Colonial Captivities*, 169–98.
13. This paragraph is based on two important works on wartime contracting: Bannerman, *Merchants and the Military*; Truxes, *Letterbook of Greg and Cunningham, 1756–1757*, esp. 3–37. The impact of army contracting on colonial economies has been largely ignored by both economic and military historians.
14. Smith, *Universal Military Dictionary*, s. v. "Quarter-Master-General." Another authority, Frenchman Pierre Joseph Bourcet, insisted that a quartermaster general should be to the army what a major was to a regiment: someone versed in every aspect of military life including intelligence gathering, and knowledge of local resources and how to organize the march so that the army could quickly move into line of battle. See Bourcet, *Principes de la guerre de montagnes*, 55–59. On St. Clair's earlier American career, see Kopperman, *Braddock*; Preston, *Braddock's Defeat*. For Loudoun's assessment of St. Clair, see Loudoun to Cumberland, Albany, October 1, 1757, *Military Affairs*, 234. A recent study of St. Clair's American career is Cubbison, *On Campaign*. On the evolution of quartermasters in European armies, see Perjes, "Army Provisioning."
15. Loudoun to Cumberland, Albany, October 2, 1756, *Military Affairs*, 234; St. Clair to Napier, Little Meadows, June 13, 1755, *Military Affairs*, 95.
16. "Rank of Provincial General and Field Officers in North America" (Kensington, May 12, 1756), *BP* 1:6; see also Pargellis, *Lord Loudoun*, chs. 2, 6, 7; Anderson, *Crucible of War*, ch. 15. On the issue of quartering, see Zimmerman, "Governor Denny"; Greene, "South Carolina Quartering Dispute."
17. Loudoun to Cumberland, Albany, October 3, November 12, 1757, *Military Affairs*, 241, 273 (quote); Hardy to Earl of Halifax, New York, May 7, 1756, *Military Affairs*,

171. French professional soldiers in Canada at the same time were making similar complaints about the colonists they encountered. See, for example, Hamilton, *Adventure in the Wilderness*, 55, 64, 83, 102.
18. Colley, *Britons*, 134 (quote); St. Clair to Braddock, Williamsburg [?] c. February 9, 1755, in *Military Affairs*, 64; Wolfe to Lord George Sackville, Louisbourg, July 30, 1758, in Willson, *James Wolfe*, 392; Burnaby, *Travels through the Middle Settlements*, 61. Wolfe was serving in an army that consisted wholly of regular troops. Lyttelton accuses Bouquet of attempting to acquire estates in South Carolina. Lyttelton to Loudoun, Charles Town, December 10, 1757, in *BP* 1:256. For Gage, see Wise, "Gage, Thomas," in Brown, *Dictionary of Canadian Biography*, 4:278–79. On the war and "otherness," see Bannister, "Oriental Atlantic," 154. On the broader issue of "otherness," especially shifting attitudes within Britain, see Greene, *Evaluating Empire*, esp. chs. 2–3.
19. For wartime smuggling, see Truxes, *Defying Empire*. For smuggling as a traditional element of the Atlantic economy, see Chet, *Ocean Is a Wilderness*, 23–25, 31. On wagons, see for example, Forbes to Bouquet, Philadelphia, June 10, 1758, in *Writings of Forbes*, 111.
20. Daniel Dulany cited from "Military Affairs in the Middle Colonies in 1755," *Pennsylvania Magazine of History and Biography* 3 (1879): 12.
21. Leach, *Roots of Conflict*, 113 ("slaves to their Officers"); Fitch, *Diary of Jabez Fitch*, 113 (execution). See Anderson, *People's Army*, 133–35, on provincial officers and courts-martial. On colonial Americans' fear of governmental power, see Bailyn, *Origins of American Politics*; Roger, *Empire and Liberty*. One historian has recently observed that "Early Modern empires were ... made by 'decentralized' and improvised decisions of individuals geographically and politically distinct from metropolitan institutions." Koot, *Biography of a Map*, 8. See also Games, "Accidental Empire"; Mancke, "Negotiating an Empire."
22. Bowen, *Britain's Oceanic Empire*, 5 ("reciprocal sovereignty"). Hancock makes much the same point regarding the transatlantic market for Madeira wine. Hancock, *Oceans of Wine*, xiv–xxv.
23. Hornsby, *British Atlantic*, 38; Shy, "American Colonies," 308.
24. Greene, *Pursuits of Happiness*, 178–79, table 8. 1. See also Fogelman, "Migration to the Thirteen British North American Colonies." Colonial peoples almost immediately altered English law and custom to suit their own particular needs. For an insightful example of this process, see Pagan, *Anne Orthwood's Bastard*.
25. On eighteenth-century populations, see Butler, *Becoming American*, ch. 1. On ethnic complexity, see the essays in Bailyn and Morgan, *Strangers within the Realm*; also Wokeck, *Trade in Strangers*; MacMaster, "Searching for Order"; Goodfriend, *Before the Melting Pot*.
26. On convict transportation, see Ekirch, *Bound for America*.
27. On plantation societies and slavery, see especially Wood, *Black Majority*; Morgan, *Slave Counterpoint*; Sobel, *World They Made Together*. On natives, see Merrell, "Customs of Our Country"; Mandell, *Behind the Frontier*; Richter, *Facing East*, esp. 171–74. On convicts, see Ekirch, *Bound for America*, chs. 4–6.
28. Historical geographers have been in the forefront of defining and studying the regional contours of British America. See especially Meinig, *Shaping of America*, vol. 1; Hornsby, *British Atlantic*. For historians' take on regional variations, see the es-

says in Greene and Pole, *Colonial British America*; Greene, *Pursuits of Happiness*; Taylor, *American Colonies*; Butler, *Becoming American*. On the development of the "backcountry," see Hofstra, "Extension of His Majesty's Dominions"; Bushman, "Markets and Composite Farms"; Ridner, *A Town In-Between*. Economic diversity and development in the colonies is covered in McCusker and Menard, *British America*. Transatlantic connections and their role in colonial economies can be found in Steele, *English Atlantic*; see also McClusky and Squire, "Pennsylvania Credit."

29. Nash, *Urban Crucible*; Smith, *Lower Sort*; Levy, "Levelers and Fugitives"; Johnson, "What Must Poor People Do?" On slavery, see Wood, *Black Majority*. On rural New England, see Gross, *Minutemen and Their World*; Anderson, *People's Army*, chs. 1–2. On the Great Awakening, see Bonomi, *Under the Cope of Heaven*. On consumerism in the colonies, see Breen, "An Empire of Goods"; Breen, "Baubles from Britain"; Carson, "Consumer Revolution"; Bushman, *Refinement of America*. On "Anglicization," and "Americanization," see Butler, *Becoming American*, ch. 4; Kammen, *People of Paradox*, 160–61; Greene, *Pursuits of Happiness*, 174–75; Greene, *Negotiated Authorities*, 46–48. For tensions between old and new within one colony, see Smolenski, *Friends and Strangers*, 118. Hornsby, in *British Atlantic*, emphasizes the bifurcated nature of the colonies, with the staple provinces (including Virginia and South Carolina) and coastal cities more closely tied to London, while interior agricultural regions developed a more "American" character.

30. Greene, *Constitutional Origins*, esp. ch. 1.

31. On the Albany Plan of Union (1754), see Roger, *Empire and Liberty*, ch. 2; Anderson, *Crucible of War*, ch. 7. On the nature of Britain's Atlantic empire, see "Negotiated Authorities" and "Metropolis and Colonies," in Greene, *Negotiated Authorities*, 1–24, 43–77; Greene, *Peripheries and Center*, esp. ch. 3; Mancke, "Empire and State," 175–95. On the raising of provincial troops, their numbers, and British perceptions of them, see Agostini, "Provincials Will Work like Giants."

32. Murrin, *Beneficiaries of Catastrophe*. Murrin emphasizes "catastrophe" in relation to English colonization, but similar explanations apply to natives living beyond the Atlantic coast. See Richter, "War and Culture"; Calloway, *New Worlds for All*, ch. 5; Richter, *Ordeal of the Longhouse*, 2–3; Galloway, *Choctaw Genesis*, 131. See the essays in Ethridge and Shuck-Hall, *Mapping the Mississippian Shatter Zone*, especially "Catawba Coalescence and the Shattering of the Carolina Piedmont, 1540, 1675," 115–41; also the essays by Drooker, Davis, and Galloway in Ethridge and Hudson, *Transformation of the Southeastern Indians*. Especially important here is Kelton, *Epidemics and Enslavement*.

33. Kelton, *Epidemics and Enslavement*, ch. 3; Gallay, *Indian Slave Trade*; Snyder, *Slavery in Indian Country*.

34. Merrell, *Indians' New World*, esp. chs. 3–4; Calloway, *New Worlds for All*, chs. 7–9; Richter, *Facing East*, ch. 5; McConnell, *Country Between*, chs. 1–2. On Pennsylvania, see Merritt, *At the Crossroads*. On the larger issue of adaptation, see Breen, "Creative Adaptations."

35. Richter, *Facing East*, ch. 5 and map, on p. 165.

36. Peter Wraxall, quoted in Richter, *Facing East*, 164 ("modern Indian politics"); Merrell, "Customs of Our Country."

37. On the origins and development of the Covenant Chain, see Jennings, *Ambiguous Iroquois Empire*. Iroquois diplomacy is discussed in the essays by Becker, Haan,

Salisbury, and Jennings in Richter and Merrell, *Beyond the Covenant Chain*; Jennings, "Iroquois Alliances." For a continent-wide perspective on native efforts to shape relations with Europeans, see Hämäläinen, "Shapes of Power."

38. Merrell, *Indians' New World*, ch. 4.
39. Jennings, *Ambiguous Iroquois Empire*, chs. 17–19; McConnell, *Country Between*, chs. 4–5; Hinderaker, *The Two Hendricks*, ch. 3; Shannon, *Iroquois Diplomacy*, chs. 4–5; MacLeitch, *Imperial Entanglements*, 71–72.
40. On the concept of "savagery" and its political uses and implications, see Silver, *Our Savage Neighbors*. On Braddock, see McConnell, *Country Between*, 119–20; Grimes, "We 'Now Have Taken up the Hatchet against Them.'" For an alternative interpretation, see Preston, *Braddock's Defeat*, 114–15.
41. That the Ohio Indians had specific targets in mind, with the Shawnees especially intent on taking war to Virginia, see Steele, "Shawnee Origins." Attacks against Maryland and Virginia began even before Braddock's defeat; see Hunter, *Forts on the Pennsylvania Frontier*, 172.
42. Silver, *Our Savage Neighbors*; Vaughan, "From White Man to Redskin." Merrell provides a brilliant analysis of how these changes overtook Pennsylvania in *Into the American Woods*, but see also Merritt, *At the Crossroads*. On scalp bounties, see "The Moral Dilemma of Scalping," in Axtell, *Natives and Newcomers*, 259–79. On British soldiers taking up scalping, see Way, "Cutting Edge of Culture." For Braddock's scalp bounty, see "Halkett's Orderly Book," in Hamilton, *Braddock's Defeat*, 113 (order issued on June 26, 1755).

ONE. *NEW YORK AND PHILADELPHIA*, Winter–Spring 1758

Epigraph: Forbes to Pitt, Philadelphia, May 19, 1758, *Correspondence of Pitt*, 1:248.

1. Pitt led the government from 1757 until 1760; he chose to hold the office of secretary of state since this placed him in charge of both colonial affairs and the war in America. His partner in the coalition government, the Duke of Newcastle, was Lord Treasurer and thus managed the financial aspects of the war. On Pitt's rise to power, see Middleton, *Bells of Victory*, 7–21. For the letters, see Pitt to Loudoun, Pitt to Abercromby, Pitt to the governors of Massachusetts Bay, New Hampshire, Connecticut, Rhode Island, New York, New Jersey, Pitt to the governors of Pennsylvania, Maryland, Virginia, South Carolina, North Carolina, all dated Whitehall, December 30, 1757, in Kimball, *Correspondence of William Pitt* (hereafter cited as *Correspondence of Pitt*), 1:133, 134, 136, 140.
2. The numbers of troops in North America can be found in "Distribution of His Majesty's Forces in North America for the Campaign of 1758," Colonial Office Papers Class 5: America and the West Indies (hereafter cited as CO 5), 50. Naval forces at Louisbourg are provided in Boscawen, *Capture of Louisbourg*, 345–46. Troops and ships assigned to the French coast are in Beetson, *Naval and Military Memoirs*, 3:165–66, 191. The Parliamentary estimates are from Beetson, *Naval and Military Memoirs*, 3:92, 169–70.
3. Robert Hunter Morris to William Johnson, in Sullivan et al., *Papers of Sir William Johnson*. (hereafter cited as *SWJP*), 2:443 ("vast Tract"); Wallace, *Travels of John Heckewelder*, 38 ("howling wilderness," "blackened ruins").
4. Steele, *Setting All the Captives Free*, 77 ("soul-wrenching"). On the impact of the

border war on Pennsylvania, see Ward, *Breaking the Backcountry*, esp. ch. 3. On the Kittanning raid and the scalp bounty, see Barr, "Victory at Kittanning?"; McConnell, *Country Between*, 106–7, 191; Middleton, *Bells of Victory*, 54. Reminders of one of Britain's worst defeats in America kept cropping up throughout the war; as British forces took Forts Niagara, Frontenac, and finally, Montreal, they kept finding pieces of Braddock's artillery train, now used by the enemy. See Preston, *Braddock's Defeat*, 297, 298, 314; Mante, *History of the Late War*, 103n293, 163n453.

5. Examples of Forbes's work can be found in "General Orders to Lieut. Col. Bouquet," New York, December 2, 1757, Forbes to Loudoun, New York, December 10, 1757, Forbes to Simon Fraser, New York, December 20, 1757, Forbes to Captain Cosnan, New York, December 27, 1757, "Extract of Orders to Col. Prevost," New York, December 30, 1757, in *Writings of Forbes*, 19–20, 21–23, 26–27, 28–29, 30; Bouquet to Forbes, Charles Town, February 1, 1758, Forbes to Bouquet, New York, February 14, 1758, *BP* 1:288, 301. On his illness, see Forbes to Loudoun, February 3, 1758, *Writings of Forbes*, 37. A recent biography of Forbes can be found in Oliphant, *John Forbes*.

6. Forbes to Loudoun, New York, March 4, 1758, Forbes to Sharpe, New York, March 21, 1758, *Writings of Forbes*, 54, 61 ("appointed"). On the selection of younger officers, see Whitworth, *Field Marshal Lord John Ligonier*, 241, 213 ("wish you joy"). On Forbes's military career, see Steele, "Forbes, John," in Brown et al., *Dictionary of Canadian Biography*, 3:218–19.

7. On the British officer corps, see Houlding, *Fit for Service*, 99–116.

8. "Distribution of His Majesty's Forces in North America for the Campaign of 1758," CO 5/50; Forbes to Abercromby, Philadelphia, June 15, 1758, *Writings of Forbes*, 113–14. See also Bouquet to Forbes, Carlisle, June 3, 1758, *BP* 2:16. Three months later Forbes asked again for more regulars since he could look "favourably" only on the few that he had. Forbes to Abercromby, Shippensburg, September 4, 1758, *Writings of Forbes*, 201.

9. Pitt to governors of Pennsylvania, Maryland, Virginia, South Carolina, North Carolina, Whitehall, December 30, 1758, *Correspondence of Pitt*, 1:141. These new instructions concerning rank were meant to eliminate a major obstacle to the integration of regular and provincial troops into larger armies. Prior to 1758, as a result of George II's original ruling governing rank, the two forces had served separately, which complicated military planning. In addition, Pitt also gained Parliament's agreement to reimburse the colonies for most of their military costs, thus encouraging provincial governments to quickly raise and equip their troops. The problem of rank was altogether absent from Amherst's all-regular army, and Abercromby had another regular general officer, Viscount Howe, who would outrank provincial officers.

10. Dziennik, *Fatal Land*, 65. For Forbes's arrival, see Forbes to Abercromby (Philadelphia), April 20, 1758, in *Writings of Forbes*, 65.

11. Bouquet to Forbes, New York, April 23, 1758, *BP* 1:333.

12. On April 20, 1758, Forbes wrote to Abercromby, asking him to send Captain Harry Gordon immediately and any other engineers assigned to Forbes, "as there is plenty of business for them." Forbes to Abercromby (Philadelphia), April 20, 1758, *Writings of Forbes*, 65. The artillery finally arrived on June 11, weeks after Forbes's army began its march west. Forbes to Pitt, Philadelphia, June 17, 1758, *Correspondence of Pitt*, 1:278.

13. Bouquet to Dobbs, Charles Town, February16, 1758, *BP* 1:302–3; Forbes to Denny,

Philadelphia, May 3, 1758, in *Colonial Records: Minutes of the Provisional Council of Pennsylvania* (hereafter cited as *PCR*), 8:110; Forbes to Pitt, Philadelphia, May 1, 1758, *Writings of Forbes*, 77. Accounts of the companies with Bouquet, *BP* 1:292.

14. Hesse to [?], Charles Town, November 6, 1757, *BP* 1:236; "Representation of Field Officers Regarding Troops," Charles Town, December 2, 1757, *BP* 1:248–49 (state of Highlanders); Dziennik, *Fatal Land*, 64 ("quite raw men"); Grant, *New Highland Military* (1757), 17 ("never saw a Cat killed"); Forbes to Pitt, Philadelphia, May 1, 1758, *Writings of Forbes*, 77 (additional companies); Byrd to Forbes, Charles Town, March 21, 1758, Headquarters Papers of John Forbes (microfilm, hereafter cited as FHQP, with reel and folio numbers), reel 1, f. 85 (officers anxious). On the travel delays, see Sinclair to St. Clair, Charles Town, April 26, 1758, FHQP, reel 1, f. 49n1 (problems embarking); Abercromby to Forbes, Albany, June 4, 1758, FHQP, reel 2, f. 291; Forbes to Bouquet, Philadelphia, June 8, 1758, FHQP, reel 2, f. 299 (battalion arrived, will disembark next day).

15. Bouquet to Stanwix, Charles Town, June 23, 1758, *BP* 1:121; Bouquet, Remonstrance to the Assembly, Charles Town, January 19, 1757, *BP* 1:278–79 ("for no other purpose"); Loudoun to Bouquet, New York, December 25, 1757, *BP* 1:268; Bouquet to Forbes, Charles Town, February 1, 1758, *BP* 1:288; Bouquet to Stanwix, Charles Town, February 21, 1758, *BP* 1:309 ("begin to despair").

16. Forbes to Denny, Philadelphia, April 20 ("Scarcity of Arms"), 21 ("any just request"), 1758, *Writings of Forbes*, 66–67; Denny to Forbes, Philadelphia, April 25, 1758, FHQP, reel 1, f. 141. Denny had previously been a captain in the 36th Foot, whose major at the time was Archibald Montgomery. See Steward, *List of the Officers*, 58.

17. This paragraph draws on the insightful analysis of the origins of Pennsylvania society and politics in Smolenski, *Friends and Strangers*.

18. Anderson, *Crucible of War*, 161–62. Denny to Forbes, Philadelphia, April 4, 1758, GD 45/2, in Papers of General John Forbes, Dalhousie Muniments, Scottish Records Office, Edinburgh, Scotland (hereafter Forbes/SRO), reel 1 ("Money to recruit"). Pemberton and his allies created the "Friendly Association for Regaining and Preserving Peace with the Indians by Pacific Measures." On Pennsylvania's declaration of war against the Delawares and Ohio Indians, see *PCR*, 7:74–76, 88–89.

19. For Pennsylvania troops, see Hunter, *Forts on the Pennsylvania Frontier*, ch. 6, esp. 200–201. On Pennsylvania's line of forts, see Hunter, *Forts on the Pennsylvania Frontier*, ch. 5; Waddell and Bomberger, *French and Indian War*, 32–35. Strategically, these forts can be seen as a northward extension of the forts built at the same time as Forts Cumberland and Frederick in Maryland. Three of these forts—Forts Loudoun, in Winchester, Virginia, Fort Vause in Virginia, and Fort Loudoun in Pennsylvania—have been the subjects of archaeological studies. See Jolly, "Fort Loudoun, Virginia"; McBride, "The Second Fort Vause"; Warfel, "Fort Loudoun." See also George Stevenson to Richard Peters, York, May 8, 1758, in Hazard et al., *Pennsylvania Archives* (hereafter *PA*, with series, volume, and page), 1.3.392 (dispute over enlistments); Forbes to Pitt, Philadelphia, May 19, 1758, *Correspondence of Pitt*, 1:247 ("scrape together"); Bouquet to Forbes, June 8, 1758, *BP* 2:17. Heydeler appears on a list of foreign protestant officers going to America. Listed a "Bas Officier" (most likely a noncommissioned officer), Heydeler, like the others, came anticipating commissions in the new Royal American Regiment. Instead, Heydeler, who Bouquet said had spent several years at the Royal Artillery school in Woolwich, went

to Pennsylvania, joined its regiment, and continued to serve throughout the war, apparently never receiving the king's commission he sought, despite earning the favorable attention of Forbes and Bouquet. See *BP* 1:46; Bouquet to Forbes, Carlisle, May 25, 1758, *BP* 1:364 ("the two 6-pounders"). On Pennsylvania's artillery, *Pennsylvania Gazette*, December 8, 1757, mentions iron guns purchased the previous year "besides a Train of Artillery, being new Brass Field Pieces, 12 and 6 Pounders"; there was also an eight-inch mortar in *BP* 1:337.

20. Loudoun to Sharpe, New York, January 20, 1758, FHQP, reel 1, f. 33 (taking troops into royal pay). A summary of the issues involved is in Sharpe to Forbes, "Conegochiegh" (Conococheague), June 9, 1758, FHQP, reel 2, f. 301.

21. Sharpe to Abercromby, Annapolis, March 20, 1758, FHQP, reel 1, f. 81; Sharpe to Abercromby (Annapolis), March 20, 1758, in Browne et al., *Archives of Maryland*, vol. 9 (hereafter cited as *AM*), 156–57; Sharpe to Forbes, Annapolis, May 6, 1758, FHQP, reel 2, f. 181; St. Clair to Forbes, Philadelphia, May 10, 1758, FHQP, reel 2, f. 212 ("deal of Vexation"); Sharpe to Forbes, Annapolis, May 14, 1758, FHQP, reel 2, f. 219; Sharpe to Calvert, May 14, 1758, in *AM*, 179 ("money").

22. Forbes to St. Clair, Philadelphia, May 23, 1758, FHQP, reel 2, f. 249 ("I really think"); Forbes to Pitt, Philadelphia, June 17, 1758, *Correspondence of Pitt*, 1:279 ("used to the woods"); Forbes to Dagworthy (Philadelphia?), n.d., FHQP, reel 3, f. 529; Forbes to St. Clair, Philadelphia, June 16, 1768, FHQP, reel 2, f. 318; Abercromby to Forbes, Albany, June 4, 1758, FHQP, reel 2, f. 291 ("Rangers"). The costs of supporting the Maryland troops was significant. From October 8, 1757, through June 1, 1758, the estimates ran to more than seven thousand pounds sterling. See "Calculation of Pay . . . due to the Maryland Troops the 8th April 1758 . . . Expence of victualling them from the 8th Oct. to this Time," June 1, 1758, FHQP, reel 2, f. 283.

23. On raising the new Virginia regiment, see Titus, *Old Dominion*, 121–22. Byrd to Forbes, Winchester, June 3, 1758, FHQP, reel 2, f. 287 ("Indian Fashion"). Fauquier to Byrd, Williamsburg, June 19, 1758, in Tinling, *Three William Byrds*, 2:660 (French uniforms).

24. Forbes to Pitt, Philadelphia, May 1, 1758, *Writings of Forbes*, 77 ("there is nothing expected"); Blair to Forbes, Williamsburg, May 20, 1758, FHQP, reel 2, f. 236; "Return of the North Carolina Troops," Fort Loudoun (Pennsylvania), July 21, 1758, FHQP, reel 2, f. 403; St. Clair to Bouquet, Carlisle, June 30, 1758, *BP* 2:153 ("in the Clouds"); Bouquet to Forbes, Raystown, August 3, 1758, *BP* 2:313 ("pitiable"); Dobbs to Forbes, Brunswick, Cape Fear, July 31, 1758, FHQP, reel 2, f. 429. According to Halkett there were never more than 127 effectives with Forbes's army. See James Abercromby to the Committee of Correspondence of North Carolina, London, June 1, 1759, in Van Horne and Reese, *Letter Book of James Abercromby*, 294.

25. Forbes to Hugh Forbes, Manchester, October 19, 1754, Forbes to Loudoun, New York, December 10, 1757, Forbes to Abercromby, Philadelphia, April 24, 1758, Forbes to Abercromby, Raystown, October 8, 1758, in *Writings of Forbes*, 1, 21, 72, 227. By July Forbes appointed two other brigade majors: Captain Joseph Shippen for the Pennsylvania troops and Captain Abraham Bosomworth of the Royal Americans for the Virginia regiments. See Tinling, *Three William Byrds*, 2:664.

26. Russell is included in "List of Officers of His Majesty's Hospital serving in North America" (1755), CO 5/213. On Grant, see Stewart to Washington, Raystown, October 24, 1758, *GWP* 6:91n2. On "flying hospitals," see Cantlie, *History of the Army*

Medical Department, 1:45–49. On the hospital staff with Forbes's army, see "Abstract of Warrant Granted by the late Brig. General Forbes," *Writings of Forbes*, 294–95. On Sergeant Morton, see Forbes to Abercromby, Philadelphia, April 24, 1758, *Writings of Forbes*, 72 ("either as Secretary or a Clerk").

27. Orderly Book, August 14, 1758, *BP* 2:677; Abercromby to Forbes, New York, April 24, 1758, FHQP, reel 1, f. 137 ("The Engineer"); Forbes to Loudoun, New York, February 27, 1758, *Writings of Forbes*, 48 ("plenty of business"). See also Forbes to Abercromby, Philadelphia, April 20, 1758, *Writings of Forbes*, 65; Porter, *History of the Corps of Royal Engineers*, 1:163–65; Taylor, *Military Roads in Scotland*, 33, 67; Steward, *List of the Officers*, 159.
28. Cleaveland, *Royal Regiment of Artillery*, 254 (Minorca), 256 (artillery for America, 1757); Matthew Clerk to Forbes, Albany (n.d.), Forbes/SRO reel 2; Forbes to St. Clair, May 25, 1758, FHQP, reel 2, f. 265 (Hay arrives with men from New York); "Warrant to pay Dr. McLeane £40 for the care of the artillery detachment," Gratz Collection, Papers of the Royal Artillery of Pennsylvania, History Society of Pennsylvania, Philadelphia (hereafter cited as HSP). See also "Return of the Officers and Men Military and Civil of the Detachment of the Royal Artillery," June 10, 1758, Forbes/SRO, reel 2. For an idea of what a "train" included, see "A Proportion of Ordnance and Stores for Pennsylvania," June 13, 1758, Forbes/SRO, reel 2.
29. Bouquet's military career prior to America is covered in *BP* 1:xvi–xxvii. Bouquet's American career is the subject of a new study, see Smith, *Bouquet's Expedition*.
30. Bouquet to St. Clair, Philadelphia, April 18, 1757, *BP* 1:83 ("in the only regiment"). Bouquet ended his letter to St. Clair with "Farewell, my dear Sir John, do not forget me," *BP* 1:84 (cloying letter, "the only regiment"). Bouquet to Peters, Charles Town, October 22, 1757, *BP* 1:225–26. For Bouquet's land dealings, see Lyttleton to Loudoun, Charles Town, December 10, 1757, *BP* 1:256; Lyttleton to Forbes, Charles Town, May 20, 1758, *BP* 1:344.
31. Bouquet to Forbes, New York, April 23, 1758, *BP* 1:333; Forbes to Bouquet, Philadelphia, June 19, 1758, Forbes to Bouquet, Carlisle, August 2, 1758, *Writings of Forbes*, 122, 166. The incident was Bouquet's decision to permit Major James Grant to make a "reconnaissance" of Fort Duquesne in September (see chapter 7 below).
32. Forbes to Hugh Forbes, Manchester, October 19, 1755, *Writings of Forbes*, 1; Abercromby to Pitt, Albany, May 22, 1758, *Correspondence of Pitt*, 1:252–53; St. Clair to Napier, Williamsburg, February 10, 1755, *Military Affairs*, 58–65; St. Clair to Napier, Albany, November 18, 1755, Forbes/SRO, reel 1. Braddock quoted in Hildeburn, "Sir John St. Clair," 6; see also Dinwiddie to Robinson, Williamsburg, January 20, 1755, in Brock, *Records of Robert Dinwiddie*, 1:475. St. Clair's early military career can be found in Preston, *Braddock's Defeat*, 36–37.
33. Road commissioners to Morris, Fort Cumberland, April 16, 1755, in Balch, *Letters and Papers*, 36–38 ("Lion rampant"); St. Clair to Blair, Winchester, May 23, 1758, FHQP, reel 2, f. 251. See also Blair to Pitt, Williamsburg, June 29, 1758, *Correspondence of Pitt*, 1:290–91.
34. St. Clair to Napier, Will's Creek, July 22, 1755, *Military Affairs*, 102 ("indignation"); St. Clair to Napier, Fort Cumberland, August 15, 1755, Forbes/SRO, reel 1 ("moral certainty"). See also Dinwiddie to Commodore Keppel, Williamsburg, September 6, 1755, in Brock, *Records of Robert Dinwiddie*, 1:197.
35. Loudoun to Cumberland, New York, March 8, April 25, October 17, 1757, *Military*

Affairs, 318 ("he found he must die"), 346, 403; Abercromby's Orders to Clair, FHQP, reel 3, f. 534; Forbes to Abercromby, Philadelphia, June 27, 1758, *The Writings of Forbes*, 128 ("Madman").

36. Stephen to St. Clair, Fort Cumberland, September 3, 1755, Forbes/SRO, reel 1; St. Clair to Stephen, Albany, October 22, 1755, Forbes/SRO, reel 1. See also *GWP* 1:225n1.
37. Forbes to Bouquet, Shippensburg, August 28, 1758, *BP* 2:440 ("pats as a Military man"); Forbes to Abercromby, Raystown, October 16, 1758, *Writings of Forbes*, 234 ("my only plight anchor"); Forbes to Loudoun, New York, February 14, 1758, *Writings of Forbes*, 42 ("Archie").
38. Bouquet to Ellis, Charles Town, November 12, 1757, *BP* 1:238. The decision to raise new Highland troops came in early January, 1757. See MacKillop, *More Fruitful than the Soil*. Forbes was especially impressed with James Burd's Pennsylvania battalion, calling them "by far the best woodsmen of the whole." Forbes to Bouquet, Shippensburg, August 28, 1758, *Writings of Forbes*, 190.
39. The best discussion of British army training in this period can be found in Houlding, *Fit for Service*, esp. chs. 4–6. On Washington, see "Invoice," December 6, 1755, and "Address," Winchester, January 8, 1756, *GWP* 2:209, 257. Bland's treatise was republished numerous times before 1762, and Washington may have purchased the 1740 edition. *A New Exercise to be observed by His Majesty's Troops* (London, 1757).
40. Byrd to Forbes, Winchester, June 23, 1758, FHQP, reel 2, f. 327; Washington to St. Clair, Fort Loudoun (Virginia), June 23, 1758, *GWP* 5:235; Washington to Lewis, Fort Loudoun (Virginia), April 21, 1758, *GWP* 5:134 ("straightened");Bouquet to Forbes, Carlisle, June 7, 1758, *BP* 2:50 (rifles, "fine powder"); Charles Smith to Washington, Fort Loudoun (Virginia), July 30, 1758, *BP* 2:351 ("not one gun"). Photographs of cartridge boxes and pouches appear in Gale, "A Soldier-Like Way," 2, 4.
41. St. Clair to Blair, Winchester, May 19, 1758, FHQP, reel 2, f. 232; St. Clair to Sharpe, Winchester, May 30, 1758, *AM*, 192; Washington to St. Clair, Fort Loudoun (Virginia), June23, 1758, *GWP* 5:235 ("distressed"); Bouquet to Forbes, Carlisle, May 30, 1758, *BP* 2:387 ("unfit for use"); Bouquet to Forbes, Carlisle, June 7, 1758, *BP* 2:47; Bouquet to St. Clair, Carlisle, June 3, 1758, *BP* 2:22 (doesn't want troops armed with bayonets, orders hatchets instead). The best source on provincial weaponry is Mullins, *Of Sorts for Provincials*, 113 ("incredibly mixed lot"), 136–44 (Pennsylvania weapons).
42. Bouquet to Stanwix, Charles Town, February 21, 1758, *BP* 1:309.
43. Washington to Forbes, Fort Loudoun (Virginia), April 23, 1758, *GWP* 5:138 ("shabby appearance," "very bare"); Washington to Bouquet, Fort Cumberland, July 3, 1758, *GWP* 5:257; Byrd to Forbes, Winchester, May 29, 1758, in Tinling, "Some Unpublished Correspondence," 283 ("Indian Fashion"); *Pennsylvania Gazette*, August 3, 1758 (advertising for Robert Gordon, deserter from the 2d Virginia, last, seen wearing a "light coloured Cloth Waistcoat and check Trowsers"); Washington to Bouquet, Fort Cumberland, July 13, 1758, *BP* 2:203; Bouquet to Washington, Raes Town, July 14, 1758, *BP* 2:206; *Pennsylvania Gazette*, June 16, 1757 (description of a Pennsylvania deserter in a "blue Coat Faced with Red); *Pennsylvania Gazette*, June 22, 1758 (deserters wearing "honeycomb" and "black" breeches and "wide Check Trowsers"); Forbes to Bouquet, Philadelphia, June 2, 1758, *BP* 2:7 (Pennsylvania uniforms, "to save time"); "Journal of James Byrd," March 1, 1758, *PA* 1.3.356 (men not to buy uniforms); Stevenson to Peters, York, May 8, 1758, *PA* 1.3.392 (stocking, "Trows-

ers," frocks); Forbes to Abercromby, Shippensburg, September 4, 1758, *Writings of Forbes*, 200 (Shelby's volunteers); Forbes to Pitt, Fort Loudoun (Pennsylvania), September 6, 1758, *Correspondence of Pitt*, 1:341–42 ("in want of Everything"); Fauquier to St. Clair, Williamsburg, June 6, 1758, in Reese, *The Official Papers of Francis Fauquier* (hereafter cited as *PFF*, with volume and page), 1:15. A survey of uniforms worn by provincial troops can be found in Haarmann, "American Uniforms."

44. Bouquet to Forbes, Carlisle, May 30, 1758, *BP* 2:389–90 (shoes). Joseph Shippen, a captain in the Pennsylvania Regiment likewise recorded that the New Levies were to have at least two extra pairs of shoes and leather sufficient to make more. Shippen Orderly Book, June 3, 1758, HSP. "Journal of James Burd," *PA* 1.3.352, 353, 354–57; Stevenson to Bouquet, York, May 31, 1758, *BP* 1:399; St. Clair to Bouquet, Winchester, May 28, 1758, *BP* 1:376–77; Baillie to Bouquet, August 28, 1762, in Stevens and Kent, *Papers of Col. Henry Bouquet*, ser. 21648, 2:77–78 (itemized list of regular's clothing and equipment). At the same time that officers were trying to equip their men, they also took care of their own needs. Washington sent his agent a list of items to purchase for the campaign including a packsaddle, a traveling letter case with inkstands, a light shoe-boot, a hair coat, a field bed, and a half dozen china cups and saucers. See Washington to David Franks, Fort Loudoun (Virginia), May 1, 1758, *GWP* 5, 152.

45. Forbes to Fauquier, Loyalhannon, November 5, 1758, in Reese, *PFF*, 1:102.

46. This and the following paragraphs on British troops draw on Brumwell, *Redcoats*, esp. chs. 2–3 and pp. 316–19, tables 2–6; Way, "Soldiers of Misfortune"; Way, "Class and the Common Soldier." On economic and social conditions in colonial cities before and during the Seven Years' War, see Nash, *Urban Crucible*, esp. chs. 7, 9; also Smith, *Lower Sort*, 108–25. The raising of the Royal Americans can be followed in Campbell, *Royal American Regiment*, esp. chs. 1–2.

47. "A Report of the Service, Size, Age and Country . . . of Five Companys of the first Battalion of His Majesty's Royal American Regiment," Charles Town, July 24, 1757, *BP* 1:152; "A Return of the Artifficers of the Forces under the Command of Lieut. Colonel Bouquet," Camp at New Market (South Carolina), July 8, 1757, *BP* 1:135.

48. McCulloch and Todish, *Through So Many Dangers*, 33 ("impress'd men," "prime of their youth"). On the ethnic composition of Montgomery's regiment, see Brumwell, *Redcoats*, table 5; on recruiting in the Highlands, Brumwell, *Redcoats*, 273–78; Forbes to Pitt, Philadelphia, June 17, 1758, *Writings of Forbes*, 117 ("Cousins"); Dziennik, *Fatal Land*, ch. 1; Knox, *Campaigns in North America*, 1:73–74 (Highlander shot).

49. Titus, *Old Dominion*, 108–9; Stephenson, "Pennsylvania Provincial Soldiers," 202–3.

50. Stephenson, "Pennsylvania Provincial Soldiers," 202–3 ("wealed"); Ward, "Army of Servants." A comparison between Virginia and Pennsylvania forces can be found in Titus, *Old Dominion*, 81–87, tables 1–4; and Ward, *Breaking the Backcountry*, 100–122, 263–64, tables 1–4. Ward's tables are especially valuable since they include, for comparative purposes, information on Massachusetts provincials, long, seen as the norm among provincial troops. Ward, *Breaking the Backcountry*, 99–100 (servants); Ward, "Army of Servants," 92–93 (mercenaries); see also Knobloch, "Mobilizing Provincials"; Stephen to Washington, Fort Cumberland, July 25, 1756, *GWP* 3:294 ("wealed," "pissed themselves"). For a different view on Virginia, see Ferling, "Who Served?"

Notes to Pages 56–58

51. St. Clair to Forbes, Winchester, May 19, 1758, FHQP, reel 2, f. 234. On Washington's efforts, see *Lord Loudoun*, 312; Ferling, "School for Command," 201.
52. Hale, *War and Society in Renaissance Europe*, 159. There is a growing literature on these followers. Among the most insightful are Hacker, "Women and Military Institutions"; Kopperman, "British High Command and Soldiers' Wives"; Mayer, *Belonging to the Army*; Fatherly, "Tending the Army."
53. Kopperman, "British High Command and Soldiers' Wives." The number of women permitted to follow the army was fixed early in the war, with Braddock's campaign in 1755; see "Halkett's Orderly Book," in Hamilton, *Braddock's Defeat*, 89–90. Numbers of women per regiment could vary greatly depending on location; see Cormack and Jones, *Journal of Corporal William Todd*, 296n28. Bagshawe to Lord George Sackville, Cork, February, 1754, in Guy, *Colonel Samuel Bagshawe*, 135–36 ("Wives and Children"). In one rearguard action in Germany in 1761, captives taken by the French included soldiers and their families; see Cormack and Jones, *Journal of Corporal William Todd*, 207.
54. Cormack and James, *Journal of Corporal William Todd*, 60. Corporal Todd noted that his army's commander in Germany, Prince Ferdinand of Brunswick, once allowed women a full ration of bread and children a half ration. Todd thought this was "very Acceptable as the Bread we receive is not near Sufficient for several men, much Less for them that has Wifes & Children" (217).
55. "The Journal of Captain Robert Cholmley's Batman," in Hamilton, *Braddock's Defeat*, 25; "The Journal of Charlotte Brown," in Calder, *Colonial Captives*, 183–84 (Braddock's defeat); Preston, *Braddock's Defeat*, 263; Steele, *Betrayals*, 230n49 (Fort William Henry, 1757); Knox, *Campaigns in North America*, 2:338, 353 (Quebec). Regiments were allowed to create widows' funds by collecting wages for a certain number of fictitious soldiers—usually two per company, called "widow's men." The widow of Lieutenant John Billings, killed while serving in the Royal Americans with Forbes, asked Bouquet for help in applying for the pension "which is appointed for Officers Widows." Mary Billings to Bouquet, Boston, February 19, 1759, *BP* 3:134–35. A charitable organization—The Society for the Encouragement of British Soldiers in Germany and North America—was founded in 1759 and disbursed clothing, other materials, and small sums of money to soldiers' widows and orphans; regimental officers, too, might contribute small sums to soldiers' survivors; see Jonas Hadway, *Account of the Society*.
56. "A Field Return of the Maryland Forces, Encamped near Raes Town," September 11, 1758, in Balch, *Letters and Papers*, 138; "Field Return of the Division of the Sixty-second Regiment, or First Highland Battalion," Raystown, September 15, 1758, in Balch, *Letters and Papers*, 140 (additional companies); "A Daily Return of the Second Battalion of the Penna. Regiment," Rays Town, August 19, 1758, in Balch, *Letters and Papers*, 132–33 (Pennsylvania); Orderly Book, Raystown, August 8, 1758, *GWP*, 5:300 (1st Virginia Regiment).
57. I am using a multiplier of ninety companies in calculating these figures; this was the total number with the army, less the four North Carolina Companies and a later group of Maryland volunteers. For the 31st Foot and of numbers pertaining to women with the army during the Revolution, see Hagist, "Women of the British Army," http://www.revwar75.com/library/hagist/britwomen.htm.

58. McConnell, *Army and Empire*, 66 (Pensacola); Hagist, "Women of the British Army," table 1.
59. "The Journal of Charlotte Brown," in Calder, *Colonial Captives*, 178, 180; "Bouquet's Accounts," *BP* 3:245 (entry for April 16, 1759); Ourry to Bouquet, Carlisle, May 27, 1759, *BP* 3:330.
60. Martha May to Bouquet, Carlisle, June 4, 1758, *BP* 2:30 (emphasis added).
61. Cormack, *"These Meritorious Objects,"* 173, 292. On Wedge, see McConnell, *Army and Empire*, 58. Some colonies also drew on blacks or mulattos to fill the ranks; see for example DeLancey, *Muster Rolls*; Braddock to Napier, Williamsburg, March 17, 1755, *Military Affairs*, 78 ("Mulattoes"); Washington to St. Clair, Fort Loudoun (Virginia), June 14, 1758, *GWP* 5:213n214 ("Sensible Fellow"); "Bouquet's Accounts," April 16, 1759, *BP* 3:245 ("Sir John's Negro"); Washington to Bouquet, Fort Cumberland, July 3, 1758, *GWP* 5:257 (servants). A pistole was a Spanish unit of currency worth approximately seventeen shillings; see McCusker, *Money and Exchange*, 11.
62. Forbes to Pitt, Philadelphia, May 19, 1758, *Correspondence of Pitt*, 1:245–46; Bouquet to Forbes, Fort Loudoun (Pennsylvania), June 11, 1758, *BP* 2:72. Heydeler's artillery likely included the two "royal" howitzers that were cast locally on Forbes's orders. On the Pennsylvania Assembly, see Assembly to Denny, Philadelphia, May 3, 1758, Forbes to Pennsylvania Commissioners, Philadelphia, May 24, 1758, and Commissioners to Forbes, Philadelphia, May 26, 1758, all in Forbes/SRO, reel 1.
63. Pitt to Governors of Pennsylvania, Maryland, Virginia, South Carolina, North Carolina, Whitehall, December 30, 1757, *Correspondence of Pitt*, 140–41; Forbes to Stanwix, Philadelphia, May 29, 1758, *Writings of Forbes*, 102 ("Cholick"). His comment to Stanwix was one of Forbes's first references to the chronic and debilitating illness that would claim his life in March, 1759. Most modern accounts attribute Forbes's problems to stomach cancer coupled with skin infections and dysentery. Dr. Gerald Norris of Birmingham, Alabama, reviewed all known references to Forbes's health during the campaign and concluded that the general suffered from a long history of "gastrointestinal symptoms." These as well as Forbes's "musculoskeletal" complaints led Dr. Norris to suggest that Forbes might have suffered from inflammatory bowel disease and arthritis. His inability to urinate may have been due to dehydration triggered by his other illnesses. The swellings of which Forbes complained could also have been due to malnutrition triggered by his gastrointestinal problems. Personal communication, Dr. Gerald Norris, March 1, 2018. I am grateful to Dr. Norris for taking time to review the material on Forbes's health. On cancer, see Oliphant, *John Forbes*, 2.
64. For French attacks and delays, see Shippen to Halkett, Lancaster, June 23, 1758, in Shippen, "Military Letters of Joseph Shippen," 457.

Two. *FRIENDS AND ENEMIES*, Winter–Spring 1758

Epigraph: Forbes to Abercromby, Philadelphia, April 22, 1758, *Writings of Forbes*, 68.
1. Loudoun to Cumberland, Albany, August 20, 1756, *Military Affairs*, 224. On the battles at Lake George and Hendrick's death, see Hinderaker, *Two Hendricks*, 257–67. On Iroquois responses to the outbreak of war, see Parmenter, "After the Mourning Wars"; Anderson, *Crucible of War*, 115–23. On irregular warfare in America, see Ward, *Breaking the Backcountry*, 45–58; Ward, "European Method of Warring."
2. Loudoun to Cumberland, Albany, October 2, 1756, in *Military Affairs*, 237; Schumann

and Schweizer, *Seven Years War*, 109–14 (little war). See also Russell, "Redcoats in the Wilderness." This irregular mode of warfare had been characteristic of warfare in the Netherlands in the sixteenth century; see Parker, *Army of Flanders*, 9–11.

3. Loudoun to Cumberland, Albany and New York, November 22 to December 26, 1756, *Military Affairs*, 269 (feels he will be blamed for the rangers); Cumberland to Loudoun, Kensington, October 22, 1756, *Military Affairs*, 255–56 (need for regular officers with irregular forces). The development and history of Rogers's Rangers can be found in Brumwell, *White Devil*, esp. ch. 3. On British efforts to adapt to American conditions, including the raising of the 80th Light-Armed Foot, see Brumwell, *Redcoats*, 191–236.

4. Loudoun to Atkin, New York, January 14, 1758, FHQP, reel 1, f. 34; Loudoun to Lyttleton, New York, February 13, 1758, FHQP, reel 1, ff. 44 (Byrd), 45 (numbers of Cherokees); Loudoun to Atkin, New York, February 14, 1758, in Mays, *Amherst Papers*, 52 (Byrd, Bosomworth). On Bosomworth, see Piker, *Four Deaths of Acorn Whistler*, 93–95. Later in the campaign Bosomworth assumed the title of "Superintendent of Indian Affairs in the Western District," which title appears to have meant nothing in the context of British Indian affairs. Even before this, however, Forbes cautioned others not to trust Bosomworth, and Bouquet later concluded that "his opinion has no great weight with me." Bouquet to Forbes, Raystown, August 8, 1758, *BP* 2:338. See Hunter, "Barton," 458 (Bosomworth's title); Forbes to Bouquet, Philadelphia, June 6, 1758, *BP* 2:39 (no trust).

5. On the cultural geography of the Cherokees, see Oliphant, *Peace and War*, 1–8; on population, see Wood, "Changing Population," 39, table 1.

6. Oliphant, *Peace and War*, 1–2 (smallpox), 12–13 (boundary); also Wood, "Changing Population," 63–64 (smallpox and population), 38, table 1. The Cherokees were thought to have three thousand fighting men in the mid-1750s; see Jacobs, *Appalachian Indian Frontier*, 42. On the impact of European expansion in the Southeast, see Kelton, *Epidemics and Enslavement*; Browne, *The Westo Indians*; Ethridge and Shuck-Hall, *Mapping the Mississippian Shatter Zone*.

7. On the changes occurring among the Cherokees, see Hatley, "Three Lives of Keowee"; in the Southeast more generally, see Saunt, "History until 1776." On Cherokee war with Creeks, see Piker, *Okfuskee*, 445–51; on Cherokees and Iroquois, see Perdue, "Cherokee Relations."

8. Fogelson, "Cherokee in the East," 346. On the town and region as factors in Cherokee social and political life, see Boulware, *Deconstructing the Cherokee Nation*, esp. 47 (British attempts to create a Cherokee "emperor"), 30 (limits of shared Cherokee identity). See also Gearing, "Structural Poses."

9. Gearing, "Structural Poses."

10. Connecortee quoted in Hatley, "Three Lives of Keowee," 231–32.

11. Hatley, *Dividing Paths*, 95. See also Oliphant, *Peace and War*, 6–8; Richter, *Facing East from Indian Country*, 169. On Cherokee mother towns, see Fogelson, "Cherokees in the East," 342; Beck, *Chiefdoms, Collapse, and Coalescence*, 238–40.

12. A recent assessment of Glen's skills in Indian affairs can be found in Piker, *Four Deaths of Acorn Whistler*, chs. 1–2.

13. On interregional rivalries and friction, see Jacobs, *Appalachian Indian Frontier*, 49. This paragraph draws heavily from Boulware, *Deconstructing the Cherokee Nation*, esp. chs. 2, 4.

14. Bosomworth to Cherokees and Catawbas, Fort Loudoun (Virginia), 132 ("common cause," "elder Brothers, and Cherokee warriors' reply"); Lyttleton to Loudoun, CharlesTown, March 21, 1758, FHQP reel 1 f. 84 ("promise"); Byrd to Lyttleton, Little Saluda, March 31, 1758, in Tinling, *Three William Byrds*, 2:644 ("if he gets"); Byrd to Lyttleton, n.p., May 1, 1758, in Tinling, *Three William Byrds*, 2:651 ("little savage," "insolent"). Daniel J. Tortora, in *Carolina in Crisis*, offers the most recent assessment of Attakullakulla and emphasizes his bid for local power among the Cherokees while downplaying his importance and influence. See also, Kelton, "British and Indian War." Although Kelton and I agree on the idea of a "British and Indian War," our interpretations nevertheless diverge. Kelton sees the effort as a success and, indeed, credits the Cherokees for making peace with Ohio Indians possible. My own take on this, as developed in the chapters that follow, is very different.
15. Even lower-ranking officers were well aware of how important Indians were to the army's success. Virginia Captain Thomas Bullitt observed that Forbes's success "will, in a great Measure, depend on the Supporting and Spiriting up Our Friend Indians." Bullitt to Denny, Fort Loudoun (Virginia), March 31, 1758, *SWJP* 2:806–8. See Savory, *His Britannic Majesty's Army*; Reid, *Frederick the Great's Allies*, esp. 5–6 (subsidy troops). The Cherokee Middle Towns were particularly reluctant to join the army. See Byrd to Forbes, Keowee, April 30, 1758, Forbes/SRO, reel 1. On Catawba participation, see "Catawba Indians to Cherokees [sic]," March 24, 1758, *SWJP*, 9:886–87 (the message was actually directed to the Mohawks).
16. Hatley, *Dividing Paths*, 93 (on the apparent chaos of colonial politics concerning the Cherokee).
17. Forbes made clear his expectation that the Indians would not return home without permission. See Bosomworth to Cherokees and Catawbas, Fort Loudoun (Virginia), April 21, 1758, Forbes/SRO, reel 1.
18. Speech of Governor Sharpe to Cherokees, April 5, 1758, Forbes/SRO, reel 1 ("great Number"); Bosomworth to Cherokees and Catawbas, Fort Loudoun (Virginia), April 21, 1758, Forbes/SRO, reel 1 ("very desirous").
19. For an excellent account of Indian encounters with border settlers, albeit in this case of Iroquois traveling south, see Hofstra, *Planting of New Virginia*, ch. 1, esp. 44–49.
20. On the Delaware migrations, see McConnell, *Country Between*, chs. 1–2; White, *Middle Ground*, 187–89. See also Schutt, *Peoples of the River Valleys*, esp. ch. 4. On the Shawnees, see Warren, *The Worlds the Shawnees Made*, 174–79, and ch. 8. On the Delaware "royal family," see Alden, "Captivity of Hugh Gibson," 142; McConnell, "Pisquetomen and Tamaqua," 275–83. On the location of native towns in the Ohio Country, see Tanner, *Atlas of Great Lakes Indian History*, 40–41. Population estimates are derived from Conrad Weiser's census of Ohio Indians during his 1748 meeting; see *PCR* 5:351–52.
21. "A Treaty, At a Council at Philadelphia, the 13th of November, 1747," in Boyd, *Indian Treaties*, 103 ("Warriors living at Ohio"). On the events summarized in this and the following paragraph, see McConnell, *Country Between*, ch. 4; White, *Middle Ground*, 189–240.
22. "The Case of the Ohio Company Extracted from Original Papers" (facsimile), in Mulkearn, *George Mercer Papers*, 23 ("Country between"); Gipson, *British Empire*, 4:284 ("clear of settlements"). On Shingas, see McConnell, *Country Between*, 98. See also Calloway, *Shawnees*, 22–26.

23. The events summarized here, along with their political and diplomatic fallout, can be followed in detail in Anderson, *Crucible of War*, 3–73, and Baugh, *Global Seven Years War*, chs. 2–4.
24. Ian Steele has provided the best and most thorough discussion of the origins of the Shawnees' war against the British. See his *Setting All the Captives Free*, 21–30, 81–82; Steele, "Shawnees and the English."
25. On the Delawares and the emerging war for the Ohio Country, see McConnell, *Country Between*, 115–22. Ackowanothic quoted in Wallace, *Conrad Weiser*, 530. Braddock's alleged response to Shingas is in Beverly W. Bond Jr., "The Captivity of Charles Stuart," *Mississippi Valley Historical Review* 13 (1926–1927): 63. The plan of the new work is reproduced in "Defense in the Wilderness," in James and Stotz, *Drums in the Forest*, facing page 156, and in Preston, *Braddock's Defeat*, 266. Preston has called into question Shingas's account, noting that Braddock met local Indians warmly and that no British record corroborates Shingas's version of his encounter with the general. Yet Shingas went to some lengths to explain his reasons for going to war to the captive Charles Stuart; allowing for the retrospective nature of the account and Stuart's own likely misunderstanding of the details, the account does echo the Delawares' principal concern, which was their sovereignty over the land and the fear that a British army would lead to further dispossession.
26. I have borrowed the term "parallel war" from MacLeod, *Canadian Iroquois*, 19–36, esp. 21. See also Steele, "Shawnee Origins."
27. Meinig, *Shaping of America*, 1:212 ("bloody edge"). Newspaper notices come from Lucier, *French and Indian War Notices*, 2:45 (M'Cord's fort), 58 ("Indians have returned"), 82 (children missing), 84 (found dead), 214 (South Branch of Potomac), 220 (three families); Dowd, *Groundless*, 107; Lucier, *French and Indian War Notices*, 3:55 (attacks in York County). On the impact of war on border societies, see Ward, *Breaking the Backcountry*, 45–58, 77–90. The best and by far the most comprehensive treatment of casualties in this border war can be found in Steele, *Setting all the Captives Free*, esp. ch. 4 on the Ohio Country up to 1759.
28. Dinwiddie quoted in Titus, *Old Dominion*, 75. On the French neutrals, see *Pennsylvania Gazette*, February 5, April 15, July 1, 1756. See also Faragher, *Great and Noble Scheme*, esp. ch. 13. Figures are from Steele, *Setting All the Captives Free*, 115; but see the different numbers offered by Ward, in "Fighting the 'Old Women,'" 315–16.
29. Titus, *Old Dominion*, ch. 4; McConnell, *Country Between*, 122–24.
30. Merrell, *Into the American Woods*, 250.
31. Lucier, *French and Indian War Notices*, 2:59 (Cresaps); Titus, *Old Dominion*, 79 (Dinwiddie); McConnell, *Country Between*, 124. The text of Pennsylvania's declaration of war can be found in Hirsh, *EAID*, 3:25–28. Steele, *Setting All the Captives Free*, 101–2 (scalp bounties), 103–5 (Kittanning raid); Fauquier to the Board of Trade, Williamsburg, January 5, 1759, in Reese, *PFF*, 1:146. See also Silver, *Our Savage Neighbors*, ch. 4. One reason that native fighters took prisoners was to incorporate these people into their own societies (see below); another was an increasing willingness of Europeans to offer ransom; in neither case was this echoed in the case of colonial attacks on native enemies. On ransoming, see Haefeli and Sweeney, *Captors and Captives*, 147–51; Steele, *Setting All the Captives Free*, ch. 14. On the moral issues arising from colonial adoption of scalping and scalp bounties, see Axtell, "Scalping."

32. Ward, "Fighting the 'Old Women,'" 297. Numbers of dead at Kittanning from Steele, *Setting All the Captives Free*, 104. Ian Steele places the total number of Ohio Indians killed at 196 from 1755 to 1759. Steele, *Setting All the Captives Free*, 586n151.
33. McConnell, *Country Between*, 115–19; McConnell, "Kuskusky Towns." For the changing cultural landscape, see also, "The French Era, 1720–1761" and "Indian Villages and Tribal Distribution c. 1768," in Tanner, *Atlas of Great Lakes Indian History*, 40–41, 58–59.
34. A list of natives with the French in the Ohio Country in 1755 can be found in Preston, *Braddock's Defeat*, 149–50.
35. Hamilton, *Adventure in the Wilderness*, 204; O'Callaghan and Fernow, *NYCD* 10:840.
36. McConnell, "Kuskusky Towns," 49; Lambing, *Baptismal Register*, 71 (infant captive baptized; Candon); *PCR* 8:389 (Tamaqua). See also Lambing, *Baptismal Register*, 75, 77, 79, 81, 83.
37. McConnell, *Country Between*, 121. On the importance of rumor in influencing Ohio Indian decisions, see Ostler, "To Extirpate the Indians."
38. McConnell, *Country Between*, 126–27.
39. On Teedyuscung, see Wallace, *Conrad Weiser*, 409 (Honest John), 441; Jennings, *Empire of Fortune*, 263–67; Merrell, *Into the American Woods*, 88. On early negotiations in Pennsylvania, see Wallace, *Conrad Weiser*, 440–51; Jennings, *Empire of Fortune*, ch. 12; Merrell, *Into the American Woods*, 238–41.
40. Hazard, *PA*, 1.3.108–9 ("proper belts"), 1.3.147–48 ("seem'd Desirous"); *PCR* 7:514–17; *PCR* 7:725, 726 ("three Indian Men"); Denny to Johnson, Philadelphia, November 20, 1757, *SWJP* 2:752–53 ("waiting at Venango"). See also Hunter, "Provincial Negotiations." Negotiations were further complicated by Teedyuscung's claim that he spoke for "ten nations," by implication including those on the Ohio. Tamaqua and his supporters would have none of this. See Wallace, *Conrad Weiser*, 444.
41. The most comprehensive study of the marine troops is Cassel, "Troupes de la Marine"; see also Balvay, *L'Épée et la Plume*, 38–55; Chartrand, *French Soldier in Colonial America*. For the material culture of marine troops in garrison, see Miville-Deschênes, *Soldier Off Duty*. Estimated numbers of men at the outposts are drawn from Mullett, "Military Intelligence," 407–8. See also Moogk, *La Nouvelle France*, 128–29. Numbers of marines at Braddock's defeat are from Preston, *Braddock's Defeat*, 337.
42. This paragraph draws on Cassel, "Militia Legend"; Dechêne, *Le Peuple, l'État et la Guerre*, 363–65. For an earlier assessment of the militia, see Eccles, "Social, Economic, and Political Significance"; also Back and Chartrand, "Canadian Militia."
43. Marquis Duquesne to the Minister, November 2, 1753, in Stevens and Kent, *Wilderness Chronicles*, 58–59 (1753 expedition); Kent, *French Invasion*, 40–41 (1753 expedition); Peyser, *On the Eve of the Conquest*, 26 (losses in 1753); Frégault, *Canada*, 212–13; Duquesne to Minister (July 6, 1755), in Stevens and Kent, *Wilderness Chronicles*, 91; "Further Examination of Michael La Chauvignerie, Junior," October 26, 1757, and Vaudreuil to Minister, Montreal, July 12, 1757, in Stevens and Kent, *Wilderness Chronicles*, 115, 103 (quotes; emphasis added). See also Stanley, *New France*, 188; Dechêne, *Le Peuple, l'État et la Guerre*, 363; Dechêne, *Power and Subsistence*, ch. 8.
44. Vaudreuil to Minister, Montreal, July 28, 1758, in Stevens and Kent, *Wilderness*

Chronicles, 114–15; Kent and Woods, *Travels in New France*, 101 (convoy from the Illinois, 1758). Distances are taken from Captain Harry Gordon, "Distances from Fort Pitt . . . to the Mouth of the Ohio," 1766, in Hutchins, *Courses of the Ohio River*, 77.

45. Duquesne to Contrecoeur, Montreal, July 18, 1754, in Grenier, *Papiers Contrecoeur*, 219 (garrison at Fort Duquesne); Peyser, *On the Eve of the Conquest*, 92 (recommended garrisons on the Ohio).
46. McConnell, *Country Between*, 128.
47. Daniel Claus to William Johnson, Philadelphia, April 5, 1756, *SWJP* 2:439 (Delaware quote); Hamilton, *Adventure in the Wilderness*, 153 (Indians at Fort William Henry), 231 (Indians at Fort Carillon).
48. Forbes to Pitt, Philadelphia, May 19, 1758, in *Correspondence of Pitt*, 1:246–47.
49. Forbes to Pitt, Philadelphia, June 17, 1758, in *Correspondence of Pitt*, 1:280.
50. As early as 1756 word filtered back to Pennsylvania that Ohio Indians were afraid of the "southern Indians" who had already attacked them three times. See *PCR* 7:515; Charles Thompson and Christian Frederick Post's Report to Denny and Forbes, June 19, 1758, Friendly Association Papers, 2:15 (hereafter cited as FAP with volume and page). See also *PCR* 8:125–27, on fear of Cherokee/British attacks among Indians on the upper Susquehanna. Sir William Johnson strongly objected to Pennsylvania and Quaker negotiations. See Loudoun to Pitt, New York, February 14, 1758, in *Correspondence of Pitt*, 1:189; Johnson to Abercrombie, Fort Johnson, December 29, 1757, April 28, 1758, *SWJP* 2:770, 829. For Quaker contacts with Ohio Indians, see Friends' Letter to Killbuck (n.d.), FAP 1:535. Forbes was certainly aware of these contacts by the time he reached Philadelphia; see Denny to Abercromby, Philadelphia, March 24, 1758, *SWJP* 2:787–88; Richard Peters, "Indian Council," March 15, 1758, in FHQP, reel 1, f. 78. Moreover, Forbes participated in Indian councils while still in Philadelphia; see *PCR* 8:124–25, 131–32. For a summary of Pennsylvania negotiations, see Hunter, "Provincial Negotiations."

THREE. *PREPARATIONS*, May 1758

Epigraph: Forbes to Bouquet, Philadelphia, May 20, 1758, *Writings of Forbes*, 94.

1. Forbes to Pitt, Philadelphia, May 19, 1758, *Correspondence of Pitt*, 1:245–48. Contrast Forbes's letter to Pitt with that of his superior, General James Abercromby who, only three days later, reported that his own plans were moving forward without major problems. The difference may reflect the fact that, by 1758, the colonies of New York, New Jersey, and those of New England had already been actively at war for three years and had learned how to cope with the demands of the campaigning season. See Abercromby to Pitt, Albany, May 22, 1758, *Correspondence of Pitt*, 1:248–56; Grant to Bouquet, Carlisle, July 11, 1758, *Writings of Forbes*, 144 (Pennsylvania troops).
2. Forbes to Stanwix, Philadelphia, May 29, 1758, *Writings of Forbes*, 102.
3. Forbes to Bouquet, Philadelphia, May 20, 1758, *Writings of Forbes*, 94–95. For a useful comparison to the task facing Forbes in supplying his small army, see Little, "Treasury, the Commissariat." Others besides Forbes were acutely aware of the challenges inherent in an overland as opposed to a water-borne campaign. See Stanwix to Pitt, Philadelphia, June 22, 1759, *Correspondence of Pitt*, 2:134.
4. Draper Wood to Forbes, Philadelphia, May 6, 1758, FHQP, reel 2, f. 183; Pargellis,

Lord Loudoun, 293 (officers' rations); Abercromby to Forbes, New York, May 4, 1758, in FHQP, reel 2, f. 175 (officers' rations), f. 284 (suspends soldiers' payments). The money normally withheld from a soldier's pay for food was part of the "off-reckonings" that included the cost of weapons, clothing, and medical care; the soldier's actual cash pay amounted to his stated wages less these deductions. For a detailed examination of this system, see Guy, *Oeconomy and Discipline*, ch. 3 and 146–57. On Virginians, see St. Clair to Forbes, Philadelphia, May 10, 1758, FHQP, reel 2, f. 212.

5. Draper Wood to Forbes, Philadelphia, May 1, 1758, FHQP, reel 2, f. 164. By mid-May Wood had already condemned seventeen barrels of flour destined for the army. "Return of Provisions at Alexandria, belonging to the Crown," May 16, 1758, Forbes/SRO, reel 1.

6. Quantities taken from "Provision Calculation for 6,000 men," FHQP, reel 3, f. 517; Adam Hoops, "Calculation of Provisions," FHQP, reel 2, f. 345. On ovens, see Duffy, *Army of Frederick the Great*, 199 (Prussian army); Kennett, *French Armies*, 110–11 (brick ovens). The army did use portable iron ovens in Germany during the war; see Bannerman, *Merchants and the Military*, 77. St. Clair to Braddock, Williamsburg, January 15, 1755, *Military Affairs*, 61 ("portable Ovens"). See also Bannerman, *Merchants and the Military*, 36–37, 60–61.

7. Advertisement for "Wagons, Horses, Drivers, etc.," *Writings of Forbes*, 88–89.

8. Burnaby, *Travels through the Middle Settlements*, 62 (nine thousand wagons); Franklin quoted in "Wagon Advertisement" in Houston, "Benjamin Franklin," 255. A census of Northampton County, Pennsylvania, reveals that of 518 householders only 37 percent owned wagons and some 77 percent owned draft horses. In some townships (Lower Socam, Mountbethel, and Upper Milford), half or more of households owned wagons and horses; Easton Township's seven householders owned no wagons, and only 28 percent owned horses, perhaps reflecting the impact of border warfare; see *PA* 5.1.204–23. On Braddock, see Braddock to Franklin, Frederick (Maryland), April 22, 1755, in Houston, "Benjamin Franklin," 251. On the 1755 episode, see also Bell and Labaree, "Franklin and the 'Wagon Affair.'"

9. St. Clair to Forbes, York, May 12, 1758, FHQP, reel 2, f. 218 ("very few"). Franklin quoted in "Wagon Advertisement" in Houston, "Benjamin Franklin," 255, 257. See also the notice calling for forty wagons, *Pennsylvania Gazette*, May 22, 1755. The reference to St. Clair as a "hussar" was meant both to underscore his volatile temperament and to remind farmers—many from Germany and central Europe—that St. Clair would act with the same severity as the infamous Hungarian light cavalry, the hussars, who were notorious for their plundering of civilians. On the problems that attended the hiring of wagons in 1755, see William Franklin to Benjamin Franklin (May 8–9, 1755?) and William Franklin, "William's Ferry at the Mouth of Conogocheeg," May 15, 1755, in Houston, "Benjamin Franklin," 269–70, 271–72. On Cumberland County, see St. Clair to Forbes, York, May 12, 1758, FHQP, reel 2, f. 218. James T. Lemon estimates that the average Pennsylvania farm had only three or four horses and that an estimated nine thousand wagons would represent only one for every four families in the colony. There was apparently very little surplus horsepower or vehicles in one of the richest colonies in British America. See Lemon, *Poor Man's Country*, 156, 165. St. Clair complained that Maryland farmers refused to obey his press warrant for wagons and doubted if they would cooperate without a threat of force. See St. Clair to Sharpe, Frederick Town, May 29, 1758, *AM* 9:191.

10. Information about wagons is drawn from Berkebile, *Conestoga Wagons*; Sharpe to Forbes, Fort Cumberland, October 1758, *AM* 9:271 ("Shannando"). In 1755 Captain Robert Orme found that provincial wagons could only carry about fourteen hundred pounds. See "Orme's Journal," in Sargent, *History of an Expedition*, 332. On European wagon capacity, see Bannerman, *Merchants and the Military*, 29.
11. On Braddock's wagons, see Walker, *Burd Papers*; the accounts list 148 wagons and teams of which 59 were counted as lost, a rate of 39 percent. "A List of the Number of Wagons, Draught and Pack Horses from the Several Townships of the County of Northampton," June 10, 1758, in *PA* 5.1.203; St. Clair to Forbes, York, May 12, 1758, FHQP, reel 2, f. 218 (Lancaster County); Bouquet to Forbes, Carlisle, June 7, 1758, *BP* 2:47 ("enough wagons," "unfit"). On Bouquet's plan, see "Expenses of Proposed Expedition Against Fort Duquesne" (Philadelphia, March 18, 1757), *BP* 1:55–56. See also Bouquet to Forbes, Lancaster, May 22, 1758, *BP* 2:350; St. Clair to Forbes, York, May 12, 1758, Forbes to St. Clair, Philadelphia, June 16, 1758, FHQP, reel 2, ff. 218, 318. On Braddock, see advertisement for wagons, Lancaster, April 26, 1755, in Wahll, *Braddock Road Chronicles*, 156. On the requirements of the artillery train, see Forbes to Bouquet, Philadelphia, June 6, 1758, *Writings of Forbes*, 107. On packhorses, see Wahll, *Braddock Road Chronicles*, 156; Bouquet to Forbes, Juniata Camp, June 21, 1758, *BP* 2:121; St. Clair to Forbes, Carlisle, May 10, 1758, FHQP, reel 2, f. 212 (packsaddles).
12. Bouquet to Forbes, Carlisle, May 30, 1758, *BP* 1:386–87 ("obstinate" "country folk"); George Stevenson to Bouquet, York, May 31, 1758, *BP* 1:399 ("ill treated"); Edward Shippen to Joseph Shippen, Lancaster, May 28, 1758, in Balch, *Letters and Papers*, 123 ("saucy"); Ourry to Forbes, Ft. Loudoun (Pennsylvania), August 6, 1758, Forbes/SRO, reel 2 (wagon drivers unarmed). Bouquet would report on one occasion that "the roads are strewn with broken wagons." Bouquet to Forbes, Rays Town, July 11, 1758, *BP* 2:180. Figures regarding feed and water for horses come from Engels, *Alexander the Great*, 14 (consumption rates), 18 (minimum requirements of food and water).
13. "Calculations of Oats for 400 Tames[sic]," FHQP, reel 3, f. 496 (this calculation fixed each team at four horses); Bouquet to Forbes, Carlisle, May 25, 1758, *BP* 1:364 ("enough grass"); St. Clair to Forbes, York, May 12, 1758, FHQP, reel 2, f. 218 (oats); Bouquet to Forbes, Rays Town, July 21, 1758, *BP* 2:253 ("greatly diminished"); Forbes to Bouquet, Carlisle, July 14, 1758, *BP* 2:208 (rye and straw). This calculus of supply and transport needs was a familiar one; see Bannerman, *Merchants and the Military*, 77, on forage and transport requirements for British troops in training camps at home.
14. Lemon, *Poor Man's Country*, chs. 6–7. On Virginia, see Hofstra, *Planting of New Virginia*, 264–65. Hofstra notes that by mid-1759 the valley was generating rich harvests and ample numbers of livestock, much of which was sent to Fort Pitt.
15. Joshua Howell to Christopher Kilby, Philadelphia, March 21, 1758, FHQP, reel 1, f. 86; Forbes to Bouquet, Philadelphia, May 20, 1758, *Writings of Forbes*, 95. On Hoops, see also MacMaster, "Searching for Community," 79, 86, 88.
16. St. Clair to Sharpe, Winchester, May 31, 1758, *AM* 9:193; St. Clair to Washington, York, May 7, 1758, *GWP* 5:169; St. Clair to Forbes, Lancaster, May 7, 1758, FHQP, reel 2, f. 187; St. Clair to Forbes, Winchester, May 24, 26, 1758, FHQP, reel 2, ff. 256, 267 ("bound in Chains"); St. Clair to Bouquet, Winchester, May 28, 1758, *BP* 1:276; also Basset to Washington, Ft. Frederick (Maryland), April 27, 1758, *GWP* 5:149 (Bassett

assigned to road work); Bouquet to Forbes, Carlisle, May 29, 1758, *BP* 1:387 (St. Clair needed). See also Stevenson to Donnellan, York, May 25, 1758, *BP* 1:371 (convoys preparing to depart).

17. Forbes to St. Clair, Philadelphia, May 25, 1758, FHQP, reel 2, f. 265; Bouquet to Forbes, Carlisle, 30 May, 1758, *BP* 1:395. St. Clair had enjoyed a favorable reputation while serving with Braddock in 1755; his changes in temperament and behavior may have resulted in part from his wound and persistent problems with kidney stones. Interestingly, though, even before Forbes's death, St. Clair pressed the new commander in chief, Jeffery Amherst, to succeed Forbes, based on seniority and experience. Amherst confided: "It was a thought that had not entered into my head, as I had no intention a vacancy should be made for the Command to descend to him." See Amherst to Forbes, New York, February 12, 1759, *BP* 3:116–17.

18. Forbes to Abercromby, Philadelphia, May 4, 1, 1758, *Writings of Forbes*, 85 ("immensity of trouble"), 74–75 ("tollerable humour"); Hoops to Forbes, Lancaster, May 2, 1758, Forbes/SRO 45/2, reel 1 ("displeased," "Cowards and Liars"); Bouquet to Forbes, Carlisle, May 30, 1758, *BP* 1:389 (Catawbas); St. Clair to Forbes, Winchester, May 21, 1758, FHQP, reel 2, f. 240 ("all the Riches"); Washington to St. Clair, Fort Loudoun (Virginia), April 18, 1758, *GWP* 5:131 ("hearty in our cause"). Washington told Forbes that only two things would "contribute greatly to their [Indians'] ease": an early start to the campaign and "plenty of Goods." Washington to Forbes, Fort Loudoun (Virginia), April 23, 1758, *GWP* 5:138. See Washington to Stanwix, Fort Loudoun (Virginia), April 10, 1758, *GWP* 5:117 ("mercenary"); Washington to Halkett, Fort Loudoun (Virginia), May 11, 1758, *GWP* 5:175 ("cravings"). On presents, see Bosomworth to Bouquet, Shippensburg, May 30, Bouquet to St. Clair, Carlisle, May 31, 1758, *BP* 1:397 ("absolute necessity"), 401 ("miscarried").

19. Forbes to Stanwix, Philadelphia, May 29, 1758, *Writings of Forbes*, 103 ("amazing"). Abercromby took the time to notify both Johnson and Atkin about Forbes's appointment to command and ordered both to cooperate with him, instructing Atkin to correspond directly with Forbes on Indian affairs. Abercromby to Johnson, New York, April 4, 1758, *SWJP* 2:813. Forbes placed much of the blame squarely on Atkin for failing to assist with the Cherokees and urged that Pitt in London be made aware of this. Forbes to St. Clair, Philadelphia, May 25, 1758, Forbes/RSO, reel 1; Forbes to Johnson, Philadelphia, May 4, 1758, *SWJP* 12:897–98. Bosomworth made recommendations early on regarding Indian affairs, telling Forbes it was "Highly necessary" that the army have adequate and competent Indian agents. Bosomworth to Forbes, Philadelphia, May 2, 1758, Forbes/RO, reel 1.

20. Johnson to Abercromby, Fort Johnson, April 28, 1758, *SWJP* 2:825 ("Party spirit"), 828 (northern Indians).

21. Forbes to Abercromby, Philadelphia, May 4, 1758, *Writings of Forbes*, 85 ("underhand way"); Forbes to Johnson, Philadelphia, May 4, 1758, *Writings of Forbes*, 82. Forbes to Amherst, Philadelphia, February 7, 1759, *Writings of Forbes*, 289 ("Myrmidons"). In a letter, written shortly before his death, Forbes condemned Johnson's insistence on putting private affairs before public interest and his complete lack of cooperation during the campaign. Forbes to Amherst, Philadelphia, February 7, 1759, *Writings of Forbes*, 289. Johnson's efforts to vacuum up trade goods had already created problems. In April 1757, Cherokees in Virginia, expecting gifts from the government for joining Washington's regiment were disappointed when Lieutenant-Colonel

George Mercer found that Johnson's agents had cleaned out the local suppliers. See Mercer to Washington, Fort Loudoun (Virginia), April 26, 1757, in Mays, *Amherst Papers*, 13–14; Edmond Atkin to Forbes, Charles Town, May 20, 1758, FHQP, reel 2, f. 235; also Forbes to Bouquet, Philadelphia, May 25, 1758, *BP* 1:355.

22. Bouquet to Forbes, Lancaster, May 22, 1758, *BP* 1:350 ("George McGuy"); Bouquet to Forbes, Carlisle, May 30, 1758, *BP* 1:388 ("without impatience").
23. St. Clair to Forbes, Winchester, May 19, 1758, FHQP, reel 2, f. 234.
24. James Burd to Forbes, Bedford, May 21, 1758, FHQP, reel 2, f. 239.
25. Atkin to Loudoun, Charles Town, March 25, 1758, in Mays, *Amherst Papers*, 59–60; Byrd to Forbes, Bedford Court House, May 21, 1758, Forbes/SRO, reel 1 ("skirmishes"); Byrd to Lachlan Mackintosh, North Yadkin, May 12, 1758, in Tinling, *Three William Byrds*, 2:653 ("several" Indians); extract of a letter from Blair to George Mercer, Williamsburg, May 20, 1758, FHQP, reel 2, f. 237 ("some battles"); William Calloway to Washington, Bedford, May 15, 1758, *GWP* 5:183 ("which Cald themselves"); St. Clair to Blair, Winchester, May 31, 1758, FHQP, reel 2, f. 277; Forbes to Stanwix, Philadelphia, May 29, 1758, *Writings of Forbes*, 103 ("Country people").
26. St. Clair to Forbes, Winchester, May 24, 1758, FHQP, reel 2, f. 256 (can't stop them from leaving); St. Clair to Bouquet, Winchester, May 27, 1758, *BP* 1:374–75 ("Numbers go home"); Forbes to Bouquet, Philadelphia, May 25, 1758, *BP* 1:355 ("anxiety"); St. Clair to Blair, Winchester, May 23, 1758, FHQP, reel 2, f. 251 (what to do).
27. Forbes to Abercromby, Carlisle, July 18, 1758, *Writings of Forbes*, 152 ("distinguish them," "prevent accidents"). See also St. Clair to Forbes, Philadelphia, May 10, 1758, FHQP, reel 2, f. 212 (yellow pendants); "Bouquet's List of Stores," Carlisle, June 3, 1758, *BP* 2:21 ("Yellow Shalloon to distinguish our Indians").
28. Halkett to Washington, Philadelphia, May 4, 1758, *Writings of Forbes*, 83–84 ("extreamly desirous"). See also Sharpe to Forbes, March 27, 1758, *AM* 9:163; Forbes to Sharpe, New York, April 4, 1758, *Writings of Forbes*, 64; Washington to Halkett, Fort Loudoun (Virginia), May 11, 1758, *GWP* 5:175.
29. Forbes to Abercromby, Philadelphia, May 4, 1758, *Writings of Forbes*, 85 (Indians may keep captives); Bosomworth to Forbes, Lancaster, May 13, 1758, Forbes/SRO, reel 1 (gifts for scalps); Bouquet to Forbes, Carlisle, May 25, 1758, *BP* 1:363 ("compelled"); Robert Callender to St. Clair, Carlisle, May 6, 1758, FHQP, reel 2, f. 180 ("if possible"). Bouquet began instructing scouts bound for Fort Duquesne not to return without either prisoners or scalps. Bouquet to Forbes, Carlisle, May 30, 1758, *BP* 1:390.
30. Forbes to Israel Pemberton, Philadelphia, May 31, 1758, FAP 1:511. See also Thayer, *Israel Pemberton*, 153–54.
31. "A List of Guides Employed in His Majesty's Service," n.p., FHQP, reel 3, f. 505 (evaluations); St. Clair to Napier, Little Meadows, June 13, 1755, *Military Affairs*, 94. Also in 1755, Richard Peters admitted that the region west of the mountains "is entirely unknown to us." Peters to Burd, Philadelphia, July 3, 1755, in Balch, *Letters and Papers*, 44.
32. John Patten, "A Map of the Ohio country," in Brown, *Early Maps*, plate 16 and 87–88. See also Morris to St. Clair, Philadelphia, February 28, 1755, *PCR* 6:302 (Patten's map); "The computed Distance of the Road by the Indian Traders from Carlisle to Shannopin's Town," *PCR* 5:750–51. On distances, see Croghan to Peters, March 23, 1754, *PA* 1.2.132–33; "Distance from Philada. To Twightwees," *PA* 1.2.133–34; "Ac-

count of the Road to Logs Town on Allegeheney River, taken by John Harris, 1754," *PA* 1.2.135–36. Governor Morris of Pennsylvania was able to obtain "with some Difficulty" a copy of the map from Evans, which he forwarded to St. Clair. Morris to St. Clair, Philadelphia, February 28, 1755, *PCR*6:301. The standard study of Evans and his maps remains Gipson, *Lewis Evans*, esp. 55–68.

33. Vaudreuil to the Minister of Marine, Montreal, July 12, 1757, Stevens and Kent, *Wilderness Chronicles*, 103 (food shortages, flooding); Kent and Woods, *Travels in New France*, 97–98 (flood at Fort Duquesne); Bond, "Captivity Narrative of Charles Stuart," *Mississippi Valley Historical Review* 13 (1926–1927): 77 (Delawares); Johnson to Abercromby, Fort Johnson, April 28, 1758, *SWJP* 2:829–30 (Delawares).

34. Denny to Washington, Philadelphia, March 25, 1758, *GWP* 5:107 (Teedyuscung; this letter can also be found in *SWJP* 2:797–98); "Proceedings of Council of Officers," Fort Loudoun(Virginia), March 30, 1758, in *SWJP* 2:803–5; Forbes to Denny, Philadelphia, May 3, 1758, *Writings of Forbes*, 81 (Cherokees going to Philadelphia).

FOUR. *MOVING WEST,* June 1758

Epigraph: Forbes to Pitt, Philadelphia, June 17, 1758, *Correspondence of Pitt*, 1:280.

1. Forbes to Bouquet, Philadelphia, June 8, 1758, FHQP, reel 2, f. 299; Sinclair to St. Clair, Charles Town, April 26, 1758, FHQP, reel 1, f. 149 (shipping);Byrd to Forbes, Charles Town, March 21, 1758, FHQP, reel 1, f. 85 (anxious to leave South Carolina); Return taken on board ships at Charles Town, May, 24, 1758, FHQP, reel 2, f. 252; "Field Return of the 1st Highland Battalion," Philadelphia, June 13, 1758, FHQP, reel 2, f. 312; "Return of the First Highland Battalion," Philadelphia, June 24, 1758, FHQP, reel 2, f. 330.

2. Forbes to Abercromby, Philadelphia, June 7, 1758, *Writings of Forbes*, 109; Forbes to Pitt, Philadelphia, June 17, 1758, *Writings of Forbes*, 117; Smith, *Universal Military Dictionary*, 13, 245; Knox, *Campaigns in North America*, 1:347 (small-arms ammunition). A complete list of the ordnance stores sent to Forbes can be found in "A Proportion of Ordnance and Stores for Pennsylvania," June 13, 1758, Forbes/SRO, reel 2. On the role of the Ordnance Board in supplying and shipping weapons and munitions, see Syrett, *Shipping and Military Power*, ch. 3.

3. "A Return of the Officers and Men, Military and Civil . . . Commanded by Captain-lieutenant Geo. Anderson," June 13, 1758, Forbes/SRO 45/2; Andrews, *Journals of Jeffery Amherst*, 231, 361 (Michelson and Wright); Forbes to Abercromby, Philadelphia, June 7, 1758, *Writings of Forbes*, 110 (Hay); Abercromby to Forbes, Albany, June 4, 1758, FHQP, reel 2, f. 291 ("all I cou'd give you"). The lion's share of the Royal Artillery (over three hundred officers and men) was assigned to Amherst's expedition against Louisbourg. Lieutenant fireworker was the lowest commissioned rank in the Royal Artillery; bombardiers were trained to use howitzers and mortars, both of which fired explosive shells; gunners were also trained artillerymen; matrosses, the lowest enlisted rank, assisted in loading and firing the guns; miners were, as the term implies, trained to tunnel under enemy works and to lay mines to destroy fortifications. See Smith, *Universal Military Dictionary*, 89, 31, 120, 161, 176.

4. "Brass ordnance, howitzers, etc. for Halifax, New York, and Pennsylvania," CO 5/213; Forbes to Abercromby, New York, March 29, 1758, Forbes/SRO 45/2, reel 1; Matthew Clerk to Forbes, Albany, n.d., Forbes/SRO, reel 2; "Abstract of Warrants granted," *Writings of Forbes*, 293–94 (contingency funds for howitzers and car-

riages); Hunter, "Barton," 447 (entry for August 5, 1758); Sharpe to Calvert, Conecocheague, June 11, 1758, in *AM* 9:203; "An account of the Brass Ordnance and Stores, . . . left at Philadelphia, 1758," (July 24), *PA* 1.3.492–97.

5. On battalion guns, see Whitworth, *Gunner at Large*, 28, 39. British understanding of Fort Duquesne came from the now famous plan that was drawn and smuggled out of the fort by Captain Robert Stobo of the Virginia forces, one of two hostages given after the defeat of Washington's force at Fort Necessity to guarantee Virginia's compliance with the surrender terms. This very accurate plan was given to Braddock and was found among his papers by the French after the battle on July 9, 1755. Stobo was sentenced to death, but he avoided his sentence by escaping from Quebec in 1759. See Alberts, *Most Extraordinary Adventures*, esp. chs. 8, 11 (Stobo's plan of Fort Duquesne appears following p. 210).

6. Wood, *By Dint of Labour*, 9 ("Drivers"); Forbes to Bouquet, Philadelphia, June 16, 1758, *BP* 2:103 (provincials as artillery drivers). See also Bouquet to Forbes, Raystown, August 20, 1758, *BP* 2:396; Bouquet to James Burd, Raystown, August 23, 1758, *BP* 2:406; Bouquet to Burd, Stoney Creek, October 12, 1758, *BP* 2:551–52.

7. Muller, *Treatise of Artillery*, 179–80; "Distribution of wagons, drivers, and horses," Byfleet, July 12, 1756, in Cleaveland, *Royal Regiment of Artillery*, 248; entry for June 11, 1755, "Orme's Journal," in Sargent, *History of an Expedition*, 332; Forbes to Bouquet, Philadelphia, June 6, 1758, *Writings of Forbes*, 107. On the number of wagons, see Hunter, "Barton," 447 (August 5, 1758).

8. This figure is derived from detailed accounts dated June 19–30, 1758, found in Gratz Collection, HSP.

9. Ridner, *Town In-Between*, 4 ("in-between"), 16 (map 2), 19 (map 3), 81–85. Bassett's "A Plan & Profil[e] of the Line of Circumvallation now throwing up near Carlisle" (1757) can be found on p. 84. The only serious bottleneck in the army's movement to Carlisle was the Susquehanna River, which was wide and deep enough to require ferries—what Bouquet and Forbes called "flats"—to move wagons, guns, and supplies as well as troops. See, for example, Forbes to Pitt, Carlisle Camp west of Susquehanna, July 10, 1758, *Writings of Forbes*, 140. On the Great Virginia Road, see Council Minutes, February 18, 1755, *PCR* 6:318. This and the following discussions of the army's route draws on the excellent material in Waddell and Bomberger, *French and Indian War*, 38–42.

10. Braddock to Napier, Fort Cumberland, June 8, 1755, *Military Affairs*, 92. St. Clair to Morris, Williamsburg, February 14, 1755, *PCR* 6:300–301.

11. On Burd's Road, see St. Clair to Morris, Williamsburg, February 14, 1755, *PCR* 6:300–301. Also Pennsylvania Council minutes, February 18, 1755, *PCR* 6:317–318; Burd to Morris, "From the Roads leading to the Ohio," June 12, 1755, *PCR* 6:433–34; Burd to Peters, "Allogueepy's [Aliquippa's] Town," June 17, 1755, *PCR* 6:435–36 ("a general Satisfaction"); Burd to Peters, "Ray's Town," June 19, 1755, *PCR* 6:436–37 ("a good wagon road"); Burd to Morris, "From our Camp at the Top of the Allegany Mountain," July 17, 1755, *PCR* 6:484–85; William Allison and William Maxwell to Peters, "Conegouchege," June 12, 1755, *PCR* 6:434 (wagoner's account).

12. Forbes to Bouquet, Philadelphia, June 16, 1758, *BP* 2:103. "North Road" appears on George Armstrong's map of the country west of the Susquehanna River, done in July 1758; see "Major George Armstrong's draft of the country west of the Susquehanna," Brown, *Early Maps*, map 32.

13. On the Great Wagon Road, see Bailyn, *Voyagers to the West*, 14–15, and maps 1c and 1d. On the Virginia section of the road, see Hofstra, "Colonial Road."
14. Forbes to Pitt, October 20, 1758, *Correspondence of Pitt*, 1:375. Turpin, *Essay on the Art of War*, esp. 2:99–102. Turpin was widely read in French and English by British officers in the middle of the eighteenth century. See Gruber, *Books and the British Army*. J. A. Houlding calls it "the best work available ... during the eighteenth-century." Houlding, *Fit for Service*, 201.
15. Forbes to Pitt, Philadelphia, June 17, 1758, *Correspondence of Pitt*, 1:280.
16. Forbes, "Memoranda," Philadelphia, c. June 1, 1758, *BP* 2:1; Forbes to Pitt, Philadelphia, June 17, 1758, *Correspondence of Pitt*, 1:280 ("Great Channel," "every Forty Miles," "several Posts").
17. Forbes to St. Clair, Philadelphia, May 23, 1758, FHQP, reel 2, f. 249 ("a Chain"); Forbes to Bouquet, Philadelphia, June 8, 1758, FHQP, reel 2, f. 299; St. Clair to Forbes, Winchester, June 3, 1758, f. 290 (Virginia troops).
18. Bouquet to Forbes, Carlisle, May 25, 1758, *BP* 1:363 (roads from Lancaster); Bouquet to Forbes, Lancaster, May 22, 1758, *BP* 1:351 (magistrates); Bouquet to Forbes, Carlisle, May 25, 1758, *BP* 1:364 ("Flats"); St. Clair to Bouquet, Winchester, May 28, 1758, *BP* 1:376.
19. Bouquet to Forbes, Fort Loudoun (Pennsylvania), June 11, 1758, *BP* 2:73–74. See also Forbes to St. Clair, Philadelphia, June 16, 1758, FHQP, reel 2, f. 318.
20. Bouquet to Forbes, Fort Loudoun, June 11, 1758, *BP* 2:73; Reece, "Colonel Eyre's Journal," 42–45 ("zig-zags"); Bullitt to Bouquet, Carlisle, June 17, 1758, *BP* 2:105.
21. Bouquet to Forbes, "Juniata Camp," June 21, 1758, *BP* 2:121.
22. Gordon's map of Braddock's march is reproduced in *Military Affairs*, facing 94; Preston, *Braddock's Defeat*, 169. Gordon's accompanying journal is in Wahll, *Braddock Road Chronicles*. "General Forbes marching Journal to the Ohio by John Potts," Shippen Family Papers, HSP. For my discussion of the army's route I have also relied heavily on Waddell and Bomberger, *French and Indian War*, 39–49, which is perhaps the most thorough account of Forbes's route linked to present-day roads and landmarks. On Potts and his map, see also Williams, *Bouquet's March*, esp. 13–16. Portions of the map, enlarged, also appear in Williams's book. The mileage is taken from "Distance from Pittsburgh to Carlisle," dated December 1758, *BP* 2:651–52. The mileage calculations available to Forbes and Bouquet in 1758 are remarkably accurate. The total distance from Carlisle to Fort Duquesne as given in *BP* 2:651 is 199 miles; a modern Pennsylvania highway map gives approximately 187 miles allowing for improvements to eliminate the detours faced by the army.
23. Bouquet to Forbes, Fort Loudoun (Pennsylvania), June 11, 1758, *BP* 2:73–74; Bouquet to Forbes, "Juniata Camp," June 21, 1758, *BP* 2:121–23 ("wagon cannot go"); Hoops to Bouquet, Carlisle, June 23, 1758, *BP* 2:133 (wagons under contract). The logistical problems of early modern armies are discussed in Chandler, *Art of War*, 13–21. For a study of logistics in the context of one war and the armies' use of foraging to create logistical "deserts" for their enemies, see Childs, *Nine Years' War*.
24. Forbes to Bouquet, Philadelphia, June 27, 1758, *BP* 2:136. On the army's cash problem, see St. Clair to Forbes, Winchester, June 3, 1758, FHQP, reel 2, f. 290.
25. Forbes to Bouquet, Philadelphia, June 27, 1758, *BP* 2:135 (packhorses); Forbes to Bouquet, Shippensburg, August 18, 1758, *Writings of Forbes*, 182 ("making the wagons").

26. Forbes to Bouquet, Shippensburg, August 18, 1758, *Writings of Forbes*, 181. Major James Grant estimated that as much as fifteen hundred or two thousand tons of fodder could be collected from the abandoned farms around Fort Loudoun. Grant to Forbes, Fort Loudoun, August 16, 1758, FHQP, reel 3, f. 476. On St. Clair, see for example, St. Clair to Washington, York, May 7, 1758, *GWP* 5:169; St. Clair to Forbes, Winchester, May 24, 1758, FHQP, reel 2, f. 256; Forbes to Abercromby, Philadelphia, June 15, 1758, *Writings of Forbes*, 114 ("my Friend," St. Clair and expenses). Forbes to Abercromby, Philadelphia, June 27, 1758, *Writings of Forbes*, 128 ("Waggons and roads"); Forbes to St. Clair, Philadelphia, May 25, 1758, FHQP, reel 2, f. 265 (provincials and Indians); Forbes to Abercromby, Carlisle, July 3, 1758, War Office Papers, Class 34: Papers of Sir Jeffery Amherst (hereafter cited as WO 34), 44 f. 159 (packsaddles).
27. Forbes to Abercromby, Philadelphia, June 7, 1758, *Writings of Forbes*, 109 (Cherokees); Forbes to Bouquet, Philadelphia, June 27, 1758, *BP* 2:135 (negotiations).
28. Forbes to Bouquet, Philadelphia, May 23, 1758, *Writings of Forbes*, 96 ("Impatient"); Forbes to Stanwix, Philadelphia, May 29, 1758, *Writings of Forbes*, 102 ("Extreamly licentious"); Bouquet to Forbes, Carlisle, June 3, 1758, *BP* 2:15–16 ("have adopted"); Bouquet to Forbes, Fort Loudoun, June 11, 1758, *BP* 2:74 ("will not leave us"); Forbes to Bouquet, Philadelphia, May 25, 1758, *BP* 1:355 ("anxiety and unease"); Byrd to Forbes, Winchester, June 23, 1758, Forbes/SRO, reel 1 ("restless"); St. Clair to Forbes, Winchester, May 19, 1758, FHQP, reel 2, f. 234 ("plundered all along the road"); St. Clair to Bouquet, Winchester, May 31, 1758, *BP* 1:404–5 ("greatest curse"); St. Clair to Blair, Winchester, May 31, 1758, FHQP, reel 2, f. 277 (Virginians); Bouquet to Forbes, Carlisle, May 25, 1758, *BP* 1:363 ("bad humour").
29. "Bouquet's List of Stores," Carlisle, June 3, 1758, *BP* 2:21 ("Yellow Shalloon," "silver arm plates"); Forbes to Bouquet, Philadelphia, June 27, 1758; Bouquet Orderly Book, June 17, 1758, *BP* 2:656 ("Marks to distinguish them"); "Form for Suttlers' Licenses," c. June 19, 1758, *BP* 2:114 (prohibition on liquor); St. Clair: Public orders, Winchester, May 16, 1758, Forbes/SRO, reel 1 (razing houses).
30. Hugh Mercer to Bouquet, Fort Littleton, June 5, 1758, *BP* 2:34 ("no Interpreter"); Bouquet to Forbes, Raystown, June 28, 1758, *BP* 2:144 (snake bite). See also Washington to St. Clair, Fort Loudoun (Virginia), May 14, 1758, *GWP* 5:154–55; St. Clair to Forbes, Winchester, May 30, 1758, Forbes/SRO, reel 1; Bouquet to Forbes, Carlisle, May 30, 1758, *BP* 1:390 (several parties out). On Catawbas, see Halkett to Washington, Philadelphia, May 4, 1758, *Writings of Forbes*, 83–84; Washington to Halkett, Fort Loudoun (Virginia), May 11, 1758, *GWP* 5, 175.
31. Forbes to Bouquet, Philadelphia, May 20, 1758, *BP* 1:348 ("endeavouring"); Forbes to Pitt, Philadelphia, June 17, 1758, *Writings of Forbes*, 118 ("used every art"); Forbes to Abercromby, Carlisle, July 3, 1758, WO 34/44, f. 159 ("in the dark"); Bouquet to Forbes, Carlisle, May 25, 1758, *BP* 1:364; Thomas Cresap to Bouquet, Old Town (Maryland), June 19, 1758, *BP* 2:111; "Examination of John Hochstattler," in Bouquet to Forbes, Carlisle, May 30, 1758, *BP* 1:392 (Delaware information); Vaudreuil to Minister, Montreal, June 10, July 28, 1758, in Stevens and Kent, *Wilderness Chronicles*, 111, 112; Hamilton, *Adventure in the Wilderness*, 294 (Bougainville on October attack).
32. Bosomworth to Cherokees and Catawbas, Fort Loudoun (Virginia), April 21, 23, 1758, FHQP, reel 1, f. 132 (permission); Lyttleton to Loudoun, Charles Town, March

21, 1758, FHQP, reel 1, f. 84 (compensation); "Speech to Indians, Fort Loudoun (Pennsylvania), n.d., *BP* 2:101 (presents to be given at end of campaign); Trent to Forbes, Fort Loudoun (Pennsylvania), May 22, 1758, FHQP, reel 1, f. 242 ("blackened themselves"); Bosomworth to Bouquet, Shippensburg, May 30, 1758, *BP* 1:397 ("Satisfy the Indians"); Bouquet to St. Clair, Carlisle, May 31, 1758, *BP* 1:401 ("bad scituation").

33. Trent to Bouquet, Fort Loudoun (Pennsylvania), June 5, 1758, FHQP, reel 2, f. 294. See also Bosomworth to Bouquet, Winchester, June 5, 1758, FHQP, reel 2, f. 295; Sharpe to Calvert, Conecocheague, June 11, 1758, *AM* 9:205.

34. Bouquet to the Cherokees and Catawbas, Fort Loudoun (Pennsylvania), c. June 14, *BP* 2:98–101; Bouquet to Forbes, Fort Loudoun (Pennsylvania), June 16, 1758, *BP* 2:95.

35. Dowd, "Insidious Friends." As late as November, Christian Frederick Post learned that Cherokees continued to blame settlers for killing thirty men, "which they resented much"; an experience that clearly continued to haunt the warriors and must have accounted for why so many decided to leave the army. See Thwaites, *Early Western Travels* (hereafter *EWT*), 241 (Raystown, November 5, 1758).

36. Forbes to Pitt, Philadelphia, June 7, 1758, Forbes to Bouquet, Philadelphia, June 10, 1758, Forbes to Loudoun, Philadelphia, June 17, 1758, *Writings of Forbes*, 111 ("fickle"), 112 ("plague"), 119 ("wavering disposition"); Byrd to Forbes, Winchester, June 23, 1758, FHQP, reel 2, f. 327 ("insolent," "restless"); Washington to Forbes, Fort Loudoun (Virginia), June 19, 1758, *GWP* 5:224 ("discontented Temper"); Bouquet to St. Clair, Fort Loudoun (Pennsylvania), June16, 1758, *BP* 2:102 ("amazed").

37. Dowd, "Insidious Friends," 150.

38. Forbes to Bouquet, Philadelphia, June 8, 1758, FHQP, reel 2, f. 299 (Byrd, Bosomworth, and Johnson); Forbes to Pitt, July 10, 1758, *Correspondence of Pitt*, 1:295–96 (on Cherokees and Attakullakulla).

39. Bouquet to Forbes, Juniata Camp, June 21, 1758, *BP* 2:124; Forbes to Bouquet, Philadelphia, June27, 1758, Forbes to Pitt, Philadelphia, June17, 1758, *Writings of Forbes*, 125 ("in your opinion"), 118 (inability to collect intelligence); Bouquet to Forbes, Raystown, June 28, 1758, *BP* 2:144 (soldier rescued by Cherokees); Bouquet to Forbes, Raystown, August 31, 1758, *BP* 2:450–51 (failure of scouting party). On this issue, see also Preston, "To Make Indians of Our White Men."

40. St. Clair to Forbes, Winchester, May 25, 1758, FHQP, reel 2, f. 262 ("new kind of Company"); Ourry to Forbes, Fort Loudoun (Pennsylvania), August 6, 1758, FHQP, reel 2, f. 431 (Shelby and volunteers, "briskest people"); Forbes to Abercromby, Shippensburg, September 4, 1758, *Writings of Forbes*, 200 ("scalps," "harvest," concern about killing wrong Indians). See also Sharpe to Pitt, Fort Frederick, August 27, 1758, *Correspondence of Pitt*, 1:32.

41. "Report of Chas. Thomson and F. Post of Journey 1758," *PA* 1.3.412–22, submitted to Denny on June 16, 1758, *PA* 1.3.413 ("strange Indians," "800 men"), *PA* 1.3.414 (blocked roads); McConnell, *Country Between*, 126–27 (Teedyuscung and western Delawares); *PA* 1.3.421 (Neilson). On the house building, see "Meeting with Teedyuscung," April 29–May 5, 1758, in Hirsh, *EAID*, 3:369–72; "Journal of Isaac Zane's Journey to Wyoming," May 21–June 1, 1758, in Hirsh, *EAID*, 3:378–82. Zane was one of the men sent to build the houses Teedyuscung had been promised.

42. On Forbes, see *PCR* 8:128. On Post's report, see *PA* 1.3.417 ("Intelligence"); Hirsh, *EAID*, 3:373–74 (Wyandots); *PA* 1.3.417–18 (Delawares and French); *PA* 1.3.418 (rumors of fort at Wyoming); *PA* 1.3.419 (Nenacheehunt).
43. Post's report, *PA* 1.3.418 (Seneca headman and warriors); *PA* 1.3.419 ("exasperated").
44. Forbes to Bouquet, Philadelphia, June 27, 1758, *BP* 2:135.
45. Denny to Johnson, Philadelphia, June 27, 1758, *SWJP* 2:865. As early as March, Denny had complained that, while meeting with Teedyuscung, "I am under great Disadvantage" for lack of a reliable interpreter. He was "obliged to depend on Such as Teedyuscung brings along with him." Denny to Abercromby, Philadelphia, March 24, 1758, *SWJP* 2:788.
46. Denny to Proprietors, April 9, 1757, *PA* 1.3.108–9, 147–48; *PCR* 7:514–17.
47. Teedyuscung to Denny, August 30, 1757, *PCR* 7:725–26 (western Delaware contacts, 1757); Bouquet to Forbes, Carlisle, May 25, 1758, *BP* 1:364.
48. "Journal of Frederick Post's Journey from Philadelphia to Wioming, June the 20th, 1758," *PCR* 8:143 ("painted faces," "40 Strangers," "upon their Guard"), 144 ("Teeduyscung shewed me"). On the genesis of Piquetomen's trip, see McConnell, "Pisquetomen and Tamaqua, 283–85. The Cherokees' message to Teedyuscung can be found in FAP 2:39 (June 20, 1758).
49. "Journal of Frederick Post's Journey," *PCR* 8:144–45.
50. Pemberton to Forbes, Philadelphia, July 4, 1758, FAP 2:95; Halkett to Pemberton, Carlisle, July 9, 1758, FAP 2:103; Forbes to Bouquet, Carlisle, August 9, 1758, *Writings of Forbes*, 170–71 ("Bussy"). The conference between the western Delawares and provincial officials occurred between July 6 and July 12, 1758, and records of it can be found in Hirsh, *EAID*, 3:397–408.
51. Forbes to Bouquet, Carlisle, July 6, 1758, *Writings of Forbes*, 128 ("Rideing and walking," says he arrived "night before last"); Halkett to Peters, "Camp at Carlisle," July 9, 1758, *Writings of Forbes*, 133; Bouquet Orderly Book, *BP* 2:758 (orders dated from "Camp at Reas Towne," June 24, 1758).

FIVE: *RAYSTOWN*, July 1758

Epigraph: Forbes to Pitt, Carlisle, July 10, 1758, *Correspondence of Pitt*, 1:294.
1. Forbes to Pitt, "Carlisle Camp," July 10, 1758, *Correspondence of Pitt*, 1:294–95.
2. Forbes to Bouquet, Philadelphia, June 10, 1758, *Writings of Forbes*, 112 ("Cholicks"); Forbes to Loudoun, Philadelphia, June 7, 1758, *Writings of Forbes*, 120 ("come home"); Forbes to Abercromby, Carlisle, July 3, 1758, WO 34/44, f. 159 ("violent pain"); Halkett to Peters, Carlisle, July 9, 1758, *Writings of Forbes*, 133 ("Rideing"); Halkett to Bouquet, Carlisle, 31 July, 1758, *Writings of Forbes*, 161 ("Physick"); Halkett to Washington, Carlisle, August 2, 1758, *Writings of Forbes*, 163 ("extreamly weak").
3. Forbes was aware of the lack of uniforms, but according to Governor Fauquier of Virginia, "to save time General Forbes dispences with uniformity altogether." Fauquier to St. Clair, Williamsburg, June 6, 1758, in Reese, *PFF*, 1:15. The Virginians, according to St. Clair, still needed weapons, blankets, kettles, tents, and canteen. St. Clair to Bouquet, Winchester, May 28, 1758, *BP* 1:376–77; Bouquet to Forbes, Carlisle, June 3, 1758, *BP* 2:16; Shippen to Forbes, Lancaster, June 12, 1758, Shippen, "Military Letters," 456 (no blankets); Bouquet to Forbes, Carlisle, May 29/30, 1758, *BP* 1:390 (no medicine); Stephen to Bouquet, Fort Loudoun (Pennsylvania), June 7,

1758, *BP* 2:53; "Military Letters of Joseph Shippen," 456 ("Walks with Sticks," "Sore Legs"). Stephen reported that there were no stores of any kind for the sick and injured, "neither Wine, Rice, Barley, Oatmeal, or Butter." Bouquet to St. Clair, Raystown, June 30, 1758, *BP* 2:152 (Virginians demand pay).

4. Forbes, Memoranda," Philadelphia, c. June 1, 1758, *BP* 2:1–2. Orderly books were a record of daily orders and other instructions, including passwords and countersigns for sentries. These books were kept by army headquarters, by staff officers as well as regimental adjutants and company officers. See Smith, *Universal Military Dictionary*, 194.
5. Bouquet Orderly Book, *BP* 2:656–57.
6. Bouquet Orderly Book, *BP* 2:656–57.
7. Bouquet Orderly Book, *BP* 2:656–58.
8. Bouquet to Washington, Camp at Reas Town, June 27, 1758, *BP* 2:134. For initial activities at Raystown, see Bouquet Orderly Book, *BP* 2:638–39.
9. On town plans, see Ridner, *Town In-Between*, 37 (grid plans); also Hofstra, *Planting of New Virginia*, 180–85 (Winchester). For an illustration of a British military encampment, see "A View of the Camp at Coxe Heath, near Maidstone in Kent" (London, 1778), reproduced in Chandler and Beckett, *Oxford Illustrated History*, 104.
10. Bouquet Orderly Book, *BP* 2:660 (hatchet men, bark covering for weapons); *A Soldier's Journal*, 7–9 (description of regimental camp).
11. Bland, *Treatise of Military Discipline*, 247–48 (camp design, camp-color men); Bouquet Orderly Book, 2:659–60. A plan for a regimental-sized camp is reproduced in Ridner, *Town In-Between*, 84. On the arrangement of encampments and lines of battle, see also Houlding, *Fit for Service*, ch. 6.
12. Pleydell was the senior draftsman for the Board of Ordnance; it was his task to take rough plans submitted by the engineers and produce completed, colored, and scaled plans conforming to contemporary standards. On "retrenchment," see Smith, *Universal Military Dictionary*, 225. Montgomery's Regiment also had the distinction of providing security for Forbes, whose "General's House" was in the center of their camp. The French lines at Fort Carillon where Montcalm's army defeated Abercromby in July 1758 were built on the same principle. The Raystown camp was not the only one that incorporated defensive works into the troop cantonments; Abercromby's 1758 camp on the site of Fort William Henry, Lake George, was also fortified, as was Amherst's camp on the same site in 1759. See Bellico, *Empires in the Mountains*, 173 ("A Map of the retrenched Camp at Lake George in 1758," detail), 185 ("Plan of the Encampment of the Army at Lake George June 1759," detail). A good contemporary view of a military camp during the war in America is Captain Thomas Davies's watercolor of the British camp at the ruins of Fort St. Frederic on Lake Champlain, 1759, in Hubbard, *Thomas Davies*, 11.
13. Bouquet Orderly Book, *BP* 2:659 (barking trees, hunting, liquor), 660 (taking duties, weapons and gear), 663 (complaints, gambling), 664 (guards on Indian camp), 665 (hunting, divine service).
14. Bouquet Orderly Book, *BP* 2:661.
15. Francis Halkett, "Sketch of the Number of Troops," Carlisle, July 17, 1758, FHQP, reel 2, f. 386. On Forbes and the diminishing size of the army, see Forbes to Abercromby, Carlisle, August 11, 1758, *Writings of Forbes*, 175.

16. Bouquet, "Daily Return of the Troops," Raystown, July 21, 1758, FHQP, reel 2, f. 402.
17. Thomas Hutchinson, "Return of the Number of Forces . . . Provided with Provisions at Raystown," August 10, 1758, FHQP, reel 3, f. 461; Shippen to Peters, Raystown, August 16, 1758, in Shippen, "Military Letters," 461–62. See also Hunter, "Barton," 449; Bouquet to Forbes, Raystown, August 8, 1758, *BP* 2:336.
18. Bouquet to Forbes, Raystown, July 11, 1758, *BP* 2:181; Bouquet to Forbes, Raystown, July 15, 1758, *BP* 2:217 (ovens, "saws," charcoal, hay, lumber, "indulgence"); Hunter, "Barton," 444 ("a fine Fort"); Glen to Washington, "Camp Rea or Bouquetsburgh," July 19, 1758, *GWP* 5:297 ("beauty"); Shippen to Peters, Raystown, August 16, 1758, in Shippen, "Military Letters," 462; Hunter, "Barton," 456–57 (ditch, "storehouse").
19. Bouquet Orderly Book, *BP* 2:670 (August 2, provincials to train), 673, 674, 675 (regulars to train).
20. Bouquet Orderly Book, *BP* 2:670 ("Line of Battle"), 673 ("Plattoons," "two deep"); Hunter, "Barton," 449 ("in the Indian Manner," emphasis added), 449–50. On Bouquet's tactics and their application during the 1763–1764 Indian War, see Smith, *Bouquet's Expedition*.
21. Bouquet to Forbes, Raystown, August 8, 1758, *BP* 2:337 ("very raw"); Bouquet Orderly Book, *BP* 2:677 (troops to train with blank ammunition). The wider use of target firing is reflected in the experience of provincial troops in New York. See "Robert Webster's Journal," 128; also Blane to Bouquet, Fort Ligonier, March 2, 1759, *BP* 3:167 (target practice results, and reward).
22. For references to courts-martial, see Bouquet Orderly Book, *BP* 2:674, 675, 676, 678, 683, 682 (firing weapons in camp), 676 (wagoner); Bouquet to Forbes, Raystown, July 11, 1758, *BP* 2:182 ("example must be made"); *BP* 2:668 (theft as a capital offense). See also Steppler, "British Military Law."
23. Hunter, "Barton," 477 ("Number of Men"); George Washington Order Book (Toner Manuscript, Library of Congress), 9 (eight deserters); Hunter, "Barton," 482 (execution). The burning clothes suggest that the firing party was very close when they shot. This was evidently not unusual; illustrations of Admiral John Byng's execution for dereliction of duty in 1757 clearly show the firing party of marines shooting the admiral with the muzzles of their muskets only a foot or so from his chest. One such illustration is reproduced in Ireland, *Naval Warfare in the Age of Sail*, 29. Essays by Arthur N. Gilbert are still the place to begin any study of British military justice in the eighteenth century; see in particular "Regimental Court Martial," "Changing Face of British Military Justice," and "British Military Justice." See also Frey, "Courts and Cats"; Hay, "Property, Authority and the Criminal Law." On the larger issue of authority in the British army, see Tatum, "Soldiers Murmured Much."
24. *A Soldier's Journal*, 3 ("our ground"), 4 (tenting arrangements). See also Kopperman, "Medical Service in the British Army."
25. On disease in early modern armies, see Tallett, *War and Society*, 106–8, 111–13. On inoculation, see for example, Loudoun to Cumberland, New York, December 26, 1756, *Military Affairs*, 280; Duffy, *Epidemics in Colonial America*, 229 ("jail fever"); Pringle, *Observations*, 53; McCrae, *Saving the Army*. Pringle's book was known to and read by British officers; see Gruber, *Books and the British Army*, 207. Other books appearing at the same time include Ranby, *Method of Treating Gun Shot Wounds*; Hamilton, *Duties of a regimental surgeon considered*.

26. Bouquet Orderly Book, *BP* 2:658–59, 666 (horses).
27. Bouquet Orderly Book, *BP* 2:659 (latrines, kitchens), 664 (latrines); *A Soldier's Journal*, 4. On the building and appearance of field kitchens, see Rees, "As Many Fireplaces as You Have Tents."
28. On weather, see *BP* 2:235 ("heavy rain"), 238, 239, 240–41 ("dark cloudy"), 293; see also Thwaites, *EWT*, 189; *Correspondence of Pitt*, 1:294 ("hot weather"); Bouquet Orderly Book, *BP* 2:681 (reference to a "second camp").
29. Washington to Bouquet, Fort Cumberland, August 18, 1758, *BP* 2:387–88. The averages are derived from monthly field returns of both regiments.
30. Lieutenant Peter Bard to Burd, Fort Augusta, July 20, 1758, in Balch, *Letters and Papers*, 125, where the detached Pennsylvanians are described as the "leavings of the battalion; some dragging their legs after them, others with their arms in slings, several sick." Governor Sharpe of Maryland reported in August that "The Army in general is very healthy the Pensilvania New Levies & those that came from North Carolina are the only Corps that have any Reason to complain of Sickness." Sharpe to Pitt, Fort Frederick, August 27, 1758, *Correspondence of Pitt*, 1:328. Returns of the provincial troops with Forbes are incomplete. The summary presented here and in the previous paragraph is based on the following: "A Weekly Return of the 2d Virginia Regt," August 21, 1758, "A Daily Return of the Virginia Companies," Fort Cumberland, July 19, 1758, "A Weekly Return of Five companies of the 2d Virginia Regiment," July 19, 1758, "A Weekly Return of the 2d Virginia Regiment," Fort Cumberland, July 24, 1758, "A Daily Return of the Virginia Detachment under Lieutenant-Colonel Stephen," Raystown, August 2, 1758, "A Daily Return of the Virginia Detachment," Raystown, July 30, 1758, "A Return of the Six Companies of the 1st Virginia Regiment," Raystown, July 12, 1758, "A Daily Return of the Virginia Companies," Raystown, July 6, 1758, all in George Washington Papers, Library Congress (hereafter GWLC), series 4; "A Return of the Augusta Regiment," January 1, 1758, *PA* 5.1.102; "Return of the Augusta Regiment," February 1, 1758, *PA* 5.1.102; "Return of the Maryland Forces at Raystown," September 11, 1758, in Balch, *Letters and Papers*, 138; "A Return of His Majesty's Forces under the Command of Brigadier General Forbes, September 25 1758 Camp Rays Town," in "Army Statistics," Shippen Papers, HSP; "An Effective Return of His Majesty's Forces Incamped at Loyal Hannon November 4th, 1758," *GWP* 6:109.
31. Halkett, "A General Sketch of the Numbers of Troops," Shippensburg, September 1, 1758, FHQP, reel 3, f. 487; *PA* 5.1.354–55 ("left behind"). For additional companies, see "A Field Return of the Division of the Sixty-second, or First Highland Battalion," Raystown, September 15, 1758, in Balch, *Letters and Papers*, 140. On Montgomery's regiment, see "Field Return of the 1st Highland Battalion," Philadelphia, June 13, 1758, FHQP, reel 2, f. 312; "Return of the First Highland Battalion," Philadelphia, June 24, 1758, FHQP, reel 2, f. 330; on the Royal Americans, "Field Return of the Second Division, First Battalion, of the Royal American Regiment," "on the March," August 24, 1758, in Balch, *Letters and Papers*, 136. On the army's condition, see "Daily Return of the Troops," Raystown, July 21, 1758, FHQP, reel 2, f. 400; "Return of the Army at Loyal Hannon," November 4, 1758, *GWP* 6:109. We should recognize that Forbes's army was campaigning in the middle of the Little Ice Age, the general cooling of the Northern Hemisphere that began c. 1300 and lasted until the 1850s. Aside from the cooler, wetter weather, what characterized the Little Ice Age was climatic instability

and short-term fluctuations in weather patterns and temperatures. The persistent rain in the Ohio Country followed by the onset of colder conditions that emerged gradually during Little Ice Age may reflect this. The literature on climate change history and the Little Ice Age in particular is vast, but see the excellent introduction in Fagan, *The Little Ice Age*, and the comprehensive treatment in Brooke, *Climate Change and the Course of Global History*; Lamb, *Climate History and the Modern World*. White, in *Cold Welcome*, examines climate, weather, and seventeenth-century North American colonization. Nothing comparable to White's work has been done for the eighteenth century, though Zilberstein, in *Temperate Climate*, looks at colonial and European efforts to make sense of the climates encountered in North America. See also the essays on North American climate by Bell, "Historic Climate Records," and Cook et al., "Dendroclimatic Evidence."

32. Stephen to Washington, Raystown, August 2, 1758, *GWP* 5:363 (smallpox); Bouquet to Forbes, Raystown, August 8, 1758, *BP* 2:337 (smallpox and efforts to contain), August 10, 1758, *BP* 2:384 (smallpox), August 8, 1758, *BP* 2:337 (flux); Hunter, "Barton," 452; Forbes to Bouquet, Carlisle, August 2, 1758, *BP* 2:305 ("general Distemper," lime); Wahll, *Braddock Road Chronicles*, 282 (fluxes in Braddock's army). See also Wells to Forbes, Fort Loudoun (Pennsylvania), July 22, 1758, FHQP, reel 2, f. 409.

33. Pringle, *Observations*, 34,38; Peebles, "A Return of the Sick in the Hospital and the Camp," September 5, 1758, GWLC, series 4; Mercer to Washington, "6 Miles from Fort Cumberland," July 12, 1758, *GWP* 5:280 ("Ague & Fever"); Bouquet to Forbes, Raystown, August 20, 1758, *BP* 2:398 (no men for escorts); Ramsay to Washington, Raystown, August 29, 1758, *GWP* 5:427 ("die fast"); Bouquet to Washington, Raystown, August 17, 1758, *BP* 2:375 ("very Sickly"); Armstrong to Bouquet, "Redoubt near Stoney Creek," September 2, 1758, *BP* 2:463; Washington to Robinson, Fort Cumberland, September 1, 1758, *GWP* 5:432; "Unpublished Correspondence of William Byrd," 289 (Fort Cumberland, August 24); Bouquet to Forbes, Raystown, August 31, 1758, *BP* 2:450 (Pennsylvanians); St. Clair to Bouquet, "Foot of Allegany," August 12, 1758, *BP* 2:359 (Highland officers); St. Clair to Bouquet, Edmunds Swamp, August 23, 1758, *BP* 2:412 (Armstrong). Venereal disease seems not to have been a major problem in Forbes's army. Although Peebles cited six cases, the only mention in official records comes in October orders, which note that a woman suspected of being infected was to be sent to the hospital for examination. See Orderly Book, Raystown, October 4, 1758, *GWP* 6:60.

34. Hunter, "Barton," 471–721 ("perfect Skeleton"), 481 ("Wild Geese"); Washington to Bouquet, Fort Cumberland, August 18, 1758, *BP* 2:387–88 ("depression of Spirits"). A British officer in 1755 described the "Inconveniency" of moving through woods infested with "a Kind of tick, or Forest Bug" whose bite led to "Inflammations and Ulcers." Wahll, *Braddock Road Chronicles*, 181.

35. Washington to Forbes, Chestnut Ridge, November 16, 1758, *GWP* 6:130–31 (falling tree); Stephen to Washington, Raystown, July 14, 1758, *GWP* 5:289 (broken leg and cut). The Fort William Henry skeletons, dating to 1757, have been summarized in Liston and Baker, "Reconstructing the Massacre," esp. 29–34. Recent analysis of nearly three dozen skeletons from Fort Erie, Ontario (although dating from the War of 1812), remains one of the most complete studies of military pathology from the preindustrial era, and the results are suggestive of what befell Forbes's soldiers more than fifty years earlier. See Owsley et al., "Injuries, Surgical Care and Disease";

Sledzik and Moore-Jansen, "Dental Pathology." On accidental drowning, see for example, "Captain William Sweat's Personal Diary," 46–47.

36. Kopperman, *Theory and Practice*, 659 (balsam), 663–64 (brandy), 667 (candle wax).
37. Halkett Orderly Book, in Hamilton, *Braddock's Defeat*, 94 (court-martial); *Pennsylvania Gazette*, October 21, 1756 (adjutant killed); "Reverend Samuel Cleaveland's Journal," *Bulletin of the Fort Ticonderoga Museum* 10 (1959), 195, 211 ("Melancholy Accident," soldier killed); Morgan to Bouquet, Juniata Crossing, July 13, 1758, *BP* 2:200 ("Some Dispute"); Hunter, "Barton," 466 (Hambright); Orderly Book, *GWP* 6:36 (Highlander); Hunter, "Barton," 480 (Kirkpatrick), 467 (artillery).
38. Hunter, "Barton," 447 (twenty wagons), 457 (building hospital, planting gardens); "Journal of Charlotte Brown," in Calder, *Colonial Captives*, 177 (wagons as shelters for medical personnel); Bouquet to Washington, September 4, 1758, *BP* 2:475 (no room in hospital); Bouquet Orderly Book, *BP* 2:679 (guards for the "new Hospital" at Raystown); Wahll, *Braddock Road Chronicles*, 114 (orders regarding women serving in the hospital, 1755); Bouquet Orderly Book, *BP* 2:680 (women to attend the sick for two weeks and wages), For references to women being paid by the army, see "Bouquet's Accounts," April 16, 1759, *BP* 3:245 (two pounds seven shillings paid to "Texter's Wife" and one pound sterling to "Heil's Widow"). On military hospitals, see also Monro, *Means of Preserving the Health of Soldiers*, vol, 1, part 2. On army medical treatment, see Kopperman, "Medical Service in the British Army"; Kopperman, "Medical Aspects"; Kopperman, *Regimental Practice*. For a more detailed look at women and army medical services, see Fatherly, "Tending the Army."
39. Armstrong to Bouquet, Stoney Creek, September 17, 1758, *BP* 2:525 ("Physick"); Bouquet to Forbes, Raystown, July 21, 1758, *BP* 2:254 (no medicines); Pringle, *Observations*, 303 (sulfur); Cuthbertson, *Compleat Interior Management and Oeconomy*, 36 ("have such a dislike"). An extensive pharmacopeia is included in Monro, *Means of Preserving the Health of Soldiers*, 2:288–322. On the treatment of gunshot wounds, see Ranby, *Method of Treating Gun Shot Wounds*, esp. 5–7, 8–10, 11–12 (allowing wound to heal without extraction).
40. Pringle, *Observations*, 93 (bathing), 242 (itch), 96–97 ("ventilators"); Bouquet Orderly Book, *BP* 2:667 (digging fresh latrines), 668 (maintenance of latrines), 669 (punishment for not using latrines), 682 (relocating campsites); 686 (striking and airing tents). On relocating campgrounds, see Hunter, "Barton," 458; Ramsay to Washington, Raystown, August 29, 1758, GWLC, series 4. Corporal William Todd, serving with British forces in France and Germany during the war, commented that the rear of his encampment "smells very Noisome with the Offal laying so thick and unburried" in the hot sun. He, too, also wrote of not changing clothes for days at a time. See Cormack and Jones, *Journal of Corporal William Todd*, 82, 83.
41. "Robert Webster's Journal," 131; "Captain William Sweat's Personal Diary," 41, 51, 53.
42. On the prescribed food allowance, see Wood, "Allowance of Provisions for One Man for Seven Days," Carlisle, June 15, 1758, FHQP, reel 2, f. 315; Bouquet Orderly Book, *BP* 2:678. I have relied here on two studies that explore soldiers' diets: Anderson, *People's Army*, 84–88; Coss, *All for the King's Shilling*, 272–87. See also McConnell, *Army and Empire*, ch. 6. Medical experts like Pringle believed that the army's ration allowance was adequate to maintaining good health among soldiers, provided they properly cooked and consumed their food rather than liquor. Pringle, *Observations*, 86–87; Cuthbertson, *Compleat Interior Management and Oeconomy*,

19–23; Bouquet Orderly Book, *BP* 2:666 (messes). On gardens, see Hunter, "Barton," 449 ("Piece of Ground"), 468–69 ("fine Gardens"); see also McConnell, *Army and Empire*, 105–6.

43. Cormack and Jones, *Journal of Corporal William Todd*, 198 ("utmost want"), 199 ("Bread Waggons"), 192 (cost of food); Stephen to Bouquet, Fort Loudoun (Pennsylvania), June 7, 1758, *BP* 2:53 (complaint about rations); Bouquet to Forbes, Raystown, July 21, 1758, *BP* 2:253. If short rations produced discontent and complaints, a generous issue could just as easily boost morale. In November 1761, Prince Ferdinand of Brunswick, commander of the British-allied army in Germany, gave each regiment additional food and also gave extra rations to women and children. Cormack and Jones, *Journal of Corporal Todd*, 217. At the same time, however, the army made clear that persistent or vocal complaints about food would be treated as acts of sedition and punished accordingly. See Knox, *Campaigns in North America*, 2:282. On the inspection and condemnation of foodstuffs, see Bouquet to Burd, Carlisle, June 6, 1758, FHQP, reel 2, f. 297. For a study of British soldiers' diet during the war, see also Yagi, "Surviving the Wilderness."

44. "Return of Provisions at Raystown, on the Road and at other Places, now Ready," July 14, 1758, FHQP, reel 2, f. 368; "Stores rec'd and Issued," Raystown, July 20,1758, Forbes/SRO, reel 1 (liquor); Forbes to Abercromby, Carlisle, July 25, 1758, *Writings of Forbes*, 160.

45. Wood, "A Calculation of Provisions to Serve Six Thousand Men three Months or 84 Days," Carlisle, July 9, 1758, Forbes/SRO, reel 1; "Return of Provisions at Raystown, on the Road and at other Place, now Ready," July 14, 1758, FHQP, reel 2, f. 368 (oxen and sheep); "Return of Provisions," Fort Cumberland, August 23, 1758, GWLC, series 4 (amount of meat from cattle), Bouquet observed that the cattle arriving from Fort Cumberland "are Extremely bad" and hoped to received "no more Such Cattle" in the future, Bouquet to Washington, Raystown, August 26, 1758, *BP* 2:425–26. British officers in 1755 were not impressed by the quality of cattle from Virginia. See Wahll, *Braddock Road Chronicles*, 203; "State of Provisions at Carlisle, July, 1758," Forbes/SRO, reel 1 (bulk supplies of cornmeal); Wood to Forbes, Carlisle, June 9, 1758, FHQP, reel 2, f. 304 (North Carolina pork); "Return of Provisions at Carlisle belonging to the Contractors, July 14, 1758, FHQP, reel 2, f. 367 (bad cornmeal).

46. St. Clair to Calvert, Fort Frederick, July 10, 1758, *AM* 9:229 (200 wagons, condition of road); Bouquet to Forbes, Raystown, July 11, 1758, *BP* 2:180 ("broken wagons," wagon masters "good for nothing"); Ourry to Forbes, Fort Loudoun, August 6, 1758, Forbes/SRO, reel 2 (drivers without firearms).

47. Bouquet to Forbes, Raystown, July 21, 1758, *BP* 2:254 (Hoops); Bouquet to Forbes, camp near Raes Town, July 11, 1758, *BP* 2:180 ("good horses," "nags"); "Calculation of Oats for 400 Tames [*sic*]," FHQP, reel 3, f. 496 (oats); Forbes to Bouquet, Carlisle, July 14, 1758, *BP* 2:208 ("Intire Stop"); Bouquet to Forbes, Raystown, July 21, 1758, *BP* 2:253 ("as if they were gold"); Bouquet to Forbes, Raystown, August 8, 1758, *BP* 2:337 (artillery teams). As early as July 5, Forbes ordered his officers to take as little personal baggage as possible "[a]s the Nature of the Country makes it impossible to provide Magazines of Forage" in the backcountry. Shippen Orderly Book, Shippen Papers, HSP. On August 2, Forbes also ordered that all available forage was to be collected from the local fields as the army passed. Forbes to Bouquet, Carlisle, August 2, 1758, *BP* 2:304. See also Grant to Forbes, Fort Loudoun (Pennsylvania), Au-

gust 16, 1758, Forbes/SRO, reel 2 (forage from abandoned farms). The forage problem added to the army's burdens in other ways. Grazing animals had to be guarded while at pasture by "grass guards" drawn from available troops; teams sent miles from camp to feed required larger escorts and risked attack before reinforcements could arrive. These daily guards occupied manpower that might have been used to escort convoys or work on the road; see Bouquet to Forbes, Raystown, July 31, 1758, *BP* 2:292 ("a heavy guard" to escort cattle to fields); Bouquet Orderly Book, *BP* 2:665 (July 14), 666 (July 20), 673 (August 7).
48. Forbes to Abercromby, Carlisle, July 9, 1758, *Writings of Forbes*, 139; Bouquet to Washington, Raystown, July 27, 1758, *BP* 2:282 (St. Clair). See also Forbes to Bouquet, Carlisle, July 14, 1758, *BP* 2:208.
49. Forbes to Abercromby, Carlisle, July 25, 1758, *Writings of Forbes*, 160 (orders St. Clair to Raystown); Bouquet to Forbes, Raystown, July 31, 1758, *BP* 2:291 (St. Clair's arrival and preparations for road survey). We should also note that, between May and August, St. Clair was constantly on the move as he worked to get troops and transport organized. He was also dealing with the arrival and departure of Cherokees and Catawbas. He was in Philadelphia, Carlisle, Fort Loudoun (Pennsylvania), Fort Loudoun (Virginia), Fort Cumberland, and Raystown; no other member of Forbes's staff logged so many miles and none suffered from kidney stones and a bladder infection as St. Clair did.

SIX: *FORBES'S ROAD*, July–August 1758

Epigraph: Forbes to Pitt, Carlisle, July 10, 1758, *Correspondence of Pitt* 1:295.
1. Forbes to Pitt, Philadelphia, May 1, 1758, *Writings of Forbes*, 78; Forbes to Stanwix, Philadelphia, May 29, 1758, *Writings of Forbes*, 103 ("open the road"); Forbes to Abercromby, Philadelphia, June 27, 1758, *Writings of Forbes*, 126–27; Bouquet to Forbes, Fort Loudoun (Pennsylvania), June 14, 1758, *BP* 2:87–88 (Bouquet's concerns); Forbes to Bouquet, Philadelphia, June 19, 1758, *BP* 2:112 (scout road beyond Raystown); Bouquet to Forbes, Juniata Crossing, June21, 1758, *BP* 2:121 ("season is too far advanced"), *BP* 2:123 (sending survey parties); Forbes to Bouquet, Carlisle, July 6, 1758, *BP* 2:164–65 ("most Certainly"); Forbes to Abercromby, Carlisle, July 9, 1758, *Writings of Forbes*, 139 ("directly across the Allegany," "by Fort Cumberland"). Forbes's determination to make a new road to the Ohio is further supported by Major James Grant, who told Bouquet that Forbes "is unwilling to be put under the necessity of making any Detour." Grant to Bouquet, Carlisle, July 11, *BP* 2:185. Forbes's own wait-and-see attitude to the road is reflected in his comments to Abercromby, that although Bouquet was "making the projected Route over the Laurel Mountain" and despite his plans for another post west of Laurel Mountain, Forbes also said he would not concentrate the whole army at Raystown "till the Route is finally determined." Forbes to Abercromby, Carlisle, July 25, 1758, *Writings of Forbes*, 160. See also Anderson, "General Chooses a Road."
2. Forbes to Bouquet, Philadelphia, June 16, 1758, *BP* 2:103; Forbes to Bouquet, Carlisle, July 6, 1758, *BP* 2:164–65.
3. Forbes to Bouquet, Carlisle, July 23, 1758, *BP* 2:264–65.
4. Sharpe to Calvert, Conecocheague, June 11, 1758, *AM* 9:205; Armstrong to Bouquet, Carlisle, June 28, 1758, *BP* 2:145; Sharpe to Tasker, June 29, 1758, *AM* 9:217. In a letter of July 10, 1758, for example, Sharpe reported that Bouquet had "intimated" he

was worried about opening a new road as Forbes had ordered. Sharpe to Calvert, Fort Frederick, July 10, 1758, *AM* 9:229. Sharpe's views were evidently reinforced by Bouquet who shared his own misgivings about the route through Pennsylvania; see Sharpe to Calvert, Fort Frederick, July 10, 1758, *AM* 9:229.

5. Sharpe to Lord Baltimore, Fort Frederick, July 9, 1758, *AM* 9:226. A recent assessment of Washington's role in the Forbes campaign can be found in Brumwell, *Gentleman Warrior*, ch. 4.

6. Sharpe to Calvert, Fort Frederick, July 10, 1758, *AM* 9:230; Edward Shippen to Joseph Shippen, Lancaster, August 5, 1758, in Balch, *Letters and Papers*, 129–30; Hunter, "Barton," 480 (Raystown, September 24, 1758).

7. Washington to Fairfax, Winchester, May 5, 1755, *GWP* 1:262–63 ("now open," "satisfaction"); Washington to Carlyle, Fort Cumberland, May 14, 1758, *GWP* 1:274; Washington to Stanwix, Fort Loudoun (Virginia), April 10, 1758, *GWP* 5:118; Washington to St. Clair, Fort Loudoun (Virginia), April 18, 1758, *GWP* 5:131 ("some disgust"); St. Clair to Bouquet, Winchester, June 9, 1758, *BP* 2:60–61 ("Virginians are dissatisfied"). Washington was characterized as "a good deal Sanguine & Obstinate" on choice of road. Armstrong to Peters, October 3, 1758, *PA* 1.3.552.

8. Washington to Bouquet, Fort Cumberland, July 7, 1758, *GWP* 5:267 ("all hands," "absolutely refuse"); Byrd to Bouquet, July 9, 1758, "Minute of the Governor and Council," Williamsburg, August 3, 1758, and Fauquier to Byrd, Williamsburg, August 17, 1758, in Tinling, *Three William Byrds*, 2:662, 664, 666; Ramsay to Washington, Raystown, August 17, 1758, *GWP* 5:397 ("Steep, Stony"); Ramsay to Washington, Raystown, August 19–20, 1758, *GWP* 5:404 ("injur'd Colony"); Kirkpatrick to Washington, Alexandria, August 23, 1758, *GWP* 5:413–14 ("headstrong prejudice," "Crafty Neighbors," "Injustice"); Washington to Bouquet, Fort Cumberland, July 16, 1758, *BP* 2:222 ("particular pains"); Washington to Bouquet, Fort Cumberland, July 24, 1758, *GWP* 5:318 ("officious"); Washington to Bouquet, Fort Cumberland, July 25, 1758, *BP* 2:273–74 ("Chearfully," "will of my own"); Washington to Jones, Fort Cumberland, July 29, 1758, *GWP* 5:350 ("warmly urge").

9. Halkett to Washington, Philadelphia, June 25, 1758, *GWP* 5:243 (emphasis added); Halkett to Bouquet, Carlisle, July 31, 1758, *Writings of Forbes*, 161 ("extremely surpris'd"); Bouquet to Forbes, Raystown, July 11, 1758, *BP* 2:179–80 ("letters I receive," "matter of politics"); Bouquet to Forbes, Raystown, July 21, 1758, *BP* 2:252 ("double caution"); Bouquet to Forbes, Raystown, July 31, 1758, *BP* 2:291 ("a party and an army"). Memories of dealing with the Virginians and their arguments evidently stayed with Bouquet. As late as the spring of 1760 he was proposing a detailed plan for a "new road" that, he hoped, would "avoid giving any Jalousie" to any interested colony. His calculations of distance and terrain were painstaking and suggest how much he wished to avoid intercolonial politics. See Bouquet to Stanwix, Philadelphia, April 26, 1760, *BP* 4:541.

10. Forbes to Bouquet, Carlisle, July 23, 1758, *BP* 2:264–65 ("As I disclaim," "drive us into the Road"); Forbes to Bouquet, Carlisle, July 14, 1758, *Writings of Forbes*, 145 ("some foolish people"); Forbes to Bouquet, Raystown, September 23, 1758, *BP* 2:536–38 ("told them plainly"). Forbes's hostility to factions among his officers was likely fueled by learning that Abercromby's army was beset by "parties" and that this contributed to Abercromby's own defeat at Fort Ticonderoga. See Forbes to Bouquet, Shippensburg, August 18, 1758, *BP* 2:383.

11. Bouquet to Washington, Raystown, July 27, 1758, *BP* 2:281–82 (asks to meet Washington). The letters from Washington that evidently prompted the meeting are Washington to Bouquet, Fort Cumberland, July 24, 25, 1758, *GWP* 5:318, 324–25. Bouquet had earlier indicated that he believed Forbes would stand by his decision; see Bouquet to Washington, Raystown, July 24, 27, 1758, *BP* 2:268–69, 281 ("generous dispositions," "candid Exposition"); Bouquet to Forbes, Raystown, July 31, 1758, *BP* 2:291 ("I learned nothing," "everything easy").
12. Washington to Halkett, Fort Cumberland, August 2, 1758, *GWP* 5:360–61; Forbes to Bouquet, Carlisle, August 9, 1758, *Writings of Forbes*, 171; Forbes to Abercromby, Carlisle, August 11, 1758, *Writings of Forbes*, 173 (emphasis added); Forbes to Bouquet, Shippensburg, September 4, 1758, *Writings of Forbes*, 199. It is not clear whether Halkett deliberately showed Washington's letter to Forbes or merely left it in view. Given his close relationship with Forbes and the general's increasing reliance on his help and judgment, and the professional ethics they both shared, it seems likely that Halkett did, in fact, share the letter with Forbes.
13. Forbes to St. Clair, Philadelphia, June 16, 1758, FHQP, reel 2, f. 318 (complaint about Gordon); Gordon, "Memorial Concerning the Back Forts in North America," December 17, 1765, *Military Affairs*, 470–71. Gordon's 1755 journal covering the march from June 2 to July 8, 1755, can be found in Wahll, *Braddock's Road Chronicles*, 243, 280–81, 292, 293, 296, 299, 303–4, 306–7, 311, 313, 317, 319, 322, 326, 332, 336, 341.
14. Bouquet to Washington, Raystown, August 10, 1758, *BP* 2:351; Bouquet to William Allen, Fort Duquesne, November 25, 1758, *BP* 2:611; Washington to Bouquet, Fort Cumberland, August 13, 1758, *GWP* 5:389 ("your"); Washington to Bouquet, Fort Cumberland, August 24, 1758, *GWP* 5:416 ("am glad the New Road turns out so much to your Liking"); Washington to Fauquier, Fort Cumberland, September 2, 1758, *GWP* 5:439–41 ("Pennsylvanians"); Robert Stewart to Washington, Cresap's, August 5, 1758, *GWP* 5:375 ("well grounded hopes"). Washington continued to write about the road until the very end of the campaign in November, corresponding not only with Forbes and Bouquet but also fellow Virginia officers, as well as Governor Fauquier and others in Williamsburg.
15. St. Clair to Bouquet, Winchester, June 11, 1758, *BP* 2:76–77 ("labour & time"); Bouquet to Forbes, Fort Loudoun (Pennsylvania), June 16, 1758, *BP* 2:96 ("often deceived"); "Instructions for Captains Ward & Clayton," Raystown, July 7, 1758, FHQP, reel 2, f. 352 ("the Bearings").
16. "Instructions for Captains Ward & Clayton," Raystown, July 7, 1758, FHQP, reel 2, f. 352; "A Report of Captain Ward sent to Reconnoiter the Road to the Westward" (July 1758), *BP* 2:243–46; "Ward's Journal of Distances," July 1758], *BP* 2:237–42 (Myers).
17. "James Patterson's Journal," August 1758, *BP* 2:327–29; Armstrong to Bouquet, Drownding Creek (Quemahoning), July 26, 1758, *BP* 2:280. In a subsequent letter Armstrong told Bouquet that his comment about scouting for land was "no more than a Jock [joke]"—but one wonders. In all events the subsequent history of the Ohio Country suggests that others shared the land hunger expressed by Armstrong. See Armstrong to Bouquet, Drownding Creek (Quemahoning), July 30, 1758, *BP* 2:286." Cock Eye's Cabin" is just south of present-day Export, Westmoreland County, Pennsylvania, the other two landmarks mentioned cannot be identified; see *BP* 2:330n10.

18. "Baker, Report on Road to Raystown," July 1758, *BP* 2:234–36; Armstrong to Bouquet, Edmund's Swamp, July 25, 1758, FHQP, reel 2, f. 419; Rhor to Bouquet (c. July 31), *BP* 2:294 ("trading path"); Bouquet to Forbes, Raystown, August 8, 1758, *BP* 2:336 (St. Clair; "how right you were"). Rhor's reference to the "Old trading path" and mention of landmarks like "Cock Eye's Cabin" are reminders that Forbes's army was not so much pioneering a way through a "wilderness" as they were navigating along older well-used native paths. For the older view, see Stotz, "Forbes Conquers the Wilderness."
19. Forbes to Bouquet, Shippensburg, August 18, 1758, *BP* 2:383 ("small Road"). On Braddock, see Robert Orme, "A Plan of the Encampment of the Detachment from the Little Meadows," and Orme, "A Plan of the Disposition of the Advanced Party, consisting of 400 Men," in Hamilton, *Braddock's Defeat*, 203, 212; also Patrick Mackellar, "A Sketch of the Field of Battle of the 9th of July Upon the Monongahela," in Hamilton, *Braddock's Defeat*, plate 17, for the use of flanking parties on Braddock's march and what Forbes likely had in mind.
20. This and subsequent discussions of the road draw on Waddell and Bomberger, *French and Indian War*, 43–47. On the weather in late July and early August, see *BP* 2:293 (July 31, "it rained all day"); *BP* 2:328 (August 1, Youghiogheny River high); *BP* 2:238 (thick fog, couldn't see Fort Duquesne); *BP* 2:349 (August 10, rain at Edmund's Swamp); Thwaites, *EWT*, 192 (Post journal: August 9, heavy rain night and day); Armstrong to Bouquet, "from Kicknepaulin's," July 26, 1758, FHQP, reel 2, f. 419 ("Indian halloes"). The elevation data comes from Briggs, "Conquest of the Allegheny Mountains," 407–8.
21. Bouquet to Forbes, Raystown, August 8, 1758, *BP* 2:336 (numbers of men); Bouquet Orderly Book, *BP* 2:671 (men assigned to roadwork, bakers); on the weather, see *BP* 2:293 (rain, end of July); *BP* 2:328 (high water in Youghiogheny River, August 1; thick fog, August 2). In the absence of any other evidence, I have assumed that scouting parties marked the correct route by cutting notches in trees; Bouquet's instructions to Ward and Clayton state that they were to "mark" the road so others could find it. See "Instructions to Captains Ward & Clayton," Raystown, July 7, 1758, FHQP, reel 2, f. 352. For a detailed summary of the route, see Waddell and Bomberger, *French and Indian War*, 38–49.
22. Bouquet to Forbes, Raystown, August 8, 1758, *BP* 2:336; Forbes to Bouquet (Carlisle, August 9, 1758), *BP* 2:344 ("advances briskly"); Bouquet Orderly Book, Raystown, August 14, 1758, *BP* 2:677 (Highlanders and other troops sent out).
23. Taylor, *Military Roads in Scotland*, 34; Mercer to Washington, July 12, 1758, *GWP* 5:280; Washington to Bouquet, Fort Cumberland, July 13, 1758, *GWP* 5:282 (width of road).
24. Bouquet to Forbes, Camp near Raystown, August 3, 1758, BP 2: 313; Armstrong to Bouquet, Drownding Creek, August 7, 1758, *BP* 2:320; Forbes to Bouquet (Carlisle, August 9, 1758), *BP* 2:344 (refers to "different partys" working "at the same Time"); St. Clair to Bouquet, "Foot of Allegheny," August 12, 1758. *BP* 2:359–60 (building a redoubt at Shawnee Cabins); St. Clair to Bouquet, Allegheny Mountain, August 16, 1758, *BP* 2:372–73 ("small retrenchment" at Kicknepauling).
25. Stephen to Bouquet, Edmund's Swamp, August 8, 1758, *BP* 2:341–42 ("extreamly troublesome," clearing camp, reservoir, "Shades of Death," "a dismal place"); Ste-

phen to Bouquet, Edmund's Swamp, August 10, 1758, *BP* 2:349 ("I shall not believe you," "glorious"). Stephen's reports suggest he did not share Washington's opinion that the new road was an impossibility.

26. Stephen to Bouquet, Edmund's Swamp, c. August 12, 1758, *BP* 2:361 (detour, logs "as hard as iron"); Sharpe to St. Clair, Fort Frederick, July 8, 1758, *AM* 9:222 (axes); Bouquet to Forbes, Raystown, August 3, 1758, *AM* 9:313 ("five or six days"); St. Clair to Bouquet, "Foot of Allegheny," August 12, 1758, *AM* 9:359–60 ("immence"); Bouquet to Washington, Raystown, August 17, *GWP* 5:395 ("over the Mountains"); Bouquet to Washington, Raystown, August 21, 1758, *GWP* 5:406 (number of troops at Raystown). See also Briggs, "Conquest of the Allegheny Mountains," 412–13.

27. Stephen to Bouquet. Edmund's Swamp, August 13, 1758, *BP* 2:363–64; St. Clair to Bouquet, Allegheny Mountain, August 16, 1758, *BP* 2:372–73 ("the labour is immence"); Bouquet to Forbes, Raystown, July 31, 1758, *BP* 2:290–91 ("very different"); Rhor, "Report on the Road," n.d., Forbes/SRO, reel 2 (Rhor's Gap); Bouquet to Forbes, Raystown, August 18, 1758, *BP* 2:380 ("long Task," working parties); Forbes to Bouquet, Shippensburg, August 28, 1758, *BP* 2:439 ("to the quick," "wrong head," "heart as well").

28. Stephen to Bouquet, Edmund's Swamp, August 8, 1758, *BP* 2:341–42 (bridging the Swamp); Stephen to Bouquet (Edmund's Swamp, c. August 12), *BP* 2:361 ("Fat Beef"); Stephen to Bouquet (Stony Run, August 18, 1758), *BP* 2:386 (calls for more rum). In mid-September Bouquet called such bridges "worthless," suggesting that many began to deteriorate only a month after being built. Bouquet to Forbes, Loyal Hannon, September 11, 1758, *BP* 2:492.

29. Stephen was concerned that, in the absence of fresh venison, cooking the salt rations threatened to dry up the local springs. Stephen to Bouquet (Edmund's Swamp, c. August 12, 1758), *BP* 2:361. For injuries suffered by common soldiers, see also Kopperman, *Theory and Practice*, appendix B.

30. Bouquet to Forbes, Raystown, August 20, 1758, *BP* 2:395–96 (road open, Rhor, Loyal Hannon post); Major Armstrong to Forbes, Kicknepaulin's, July 26, 1758, Forbes/SRO, reel 2 ("a very pretty place"); Bouquet to Washington, Raystown, August 21, 1758, *BP* 2:404 ("very good Road"); Ramsay to Washington, Raystown, August 17, 1758, *GWP* 5:397 ("Alpine difficulties," "difficult access"); Bouquet to Washington, Raystown, August 21, 1758, *BP* 2:404 (wagons over mountain); Forbes to Bouquet, Carlisle, July 23, 1758, *BP* 2:265 ("Bugbear"); Forbes to Peters, Shippensburg, August 28, 1758, *Writings of Forbes*, 191 ("that impossible Road); St. Clair to Bouquet, Kickenpaulin's, August 23, 1758, *BP* 2:414 (predicted schedule, needs more men).

31. St. Clair to Forbes, August 8, 1758, FHQP, reel 3, f. 157 ("party of pleasure"); Glen to Forbes, "Camp at Raes Town," August 8, 1758, FHQP, reel 3, f. 456 (St. Clair's appearance); Bouquet to Washington, Raystown, August 26, 1758, *BP* 2:426 (first division of artillery); Burd to Bouquet, Quemahoning, August 29, 1758, *BP* 2:445 (pace of work); Bouquet to Forbes, Loyal Hannon, September 11, 1758, *BP* 2:494 ("a less frightful pass"). On the problems with the Laurel Mountain road, see Bouquet to Burd, Stony Creek, October 12, 1758, *BP* 2:551 (Bouquet finds the road "impassable"); Washington to Fauquier, Loyal Hannon, October 30, 1758, *GWP* 6:99 ("accidental" discovery of new route); Bouquet to Washington, "Camp at the East Side of Laurel Hill," November 1, 1758, *GWP* 6:103 (need to cut a new way across mountain—old route "impracticable").

32. Stephen to Washington, Loyalhannon, September 9, 1758, *GWP* 6:6–7.
33. Stephen to Bouquet, Quemahoning, August 26, 1758, *BP* 2:430–32 (to his "Commanding Officer," "Usd me Extreamly ill"). The sequence of events as related by Stephen comes from Stephen's letter to "my Friend." Stephen to Bouquet, Quemahoning, August 26, *BP* 2:430–33. St. Clair to Bouquet, Kikoney Paulins, August 27, 1758, *BP* 2:434 ("he woud brake his Sword in pieces").
34. St. Clair to Bouquet, Kikoney Paulins, August 27, 1758, *BP* 2:434–36.
35. The fact that copies of what passed between Stephen and St. Clair in 1755 appear in Forbes's papers suggest both that the general knew of the earlier incident and anticipated further trouble between the two men.
36. Bouquet to St. Clair, Raystown, August 28, 1758, *BP* 2:435–36; Bouquet to Forbes, Raystown, September 4, 1758, *BP* 2:475 (intercession by Burd and Grant); Ramsay to Washington, Raystown, September 3, 1758, *GWP* 5:454 ("public justification"); Bouquet to Forbes, Raystown, September 4, 1758, BP 2:475; Ramsay to Washington, Raystown, September 3, 1758, *GWP* 5:454 ("Sir John Wildair," "B—ly"); Hunter, "Barton," 467 ("rank"); Stephen to Washington, Loyal Hannon, September 14, 1758, *GWP* 6:17 (Stephen reinstated); Forbes to Bouquet, Raystown, September 23, 1758, *BP* 2:538 (St. Clair to acknowledge error).

SEVEN. *LOYALHANNON AND FORT DUQUESNE*, September 1758

Epigraph: Forbes to Pitt, Fort Loudoun (Pennsylvania), September 6, 1758, *Correspondence of Pitt*, 1:339.

1. McConnell, "Pisquetomen and Tamaqua," 286 ("truth of affairs"). See also "Post Journal," FHQP, reel 2, f. 376; Stephen to Bouquet, Edmund's Swamp, August 13, 1758, *BP* 2:363–64 (on work crews' concern they will attract raiding parties).
2. FHQP, reel 2, f. 372 (Denny asks Forbes to assist and protect Post, c. July 25, 1758). See also Peters to Weiser, Philadelphia, July 28, 1758, FHQP, reel 2, f. 427.
3. "The Journal of Charles [sic] Frederick Post," Thwaites, *EWT*, 195. Post also noted that "the Jealousy that Subsists amongst the Indians is not to be described," in part because many of them thought him a spy. Thwaites, *EWT*, 201.
4. "Journal of Post's Journey to Allegheny," in Hirsh, *EAID*, 3:412 ("unreasonable"), 409 ("never expected to see"), 410 (Teedyuscung), 411 ("nothing to say"). The Delawares were eager to drive this point home, saying "they again told me to lay aside *Teedyuscung*" and would have nothing to do with his negotiations. Hirsh, *EAID*, 3:411. Italics in this and following references are from the original.
5. Hirsh, *EAID*, 3:411 ("sunrise to the sunset," Delaware George), 410 (French building houses), 411 ("*French* captain appeared low spirited"). The French made an attempt to have the Indians surrender Post to them, which was rebuffed as a violation of diplomatic protocol. See "Post Journal," FHQP, reel 2, f. 376.
6. "Journal of Posts Journey to the Allegheny," Hirsch, *EAID*, 3:413–14 (number of French and Indians present). By holding the council within sight of Fort Duquesne the natives sent a message to the French that they were acting independently and would not be interfered with. See also Raffle, *Malartic Journals*, 187.
7. "Journal of Posts Journey to the Allegheny," in Hirsch, *EAID*, 3:414.
8. "Journal of Posts Journey to the Allegheny," in Hirsch, *EAID*, 3:415.
9. Post Journal, FHQP, reel 2, f. 376. Tamaqua's efforts to build consensus were bearing fruit; the Delawares' reply to Pennsylvania's message was endorsed by fourteen men,

representing all three western Delaware social divisions. See Hirsch, *EAID*, 3:418. For another pointed indictment of British and French culpability in causing the war, see "Speech of Ackowanothio," (September 1758), in Hirsch, *EAID*, 3:423–25.
10. Hirsch, *EAID*, 3:418–19.
11. Bouquet to Hamilton, Loyalhannon, September 13, 1758, *BP* 2:495 (Fort Dewart, Fort Dudgeon, post at Stoney Creek).
12. Bouquet to Forbes, Raystown, July 21, August 8, 1758, *BP* 2:252, 335–36 ("140 miles").
13. Forbes to Bouquet, Shippensburg, August 28, 1758, *BP* 2:340.
14. Bouquet to Burd, Raystown, August 23, 1758, *BP* 2:407.
15. Burd to Bouquet, Fort Dewart, August 26, 1758, *BP* 2:427 (wagons and artillery); Burd to Bouquet, Quemahoning, August 28, 1758, *BP* 2:438; Bouquet to Sinclair, Loyal Hannon, September 9, 1758, *BP* 2:482 ("most infernal one," "uneasy").
16. Bouquet to Grant, Reas Town camp, August 26, 1758, Papers of the McPherson-Grant Family of Ballindalloch, Banffshire, Gifts and Deposits (GD) 494/1/31/15/9, typescript provided by the Fort Ligonier Association; Bouquet to Forbes, Raystown, August 26, 1758, *BP* 2:423–24.
17. Forbes to Bouquet, Shippensburg, August 28, 1758, in *Writings of Forbes*, 188–89; Bouquet to Burd, Reas Town Camp, August 29, 1758, *BP* 2:444 ("traverses"). For the weather: Hunter, "Barton," 459, 460, 465–67, 471 (falling leaves and frost); *BP* 2:478 (hard rain, unsettled weather).
18. Bouquet's additional orders to Burd are in "Instructions for Colonel Burd, Camp at Loyal Hannon," September 25, 1758, *BP* 2:543–44 ("Fort of Logs").
19. Forbes to Bouquet, Rays Town, October 10, 1758, *BP* 2:550. British engineers in America seem to have acquired a poor reputation, with problems evident at Abercromby's attack of Fort Carillon in 1758 and again the following year during the British siege of Fort Niagara. On Carillon, see Westbrook, "Like Roaring Lions," 62–63, 74–75; on Niagara, see Dunnigan, *Siege 1759*, 48–49, 53–54.
20. "Plan of Fort Ligonier [1759]," Amherst A55, RUSI Maps, vol. 79 (no. 11), British Library Additional Manuscripts, 57714. My thanks to Brian Dunnigan for his help in locating and identifying this plan.
21. Bouquet to Forbes, Raystown, July 21, 1758, *BP* 2:253 ("greatly diminished"); Forbes to Abercromby, Carlisle, August 11, 1758, *Writings of Forbes*, 173 ("distress"); Bouquet to Forbes, Raystown, August 8, 1758, *BP* 2:337 ("suffered a great deal"); Bouquet Orderly Book, *BP* 2:673, 680, 687 (size of covering parties).
22. Bouquet to Forbes, Loyal Hannon, September 11, 1758, *BP* 2:494 ("excellent pastures"); Grant to Forbes, Fort Loudoun (Pennsylvania), August 16, 1758, Forbes/SRO 45/2 ("extremely bad"); Forbes to Howell, Shippensburg, August 15, 1758, FHQP, reel 3, f. 47 (contractors); Howell to Forbes, Shippensburg, August 23, 1758, FHQP, reel 3, f. 484; Forbes to Howell, Shippensburg, August 26, 1758, FHQP, reel 3, f. 485; Bouquet to Forbes, Raystown, September 4, 1758, *BP* 2:471; Forbes to Pitt, Fort Loudoun (Pennsylvania), September 6, 1758, *Correspondence of Pitt*, 1:340 ("real hindrance," "distress"); Halkett to Sharpe, Raystown, September 16, 1758, *AM* 9:266 (Washington); Forbes to Denny, Fort Loudoun, September 9, 1758, *Writings of Forbes*, 207 (confiscations); Forbes to Abercromby, Raystown, October 24, 1758, *Writings of Forbes*, 244–45.
23. Forbes to Abercromby, Raystown, October 24, 1758, *Writings of Forbes*, 244 ("diligence and application," "better footing"); Forbes to Sharpe, Shippensburg, Septem-

ber 3, 1758, *Writings of Forbes*, 198 ("neglect"); Forbes to Abercromby, Raystown, October 8, 1758, *Writings of Forbes*, 225 ("immense confusion," "certain dexterity," "solemn face"); Forbes to Bouquet, Shippensburg, September 4, 1758, *Writings of Forbes*, 199 ("odd man," "any Concerns").

24. Forbes to Bouquet, Shippensburg, August 28, 1758, *Writings of Forbes*, 188 ("must be sick"); Forbes to Howell, Shippensburg, August 26, 1758, FHQP, reel 3, f. 485 ("pain," "want of health"); Bouquet to Stephen, Loyal Hannon, September 13, 1758, *BP* 2:496 (Forbes not to be involved in dispute); Forbes to Bouquet, Shippensburg, August 18, 1758, *Writings of Forbes*, 181 ("excruciating pain"); Halkett to Bouquet, Carlisle, August 2, 1758, *Writings of Forbes*, 162 ("most painful symptoms"); Forbes to Bouquet, Shippensburg, September 2, 1758, *Writings of Forbes*, 193 ("have been worse"); Forbes to Pitt, Fort Loudoun (Pennsylvania), September 6, 1758, *Correspondence of Pitt*, 1:343 ("extreamly precarious"); Forbes to Abercromby, Shippensburg, September 4, 1758, *Writings of Forbes*, 199 ("excruciating pains"); Young to Bouquet, Raystown, September 10, 1758, *BP* 2:489 (believes Forbes near death); Abercromby to Stanwix, Camp at Lake George, September 7, 1758, in Preston and La Montagne, *Royal Fort Frontenac*, 265 ("Reports he is dead"). Part of Forbes's chronic pain may have been the result of severe constipation. In late August he asked Richard Peters to send him prunes "by way of a laxative." Forbes to Peters, Shippensburg, August 28, 1758, *Writings of Forbes*, 193.
25. Forbes to Washington, Raystown, September 16, 1758, *GWP*, 6:23.
26. Washington to Bouquet, Fort Cumberland, July 13, 1758, *BP* 2:203–6; Stephen to Bouquet, Edmund's Swamp, August 13, 1758, *BP* 2:363; Forbes to Peters, Shippensburg, August 28, 1758, *Writings of Forbes*, 191–92.
27. "James Patterson Journal" (August) 1758, *BP* 2:327–29 (food, tobacco, paint); Forbes to Bouquet, Shippensburg, August 15, 1758, *BP* 2:367 ("still of opinion"); Forbes to Bouquet, Raes town, September 17, 1758, *Writings of Forbes*, 214 (Armstrong's suggestion and Forbes's doubts); Hunter, "Barton," 464 ("unsuccessful," "coldly received"); Bouquet to Burd, Raystown, August 26, 1758, *BP* 2:419 ("acute hearing," "knocked on the head"). Bouquet also recommended that Burd's men refrain from scalping since this would only make Indians more vigilant.
28. *Pennsylvania Gazette*, August 31, 1758 (wagons attacked between Loudoun and Littleton and on Sideling Hill; attack near Shippensburg); Halkett to Bouquet, Shippensburg, August 26, 1758, *BP* 2:428–29 ("infest us"); Forbes to Sharpe, Shippensburg, August 23, 1758, *AM* 9:242 ("within a mile"); Hunter, "Barton," 448 (Fort Littleton); St. Clair to Bouquet, Allegheny Mountain, August 16, 1758, *BP* 2:373 ("Enemy all round us," "take all the care"); Bouquet to Washington, Raystown, August 17, 1758, *GWP* 5:395 ("Woods about us"); Washington to Bouquet, Fort Cumberland, August 7, 1758, *BP* 2:324; "Journal of Charles [sic] Frederick Post," in Thwaites, *EWT*, 223 (Kuskuskies); Hunter, "Barton," 458 (Delawares say they were Cherokees); Washington to Bouquet, Fort Cumberland, August 24, 1758, *BP* 2:416 (Bullen and French, burials).
29. Vaudreuil to Massiac, Montreal, September 28, 1759 (sic), *PA* 2.6.558.
30. Hunter, "Barton," 471 (attack at Loyalhannon); Bouquet to Forbes, Camp at Loyalhanna, September 11, 1758, *BP* 2:494 ("some scalping"); Bouquet to Hugh Mercer, Loyal Hannon, September 14, 1758, *BP* 2:498 ("Strong Parties").
31. Bouquet to Forbes, Loyal Hannon, September 11, 1758, *BP* 2:492–93 ("rabble"); Bou-

quet to Forbes, Loyal hannon, September 17, 1758, *BP* 2:517–20 (Grant's objection and plan); Grant to Bouquet, Fort Duquesne, c. September 14, 1758, *BP* 2:499–504 ("long projected Scheme"); Bouquet to Forbes, Loyalhannon, September 11, 1758, *BP* 2:493 ("good lesson," Rhor, "secret orders"); Grant to Bouquet Fort Duquesne, c. September 14, 1758, *BP* 2:501 ("coup de main").

32. Bouquet to Forbes, Loyalhannon, September 11, 1758, *BP* 2:493 ("large party," "pick of the troops"); Hunter, "Barton," 471 (Dagworthy ordered to Loyal Hannon); Peckham, "Thomas Gist's Indian Captivity," 289–90 ("bush fighting"); Bouquet to Forbes, Loyal Hannon, September 11, 1758, *BP* 2:493–94 ("detained by an oversight," Grant's departure, "splendid order," "their best," "somewhat hazardous," "necessary"); Peckham, "Thomas Gist's Indian Captivity," 290. Losses can be found in "List of Casualties from Action Near Fort Duquesne," *BP* 2:508–9. The detachment numbered 803 officers and men.

33. Hunter, "Barton," 471 (McLean); Peckham, "Thomas Gist's Indian Captivity," 290 ("different opinions," "Major Lewis").

34. Peckham, "Thomas Gist's Indian Captivity," 291.

35. Peckham, "Thomas Gist's Indian Captivity," 291–92n16; Kirk, *Memoirs and Adventures*, 6.

36. Grant to Forbes (Fort Duquesne), c. September 14, 1758, *BP* 2:501.

37. Peckham, "Thomas Gist's Indian Captivity," 292 ("platoons"); Kirk, *Memoirs and Adventures*, 6 ("platoon firing"); Grant to Forbes (Fort Duquesne), c. September 14, 1758, *BP* 2:503 ("I was told"); Bouquet to Forbes, Loyalhannon, September 17, 1758, *BP* 2:520 ("My heart is broke"); Grant to Forbes (Fort Duquesne), c. September 14, 1758, *BP* 2:504 (retreat and Landers). After cataloguing the events that led to the destruction of his command and his own captivity, Grant ended by expressing the hope that these events would not prejudice him on the seniority list if vacancies and promotions came available and asked that Forbes expedite his exchange. See Grant to Forbes (Fort Duquesne), c. September 14, 1758, *BP* 2:504. Anyone wishing to read a detailed tactical reconstruction of the battle should consult McCulloch, *Sons of the Mountains*, 119–29. Readers should note, however, that McCulloch dates the events to September 13, not September 14.

38. Peckham, "Thomas Gist's Indian Captivity," 294 (killing prisoners); official casualty figures can be found in "A List of the Officers & Soldiers killed, missing & Returned," *BP* 2:508–9. On the Virginia Regiment, see "List of Casualties in the First Virginia Regiment," *GWP* 6:46–47; Washington to Fauquier, Raystown, September 25, 1758, *GWP* 6:44. In this and other letters Washington assumed that Lewis had been killed; only later did the French release the names of those held prisoner. See Lignery to Bouquet, Fort Duquesne, September 27, 1758, *BP* 2:533–35. Stephen to Bouquet, September 15, 1758, *BP* 2:512 (French summon Grant).

39. Bouquet to Forbes, Loyalhannon, September 17, 1758, *BP* 2:517–20 ("make no apology"); Armstrong to Bouquet, Stoney Creek, September 24, 1758, *BP* 2:542 ("very uneasy"); Forbes to Bouquet, Raystown, September 23, 1758, *BP* 2:535–38 ("no less surprise," "lame," Rhor); Forbes to Abercromby, Raystown, September 21, 1658, *Writings of Forbes*, 215–18 ("severe check," "Endeavours," "rashness and ambition"); Forbes to Pitt, Raes Town Camp, October 20, 1758, *Correspondence of Pitt*, 1:371 ("most terrible check"); William Peters to Richard Peters, Philadelphia, September 29, 1758, *PA* 1.3.547 (Halkett's letter); Armstrong to Richard Peters, Raystown, Octo-

ber 3, 1758, *PA* 1.3.551–52 ("Quixot Expedition"); Washington to Fauquier, Raystown, September 28, 1758, in Reese, *PFF* 1:82 ("ill-concerted").
40. Hamilton, *Adventure in the Wilderness*, 295 ("an engineer"); Doriel to Belle Isle, Quebec, October–November 3, 1758, *PA* 2.6.447–48 (almost caught by surprise); Bougainville to de Cremille, Quebec, November 8, 1758, *PA* 2.6.449–50 ("very different road," "chain of posts," "more than probable"); Bougainville to de Cremille, Quebec, November 8, 1758, *NYCD* 10:888 ("fortunate adventure"); Peckham, "Thomas Gist's Indian Captivity," 295–96 ("my lott," "confirmation of friendship"); Raffle, *Malartic Journals*, 190.
41. Bradstreet to Abercromby, Oswego, August 31, 1758, in Preston and La Montagne, *Royal Fort Frontenac*, 262, 71–82 (details of Bradstreet's raid); Forbes to Abercromby, Raystown, September 21, 1758, *Writings of Forbes*, 215 ("a good deal damped"). Forbes may have received news on or before September 17 since he made a brief note about it in a letter of that date to Bouquet. *Writings of Forbes*, 214. Joseph Shippen to Edward Shippen, Raystown, September 19, 1758, *BP* 2:527–28 ("breathe nothing but Revenge"); Washington to Fairfax, Camp at Rays Town, September 25, 1758, *GWP* 6:39 ("one People").
42. Forbes told Bouquet that he arrived at Raystown "night before last"; given the date of his letter this would be September 15. Forbes to Bouquet, Raes Town, September 17, 1758, *BP* 2:522.
43. Stephen to Washington, Camp at Loyal Hannon, September 8, 1758, *GWP* 6:6–7 (clothing).

EIGHT. *LOYALHANNON*, October 1758

Epigraph: Forbes to Pitt, Raes Town, October 20, 1758, *Correspondence of Pitt*, 1:374.
1. Forbes to Pitt, October 20, 1758, *Correspondence of Pitt*, 1:371; Armstrong to Bouquet, Stony Creek, September 24, 1758, *BP* 2:542 ("uneasy," "Shock"); Forbes to Pitt, October 20, 1758, *Correspondence of Pitt*, 1:373–74.
2. Forbes to Abercromby, Raystown, October 8, 1758, *Writings of Forbes*, 226 ("briars and thorns"); Mercer to Washington, Raystown, September 15, 1758, *GWP* 6:21; Halkett to Sharpe, Raystown, September 16, 1758, *AM* 9:266; Forbes to Washington, Raystown, September 16, 1758, *GWP* 6:23; Forbes to Denny, Raystown, October 24, 1758, *Writings of Forbes*, 242; Forbes to Abercromby, Raystown, October 24, 1758, *Writings of Forbes*, 247. Reverend Barton dined with Forbes in late September and found him "very facetious & in high Spirits" but at the same time "extremely weak & in a low State of Health." Hunter, "Barton," 480.
3. Forbes to Bouquet, Raystown, October 25, 1758, *Writings of Forbes*, 248; Hunter, "Barton," 449–50 (August 13, 14) ("This Morning the Tents & were cover'd with a Hore-Frost; & some say there was ice"); Bouquet to Forbes, Raystown, August 18, 1758, *BP* 2:381; St. Clair to Bouquet, Stoney Creek, August 23, 1758, *BP* 2:413; Andrew Stephen to Washington, Loyalhannon, September 9, 1758, *GWP* 6:6 (Stephen also recommended having blanket coats made for the troops, *GWP* 6:15; Hunter, "Barton," 451–52 (August 18, 19); *BP* 2:421 (September 11, 12) (Hore-Frost); *BP* 2:475 (September 18) ("very cold Morning"); *BP* 2:466 (September 2) (the cold and fog are making people sick). Washington to Fauquier, Raystown, September 18, 1758, *GWP* 6:53 ("face of nature").
4. Forbes to Peters, Shippensburg, August 28, 1758, *Writings of Forbes*, 192 ("learn

nothing"); Forbes to Pitt, Fort Loudoun (Pennsylvania), September 6, 1758, *Writings of Forbes*, 204 ("number of posts"). Forbes also worried that, since Abercromby's defeat at Fort Carillon/Ticonderoga, he would now face a reinforced garrison at Fort Duquesne; see Forbes to Lyttleton, Shippensburg, August 16, 1758, FHQP, reel 3, f. 475. Washington arrived at Raystown on the evening of September 16, 1758; see Halkett to Sharpe, Camp at Raystown, September 16, 1758, *Writings of Forbes*, 209; Washington to Fauquier, Fort Cumberland, September 2, 1758, Reese, *PFF*, 1:67.

5. Forbes to Abercromby, Carlisle, July 3, 1758, WO 34/44 f. 159; Forbes to Bouquet, Carlisle, August 9, 1758, *Writings of Forbes*, 171.
6. Bouquet to Forbes, Raystown, August 20, 1758, *BP* 2:396. On escorts, see Bouquet Orderly Book, Raystown, August 22, 1758, *BP* 2:681, and George Washington Order Book (Toner Manuscript, Library of Congress), 64. Burd to Bouquet, Loyal Hannon, September 6, 1758, *BP* 2:478; Burd to Bouquet, September 11, 1758, *BP* 2:494; St. Clair to Forbes, n.d., Fort Loudoun (Pennsylvania), Forbes/SRO, reel 2 (repairing axle trees); Hunter, "Barton," 467 (new carriages); Halkett to Sharpe, Raystown, October 2, 1758, *Writings of Forbes*, 222 ("spair Wheels"); Bouquet to Forbes, Raystown, August 20, 1758, *BP* 2:396 (horses); James Sinclair to Bouquet, Raystown, September 14, 1758, *BP* 2:506 (horses).
7. Orderly Book, October 4, 1758, *GWP* 6:59; Orderly Book, October 22, 1758, *GWP* 6:77; Stewart to Washington, Camp at Raes Town, October 25, 1758, *GWP* 6:93 (Highlanders and Byrd's regiment). The artillery escorted by Washington's troops did not arrive at Loyalhannon until c. October 22, 1758; see *GWP* 6:80n1. Forbes to Abercromby, Raystown, October 8, 1758, *Writings of Forbes*, 226.
8. Forbes to Abercromby, Raystown, October 8, 1758, *Writings of Forbes*, 226; Bouquet to Burd, Stoney Creek, October 12, 1758, *BP* 2:551 (new road over Laurel Mountain); Armstrong to Peters, Raystown, October 3, 1758, *PA*1.3.552 ("dry weather"); Forbes to Abercromby, Raystown, October 24, 1758, *Writings of Forbes*, 245, 246–47 ("extraordinary rains"). The experience of the Highlanders and Byrd's Virginia regiment reflect the slow pace of the advance. They left Raystown on October 23 but had to stop at Shawnee Cabins because of heavy rain. See also Forbes to Bouquet, Stoneycreek, October 30, 1758, *BP* 2:590.
9. Orderly Book, October 16, 1758, *GWP* 6:79; Bouquet to Forbes, Raystown, August 31, 1758, *BP* 2:450 ("idling in the Forts"). The number of dead and missing is from *PA*5.1.354–55. Bouquet to Burd, Reas Town Camp, September 1, 1758, *BP* 2:458 ("cannot account"); (Halkett), "A General Sketch of the number of Troops," Shippensburg, September 1, 1758, FHQP, reel 3, f. 487. Orderly Book, September 28, 1758, *GWP* 6:51, cites orders from Forbes that include "Considering the few numbers our Army consists of"; Forbes to Fauquier, Raystown, October 22, 1758, in Reese, *PFF*, 1:94 ("King's Troops"). On paper, the 60th and 77th numbered roughly seventeen hundred men at the beginning of the campaign.
10. "A Return of the Sick in the Hospital and in Camp" (Raystown), September 5, 1758, GWLC, Series 4; Bouquet to Forbes, Raystown, August 31, 1758, *BP* 2:450 ("greatest number"); Forbes to Abercromby, Raystown, October 22, 1758, *Writings of Forbes*, 24 (flux and fevers); Forbes to Denny, Raystown, October 22, 1758, *Writings of Forbes*, 243.
11. Orderly Book, Camp at Reas Town, September 24, 1758, *GWP* 6:36–37 (deserters

and punishment); Washington to Forbes, Chestnut Ridge, November 16, 1758, *GWP* 6:130 (Lower Counties); Orderly Book, Loyal Hannon, November 3, 1758, *GWP* 6:104 ("cut Firing"); Bouquet to Forbes, Raystown, September 4, 1758, *BP* 2:471 ("bored"); Hunter, "Barton," 470 ("dejected"); Bouquet to Forbes, Loyal Hanna, October 28, 1758, *BP* 2:588–89.

12. "An Inventory, of ye Officers & Soldiers Effects . . . of ye 2 Division 1st Battn of ye Royal American Regt," September 20, 1758, *BP* 2:531 (Billings and Jenkins), 532 (enlisted men); "The Effects of Several Officers of the first Virginia Regiment, which were lost with Major Grant to be sold to morrow," in Orderly Book, Loyal Hannon, October 29, 1758, *GWP* 6:97; Grimm, *Archaeological Investigation*. On the size of the collections, Martin West, personal communication, November 13, 2016. Not all of the material found at Fort Ligonier dates from the Forbes campaign, of course. The post was occupied for eight years and saw much traffic, both military and civilian. However, features clearly associated with Forbes's army: the creek bed west of the camp, portions of both the inner fort and outer retrenchment, a fascine battery constructed in late autumn, and sections of Forbes' road were all systematically excavated.

13. Grimm, *Archaeological Investigation*, 128–44 (shoes described), 100–101, 103, 105, 107, 110 (shoes illustrated), 56–58 (shoe buckles described), 52, 54 (buckles illustrated), 70 (cuff links described), 59, 61 (cuff links illustrated). My comments regarding "signaling" and consumer behavior are based on Breen, "Baubles from Britain"; Calvert, "Function of Fashion"; Carson, "Consumer Revolution"; Breen, *Marketplace of Revolution*, esp. chs. 1–3. Descriptions of runaway servants in Pennsylvania during the mid-1750s frequently include references to new shoes, good shoes, or old shoes with brass, steel, or "yellow" buckles for both men and women; see Boyle, *"Apt to get drunk,"* esp. 284–85, 287–89, 290–91, 294–95, 297–99.

14. I have drawn this brief discussion from Mayer, "From Forts to Families," esp. 32–33; a photograph of women's shoes appears on page 32. On this particular style of shoe, see also Baumgarten, *What Clothes Reveal*, 92.

15. Grimm, *Archaeological Investigation*, 98 (moccasin illustrated); Bouquet to Forbes (Loyalhannon), October 20, 1758, *BP* 2:582.

16. Grimm, *Archaeological Investigation*, 72, 74, 78 (cartridge box flap), 115 (gun parts), 145 (shot pouch). On broken arms, see Bouquet to Forbes, Camp at Loyalhanna, September 17, 1758, *BP* 2:520.

17. Grimm, *Archaeological Investigation*, 117, 119–20, 122, 124, 126, 129–30, 132–33, 138–41 (leather harness gear).

18. Grimm, *Archaeological Investigation*, 97 (toys, personal items, pencils), 150 (case bottle, rum bottle), 148 (candleholders, forks, spoons), 166–69 (metal cups, pails, canteens), 156, 158–65 (ceramics), 153 (medicine vials), 163 (pill tile).

19. Forbes to Pitt, Fort Loudoun (Pennsylvania), September 6, 1758, *Writings of Forbes*, 203 ("provisions"); Forbes to Bouquet, Camp at Raystown, October 21, 1758, *BP* 2:582 ("plenty"); Forbes to Abercromby, Raestown, October 24, 1758, *Writings of Forbes*, 244. There is no mention in his correspondence that would suggest Forbes directed any apology to St. Clair.

20. Forbes to Bouquet, Shippensburg, August 18, 1758, *Writings of Forbes*, 182 ("less provisions"); Forbes to Bouquet, Reastown Camp, October 10, 1758, *BP* 2:550 (im-

pressing wagons); James Sinclair to Bouquet, Rays Town, October 13, 1758, *BP* 2:557 (cost of transport, "fair means," "Compulsion"); Forbes to Abercromby, Raestown, October 24, 1758, *Writings of Forbes*, 247 (Allegheny Mountain).

21. Bouquet to Forbes, Dudgeon, October 13, 1758, *BP* 2:555 ("impracticable"); Forbes to Bouquet, Raystown, October 21, 1758, *Writings of Forbes*, 241 (packhorses); James Sinclair to Bouquet, Camp at Rays Town, October 18, 1758, *BP* 2:568 ("Crowd so fast"); Bouquet to Forbes, Stoney Creek, October 15, 1758, *BP* 2:560 (work on road); Bouquet to Forbes, Camp at Loyalhanna, October 20, 1758, *BP* 2:573 (good forage, Quemahoning Creek), *BP* 2:574 ("cannot leave troops").

22. Forbes to Bouquet, Camp at Raystown, October 21, 1758, *BP* 2:583 ("Disorder"); Forbes to Bouquet, "Stonycreek," October 30, 1758, *BP* 2:590 (Allegheny Mountain road).

23. C. J. Russ, "Le Marchand de Lignery, François-Marie," *Dictionary of Canadian Biography*, 3:378. On the economic situation in New France, see Dechêne, *Power and Subsistence*, 121–27, and appendix E; Little, *Esther Wheelwright*, 189; "Examination of John Hockstattler," Shamokin, May 5, 1758, in Stevens and Kent, *Wilderness Chronicles*, 120 (food shortages on the Ohio).

24. Burd to Bouquet, Camp at Loyal Hannon, October 12, 1758, *BP* 2:552. Forbes noted in his report to Abercromby that, along with the firing, the British troops heard "the Indian Halloo," upon which sixty of the Maryland troops went out after the enemy; when they were being surrounded Burd sent out additional forces to support them. See Forbes to Abercrombie, Raystown, October 16, 1758, *Writings of Forbes*, 232–33; Raffle, *Malartic Journals*, 193.

25. Burd to Bouquet, Camp at Loyal Hannon, October 12, 1758, *BP* 2:552; Pouchot, *Memoirs of the Late War*, 168 (number of French engaged). Louise Dechêne gives the number of French at 650; see *Le Peuple, l'État*, 504. On French and Indian numbers, see below for the French prisoner's information, which put the numbers much closer to Burd's original estimate. Burd Journal, October 12, 1758, notes that the French attempted to assault one of the redoubts at 8 pm but were stopped by the artillery. Burd specifically mentioned the attack was on "Redoubt 3," which would have been the small redoubt shown on the Pleydell and McDonald plans situated near the road on the east side of the encampment. There thus seem to have been two phases to the attack: the initial firing lasting into the afternoon, followed by an attempted assault on the redoubt. Fragment of a journal kept by Col. Burd while commanding the troops at Loyal Hannon, October 12–17, 1758, Shippen Family Papers, HSP; Forbes to Abercromby, Raystown, October 16, 1758, *Writings of Forbes*, 232. On Gordon's role, see Burd to Bouquet, Camp at Loyal Hannon, October 13, 1758, *BP* 2:556; Bouquet to Burd, Fort Dudgeon, October 13, 1758, *BP* 2:553; "A Return of the Killed Wounded and Missing in defence of the Camp at Loyal Hannon," October 12, 1758, facsimile, *BP* 2: opposite 552 (Wright). Wright's wound may, in fact, have been more serious than reported, as he was reported dead at new Fort Pitt in December the following year. Andrews, *Journals of Jeffery Amherst*, 2:361.

26. "A Return of the Killed, Wounded and Missing in defence of the Camp at Loyal Hannon," October 12, 1758, *BP* 2: opposite 552. This material is abstracted in *BP* 2:567. Forbes to Pitt, Raes Town Camp, 20 October, 1758, *Writings of Forbes*, 239. On French dead, see Burd Journal, October 12–17, 1758, Burd-Shippen Papers, American Philosophical Society (hereafter APS) (entry for October 14); Pouchot, *Memoirs*

of the Late War, 168 (French losses); Bouquet to Forbes, Dudgeon, October 13, 1758, *BP* 2:555 (French losses). The French were evidently surprised that, given their numerical superiority, the garrison did not launch a sortie; see Raffle, *Malartic Journals*, 193.

27. "Fragment of a diary at a fort in western Pennsylvania," Burd-Shippen Papers, Military, APS (October 19); Burd Journal, October 12–17, Burd-Shippen Papers, APS (October 13, crossed path, heard yelling); Forbes to Abercromby, Raystown, October 16, 1758, *Writings of Forbes*, 232–33; Forbes to Pitt, Raystown, October 20, 1758, *Correspondence of Pitt*, 1:372;Pouchot, *Memoirs of the Late War*, 168.
28. Bouquet to Forbes, Stoney Creek, October 15, 1758, *BP* 2:560; Forbes to Abercromby, Raystown, October 16, 1758, *Writings of Forbes*, 232–33 ("great action"). In the same letter Forbes enclosed a casualty list but asked Abercromby to keep it to himself, perhaps because Forbes anticipated ridicule from fellow officers in New York. Bouquet to Forbes, Stoney Creek, October 15, 1758, *BP* 2:560; Forbes to Pitt, Raystown, October 20, 1758, *Correspondence of Pitt*, 1:372 ("extreamly angry"); Forbes to Bouquet, Raystown, October 15, 1758, *Writings of Forbes*, 229 ("very glad").
29. "Declaration of Martin Discentio," n.d., Box 7, Burd-Shippen Papers, Military, APS.
30. Bouquet to Forbes, Stoney Creek, October 15, 1758, *BP* 2:560; Bouquet to Burd, Stoney Creek, October 16, 1758, *BP* 2:565. See also "Last Official Report of the French Posts in the Northern Part of North America," *Pennsylvania Magazine of History and Biography* 56 (1932): 63 ("le Fort Duquesne").
31. "Extract of a Letter from Rays-town, October 16, 1758," *BP* 2:567 (Highland losses on October 12); Kalter, *Benjamin Franklin*, 290 (conference convened on October 7); Raffle, *Malartic Journals*, 194.

NINE. *EASTON AND THE KUSKUSKIES*, October–November 1758

Epigraph: Forbes to Pitt, Raes Town, October 20, 1758, *Correspondence of Pitt*, 1:371.
1. Forbes reached the Raystown camp on October 15, 1758; he was now about fifty miles from the head of his army, closer than he had been since the campaign started. Forbes to Denny, Raystown, October 22, 1758, *Writings of Forbes*, 242 ("precarious"); Bouquet to Burd, Stoney Creek, October 12, 1758, *BP* 2:551 ("a Pace"); Forbes to Abercromby, Raystown, October 24, 1758, *Writings of Forbes*, 247. Forbes had done everything he could to ensure that the Ohio Indians accepted the peace offers from Easton, going so far as to order Bouquet to keep the troops east of the Ohio River and not offer any provocation unless the western Indians persisted in their attacks.
2. Denny to Johnson, Philadelphia, August 30, 1758, *SWJP* 2:891. This information would have upset Johnson, who was always jealous of his prerogatives as the crown's Indian agent for the northern colonies. News from Pennsylvania appearing in 1759 reported on the success of the Easton conference during which "peace hath since, *by the intervention of brigadier general Forbes*, been acceded to" by the Ohio Indians (emphasis mine). *Gentleman's Magazine* 28 (April 1759): 220. The centrality of Delawares to the success of the campaign was shared by others. Washington, for example, thought that should the Delawares make peace "other tribes will follow their example." Washington to Fauquier, "Camp at Fort d'Quesne," November 28, 1758, in Reese, *PFF*, 1:116.
3. Post to Forbes, c. August 1758, *BP* 2:371; also Forbes to Bouquet, Carlisle, August 9, 1758, *Writings of Forbes*, 171. A copy of Post's journal, beginning on July 15, 1758, can

be found in FHQP, reel 2, f. 376. Post's journal of his trip to the Kuskuskies offers clear evidence of Delaware attitudes by midsummer; but see also Thompson and Post's Report to Denny and Forbes, June 19, 1758, FAP 2:15, on the suspicions they encountered at Wyoming. For another native indictment of the British, see "Speech of Ackowanothio," September 1758, in Hirsh, *EAID*, 3:423–25.

4. Fred Anderson argues that Abercromby specifically "authorized" Forbes to open negotiations with the Ohio Indians, saying that this "took a kind of courage" on Abercromby's part. Anderson, *Crucible of War*, 267. Having read the relevant letters, especially Abercromby to Forbes, Lake George, July 23, 1758, FHQP, reel 2, f. 415, I can find no evidence to support this. In this letter Abercromby merely offers Forbes tacit approval for his actions based on the latter's role as commander in chief in the southern colonies and pledges to support him "to the utmost of my power." See also Abercromby to Forbes, Albany, June 4, 1758. Abercromby's reluctance to lock horns with Johnson may have been due, in part, to the general's recent and spectacular defeat at Fort Carillon (Ticonderoga)and his concern about Johnson's own channels to the ministry in London as well as his own preoccupation with military affairs in New York in the wake of the Carillon campaign. The correspondence that passed between Forbes and Abercromby tends to emphasize the latter's expectation of timely replies to his letters but little constructive observations regarding Indian affairs in Pennsylvania. On Forbes's relationship with the Friendly Association, see Jennings, *Empire of Fortune*, ch. 17.

5. For other interpretations of the Easton conference, see Anderson, *Crucible of War*, 274–79; Merritt, *At the Crossroads*, 250–51; Jennings, *Empire of Fortune*, 396–404. The Quakers listed 508 natives from fourteen nations. See FAP2:259.

6. Pemberton to Forbes, Philadelphia, July 19, 1758, FHQP, reel 2, f. 395.

7. Johnson to Abercromby, Fort Johnson, April 28, 1758, *SWJP* 2:824–30; see also Richard Peters, report on Indian Council, March 15, 1758, FHQP, reel 1, f. 78, on Teedyuscung's claims. On the conflict between Quakers and the Proprietors, see Thayer, *Israel Pemberton*, esp. 201–4; Jennings, *Empire of Fortune*, 379–83.

8. "Extract of a Letter from Sir William Johnson to Major-General Abercromby," Fort Johnson, June 18, 1758, FHQP, reel 2, f. 321 ("Counter Workings"); Johnson to Abercromby, Fort Johnson, December 29, 1757, *SWJP* 2:770 ("entirely interfere"); Denny to Johnson, Easton, October 24, 1758, *SWJP* 3:10–11 ("counteract"); Peters to Johnson, Philadelphia, September 30, 1762, *SWJP* 10:537–38 ("same Game"). Some additional insight into the friction between the Quakers and provincial and crown authorities can be found in "Benjamin Chew's Journal of a Journey to Easton, 1758," in Boyd, *Indian Treaties*, 312–18.

9. Johnson to de Lancey, Fort Johnson, September 10, 1758, *SWJP* 2:896 (not attending, "forbidding," "warm Applications"); Johnson to Denny, Fort Johnson, July 21, 1758, FHQP, reel 2, f. 404 (invitation to Six Nations, sending Croghan and Andrew Montour to "assist" in the conference). "Instructions for George Croghan," Fort Johnson, July 21, 1758, *SWJP* 9:951–52, state that (Croghan's principal task is to protect "His Majesty's Interests"—which Croghan undoubtedly understood as to be the same as Johnson's and the Six Nations' interest. See also Johnson to Six Nations, Fort Johnson, July 22, 1758, *SWJP* 9:954 (asks them to send delegates to Easton and to help guide proceedings for "our common Welfare"). On Johnson's efforts to make contact with the western Delawares, see message carried by "Joseph Peppy [*sic*], A

Delaware," July 21, 1758, *SWJP* 2:875–77; Johnson to Abercromby, Fort Johnson, July 21, 1758, *SWJP* 2:827. A grateful Forbes, upon learning that Croghan would attend the conference, expressed the hope that Croghan would see to it that "selfish, provincial, or Proprietary Views" would not dominate the talks. He hoped the Indian agent would learn as much as he could about circumstances in the Ohio Country. See Forbes to Denny, August 26, 1758, *SWJP* 9:970. Forbes also insisted that Croghan join the army with as many Indians as he could muster as soon as the Easton conference ended; see Croghan to Johnson, Easton, September 21, 1758, *SWJP* 2:4.

10. "Minutes of Conferences, Held at Easton, In October, 1758," in Kalter, *Benjamin Franklin*, 292.

11. For details concerning the negotiating process, see Merrell, *Into the American Woods*, esp. ch. 7; Merrell, "I Desire All that I Have Said"; also Foster, "On Who Spoke First."

12. Kalter, *Benjamin Franklin*, 291–92 (roster of conference attendees, both colonial and Indian), 301–3 (Pisquetomen, message from the western Delaware headmen), 299 (Denny acknowledges the Delawares' arrival). Forbes mentioned that "Frederick Post has been here some time." Forbes to Peters, Raystown Camp, October 16, 1758, *Writings of Forbes*, 235. On the journey to Fort Augusta, see "Two Journals," 225–30. On Pisquetomen's age, see Strang, "Mason-Dixon and Proclamation Lines," 18.

13. Kalter, *Benjamin Franklin*, 294–96.

14. Kalter, *Benjamin Franklin*, 296–300, 303–7, 312–13 (Iroquois walk out on Teedyuscung). See also Jennings et al., *Iroquois Diplomacy*, 156; Jennings, *Empire of Fortune*, 396–400. For the Quakers, see Thayer, *Israel Pemberton*, ch. 12. Among the matrilineal Iroquois, "nephew" referred to a sister's son; and the brother or brothers of a woman became the surrogate fathers of her children. The term thus reflects not only subordination but the duty of the "father." Such kinship terms carried much meaning for natives, if not for colonists; for example, the Iroquois insisted on referring to colonial leaders as "brother" (that is, equals), while they continued to refer to the governors of New France as "father" (underscoring the protectiveness and generosity they expected from such a figure, not their presumed subordination to him as "children"). For more on this, see Richter, *Ordeal of the Longhouse*, ch. 2.

15. Kalter, *Benjamin Franklin*, 301–3.

16. Kalter, *Benjamin Franklin*, 303. Denny was aware of what it would take to restore peace with the Ohio Indians; Johnson had earlier recommended that Pennsylvania address land issues, including a boundary between natives and colonists, and a fair and regulated trade. These, he believed, would be the best way to undermine the French and restore peace. See Johnson to Denny, Fort Johnson, July 21, 1758, FHQP, reel 2, f. 404; also Pemberton to Forbes, Easton, October 26, 1758, FAP 2:279; "Notes on the Treaty of 1758," FAP 2:247. For the fact that the western Delawares were not yet ready to embrace any peace offer put before them, see their insistence that Post not discuss the 1757 peace treaty between Teedyuscung and Pennsylvania, telling him "they had nothing to say to any treaty, or league of peace" that others had agreed to. See "Two Journals," 197–98.

17. Kalter, *Benjamin Franklin*, 311–12.

18. Kalter, *Benjamin Franklin*, 316. For a Quaker assessment of the causes of the war, see also Thomson, *Enquiry into the Causes*.

19. Kalter, *Benjamin Franklin*, 322 ("came to take their Leave"), 323 ("Persons appointed," "Belts and Strings").
20. "Two Journals," 234 ("Having received orders"), 238 ("some of the Irish people," "in a friendly manner," "to get them off clear").
21. Kalter, *Benjamin Franklin*, 317–19. See also McConnell, *Country Between*, 132–35; Jennings, *Empire of Fortune*, 403–4.
22. "Two Journals," 240.
23. "Two Journals," 241–42 ("one of the worst roads"), 242 ("great mischief," "conduct to our people"), 243 ("such usage," "they were not afraid").
24. "Two Journals," 243 ("expressed his joy," desired them that had any love"), 244 ("any accident," "enemy will follow"), 245 ("in Indian dress," "Indian halloo"). Forbes's message is in *Writings of Forbes*, 252–53; another draft of Forbes's message is in FAP 2:291.
25. "Two Journals," 245 ("rolled down the hill," "weeds, briars and bushes"), 246 ("grumbled," "Indians were so slightly fitted out"), 248 ("could find no writing," "seemed much concerned"). Not being able to accurately speak the message associated with the belt would, at the least, be embarrassing for a seasoned leader such as Pisquetomen; at worst it could lead to suspicion, confusion, or delay in returning answers that the senders certainly expected.
26. "Two Journals," 249 ("the French," "no body was home"), 250 ("burnt," "hard matter"), 251 ("good news"), 252 ("many of the warriors"), 253 ("fall upon the Indians"). Post's reference to "our party" may mean Forbes's army at Loyalhannon. A mixed French and Indian force that certainly included some of these Delaware warriors did, in fact, attempt another raid on the encampment on November 12 (see chapter 10).
27. On the Delaware move west, see McConnell, "Kuskusky Towns," 53. Within three years of Post's second visit, the Kuskuskies and nearby towns were all but abandoned, as the Ohio Indians—Delawares, Shawnees, and Iroquois—had moved to the Muskingum and Scioto River Valleys or farther up the Allegheny River toward Seneca country.
28. "Two Journals," 254–56.
29. "Two Journals," 257–60, 240 (Pisquetomen).
30. "Two Journals," 270 (Delaware to remain at home), 258 (Post on Indians' concern), 264–67 (Forbes's message), 274–75 (Tamaqua urges Forbes to go home), 278 (Keekyuscung), 269 ("English had the field").
31. "Two Journals," 271.
32. "Two Journals," 277–78, (expect good treatment from British, "Good news," Tamaqua urges Denny to "be strong"), 268 ("cousins"). On the status of the Ohio Indians, see McConnell, *Country Between*, esp. chs. 1–5.
33. The most recent discussion of the boundary issue, albeit from a British imperial perspective, can be found in Edelson, *New Map of Empire*, ch. 4. For the long-term implications of the return of the western lands to the Iroquois, see also Campbell, *Speculators in Empire*.
34. "Two Journals," 278–79, 282–83 ("no inclination"); "Conference with the Delaware Indians," Pittsburgh, December 4, 1758, *BP* 2:622 ("extensive Trade"), 623–24 ("No Body," "None of your People Straggle"). For a second version of this meeting, recounted by the Munsee headman Custaloga to the French, see *BP* 2:624–26.

35. "Two Journals," 279–80, 281; "Conference with the Delaware Indians," Pittsburgh, December 4, 1758, BP 2:621–22.

TEN. *LOYALHANNON AND FORT DUQUESNE*, October–November 1758

Epigraph: Forbes to Pitt, Pittsbourgh, November 27, 1758, *Writings of Forbes*, 267.
1. Forbes to Pitt, Rays Town Camp, October 20, 1758, *Writings of Forbes*, 240–41.
2. On Forbes's arrival at Loyalhannon, *BP* 2:592.
3. Forbes to Fauquier, Loyalhannon, November 5, 1758, in Reese, *PFF* 1:102–3; "An Effective Return of his Majesty's Forces Incamped at Loyal Hannon November the 4th 1758," *GWP* 6:109; Orderly Book, October 30, 1758, *GWP* 6:98 ("an Hospital"); *GWP* 6:121 (Maryland sick relocated). The army's "flying hospital" under Doctor Russell had also moved from Raystown to Loyalhannon; see Orderly Book, November 3, 1758, in *GWP* 6:107. The number of men sick or hospitalized should be taken as a minimum. Desertions must have continued, especially from those men detached or "on command" along the road, though specific numbers do not exist. In late September the army consisted of 6,722 men, including 199 sick and wounded; these figures do not reflect the casualties from September 14, 1758, however. See return of the army at Rays Town, September 25, 1758, in "Military Statistics," Shippen Family Papers, HSP. According to the November return, there were twelve surgeons and mates available to individual regiments.
4. The proposal and details are in *BP* 2:594–96.
5. Forbes to Abercromby, Raystown, October 24, 1758, *Writings of Forbes*, 244. Bouquet's figures are found in "Calculation for Carriages of Supplies," c. May 15, 1759, in *BP* 3:287–88; "State of Provisions at Lancaster," December 15, 1758, *BP* 2:630.
6. Forbes to Bouquet, Raystown, October 20, 1758, *BP* 2:585. Concerned about the dwindling numbers and condition of his regulars, Forbes also asked the governors to provide garrisons for the forts and had already calculated how many men he would need to hold the posts along the road. See Forbes to Denny, Raystown Camp, October 22, 1758, *Writings of Forbes*, 242–43. Forbes's successor, General John Stanwix, faced serious difficulties in raising troops and supplies for the 1759 campaign and ended up with a force less than half the size anticipated. See Stanwix to Pitt, Philadelphia, June 22, 1759, *Correspondence of Pitt*, 2:130–34; also Fauquier to Pitt, Williamsburg, April 3, 1759, Sharpe to Pitt, Annapolis, April 18, 1759, Dobbs to Pitt, New Bern, May 18, 1759, in *Correspondence of Pitt*, 2:80, 91, 108.
7. Bouquet, Council of War (Pittsburgh), November 11, 1758, *BP* 2:600–601. The use of "Pittsburgh" suggests that Forbes had tentatively adopted that name for the post at Loyalhannon.
8. Orderly Book, November 12, 1758, *GWP* 6:120.
9. "Questions and Answers about Fort Ligonier," Camp at Loyalhannon, November 16, 1758, *BP* 2:602. The engineers were Captain Harry Gordon and Lieutenant Richard Dudgeon. In 1758 the magazine was an above ground structure within the inner fort; a subterranean magazine was later built to replace this wooden structure, which then seems to have become a soldiers' barracks or guardroom.
10. The first reference to Washington's troops at the camp is in Orderly Book, "Camp at Loyal Hannon," October 23, 1758, *GWP* 6:89. On the road issue, see Forbes to Bouquet, "Raestown" September 23, 1758, *Writings of Forbes*, 219.

11. *Pennsylvania Gazette*, November 30, 1758.
12. Forbes to Abercromby, "Loyall Hanning," November 17, 1758, *Writings of Forbes*, 255; Orderly Book, "Camp at Loyall Hannon," November 13, 1758, *GWP* 6:121. See also *GWP* 6:121–23n1; Anderson, *George Washington Remembers*, 23 ("circumstance"); and for another examination of the event, Brumwell, *Gentleman Warrior*, 144–45.
13. Anderson, *George Washington Remembers*, 23 ("presented"). On Virginians' earlier losses, see "List of Casualties from Action Near Fort Duquesne," *BP* 2:508–9; "A Return of the Killed, Wounded and Missing," October 12, 1758, *BP* 2: facing 552. The issue that continues to stir discussion among those who have closely studied the Forbes campaign is the contradiction between the newspaper account and Washington's own recollections. In the former, Washington led the initial force with Mercer coming to *his* assistance; the latter reverses these crucial roles, with Washington coming out to relieve Mercer's command. If, as seems logical, it was the first detachment of Virginians, already engaged with an unknown number of the enemy, that was prepared to continue firing, the second detachment seems to have marched into their comrades' line of fire and provoked a volley. If, in fact, Washington had led the initial sortie, then the onus of the outcome would have fallen on him, not Mercer. At least one of Washington's officers, Captain Thomas Bullitt (a survivor of Grant's defeat), blamed Washington for the affair and the resulting casualties. See Lengel, *General George Washington*, 75. Forbes, of course, wrote nothing about who led what detachment, and there are no other contemporary accounts.
14. *Pennsylvania Gazette*, November 30, 2758 (prisoner Johnson); Forbes to Abercromby, "Loyall Hanning," November 17, 1758, *Writings of Forbes*, 255 ("only Intelligence"); Sharpe to Pitt, Annapolis, November 28, 1758, *AM* 9:303 ("imagining"); Orderly Book, "Loyall Hannon," November 12, 1758, *GWP* 6:121(detachments ordered out), November 13, 1758, *GWP* 6:123 ("The line"), November 14, 1758, *GWP* 6:125–26 ("Disposition," march the following morning).
15. Bouquet to Allen, Fort Duquesne, November 25, 1758, *BP* 2:610 ("light-train"); Orderly Book, "Camp at Loyal Hannon," November 14, 1758, *GWP* 6:125–26, 127 (officers ordered to take only their fittest men). The individual brigades must have varied in size, but all were small; Washington's command included just 718 officers and men, see *GWP* 6:127n1. The brigade majors are listed in Orderly Book, November 21, 1758, *GWP* 6:151.
16. Washington to Forbes, October 8, 1758, *GWP* 6:66–67. The plan itself was drawn on the reverse of this letter and is reproduced on *GWP* 6:68–69. See also "Explanation of an Order of March," FHQP, reel 3, f. 499; "Explanation to the Plan of the Line of Battle," FHQP, reel 3, f. 500.
17. Forbes to Abercromby, Loyal Hannon, November 17, 1758, *Writings of Forbes*, 255 ("greatest anxiety"); Forbes to Denny, Raystown, October 22, 1758, *Writings of Forbes*, 242 ("Health continues precarious"); Forbes to Abercromby, Raystown, October 24, 1758, *Writings of Forbes*, 247 ("present situation of my health"); Forbes to Denny, Pittsburgh, November 26, 1758, *Writings of Forbes*, 365 (emphasis added); Bouquet to Washington, Loyal Hannon, November 16, 1758, *GWP* 6:133 (asking Washington to "get a chimney built" for Forbes in each of the encampments); Forbes to Abercromby and Amherst, Pittsburgh, November 26, 1758, *Writings of Forbes*, 263 ("my stomach, Midriff and Liver").

18. Council of War, Pittsburgh, November 11, 1758, *BP* 2:600 (artillery); MacGregor and Pawlikowowski, "Lindenmuth," 381.
19. Fauquier to the Board of Trade, Williamsburg, June 11, 1758, in Reese, *PFF*, 1:24; Forbes to St. Clair, Philadelphia, June 16, 1758, FHQP, reel 2, f. 318; George Turner to Byrd, Fort Loudoun(Virginia), June 23, 1758, FHQP, reel 2, f. 325; Turner to Byrd, Winchester, August 4, 1758, Tinling, *Three William Byrds*, 2:665 (shaman); Forbes to Bouquet, Raystown, October 10, 1758, *BP* 2:550; Bouquet to Burd, Stoney Creek, October 16, 1758, in Balch, *Letters and Papers*, 146.
20. Forbes to Bouquet, Raystown, October 15, 1758, *BP* 2:562 ("bullying," "the Famous Little Carpenter"); Forbes to Abercromby, Raystown, October 16, 1758, *Writings of Forbes*, 233 ("stupid speeches," "Rascal"); Forbes to Bouquet, Raystown, October 25, 1758, *Writings of Forbes*, 248 (believes he has persuaded Cherokees); Bouquet to Washington, "Camp at the East Side of Lawrell Hill," November 1, 1758, *GWP* 6:103 ("Seven Guns").
21. "Fragment of a diary at a fort in western Pennsylvania," Burd-Shippen Papers, Military, APS, notes that Forbes left Loyalhannon on November 18, 1758; Forbes to Burd, New Camp, November 19, 1758, *Writings of Forbes*, 256–57. On Attakullakulla's possible motives, see Oliphant, *Peace and War*, 67.
22. Forbes to Burd, New Camp, November 19, 1758, *Writings of Forbes*, 256–57; Washington to Fauquier, Fort Duquesne, November 28, 1759, *GWP* 6:159; Fauquier to Lyttleton, Williamsburg, December 14, 1758, in Reese, *PFF*, 1:134 ("scandalous Behaviour"); Davies cited in Williams, "An Account of the Presbyterian Mission," 134 ("northward," "his arms had been taken"), 137 ("railed much," "hate all that comes from it"). By the middle of the eighteenth century, native men throughout eastern America had adopted firearms as an important part of their fighting and hunting repertoire; the importance of muskets is underscored by the habit among traders and government agents in the southern colonies of counting the numbers of "gunmen" among the various nations. For the symbolic importance of firearms to Indians and the importance of disarming a man such as Attakullakulla, see Silverman, *Thundersticks*, esp. 9–12.
23. See *GWP* 6:134n2 on arrangements for the advance, also *GWP* 6:150n4; Washington to Forbes, Camp on Chestnut Ridge, November 15, 1758, *GWP* 6:129; Halkett to Burd, "New Camp," November 20, 1758, *GWP* 6:258 (distance to camp); Forbes to Bouquet, November 22, 1758, *Writings of Forbes*, 261 (artillery); "Fragment of a diary at a fort in western Pennsylvania," November 19, 1758, Burd-Shippen Papers, Military, APS. On the issue of time, see Forbes to Bouquet, Raestown, October 25, 1758, *Writings of Forbes*, 249.
24. Bouquet to Washington, Camp at Loyal Hannon, November 16, 1758, *GWP* 6:132–33 (Armstrong); Washington to Forbes, "Camp, on Chestnut-Ridge," November 15, 1758, *GWP* 6:129 (delays, shortage of tools); Washington to Bouquet, "Camp West of bushy Run," November 17, 1758, *GWP* 6:137 ("want of a guide"); Washington to Forbes, November 17, 1658, *GWP* 6:138 ("opened the Road"); Washington to Forbes, Chestnut Ridge, November 16, 1758, *GWP* 6:130–31 (desertions, injuries).
25. Washington to Forbes, November 17, 1758, *GWP* 6:139 ("high spirits," "anxious"); Orderly Book, November 18, 1758, *GWP* 6:139 (at Armstrong's camp), 140–41 (tools available); Washington to Forbes, "Colo. Armstrong's Camp," November 18, 1758,

GWP 6:141–42 ("deceived"); Forbes to Washington, "From the Camp where they are Building the Redouts," November 19–20, 1758, *GWP* 6:144–45.

26. Washington to Forbes, "Colo. Armstrong's Camp," November 18, 1758, *GWP* 6:142–43 (enemy party, "Croghan"); Orderly Book, November 18, 1758, *GWP* 6:140 ("Carolina & Maryland Companies"); Forbes to Washington (New Camp), November 19–20, 1758, *GWP* 6:144 ("never doubted").

27. Vaudreuil to Minister of Marine, Montreal, January 20, 1759, in Stevens and Kent, *Wilderness Chronicles*, 126 (Lignery's scouts, cannon fire, decision to destroy/abandon Fort Duquesne); Doriel to Belle Isle, Quebec, August 31, 1758, *NYCD* 10:821–22 ("fall of themselves"); Daine to Belle Isle, Quebec, November 3, 1758, *NYCD* 10:884 (expects Fort Duquesne to fall). On the logistical problem, see report from Governor Kerlerac, New Orleans, December 12, 1758, in Rowland and Sanders, *Mississippi Provincial Archives* 5:209–9; Vaudreuil to Massaic, Montreal, November 28, 1758, *NYCD* 10:924. On Indians, see Vaudreuil to the Minister of Marine, Montreal, February 15, 1759, and Vaudreuil to Berryer, Montreal, March 30, 1759, in Stevens and Kent, *Wilderness Chronicles*, 131–32, 140–41.

28. Forbes to Washington ("New Camp"), November 19–20, 1758, *GWP* 6:145; Orderly Book, "Washington's Camp," November 21, 1758, *GWP* 6:151 (full rations).

29. Orderly Book, *GWP* 6:151. This admittedly speculative account of Forbes's plans is based on material concerning the Braddock campaign uncovered in Preston, *Braddock's Defeat*, esp. 227, 229. On Forbes's scouts, see entry for November 20, 1758, "Fragment of a diary at a fort in western Pennsylvania," Burd-Shippen Papers, Military, APS (Grant's field).

30. Entry for November 20, 1758, "Fragment of a diary at a fort in western Pennsylvania," Burd-Shippen Papers, Military, APS ("any Soldier"); Orderly Book, *GWP* 6:128 (women), 156 (dogs).

31. *Pennsylvania Gazette*, December 7, 1758 ("heavy Firing"); Vaudreuil to Minister of Marine, Montreal, January 20, 1759, in Stevens and Kent, *Wilderness Chronicles*, 126 (Lignery); Forbes to Abercromby and Amherst, "Fort Duquesne now Pittsbourg," November 26, 1758, *Writings of Forbes*, 262. See also Bouquet to Allen, Fort Duquesne, November 25, 1758, *BP* 2:610. Washington to Fauquier, Fort Duquesne, November 28, 1758, *GWP* 6:158; *New York Mercury*, December 13, 1758 (artillery); Raffle, *Malartic Journals*, 195, 200.

ELEVEN. NOVEMBER 1758–MARCH 1759

Epigraph: Forbes to Abercromby and Amherst, "Fort Duquesne now Pittsbourg," November 26, 1758, *Writings of Forbes*, 262.

1. "Letter from General Forbes' Army, Pittsburgh (formerly Fort Duquesne)," *Pennsylvania Gazette*, December 14, 1758, *BP* 2:613 ("publick Thanksgiving"); "Extract of Letter from Pittsburgh (lately Fort Duquesne)," November 26, 1758, *Pennsylvania Gazette*, December 14, 1758, in *BP* 2:613 (*feu de joie*, bodies on Grant's field, no tents or "Conveniency"). Post, upon his arrival at the Forks, likewise commented on the artillery fire, which alarmed his Delaware escort. "Two Journals," 282.

2. Forbes to Abercromby and Amherst, "Fort Duquesne now Pittsbourg," November 26, 1758, *Writings of Forbes*, 263; Forbes to Denny, "Fourt Duquesne, or now Pittsburgh," November 26, 1758, *Writings of Forbes*, 265 (barracks for regulars). Forbes did not neglect the opportunity to strengthen his patronage ties to powerful men

at home. He informed Pitt that not only had he renamed Fort Duquesne in the prime minister's honor but he had renamed Loyalhannon Fort Ligonier after Field Marshal Sir John Ligonier, and Raystown became Fort Bedford, named for Lord Bedford, on January 21, 1759. See *Writings of Forbes*, 269; also Forbes to Fauquier, "Fort Duquesne now Pittsburgh," November 26, 1758, in Reese, *PFF* 1:114.

3. Forbes to Abercromby and Amherst, "Fort Duquesne now Pittsbourg," November 26, 1758, *Writings of Forbes*, 263. The mounting costs of the campaign clearly weighed on Forbes; see Forbes to Lords Commissioners of His Majesty's Treasury, Philadelphia, January 18, 1759, *Writings of Forbes*, 280–83, and "Abstracts of Warrants Granted by the Late Brigadier General Forbes, during the Campaign 1758," *Writings of Forbes*, 293–99.

4. Forbes to Bouquet, Carlisle, January 8, 1759, *Writings of Forbes*, 276; Washington to Fauquier, Loyalhanna, December 2, 1758, *GWP* 6:161. See also McCusker, *Money and Exchange*, 185, table 3.7. One important explanation for the rising costs of hiring transportation was the army's tendency to destroy both wagons and horses through hard usage and overwork. Forbes's successor in the Ohio Country, General John Stanwix, complained that this, and the army's slowness to compensate owners, threatened his own efforts to raise transportation in 1759. See Stanwix to Pitt, Philadelphia, June 22, 1759, *Correspondence of Pitt*, 2:130–31.

5. Bouquet to Stanwix, Fort Duquesne, November 25, 1758, *BP* 2:609 ("our officers," "greatly reduced," no clothes or shoes); Bouquet to the Duke of Portland, "Fort Du Quesne," December 3, 1758, *BP* 2:620 ("sad state of affairs"); "A Monthly Return of the 2d Div," York, March 24, 1759, *BP* 3:216. See also "Return of the Six Companies," Albany, February 24, 1759, *BP* 3:146; Major John Tulleken to Bouquet, New York, December 16, 1758, *BP* 2:633 (state of six companies in New York).

6. Ourry to Bouquet, Fort Bedford, December 16, 1758, *BP* 2:632 (Blane and sick troops); Armstrong to Bouquet, Raystown, December 16, 1758, *BP* 2:631 ("falling sick"); Armstrong to Bouquet, Fort Bedford, December 27, 1758, *BP* 2:646 ("residue"); Archibald Blane to Bouquet, Fort Ligonier, March 2, 1759, *BP* 3:167 ("behave so bad"); "Inquiry Concerning a Quarrel Between Sergeants," York, January 29, 1759, *BP* 3:95; Lander to Bouquet, Fort Duquesne, November 30, 1758, *BP* 2:615.

7. Campbell to Bouquet, Fort Bedford, December 20, 1758, *BP* 2:637 ("deplorable condition"); Halkett to Bouquet, Fort Loudoun (Pennsylvania), January 4, 1759, *BP* 3:13 (blankets): Robertson to Bouquet, Pittsburgh, August 6, 1759, *BP* 3:504–5 ("Coats were all in Raggs"); Campbell to Bouquet, Fort Bedford, December 20, 1758, *BP* 2:637 (357 sick, "Scarce able to drag"). See also McKenzie to Bouquet, Fort Ligonier, May 12, 1759, *BP* 3:281; Bouquet to Robertson, Fort Bedford, August 10, 1759, *BP* 3:534–35. The casualties are drawn from returns in *BP* 2:508–9 and opposite 552.

8. Entry for November 19, 1758, "Fragment of a diary at a fort in western Pennsylvania," Burd-Shippen Papers, Military, APS ("great numbers of Sick"). See Washington to Bouquet, Pittsburgh, November 29, 1758, *GWP* 6:160; Washington to Fauquier, Loyalhannon, December 2, 1758, *GWP* 6:161; "A Return of the Invalids of the . . . 1st Virginia Regiment left at Loyalhannon," n.d., *GWLC*; also Craik to Washington, Winchester, December 20, 1758, *GWP* 6:169–70; Stewart to Washington, Fort Loudoun (Virginia), December 20, 1758, *GWP* 6:171–72; Forbes to Pitt, Ft. Loudoun (Pennsylvania), September 6, 1758, *Correspondence of Pitt*, 1:341–42 (state of North Carolina troops). "A Return of the Sick in the General Hospital," Loyalhannon, December 5,

1758, Burd-Shippen Papers, Military, APS, lists 114 sick from several regiments in the Maryland Hospital directed by surgeon Henry Heinsman. It is likely that most of the sick and injured were being treated by their regimental surgeons in the field.

9. These figures are taken from the casualty returns for September 14 and October 12, 1758, found in *BP* 2:508–9, opposite 552, and "Rosters of Maryland Troops, 1757–1759," *Maryland Historical Magazine* 5 (1910): 271–89. See also Halkett to Bouquet, "Camp at the Foot of the East Side of the Alleganey," December 29, 1758, *Writings of Forbes*, 272 (Maryland troops deserting "in great numbers" from Fort Cumberland).

10. Armstrong to Bouquet, Rays Town, December 16, 1758, *BP* 2:631 ("great Mortifycation"); Ourry to Bouquet, Fort Bedford, December 20, 1758, *BP* 2:637–38. Some of the provincials were undoubtedly aware that their terms were up. For example, the Virginia House of Burgesses resolved to disband Byrd's regiment while maintaining Washington's beyond December 1. See McIwaine, *Journals of the House of Burgesses*, 49–52. At least one thief was caught and court-martialed; see "At a Court of Inquiry held by Order to Col. Bouquet, at Fort Bedford," January 20, 1759, *BP* 3:62–63.

11. Bouquet to Forbes, Bedford, January 13, 1759, *BP* 3:43 (Pennsylvania officers); Forbes to Amherst, Philadelphia, January 18, 1759, *Writings of Forbes*, 282. See also "Places for Magazines between Lancaster & Will's Creek or Fort Cumberland," n.d., "Posts for the Security & Convoy of the above Magazines," n.d., in FHQP, reel 3. f. 520; Raffle, *Malartic Journals*, 198, 202–3.

12. McKenzie to Bouquet, Fort Bedford, January 6, 1759, *BP* 3:18. Details about Mercer's fort including contemporary plans are in James and Stotz, *Drums in the Forest*, 140–52.

13. McConnell, *Country Between*, 138–39. On the relocation of Ohio Indians, see Tanner, *Atlas of Great Lakes Indian History*, 39–47, map 9 ("The French Era, 1720–1761"), and map 13 ("Indian Villages and Tribal Distributions c. 1768").

14. See Thwaites, *EWT*, 252–54 (differences within Delaware society, suspicion), 256 ("river Ohio," "go back over the mountain"), 278 (Keekyuscung); see also the Delawares' reply to the November 9 message in FAP 3:311. On the number of captives held in Ohio Indian towns, see Steele, *Setting All the Captives Free*, 435, table 2.

15. All quotes are from "A Conference held by Colonel Bouquet with the Chiefs of the Delaware Indians," Pittsburgh, December 4, 1758, BP 2:621–24. There exists another version of this council, provided to the French by Custaloga, a Munsee headman whose village was near Fort Venango, that was taken down and sent by Captain Lignery to Governor General Vaudreuil. It differs in tone from Bouquet's official version. In Custaloga's telling, the British were fairly apologetic about their arrival at the Forks and, instead of expecting the captives to be returned, dismissed the issue, telling the natives that those already adopted or married could remain, anticipating only that the aged would be returned once peace was confirmed. This version also has Bouquet openly soliciting Delaware aid in convincing the French to abandon the Ohio Country. Whether Custaloga was present on December 4 is unclear (the only person named is Tamaqua), and it is also unclear whether he got this version from someone else or was, in fact, telling the French what he thought they wanted to hear. This version is in Stevens and Kent, *Wilderness Chronicles*, 134–38. It is likely that Post, upon his arrival at the Forks from the Kuskuskies on December 3, recounted for Bouquet the Delaware speeches in answer to Denny's and Forbes's messages; see also Raffle, *Malartic Journals*, 196.

16. Forbes to Denny, "Fourt Duquesne, or now Pittsburgh," November 26, 1758, *Writings of Forbes*, 265; Forbes to Amherst, Shippensburg, January 6, 1759, *Writings of Forbes*, 275; Forbes to Amherst, Lancaster, January 13, 1759 (need for Amherst in Philadelphia), *Writings of Forbes*, 278; Forbes to Amherst, Philadelphia, January 26, February 7, 1759, *Writings of Forbes*, 283 ("I dare venture"), 289 ("not generally understood," "Myrmidons"); Amherst to Forbes, New York, February 4, 1759, in Middleton, *Amherst and the Conquest of Canada*, 21.
17. Forbes to Abercromby and Amherst, "Fort Duquesne now Pittsbourg," November 26, 1758, *Writings of Forbes*, 263 ("inflammation"); Forbes to Denny, "Fourt Duquesne, or now Pittsburgh," November 26, 1758, *Writings of Forbes*, 265; Forbes to Pitt, Pittsburgh, November 27, 1758, and Philadelphia, January 21, 1759, *Writings of Forbes*, 268; Forbes to Amherst, Lancaster, January 13, 1759, *Writings of Forbes*, 279 (Dr. Huck); Forbes to Amherst, Philadelphia, January 26, 1759, *Writings of Forbes*, 285 ("infirmity & Distemper"). See also Armstrong to Bouquet, Fort Bedford, January 1, 1759, *BP* 3:2 (Forbes "in good humour but feeble & weak"); Amherst to Whitmore, New York, January 16, 1759, in Middleton, *Amherst and the Conquest of Canada*, 15 ("by all that I hear of him, he is in a very bad way & 'tis not thought he can recover").
18. Halkett to Bouquet, "Tomhach Camp," December 28, 1759, *Writings of Forbes*, 271 (no fire, snowstorm); Halkett to Bouquet, Fort Bedford, December 31, 1758, *Writings of Forbes*, 273 ("tolerably well"). On logistics, see for example, Forbes to Bouquet, Bouquet's Camp, December 4, 1758, *Writings of Forbes*, 270; Forbes to Bouquet, Carlisle, January 8, 1759, *Writings of Forbes*, 276–77; Forbes to Bouquet, January 14, 1759, *Writings of Forbes*, 279–80. Soon after arriving in Philadelphia, Forbes learned that St. Clair was trying to gain command of the southern (Forbes's) army and was being "extremly liberal in his criticisms, remarks, and observations," especially to the new commander in chief, Amherst. Anticipating trouble Forbes quickly wrote to Bouquet (then at York, Pennsylvania), asking for any views the colonel might have on St. Clair's behavior during the campaign. Bouquet's reply came in the form of a damning bill of particulars. It began by emphasizing St. Clair's failure to provide the army with adequate forage and his mismanagement of transportation, which "brought us within a hair's breadth of disaster." To this Bouquet added the altercation with Colonel Stephen and St. Clair's generally incompetent behavior, and he concluded by stating that a sense of professionalism and personal honor would not allow him to again serve with St. Clair. See Halkett to Forbes, New York, February 5, 1759, *BP* 3:104; Forbes to Bouquet, Philadelphia, February 8, 1759, *BP* 3:110; Bouquet to Forbes, York, February 14, 1759, *BP* 3:122–24.
19. Forbes to Bouquet, Philadelphia, February 8, 1759, *BP* 3:291 ("rubs and hinderances"); Forbes's will, *BP* 3:299–300; Bouquet to Amherst, Philadelphia, March 1, 1759, in Middleton, *Amherst and the Conquest of Canada*, 24 ("So far gone"); Pitt to Forbes, Whitehall, March 15, 1759, *Correspondence of Pitt*, 2:68. Pitt had written earlier, on January 23, 1759, offering his and the king's congratulations on his successful campaign; this letter likewise never reached Forbes, *Correspondence of Pitt*, 2:16–18.

CONCLUSIONS

1. On the course of the war in America in 1759 and 1760, see Anderson, *Crucible of War*, 344–410. On British concerns about the French, see for example, Mercer to

Bouquet, "Pittsbg.," January 19, 1759, *BP* 3:58; Croghan to Stanwix, Pittsburgh, July 15, 1759, *BP* 3:417; "Indian Intelligence," Pittsburgh, August 4, 1759, *BP* 3:493. On Lignery, see Russ, "Le Marchand de Lignery, François-Marie," *Dictionary of Canadian Biography*, 3:378; on Lignery and Fort Niagara see Dunnigan, *Siege 1759*, 83–99.

2. Stanwix to Bouquet, Philadelphia, May 1, 1759, *BP* 3:265 (acting as quartermaster); Bouquet to Forbes, February 14, 1759, *BP* 3:124 ("war of scalps"). On Bouquet's later career and his activities during the 1763 Indian war, see Smith, *Bouquet's Expedition*, esp. 165–234, and editor's Appendix 3 (on Bouquet's death). St. Clair continued to serve as a deputy quartermaster general in America, though he had little to do with active operations in the field. He died in America in 1767. See Gage to Ellis, New York, May 29, 1765 (St. Clair as deputy quartermaster general) and Gage to Barrington, New York, December 8, 1767 (death of St. Clair), in Carter, *General Thomas Gage*, 2:289, 441.

3. Studies of Washington and especially his military careers are legion; among the best is Brumwell, *Gentleman Warrior*; Anderson, *George Washington Remembers*, 23 (on Washington's health). On Washington's continued belief in the importance of the Ohio Country to Virginia and his concerns about Pennsylvania, see for example, Washington to Fauquier, Loyalhanna, December 2, 1758, *GWP* 6:162. For a discussion of lessons learned by Washington during the Seven Years' War, see Ferling, "School for Command."

4. Kenny quoted in McConnell, *Country Between*, 180.
5. McConnell, *Country Between*, 160–61.
6. Bouquet to Allen, Fort Duquesne, November 25, 1758, *BP* 2:611 ("knocked on the head"); Netawatwees quoted in McConnell, *Country Between*, 181. On the Great Lakes, see White, *Middle Ground*, chs. 6 and 7.
7. On Pontiac and the 1763 war, see Dowd, *War under Heaven*.
8. Richter, *Before the Revolution*, 389 (racialized frontier). A recent study of the Black Boys, which sets them at the center rather than the periphery of frontier history, is Patrick Spero, *Frontier Rebels*.
9. The Iroquois involvement in the Treaty of Fort Stanwix can be followed in Campbell, *Speculators in Empire*. For the issue of boundaries in America, see Edelson, *New Map of Empire*, esp. ch. 4.

BIBLIOGRAPHY

PRIMARY SOURCES

Manuscript Collections

Alderman Library, University of Virginia, Charlottesville, Virginia
Headquarters Papers of John Forbes (microfilm, 3 reels)

American Philosophical Society, Philadelphia, Pennsylvania
Burd-Shippen Papers, Military

Bryn Mawr College, Bryn Mawr, Pennsylvania
The Friendly Association Papers. https://www.brynmawr.edu/cdm/landingpage/collections/HC_Friendly/

Fort Ligonier Association, Ligonier, Pennsylvania
Papers of the McPherson-Grant Family of Ballindalloch (typescript)

Historical Society of Pennsylvania, Philadelphia, Pennsylvania
Gratz Collection
Papers of the Royal Artillery of Pennsylvania
Shippen Family Papers

Huntington Library, San Marino, California
Loudoun Papers
"The New laied our Roads by Order of ye Assembly of Pennsylvania From Shippensburg to a Branch of the Yohiogenni" (James Burd) [LO530]

Library of Congress, Washington, D.C.
George Washington Order Book, Toner Manuscript, Joseph M. Toner Collection
George Washington Papers, available online at https://www.loc.gov/george-washington-papers/
"Orderly Book—Expedition of General John Forbes to Fort Duquesne (1758)"

The National Archives, Kew, London, England
Colonial Office Records, Class 5: America and the West Indies (microfilm)
War Office Papers, Class 34: The Sir Jeffery Amherst Papers (microfilm)

Scottish Records Office, Edinburgh, Scotland
Dalhousie Muniments, GD45/2: Papers of General John Forbes (microfilm)

Periodicals

The Gentleman's Magazine and Historical Chronicle
New York Mercury
Pennsylvania Gazette

PRIMARY SOURCES

Abbott, W. W., et al., eds. *The Papers of George Washington, Colonial Series*. Vols. 5–6. Charlottesville: University of Virginia Press, 1988.

Alden, Timothy, ed. "An Account of the Captivity of Hugh Gibson among the Delaware Indians of the Big Beaver and Muskingum from the latter part Of July 1756 to the Beginning of April, 1759." *Collections of the Massachusetts Historical Society*, 3d ser., 6 (1837): 140–53.

Anderson, Fred. *George Washington Remembers: Reflections on the French and Indian War*. Lantham, Md.: Rowman and Littlefield, 2004.

Andrews, Robert J., ed. *The Journals of Jeffery Amherst, 1757–1763*. 2 vols. East Lansing: Michigan State University Press, 2015.

Balch, Thomas, ed. *Letters and Papers Relating Chiefly to The Provincial History of Pennsylvania: with some notices of the Writers*. Philadelphia: Crissy and Markley, 1855.

Beetson, Robert, ed. *Naval and Military Memoirs of Great Britain from 1727 to 1782*. 6 vols. London: Longman, Hurst, Rees and Orme, 1804.

Bland, Humphrey. *A Treatise of Military Discipline*. London, 1727.

Bond, Beverly W. "The Captivity Narrative of Charles Stuart, 1755–1758." *Mississippi Valley Historical Review* 13 (1926–1927): 58–81.

Bourcet, Pierre Joseph. *Principes de la guerre de montagnes*. Paris, 1775.

Boyd, Julian P., ed. *Indian Treaties Printed by Benjamin Franklin, 1736–1762*. Philadelphia: Historical Society of Pennsylvania, 1938.

Boyle, Joseph Lee, ed. *"Apt to Get Drunk at all Opportunities": White Pennsylvania Runaways, 1750–1762*. Baltimore: Clearfield, 2015.

Brock, R. A., ed. *The Official Records of Robert Dinwiddie, Lieutenant-governor of The Colony of Virginia, 1751–1758*. 2 vols. Richmond: Virginia Historical Society, 1887.

Browne, William Hand, et al., eds. *Archives of Maryland*. Vol. 9, *Correspondence of Horatio Sharpe*. Baltimore, 1883.

Burnaby, Andrew. *Travels through the Middle Settlements in North America in the Years 1759 and 1760*. Ithaca, N.Y.: Cornell University Press, 1963.

Calder, Isabel M., ed. *Colonial Captives, Marches and Journeys*. New York: MacMillan, 1935.

"Captain William Sweat's Personal Diary of the Expedition against Ticonderoga, May 2–November 7, 1758." *Essex Institute Historical Collections* 93 (1957): 36–57.

Carter, Clarence Edwin, ed. *The Correspondence of General Thomas Gage with the Secretaries of State, and with the War Office and the Treasury 1763–1775*. 2 vols. New York: Archon Books, 1969. Originally published, New Haven, Conn.: Yale University Press, 1933.

Colonial Records: Minutes of the Provincial Council of Pennsylvania. 16 vols. Harrisburg, Pa.: 1838–1853.

Cormack, Andrew, and Alan Jones, eds. *The Journal of Corporal William Todd, 1745–1762*. London: Army Records Society, 2001.
Cuthbertson, Bennett. *A System for the Compleat Interior Management and Oeconomy Of a Battalion of Infantry*. Dublin, 1768.
D'Aulney, Louis Dupré. *Traité General des Subsistances Militaires*. Paris, 1745.
DeLancey, Edward F., ed. *Muster Rolls of New York Provincial Troops, 1755–1764*. New York: New York Historical Society, 1891.
Dulaney, Daniel. "Military and Political Affairs in the Middle Colonies in 1755." *Pennsylvania Magazine of History and Biography* 3 (1879): 11–31.
Fitch, Jabez Jr. *The Diary of Jabez Fitch, Jr. in the French and Indian War, 1757*. Glen Falls, N.Y.: Rogers Island Historical Association, 1968. Publication no. 1.
Frearson, C. W., ed. *"To Mr. Davenport": being letters of Major Richard Davenport (1714–1760) to his brother during service in the 4th Troop of Horse Guards And the 10th Dragoons, 1742–1760*. London: Society for Army Historical Research, 1968. Special publication no. 9.
Graham, Gerald S., ed. *The Walker Expedition to Quebec, 1711*. Toronto: Champlain Society, 1953.
Grant, George. *The New Highland Military Discipline*. Bloomfield, Ont.: Museum Restoration Service, 1967. Originally published 1757.
Grenier, Fernand, ed. *Papiers Contrecoeur et Autres Documents Concernant le Conflit Anglo-Francaise sur l'Ohio de 1745 á 1756*. Quebec: Les Presses Universitaires Laval, 1952.
Guy, Alan, ed. *Colonel Samuel Bagshawe and the Army of George II, 1731–1762*. London: Army Records Society, 1990.
Hadway, Jonas. *An Account of the Society for the Encouragement of British Troops in Germany and North America*. London, 1762.
Hamilton, Charles, ed. *Braddock's Defeat: The Journal of Captain Robert Chomley's Batman; the Journal of a British Officer; Halkett's Orderly Book*. Norman: University of Oklahoma Press, 1959.
Hamilton, Edward P., trans and ed. *Adventure in the Wilderness: The American Journals of Louis Antoine de Bougainville, 1756–1760*. Norman: University of Oklahoma Press, 1964.
Hamilton, Robert. *The Duties of a Regimental Surgeon Considered: with observations On his general qualifications: and hints relative to a more respectable Practice and better regulation of that department*. 2 vols. London, 1787.
Hayter, Tony, ed. *An Eighteenth-Century Secretary at War: The Papers of William, Viscount Barrington*. London: Army Records Society, 1988.
Hazard, Samuel, et al., eds. *Pennsylvania Archives, Selected and Arranged from Original Documents*. 138 vols. in 9 series. Harrisburg,1838–1935.
Hirsh, Alison Duncan, ed. *Early American Indian Documents: Treaties and Laws, 1607–1789, Pennsylvania Treaties*. Vol. 3, *1756–1775*. Washington, D.C.: University Publications of America, 1979.
Hunter, William A., ed. "Thomas Barton and the Forbes Expedition." *Pennsylvania Magazine of History and Biography* 195 (1971): 431–83.
Hutchins, Thomas. *The Courses of the Ohio River, taken by Lt. T. Hutchins, Anno 1766, And Two Accompanying Maps*. Edited by Beverly W. Bond Jr. Cincinnati: Historical and Philosophical Society of Ohio, 1942.

Jacobs, Wilbur R., ed. *The Appalachian Indian Frontier: The Edmond Atkin Report and The Plan of 1755*. Lincoln: University of Nebraska Press, 1967.

James, Alfred Proctor, ed. *Writings of General John Forbes Relating to His Service in North America*. Menasha, Wisc.: Collegiate Press, 1938.

Jordan, John W., ed. "Journal of James Kenny, 1761–1763." *Pennsylvania Magazine of History and Biography* 37 (1913): 1–47, 152–201.

"Journal of Rev. John Cleaveland, June 14, 1758–October 25, 1758." *Bulletin of the Fort Ticonderoga Museum* 10 (1959): 192–233.

Kalter, Susan, ed. *Benjamin Franklin, Pennsylvania, and the First Nations: The Treaties of 1736–1762*. Urbana: University of Illinois Press, 2006.

Kent, Donald H., and Emma Edith Woods, eds. *Travels in New France by JCB*. Harrisburg: Pennsylvania Historical Commission, 1941.

Kimball, Gertrude Selwyn, ed. *Correspondence of William Pitt when Secretary of State with Colonial Governors and Military and Naval Commissioners in North America*. 2 vols. New York: Macmillan, 1906.

Kirk, Robert. *The Memoirs and Adventures of Robert Kirk, Late of the Royal Highland Regiment*. Limerick, 1775(?).

Knox, John. *An Historical Journal of the Campaigns in North America for the Years 1757, 1758, 1759, and 1760*. 3 vols. Edited by Arthur Doughty. Freeport, N.Y.: Books for Libraries, 1970. Originally published 1769.

Kopperman, Paul, ed. *Regimental Practice by John Buchanan, M.D.: An Eighteenth-Century Medical Diary and Manual*. New York: Routledge, 2012.

Kopperman, Paul E., ed. *Theory and Practice in Eighteenth-Century British Medicine: "Regimental Practice" by John Buchanan, M.D.* 2013. https://www.ir.library.oregonstate.edu/downloads/3j3332791/.

Lambing, A. A., ed. *The Baptismal Register of Fort Duquesne (from June, 1754 to Dec., 1756)*. Pittsburgh: Myers, Shinkle & Co., 1885.

Lucier, Armand Francis, ed. *French and Indian War Notices Abstracted from Colonial Newspapers*. 4 vols. Bowie, MD: Heritage Books, 1999.

MacGregor, Doug, and Melissah Pawlikowowski, eds. "'This Wretched World': The Journal of John Michael Lindenmuth." *Pennsylvania History* 74 (2007): 374–93.

Mante, Thomas. *The History of the Late War in North America, and the Islands of The West Indies, Including the Campaigns of MDCCLXIII and MDCCLXIV Against His Majesty's Indian Enemies*. London, 1772.

Mays, Edith, ed. *Amherst Papers, 1756–1763: The Southern Sector: Dispatches from South Carolina, Virginia and His Majesty's Superintendent of Indian Affairs*. Bowie, Md.: Heritage Books, 1999.

McCulloch, Ian, and Timothy Todish, eds. *Through So Many Dangers: The Memoirs and Adventures of Robert Kirk, Late of the Royal Highland Regiment*. Fleischmanns, N.Y.: Purple Mountain Press, 2004.

McIlwaine, H. R., ed. *Journals of the House of Burgesses of Virginia, 1758–1761*. Richmond: Virginia State Library, 1908.

Middleton, Richard, ed. *Amherst and the Conquest of Canada*. London: Army Records Society, 2003.

Monro, Donald. *Observations on the Means of Preserving the Health of Soldiers*. 2 vols. London, 1780.

Mulkearn, Lois, ed. *George Mercer Papers Relating to the Ohio Company of Virginia*.

Pittsburgh: University of Pittsburgh Press, 1954.
Muller, John. *A Treatise of Artillery*. London, 1757.
O'Callaghan, Edmund B., and Berthold Fernow, eds. *Documents Relative to the Colonial History of the State of New York*. 14 vols. Albany, N.Y.: Weed, Parsons,1856–1887.
Pargellis, Stanley McCrory, ed. *Military Affairs in North America, 1748–1756: Selected Documents from the Cumberland Papers in Windsor Castle*. New York: Appleton-Century, 1936.
Peckham, Howard H., ed. "Thomas Gist's Indian Captivity, 1758–1759." *Pennsylvania Magazine of History and Biography* 80 (1956): 285–311.
Peyser, Joseph L., ed. *On the Eve of the Conquest: The Chevalier de Raymond's Critique of New France in 1754*. East Lansing: Michigan State University Press, 1997.
Pouchot, Pierre. *Memoirs of the Late War in North America between France and England*. Edited by Brian Dunnigan. Translated by Michael Cardy. 2d ed. Youngstown, N.Y.: Old Fort Niagara Association, 2004.
Preston, Richard A., and Leopold La Montagne, eds. *Royal Fort Frontenac*. Toronto: Champlain Society, 1958.
Pringle, Sir John. *Observations on the Diseases of the Army*. Philadelphia, Pa.: Edward Earle, 1810.
Raffle, William, ed. *Glories to Useless Heroism: The American Journals of Comte Maures de Malartic, 1755–1760*. Solihull, England: Helion, 2017.
Ranby, John. *The Method of Treating Gun Shot Wounds*. London, 1760.
Reece, Frances R., ed. "Colonel Eyre's Journal of His Trip from New York to Pittsburgh, 1761." *Western Pennsylvania Historical Magazine* 27 (1944): 37–50.
Reese, George, ed. *The Official Papers of Francis Fauquier, Lieutenant-Governor of Virginia, 1758–1768*. 3 vols. Charlottesville: University of Virginia Press, 1983.
"Robert Webster's Journal, April 5 to November 23, 1759." *Bulletin of the Fort Ticonderoga Museum* 2 (1931): 120–53.
"Roster of Maryland Troops, 1757–1759." *Maryland Historical Magazine* 5 (1910): 271–89.
Rowland, Dunbar, and A. G. Sanders, eds. *Mississippi Provincial Archives*. Vol. 5, *French Dominion, 1749–1763*. Revised by Patricia Kay Galloway. Baton Rouge: Louisiana State University Press, 1984.
Sargent, Winthrop, ed. *The History of an Expedition Against Fort Duquesne*. Philadelphia: Historical Society of Pennsylvania, 1855.
Shippen, Joseph. "Military Letters of Captain Joseph Shippen in the Provincial Service, 1756–1758." *Pennsylvania Magazine of History and Biography* 36 (1912): 367–78, 385–463.
Smith, George. *An Universal Military Dictionary*. Ottawa: Museum Restoration Service, 1969. Originally published London, 1779.
Smith, William. *Bouquet's Expedition against the Ohio Indians in 1764 by William Smith*. Edited with introduction and annotations by Martin West. Kent, Ohio: Kent State University Press, 2017.
A Soldier's Journal. London, 1770.
Stevens, Sylvester K., and Donald H. Kent, eds. *The Papers of Col. Henry Bouquet*. Series 21630–60. 19 vols. Harrisburg: Pennsylvania Historical Commission, 1940–1943.
Stevens, Sylvester K., and Donald H. Kent, eds. *Wilderness Chronicles of Northwestern Pennsylvania*. Harrisburg: Pennsylvania Historical Commission, 1941.

Stevens, Sylvester K., et al., ed. *The Papers of Henry Bouquet*. 6 vols. Harrisburg: Pennsylvania Historical and Museum Commission, 1951–1994.
Steward, Nicholas, ed. *A List of the Officers of the British Army to August 1755 (with an Appendix to October 1755)*. Dublin, 1755. Salem, Mass.: Steward Archives, 2015.
Sullivan, James, et al., eds. *The Papers of Sir William Johnson*. 14 vols. Albany: The University of the State of New York, 1921–1965.
Thomson, Charles. *An Enquiry into the Causes of the Alienation of the Delaware And Shawanese Indians*. London, 1759.
Thwaites, Reuben Gold, ed. *Early Western Travels, 1748–1846*. Vol. 1. Cleveland, Ohio: Arthur H. Clark, 1904.
Tinling, Marion, ed. *The Correspondence of the Three William Byrds of Westover, Virginia, 1684–1776*. 2 vols. Charlottesville: University of Virginia Press, 1977.
Tinling, Marion, ed. "Some Unpublished Correspondence of William Byrd III." *Virginia Magazine of History and Biography* 88, no. 3 (1980): 277–300.
Truxes, Thomas M., ed. *The Letterbook of Greg and Cunningham 1756–1757: Merchants of New York and Belfast*. Oxford: Oxford University Press for The British Academy, 2001.
Turpin de Crissé. *An Essay on the Art of War Translated from the French of Count Turpin by Captain Joseph Otway*. Paris, 1754. 2 vols. London, 1761.
"Two Journals of Western Tours." In *Early Western Travels, 1748–1846*, edited by Reuben Gold Thwaites, 1:197–283. Cleveland, Ohio: Arthur H. Clark, 1904.
Van Horne, John C., and George Reese, eds. *The Letter Book of James Abercromby Colonial Agent*. Richmond: Virginia State Library and Archives, 1991.
Wahll, Andrew J, ed. *Braddock Road Chronicles*. Westminster, Md.: Heritage Books, 2006.
Walker, Lewis B., ed. *The Burd Papers: The Settlements of the Waggoners' Accounts Relating to General Braddock's Expedition*. Pottsville, Pa.: Standard Publishing, 1899.
Wallace, Paul A. W., ed. *The Travels of John Heckewelder in Frontier America*. Pittsburgh: University of Pittsburgh Press, 1985.
Whitworth, Rex, ed. *Gunner at Large: The Diary of James Woods, R.A., 1746–1765*. London: Leo Cooper, 1988.
Williams, Edward G, ed. *Bouquet's March to the Ohio: The Forbes Road*. Pittsburgh: Historical Society of Western Pennsylvania, 1975.
Williams, Samuel C., ed. "An Account of the Presbyterian Mission to the Cherokees,1757–1759." *Tennessee Historical Magazine*2d ser., no. 1 (1930–1931): 125–38.
Wood, Stephen, ed. *By Dint of Labour and Persverence . . . : A Journal Recording Two Months in Northern Germany kept by Lieutenant-Colonel James Adolphus Oughton, Commanding 1st Battalion 37th Regiment of Foot, 1758*. London: Society for Army Historical Research, 1997. Special publication no. 14.

Secondary Sources

Agostini, Thomas. "'The Provincials Will Work like Giants': British Imperialism, American Colonial Troops, and the Trans-Atlantic Labor Economies during the Seven Years' War." *Early American Studies* 15 (2017): 64–98.
Alberts, Robert C. *The Most Extraordinary Adventures of Major Robert Stobo*. Boston: Houghton Mifflin, 1765.

Anderson, Fred. *Crucible of War: The Seven Years' War and the Fate of Empire in British North America*. New York: Alfred A. Knopf, 2000.

Anderson, Fred. *A People's Army: Massachusetts Soldiers and Society in the Seven Years' War*. Chapel Hill: University of North Carolina Press, 1984.

Anderson, Fred. "Why Did Colonial New Englanders Make Bad Soldiers? Contractual Principles and Military Conduct during the Seven Years' War." *William and Mary Quarterly*, 3d ser., 38 (1981): 395–417.

Anderson, Niles. "The General Chooses a Road." *Western Pennsylvania Historical Magazine* 42, no. 2 (1959): 100–138.

Armitage, David, and Michael J. Braddick, eds. *The British Atlantic World, 1500–1800*. New York: Palgrave MacMillan, 2002.

Axtell, James. *The European and the Indian: Essays in the Ethnohistory of Colonial North America*. New York: Oxford University Press, 1982.

Axtell, James. "The Moral Dilemma of Scalping." In Axtell, *Natives and Newcomers*, 259–79.

Axtell, James. *Natives and Newcomers: The Cultural Origins of North America*. New York: Oxford University Press, 2001.

Axtell, James. "Scalping: The Ethnohistory of a Moral Question." In Axtell, *European and the Indian*, 207–41.

Babits, Lawrence E., and Stephanie Gandulla, eds. *The Archaeology of French and Indian War Frontier Forts*. Gainesville: University Press of Florida, 2013.

Back, Francis, and Rene Chartrand. "Canadian Militia, 1750–1760." *Military Collector and Historian* 36 (1984): 19–21.

Bailyn, Bernard. *The Origins of American Politics*. New York: Random House, 1965.

Bailyn, Bernard. *Voyagers to the West: A Passage in the Peopling of America on the Eve of the Revolution*. New York: Alfred A. Knopf, 1986.

Bailyn, Bernard, and Philip D. Morgan, eds. *Strangers within the Realm: Cultural Margins of the First British Empire*. Chapel Hill: University of North Carolina Press, 1991.

Balvay, Arnaud. *L'Épée et la Plume: Amerindiens et soldats des troupes de la Marine en Louisiane et au Pays d'en Haut (1683–1763)*. Quebec: Les Presses de l'Université Laval, 2006.

Bamford, Andrew. *Sickness, Suffering and the Sword: The British Regiment on Campaign, 1808–1815*. Norman: University of Oklahoma Press, 2013.

Bannerman, Gordon E. *Merchants and the Military in Eighteenth-Century Britain*. London: Pickering and Chatto, 2008.

Bannister, Jerry. "The Oriental Atlantic: Governance and Regulatory Frameworks in the British Atlantic World." In Bowen et al., *Britain's Oceanic Empire*, 151–76.

Barr, Daniel, ed. *The Boundaries between Us: Natives and Newcomers along the Frontiers of the Old Northwest Territory, 1750–1850*. Kent, Ohio: Kent State University Press, 2006.

Barr, Daniel. "Victory at Kittanning? Reevaluating the Impact of Armstrong's Raid on the Seven Years' War in Pennsylvania." *Pennsylvania Magazine of History and Biography* 131, no. 1 (2007): 5–32.

Barr, Juliana, and Edward Countryman, eds. *Contested Spaces of Early America*. Philadelphia: University of Pennsylvania Press, 2017.

Baugh, Daniel. *The Global Seven Years War, 1754–1763*. London: Longman/Pearson, 2011.

Baumgarten, Linda. *What Clothes Reveal: The Language of Clothing in Colonial and Federal America*. New Haven, Conn.: Yale University Press for the Colonial Williamsburg Foundation, 2002.

Beck, Robin. *Chiefdoms, Collapse and Coalescence in the Early American South*. New York: Cambridge University Press, 2013.

Berkebile, Don H. *Conestoga Wagons on Braddock's Campaign 1755*. Contributions from the Museum of History and Technology, paper no. 9. Washington, D.C.: Smithsonian Institution, 1959.

Bell, T. F. "Historical Climate Records from Northeastern North America, 1640–1900." In Bradley and Jones, *Climate since A.D. 1500*, 74–91.

Bell, Whitfield J. Jr., and Leonard W. Labaree. "Franklin and the 'Wagon Affair,' 1755." *Proceedings of the American Philosophical Association* 101 (1957): 551–58.

Bellico, Russell P. *Empires in the Mountains: French and Indian War Campaigns and the Forts in the Lake Champlain, Lake George, and Hudson River Corridor*. Fleischmanns, N.Y.: Purple Mountain Press, 2010.

Bonomi, Patricia U. *Under the Cope of Heaven: Religion, Society and Politics in Colonial America*. New York: Oxford University Press, 1986.

Boscawen, Hugh. *The Capture of Louisbourg, 1758*. Norman: University of Oklahoma Press, 2011.

Boulware, Tyler. *Deconstructing the Cherokee Nation: Town, Region, and Nation among Eighteenth-Century Cherokees*. Gainesville: University Press of Florida, 2011.

Bowen, H. V., et al., eds. *Britain's Oceanic Empire: Atlantic and Indian Ocean Worlds, c. 1550–1850*. New York: Cambridge University Press, 2012.

Bowen, H. V., et al. "Introduction: Britain's Oceanic Empire." In Bowen et al., *Britain's Oceanic Empire*, 1–11.

Bowler, R. Arthur. *Logistics and the Failure of the British Army in America, 1775–1783*. Princeton, N.J.: Princeton University Press, 1975.

Bradley, Raymond S., and Philip D. Jones, eds. *Climate since A.D. 1500*. London: Routledge, 1990.

Breen, T. H. "Baubles from Britain: The American and Consumer Revolutions of the Eighteenth Century." *Past and Present* 119 (May 1988): 73–104.

Breen, T. H. "Creative Adaptations: Peoples and Cultures." In Greene and Pole, *Colonial British America*, 195–232.

Breen, T. H. "An Empire of Goods: The Anglicization of Colonial America, 1690–1776." *Journal of American Studies* 25 (1980): 467–99.

Breen, T. H. The *Marketplace of Revolution: How Consumer Politics Shaped American Independence*. New York: Oxford University Press, 2004.

Brewer, John. *The Sinews of Power: War, Money and the English State, 1688–1783*. New York: Alfred A. Knopf, 1989.

Briggs, Reginald P. "Conquest of the Allegheny Mountains." *Environmental and Engineering Geoscience* 4 (1998): 397–414.

Brooke, John L. *Climate Change and the Course of Global History: A Rough Journey*. New York: Cambridge University Press, 2014.

Brown, George W., et al., eds. *Dictionary of Canadian Biography*. Vol. 3. Toronto: University of Toronto Press, 1974.

Brown, Lloyd Arnold. *Early Maps of the Ohio Valley*. Pittsburgh: University of Pittsburgh Press, 1959.

Browne, Eric E. *The Westo Indians: Slave Traders of the Early Colonial South*. Tuscaloosa: University of Alabama Press, 2005.

Brumwell, Stephen. *George Washington: Gentleman Warrior*. London: Quercus, 2012.

Brumwell, Stephen. "Rank and File: A Profile of One of Wolfe's Regiments." *Journal of the Society for Army Historical Research* 79 (2001): 3–24.

Brumwell, Stephen. *Redcoats: The British Soldier and War in the Americas, 1755–1763*. New York: Cambridge University Press, 2002.

Brumwell, Stephen. *White Devil: A True Story of War, Savagery, and Vengeance in Colonial America*. Cambridge, Mass.: Da Capo Press, 2004.

Bushman, Richard. "Markets and Composite Farms in Early America." *William and Mary Quarterly*, 3d ser., 55 (1998): 351–74.

Bushman, Richard L. *The Refinement of America: Persons, Houses, Cities*. New York: Random House, 1992.

Butler, Jon. *Becoming American: The Revolution before 1776*. Cambridge, Mass.: Harvard University Press, 2000.

Calloway, Colin. *New Worlds for All: Indians, Europeans, and the Remaking of Early America*. Baltimore: Johns Hopkins University Press, 1997.

Calloway, Colin. *The Scratch of a Pen: 1763 and the Transformation of North America*. New York: Oxford University Press, 2006.

Calloway, Colin. *The Shawnees and the War for America*. New York: Viking, 2007.

Calvert, Karin. "The Function of Fashion in Eighteenth-Century America." In Carson et al., *Of Consuming Interests*, 252–83.

Campbell, Alexander V. *The Royal American Regiment: An Atlantic Microcosm*. Norman: University of Oklahoma Press, 2010.

Campbell, William J. *Speculators in Empire: Iroquoia and the 1768 Treaty of Fort Stanwix*. Norman: University of Oklahoma Press, 2012.

Cantlie, Sir Neil. *A History of the Army Medical Department*. 2 vols. London: Churchill Livingstone, 1974.

Carson, Cary. "The Consumer Revolution in Colonial British America: Why Demand?" In Carson et al., *Of Consuming Interest*, 483–697.

Carson, Cary, et al., eds. *Of Consuming Interests: The Style of Life in the Eighteenth Century*. Charlottesville: University of Virginia Press, 1994.

Cassel, Jay. "The Militia Legend: Canadians at War, 1665–1760." In Tremblay, *Canadian Military History*, 59–68.

Cassel, Jay. "The Troupes de la Marine in Canada: Men and Materiel, 1683–1760." PhD dissertation, University of Toronto, 1987.

Cayton, Andrew L., and Frederika Teute, eds. *Contact Points: American Frontiers from the Mohawk Valley to the Mississippi, 1750–1830*. Chapel Hill: University of North Carolina Press, 1998.

Chandler, David. *The Art of War in the Age of Marlborough*. New York: Hippocrene, 1976.

Chandler, David, and Ian Beckett, eds. *The Oxford Illustrated History of the British Army*. New York: Oxford University Press, 1994.

Charters, Erica. *Disease, War, and the Imperial State: The Welfare of the British Armed Forces during the Seven Years' War*. Chicago: University of Chicago Press, 2014.

Chartrand, Rene. *The French Soldier in Colonial America*. Bloomfield, Ont.: Museum Restoration Service, 1984.
Chet, Guy. *The Ocean Is a Wilderness: Atlantic Piracy and the Limits of State Authority, 1688–1856*. Amherst: University of Massachusetts Press, 2014.
Childs, John. *The Nine Years' War and the British Army, 1688–97: The Operations in the Low Countries*. Manchester, England: Manchester University Press, 1991.
Cleaveland, Colonel, ed. *Notes on the Early History of the Royal Regiment of Artillery*. Uckfield, England: Naval and Military Press, n.d.
Colley, Linda. *Britons: Forging the Nation, 1707–1837*. New Haven: Yale University Press, 1992.
Cook, E. E., et al. "Dendroclimatic Evidence from Eastern North America." In Bradley and Jones, *Climate since A.D. 1500*, 331–48.
Cormack, Andrew Edward. *"These Meritorious Objects of the Royal Bounty": The Chelsea Out-Pensioners in the Early Eighteenth Century*. Published by the author, 2017.
Coss, Edward J. *All for the King's Shilling: The British Soldier under Wellington, 1808–1814*. Norman: University of Oklahoma Press, 2010.
Cubbison, Douglas R. *The British Defeat of the French in Pennsylvania, 1758: A Military History of the Forbes Campaign against Fort Duquesne*. Jefferson, N.C.: McFarland, 2010.
Cubbison, Douglas R. *On Campaign against Fort Duquesne: The Braddock and Forbes Expeditions, 1755–1758, through the Experiences of Quartermaster Sir John St. Clair*. Jefferson, N.C.: McFarland, 2015.
Daniels, Christine, and Michael V. Kennedy, eds. *Negotiated Empires: Centers and Peripheries in the Americas, 1500–1820*. New York: Routledge, 2002.
Daunton, Martin, and Rick Halpern, eds. *Empire and Others: British Encounters with Indigenous Peoples, 1600–1830*. Philadelphia: University of Pennsylvania Press, 1999.
Dechêne, Louise. *Le Peuple, l'État et la Guerre au Canada sous le Régime français*. Edited by Hélène Paré, Sylvie Dépatie, Catherine Desbarats, Thomas Wren. Quebec: Les Editions du Boréal, 2008.
Dechêne, Louise. *Power and Subsistence: The Political Economy of Grain in New France*. Translated by Peter Feldstein. Montreal: McGill-Queen's University Press, 2018. Originally published as *Le Partage des subsistances au Canada sous le Régime français*. Quebec: les Editions Boréal, 1994.
Dowd, Gregory Evans. *Groundless: Rumors, Legends, and Hoaxes on the Early American Frontier*. Baltimore: Johns Hopkins University Press, 2015.
Dowd, Gregory Evans. "'Insidious Friends': Gift-Giving and Cherokee–British Alliance in the Seven Years' War." In Cayton and Teute, *Contact Points*, 114–50.
Dowd, Gregory Evans. *War under Heaven: Pontiac, the Indian Nations and the British Empire*. Baltimore: Johns Hopkins University Press, 2002.
Duffy, Christopher. *The Army of Frederick the Great*. 2d ed. Chicago: Emperor's Press, 1996.
Duffy, John. *Epidemics in Colonial America*. Baton Rouge: Louisiana State University Press, 1971.
Duncan, Francis. *History of the Royal Regiment of Artillery*. London: John Murray, 1872.
Dunnigan, Brian Leigh. *Siege 1759: The Campaign against Niagara*. Youngstown, N.Y.: Old Fort Niagara Association, 1996.

Dziennik, Matthew P. *The Fatal Land: War, Empire, and the Highland Soldier in British America*. New Haven: Yale University Press, 2015.
Eccles, W. J. "The Social, Economic, and Political Significance of the Military Establishment in New France." In W. J. Eccles, *Essays on New France*, 110–24. New York: Oxford University Press, 1988.
Edelson, S. Max. *The New Map of Empire: How Britain Imagined America before Independence*. Cambridge, Mass.: Harvard University Press, 2017.
Ekirch, A. Roger. *Bound for America: The Transportation of British Convicts to the Colonies, 1718–1775*. Oxford: Clarendon Press of Oxford University Press, 1990.
Engels, Donald W. *Alexander the Great and the Logistics of the Macedonian Army*. Berkeley: University of California Press, 1978.
Ethridge, Robbie, and Charles Hudson, eds. *The Transformation of the Southeastern Indians, 1540–1760*. Oxford: University Press of Mississippi, 2008.
Ethridge, Robbie, and Sheri M. Shuck-Hall, eds. *Mapping the Mississippian Shatter Zone: The Colonial Indian Slave Trade and Regional Instability in the American South*. Lincoln: University of Nebraska Press, 2009.
Fagan, Brian. *The Little Ice Age: How Climate Made History, 1300–1850*. New York: Basic Books, 2000.
Faragher, John Mack. *A Great and Noble Scheme: The Tragic Story of the Expulsion of the French Acadians from Their American Homeland*. New York: W. W. Norton, 2005.
Fatherly, Sara. "Tending the Army: Women and the British General Hospital in North America, 1754–1763." *Early American Studies* 10, no. 2 (2012): 566–99.
Ferling, John E. "School for Command: Young George Washington and the Virginia Regiment." In Hofstra, *George Washington*, 195–222.
Ferling, John E. "Who Served in the French and Indian War?" *Virginia Magazine of History and Biography* 94, no. 3 (1986): 307–28.
Flavell, Julie, and Stephen Conway, eds. *Britain and America Go to War: The Impact of War and Warfare in Anglo-America, 1754–1815*. Gainesville: University Press of Florida, 2004.
Fogelman, Eric. "Migrations to the Thirteen British North American Colonies, 1700–1775: New Estimates." *Journal of Interdisciplinary History* 22 (1992): 691–709.
Fogelson, Raymond. "Cherokee in the East." In Fogelson, *Handbook*, 14: 337–53.
Fogelson, Raymond, ed. *Handbook of North American Indians*. Vol. 14, *Southeast*. Washington, D.C.: Smithsonian Institution, 2004.
Foster, Michael K. "On Who Spoke First at Iroquois-White Councils: An Exercise in the Method of Upstreaming." In Foster et al., *Extending the Rafters*, 183–207.
Foster, Michael K., et al., eds. *Extending the Rafters: Interdisciplinary Approaches to Iroquoian Studies*. Albany: The State University of New York Press, 1984.
Frégault, Guy. *Canada: The War of the Conquest*. Translated by Margaret M. Cameron. Toronto: Oxford University Press, 1964.
Frey, Silvia. *The British Soldier in America: A Social History of Military Life in the Revolutionary Period*. Austin: University of Texas Press, 1981.
Frey, Silvia. "Courts and Cats: British Military Justice in the Eighteenth Century." *Military Affairs* 43, no. 7 (1979): 5–11.
Gale, R. R. *"A Soldier-Like Way": The Material Culture of the British Infantry, 1751–1768*. Elk River, Minn.: Track of the Wolf, 2007.

Gallay, Alan. *The Indian Slave Trade: The Rise of the English Empire in the American South, 1670–1717*. New Haven: Yale University Press, 2002.
Galloway, Patricia. *Choctaw Genesis, 1500–1700*. Lincoln: University of Nebraska Press, 1995.
Gallup-Diaz, Ignacio, et al., eds. *Anglicizing America: Empire, Revolution, Republic*. Philadelphia: University of Pennsylvania Press, 2015.
Games, Allison. "Accidental Empire." *Reviews in American History* 28 (2000): 341–50.
Gearing, Fred. "Structural Poses of Eighteenth-Century Cherokee Villages." *American Anthropologist* 60 (1958): 1148–57.
Gilbert, Arthur N. "British Military Justice during the American Revolution." *Eighteenth Century* 2 (1979): 24–38.
Gilbert, Arthur N. "The Changing Face of British Military Justice, 1757–1783." *Military Affairs* 49, no. 2 (1985): 80–84.
Gilbert, Arthur N. "The Regimental Court-Martial in the Eighteenth Century." *Albion* 8 (1976): 50–66.
Gipson, Lawrence Henry. *The British Empire before the American Revolution*. Vol. 4, *Zones of International Friction: North America, South of the Great Lakes Region, 1748–1754*. New York: Alfred Knopf, 1958.
Gipson, Lawrence Henry. *The British Empire before the American Revolution*. Vol. 7, *The Great War for the Empire: The Victorious Years, 1758–1760*. New York: Alfred Knopf, 1967.
Goodfriend, Joyce. *Before the Melting Pot: Society and Culture in Colonial New York City, 1664–1750*. Princeton, N.J.: Princeton University Press, 1992.
Greene, Jack P. *The Constitutional Origins of the American Revolution*. New York: Cambridge University Press, 2011.
Greene, Jack P. *Evaluating Empire and Confronting Colonialism in Eighteenth-Century Britain*. New York: Cambridge University Press, 2013.
Greene, Jack P. *Imperatives, Behaviors & Identities: Essays in Early American Cultural History*. Charlottesville: University of Virginia Press, 1992.
Greene, Jack P. *Interpreting Early America: Historiographical Essays*. Charlottesville: University of Virginia Press, 1996.
Greene, Jack P. "Metropolis and Colonies: Changing Patterns of Constitutional Conflict in the Early British Empire, 1607–1763." In Greene, *Negotiated Authorities*, 43–77.
Greene, Jack P. *Negotiated Authorities: Essays in Colonial Political and Constitutional History*. Charlottesville: University of Virginia Press, 1994.
Greene, Jack P. "Negotiated Authorities: The Problem of Governance in the Extended Polities of the Early Modern Atlantic World." In Greene, *Negotiated Authorities*, 1–24.
Greene, Jack P. *Peripheries and Center: Constitutional Development of the Extended Polities of the British Empire and the United States, 1607–1788*. New York: W. W. Norton, 1986.
Greene, Jack P. *Pursuits of Happiness: The Social Development of Early Modern British Colonies and the Formation of American Culture*. Chapel Hill: University of North Carolina Press, 1988.
Greene, Jack P. "The South Carolina Quartering Dispute, 1757–1758." *South Carolina Historical Magazine* 60 (1954): 193–204.

Greene, Jack P., and J. R. Pole, eds. *Colonial British America: Essays in the New History of the Early Modern Era*. Baltimore: Johns Hopkins University Press, 1984.

Grimes, Richard S. "We 'Now Have Taken Up the Hatchet Against Them': Braddock's Defeat and the Martial Liberation of the Western Delawares." *Pennsylvania Magazine of History and Biography* 137 (2013): 227–59.

Grimm, Jacob L. *Archaeological Investigation of Fort Ligonier, 1960–1965*. Annals of the Carnegie Museum, no. 42. Pittsburgh: Carnegie Museum of Natural History, 1970.

Gross, Robert. *The Minutemen and Their World*. New York: Hill and Wang, 1976.

Gruber, Ira D. *Books and the British Army in the Age of the American Revolution*. Chapel Hill: University of North Carolina Press, 2010.

Guy, Alan. *Oeconomy and Discipline: Officership and Administration in the British Army, 1714–1763*. Manchester, England: Manchester University Press, 1985.

Guy, John. "'That Stubborn English Spirit': Officer Discipline and Resistance to Authority, 1727–1750." *Army Museum* (1984): 31–42.

Haarmann, Albert. "American Uniforms during the French and Indian War, 1754–1763." *Military Collector and Historian* 32, no. 2 (1985): 58–66.

Hacker, Barton. "Women and Military Institutions in Early Modern Europe: A Reconnaissance." *Journal of Women in Culture and Society* 6 (1981): 643–71.

Haefeli, Evan, and Kevin Sweeney. *Captors and Captives: The 1704 French and Indian Raid on Deerfield*. Amherst: University of Massachusetts Press, 2003.

Hagist, Don N. "The Women of the British Army in America." http://www.Revwar.75.com/library/hagist/britwomen.btm/.

Hale, J. R. *War and Society in Renaissance Europe, 1450–1620*. Baltimore: Johns Hopkins University Press, 1985.

Hämäläinen, Pekka. "The Shapes of Power: Indians, Europeans, and North American Worlds from the Seventeenth to the Nineteenth Century." In Barr and Countryman, *Contested Spaces*, 31–68.

Hancock, David. *Oceans of Wine: Madeira and the Emergence of American Trade and Taste*. New Haven: Yale University Press, 2009.

Hatley, Thomas. *The Dividing Paths: Cherokees and South Carolinians through the Era of Revolution*. New York: Oxford University Press, 1995.

Hatley, Thomas. "The Three Lives of Keowee: Loss and Recovery in Eighteenth-Century Cherokee Villages." In Waselkov et al., *Powhatan's Mantle*, 223–48.

Hay, Douglas. "Property, Authority and the Criminal Law." In Hay et al., *Albion's Fatal Tree*, 17–63.

Hay, Douglas, et al., eds. *Albion's Fatal Tree: Crime and Society in Eighteenth-Century England*. New York: Verso, 2011.

Henderson, Rodger C. *Community Development and the Revolutionary Transition in Eighteenth-Century Lancaster County, Pennsylvania*. New York: Garland, 1989.

Henretta, James A. *"Salutary Neglect": Colonial Administration under the Duke of Newcastle*. Princeton, N.J.: Princeton University Press, 1972.

Henshaw, Victoria. *Scotland and the British Army, 1700–1750*. New York: Bloomsbury, 2014.

Hildeburn, Charles R. "Sir John St. Clair, Baronet, Quarter-Master-General in America, 1755 to 1767." *Pennsylvania Magazine of History and Biography* 9, no. 1 (1885): 1–14.

Hinderaker, Eric. *Elusive Empires: Constructing Colonialism in the Ohio Valley,1673–1800*. New York: Cambridge University Press, 1992.

Hinderaker, Eric. *The Two Hendricks: Unraveling a Mohawk Mystery.* Cambridge, Mass.: Harvard University Press, 2010.

Hoffman, Ronald, et al., eds. *Through a Glass Darkly: Reflections on Personal Identity in Early America.* Chapel Hill: University of North Carolina Press, 1997.

Hofstra, Warren. "The Colonial Road." In *The Great Valley Road of Virginia: Landscape from Prehistory to the Present.*, edited by Warren R. Hofstra and Karl Reitz, 79–108. Charlottesville: University of Virginia Press, 2011

Hofstra, Warren R., ed. *Cultures in Conflict: The Seven Years' War in North America.* Lanham, MD: Rowman and Littlefield, 2007.

Hofstra, Warren. "'The Extension of His Majesty's Dominions': The Virginia Backcountry and the Reconfiguration of Imperial Frontiers." *Journal of American History* 84 (1998): 1281–312.

Hofstra, Warren, ed. *George Washington and the Virginia Backcountry.* Madison, Wis.: Madison House, 1998.

Hofstra, Warren R. *The Planting of New Virginia: Settlement and Landscape in the Shenandoah Valley.* Baltimore: Johns Hopkins University Press, 2004.

Hofstra, Warren R., ed. *Ulster to America: The Scots-Irish Migration Experience, 1680-1830.* Knoxville: University of Tennessee Press, 2011.

Hornsby, Stephen J. *British Atlantic, American Frontier: Spaces of Power in Early Modern British America.* Hanover, N.H.: University Press of New England, 2005.

Houlding, J. A. *Fit for Service: The Training of the British Army, 1715–1795.* Oxford: Clarendon Press of Oxford University Press, 1981.

Houston, Alan. "Benjamin Franklin and the 'Wagon Affair' of 1755." *William and Mary Quarterly*, 3d ser., 66 (2009): 225–86.

Hubbard, R. H., ed. *Thomas Davies in Early Canada.* Ottawa: Oberon Press, 1973.

Hudson, Geoffrey L, ed. *British Military and Naval Medicine, 1600–1830.* Wellcome Series in the History of Medicine. New York: Rodolphi, 2007.

Hulbert, Archer Butler. *The Old Glade (Forbes's) Road.* Cleveland, Ohio: Arthur H. Clark,1903.

Hunter, William A. *Forts on the Pennsylvania Frontier, 1753–1758.* Harrisburg: Pennsylvania Historical and Museum Commission, 1960.

Hunter, William A. "Provincial Negotiations with the Western Indians, 1757–58." *Pennsylvania History* 18 (1951): 213–29.

Ireland, Bernard. *Naval Warfare in the Age of Sail: War at Sea, 1756–1815.* New York: W. W. Norton, 2000.

James, Alfred Proctor, and Charles Morse Stotz. *Drums in the Forest.* Pittsburgh: Historical Society of Western Pennsylvania, 1958.

Jennings, Francis. *The Ambiguous Iroquois Empire: The Covenant-Chain Confederation of Indian Tribes with English Colonies from Its Beginning to the Lancaster Treaty of 1744.* New York: W. W. Norton, 1984.

Jennings, Francis. *Empire of Fortune: Crowns, Colonies, and Tribes in the Seven Years' War in America.* New York: W. W. Norton, 1988.

Jennings, Francis. "Iroquois Alliances in American History." In Jennings et al., *History and Culture,* 37–66.

Jennings, Francis, et al., eds. *The History and Culture of Iroquois Diplomacy.* Syracuse, N.Y.: Syracuse University Press, 1985.

Johnson, Daniel. "'What Must Poor People Do': Economic Protest and Plebian Culture in Philadelphia, 1682–1754." *Pennsylvania History* 79 (2012): 117–53.
Jolly, Robert L. "Fort Loudoun, Virginia: A French and Indian War Period Fortification Constructed by George Washington." In Babits and Gandulla, *Archaeology*, 102–21.
Jones, Dorothy V. *License for Empire: Colonialism by Treaty in Early America*. Chicago: University of Chicago Press, 1982.
Kammen, Michael. *People of Paradox*. Ithaca, N.Y.: Cornell University Press, 1977.
Kelton, Paul. "The British and Indian War: Cherokee Power and the Fate of Empire in North America." *William and Mary Quarterly*, 3d ser., 69 (2012): 763–92.
Kelton, Paul. *Epidemics and Enslavement: Biological Catastrophe in the Native Southeast, 1492–1715*. Lincoln: University of Nebraska Press, 2007.
Kennett, Lee. *The French Armies in the Seven Years' War: A Study in Military Organization and Administration*. Durham, N.C.: Duke University Press, 1967.
Kent, Donald H. *The French Invasion of Western Pennsylvania, 1753*. Harrisburg: Pennsylvania Historical and Museum Commission, 1981.
Knoblauch, Edward H. "Mobilizing Provincials for War: The Social Composition of New York Forces in 1760." *New York History* 78, no. 2 (1997): 147–72.
Koot, Christian J. *A Biography of a Map in Motion: Augustine Herman's Chesapeake*. New York: New York University Press, 2018.
Kopperman, Paul E. *Braddock on the Monongahela*. Pittsburgh, Pa.: University of Pittsburgh Press, 1977.
Kopperman, Paul E. "The British High Command and Soldiers' Wives in America,1755–1783." *Journal of the Society for Army Historical Research* 60 (1982): 14–34.
Kopperman, Paul E. "The Medical Aspects of the Braddock and Forbes Expeditions." *Pennsylvania History* 71 (2004): 257–84.
Kopperman, Paul E. "Medical Service in the British Army, 1742–1783." *Journal of the History of Medicine and Allied Sciences* 34 (1979): 428–55.
Kummerow, Burton, et al. *Pennsylvania's Forbes Trail: Gateway and Getaways along the Legendary Route from Philadelphia to Pittsburgh*. New York: Rowman and Littlefield, 2008.
Lamb, H. H. *Climate, History and the Modern World*. 2d ed. New York: Routledge, 2002.
Lawson, Cecil C. P. *A History of the Uniforms of the British Army*. Vol 2, *From the Beginnings to 1760*. London: Norman Military Publications, 1963.
Leach, Douglas Edward. *Roots of Conflict: British Armed Forces and Colonial Americans, 1677–1763*. Chapel Hill: University of North Carolina Press, 1986.
Lemon, James T. *The Best Poor Man's Country: A Geographical Study of Early Southeastern Pennsylvania*. New York: W. W. Norton, 1971.
Lengel, Edward G. *General George Washington: A Military Life*. New York: Random House, 2007.
Levy, Barry. "Levelers and Fugitives: Runaway Advertisements and the Contrasting Political Economics of Mid-Eighteenth-Century Massachusetts and Pennsylvania." *Pennsylvania History* 78 (2011): 1–32.
Linch, Kevin, and Matthew McCormack, eds. *Britain's Soldiers: Rethinking War and Society, 1715–1815*. Liverpool, England: Liverpool University Press, 2014.
Liston, Maria, and Brenda Baker. "Reconstructing the Massacre at Fort William Henry, New York." *International Journal of Osteoarchaeology* 6 (1996): 28–41.

Little, Ann M. *The Many Captivities of Esther Wheelwright.* New Haven: Yale University Press, 2016.
Little, Hamish MacDonald. "The Treasury, the Commissariat and the Supply of the Combined Army in Germany during the Seven Years' War (1756–1763)." PhD dissertation, University College, London, 1981.
Lynn, John A. II, ed. *Feeding Mars: Logistics in Western Warfare from the Middle Ages to the Present.* Boulder, Colo.: Westview Press, 1992.
Lynn, John A. II. *Women, Armies, and Warfare in Early Modern Europe.* New York: Cambridge University Press, 2008.
Mackillop, Andrew. *More Fruitful than the Soil: Army, Empire and the Scottish Highlanders, 1715–1815.* London: Birlinn, 2001.
MacLeitch, Gail D. *Imperial Entanglements: Iroquois Change and Persistence on the Frontiers of Empire.* Philadelphia: University of Pennsylvania Press, 2016.
MacLeod, Peter. *The Canadian Iroquois and the Seven Years' War.* Canadian War Museum Historical Publication no. 29. Toronto: Dundurn Press, 1996.
MacMaster, Richard K. "Searching for Community: Carlisle, Pennsylvania, 1750s–1780s." In Hofstra, *Ulster to America*, 77–104.
MacMaster, Richard K. "Searching for Order: Donegal Springs, Pennsylvania, 1720s–1730s." In Hofstra, *Ulster to America*, 51–76.
Mancke, Elizabeth. "Empire and State." In Armitage and Braddick, *British Atlantic World*, 175–95.
Mancke, Elizabeth. "Negotiating an Empire: Britain and Its Overseas Peripheries,1550–1780." In Daniels and Kennedy, *Negotiated Empires*, 235–66.
Mandell, Daniel R. *Behind the Frontier: Indians in Eighteenth-Century Eastern Massachusetts.* Lincoln: University of Nebraska Press, 1996.
Marshall, P. J., ed. *The Oxford History of the British Empire.* Vol. 2, *The Eighteenth-Century.* New York: Oxford University Press, 1998.
Mayer, Holly. *Belonging to the Army: Camp Followers and Community in Revolutionary America.* Columbia: University of South Carolina Press, 1996.
Mayer, Holly. "From Forts to Families: Following the Army into Western Pennsylvania." *Pennsylvania Magazine of History and Biography* 130 (2006): 5–43.
McBride, Kim A. "The Second Fort Vause: A Critical French and Indian War Fort in the Roanoke Valley of Virginia." In Babits and Gandulla, *Archaeology*, 122–38.
McClusky, Turk, and James C. Squire. "Pennsylvania Credit in the Virginia Back-Country, 1746–1754." *Pennsylvania History* 81 (2014): 207–25.
McConnell, Michael N. *Army and Empire: British Soldiers on the American Frontier, 1758–1775.* Lincoln: University of Nebraska Press, 2004.
McConnell, Michael N. *A Country Between: The Upper Ohio Valley and Its Peoples,1724–1774.* Lincoln: University of Nebraska Press, 1992.
McConnell, Michael N. "Kuskusky Towns and Early Western Pennsylvania Indian History, 1748–1778." *Pennsylvania Magazine of History and Biography* 116 (1992): 33–49.
McConnell, Michael N. "Pisquetomen and Tamaqua: Mediating Peace in the Ohio Country." In *Northeastern Indian Lives, 1632-1816.*, edited by Robert S. Grumet, 273–94. Amherst: University of Massachusetts Press, 1996.
McCrae, Morrice. *Saving the Army: The Life of Sir John Pringle.* Edinburgh, Scotland: John Donald, 2014.
McCulloch, Ian Macpherson. *Sons of the Mountains: The Highland Regiment in the*

French and Indian War, 1756–1767. 2 vols. Fleishmans, N.Y.: Purple Mountain Press, 2006.
McCusker, John J. *Money and Exchange in Europe and America, 1600–1775: A Handbook*. Chapel Hill: University of North Carolina Press, 1978.
McCusker, John J., and Russell R. Menard. *The Economy of British North America,1607–1789*. Chapel Hill: University of North Carolina Press, 1985.
Meinig, D. W. *The Shaping of America: A Geographical Perspective on Five Hundred Years of History*. Vol 1, *Atlantic America, 1492–1800*. New Haven: Yale University Press, 1986.
Merrell, James H. "'The Customs of Our Country': Indians and Colonists in Early America." In Bailyn and Morgan, *Strangers within the Realm*, 117–56.
Merrell, James H. "'I Desire All That I Have Said . . . May Be Taken down Aright': Revisiting Teedyuscung's 1756 Treaty Council Speeches." *William and Mary Quarterly*, 3d ser., 63 (2006): 777–826.
Merrell, James H. *The Indians' New World: Catawbas and Their Neighbors from European Contact through the Era of Removal*. Chapel Hill: University of North Carolina Press, 1989.
Merrell, James H. *Into the American Woods: Negotiators on the Pennsylvania Frontier*. New York: W. W. Norton, 1999.
Merritt, Jane T. *At the Crossroads: Indians and Empires on a Mid-Atlantic Frontier*. Chapel Hill: University of North Carolina Press, 2003.
Middleton, Richard. *The Bells of Victory: The Pitt-Newcastle Ministry and the Conduct of the Seven Years' War, 1757–1762*. New York: Cambridge University Press, 1985.
Miville-Deschênes, Francois. *The Soldier Off Duty: Domestic Aspects of Military Life at Fort Chambly under the French Regime as Revealed by Archaeological Objects*. Ottawa: Environment Canada, 1987.
Moogk, Peter N. *La Nouvelle France: The Making of French Canada—A Cultural History*. East Lansing: Michigan State University Press, 2000.
Morgan, Philip D. *Slave Counterpoint: Black Culture in the Eighteenth-Century Chesapeake and Lowcountry*. Chapel Hill: University of North Carolina Press, 1998.
Mullett, Charles F. "Military Intelligence on Forts and Indians in the Ohio Valley,1756–1757." *William and Mary Quarterly*, 3d ser., 3 (1946): 398–410.
Mullins, Jim. *Of Sorts for Provincials: American Weapons of the French and Indian War*. Elk River, Minn.: Track of the Wolf, 2008.
Murrin, John M. *Beneficiaries of Catastrophe: The English Colonies in America*. Washington, D.C.: American Historical Association, 1997.
Nash, Gary B. *The Urban Crucible: Social Change, Political Consciousness and the Origins of the American Revolution*. Cambridge, Mass.: Harvard University Press, 1979.
Nelson, Paul David. *General James Grant: Scottish Soldier and Royal Governor of East Florida*. Gainesville: University Press of Florida, 1993.
Oliphant, John. *John Forbes: Scotland, Flanders and the Seven Years' War, 1707–1759*. New York: Bloomsbury, 2015.
Oliphant, John. *Peace and War on the Anglo-Cherokee Frontier, 1756–1763*. Baton Rouge: Louisiana State University Press, 2001.
Ostler, Jeffrey. "'To Exterpate the Indians': An Indigenous Consciousness of Genocide in the Ohio Valley and Lower Great Lakes, 1750–1810." *William and Mary Quarterly*, 3d ser., 72 (2015): 587–622.

Owsley, Douglas, et al. "Injuries, Surgical Care and Disease." In Pfeiffer and Williamson, *Snake Hill*, 198–226.
Pagan, John Ruston. *Anne Orthwood's Bastard: Sex and Law in Early Virginia*. New York: Oxford University Press, 2003.
Pargellis, Stanley McCrory. *Lord Loudoun in North America*. New Haven, Conn.: Yale University Press, 1933.
Parker, Geoffrey. *The Army of Flanders and the Spanish Road, 1567–1659*. 2nd ed. New York: Cambridge University Press, 2004.
Parmenter, Jon. "After the Mourning Wars: The Iroquois as Allies in North American Campaigns, 1676–1760." *William and Mary Quarterly*, 3d ser., 64 (2007): 39–82.
Pencak, William A., and Daniel K. Richter, eds. *Friends and Enemies in Penn's Woods: Indians, Colonists, and the Racial Construct of Pennsylvania*. University Park: Pennsylvania State University Press, 2004.
Perdue, Theda. "Cherokee Relations with the Iroquois in the Eighteenth Century." In *Beyond the Covenant Chain: The Iroquois and Their Neighbors in Indian North America, 1600-1800*, edited by Daniel K. Richter and James H. Merrell, 135–49. Syracuse, N.Y.: Syracuse University Press, 1987.
Perjes, G. "Army Provisioning, Logistics and Strategy in the Second Half of the Seventeenth Century." *Acta Historia Academiae Scientiarum Hungarae* 15 (1970): 1–52.
Pfeiffer, Susan, and Ronald Williamson, eds. *Snake Hill: An Investigation of a Military Cemetery from the War of 1812*. Toronto: Dundurn, 1991.
Piker, Joshua. *The Four Deaths of Acorn Whistler: Telling Stories in Colonial America*. Cambridge, Mass.: Harvard University Press, 2013.
Piker, Joshua. *Okfuskee: A Creek Indian Town in Colonial America*. Cambridge, Mass.: Harvard University Press, 2004.
Porter, W. *The History of the Corps of Royal Engineers*. 3 vols. N.p., 1889.
Preston, David. *Braddock's Defeat: The Battle of the Monongahela and the Road to Revolution*. New York: Oxford University Press, 2015.
Preston, David. "'To Make Indians of Our White Men': British Soldiers and Indian Warriors from Braddock's to Forbes's Campaigns, 1755–1758." *Pennsylvania History* 74 (2007): 280–306.
Rees, John U. "'As Many Fireplaces as You Have Tents': Earthen Camp Kitchens." *Continental Soldier* 11, no. 3 (Summer 1998): 26–32.
Reid, Stuart. *Frederick the Great's Allies, 1756–1763*. Oxford, England: Osprey, 2010.
Richter, Daniel K. *Before the Revolution: America's Ancient Pasts*. Cambridge, Mass.: Harvard University Press, 2011.
Richter, Daniel K. *Facing East from Indian Country: A Narrative History of Early America*. Cambridge, Mass.: Harvard University Press, 2001.
Richter, Daniel K. *The Ordeal of the Longhouse: The Peoples of the Iroquois League in the Era of European Colonization*. Chapel Hill: University of North Carolina Press, 1992.
Richter, Daniel K. "'War and Culture': The Iroquois Experience." *William and Mary Quarterly*, 3d ser., 40 (1982): 528–59.
Richter, Daniel K., and James H. Merrell, eds. *Beyond the Covenant Chain: The Iroquois and Their Neighbors in Indian North America, 1600–1800*. Syracuse, N.Y.: Syracuse University Press, 1987.

Ridner, Judith. *A Town In-Between: Carlisle, Pennsylvania, and the Early Mid-Atlantic Interior*. Philadelphia: University of Pennsylvania Press, 2010.

Roger, Alan. *Empire and Liberty: American Resistance to British Authority, 1755–1763*. Berkeley: University of California Press, 1974.

Russell, Peter E. "Redcoats in the Wilderness: British Officers and Irregular Warfare in Europe and America, 1740–1760." *William and Mary Quarterly*, 3d ser., 35 (1978): 629–52.

Saunt, Claudio. "History until 1776." In Fogelson, *Handbook*, 14: 128–38.

Savory, Sir Reginald. *His Britannic Majesty's Army in Germany during the Seven Years' War*. Oxford: Clarendon Press of Oxford University Press, 1966.

Schumann, Matthew, and Karl Schweizer. *The Seven Years War: A Transatlantic History*. New York: Routledge, 2008.

Schutt, Amy C. *Peoples of the River Valleys: The Odyssey of the Delaware Indians*. Philadelphia: University of Pennsylvania Press, 2013.

Scouller, R. E. *The Armies of Queen Anne*. Oxford: Clarendon Press of Oxford University Press, 1966.

Shannon, Timothy J. *Indians and Colonists at the Crossroads of Empire*. Ithaca, N.Y.: Cornell University Press, 2002.

Shannon, Timothy J. *Iroquois Diplomacy on the Early American Frontier*. New York: Penguin Books, 2008.

Shoemaker, Nancy. *A Strange Likeness: Becoming Red and White in Eighteenth-Century North America*. New York: Oxford University Press, 2004.

Shy, John. "The American Colonies in War and Revolution, 1748–1783." In Marshall, *Oxford History*, 2:300–324.

Shy, John. "Logistical Crisis and the American Revolution: A Hypothesis." In Lynn, *Feeding Mars*, 161–79.

Shy, John. *Toward Lexington: The Role of the British Army in the Coming of the American Revolution*. Princeton, N.J.: Princeton University Press, 1965.

Silver, Peter. *Our Savage Neighbors: How Indian War Transformed Early America*. New York: W. W. Norton, 2008.

Silverman, David J. *Thundersticks: Firearms and the Violent Transformation of Native America*. Cambridge, Mass.: Belknap Press of Harvard University Press, 2016.

Sledzik, Paul S., and Peer H. Moore-Jansen. "Dental Pathology." In Pfeiffer and Williamson, *Snake Hill*, 227–46.

Smith, Billy G. *The "Lower Sort": Philadelphia's Laboring People, 1750–1800*. Ithaca, N.Y.: Cornell University Press, 1994.

Smith, Thomas H. *The Mapping of Ohio*. Kent, Ohio: Kent State University Press, 1977.

Smolenski, John. *Friends and Strangers: The Making of a Creole Culture in Colonial Pennsylvania*. Philadelphia: University of Pennsylvania Press, 2010.

Snyder, Christina. *Slavery in Indian Country: The Changing Face of Captivity in Early America*. Cambridge. Mass.: Harvard University Press, 2010.

Sobel, Mechal. *The World They Made Together*. Princeton, N.J.: Princeton University Press, 1987.

Spero, Patrick. *Frontier Country: The Politics of War in Early Pennsylvania*. Philadelphia: University of Pennsylvania Press, 2016.

Spero, Patrick. *Frontier Rebels: The Fight for Independence in the American West, 1765–1775*. New York: W. W. Norton, 2018.

Stanley, George F. G. *New France: The Last Phase, 1744–1760.* Toronto: McClelland and Stewart, 1968.

Steele, Ian K. *Betrayals: Fort William Henry and the "Massacre.* New York: Oxford University Press, 1990.

Steele, Ian K. *The English Atlantic, 1675–1740: An Exploration of Communication and Community.* New York: Oxford University Press, 1986.

Steele, Ian K. *Setting All the Captives Free: Captives, Adjustment, and Recollection in Allegheny Country.* Kingston, Ont.: McGill-Queen's University Press, 2013.

Steele, Ian K. "The Shawnee Origins of their Seven Years' War." *Ethnohistory* 53 (2006): 657–87.

Steele, Ian K. "The Shawnees and the English: Captives and War, 1753–1765." In Barr, *Boundaries between Us*, 1–24.

Steele, Ian K. *Warpaths: Invasion of North America.* New York: Oxford University Press, 1994.

Stephenson, R. Scott. "Pennsylvania Provincial Soldiers in the Seven Years' War." *Pennsylvania History* 63 (1993): 196–212.

Steppler, Glenn A. "British Military Law, Discipline and the Conduct of Regimental Courts-Martial in the Late Eighteenth Century." *English Historical Review* 102, no. 405 (1987): 859–86.

Steppler, Glenn A. "The Common Soldier in the Reign of George III, 1760–1793." PhD dissertation, Exeter College, Oxford, 1984.

Stotz, Charles M. "Forbes Conquers the Wilderness." *Western Pennsylvania Historical Magazine* 67 (1984): 309–22.

Stotz, Charles M. *Outposts of the War for Empire: The French and English in Western Pennsylvania, Their Armies, Their Forts, Their People, 1749–1764.* Pittsburgh: Historical Society of Western Pennsylvania, 1985.

Strang, Cameron B. "The Mason-Dixon and Proclamation Lines: Land Surveying and Native Americans on Pennsylvania's Borderlands." *Pennsylvania Magazine of History and Biography* 136, no. 1 (2012): 5–23.

Syrett, David. *Shipping and Military Power in the Seven Years War: The Sails of Victory.* Exeter: University of Exeter Press, 2008.

Tallett, Frank. *War and Society in Early Modern Europe, 1495–1715.* New York: Routledge, 1992.

Tanner, Helen Hornbeck. *Atlas of Great Lakes Indian History.* Norman: University of Oklahoma Press, 1987.

Tatum, William P. III. "'The Soldiers Murmured Much on Account of this Usage': Military Justice and Negotiated Authority in the Eighteenth-Century British Army." In Linch and McCormack, *British Soldiers*, 95–113.

Taylor, Alan. *American Colonies.* New York: Viking, 2001

Taylor, William. *The Military Roads in Scotland.* Argyle, Scotland: House of Lochar, 1996.

Thayer, Theodore. *Israel Pemberton: King of the Quakers.* Philadelphia: Historical Society of Pennsylvania, 1943.

Titus, James. *The Old Dominion at War: Society, Politics and Warfare in Late Colonial Virginia.* Columbia: University of South Carolina Press, 1991.

Tortora, Daniel J. *Carolina in Crisis: Cherokees, Colonists, and Slaves in the American Southeast, 1756–1763.* Chapel Hill: University of North Carolina Press, 2015.

Tremblay, Yves, ed. *Canadian Military History since the Seventeenth Century.* Ottawa: Department of National Defence, 2001.

Truxes, Thomas M. *Defying Empire: Trading with the Enemy in Colonial New York.* New Haven, Conn.: Yale University Press, 2008.

Van Crefeld, Martin. *Supplying War: Logistics from Wallenstein to Patton.* New York: Cambridge University Press, 1972.

Vaughan, Alden T. "'From White Man to Redskin': Changing Anglo-American Perceptions of the American Indian." *American Historical Review* 87, no. 4 (1983): 913–53.

Vaughan, Alden. *Transatlantic Encounters: American Indians in Britain, 1500–1775.* New York: Cambridge University Press, 2006.

Von Arni, Gruber. *Hospital Care and the British Standing Army, 1660–1714.* Aldershot, England: Ashgate, 2006.

Waddell, Louis M., and Bruce D. Bomberger. *The French and Indian War in Pennsylvania, 1753–1763: Fortification and Struggle during the War for Empire.* Harrisburg: Pennsylvania Historical and Museum Commission, 1996.

Wallace, A. F. C. *Teedyuscung: King of the Delawares.* Philadelphia: University of Pennsylvania Press, 1949.

Wallace, Paul A. W. *Conrad Weiser, 1696–1760: Friend of Colonist and Mohawk.* Philadelphia: University of Pennsylvania Press, 1945.

Wallace, Paul A. W. *Indian Paths of Pennsylvania.* Harrisburg: Pennsylvania Historical and Museum Commission, 1965.

Ward, Matthew. "An Army of Servants: The Pennsylvania Regiment during the Seven Years' War." *Pennsylvania Magazine of History and Biography* 119 (1995): 75–93.

Ward, Matthew. *Breaking the Backcountry: The Seven Years' War in Virginia and Pennsylvania, 1754–1765.* Pittsburgh: University of Pittsburgh Press, 2003.

Ward, Matthew. "'The European Method of Warring Is Not Practiced Here': The Failure of British Military Policy in the Ohio Valley, 1755–1759." *War in History* 4, no. 3 (1997): 247–63.

Ward, Matthew. "Fighting the 'Old Women': Indian Strategy on the Virginia and Pennsylvania Frontier, 1754–1758." *Virginia Magazine of History and Biography* 103 (1995): 297–320.

Warfel, Stephen G. "Fort Loudoun: A Provincial Fort on the Mid-Eighteenth-Century Pennsylvania Frontier." In Babits and Gandulla, *Archaeology*, 158–73.

Warren, Stephen. *The Worlds the Shawnees Made: Migration and Violence in Early America.* Chapel Hill: University of North Carolina Press, 2016.

Waselkov, Gregory, et al., eds. *Powhatan's Mantle: Indians in the Colonia lSoutheast.* Lincoln: University of Nebraska Press, 1989.

Way, Peter. "Class and the Common Soldier in the Seven Years' War." *Labor History* 44 (2003): 455–81.

Way, Peter. "The Cutting Edge of Culture: British Soldiers Encounter Native Americans in the French and Indian War." In Daunton and Halpern, *Empire and Others*, 123–48.

Way, Peter. "'Soldiers of Misfortune': New England Regulars and the Fall of Oswego, 1755–1756." *Massachusetts Historical Review* 3 (2001): 49–88.

Westbrook, Nicholas, ed. "'Like Roaring Lions Breaking from Their Chains': The Highland Regiment at Ticonderoga." *Bulletin of the Fort TiconderogaMuseum* 16 (1998): 16–91.

White, Richard. *The Middle Ground: Indians, Empires and Republics in the Great Lakes Region, 1650–1815.* New York: Cambridge University Press, 1991.

White, Sam. *A Cold Welcome: The Little Ice Age and Europe's Encounter with North America.* Cambridge, Mass.: Harvard University Press, 2017.

Whitworth, Rex. *Field Marshal Lord Ligonier: A Story of the British Army, 1700–1770.* Oxford: Clarendon Press of Oxford University Press, 1958.

Willson, Beckles. *The Life and Letters of James Wolfe.* London, 1909.

Wokeck, Marianne S. *Trade in Strangers: The Beginnings of Mass Migration to North America.* University Park: Pennsylvania State University Press, 1999.

Wood, Jerome. *Conestoga Crossroads: Lancaster Pennsylvania, 1750–1790.* Harrisburg: Pennsylvania Historical and Museum Commission, 1979.

Wood, Peter. *Black Majority: Negroes in Colonial South Carolina from 1670 through the Stono Rebellion.* New York: Alfred A. Knopf, 1974.

Wood, Peter. "Changing Population of the Colonial South: An Overview by Race and Region, 1685–1790." In Waselkov et al., *Powhatan's Mantle*, 35–103.

Yagi, George. *The Struggle for North America, 1754–1758: Britannia's Tarnished Laurels.* New York: Bloomsbury, 2016.

Yagi, George. "Surviving the Wilderness: The Diet of the British Army and the Struggle for Canada, 1754–1760." *Journal of the Society for Army Historical Research* 89 (2011): 66–86.

Zilberstèn, Anya. *A Temperate Climate: Making Climate Change in Early America.* New York: Oxford University Press, 2016.

Zimmerman, John J. "Governor Denny and the Quartering Act of 1756." *Pennsylvania Magazine of History and Biography* 91 (1967): 266–81.

INDEX

Note: Page references in *italics* indicate illustrative material.

Abenakis, 23
Abercromby, James, *30*; appointed commander in chief, 29; artillerymen assignments, 113; campaign preparations, 317n1; colonial relations, 39, 40; on Forbes's health, 210–11; Indian affairs, 243–44, 348n4; light infantry, 63; Montreal campaign, 33; recruitment advice for Forbes, 45; supply concerns, 92
Acadia, 7, 78
Ackowanothic (Delaware), 76
Admiralty Board, 13
African Americans: as slaves, 19; as soldiers, 60
agriculture, and army supplies, 12–13, 94
Albany Plan of Union, 22
Allegheny Country, *32*
Allegheny Mountain, 185–88, 190–93
Allen, William, 184
Amherst, Jeffery, 29, 33, 34, 222, 289–90, 320n17
ammunition. *See* weapons and ammunition
Anderson, Fred, 348n4
Anderson, George, 112
animals: horses, 96, 97–98, 116, 126, 159, 170–71, 209, 225, 318n9; livestock, 159, 169, 208–9, 239, 333n45
archaeological remains, 229–33
Armstrong, John: army health concerns, 163, 283; on Forbes, 222; Fort Duquesne advance logistics, 268, 274–75; and officer rank, 34; raiding efforts, 31, 38, 80, 212; road construction, 119–20, 203; route logistics involvement, 178, 179, 186, 187, 336n17; logistics, 285, 286; with Forbes's army, 48.
army, British regular and provincial: administrative structure, 13–16; campaign recruitment, 34–36, 38–41, 305n8; demographics, 53–55; desertion, 55, 145, 157, 215, 228, 275, 284–85, 309n43, 351n3; discipline and training, 49–50, 55–56, 145–46, 151, 154–57; drafting, 11, 300n5; equipment, overview, 50–52; Fort Duquesne advance logistics, 268–71, *270*, 274–79; garrison assignments, 90–91, 281, 285–86; Loyalhannon logistics, 204–5, 224–26, 234–35, 253, 344n8; morale, 218–19, 228, 283; population and losses, 153–54, 227, 262, 282–85, 351n3; provincial soldiers as "others," 17–18; Raystown advance logistics, 122–28, 144–46. *See also* health; Highland Regiments; Pennsylvania Regiment; Royal American Regiment; supplies; Virginia Regiments; weapons and ammunition
army, French: challenges of Ohio Country defense, 85–87; demographics, 84–85. *See also* Indian-French relations
artillery: train and personnel, 112; weapons, 113–14
Atkin, Edmond, 25, 63–64, 70, 100–101, 102, 103, 320n19
Attakullakulla (The Little Carpenter) (Cherokee), 69–70, 134, 271–74, 314n14
Aubry, Charles Philippe, 236
Augustus, George, 33

Bagshawe, Samuel, 56–57
Baker, James, 187
Barton, Thomas, 113, 116, 154, 162, 163, 168, 179, 197, 214
Basset, Thomas, 91, 124, 206
Bernard, Sir Francis, 249
Billings, John, 229
Billings, Mary, 217, 311n55
Black Boys, 296
Blainville, Céleron de, 74

381

Blair, John, 40, 47, 70, 99, 103
Bland, Humphrey, *A Treatise of Military Discipline*, 50, 146, 147
Blane, Archibald, 283
Board of Admiralty, 13
Board of Ordnance, 13–14
Board of Treasury, 14
Bosomworth, Abraham: Cherokee peace efforts, 69, 70, 100–102, 131, 134; Indian emissary appointment, 64, 243, 313n4; Virginia regiment appointment, 307n25
Boston, 53
Bouquet, Henry, *44*; appointed second in command, 35, 43, 45; army health concerns, 159, 162, 163, 165; on Bosomworth, 313n4; challenges with raiders, 212; colonial relations, 17, 36, 45; conflict with St. Clair, 99, 196–97, 357n18; criticism of provincial soldiers, 41; on Forbes's health, 291; Fort Duquesne advance logistics, 269, 275, 278; and French raid on Loyalhannon, 239–40; on Gordon, 42; and Grant's defeat, 217–18; Indian affairs, 102, 128–34, 259–60, 288, 321n29, 356n15; intelligence gathering, 212, 213–14; Loyalhannon logistics, 224–25; Loyalhannon encampment preparation, 203–4, 205–7; military background, 43–44; on officer losses, 282; post-campaign duties, 293; Raystown logistics, 123–26, 144–46; Raystown encampment preparation, 146–53, 154; recruitment of skilled laborers, 13, 151–52; route, 178, 181–84, 187–94, 204–5, 235, 335n9; supplies, 50, 91, 96, 97, 168, 208; training and disciplinary regimen, 145–46, 154–57; widows' funds, 59, 311n55
Bourcet, Pierre Joseph, 301n14
Braddock, Edward: campaign logistics compared to Forbes, 96, 121; defeat near Fort Duquesne, 7, 31, 47, 94; Indian affairs, 26, 76, 315n25; preference for Pennsylvania as base, 118; regiments, 11; scalp bounties, 26; on St. Clair, 45–46
Braddock's Road, 120, 173, 176, 178–84, 221, 266
Bradstreet, John, 15, 45, 219

British army. *See* army, British regular and provincial
British-Indian relations. *See* Indian-British relations
British Mutiny Act, 55
Brown, Charlotte, 58–59
Brown, Samuel, 106
Buchanan, John, 164
Buchannon, William, 119
Bull, John, 251
Bullen, Captain (Catawba), 128, 212–13
Bullitt, Thomas, 124, 216, 314n15, 352n13
Burd, James: Fort Duquesne advance logistics, 269; and French raid on Loyalhannon, 236–39, 346n25; Loyalhannon logistics, 194, 202–3; Loyalhannon encampment preparation, 203–7, *204*; and officer rank, 34; road building, 119–20; logistics, 52; with Forbes's army, 48. *See also* Pennsylvania Regiment
Burd's Road, 119–20, 123–25
Burnaby, Andrew, 17
Byng, Sir John, 10, 329n23
Byrd, William, III: Fort Duquesne advance logistics, 269; Indian affairs, 64, 69–70, 103, 128, 134, 243, 271; and officer rank, 34; route involvement, 181, 266; with Forbes's army, 49. *See also* Virginia Regiments

Callender, Robert, 179
Campbell, John, 10
camps. *See* Loyalhannon; Raystown
Candon, John, 81
captives. *See* prisoners
Carlisle, 116–18, 121, 286
casualties, 77–78, 80, 237–39, 282–85, 347n28
Catawbas: alliance strategies, overview, 25; cultural differences and misunderstandings with British, 100, 102, 128, 132, 133; emergence, 23; as intelligence gatherers, 99, 104–5, 129; raids against, 212–13
cattle, 159, 169, 209, 239, 333n45
Cayugas, 62, 252, 254–55, 259
Champlain Valley, 7
Cherokees: British peace efforts, 63–64, 67–71, 271–74; conflict among, 68–69;

conflict with colonists, 103–4, 326n35; conflict with Ohio Indians, 89, 101, 102–3, 107, 317n50; cultural differences and misunderstandings with British, 67, 69–70, 100, 102, 128–29, 130–34, 320–21n21; diplomatic practices, 66–68; early encounters with Europeans, 22–23, 64–66; as intelligence gatherers, 99, 104–5, 122, 129–30; and route, 179–81
children, 56–57, 58, 77, 311n54
Christie, Gabriel, 15
civilian followers: clothing, 229–30; as common feature of army composition, 56–60; contractors, 14–15, 92, 97, 98; forbidden from Fort Duquesne advance, 278; Indian relations, 129; rations, 56, 57, 168, 311n54, 333n43; women's occupations, 57, 59, 166
Clayton, Asher, 185–86
Clerk, Matthew, 42, 113
coalition warfare, 27–28
colonial government. *See* Maryland; Pennsylvania; Virginia
Conestogas, 20
courts-martial, 18, 156–57, 164–65, 228
Covenant Chain, 24–25, 245, 250–51, 252
Creeks, 22–23
Cresap, David, 79
Cresap, Thomas, 79, 130
Croghan, George, 83, 101, 119, 138–39, 244–46, 249, 275–76, 348–49n9
Cumberland, William Augustus, duke of, 10, 33; *A New Exercise to be observed by His Majesty's Troops*, 50
Cunne Shote, 65
Custaloga, 82, 356n15

Dagworthy, John, 39–40, 49, 56, 135, 230, 268–69
Davies, Samuel, 273
Davison, Adam, 165
DeLancey and Watts (contracting firm), 14
Delawares: colonial captives and refugees, 81–82; in colonial territory, 20; discontent with French, 107; French peace efforts, 200; intelligence gathering for French, 130; migration and settlement in Ohio Country, 71–72, 74, 80; Pennsylvania attacks on, 79, 80, 82; Pennsylvania peace efforts, Croghan's negotiations, 83; Pennsylvania peace efforts, Fort Duquesne council, 288–90, 356n15; Pennsylvania peace efforts, Post's negotiations, 128, 135–38, 140, 198–202, 243, 252–59, 287–88, 339nn3–4 (*See also* Easton conference); Pennsylvania peace efforts, Teedyuscung's negotiations, 88–89, 101, 107, 135–41, 199, 244–45, 249–50, 339n4; raids on colonial frontier, 31, 76–77; and ramifications of Forbes campaign, 294–95; Virginia peace efforts, 107
Denny, William: Indian affairs, 70, 83, 107, 138, 198–99, 243–53, 327n45, 349n16; intelligence gathering logistics, 105; military background, 37, 306n16; resistance to quartering, 16; resistance to providing weapons, 37
desertion, 55, 145, 157, 215, 228, 273, 275, 284–85, 309n43, 351n3
diet. *See* rations and foodstuffs
Dinwiddie, Robert, 40, 46, 48, 68, 78, 79
diplomacy. *See* Indian-British relations
Discentio, Martin, 240
discipline and training, 49–50, 55–56, 145–46, 151, 154–57
disease. *See* health
Dobbs, Arthur, 40, 41
drafting, 11, 300n5
Dudgeon, Richard, 206, 351n9
Dulany, Daniel, 17
Dunmore's War (1774), 297
Duquesne, Ange de Menneville, marquis de, 75, 85

Easton conference: aims of, 244–46; Delaware peace agreement, 258–60; deliberations, 249–51; Indian protocols at, 246–48; message party at Kuskuskies, 251–58; Treaty, 140, 199–200, 288, 289
economy, global, 20–21
encampments. *See* Loyalhannon; Raystown
equipment. *See* supplies; weapons and ammunition

Evans, Lewis, 106, *119*
Evans, Lieutenant, 266–67

Fauquier, Francis, 40, 70, 79, 273
food. *See* rations and foodstuffs
forage, 97, 98, 125, 126–27, 170–71, 208–10, 334n47
Forbes, John: administrative staff appointments, 41–43, 45, 48–49, 203, 305n12; as brigadier general, 33; and colonial debates on Loyalhannon route choice, 178–85; conflict with St. Clair, 45, 99, 127–28, 197, 210, 357n18; death, 291; Fort Duquesne advance logistics, 264–66, 268–71, 274–79; and French raid on Loyalhannon, 240, 346n24, 347n28; garrison assignments, 90–91, 281, 285–86; gathers troops, 34–36, 38–41, 60–61, 90–91, 305n8; and Grant's defeat, 217–18, 222; health, 32–33, 61, 143–44, 210–11, 223, 235, 271, 281, 290–91, 312n63, 343n2; Indian affairs, Cherokees, 100–105, 128–29, 132–34, 271–74, 320n19, 320n21; Indian affairs, Delawares, 138, 140–41, 242–44, 253–54, 287–90, 317n50, 347n1, 349n9; intelligence gathering, 99–100, 105–6, 129–30, 134–35, 211–12; and Louisbourg campaign, 10; Loyalhannon logistics, 205, 207 224–26; morale concerns, 218–19, 228; praise for Pennsylvania Regiment, 309n38; Raystown logistics, 122–28; route options, 118–23, 173–78; Scottish background, 12; logistics, 37, 51–52, 98, 113–14, 169, 170–71, 209–10, 233–35, 263–64, 276–77, 333–34n47; wagon transport, 91, 93–96, 115–16, 126–27, 224
Forbes Road, *174*, *177*; colonial debate over, 178–85; conflict between St. Clair and Stephen over, 194–97; construction, 187–94, *189*; scouting parties, 185–87, *188*, 193–94, 337n21; slow advance to Loyalhannon, 204–5, 224–26, 234–35, 253, 344n8
Fort Bedford, 355n2. *See also* Raystown
Fort Carillon (Ticonderoga), 63
Fort Cumberland, 39, 153, 165, 168, 173, 179, 209, 211, 221

Fort Duquesne, *122*; Braddock's defeat, 7, 31, 47; British advance to, 268–71, *270*, 274–79; and British council of war discussions, 264–65; British garrison assigned to, 281, 285; British intelligence gathering on, 105, 137, 140, 240–41, 268; British logistics, 282; Delaware peace council at, 288–90, 356n15; French abandonment of, 278; French defense and logistics, 85–86, 106–7, 114–15, 235–36, 240–41, 276, 323n5; Grant's defeat, 211, 213–18, 342n37; transition to Fort Pitt, 294, 295, 355n2
Fort Frederick, 39
Fort Frontenac, 219
Fort Ligonier, 355n2. *See also* Loyalhannon
Fort Littleton, 122, 124, 169, 285
Fort Loudoun, 131–32, 169, 285
Fort Necessity, 7
Fort Niagara, 10, 137, 292
Fort Oswego, 10, 63, 301n6
Fort Pitt, 294, 295, 355n2
Fort Stanwix Treaty (1768), 297
Fort William Henry, 63
Franklin, Benjamin, 22, 37, 94, 245
Fraser, Simon, 11
French, Captain (Catawba), 212–13
French army. *See* army, French
French-Indian relations. *See* Indian-French relations
French occupation, North America. *See* New France
Friendly Association. *See* Quakers

Gage, Thomas, 17, 63, 296–97
Gates, Horatio, 293
George II of Great Britain, 22, 33
Georgia, 19
Gibson, Hugh, 81
gift-giving and reciprocity, 67, 69–70, 100, 102, 128–29, 130–32, 320–21n21
Gist, Christopher, 102
Gist, Thomas, 214–16, 219
Glen, James, 68, 70, 134, 154, 291
Gordon, Harry: advocacy for Braddock's Road, 183–84; appointed as Forbes's chief engineer, 42–43, 48, 305n12; artillery command, 237; campaign preparation ar-

rangements, 91; Loyalhannon construction, 207, 265, 351n9; maps by, 124
Grant, James: defeat at Fort Duquesne, 211, 213–18, 220–21, 342n37; Forbes's praise of, 48; Loyalhannon logistics, 194; route, 334n1; in Second Highland Battalion, 11–12; second in command, Burd's, 203; logistics, 325n26
guerrilla warfare, 62–63

Halkett, Francis: army health concerns, 283; challenges with Indian raiders, 212; on Forbes, 141, 210, 223, 290; as Forbes's secretary, 41; on Grant's defeat, 218; Indian affairs, 104; logistics, 181–82, 225, 336n12
Halkett, Sir Peter, 41
Hambright, Captain, 165
Hay, Charles, 12
Hay, David, 42–43, 90, 113, 116, 224
Hays, William, 251, 255
health: of Forbes, 32–33, 61, 143–44, 210–11, 223, 235, 271, 281, 290–91, 312n63, 343n2; hygiene, 159, 166–67; injuries, 164–66, 192–93; nutrition, 167–68, 332–33n42; sickness, among civilians, 57, 160; sickness, among soldiers, 35–36, 111–12, 145, 153, 158, 159–64, 193, 227–28, 283–84, 331n33, 356n8
Heinsman, Henry, 356n8
Hendrick (Mohawk sachem), 62
Hesse, Emanuel, 282
Heydeler, Martin (Heideler), 38, 113, 306–7n19
Hickman, Thomas (Delaware), 251
Highland Regiments: creation of, 11–12; Fort Duquesne advance logistics, 269; garrison assignments, 286; language barrier, 54; numbers, 262, 282, 283; rank and regimental seniority, 34, 151; Raystown logistics, 123; recruits in, 11, 35; sickness in, 35, 36, 111–12, 145, 161, 283–84; uniforms, 51
Hofstra, Warren, 319n14
Hoops, Adam, 14, 98, 119–20
Hop (Cherokee), 273
Hornsby, Stephen J., 303n29
horses, 96, 97–98, 116, 126, 159, 170–71, 209, 225, 318n9

Howarth, Colonel, 69
Howe, Viscount, 33, 305n9
Howell, Joshua, 98
howitzers, 113, 114, *114*
Huck, Richard, 290

illness. *See* health
Indian-British relations: British army peace efforts, Cherokees, 63–64, 67–71, 271–74; challenges of, overview, 25–27; Covenant Chain, 24–25, 245, 250–51, 252; cultural differences and misunderstandings, 67, 69–70, 100, 102, 128–29, 130–34, 138–39, 320–21n21; frontier raids and counterattacks, 31, 75–79, 80, 103–4; intelligence gathering, 99, 104–5, 122, 129–30; Pennsylvania peace efforts, Delaware and Croghan negotiations, 83; Pennsylvania peace efforts, Delaware and Post negotiations, 128, 135–38, 140, 198–202, 243, 252–59, 287–88, 339nn3–4; Pennsylvania peace efforts, Delaware and Teedyuscung negotiations, 88–89, 101, 107, 135–41, 199, 244–45, 249–50, 339n4; Pennsylvania peace efforts, Delawares at Fort Duquesne council, 288–90, 356n15; ramifications of Forbes campaign, 294–97; Virginia peace efforts, Delawares, 107; Virginia peace efforts, Iroquois, 74, 75. *See also* Easton conference
Indian-French relations: Cherokees, 68–69; decline, 87–88, 107, 137, 219; Delawares, 107, 130, 200; and guerrilla warfare, 62–63; raiding parties, 80, 83–84, 211–19, 220–21, 236–40, 266–67, 275–76, 346nn24–25
Indian peoples: colonial attitudes toward, 26–27, 68, 71, 78–79; diplomacy strategies and customs, 24–25, 66–68, 69, 83, 138–39, 200, 246–48, 251–52, 254–56; early encounters with Europeans, 22–23; kinship terms, 249, 252, 349n14; in mainland colonies, 20. *See also specific tribes*
intelligence gathering and reconnaissance: British assignments for Indian allies, 99, 104–5, 122, 129–30; challenges with raiders, 211–12; Forbes Road scouting parties, 185–87, 188, 193–94, 337n21;

intelligence gathering and reconnaissance (*cont.*): Forbes's plans for, 99–100, 105–6, 129–30, 134–35, 211–12; on Fort Duquesne, 105, 137, 140, 240–41, 268; provincial soldiers to scout, 63, 134–35

Iroquois Confederacy: alliance with British against New France, 72–74, 75; alliance with Delawares, 200; Covenant Chain, 24–25, 245, 250–51, 252; early encounters with Europeans, 22–23; at Easton conference, 244–46, 249–50, 251; land claims in Ohio Country, 72, 258–59, 297

Jacobs, Captain (Delaware), 80, 82
Jenkins, Edward, 229
Johnson, William, *247*; appointed superintendent for Indian affairs, 25, 70; Cherokee affairs, 100–102, 320–21n21; criticism of provincial involvement in Indian affairs, 101, 245–46, 347n2; Delaware affairs, 83, 107, 349n16; Forbes's criticism of, 100–102, 134, 243–44, 320n21; Iroquois affairs, 101, 250, 297; military involvement, 62
Jumonville, Joseph Coulon de Villiers de, 75
Juniata Crossing, 122, 124, 285

Keekuyscung (Delaware), 139–40, 257, 288
Kelton, Paul, 314n14
Kenny, James, 294
Kilby, Christopher, 14, 98
Kilby and Baker (contracting firm), 14
kinship terms, 249, 252, 349n14
Kirk, Robert, 54, 215–16
Kirkpatrick, Ensign, 165

land claims, Indian, 24–25, 72, 251, 258–59, 349n16
Lander, Francis, 283
Laurel Mountain, 185–88, 190, 193–94
Lee, Charles, 12
Leininger, Barbara, 81
Lemon, James T., 318n9
Le Roy, Marie, 81
Lewis, Andrew, 43, 195, 214–17
Lignery, François le Marchant de, 87, 213, 218, 235–36, 276, 278, 292

Ligonier, Sir John, 33
Little Ice Age, 331n31
livestock, 159, 169, 208–9, 239, 333n45. *See also* horses
Loudoun, John Campbell, fourth earl of: call for Indian recruitment, 63–64; colonial relations, 39; as commander in chief, 16; criticism of colonial government, 36; and Louisbourg campaign, 12; regiments, 10, 11; relieved of command, 29; on St. Clair, 15; supply concerns, 92
Louisbourg, 10, 12, 29, 222
Lowry, Lazarus, 106
Loyalhannon: deterioration, 265; encampment preparation, *152*, *204*, 206–7, *208*; garrison assignments, 285, 286, 288; health conditions, 227–28; march to, 224–26, 234–35, 344n8; numbers of troops at, 227, 262, 351n3; raids on, 213, 236–40, 266–67, 346nn24–25; as site of "second parallel," 223; site selection, 203–6, *238*; logistics, 207–10, 233–35, 263–64
Lyttleton, William Henry, 64, 69, 70

maps (contemporary), 106, *119*, 124–25
Marin de la Malgue, Joseph, sieur de, 86
Maryland: Covenant Chain, 24; demographics, 19; food supply from, 98; funding for troops, 39–40, 90; Indian relations, 31; interest in Forbes Road route, 179–80; troops in Forbes campaign, 34, 38–40, 49, 52, 56, 230, 284–85; weapons from, 36–37, 99
Massachusetts, 24, 26
May, Martha, 59
McDonald, Theodosius, 237
McKee, Thomas, 102
McKenzie, Alexander, 286
McLean, Allen, 214
medicine, 164, 166. *See also* health
Menatochyand (Delaware George), 82, 83, 199, 200, 255, 257
Mercer, George, 189–90, 203, 266–67, 321n21, 352n13
Mercer, Hugh, 49, 145, 223, 281, 286
Merrell, James H., 304n42

Mesquakis (Fox), 72
Metacom's War (King Philip's War; 1675–1676), 26
Miami confederacy, 72–73
Michelson, Walter (Mitchelson), 112
militia, 54. *See also* army, British regular and provincial
Mohawks, 24, 25, 62
Montgomery, Archibald, 11, 34, 35–36, 48, 203, 269. *See also* Highland Regiments
Morton, Sergeant (48th Foot), 41–42
Muller, John, 116
Munsees, 20, 72
Murrin, John M., 303n32

Native Americans. *See* Indian-British relations; Indian-French relations; Indian peoples
Neilson, Captain, 136, 137
Nenacheehunt (Delaware), 137
Netawatwees (Newcomer) (Delaware), 82, 83, 295
New France, 8–9; Ohio Country fortification challenges, 85–87, 106–7, 137; Ohio Country land claims, 25, 74–75. *See also* army, French; Indian-French relations
New Jersey, 19
New Levies, 38, 49, 52, 56, 144, 161, 285, 310n44
New York, 19, 24
New York City, 53
Norris, Gerald, 312n63
North Carolina: food supply from, 98; troops in Forbes campaign, 34, 40–41, 50, 153, 262, 284, 285
Nova Scotia, 7, 78
nutrition. *See* rations and foodstuffs

officers: officer corps, 12; rank, 16, 22, 34, 305n9; training and disciplinary regimen, 145–46
Ohio Company, 25, 74, 75, 78, 178
Ohio Country: French fortification challenges, 85–87, 106–7, 137; French land claims, 25, 74–75; Indian land claims, 24–25, 72, 251, 258–59, 349n16; Indian migration to, 72–74, 80–81

Ohio Indians: emergence, 23; ramifications of Forbes campaign for, 294–97; relations with Cherokees, 89, 101, 102–3, 107, 317n50; settlements disrupted by warfare, 80–81. *See also* Delawares; Iroquois Confederacy; Shawnees
Ojibwas, 219
Oneidas, 72
Onondagas, 62
Ontario, Lake, 7
Ordnance Board, 13–14
Orme, Robert, 116
Ottawas, 219
Ourry, Lewis, 171, 282, 285

Patterson, James, 186
Peebles, John, 162–63
Pemberton, Israel, 38, 101, 105, 136, 140–41, 244–45, 306n18
Penn, William, 37
Penn family, 24, 37–38, 72, 76, 136, 199, 245–46, 251
Pennsylvania: as base of operations, 118; conflict with Indians, 22, 31, 71, 72, 76–79, 80, 82; Covenant Chain, 24–25, 245, 250–51, 252; cultural diversity, 19; Delaware peace efforts, Croghan's negotiations, 83; Delaware peace efforts, Fort Duquesne council, 288–90, 356n15; Delaware peace efforts, Post's negotiations, 128, 135–38, 140, 198–202, 243, 252–59, 287–88, 339nn3–4 (*See also* Easton conference); Delaware peace efforts, Teedyuscung's negotiations, 88–89, 101, 107, 135–41, 199, 244–45, 249–50, 339n4; interest in Forbes Road route, 179–81, 184; scalp bounties, 26, 31, 79, 201; supplies from, 36–37, 60, 94–96, 98, 318n8. *See also* Quakers
Pennsylvania Gazette, 77
Pennsylvania Regiment: creation of, 37–38; demographics, 54–55; experience, 49; Forbes's recruitment of, 34, 38; Fort Duquesne advance logistics, 269; garrison assignments, 90–91; New Levies, 38, 49, 52, 56, 144, 161, 285, 310n44; numbers, 153, 227, 262; praise for, 309n38;

Pennsylvania Regiment (*cont.*): Raystown logistics, 122–23; sickness in, 145, 161, 227, 330n30; uniforms, 52, 310n44; weapons, 50, 51, 144

Peters, Richard, 37, 141, 246, 251

Philadelphia, 118

Pisquetomen (Delaware), 72, 82, 139–40, 198, 201, 248–49, 250–57

Pitt, William: ambitions for Forbes's campaign, 31, 61; approval of Forbes's leave, 291; army expansion efforts, 11; European military campaigns, 29; and officer rank, 34, 305n9; as secretary of state, 29, 304n1; troop funding, 40

Pleydell, J. C., 149, 155, 206, *208*, 328n12

Plumstead and Franks (contracting firm), 14

Post, Christian Frederick; and Delaware peace talks, 128, 135–38, 140, 198–202, 243, 252–59, 287–88, 339nn3–4; encounters warriors at Kuskuskies, 212–13; information on Cherokees, 326n35

Potts, John, 124, 125

Pouchot, Pierre, 238, 239

Powhatans, 20

Preston, David, 315n25

Prideaux, John, 292

Pringle, John, *Observations on the Diseases of the Army*, 158–59, 162, 166, 332–33n42

prisoners: civilian, 77, 78, 81–82; French, 129, 240, 267, 268; from Grant's defeat, 48, 216–17, 342n38; negotiations for release of Pennsylvanian, 199, 251, 288; Shawnee, 75

provincial army. *See* army, British regular and provincial; Pennsylvania Regiment; Virginia Regiments

provisions. *See* rations and foodstuffs; supplies; weapons and ammunition

punishments, 55, 156–57, 228, 329n23

Quakers: Indian affairs, 78, 83, 88, 101, 136, 140–41, 199, 243, 244–46; political influence, 37–38

quartering, 16, 36

quartermasters general, role of, 15, 301n14

rangers, 63, 135

rations and foodstuffs: for animals, 97–98, 126–27, 170–71, 208–9; for civilians, 56, 57, 168, 311n54, 333n43; forage, 97, 98, 125, 126–27, 170–71, 208–10, 334n47; logistics, 98, 169–71, 209–10, 233–35, 276–77, 282; nutritional value, 167–68, 332–33n42; for soldiers, 92–93, 167–68, 193, 263, 265, 277, 318n4, 333n43

Raystown: encampment preparation, 146–53, *150*; garrison assignments, 285, 286, 288; health conditions, 158–68; march to, 123–26, 144–46; number of troops at, 153–54, 262; planned route to, 119–20, 121–23; as site of "first parallel," 121; logistics, 169–71, 285; training at, 154–57

reciprocity and gift-giving, 67, 69–70, 100, 102, 128–29, 130–32, 320–21n21

reconnaissance. *See* intelligence gathering and reconnaissance

regular army. *See* army, British regular and provincial; Highland Regiments; Royal American Regiment

Rhor, Charles, 91, 187, 191, 193, 204–5, 214, 216, 217, 218

"River Indians," 20

Robertson, James, 15

Rogers, Robert, 63

Royal American Regiment: creation of, 11, 49; demographics, 53–54; experience, 144; Fort Duquesne advance logistics, 269; garrison assignments, 286; numbers, 153, 227, 262, 282; rank and regimental seniority, 34, 151; Raystown advance logistics, 122; sickness in, 35–36, 145, 161; uniforms, 51

Royal Navy, 14, 29–30

Russell, William, 41

scalping: cash bounties for, 26–27, 31, 79, 135, 201; in Indian scouting practice, 104–5, 129–30, 321n29

Scottish Highlanders. *See* Highland Regiments

Senecas, 62, 72, 137, 138, 249

servants, 55, 59–60, 153

Seven Years' War, outbreak and early history, 7–10
Shamokin Daniel (Delaware), 201, 243
Sharpe, Horatio: on army health, 330n30; Indian affairs, 70; logistics, 113; route, 178, 179, 191, 335n4; scout company, 135; and troop funding, 39
Sharrett, Ralph, 106
Shawnees: abandonment of French, 235; alliance with Delawares, 200; colonial captives and refugees, 81–82; conflict with southern Indians, 107; early encounters with Europeans, 22–23; migration and settlement in Ohio Country, 72, 80; raids on colonial frontier, 31, 75–76; Virginia attacks on, 79
Shelby, Evan, 52, 135
Shingas (Delaware), 72, 74, 76, 82, 139, 201, 202, 257, 315n25
Shippen, Edward, 179, 185
Shippen, Joseph, 154, 307n25, 310n44
Shippensburg, 121, 131, 285
Shirley, William, 16
sickness. *See* health
Sinclair, Lieutenant, 235
Six Nations. *See* Iroquois Confederacy
slaves, 19, 60
Smith, James, 296
Society for the Encouragement of British Soldiers in Germany and North America, 311n55
South Carolina, 36, 64, 68, 69
Stanwix, John, 351n6, 355n4
St. Clair, James (Sinclair), 172
St. Clair, Sir John, 46; challenges with raiders, 212; combative personality, 46–47, 48, 99, 320n17, 357n18; conflict with Stephen, 194–97, 210; criticism of colonists, 17, 39, 40–41, 46–47; encampment selection, 205; frequent travel, 334n49; health, 47; Indian affairs, 100, 102, 103–4, 128; and intelligence gathering, 106; logistics, 51, 52, 91, 93, 94, 96–99, 170–72, 210; military background, 45–46; post-campaign duties, 358n2; preference for Pennsylvania as base, 118; quartermaster general appointment, 15, 45, 47–48; route, 119, 123, 127–28, 176–81, 185, 187, 191–92, 193–94; Washington's troops, 56

Steele, Ian, 315n24
Stephen, Adam: challenges with raiders, 211; conflict St. Clair, 48, 194–97, 210; disciplinary regimen, 55; Raystown advance logistics, 123; road construction efforts, 190–91, 192, 203; weather concerns, 223
Stewart, Robert, 184
Stille, Isaac (Delaware), 251, 254, 256
Stobo, Robert, 323n5
Stockbridge Indians, 20
Stuart, Charles, 315n25
supplies: archaeological remains, 229–33; contractors, 14–15, 92, 97, 98; logistical concerns, overview, 12–13; shortages, 52, 98–99, 144, 209, 265, 285, 286; uniforms, 51–52, 134, 144, 229, 230, 310n44; wagon transportation, 91–92, 93–99, 95, 126–27, 170, 209–10, 234–35. *See also* rations and foodstuffs; weapons and ammunition

Tagashata (Ohio Indian), 249
Tamaqua: Delaware peace talks involvement, 72, 83, 88–89, 139, 199–200, 202, 250, 257–59, 287–89, 316n40; dissatisfaction with post-war conditions, 294–95; release of civilian captives, 82
Tanaghrisson (Seneca), 74, 80
Teedyuscung: Delaware peace talks involvement, 88, 101, 107, 135–41, 199, 244–45, 249–50, 316n40, 339n4; as interpreter, 327n45; raids on Pennsylvania, 77
Thomson, Charles, 128, 136
Tishcohan (Delaware), 73
Todd, William, 168, 311n54
Tortora, Daniel J., 314n14
training and discipline, 49–50, 55–56, 145–46, 151, 154–57
transportation. *See* wagons
Treasury Board, 14
Trent, William, 131
Turpin de Crissé, Lancelot, comte, *Essay on the Art of War*, 120–22, 223, 268, 324n14

uniforms, 51–52, 134, 144, 229, 230, 310n44

Vaudreuil, Governor-General, 130, 213
Virginia: Covenant Chain, 24; food supply from, 98; Indian relations, alliances, 68, 74, 75, 107; Indian relations, conflict, 22, 31, 71, 75–76, 77–79, 103–4; interest in Forbes Road route, 178–85; Ohio Country land claims, 74, 75; resistance to providing weapons, 37, 99; scalp bounty, 79; westward expansion, 19
Virginia Regiments: demographics, 54–56; equipment, 50–52; experience, 49, 55–56; Forbes's recruitment of, 34, 40; Fort Duquesne advance logistics, 268–69; Loyalhannon November skirmish, 266–67; numbers, 262; rations, 92; Raystown advance logistics, 123, 224; regimental seniority, 151; sickness in, 160–61, 162–63, 227, 284

Waddell, Hugh, 40
wagons: archaeological remains, 232; poor condition, 170, 234; slow pace of, 125–26, 170, 209–10, 234–35; artillery transportation, *109*, 112, 115–16. 224–25; supply transportation, 91–92, 93–99, *95*, 126–27, 170, 209–10, 234–35
Walker, John, 106, 185
Walking Purchase, 24–25, 245
wampum, 69, 83, 138–39, 200, 247–48, 251–52, 254–56
Ward, Edward, 75, 185–86
War Office, 14
Washington, George, *180*; advocacy for Braddock's Road, 178, 179–85, 266, 336n14; army health concerns, 284; campaign experience, overview, 293–94; desertion concerns, 228; in early conflict against New France, 75; Fort Duquesne advance logistics, 268, 269, 275–77, 278; Fort Necessity surrender, 7; on Grant's defeat, 218, 220; Indian affairs, 70, 100, 213, 320n18, 347n2; and Loyalhannon November skirmish, 266–67, 352n13; and officer rank, 16, 34; and slaves, 60; supply concerns, 51, 310n44; training and disciplinary regimen, 50, 55–56; weather concerns, 223; with Forbes's army, 48. *See also* Virginia Regiments

weapons and ammunition: and accidental shootings, 164–65; artillerymen, 112–13, 322n3; short supply, 37, 50–51, 99, 144; training, 156; types, 50, 113–14, *114*, *115*, *117*, 231–32; transportation logistics, 112, 115–16, 224–25
Webster, Robert, 167
Wedge, Henry, 60
Weiser, Conrad, 72, 248, 249, 251
widows, 59, 217, 311n55
Wills, Thomas, 165
Wolfe, James, 17, 33, 302n18
women: clothing, 229–30; occupations, 57, 59, 166; numbers, 57–58, 311n53; rations for, 56, 57, 168, 311n54, 333n43; widows, 59, 217, 311n55
Wood, Draper, 92–93, 169, 318n5
Wright, George, 112, 237
Wyandots, 72, 80, 137, 200, 219

www.ingramcontent.com/pod-product-compliance
Lightning Source LLC
Chambersburg PA
CBHW032024290426
44110CB00012B/655